INTRODUCTION TO
CANADIAN LAW

EDITORS AND SENIOR AUTHORS
Sherrie Barnhorst LL.B., LL.M.
Joan Mather B.A., B.Ed.

CONTRIBUTING AUTHORS
Judith Keene LL.B.
Malcolm Davidson B.A.

Prentice-Hall Canada Inc.,
Scarborough, Ontario

Canadian Cataloguing in Publication Data

Mather, Joan, 1950 —
  Introduction to Canadian law

For use in secondary schools.
Includes index.
ISBN 0-13-479171-1

I. Law — Canada. I. Barnhorst, Sherrie, 1948 —
II. Title.

KE445.M38   1985   349.71   C84-099623-3

© 1985 by Prentice-Hall Canada Inc., Scarborough, Ontario
ALL RIGHTS RESERVED

No part of this book may be reproduced in any form without permission in writing from the publisher.
Prentice-Hall, Inc., Englewood Cliffs, New Jersey
Prentice-Hall International, Inc., London
Prentice-Hall of Australia, Pty., Ltd., Sydney
Prentice-Hall of India Pvt., Ltd., New Delhi
Prentice-Hall of Japan, Inc., Tokyo
Prentice-Hall of Southeast Asia (Pte.) Ltd., Singapore
Editora Prentice-Hall do Brasil Ltda., Rio de Janeiro
Prentice-Hall Hispanoamericana, S.A., Mexico

ISBN 0-13-479171-1

  6 7 8 9 BBM 99 98 97

Printed and bound in Canada by
Best Book Manufacturers
Project Editor: Lois Rock
Production Editing: Olga V. Domján
Associate Editor: Mary Land
Production: Monika Heike
Cover Photograph: EduVision Inc.
Illustration: Pat Cupples
Composition: Trigraph Inc.

Policy Statement

Prentice-Hall Canada Inc., Educational Book Division, and the authors of *Introduction to Canadian Law* are committed to the publication of instructional materials that are as bias-free as possible. The student text was evaluated for bias prior to publication.

  The authors and publishers also recognize the importance of appropriate reading levels and have therefore made every effort to ensure the highest degree of readability in the student text. The content has been selected, organized, and written at a level suitable to the intended audience. Standard readability tests have been applied at several stages in the text's preparation to ensure an appropriate reading level.

  Research indicates, however, that readability is affected by much more than word or sentence length; factors such as presentation, format and design, none of which is considered in the usual readability tests, also greatly influence the ease with which students read a book. These and many additional features, such as a glossary, have been carefully prepared to ensure maximum student comprehension.

Disclaimer

The contents of this edition are correct and contemporary, as of the publication date. Because the law is constantly developing and is slightly different in each province, this edition should not be used as a legal handbook. A reader experiencing legal difficulty should consult a lawyer.

Contents

Acknowledgements   vii
Preface   vii
Overview   vii
Chapter Structure   viii
Understanding a Case Citation   viii
Report Series   ix

Unit 1 The Law, the Individual, and the State   *1*

1 **An Introduction to Law**   *2*
   The Functions of Law   *3*
   The Classes of Law   *6*
   Substantive and Procedural Law   *7*
   The Rule of Law   *8*
   Fundamental Justice   *12*

2 **The Development of Canadian Law**   *18*
   The Sources of Our Law   *18*
   Differences Between the Common Law
      and the Civil Law Systems   *23*
   The Lawmaking Process Today   *25*
   Lawmaking: The Judicial Process   *37*

3 **Civil Rights**   *42*
   The Source of Civil Rights and Freedom   *43*
   Is There a Limit to Our Rights?   *46*
   Civil Rights and the *Charter*   *47*
   The *Charter* — A Final Comment   *60*

4 **An Introduction to Criminal Law**   *64*
   The Basic Elements of a Crime   *65*
   Parties to the Crime   *75*
   The Presumption of Innocence and the Burden
      of Proof   *77*

5 **Criminal Procedure: Before the Trial**   *84*
   Types of Offences   *86*
   Police Powers   *87*
   Powers of Search   *95*
   Procedures Following Arrest   *99*

6 **Criminal Procedure: The Trial**   *106*
   Starting the Trial Process   *107*
   Rights of the Defendant at Trial   *108*
   The Procedure for Trying Indictable Offences   *108*

The Procedure for Trying Summary Conviction
Offences   *123*
Young Offenders   *124*

7   **Criminal Offences**   *133*
Offences against the Public Order, Part II   *134*
Offences against the Administration of Law and Justice,
Part III   *136*
Sexual Offences, Public Morals and Disorderly Conduct,
Part IV   *137*
Offences against the Person and Reputation, Part VI   *140*
Offences aginst the Rights of Property, Part VII   *153*
Wilful and Forbidden Acts in Respect of Certain Property,
Part IX   *158*
Drug Offences   *159*

8   **An Introduction to Defences**   *170*
The Incapacity of Young Children   *171*
Insanity   *172*
Automatism   *175*
Intoxication   *176*
Duress or Compulsion   *177*
Self Defence   *179*
Defence of Property   *179*
Necessity   *180*
Mistake of Fact; Mistake of Law   *180*
Double Jeopardy   *181*

Unit 2   **The Law and Private Relationships**   *188*

9   **Human Rights**   *190*
Prejudice and Discrimination   *191*
Human Rights Legislation   *194*
The Complaint Process   *200*
Affirmative Action — Cure and Prevention   *203*
Human Rights Legislation and the *Charter of Rights
and Freedoms*   *204*

10   **Private Wrongs: Torts**   *211*
Intentional Torts   *213*
Negligence   *221*
Strict Liability   *229*
Additional Types of Torts   *231*
Occupier's Liability   *237*

11   **Civil Procedure and the Civil Courts**   *246*
Young People and Civil Procedure   *247*
Before Bringing an Action   *248*
The Civil Courts   *249*

        Bringing a Civil Action   253
        Insurance against Civil Liability   263

12 An Introduction to Contracts   267
    Forms of Contracts   268
    Necessary Elements   269
    Offer and Acceptance   269
    Consideration   278

13 Contracts: Capacity, Consent, and Legal Purpose   288
    Legal Capacity   289
    Genuine Consent   296
    Legal Purpose   303

14 Completing the Contract   316
    Privity of Contract   317
    Discharge of Contract   321
    Breach of Contract   326
    Remedies for Breach   329
    The *Statute of Frauds*   332

Unit 3   The Law and the Family   340

15 Forming the Family Unit   342
    Engagement   343
    Creating a Valid Marriage   345
    After the Wedding   352
    Cohabiting Couples   354
    Domestic Contracts   356

16 Children and Their Parents   364
    The Legal Rights of Children   365
    The Legal Rights of Parents   373
    Adoption   378

17 Ending the Relationship   387
    Separation Agreements   388
    Separation and Provincial Legislation   390
    Divorce   397
    Annulment   402
    Ending the Common Law Relationship   403
    Violence in the Family   405

18 Wills and Inheritance   413
    The Law of Wills   415
    Provision for Dependants   421
    The Law of Intestacy   424
    Executors and Administrators   426

Unit 4 The Law and the Marketplace 434

19 Consumer Law 436
 The Sources of Consumer Law 437
 Consumer Problems and Legal Remedies 442
 The Prevention of Consumer Problems 449
 Buying on Credit 454

20 The Law of Bailment 468
 Creating a Bailment 469
 Taking Care of Bailed Property 469
 The Common Law Rules 470
 Legislation and Bailment 478
 Contracts and Bailment 481

21 The Law of Real Property 488
 The Meaning of Real Property 489
 Ownership of and Title to Real Property 490
 Concurrent Ownership 492
 Other Interests in Land 492
 Protecting Interests in Land — Registration Systems 494
 Restrictions on the Use of Property 496
 Transferring Title to Land 498

22 Landlord and Tenant Law 511
 Lease and Tenancy 512
 Residential *versus* Commercial Tenants 513
 The Sources of Landlord-Tenant Law 514
 The Rights and Responsibilities of Residential Landlords and Tenants 516
 Terminating the Lease 524
 Rent Review and Rent Control 527

Unit 5 The Law and The Workplace 532

23 Employment Relationships and the Law 534
 The Employment Contract 534
 Individual Bargaining and Employment Relationships 536
 Employer and Employee 536
 Principal and Agent 552
 Independent Contractor and Client 554

24 Collective Bargaining 561
 The Development of Collective Bargaining 562
 The Collective Bargaining Cycle 563

Glossary 582
Index 592
Credits 598

Acknowledgements

To all of those people who contributed time, effort, guidance, ideas, encouragement and patience, a sincere thank you. Without you, our task would have been impossible.

Preface

The study of law in Canadian secondary schools has been consistently popular in recent years. Students recognize the daily impact of law on their lives and wish to acquire greater knowledge and skill. With this in mind, we have written a text for senior secondary students across the country. An effort has been made to include those topics which have relevance to the students' lives both now and in the near future. Hypothetical situations and case illustrations have been chosen for their relevance to the needs and interests of the students, and attention has been paid to creating a text with national scope. Our federal system of government designates many areas of law as provincial concerns. Therefore, in writing this text, those principles which are common to all jurisdictions are discussed, and provincial variations are mentioned. It was not possible to canvass the law in all jurisdictions. A serious attempt to avoid excessive focussing on the law of one province has been made.

Overview

Introduction to Canadian Law was written with a one-year course in mind. The text is divided into five units each dealing with a specific type of socio-legal relationship:

Unit I   The Law, the Individual, and the State
Unit II   The Law and Private Relationships
Unit III   The Law and the Family
Unit IV   The Law and the Marketplace
Unit V   The Law and the Workplace

Chapters 1, 2, and 3 of Unit I should definitely be examined first because they introduce the student to many important principles and concepts of law upon which our system of law is founded. The content of these chapters should be thoroughly grasped before the student is introduced to more specific areas of law.

The remaining chapters of the book and units need not be examined in any particular order. However, certain chapters logically follow one another and form mini-units of study. For example, criminal law is the subject of chapters 4 to 8, contract law is discussed in chapters 12 to 14 and chapters 10 and 11 examine civil procedure and torts.

Chapter Structure

The text of each chapter presents the facts and concepts essential to a law course. It also includes numerous examples, case applications and discussion questions. These are integrated so as to involve the students, to motivate them and to give them immediate practice in applying what they have learned.

At the end of each chapter is an applications section intended to provide sufficiently diverse material to meet the various needs and abilities of the students. Most chapters include four types of activities:

1. *Summarizing Your Reading*
Numerous, detailed questions provide a notetaking guideline for students, and serve as a test review of important facts, principles and concepts.
2. *Discussing Key Issues*
Challenging discussion questions broaden the scope of the material presented in the text and ask students to examine the policy or the reasons for law.
3. *Projects and Activities*
These suggest various areas in which students may expand their knowledge of the type of law discussed in the chapter. It is not intended that all students will do all the suggested projects and activities.
4. *Resolving Cases*
Cases are provided for students to acquire a firmer grasp of the principles, and to apply their knowledge of legal facts and principles to real situations. These are intended to give students practice in developing logical and well-reasoned answers.

Understanding a Case Citation

The decisions of courts in particular cases are extremely important to our legal system. A variety of report series exists across the country to record these decisions. It is very useful for every student of law to understand how to read the case citations contained in the reports. The following is an example of a criminal law case citation:

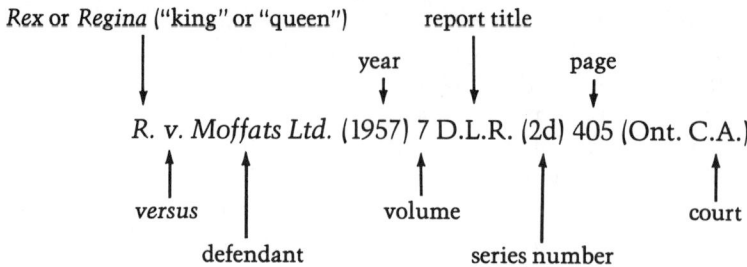

The following is an example of a civil law case citation:

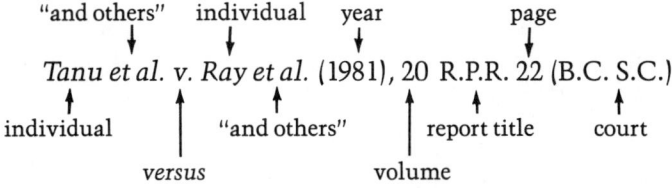

Report Series

The following list represents the report series from which the cases in the text have been taken.

A.C.W.S.	All Canada Weekly Summaries
A.R.	Alberta Reports
All E. R.	All England Reports
Alta. L. R.	Alberta Law Reports
B.C.L.R.	British Columbia Law Reports
C.C.C.	Canadian Criminal Cases
C.C.L.T.	Canadian Cases on the Law of Torts
C.H.R.R.	Canadian Human Rights Reporter
C.L.L.C.	Canadian Labour Law Cases
C.L.L.R.	Canadian Labour Law Reports
C.L.R.B.R.(N.S.)	Canadian Labour Relations Board Reports (New Series)
C.P.R.	Canadian Patent Reporter
C.R.	Criminal Reports
C.R.D.	Charter of Rights Digest
C.R.N.S.	Criminal Reports New Series
D.L.R.	Dominion Law Reports
M.P.R.	Maritime Provinces Reports
N.B.R.	New Brunswick Reports
Nfld. & P.E.I.R.	Newfoundland and Prince Edward Island Reports
N.R.	National Reporter
N.S.R.	Nova Scotia Reports
O.H.R.C.	Ontario Human Rights Commission
O.R.	Ontario Reports
O.W.N.	Ontario Weekly Notes
Q.B.	Queen's Bench (British report series)
R.F.L.	Reports of Family Law
R.P.R.	Real Property Reports
S.C.	Supreme Court
S.C.R.	Supreme Court Reports
S.R.	Saskatchewan Reports
W.W.R.	Western Weekly Reports

UNIT 1

The Law, the Individual, and the State

1. An Introduction to Law
2. The Development of Canadian Law
3. Civil Rights
4. An Introduction to Criminal Law
5. Criminal Procedure—Before the Trial
6. Criminal Procedure—The Trial
7. Criminal Offences
8. An Introduction to Defences

1

An Introduction to Law

> The Functions of Law
> The Classes of Law
> Substantive and Procedural Law
> The Rule of Law
> Fundamental Justice

Law is such a major part of our everyday lives that we cannot possibly escape from it. In fact, you probably already know a great deal about the law. Newspapers, magazines, television, and experience all help to educate us about the law and our legal system. For example, do you know at what age you can do the following?

1. get your driver's licence
2. legally drink alcoholic beverages
3. quit school
4. leave home
5. vote in a federal or provincial election

You may well know the answers to some or even all of these questions, because they relate to areas of law that might affect your life right now or in the near future. Although you may never have thought about it, you already have a head start on your study of law. As you read the chapters in this text, you will discover a great deal more about the law and its effect on your life and on the society in which you live.

Figure 1-1 Which of the signs set out rules which maintain order and regulate our conduct?

The Functions of Law

What would happen if there was no law? You might enjoy imagining a world of total freedom where everyone gets to do exactly as he or she pleases, but let's consider this situation further and examine an hour without law.

You decide to go skiing with some friends. You borrow your parent's car and head off looking forward to a great day on the slopes. Unfortunately, just as you drive out of your neighbourhood, you are involved in a huge traffic jam. Motorists are not obeying traffic lights, stop signs, or any other rule of the road. Drivers honk their horns furiously. You can see several cars that are badly battered. "Where are the police?" you wonder. Then you remember: if there are no laws to enforce, there is no need for the police.

So much for your skiing trip! You'll be lucky to get yourself and the car out of this mess in one piece.

Figure 1-2 Knowing and following the rules helps make a game more enjoyable.

In many situations, individuals are able to work things out between themselves, out of a desire to be fair and helpful. But as situations grow more complex, or greater numbers of people are involved, rules providing guidelines for the interaction of people are essential. For instance, have you ever tried to play a game with someone who did not know the rules? What happened? Or think about what happens in a game when a player ignores the rules. It is the law that sets out these rules governing human interaction. Law is therefore necessary to maintain order and to regulate the way in which we live and conduct ourselves. The many functions of law are examined in detail below.

Regulates Conduct

Although the main function of law is to regulate the conduct of individuals, businesses, and governments, it should be kept in mind that this regulation is not always negative. That is, the law does far more than forbid us to do certain things or restrict our activities.

Avoids or Settles Disputes

First, the law helps us to avoid or settle disagreements. It is a problem-solving tool. For example, the law sets out rules for making and enforcing agreements. These rules are called *contract law*. When you buy a new car, the contract of sale will set out the terms of the agreement, such as method of payment, the price of the car, optional equipment included, warranties, and so forth. The written contract will probably follow a certain format which, from experience, car dealers know the courts will consider valid. In this way the seller uses knowledge of the law to avoid disputes.

However, misunderstandings over the exact terms of the contract may still arise. Perhaps your understanding was that the car included an AM/FM radio, but when you receive the car, the radio is AM only.

If you and the dealer cannot settle the dispute, you can go to court and ask a judge to interpret the contract. In this way the law helps you to settle a disagreement.

Contracts of sale, employment contracts, and service contracts are an important part of our everyday lives. It is therefore extremely useful for us to know about the rules for making a valid contract that a court will enforce.

Sets Out Rights and Obligations

Another function of law is to set out rights and obligations between individuals and between the government and its citizens. *Family law*, for instance, establishes the obligations that parents have to their children, such as the duty to support them. It also sets out the rights and obligations between spouses. *Labour law* sets out the rights and duties that exist between employers and employees; for instance, the right of employees to form unions. *Tax law* obligates people and businesses to pay a certain amount of their earnings each year to the government. The ***Charter of Rights and Freedoms*** limits the authority of the government to make laws that would violate certain rights of the individual.

Provides Remedies

The law also gives us remedies if our rights are violated. For example, every province and territory in Canada has **human rights legislation** which protects people from various forms of discrimination. If a person has been illegally discriminated against, the legislation tells that person how to go about seeking a remedy and what compensation is available.

Maintains Order and Provides Protection

Criminal law serves the purpose of maintaining order and protecting the public. This area of law prohibits certain types of conduct, among them murder, theft, assault, and impaired driving. Criminal law also sets out penalties, such as fines and imprisonment, for people who are found guilty of breaking the law.

Sets up the Structure of the Government

A very important function of the law is to set up the structure of our government. *Constitutional law* establishes the form of our government and assigns powers and duties to the various branches of government.

Directs How to Make Laws

Perhaps most importantly, there is an area of law which regulates the making of laws. As you will learn in the next chapter, the process by which a **statute** is enacted (a law is passed by the government) is regulated by law.

As you can see, laws play a large part in our lives, even though we may not be aware of them. Given the many functions of law, is it possible to come up with a single definition of law?

—Can you try to define "law"? How is law different from the rules of a club to which you belong or the rules of your favourite sport? How is it the same?

The main difference between law and the other rules we live by is that laws are made by our governments—federal, provincial, and municipal—and by our courts. In other words, law can be defined as those rules made and enforced by government and the courts which cannot be broken without a penalty.

The Classes of Law

Since the law covers such a wide range of human concerns, it may be useful to classify the different areas of law. The two main classes into which law is most often divided are **public** and **private** law. Figure 1-3 indicates some of the types of law in these two classes.

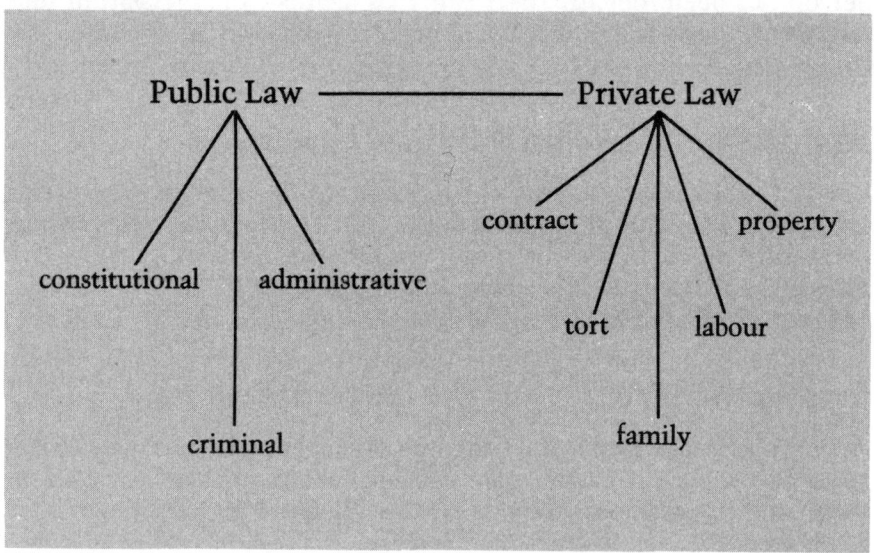

Figure 1-3 Types of Public Law and Private Law

Public Law

Public law deals with the relationships between government and individuals, and among the various branches of government. Another way of defining public law is to say it always concerns the public in general or the public interest.

Under public law, there are three types of law: constitutional, administrative, and criminal law. Constitutional and criminal law were defined earlier in this chapter. It should be noted that criminal law is considered to be public law both because the federal government decides what conduct is prohibited and because the public has an interest in preventing and controlling crime.

Administrative law concerns the activities of various government agencies, such as the provincial Workers' Compensation Boards or the federal Environmental Protection Board. The laws which set up and regulate such boards, together with their decisions, make up the body of administrative law.

Private Law

Private law is also called **civil law**. In contrast to public law, it concerns only the interests of private individuals. Some of the types of law that fall under this classification have been discussed earlier: contract law, family law, and labour law. *Tort law* is a type of private law that defines private wrongs and gives remedies to those who have been injured by the intentional or negligent actions of others. That is, if you are hurt in a car accident because of the negligence of another person, the law says that if you can prove the negligence in court, you are entitled to compensation for your injuries.

Another type of private law is *property law*. The rules about how to buy a house, how to obtain a mortgage, and what happens to the house when you die are just a few of the areas covered by property law.

Substantive and Procedural Law

Each type of law can be further divided into substantive and procedural. *Substantive law* consists of the actual rights and obligations to which each of us is subject. *Procedural law* sets out the methods by which these rights and obligations are enforced. For example, recent federal legislation gave certain homeowners the right to receive a grant of money for the purpose of insulating their homes. The method of applying for the grant—the forms to be filled out, deadlines for applying, and so forth—fall under procedural law. On the other hand, the rules that describe who is eligible for the grant, and what kind of work the grant covers fall under substantive law.

Many other types of law not mentioned here will be discussed in the following chapters. As you learn about each type, remember to note whether it falls under public or private law. Also analyze whether the rules discussed for each type are procedural or substantive law.

The Rule of Law

At the beginning of this chapter, you read about a world without law. Recall that total chaos prevailed. To prevent such chaos, our society recognizes and uses an important legal principle: the **rule of law**. This principle is referred to in the preamble to the *Charter of Rights and Freedoms*:

> **Whereas Canada is founded upon principles that recognize the Supremacy of God and the rule of law...**

Many legal writers and judges have tried to define the rule of law. We can summarize their efforts briefly in the following four points:

1. Individuals in society must recognize and accept that law is necessary for the regulation of society.
2. People are governed by law and not by arbitrary power.
3. The law applies equally to all members of society, including the government.
4. There must be a procedure for changing the law in a peaceful and orderly fashion.

Acceptance of Law

There is very little point in passing a law that cannot be enforced. Enforcement of the law depends on acceptance by a majority of the members of society of the need for law in general, and of the need for a particular law.

—Can you imagine what might happen if a law were passed tomorrow that made it a crime to smoke tobacco?
—Is it likely that this law could be enforced? Explain your answer.

In order for society to accept and abide by a given law, it must be seen as fair. When asked about the law making smoking of tobacco illegal, you probably thought, "But that's not fair!" The freedom to pursue our activities as long as they do not unreasonably interfere with others is something we all value; to take away this freedom seems very unjust.

Laws generally reflect the values and moral attitudes of society. Some laws do so more directly than others. For instance, a law restricting gambling gives greater evidence of the values of society than a law requiring motorists to be licensed to drive. If a law strays too far from the values of a majority of the members of society, it runs the risk of being seen as an unfair law, and becomes unenforceable.

Figure 1-4 What values of society are discussed in this article? Do you feel that raising the drinking age would decrease the number of drinking drivers? What, in your opinion, would be effective ways of dealing with such drivers?

Why raise drinking age?

It would be pointless, and unfair, to raise the legal drinking age from 19 to 21 at this stage. A majority of the public would favor such a change, according to a recent Gallup Poll. But there's no persuasive evidence that it would be an effective way to combat the problem of drunken driving.

For one thing, 19- and 20-year-olds aren't the age group where the problem of drinking and driving is most acute. The largest number of traffic accidents involving alcohol in Ontario occurs among drivers aged 25 to 34. Drivers in the 21-24 age group have the second-highest number of alcohol-related accidents. Those aged 35 to 44 have the third-highest. The 19-and 20-year-olds trail behind.

It's also unlikely that raising the legal age would effectively deter 19- and 20-year-olds from drinking. Much of the drinking in this age group occurs not in bars but at private parties, where it is virtually impossible for any authorities to enforce the age restriction.

For a law to be respected, it must be seen as generally fair and sensible. But in a society that treats them as adults in virtually every other way, many people who are 19 or 20 would be unlikely to accept that there's any harm in drinking alcohol on private premises. After all, they are by that age considered mature enough to vote, to get married, to drive, to serve in the armed forces — what's the logic or fairness of treating them as children only with regard to alcohol?

Practical experience doesn't confirm that this approach would be effective. In 1979, Ontario raised the legal drinking age from 18 to 19 — but the number of alcohol-related accidents involving 18-year-olds didn't go down. In 1978, when they could drink legally, there were 1,891 such accidents; in 1979, when they couldn't, there were 1,920.

That single experience isn't necessarily the final word on the subject. But until there is some persuasive reason to believe that raising the drinking age is necessary and would do some good, that approach shouldn't be pursued.

Rather, the emphasis in the battle against drinking and driving should be on education, detection and punishment.

People need to be educated to recognize driving under the influence of alcohol as a profoundly antisocial act, one that claimed 1,275 lives and injured 35,360 Canadians in 1981.

People need to be made to feel — through increased use of police spot checks — that they are likely to be caught if they do drink and drive.

And they need to be made to feel — through the imposition of tougher penalties on people convicted of drunken driving — that the consequences of being caught are too unpleasant to risk.

—What is a "value"?
—Can you think of other laws that directly reflect the values of our society? Explain your answer.

AN INTRODUCTION TO LAW 9

Government by Law

No one in our society has the authority to take away rights or impose obligations except in accordance with law. In other words, we do not allow government officials to exercise *arbitrary* or unlimited power. They must act according to the law; that is, we in Canada have a right to **due process of law**. The *Canadian Bill of Rights* states:

> 1. It is hereby recognized and declared that in Canada there have existed and shall continue to exist without discrimination by reason of race, national origin, colour, religion, or sex, the following human rights and fundamental freedoms, namely,
>   (a) the right of the individual to life, liberty, security of the person and enjoyment of property, and the right not to be deprived thereof except by due process of law.

This is a basic principle of justice that many of us probably expect without even thinking about it. However, there have been attempts to violate it. Consider the following case:

Roncarelli v. Duplessis [1959] S.C.R. 121

In the 1940s, there was considerable friction between persons in the religious group known as Jehovah's Witnesses and the Roman Catholic population in Québec. The Jehovah's Witnesses attempted to spread their beliefs through the distribution of periodicals and word of mouth. As a result, there were many violent confrontations between Witnesses and Québec Catholics. In the mid-40s, the Québec government stepped in to stop what it considered an insult to the Catholic population. Almost 1000 Witnesses were arrested under municipal by-laws for selling their publications without a licence.

Roncarelli was a well-respected restaurant owner in Montréal who was also a Jehovah's Witness. His restaurant had been licenced for over thirty-four years to sell alcohol. Roncarelli was able to put up bail for almost 400 of the arrested Witnesses.

Maurice Duplessis was the Premier and Attorney-General of Québec at that time. When he was informed of Roncarelli's activities by the Liquor Commission, he ordered that Roncarelli's licence be cancelled. The liquor legislation stated that licences could be cancelled at the Commission's discretion. Roncarelli sued Duplessis for damages for improperly cancelling his licence and for his loss of business.

The court found that the purpose of cancelling the licence was to stop the activities of the Witnesses, to punish Roncarelli, and to warn others that they would be stripped of privileges if they were involved with the Witnesses.

The Supreme Court of Canada held that Duplessis' action was a "gross abuse of legal power expressly intended to punish him [Roncarelli] for an act wholly irrelevant to the statute." Roncarelli was awarded $33 123.53 in damages.

—**Why do you think the court held Duplessis' action to be a "gross abuse of power"?**

Equal Application of the Law

It is easy to understand what is meant by the equal application of the law—no one, not even governments or government officials, is above the law. In other words, the law applies equally to everyone, regardless of his or her position in society. This is a basic principle of justice. Consider this situation: your parents have rules about the penalty that will be imposed if you or your sister break curfew. If you both come in late one night and only you are punished, you will likely feel that your parents are being very unjust.

You're grounded!

Figure 1-5 Would you feel that the principle of equal application of the law was being followed if this happened to you?

—**Can you give any examples where the law does not seem to have been applied equally? Is this the fault of the law? How can you explain this occurrence?**

Procedure for Change

The final point in our definition of the rule of law is that there must be a method for the peaceful and orderly *reform* (change) of the law. Reform is necessary to keep the law alive and flexible, so that it may serve the society for which it is designed. For instance, with the rapid technological change that has been occurring in our society, new crimes have been developed. Computer fraud is one crime unheard of only a few years ago. Society needs to be protected from new crimes, and the law must be able to adapt to these new situations.

Similarly, in 1976, the federal government abolished the death penalty because it felt that this law no longer reflected the values of society. While this topic remains a controversial one, it is an important example of the ability of the law to adapt.

—What do you think the average citizen can do to help change the law?

Fundamental Justice

A legal principle equal in importance to the rule of law which our society recognizes is that legal proceedings which decide the rights or obligations of individuals must follow the principles of **fundamental** or **natural justice**. Briefly, these rules are as follows:

1. Everyone has the right to be heard, in other words, to have "a day in court".
2. Everyone has the right to be treated with impartiality by people free of bias.

These rules were developed by the courts to apply to the courts themselves. Their purpose is to protect the individual against abuses of **judicial** (judges') **authority**. Today, the rules of fundamental justice apply not only to the courts, but also to **quasi-judicial** bodies. Examples of the latter are the government boards or agencies which make decisions affecting individual rights and obligations, such as the Unemployment Insurance Commission and the Workers' Compensation Board.

The Right to be Heard

The exact extent of the rules of fundamental justice depends upon the nature of the right in question. For example, in a criminal case where a person's liberty is at stake, the right to be heard includes the right to be given **notice** of the hearing, the right to appear in person to make a defence, the right to *counsel* (a lawyer), and the right to cross-examine witnesses. On the other hand, where a less important right is under consideration, a person may only have the right to notice and the right to submit a written argument. The general rule is that every individual has the right to what seems fair under the circumstances. Consider the following case:

Re Nicholson and Haldimand–Norfolk Regional Board of Commissioners of Police (1979) S.C.R. 111

Nicholson had been a police constable for fifteen months when he was dismissed without being given any reasons. Regulations under the Ontario *Police Act* provided a procedure for dismissing constables who had served more than the eighteen-month probationary period. Regular constables were entitled to a hearing and could appeal the decision. Probationers had no such rights under the *Act*.

The Supreme Court of Canada held that the rules of natural justice applied and that Nicholson was entitled to be told why he was being fired and to respond orally or in writing to the charges.

Although the rules of fundamental justice were developed by the courts, today there are many statutes which cover specific situations. The *Police Act* discussed above, for example, sets out the procedure that has to be followed before a police constable who has worked beyond the probationary period can be dismissed. In addition, there is legislation intended for general situations. The *Canadian Bill of Rights* states:

> **No law in Canada shall...**
> **(2) (e) deprive a person of the right to a fair hearing in accordance with the principles of fundamental justice for the determination of his rights and obligations.**

The *Charter of Rights and Freedoms* also guarantees everyone fundamental justice:

> **7. Every one has the right to life, liberty and security of the person and the right not to be deprived thereof except in accordance with the principles of fundamental justice.**

The phrase "life, liberty and security of the person" is open to interpretation by the courts to some degree. For example, if the death penalty were ever re-enacted, the rules of fundamental justice would have to be followed before a person's life could be taken. "Liberty" refers to the *physical* liberty of the person, at the very least. That is, before a person can be imprisoned, the principles of fundamental justice must be followed. "Security of the person" likely refers to interference with a person's physical integrity. A decision to operate on a person without that person's consent, for instance, would have to be made following the rules of fundamental justice.

Cross-examination blocked
Wrong to cut off hearing, judge rules

By KIRK MAKIN

A Provincial Court judge was wrong in cutting short a preliminary inquiry after examining in his chambers statements an accused man allegedly made to police, a Supreme Court of Ontario judge has concluded.

Mr. Justice John G. White said further that it was "a fundamental breach of fairness" for Provincial Court Judge A. E. Charlton to refuse to let a defence lawyer cross-examine Crown witnesses about statements.

Judge White quashed committals for trial on 20 robbery charges against Donald Charrier and ordered Judge Charlton to resume the preliminary inquiry "forthwith and as a matter of high priority."

He instructed the judge to "comply with the basic requirements of conducting a fair hearing, including affording to defence counsel the right to cross-examine Crown witnesses."

The purpose of the preliminary inquiry, held last January in Newmarket, was to determine whether there was enough evidence to send Mr. Charrier to trial.

A voir dire (a trial within a trial) had just been held over the admissibility of the statements when Judge Charlton ended the hearing.

Judge Charlton himself had decided they would be introduced as exhibits at the hearing, recessed the hearing so he could read them in his chambers, and returned to the court to say he had decided there was enough evidence to commit Mr. Charrier to trial on all 20 counts.

Judge White noted that the Provincial Court judge introduced the statements "without so much as a proffering of those statements by the Crown as part of the Crown's case, and without affording the accused or his counsel an opportunity to cross-examine the witnesses who gave evidence as to the making of those statements by the accused."

Figure 1-6 Why did the Supreme Court of Ontario overturn the decision of the provincial court judge?

Impartiality

As we have said, everybody has the right to have his or her rights and obligations determined impartially by someone free of bias. Whether a case is heard by a judge or a judge and jury, the rule of **impartiality** is very important. This means, for instance, that a juror cannot know the accused in a criminal trial, and that the juror should not have formed an opinion of guilt or innocence before the facts are presented. It also means that a judge or juror cannot have a personal interest in the results of a particular case. For instance, a judge hearing an application to rezone a large area of land from agricultural to commercial use would have a **conflict of interest** if he or she owned a small farm within the area, and so could not give an impartial decision in the case.

A principle that goes hand in hand with impartiality is the independence of the judiciary. In Canada, judges in the lower courts are appointed by the provincial governments, while superior court judges are federally appointed. Once appointed to the bench, a judge is free of the influence of both the government that made the appointment and society. A judge must answer only to the law and to his or her own conscience. For these reasons, judges are appointed for life. They can be disciplined or removed from the bench for a serious breach of duty only, not because of the unpopularity of a particular decision.

The Adversarial System

The rule of impartiality is particularly important because of the method used in our courts to resolve disputes—the **adversarial system** or **process**.

Centuries ago, when two people had a dispute, the law often allowed them to fight it out in physical combat. The winner of such a trial by battle was the victor in the legal dispute. Today, people fight their battles with words, in courtrooms. The essential characteristic of the adversarial system is that two opposing sides (adversaries) put forth their case in the best possible light. The judge, an impartial referee of the "battle", decides what rules apply. If there is a jury, the jurors observe and listen in silence. Neither the jury nor the judge can question witnesses or decide whom they would like to hear. It is up to each side to plan its own case: what witnesses to call, what arguments to make, and so forth. The judge and jury must base their decisions on the evidence that the adversaries present.

Figure 1-7 In theory, the intent of the adversarial system is that the judge or jury make a decision when each adversary has had an opportunity to put forth his or her best possible case. Do you agree with this theory? Can you see any flaws in it?

SUMMARIZING YOUR READING

1. Explain what is meant by the statement, "The law is a problem-solving tool."

2. List and explain six functions of law.

3. Define "law". How is it different from other rules we live by?

4. Explain the distinction between public and private law.

5. Name and briefly define two types of law which are classified as public law.

6. Name and briefly define two types of law which are classified as private law.

7. What is the difference between procedural and substantive law?

8. List and explain the four points that summarize the rule of law.

9. What are the rules of fundamental justice? Give an example of fundamental justice in action.

10. Are the rules of fundamental justice the same in every situation? Explain.

11. Where are the rules of fundamental justice set out?

12. How does the law ensure the impartiality of judges?

13. Explain how the adversarial system works.

DISCUSSING KEY ISSUES

1. You may be surprised at how much law there is in our society. Some cultures may not need such extensive laws and may be able to rely on unwritten customs handed down from generation to generation for deciding how to manage their affairs.

   Why do you think we can't rely on custom or common sense? Why do we need so much law?

2. What is justice, in your opinion? Can you think of a situation that is (or was) legal, but that in your opinion is (or was) not morally just? On the other hand, can you think of a situation that is (or was) morally just in your opinion, but that is (or was) not legal?

PROJECTS AND ACTIVITIES

1. Clip articles about law from the newspaper and magazines. For each article, state whether the class of law is public or private, and what specific type of law it discusses.

2. Make a list of your activities for one day. How many times do you think your day was influenced by law? What classes of law and what specific types of law influenced you? How do you feel about the effect that these laws have on your life?

RESOLVING CASES

Two weeks after Stephen Dawson was born, he contracted spinal meningitis. The disease left him severely retarded, blind, almost deaf, and suffering from cerebral palsy. When Stephen was two years old, his parents placed him in a hospital where he would receive appropriate care. Eventually, it became necessary to operate to install an apparatus called a brain shunt. Its purpose was to drain fluid from Stephen's brain.

When Stephen was six years old, this shunt became blocked, and doctors wanted to operate again to repair this situation. Stephen's parents refused to consent to the operation. They argued that their son had no opportunity to lead a normal life and that he should be allowed to die with dignity. The British Columbia Association for the Mentally Retarded sought custody of the boy so that consent could be given for the operation.

— Who should be able to decide whether Stephen should have this operation: his parents, his doctors, the courts?
— If you were the judge who heard this case, what factors would you consider in deciding whether or not Stephen should have the operation?
— Which of the factors in the preceding question would you consider in the following situations?
  (a) An eighty-year-old man with a bad heart asks his family and doctors not to use any extraordinary measures to prolong his life.
  (b) A forty-year-old woman is in constant and excruciating pain from an incurable disease. She is kept alive by being "hooked up" to a machine which purifies her blood. She wants the machine disconnected.
  (c) A twenty-year-old woman lapses into a coma after taking a combination of alcohol and drugs. Her parents want the life support systems disconnected after she is declared brain-dead.
— How can you distinguish each of these situations from Stephen's case?

2

The Development Of Canadian Law

> The Sources of Our Law
> Differences Between the Common Law and Civil Law Systems
> The Lawmaking Process Today
> Lawmaking: The Judicial Process

New laws are constantly being made to deal with the rapid changes in our society. However, our legal system has a long history and many of the rules we use today were first developed hundreds of years ago. This chapter will look at the historical development of Canadian law and then closely examine lawmaking today in our legislatures and in our courts.

The Sources of Our Law

Canada actually has two legal systems. Thus, our law has come to us from two distinct sources: the **civil law system** and the **common law system**.

The Civil Law System

We shall look first at how the civil law developed, since it is the older system. Québec is the only province in Canada which uses the civil law system. This system has its roots in Roman law. In 528 A.D., the Roman Emperor Justinian decided to *codify* (systematize) the law that had developed over the many centuries of the existence of the Roman Empire. He had all the law put into one document which became known as *Justinian's Code*. From then onwards, all legal disputes anywhere in the Roman Empire had to be resolved by looking at the Code, not at any other legal document.

Justinian's Code was forgotten after the fall of the Roman Empire. However, in the 1100s, it was re-discovered. Legal scholars began to study the Code once again, and it came to influence much of their thinking about the law and legal systems.

In the early nineteenth century, Napoléon Bonaparte revised the law of France. He ordered the writing of the *Napoleonic Code*. It was based primarily on French law, but went back to Roman law as well. This Code was used in many other European countries. The legislators responsible for enacting the Québec *Civil Code* were also influenced by the Napoleonic Code.

Today, Québec has two codes of law: the Civil Code, which contains the substantive law, and the *Code of Civil Procedure*, which sets out the procedural law. These codes apply only to the lawmaking areas given to the provincial government by Canada's Constitution. Some areas of law which fall within provincial jurisdiction are civil rights and property law. Those areas which fall within the federal government's lawmaking power, such as criminal law, apply across Canada, including Québec.

Notice that the term "civil law" has been used in this text in two distinct ways. It can refer to the civil law system as used in Québec and described above. In addition, it can be used as it was in Chapter 1 to refer to private law affecting the relationship between individuals, as in tort law or contract law.

The Common Law System

The common law system is used in all of the provinces except Québec, as well as by the federal government. Indeed, this is the system used in most of the English-speaking world. The common law system originated in England in the eleventh century.

After the Romans left England in the early fifth century A.D., the country was occupied by various Anglo-Saxon tribes from northern Europe, each of which had its own customs and laws. Then in 1066 the Normans under William Duke of Normandy invaded and conquered England. To control his vast holdings, he set up a centralized government which included a court system. The King would select judges from his court. These judges would then travel from village to village to hear cases and settle disputes. At first, they applied the law

Figure 2-1 *The son of William the Conqueror, Henry I, instituted a system of travelling judges.*

of the community. In fact, one of the roles of early juries was to inform the judges of local customs. If local law did not apply to the situation, the judge could use Norman law—or common sense.

When the travelling judges returned to the King's court, they must have compared cases. Eventually they started following past decisions of their own and of other judges, instead of local custom or Norman law or common sense. If a case had facts similar to a case decided previously, the judge would use the same rule of law and give the same decision as in the earlier case. In this way, a uniform body of law, common to all of England, developed—the common law.

Over centuries, the practice of following earlier decisions became a strict rule called the doctrine of *stare decisis*, a Latin phrase meaning "to stand by former decisions". The rules developed in earlier cases which were applied in later cases were called **precedents**. Thus, the principle of *stare decisis* is also known as the **rule of precedent**.

In many ways, following precedent is common sense. Consider this example of how precedents are set in a family situation.

Viktor has just got his driver's licence and has started to use the family car frequently. His parents begin to feel that the car is never there when they need it. The family sits down together to work out some rules. This is what they decide:

Viktor can have the car one weekend-night every other weekend if he gives a week's notice of when he needs the car. He can use the car one night during the week with two days' notice. If he uses the car without permission or proper notice, his allowance gets docked.

The next year, when Anita, Viktor's sister, obtains her driver's licence, the rules agreed to for Viktor can be applied to her. In other words, the rules in Viktor's case become a precedent to be followed in Anita's case.

—**What do you think are the advantages of following precedent? What might be some disadvantages?**

Equity

While the royal courts were developing the common law, there were other bodies of law growing in other courts. The most important of these was the law of **equity**. Over time, the common law courts became too rigid. Society was changing, but the courts failed to recognize that precedents which had originally been fair no longer were. In other words, by following the rule of *stare decisis* too closely, the law had stopped developing. The common law courts were therefore limited in the kinds of remedies they would give and the types of cases they would hear. People who were dissatisfied with the courts' decisions would appeal to the King, asking for justice. The King eventually assigned the task of hearing these complaints to his chancellors, who were usually high-ranking clerics (clergymen). They were to act as the King's conscience and do what was *equitable* (just) in the circumstances. Finally, *Courts of Chancery* or *Courts of Equity* were set up. These courts were not bound by the rules of common law. Like the common law courts, however, the Courts of Chancery started following their own precedents and developed the body of law called equity. People could choose to take their complaint to either a common law court or a Court of Chancery, whichever they believed would give them the result they wanted. As mentioned, one difference between the common law and equity was the kinds of remedies available to the injured party. In a common law court, an injured person could ask only for a money award as compensation. A court of equity could order other remedies, including **specific performance**. Specific performance is a court order telling a person to do something; generally it orders a wrongdoer to compensate the injured person in some specified manner.

Your parents have just found their dream house. Their offer to purchase is accepted and everyone starts packing. A few days before the deal is supposed to close, the sellers call to say that they have changed their minds and don't want to sell the house after all. Your parents decide to sue.

—Why would money be an inadequate remedy?
—What remedy should your parents ask for?

In the nineteenth century, in England and Canada, the two court systems, common law and equity, were united. A person no longer chooses which court system to use. A single court gives both equitable and common law remedies. However, when you go to court, you must specify the type of remedy you are seeking. For example, assume that your parents in the above example asked for specific performance and not monetary damages (compensation). If a court finds that they are not entitled to specific performance, it cannot order damages instead, since your parents did not ask for that remedy.

Canon (Ecclesiastical) Law

At the time that the common law was developing, the Church had a great deal of lawmaking power over certain areas, such as matters involving the family. The Church had its own body of law, **canon** (ecclesiastical) **law**, and its own court system. In fact, canon law is an area through which Roman law influenced English law; the Christian Church, before the Reformation, was centered in Rome. Even today many of the rules regarding marriage can be traced directly to canon law.

Mercantile Law

Medieval England was a rural society whose primary occupation was agriculture. Much of the common law, therefore, concerned problems involving land. Gradually the villages and towns grew, and businesses began to develop. The common law could not deal adequately with commercial problems, so merchants set up their own courts to handle these matters. Out of these courts came much of our business law. For example, the laws concerning the sale of goods, and *bills of exchange* (such as cheques and promissory notes) developed in these early *mercantile courts*.

The Meaning of Common Law Today

Eventually, the common law courts took over the functions of the mercantile and ecclesiastical courts, so that these areas of law became part of the common law. Today, the term "common law" has three meanings. It may mean **case law**, law based on the decisions of judges, as distinct from **statute law**, laws passed by governments. It may refer to the common law system used in English-speaking countries; in this sense, it includes *all* of a country's law, both statute law and case law. Finally, the term is also used to refer to decisions of judges, which are based on common law rules rather than equitable rules.

Differences between the Common Law and Civil Law Systems

You have seen that the civil law system is based on a written code. The Québec Civil Code is legislation enacted by the Québec government. The common law, however, consists in part of case law—judge-made law. The most important court decisions are recorded in legal volumes called **reports**.

A code contains general principles, while case law consists of specific rules for particular situations. When Viktor's parents were making rules for the use of the car, they may have said, "The general rule is that you can use the car a reasonable number of times each week. What is reasonable depends on your needs and the needs of the family." If so, they would have been using the method used by the civil law system. A judge in Québec who has to make a decision will go to the Civil Code to see what general principle applies to the facts of the case.

A common law judge, on the other hand, will try to find the previous case which has facts that most closely resemble the facts of the case before the court. When the judge finds that case, he or she will take the rule which was applied in it and apply it to the case at hand. This means that the common law judge will probably look at many related cases to distinguish between them with regard to the facts. That is, the judge will look at the facts of each case individually, and if they are not the same as or very similar to those in the case before the court, the rule in the earlier similar case will not be used. Let's look again at the example with Viktor and Anita.

By the time Anita obtains her driver's licence, the family situation has changed. The family has moved to a house that is quite close to a subway line. Anita's mother has started working as a real estate agent and often needs the car at night. Also, there are now four people instead of three wanting to use the car. The facts are different from those that applied when Viktor started driving the family car. Therefore, the old rules cannot be applied in this new situation.

Since two situations are rarely exactly the same, the common law has had to continue to develop new rules or modify old ones. Thus, the common law is constantly growing and evolving.

What about case decisions under the civil law system in Québec? The Québec judge does not ignore previous court decisions. It is still useful to see how other courts have applied the general rules in cases that are similar. However, the Québec judge is not bound by precedent: the decisions in previous cases do not have to be followed. In practice, though, judges often do follow decisions in other, similar cases, since they realize that it is important for the law to be consistent.

In some ways, therefore, the two systems of law are not as different as they first seem. There is yet another point of similarity between the civil and common law systems. Although the common law system of judge-made rules was the main source of law in English-speaking regions for centuries, today **legislation** is far more important as a source of our law. You probably know that legislation consists of the statutes enacted by the federal and provincial governments. Under our parliamentary form of government, legislation generally overrides judge-made law. Therefore, whenever a statute is passed which covers an area of case law, a judge will thenceforth refer to that statute rather than to previous cases. Since statutes consist of general principles, a common law judge acts much like a civil law judge when applying a statute to a case that is before the court.

Figure 2-2 The Different Meanings of Common Law

Common law = Case law

Common Law = The legal system used in most English-speaking countries

Common law = Decisions of judges based on rules of common law, not equity

The Lawmaking Process Today

You have seen that the legal system in Canada has developed over a long period, stretching back to the days of the Roman Empire. In this section, we will take a detailed look at the lawmaking process in our legislatures and our courts today.

A **constitution** is the body of laws which sets out who has the authority to make law. It is therefore the supreme law of the country. In Canada the Constitution consists of several statutes. Chief among them are the *Constitution Act, 1867* (formerly called the *British North America Act*), and the *Constitution Act, 1982*, which contains the *Charter of Rights and Freedoms*, amendments to the statutes, and case law interpreting the statutes. In addition, we have inherited many unwritten British traditions as part of our Constitution.

On April 17, 1982, a very significant event in Canadian history took place—our Constitution was **patriated**. The British Parliament passed the *Canada Act*, giving Canada the authority to amend its own Constitution for the first time in its history.

—Examine section 38 of the *Constitution Act, 1982* and explain in your own words the procedure for amending our Constitution.

The Federal System

The *Constitution Act, 1867* sets out our basic system of government, which is a **federal system**. This means that we have two major levels of government, federal and provincial. Each level can make law within certain areas of authority or **jurisdiction**, as granted by the Constitution. As our first Prime Minister, Sir John A. MacDonald, described it, a federal system provides "a general government and legislature for general purposes with local governments and legislatures for local purposes."

The Jurisdiction of the Federal Government

The jurisdiction of the federal government to make law is set out in section 91 of the *Constitution Act, 1867*. This section established twenty-nine areas of federal jurisdiction, including the following:

(a) the public debt and property
(b) the regulation of trade and commerce
(c) the raising of money by any mode or system of taxation
(d) the postal service
(e) militia, military, and naval service and defence
(f) seacoast and inland fisheries

(g) currency and coinage
(h) weights and measures
(i) Aboriginal Peoples and lands reserved for them
(j) marriage and divorce
(k) the criminal law, except the constitution of courts of criminal jurisdiction, but including the procedure in criminal matters
(l) the establishment, maintenance, and management of penitentiaries

Section 91 does not limit the power of the federal government to the twenty-nine areas of jurisdiction specifically mentioned, however. The federal government also has **residual power**. That is, it has the authority "to make laws in areas not specifically assigned to the provincial legislatures." An example of the use of residual power is the federal government's authority over broadcasting and aeronautics. These two areas were, of course, not even dreamed of in 1867.

The Jurisdiction of the Provincial Governments

What, then, are the "subjects assigned exclusively" to the provinces? Section 92 outlines fifteen areas of provincial jurisdiction, including

(a) direct taxation within the province for the raising of revenue for provincial purposes
(b) the establishment, maintenance, and management of prisons in and for the province
(c) the solemnization of marriage in the province
(d) property and civil rights in the province
(e) the administration of justice in the province, including the constitution, maintenance, and organization of provincial courts, both civil and criminal jurisdiction, and including procedure in civil matters in these courts
(f) generally all matters of a merely local or private nature in the province

Each level of government must restrict its legislation to the areas of authority granted by the Constitution. For example, it would be unconstitutional for a province to pass a new criminal law or to set its own grounds for divorce, as these are clearly federal matters. Similarly, the federal government could not pass a law stating that all young people must attend school to the age of eighteen, because education is an area of provincial authority. The courts are responsible for striking down any legislation which is *ultra vires*, that is, "beyond the power" of the particular government in question.

Ottawa has no authority over textbooks, PM says

The federal Government has no power to force primary and secondary schools to use textbooks written and published in Canada that reflect a Canadian viewpoint, Prime Minister Pierre Trudeau says.

Education matters are under provincial jurisdiction and the federal Government cannot influence the choice of textbooks or their contents, Mr. Trudeau told the House of Commons in Ottawa yesterday.

He was responding to a question by Progressive Conservative MP James Hawkes about a national study which found little progress in the use of Canadian learning materials in elementary and secondary schools in the past 15 years.

The three-year research project, released over the weekend, found most print materials used in Canadian schools are neither written nor published by Canadians and do not reflect a Canadian point of view.

The study, a joint project of the Association of Canadian Publishers and the Canadian School Trustees Association, noted that curriculum developments through the 1970s reflected a growing emphasis on Canadian studies, but non-Canadian reading materials continue to dominate the educational system.

Figure 2-3 What would be the response of the courts if the federal government decided to pass a law concerning education?

The Jurisdiction of the Municipal Governments

Although the *Constitution Act, 1867* established two levels of government, in fact there is also a third level—municipal government. Municipalities can be cities, towns, villages, counties, or districts. These truly local governments do not have any constitutional authority. Rather, they operate under authority delegated to them by the government of the province in which they are located. Within the areas of jurisdiction granted by each province, municipalities pass rules called **by-laws** to govern certain activities.

—Why is a third level of government necessary?
—Can you list three areas of authority in which municipalities can enact by-laws?

The Parliamentary System

The federal lawmaking body in Canada is Parliament, which consists of the Queen (or the Governor-General as her representative), and two houses—the House of Commons (the lower house) and the Senate (the upper house). Each provincial parliament consists of a Lieutenant-Governor as the Queen's representative and one house, the legislative assembly or legislature.

The Governor-General

The Governor-General is appointed by the Queen on the advice of the federal Cabinet. The *Constitution Act, 1867* would seem to grant immense power to this position. In fact, the function of the Governor-General as the representative of the monarch is largely symbolic and ceremonial. The Governor-General must give *Royal Assent* to any new law passed by Parliament by signing the Act. However, he or she does not have the authority to refuse to sign an Act of Parliament.

Royal Assent to all provincial laws is given on the Queen's behalf by the Lieutenant-Governor of each province.

The Senate

The Fathers of Confederation designed the Senate with the intention of providing some measure of equal representation to the less heavily populated areas of the country. At the time, the Maritime provinces were concerned that their voice would be ineffective in the House of Commons, where representation is based on population.

Today, there are 104 seats in the Senate, apportioned in the following manner:

Figure 2-4 The Apportionment of Seats in the Senate

Ontario	24		
Québec	24		
Maritime Provinces	24	Nova Scotia	10
		New Brunswick	10
		Prince Edward Island	4
Western Provinces	24	Manitoba	6
		Saskatchewan	6
		Alberta	6
		British Columbia	6
Newfoundland	6		
Northwest Territories and the Yukon	2		

Senators are appointed by the Governor-General, on the recommendation of the Prime Minister and the Cabinet. Once appointed, they may serve indefinitely. However, they must retire at the age of seventy-five.

Proposed laws (called **bills**) can originate in the Senate, except for bills concerning money. However, the usual procedure is for a bill to pass three readings in the House of Commons before it follows the same procedure in the Senate. Senate approval is necessary before a bill can become law, but it is very seldom that the Senate rejects a bill.

—Why do you think the Senate cannot initiate a bill dealing with the expenditure of money?
—Should an appointed Senate have the power to reject a bill passed by an elected House of Commons?

SENATE   HOUSE OF COMMONS

Special Joint Committee on
SENATE REFORM

The Special Joint Committee of the Senate and of the House of Commons on Senate Reform will hold hearings to consider and report upon ways by which the Senate of Canada could be reformed in order to strengthen its role in representing people from all regions of Canada and to enhance the authority of Parliament to speak and act on behalf of Canadians in all parts of the country.

In its final report the Committee will include recommendations concerning the method of selection, powers, length of term for Senators, distribution of seats and other matters that the Committee considers relevant to the reform of the Senate.

Individuals and organizations may forward requests to appear before the Committee until July 15, and written submissions should be received by August 15. Written submissions may be made in English, in French or in both official languages. If possible, submissions should be typed on 28 cm by 22 cm paper with margins of 3 cm by 2 cm.

The Committee reserves the exclusive right of selecting the witnesses who will be invited to appear before it.

All briefs, correspondence or inquiries should be addressed to:

Joint Clerks of the Committee
Special Joint Committee on Senate Reform
Houses of Parliament
Ottawa, Ontario
K1A 0A4

Joint Chairmen
Senator Gildas Molgat
Roy MacLaren, M.P.

Figure 2-5 From time to time, it has been suggested that the Senate should be reformed or abolished. The federal government has held public hearings to examine the matter. This type of hearing allows the public to make their opinions known to the government.

The Senate fulfills two main functions. The first of these is the "fine-tuning" of bills forwarded from the House of Commons. Committees of the Senate hold hearings to listen to evidence from groups that will be affected by the proposed legislation. The Senate then conducts a clause-by-clause debate of the bill. Senators are appointed because of their experience and expertise as former cabinet ministers, former premiers, lawyers, judges, labour leaders, among others. Although the Senate rarely advocates an amendment to the principle of a bill, senators do use their experience and expertise to clarify and simplify the language of the bill.

The other major task of the Senate which has developed in recent years is the investigation of important national problems such as inflation, poverty, and unemployment, to name just a few. The reports issued after these investigations can be of great assistance to the government in making policy and developing legislation.

The provincial parliaments do not have an upper house or Senate.

The House of Commons

The House of Commons is the major lawmaking body of Parliament: most legislation originates here. All members of the House are elected by the people living in the various electoral districts called *constituencies* or *ridings*. The political party which has the greatest number of members elected to the House forms the government. The leader of this party becomes the Prime Minister. A Cabinet is selected from the party *caucus* (all of the members of that party elected to the House) to assist the Prime Minister.

The party that has the second largest number of members elected to the House forms Her Majesty's Loyal Opposition. A Speaker is elected by the House at the start of each session of Parliament. The role of the Speaker is to ensure that all members conduct themselves in the House according to established rules of procedure.

The Prime Minister and the Cabinet are the *executive members* of the government. This group is largely responsible for setting government policy, introducing legislation, and administering government departments.

Cabinet ministers are appointed by the Governor-General on the advice of the Prime Minister. Some cabinet ministers are assigned a *portfolio* making them responsible for a particular department, for example, Finance or Defence. The day-to-day running of the various government departments is carried on by trained and skilled employees of the government called *public* or *civil servants*. Senior public servants in each department keep the minister informed and offer advice, but the ultimate responsibility for the operation of the department rests with its minister, who must make regular reports to the House of Commons.

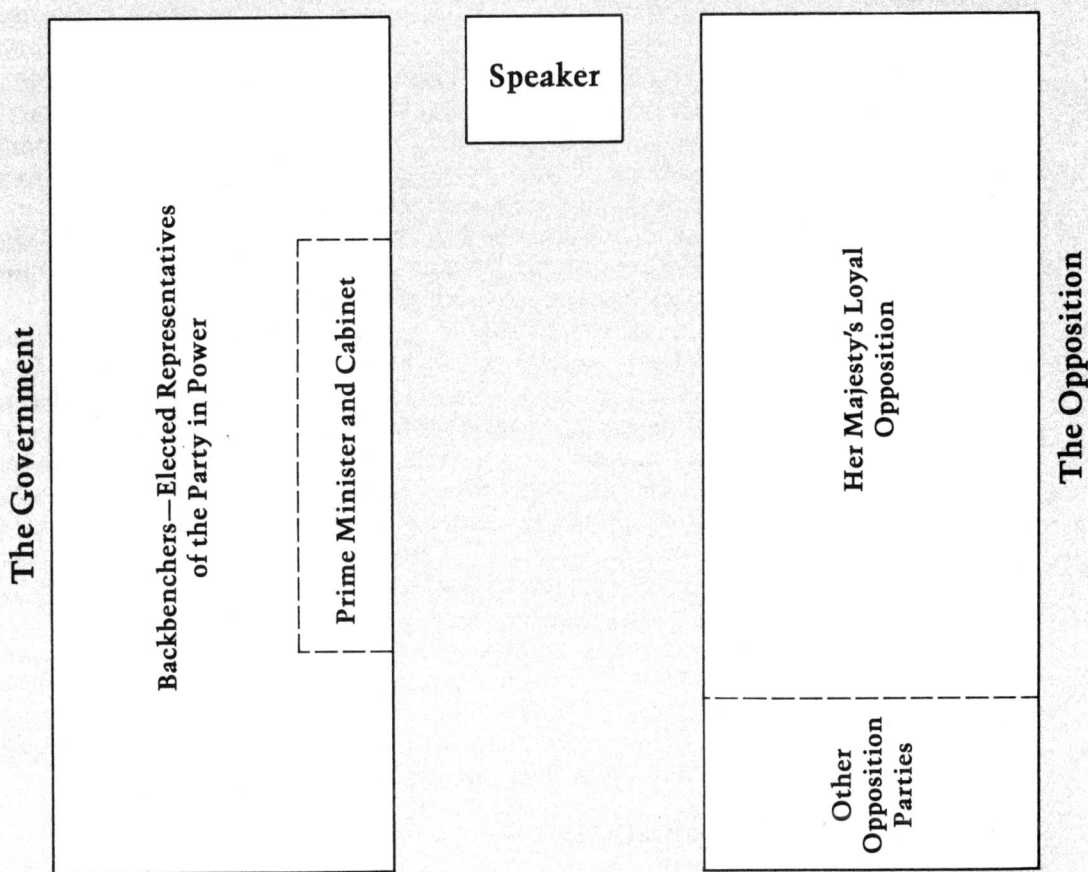

The role of the opposition parties is to be the watchdog of the government—to examine and to criticize proposed legislation carefully. In short, their function is to try to ensure the effective governing of the country.

The provincial legislatures are similar to the House of Commons. Members are elected from constituencies or ridings set up by the province according to population. The party obtaining the most seats forms the government. The leader of the government is called the Premier, and a Cabinet is selected to assist the Premier.

Figure 2-6 The Organization of the House of Commons

Passing a Statute

You will recall that a bill or proposed law can originate in the Senate as a private bill or, as is more usually the case, in the House of Commons. Any member of the House can introduce a *private member's bill* as a means of beginning a debate in the Commons about a matter of concern to that member. As you can imagine, however, unless the bill has the backing of the government or party in power, there is little chance for it to become law. Private member's bills are allowed only a very short time for debate in the House. As a result, they usually "die" before a vote is ever taken.

It is the bills introduced and backed by the government, *public bills*, that stand the greatest chance of becoming law. Let's examine the procedure for passing a hypothetical public bill.

The government decides that it is a matter of national importance to pass legislation protecting the quality of drinking water. The Cabinet minister responsible for Health and Welfare suggests that a *Safe Drinking Water Act* is necessary. The minister claims that this is an appropriate matter for the federal government to undertake, based on two factors: the federal authority to pass laws for the "peace, order and good government" of the country, and the federal jurisdiction over criminal law, which has been interpreted by the Supreme Court of Canada to include laws for the preservation of "public peace, order, security, health, and morality".

The Cabinet gives approval to the minister's proposal. Now the real work begins. The task of investigating and then drafting appropriate legislation is given to lawyers and environmental experts working for the Ministry involved. Public hearings might be held. The bill will be drafted to include at least the following principles:

1. the purpose of the *Act*
2. definitions of terms used within the *Act*—for example, what is a "contaminant"?
3. regulations and standards relating to the quality of drinking water
4. the enforcement process and penalties for a violation of the law
5. a federal/provincial cost sharing arrangement for enforcement of the *Act*

Once the bill has been drafted to the satisfaction of the Cabinet, it will be introduced in the House of Commons and given first reading. After this the bill can be printed and distributed to members of the House and the public.

When the bill comes back to the House for second reading, it is debated in principle. The House will examine such things as the need for the legislation, the feasibility of introducing a law of this nature, and the general principles outlined in the bill. A bill which passes a

Figure 2-7 After first reading, a bill is distributed and opened to public comment.

THE HOUSE OF COMMONS
STANDING COMMITTEE ON

HEALTH, WELFARE AND SOCIAL AFFAIRS

The Standing Committee on Health, Welfare and Social Affairs will be holding meetings on the subject matter of Bill C-221, An Act to Amend the Narcotic Control Act (therapeutic use of heroin).

The Committee invites organizations or individuals who are interested in the question of whether or not the therapeutic use of heroin should be permitted to submit briefs to the Clerk of the Committee by 5:00 p.m., **Monday, May 28**.

Briefs may be submitted in English, French or both official languages; preferably typed on 22 by 28 cm paper with margins of 1 by 3 cm. Public distribution of all submissions is left to the discretion of the Committee, unless otherwise requested.

All briefs, correspondence or inquiries should be addressed to:

The Clerk,
Standing Committee on Health, Welfare and Social Affairs,
House of Commons,
Ottawa, Ontario
K1A 0A6
Tel: (613) 992-3150

**DAVID WEATHERHEAD, M.P.
Chairman**

---

second reading vote has been approved in principle and goes next to committee.

Most bills go to a *standing committee* composed of members of Parliament, including members of the opposition. These members are elected at the beginning of a session of Parliament to examine all proposed legislation relating to a particular subject. In our example, a bill relating to safe drinking water might go to a standing committee on Health and Welfare, or on the Environment. The committee is responsible for debating the bill clause by clause and for hearing the evidence of witnesses. These witnesses could include environmental experts, physicians, or concerned members of the public. Amendments are proposed and voted upon. Each clause of the bill must be accepted by the committee.

The *report stage* of a bill occurs when the bill has passed through committee, and the chairperson of the committee brings it back to the House of Commons to report on the results of the examination and debate. Further amendments can be proposed and voted upon by the House.

The bill now moves to third reading. During the third reading debate, members of the House vote on the acceptance or rejection of the amended bill. A rejected bill can be sent back to committee for further amendment. A bill accepted after third reading must go through a similar procedure in the Senate.

There is an exception to this procedure, however. Bills relating to taxation stay within the House of Commons for examination and debate by the *Committee of the Whole* (all members of the House). No witnesses are called during the debate of a money bill. A bill passed by the Committee of the Whole goes directly to third reading, omitting the further amendments which can take place during the report stage.

Finally, the bill is presented to the Governor-General (Lieutenant-Governor in the provincial legislatures) for Royal Assent. At this point the bill becomes known as a statute or Act; that is, it becomes law. The statute comes into force or becomes effective in one of the following ways:

1. on a date specified in the statute
2. on the day it receives Royal Assent, or
3. on the day of *proclamation*, which is a public announcement that the bill has become a statute

The statute will indicate the method by which it will come into force.

Figure 2-8
Passing a Statute

Bill proposed	Private bill, private member's bill, or public bill
Bill drafted	Ministry lawyers and experts study proposals.
	Public hearings might be held.
	Bill drafted.
	Cabinet approves draft.

First reading of the bill	Bill presented to the House of Commons.
	Bill printed and distributed to members of the House after the first reading and to the public. No discussion at this stage, to give MPs a chance to study the bill and prepare for later debate.
Second reading of the bill	Bill debated in principle.
	If bill is not approved, drafters of the legislation must start again.
	Bill must be re-thought and re-drafted before being presented again. Or, bill may simply die and not reappear.
Bill approved in principle; goes to committee.	Committee debates each clause of the bill.
	Committee hears evidence of witnesses.
	Amendments proposed and voted on.
Report stage	Committee chairperson reports on the progress of the bill in committee to the House of Commons.
Third reading of the bill	House of Commons votes to accept or reject amended bill.
Accepted bill goes to the Senate	Senate hears three readings of the bill. Senators clarify language of the bill, and vote on whether to accept or reject it.
Bill presented to the Governor-General	Governor-General gives Royal Assent.
Bill becomes a statute, that is, a law:	a) on a date specified in the bill; or b) when it receives Royal Assent; or c) upon proclamation.

Sometimes, portions of a bill do not take effect when the new law comes into force. An important example of this is the equality rights section of the *Charter of Rights and Freedoms*. Although the *Constitution Act*, including the *Charter*, was proclaimed on April 17, 1982, there was a provision that section 15 would not take effect until April 17, 1985.

> 32. (2) Not withstanding subsection (1), section 15 shall not have effect until three years after this section comes into force.
>
> 15. (1) Every individual is equal before and under the law and has the right to the equal protection and benefit of the law without discrimination and, in particular, without discrimination based on race, national or ethnic origin, colour, religion, sex, age or mental or physical deficiency.

—Why do you think this three-year delay was provided for s. 15?

Regulations under a Statute

Statutes are worded in such a way as to convey basic principles expressed in general language. To carry out the purposes of the legislation, each statute usually includes a section near the end which authorizes the minister who will be administering the Act to make **regulations** to enforce it. Regulations deal with details that may need to be changed over time. In other words, the statute contains the general rules, while the regulations contain the detailed instructions for carrying out the rules. Although they may be very important to the people affected by the statute, regulations are made by administrators; they are not voted on by Parliament. The following section from Ontario's *Education Act* grants authority to the Minister of Education to pass regulations.

> 10. (1) Subject to the approval of the Lieutenant-Governor in Council, the Minister may make regulations in respect of schools or classes established under this Act, or any predecessor of this Act, and with respect to all other schools supported in whole or in part by public money...

The Ontario *Education Act* goes on to list thirty-three areas in which the minister is empowered to make regulations under the *Act*, including the following:

1. listing the textbooks that are selected and approved for use in schools

2. prescribing the duties of pupils
3. governing the provision of religious exercises and religious education in public and secondary schools

Statutes and regulations are published by the federal and provincial governments, and can either be purchased or found in libraries.

Lawmaking: The Judicial Process

Statute law has become increasingly important in modern times, but case law continues to play a key role in our legal system. Judge-made law remains a significant source of law. For instance, it is still valid law in areas not covered by statute, such as most of tort law and contract law.

Additionally, case law is necessary for interpreting statutes. Once a court makes a decision on the meaning of a statute, that decision becomes a precedent. Thus, the rule of *stare decisis* is still followed by our courts. The result is that lower courts are bound by the decisions of higher courts, while courts at the same level always try to follow each other's decisions. For instance, the decisions of the Supreme Court of Canada, our highest court, must be followed by every other court in Canada; the various provincial Courts of Appeal, which are the highest courts in each province, try to follow each other's decisions.

Let's take a look at an important statute that the courts will be interpreting in the coming years.

> 1. The *Canadian Charter of Rights and Freedoms* guarantees the rights and freedoms set out in it subject only to such reasonable limits prescribed by law as can be demonstrably justified in a free and democratic society.

—What are "reasonable limits"?
—What acts of government can be "demonstrably justified"?
—In fact, what does "demonstrably justified" mean?

You probably cannot give definite answers to these questions, but these are precisely the kinds of issues that courts are faced with every day. Each of the above questions will have to be answered by the Supreme Court of Canada before we can know with any certainty what section 1 of the *Charter* actually means. Interpreting the various clauses of the *Charter* will keep our courts very busy over the next few years. This task is but one example of the important role the courts fill in our legal system.

Throughout this text, you will be examining decisions made by courts as they carry out their functions. The structure of the criminal and civil courts will be examined in Chapters 5 and 11. However, you should have a general understanding of court structure as you begin your study of law.

Canadian Court Structure

The Supreme Court

The highest court in this country is the Supreme Court of Canada. This is an **appellate court**, which means that the court handles appeals, not trials. Moreover, it does not hear all appeals which are brought to it, just those which the court feels are of importance in the interpretation of law. Appeals arise in the lower courts, in cases where it is claimed that an erroneous decision has been made. A panel of Supreme Court justices hears briefs presented by lawyers, then gives a written or oral decision on a given case. Since several judges (up to nine for very important cases) hear the case, they may not agree on whether the appeal should be *allowed* or *dismissed*. However, the decision will be decided by a simple majority. Important or complicated decisions will be given in writing rather than orally. Usually one judge will be selected to write the **majority opinion**. The dissenting judges may also write their reasons for disagreeing with the majority. The majority decision becomes a precedent for all the other courts in Canada to follow when similar cases come before them.

The Federal Court

The Federal Court of Canada plays an important role in federal/provincial relations by hearing disputes among the provinces and between the provinces and Ottawa. It also deals with cases involving claims by or against the federal government, and matters dealing with taxation, trademarks, copyrights and patents, admiralty law, and aeronautics cases, among others.

The Federal Court of Canada has both an appellate and a trial division. It hears appeals from its own trials division, and from the decisions of various federal boards and commissions, such as the Canada Employment and Immigration Commission and the Canada Labour Relations Board.

Provincial Courts

Within each province, the following three levels of courts usually exist:

1. the superior or supreme court of the province, including both a trials and an appeals division
2. county or district courts
3. provincial or magistrate's courts

As you will learn later in this text, each of these levels of courts has both criminal and civil jurisdiction. The limits of their powers are set out by the *Judicature Act* of each province and by various other provincial statutes.

Specialty Courts

There are also a number of specialty courts within our legal system. Two examples of courts that fill a special function are the surrogate or probate court and the coroner's court. The surrogate court is responsible for all matters dealing with the estates of dead persons. Coroner's courts sit from time to time to inquire into any death which has occurred in unnatural circumstances and to make recommendations to the government.

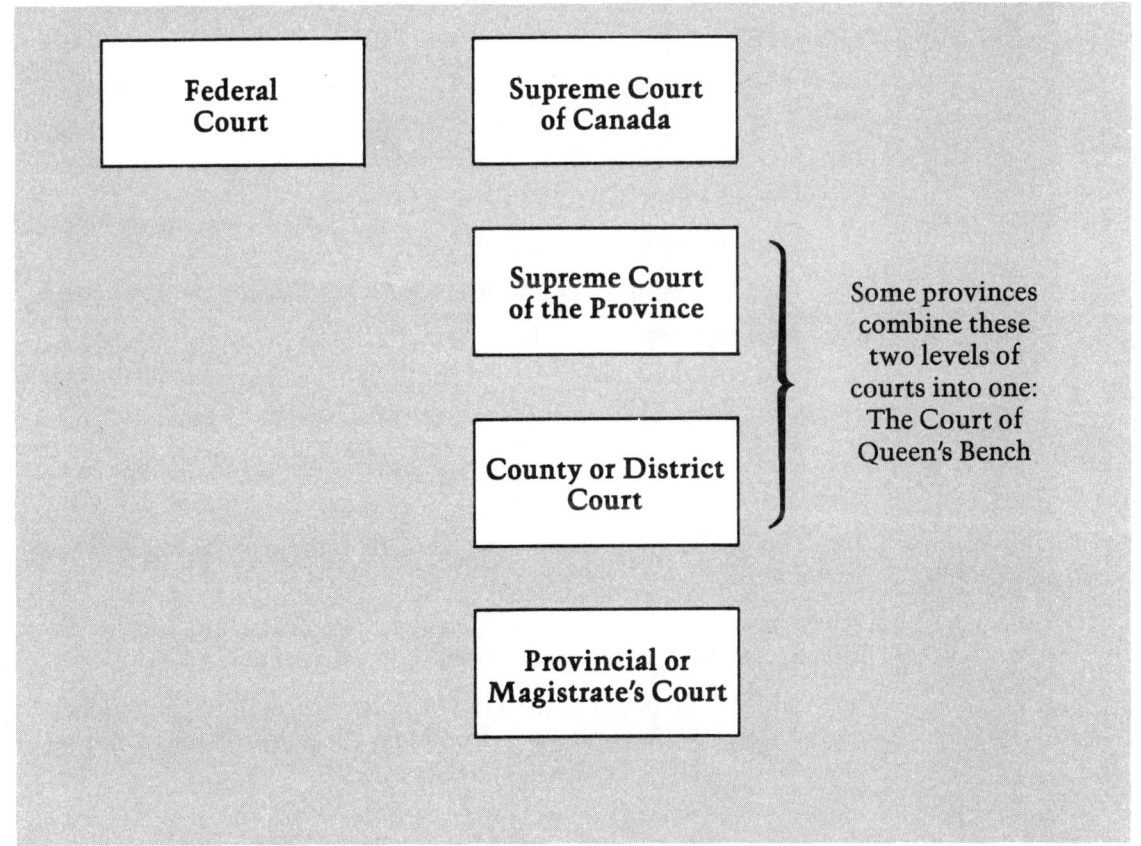

Figure 2-9 Court Structure in Canada

SUMMARIZING YOUR READING

1. Name the two systems of law that exist in Canada.

2. What does the term "common law" refer to?

3. Briefly review the development of the common law.

4. Explain the principle of *stare decisis*.

5. Briefly review the development of equity.

6. What are two historical sources of Canadian law other than equity?

7. What is the main distinction between the civil law system and the common law system?

8. Does a Québec judge use precedents?

9. What effect does statute law have on common law?

10. What is a Constitution?

11. Why is April 17, 1982 an important date in Canadian history?

12. Define "federal system of government".

13. Define "jurisdiction", and give two examples of federal jurisdiction under the *Constitution Act, 1867*.

14. What does it mean to say that the federal government has "residual power"?

15. What does *ultra vires* mean?

16. How do municipal governments fit into the federal system?

17. What elements does the federal Parliament consist of? How does this structure differ from that of the provincial legislatures?

18. What is the major function of the Governor-General?

19. What was the original purpose of the Senate? Describe the two main functions of the Senate.

20. Why is the House of Commons the main lawmaking body of Parliament?

21. What does it mean to say that the Prime Minister and the Cabinet are the executive members of the government?

22. Outline the procedure that a bill goes through in the federal Parliament before it becomes law. How does this differ from the procedure in the provincial legislatures?

23. What are regulations? How do they differ from the other two main sources of law, case law and statute law?

24. Briefly explain the interpretive role of the courts.

25. What is an appellate court? How does its function differ from that of a trial court?

PROJECTS & ACTIVITIES

1. Prepare a chart indicating the names of the following:

Federal
— Governor-General of Canada
— Prime Minister of Canada
— Leader of Her Majesty's Loyal Opposition
— Leaders of other opposition parties
— Speaker of the House
— Two cabinet ministers (and their portfolios)
— Your federal member of Parliament
— The constituency in which you live

Provincial
— Lieutenant-Governor of the Province
— Premier of the Province
— Leader of the Official Opposition
— Leaders of other opposition parties
— Speaker of the House
— Two provincial cabinet ministers (and their portfolios)
— Your member of the provincial legislature
— The constituency or riding in which you live

Municipal
— Your Municipality
— Mayor or reeve of the municipality
— Your councillor or alderman
— Your constituency or ward

2. Set up a student grievance system in your class. What rights should students have? What obligations? Include a procedure to enforce rights and obligations. Consider the following points: How can a student or teacher complain? Who decides whether the complaint is justified? Is there an appeal procedure? What penalties should there be for violating the rules? What compensation is the wronged person entitled to?

Draft your student grievance bill, debate it, and have it passed by a majority of your classmates.

3. Write a research paper tracing the patriation of Canada's Constitution. Why did the patriation process take so long? What compromises had to be made in order to achieve it?

3

Civil Rights

> The Sources of Civil Rights and Freedoms
> Is There a Limit to Our Rights?
> Civil Rights and the *Charter*
> The *Charter* — A Final Comment

Figure 3-1

Have you ever heard people say that they know their rights? Have you ever said it yourself?

When we make a statement like this, we may be referring to a type of right called a **civil right**. Civil rights and freedoms limit the power of government to act in certain areas that affect our lives.

A *right* is something guaranteed by law, such as the right of Canadian citizens to vote in elections. A statute which prevents certain Canadians from voting may violate this right. We say *may*, because as you will see in this chapter there are no *absolute* rights. All rights have certain limitations. In the case of voting, people under a certain age are not allowed to vote. Rights must also be balanced by responsibilities. A citizen has not only the right to vote, but also the responsibility to be well-informed when taking part in the democratic process by casting a ballot on election day.

Another type of right is known as a **human right**. It is important to note the distinction between civil rights and human rights. If you have been turned down for a job you really wanted and you suspect it was because of your sex, race, colour, or perhaps your religion, and not because of your qualifications for the job, your human rights may have been violated. Human rights, in general, protect us from being unfairly discriminated against by private persons, while civil rights protect us from being treated unfairly by the government. Human rights will be examined in detail in Chapter 9.

When we speak of civil rights, we also have to include civil *freedoms*. Freedoms are those things that an individual can do which cannot be prohibited by law. For instance, a statute which stated that newspapers cannot print letters critical of the government would most likely violate our freedom of expression and freedom of the press.

The Sources of Civil Rights and Freedoms

The *Charter of Rights and Freedoms*

When the *Constitution Act, 1982* was passed, Canadians gained for the first time an *entrenched Charter of Rights and Freedoms*. "Entrenchment" indicates that our civil rights are now part of our written Constitution, and that they can be changed by a constitutional amendment only. Section 38 of the *Constitution Act, 1982* states that an amendment requires the consent of two-thirds of the provinces, representing at least fifty percent of the population, as well as the approval of Parliament. You probably know that it is not always an easy task to get the various provincial governments and the federal government to agree. We can, therefore, assume that our rights cannot be lightly interfered with now that they are entrenched.

However, in section 33 of the *Charter*, there is a qualification to the guarantee of our civil rights:

> 33. (1) Parliament or the legislature of a province may expressly declare in an Act of Parliament or of the legislature, as the case may be, that the Act or a provision thereof shall operate notwithstanding a provision included in section 2 or sections 7 to 15 of this *Charter*.

Section 33 is known as the "override" clause. It allows the federal or provincial governments to enact legislation that is not subject to the *Charter*. In other words, a provincial government or the federal government may pass a statute that violates a right or freedom guaranteed by the *Charter*.

There are some limitations on the "override" clause that you should be aware of:

1. The government must expressly state, probably in the statute itself, that the *Charter* does not apply to that particular Act.
2. Section 33 applies only to those rights and freedoms found in sections 2 and 7 to 15. Other rights and freedoms are absolutely protected.
3. Legislation that operates "notwithstanding" the *Charter* is valid for up to five years only. At the end of that time, it must be re-enacted. This ensures that the legislature will have to review the statute and vote on it again.

—Why do you think section 33 was included in the *Charter*?
—Is it a good idea to have included it? Explain.
—Do you think it will be used very often? Why or why not?

The *Bill of Rights*

Prior to the passing of the *Charter of Rights and Freedoms*, the *Canadian Bill of Rights* was the written statement of our civil rights. This statute was passed by the federal government in 1960. It did not establish any new rights for Canadians, but simply recognized in statute form those traditional rights, such as freedom of speech and religion, that came to us from common law.

The *Bill of Rights* has not been *repealed* (withdrawn) and is still, therefore, a part of our law. Why, then, did we need the *Charter*? There are several reasons.

First, the *Bill of Rights* is a federal statute that applies only to the powers of and legislation passed by the federal government, not to the provinces. The *Charter of Rights and Freedoms* specifically applies to both levels of government.

Re Ward et al. and Board of the Blaine Lake School Unit No. 57 (1971) 20 D.L.R. (3d) 651 (Sask. Q.B.)

A student was suspended from school because he would not get his hair cut to comply with school board regulations about hair length for males. His parents appealed the school board's decision to the court, claiming that their son's right to freedom of expression under the *Bill of Rights* was being denied. The court ruled that school boards are authorized by provincial legislation to set regulations and, therefore, the *Bill of Rights* did not apply.

A second shortcoming of the *Bill of Rights* is that because it is not a part of the Constitution, it can be amended or repealed by a simple majority in Parliament, as any other statute can. Many people found this situation disturbing.

Third, many people were unhappy with the way the courts were using the *Bill of Rights*. The Supreme Court of Canada in particular has been very reluctant to use the *Bill of Rights* to strike down federal statutes which, some people felt, violated individual rights. In fact, in twenty years, the *Bill of Rights* was used only once to strike down a statute. This reluctance of the courts stems partly from the fact that the *Bill of Rights* is not a constitutional document. Courts are very hesitant to use one statute to void another. However, the most important reason for the courts' restrained approach is that a basic principle of our government has been the supremacy of Parliament. This principle has meant that Parliament, and not the Supreme Court of Canada, has been the highest lawmaking body in the country. If the courts have the power to strike down legislation that they believe offends certain rights, an important limitation has been put on the principle of the supremacy of Parliament. The *Constitution Act*, which includes the *Charter*, very specifically states this limitation in section 52:

> 52. (1) The Constitution of Canada is the supreme law of Canada, and any law that is inconsistent with the provisions of the Constitution is, to the extent of the inconsistency, of no force or effect.

Because the *Constitution Act* is a constitutional document, and not merely another statute, there is no reason for the courts to hesitate to use it to void statutes where they feel it is necessary.

Finally, the only action the courts can take under the *Bill of Rights* is to rule on the validity or meaning of a statute. They cannot give any other remedy, such as money damages, to a person whose rights have been violated. The *Charter* goes a step further and allows the courts to award any remedy, including money damages, they consider appropriate under the circumstances. In addition, the *Charter* provides a special remedy in section 24 for persons accused of crimes: when evidence has been obtained in a way that violates a *Charter* right or freedom (for example, by an illegal search), the courts may exclude such evidence, if "having regard to all the circumstances, the admission of it...would bring the administration of justice into disrepute."

Is There a Limit to Our Rights?

We have already mentioned that no right can exist without some limits. You have a responsibility to respect the rights of others, and doing so will often result in a limit being placed on your own freedom. Look at the situation in your classroom for a moment. In consideration of the rights of others, you should not mumble and mutter at the back of the room while a classmate or your teacher is speaking. This, of course, limits your freedom of expression, but it allows the speaker to talk without interruption and lets others in the room hear clearly what he or she is saying. Imagine how you would feel when it is your turn to speak in class if others were having their own private conversations.

The *Charter* recognizes in section 1 that rights and freedoms cannot be without limitation:

> **1. The *Canadian Charter of Rights and Freedoms* guarantees the rights and freedoms set out in it subject only to such reasonable limits prescribed by law as can be demonstrably justified in a free and democratic society.**

Thus, even if a *Charter* right or freedom appears to be violated, a court may find that the limitation is a reasonable one given the circumstances. Consider the following situations:

—The *Charter of Rights and Freedoms* guarantees "freedom of expression", yet the *Criminal Code* makes it an offence to publish "obscene material". Is this a reasonable limitation on freedom of expression? There also exist provincial censorship boards that review movies. Is it reasonable, in your opinion, to limit the freedom of expression of film-makers?

—The *Charter* guarantees a person accused of a crime the right to a fair and public hearing. Section 442 of the *Criminal Code* allows a judge to exclude the public if it would be in the interests of "public morals, the maintenance of order or the proper administration of justice." This section might be used, for example, in the case of an accused on trial for the sexual assault of a child, when the child testifies. Do you think this is a reasonable limitation on the right to a public trial?

As you can see, the courts are going to have the very difficult task of interpreting s. 1 of the *Charter* and determining what exactly is meant by "reasonable limits" and "demonstrably justified in a free and democratic society".

—What factors do you think the courts will consider in applying s. 1? Do you think they might look at such things as whether the legislation is in the public interest; for public safety, health, or morals; for national security; or for the prevention of crime?

It is far too early to tell what kind of tests the courts will use to apply s. 1. However, many of the rights in the *Charter* are also contained in the *Bill of Rights*. It is reasonable to assume that some of the case law which interpreted the meaning of rights under the *Bill* will be used in interpreting the same rights in the *Charter*. Remember, though, that the *Charter* contains rights not listed in the *Bill* and that in many instances, the *Charter* uses different terms for describing the rights contained in both. For these reasons, case law referring to the *Bill of Rights* should be used cautiously. In the end, it will be up to the Supreme Court of Canada to establish just how far the *Charter* rights go in protecting individuals.

Civil Rights and the *Charter*

You've heard the statement, "I know my rights!" Well, do you? A review of the *Charter* should help you to have a much clearer picture of your civil rights.

The *Charter* classifies our rights according to the following categories. These form the subject of the remainder of this chapter.

1. fundamental freedoms
2. democratic rights
3. mobility rights

4. legal rights
5. equality rights
6. official languages and minority language education rights
7. enforcement
8. general matters

Fundamental Freedoms

> 2. Everyone has the following fundamental freedoms:
>   *(a)* freedom of conscience and religion;
>   *(b)* freedom of thought, belief, opinion and expression, including freedom of the press and other media of communication;
>   *(c)* freedom of peaceful assembly; and
>   *(d)* freedom of association.

—Obtain a copy of the *Bill of Rights*. Examine s. 1 (c)-(f). How does the language outlining fundamental freedoms differ from that used in s. 2 of the *Charter of Rights and Freedoms*?

The fundamental freedoms guaranteed by the *Bill of Rights* are also in the *Charter*, but the language of the *Charter* is slightly more elaborate. It is unlikely that our rights in this area will change significantly under the *Charter*, however.

Freedom of Conscience and Religion

Freedom of religion in the *Bill of Rights* has been interpreted by the Supreme Court of Canada to mean freedom from the imposition of religious dogma. In other words, the religious beliefs of the majority cannot be imposed upon the minority. Freedom of religion in Canada is essentially the freedom to worship in the way you wish, or not to worship at all.

—Interview your school principal to find out what your school board's policy is on the reading of the Lord's Prayer in class. If your school board allows the Lord's Prayer to be read, what provision does it make for the various religious minorities in your school?
—What do you think freedom of conscience might mean? Why has it been added to the *Charter*?

Freedom of Expression

Section 2(b) of the *Charter* combines the *Bill of Rights* guarantees of freedom of speech and freedom of the press, and expands the language of both of these rights to reflect case law. In other words, even before the *Charter* was passed, a television news commentator had the same guarantee of freedom of expression that a newspaper journalist had. The language of the *Charter* states this explicitly, putting case law into statute form.

Freedom of Peaceful Assembly

Freedom of peaceful assembly and of association allows you, for instance, to join an organization whose purpose is to demonstrate peacefully against certain government policies with which your group disagrees.

Figure 3-2 Freedom of peaceful assembly is one of the fundamental freedoms of Canadians. What are some of our other fundamental freedoms?

Democratic Rights

> 3. Every citizen of Canada has the right to vote in an election of members of the House of Commons or of a legislative assembly and to be qualified for membership therein.
> 4. (1) No House of Commons and no legislative assembly shall continue for longer than five years from the date fixed for the return of the writs at a general election of its members.
>   (2) In time of real or apprehended war, invasion or insurrection, a House of Commons may be continued by Parliament and a legislative assembly may be continued by the legislature beyond five years if such continuation is not opposed by the votes of more than one-third of the members of the House of Commons or the legislative assembly, as the case may be.
> 5. There shall be a sitting of Parliament and of each legislature at least once every twelve months.

Sections 3, 4, and 5 of the *Charter* are not covered in the *Bill of Rights*. However, the right to vote (s.3) is protected by various provincial and federal statutes in addition to the *Charter*. As well, the *Constitution Act, 1867* and other statutes have set limits on how long the House of Commons and legislative assemblies can continue to sit without calling an election (s.4) and how often there must be a sitting of each legislative body (s.5).

Notice that the *Charter* guarantees the right to vote to "citizens" of Canada. Under present election statutes there are several types of persons who are not entitled to vote. Under the *Canada Elections Act*, the following persons cannot vote:

1. federally appointed judges
2. inmates in penal institutions
3. persons who are restrained of liberty or deprived of management of their property because of mental disease

In addition, most provinces and the federal government set the voting age at eighteen, while British Columbia, the Yukon, and the Northwest Territories set the voting age at nineteen. It is likely that the Supreme Court of Canada will be using s. 1 to decide whether these restrictions are reasonable.

—Do you think it is a justifiable "reasonable limit" to exclude inmates in penal and mental institutions and judges from voting? Explain your answer.

—Is it reasonable to have different minimum ages for voting across the country, in your opinion?

You should know that the democratic rights contained in the *Charter* are not covered by s. 33, the "override" clause.

—**Why do you think the *Charter* protects democratic rights from s. 33?**

Figure 3-3 Mobility rights are among the new rights under the Charter.

Mobility Rights

> 6. (1) Every citizen of Canada has the right to enter, remain in and leave Canada.
> (2) Every citizen of Canada and every person who has the status of a permanent resident of Canada has the right
> *(a)* to move to and take up residence in any province; and
> *(b)* to pursue the gaining of a livelihood in any province.

Mobility rights are new rights under the *Charter*. They are also exempted from s. 33.

Federal Republic of Germany v. Rauca (1983) 41 O.R. (2d) 225 (Ont. C.A.)

Helmut Rauca, a naturalized citizen of Canada, was alleged to be a former member of the Nazi Gestapo. The Federal Republic of Germany charged him with the murder of approximately 11 500 people in Lithuanian concentration camps between August, 1941 and December, 1943. The Federal Republic of Germany requested that Canada extradite Rauca under the terms of a treaty between the two countries.

As a citizen of Canada, Rauca fought the extradition process as a violation of his rights under s. 6(1). The court stated that Canada had international obligations. The extradition process does not determine guilt or innocence, but the court must be satisfied (a) that the fugitive is the person who allegedly committed the extradition crime, (b) that the offences charged are offences under the criminal law of the requested state and the requesting state and under the treaty, (c) that the offences were committed within the jurisdiction of the requesting state, and (d) that there is sufficient evidence to substantiate the charges. The court was satisfied on all counts, and granted the extradition order.

(Helmut Rauca died in prison before his trial for war crimes could take place.)

—In what way did s. 1 of the *Charter* have a bearing on this case? Explain.

Legal Rights

> 7. Everyone has the right to life, liberty and security of the person and the right not to be deprived thereof except in accordance with the principles of fundamental justice.

This section guarantees that no one's life, liberty, or security of the person can be interfered with unless the principles of fundamental justice are followed. You will recall from Chapter 1 that the principles of fundamental justice are rules that the courts have developed over the years to ensure that a person receives a fair hearing. Such rights as the right to be heard and the right to be informed of the charges against you are examples of the principles of fundamental justice.

Section 7 is raised most often in criminal cases. However, it may also be used in other areas of law. For example, it could be used to challenge provincial laws that permit the non-voluntary commitment of the mentally ill. Alberta until 1972 and British Columbia until 1973 had statutes that permitted the sterilization of certain people without their consent. These types of laws, if they existed today, could also be challenged under this section of the *Charter*.

Section 7 represents one area of the *Charter* that does not go as far as the *Bill of Rights*. Section 2(e) of the *Bill* gives every person "a right to a fair hearing in accordance with the principles of fundamental justice", whenever the person's "rights and obligations" are at issue. This is a much broader right to a fair hearing, since "rights and obligations" covers more than life, liberty, and security of the person. For instance, if you wish to object to the **expropriation** (takeover) of your property under a federal statute, under the *Charter* you are not guaranteed the right to a fair hearing. Luckily, however, the *Bill of Rights* was not repealed when the *Charter* was enacted. Therefore, you can still rely on the *Bill of Rights* in an area such as this, which has not been duplicated in the *Charter*. In fact, s. 1(a) of the *Bill* specifically protects the right to the enjoyment of property and the right to not be deprived of that right to enjoyment except by the due process of law.

Sections 8 to 14 of the *Charter* are generally of importance to those who have been charged with criminal offences. They include such rights as the right to be secure against unreasonable search and seizure, the right to be informed of the reason for arrest, and the right to be tried within a reasonable time. These sections will be discussed in detail in the chapters on criminal law.

Equality Rights

> 15. (1) Every individual is equal before and under the law and has the right to the equal protection and equal benefit of the law without discrimination and, in particular, without discrimination based on race, national or ethnic origin, colour, religion, sex, age or mental or physical disability.
> (2) Subsection (1) does not preclude any law, program or activity that has as its object the amelioration of conditions of disadvantaged individuals or groups including those that are disadvantaged because of race, national or ethnic origin, colour, religion, sex, age or mental or physical disability.
> 28. Notwithstanding anything in this *Charter*, the rights and freedoms referred to in it are guaranteed equally to male and female persons.

Sections 15 and 28 contain the anti-discrimination clauses of the *Charter*. They protect individuals from the discriminatory actions of government only, not from discrimination by other individuals. This subject will be discussed in detail in Chapter 9, on human rights, but it is important to note here that s. 15 did not take effect along with the rest of the *Charter* in April, 1982. Rather, it came into force three years later—in April, 1985. The federal and provincial governments needed this time to examine existing legislation for violations of this *Charter* right.

R. v. Johns [1982] 1 C.R.D. 350.70-01 (Ont. C.C.)

The defendant was charged under s. 256 of the *Criminal Code*, which sets out that "every male person who procures a feigned marriage between himself and a female person is guilty of an indictable offence."

Johns argued that this section of the *Code* is discriminatory. As it applied only to males, he claimed that it violated s. 15(1) of the *Charter*.

The court dismissed his argument because s. 15 was not yet in force and, therefore, s. 256 of the *Criminal Code* was still valid law.

A similar right to freedom from discrimination can be found in the *Bill of Rights*:

> **1. It is hereby recognized and declared that in Canada there have existed and shall continue to exist without discrimination by reason of race, national origin, colour, religion or sex, the following human rights and fundamental freedoms, namely,**
> *(a)* **the right of the individual to life, liberty, security of the person and enjoyment of property, and the right not to be deprived thereof except by due process of law;**

—What prohibited grounds of discrimination have been added by the *Charter*?

Notice that the *Charter* expands the wording to include not only equality "before the law" but also "under the law" and "equal protection and equal benefit of the law". These added phrases should broaden the protection given to individuals. The term "equality before the law" has been given a very restricted meaning by the Supreme Court of Canada, as the following case indicates:

The Attorney General of Canada and Lavell [1974] S.C.R. 1349

Before her marriage, Lavell was a registered member of the Wikwemikong band. Her name was removed from the Indian register when she married a non-Indian, because of section 12(1) (b) of the *Indian Act*. This loss of Indian status for marrying outside of her race applied only to women. It meant, among other things, that the woman no longer had a right to live on reserve land, even if her marriage subsequently broke up.

Lavell applied to the court to have s. 12(1) (b) struck down because it denied equality before the law as guaranteed by the *Bill of Rights*. The Supreme Court of Canada ruled that "equality before the law" means "equality of treatment in the enforcement and application of law." As long as Lavell was treated the same as all other Indian women who marry non-Indians, she had not been denied equality before the law.

—What is your opinion of this decision?

Figure 3-4 Follow-up to the Lavell Case

Law to repeal status clause nearly finished

OTTAWA (CP) — Legislation repealing a discriminatory section of the Indian Act affecting native women will be introduced as a separate bill at the same time as other bills on Indian self-government, Judy Erola, minister responsible for the status of women, told the House of Commons yesterday.

Mrs. Erola told reporters later the bills do not need to be passed at the same time, but would be tabled together because they deal with related issues.

Justice Department officials have almost finished drafting the bills, which should be introduced in the Commons "within the next few weeks," she said.

The Commons recesses for the summer at the end of June. Many observers believe a new Liberal leader could dissolve Parliament shortly after the party's mid-June leadership convention and call an election.

All parties have pledged to cooperate to speed passage of legislation repealing a section of the century-old federal act which discriminates against Indian women.

Under the section, an Indian woman who marries a non-Indian loses her Indian status and associated rights for herself and her children. The same does not apply to Indian men, whose non-Indian wives can receive Indian status.

A status Indian is entitled to land, housing and education on reserves — benefits that are denied to Indians who have lost their status.

Up to 23,000 women and 40,000 children who have lost their status as Indians could be affected by the legislation.

Prime Minister Pierre Trudeau used the occasion of International Women's Day last May 8 to announce to federal, provincial and native leaders that the Government was determined to introduce a bill to repeal the offending section of the act "shortly."

The definition given to "equality before the law" in the Lavell case by the Supreme Court is known as **procedural equality**. As long as the law is applied equally to all the people it affects, there has been no unfair treatment. The Supreme Court refused to consider whether it was unfair to treat Indian women differently from Indian men.

By adding the phrases "equality under the law" and "equal protection of the law" it is hoped that the courts will go beyond procedural equality to examine whether a given law itself is unfair.

The "equal benefits of the law" phrase was added in response to another interpretation given to "equality before the law" by the courts.

Bliss v. Attorney General of Canada [1979] 1 S.C.R. 183

Bliss, who was pregnant, was not eligible for maternity benefits under the *Unemployment Insurance Act* because she had not worked the required number of weeks. She was turned down for regular unemployment benefits because she was pregnant, even though she had worked enough weeks to qualify for regular benefits. It was assumed that she was unavailable for work because of her pregnancy. Being ready and able to work are necessary conditions for collecting unemployment insurance.

Bliss challenged the *Act* on the grounds that she was being denied equality before the law because of her sex. The Supreme Court of Canada held that "equality before the law" is violated only where legislation treats one group more harshly than another. In this case, the legislation provided special maternity benefits to women who qualified, so no denial of equality before the law was present.

—**"Sex" is a prohibited ground of discrimination in s. 15. However, women's groups lobbied very hard for the inclusion of s. 28 in the *Charter*. Why do you think this is so? In considering this question, remember the court decisions in the *Lavell* and *Bliss* cases.**

Official Languages and Minority Language Education Rights

Official Languages

Canada is a multicultural society, and the *Charter* reflects this in the special protection it gives to Canada's two official languages: English and French. The equality of these languages has long been recognized at the federal level, as evidenced by the *Constitution Act, 1867*. For example, s. 133 of that *Act* sets out the requirement for using Canada's two official languages:

> 133. Either the English or the French language may be used by any Person in the Debates of the Houses of Parliament of Canada and of the Houses of the Legislature of Quebec; and both those Languages shall be used in the respective Records and Journals of those Houses; and either of those Languages may be used by any Person or in any pleading or process in or issuing from any Court in Canada established under this Act, and in or from all or any of the Courts of Quebec.

Section 16(1) of the *Charter* extends the language rights under s. 133.

> 16. (1) English and French are the official languages of Canada and have equality of status and equal rights and privileges as to their use in all institutions of the Parliament and government of Canada.

Figure 3-5 *French and English have equal status as official languages of Canada. All government publications, for instance, must be printed in both languages.*

Not only must Parliament and the federal courts be bilingual, but departments and agencies of government, Crown corporations, and so forth, must also ensure the equal status of both languages. This does not mean that all federal employees must be bilingual, but it may mean that a federal employee has a right to use either French or

English in the course of work. The sections which follow s. 16 cover more specific situations where both languages must be used. Section 20, for instance, provides that

> 20. (1) Any member of the public in Canada has the right to communicate with, and to receive available services from, any head or central office of an institution of the Parliament or government of Canada in English or French, and has the same right with respect to any other office of any such institution where
> (a) there is a significant demand for communications with and services from that office in such language; or
> (b) due to the nature of the office, it is reasonable that communications with and services from that office be available in both English and French.

The sections on language rights (16-22) are not subject to s. 33, the "override" clause.

Minority Language Education Rights

> 23. (1) Citizens of Canada
> (a) whose first language learned and still understood is that of the English or French linguistic minority population of the province in which they reside, or
> (b) who have received their primary school instruction in Canada in English or French and reside in a province where the language in which they received that instruction is the language of the English or French linguistic minority population of the province,
> have the right to have their children receive primary and secondary school instruction in that language in that province.

Section 23 guarantees to the French- and English-speaking minority groups within each of the provinces the right to have their children educated in either of these languages, wherever there are sufficient numbers of students to make this financially feasible. Note that this right applies only to "citizens of Canada", however. A French family who emigrates from Paris to a city in Ontario would not have the right to have its children educated in French. By the same token, a family moving from Rome to Québec would not have the right to have its children educated in English.

Finally, although French and English are the official languages of Canada, people from many nations and ethnic backgrounds live here. Section 27 of the *Charter* recognizes this:

> 27. This *Charter* shall be interpreted in a manner consistent with the preservation and enhancement of the multicultural heritage of Canadians.

Enforcement

> 24. (1) Anyone whose rights or freedoms, as guaranteed by this *Charter*, have been infringed or denied may apply to a court of competent jurisdiction to obtain such remedy as the court considers appropriate and just in the circumstances.
> (2) Where, in proceedings under subsection (1), a court concludes that evidence was obtained in a manner that infringed or denied any rights or freedoms guaranteed by this *Charter*, the evidence shall be excluded if it is established that, having regard to all the circumstances, the admission of it in the proceedings would bring the administration of justice into disrepute....

As mentioned previously, the *Charter* allows a court to award whatever remedy it considers appropriate when a person's rights have been violated. As well, a court may exclude evidence whose admission would bring the administration of justice into disrepute.

General Matters

> 25. The guarantee in this *Charter* of certain rights and freedoms shall not be construed so as to abrogate or derogate from any aboriginal, treaty or other rights or freedoms that pertain to the aboriginal peoples of Canada including
>   (a) any rights or freedoms that have been recognized by the Royal Proclamation of October 7, 1763; and
>   (b) any rights or freedoms that may be acquired by the aboriginal peoples of Canada by way of land claims settlement.
> 26. The guarantee in this *Charter* of certain rights and freedoms shall not be construed as denying the existence of any other rights or freedoms that exist in Canada.

> 27. This *Charter* shall be interpreted in a manner consistent with the preservation and enhancement of the multicultural heritage of Canadians.
> 28. Notwithstanding anything in this *Charter*, the rights and freedoms referred to in it are guaranteed equally to male and female persons.
> 29. Nothing in this *Charter* abrogates or derogates from any rights or privileges guaranteed by or under the Constitution of Canada in respect of denominational, separate or dissentient schools.
> 30. A reference in this *Charter* to a province or to the legislative assembly or legislature of a province shall be deemed to include a reference to the Yukon Territory and the Northwest Territories, or to the appropriate legislative authority thereof, as the case may be.
> 31. Nothing in this *Charter* extends the legislative powers of any body or authority.

Sections 27 and 28 under the General heading in the *Charter* have already been discussed above. Section 25 establishes that aboriginal (Indian, Inuit, and Métis) rights and freedoms are not affected by the *Charter*.

Section 29 specifically recognizes the existing rights of denominational and separate schools.

Perhaps the most important section under the general heading is s. 26. It would have been very difficult indeed to list in the *Charter* every right enjoyed by Canadians. It is important, therefore, that s. 26 clearly states that the *Charter* does not deny the existence of other rights. This is why the previously mentioned sections of the *Bill of Rights* which have not been duplicated in the *Charter* are still in effect. There are also other statutes, both provincial and federal, that protect other rights. The *Charter* does not invalidate them. However, the *Charter* is the supreme law, so if another "rights" statute were to conflict with the *Charter*, the other statute would become void.

The *Charter* – A Final Comment

The *Bill of Rights* has had only limited success in protecting the rights of Canadians. The coming years will be an extremely interesting period in Canada, as we watch what the courts, especially the Supreme Court of Canada, do with the *Charter*.

One final benefit of an entrenched *Charter* should be mentioned. Since the *Charter* is a part of the Constitution, people should be more aware of it than they have been of other civil rights statutes. The great public debate which preceded the *Charter's* enactment and the interest displayed by the media towards cases which have relied on the *Charter* have attracted and will continue to attract our attention to it. This means that all of us will be more aware of our rights, freedoms, and responsibilities, and in the end will be encouraged to use and protect our rights. In sum, therefore, the *Charter* is a very valuable educational tool.

SUMMARIZING YOUR READING

1. From what kind of interference do civil rights laws protect us?

2. How do civil rights differ from human rights?

3. What are the two main statutes that define our civil rights?

4. Define "entrenchment".

5. What are some important advantages of having our civil rights entrenched in the Constitution?

6. What are the limitations of the *Bill of Rights*?

7. Explain why rights cannot be without limitation.

8. In what way does the *Charter of Rights and Freedoms* recognize that rights must be limited?

9. What important role will the courts play with respect to the *Charter*?

10. What does "supremacy of Parliament" mean? How might the *Charter* have changed this principle?

11. Section 24 provides remedies for violations of the *Charter*. What form(s) might these remedies take?

12. What is the significance of s. 33 of the *Charter*?

13. What are the four fundamental freedoms enjoyed by Canadians?

14. What are our democratic rights?

15. What rights are provided by s. 6 of the *Charter*?

16. To what situations does s. 7 apply? What are principles of fundamental justice?

17. What important guarantee is provided by the *Bill of Rights* but does not appear in the legal rights section of the *Charter*?

18. Did s. 15 become law at the same time as the rest of the *Charter*? Explain.

19. How do the guarantees under s. 15 of the *Charter* differ from the *Bill of Rights* protection?

20. Explain the minority language education rights found in the *Charter*.

21. What is the significance of s. 26 of the *Charter*?

DISCUSSING KEY ISSUES

1. Those who opposed an entrenched *Charter of Rights and Freedoms* argued that an unelected body (judges) should not tell an elected body (legislatures) what the law should be. Discuss the pros and cons of allowing the Supreme Court of Canada to become the final lawmaker in our society.

2. Several convicted murderers have recently written books about their crimes. Suppose that the government passed a law which prohibited anyone convicted of a crime from publishing for profit any material about the crime. Would this law violate the convicted person's right to freedom of expression? How might section 1 of the *Charter* apply to this law?

PROJECTS AND ACTIVITIES

1. During your study of this unit, clip as many newspaper and magazine articles relating to the *Charter* as you can find. Share these with the class and create a bulletin board display.

2. Prepare a research paper on the process that resulted in the patriation of the Constitution on April 17, 1982. What was the position of the various provinces, particularly Québec? What were the attitudes of the women's rights movement and the Native rights movement towards the *Charter*?

3. Part II, section 35 of the *Constitution Act, 1982* deals with aboriginal rights. Prepare a research paper on the Native rights movement and on how this section affects Native People.

4. What is the *War Measures Act* (more recently called the *Public Order (Temporary Measures) Act*)? On what occasions has it been used? What effect does it have on civil rights? What effect, if any, will the *Charter* likely have on this *Act*?

5. Retired Supreme Court of Canada Justice Emmett Hall once said: "In the space of three years from the Supreme Court of Canada *Drybones* decision (1970) to *Lavell* (1973) the *Bill of Rights* went from a high point of great expectancy down a short steep slope to near oblivion...*Drybones* and *Lavell* were decided by the same court. The two decisions are incompatible."

The *Lavell* case has been discussed in this chapter. Look up the *Drybones* case ([1970] S.C.R. 282) and write a paper explaining what Justice Hall meant.

An Introduction to Criminal Law

The Basic Elements of a Crime
Parties to the Crime
The Presumption of Innocence and the Burden of Proof

You saw in Chapter 1 that criminal law is a type of public law. Criminal law states what actions are prohibited, sets out the rules for enforcement, and establishes the penalties for committing prohibited actions.

A store is broken into. The police investigate and eventually question a suspect who is charged with break, enter, and theft. When the accused is arrested, the police search him and his apartment, seizing items taken from the store. At the accused's bail hearing the next day, he is released on his personal promise to appear for trial. At his trial, he pleads not guilty and raises the defence of intoxication. The Crown prosecutor, however, proves his case against the accused **beyond a reasonable doubt**. The accused is found guilty as charged and sentenced to three years in prison. He appeals the sentence, arguing that it is too harsh. The appeal court agrees, since he is a first offender, and reduces the sentence to one year.

Figure 4-1

This case illustrates the two main types of criminal law. The powers of the police to investigate the crime and their authority to arrest and search the accused, and the rules governing the bail hearing, the trial, and the appeal are matters of **criminal procedure**; the law which prohibits certain actions, such as break, enter, and theft, defines the defences available to the accused, and sets out penalties for breaking the law are **substantive criminal law**. In short, criminal procedure consists of the rules by which substantive criminal law is enforced.

This chapter will look at some general principles of substantive criminal law: the basic elements of a crime (What exactly is a crime? Has a crime been committed?), and the decision as to who is responsible (Who are the parties to a crime?).

The Basic Elements of a Crime

What Exactly is a Crime?

A crime is either a prohibited action or the omission of an action which is considered to be a wrong against society and usually against a victim as well. Although most crimes involve the actual performance of a prohibited action, such as theft or assault, there are a few situations where it is a crime *not* to perform an action. For example, parents have a duty to provide the "necessaries of life" for their children who are under the age of sixteen. Failure to provide necessaries (the omission) is a crime.

When a crime is committed not only the victim, but also the community, suffers. This is why we say that a crime is a wrong against society. One of the reasons that certain actions are prohibited is to allow people to feel safe in their homes and on the streets. When the crime rate goes up, everyone feels less secure. Therefore, crime is a public concern.

It is important for you to understand that criminal law is primarily concerned with protecting the public and maintaining the peace, and not with compensating victims of crime. When a person is charged and tried for an offence, the police and the Crown Attorney, the prosecutor, are acting on behalf of the state, not for the victim. This explains the method used for naming criminal cases: *Regina v. Smith* means that the Queen (*Regina*) is proceeding against (*v.* = *versus*) Smith. The purpose of imposing a penalty on a person found guilty of breaking the law is to punish, and, it is hoped, to rehabilitate the offender, while at the same time providing an example for others that may deter them from criminal activity. Compensation for the victim is left to private law, primarily tort law, which is covered in a later chapter.

Figure 4-2

Suppose your local park has recently been the scene of several muggings.
— In what way does the community suffer because of these crimes?
— How do the muggings affect the lives of people who are not the actual victims?
— Can you think of crimes for which there are no individual victims?
— Why should such actions be prohibited?
— How does their commission affect the community?

Although some actions, such as murder and theft, have always been crimes, the actions which are defined as crimes may change over time because of changes in public feelings and values, or because of other changes in society. For example, in the late 1960s the hijacking of aircraft became an international threat. Since it was a new problem, our criminal law did not specifically deal with it. As a result, in 1972, Parliament passed a criminal law to prohibit the unlawful seizure or control of an aircraft.

Today, computers have opened up a whole new area of criminal activity to which the criminal law has not yet responded.

Jurisdiction

Canada's *Constitution Act, 1867* granted the authority to make criminal law to the federal government. For this reason, criminal law, including the rules of criminal procedure, is the same in every province and territory in Canada. Thus, an offence in Newfoundland is also an offence in British Columbia, and the police have the same powers to search and arrest in Alberta as in Prince Edward Island.

On the other hand, the provinces were granted the responsibility for the "administration of justice". This includes responsibility for maintaining a police force. However, only Québec and Ontario actually have provincial police forces. Some provinces have handed on the task of maintaining a police force to the municipalities, which may have municipal police. Those provinces and municipalities that do not have their own police contract to use the services of the Royal Canadian Mounted Police (R.C.M.P.). Of course, the R.C.M.P. also operates as a federal police force, enforcing other federal statutes as well as the *Criminal Code*, policing the Northwest Territories and the Yukon, and protecting national security.

The provinces also have responsibility for the organization of the provincial courts and the appointing of judges to these courts. However, it is the federal government that appoints and pays the salaries of the judges of the county, district, and superior courts of each province. As well, the federal government maintains the Supreme Court of Canada and other federal courts.

The federal government was granted the authority to establish penitentiaries, while the provinces may establish prisons and reformatories. Provincial offenders and persons who violate federal criminal law and are sentenced to less than two years are imprisoned in provincial institutions.

At one time much of our criminal law was part of the common law; that is, it was contained in cases rather than in statutes. In 1892, the federal government passed the *Criminal Code*. It served to **codify** many parts of the criminal law, particularly what actions are crimes. Other federal statutes also contain criminal law. For example, the *Narcotic Control Act* makes it an offence to possess or traffic certain drugs. However, the *Criminal Code* is the most important criminal statute.

The *Constitution Act, 1867* also gave the provinces authority to make laws in certain areas, such as property and civil rights. The provinces also have the authority to impose penalties on violators of these provincial laws. Strictly speaking, a violation of a provincial law is not a crime. However, the penalties for committing provincial offences, or **quasi-criminal offences** as they are sometimes called, are very similar to those for committing crimes: fines or imprisonment for up to two years less a day. In addition, the procedure for trying someone accused of committing a provincial offence is substantially the same as criminal procedure, and the same courts are used.

People can also be prosecuted for breaking municipal by-laws.

Examples of provincial and municipal offences follow:

Bill runs a red light and is given a ticket for violating his province's *Highway Traffic Act*. He appears in court and pleads guilty. He is fined $50 and loses his licence for twelve months because of the number of demerit points he has accumulated.

While her parents are away, Jill throws a party that gets out of hand. She is charged under a municipal anti-noise by-law. She is found guilty when the police tell the judge under oath, that noise from the party could be heard a block away at 4 a.m. She is fined $100.

Unless you know which statute contains a given offence, you may have difficulty in telling a provincial offence from a federal crime. In general, crimes are more serious and involve greater penalties than provincial offences. Also, a conviction for a crime leads to a criminal record.

Federal Crimes	Provincial Offences*	Municipal By-laws*
Theft under $200	Careless driving	Parking violations
Assault	Serving alcohol to minors	Noise control violations
Driving while impaired	Trespassing	Littering on a public street

*Provincial offences and municipal by-laws vary from place to place.

Figure 4-3 Types of Offences. Provincial offences and municipal by-laws vary from place to place.

Has a Crime Been Committed?

Although there are many different types of crimes, ranging from assaults to sophisticated computer frauds, in general every crime has two basic elements:

1. a physical element known as *actus reus*, Latin for "guilty action" and
2. a mental element called *mens rea*, Latin for "guilty mind".

In other words, in deciding whether a person has committed a crime, we must ask: "Was the action performed voluntarily?" and "Did the actor realize what the consequences of the action would be?"

Let's look at these two parts of a crime more closely.

The Physical Element—*Actus Reus*

Most offences require a physical action, although sometimes a failure to act (an omission) can be the *actus reus* in the offence. The action or omission must be voluntary. For example, a person who has an epileptic seizure and strikes someone has not acted voluntarily. A few offences require neither an action nor an omission, but rather a state of being. Being in possession of stolen property is an example of a state of being which can be an offence if the other elements of the offence exist.

Often the *Criminal Code* does not say what specific action is forbidden, but requires a certain consequence instead. A person can be charged with murder by unlawfully causing the death of a human being by means of many different types of actions. It is the consequence of unlawfully causing death that makes the offence murder. It will not matter whether the death has been caused by shooting, stabbing, or strangling, for instance.

Julia and Miguel have been arguing over who should have custody of their children when they separate. During a particularly heated moment, Julia picks up a butcher knife from the kitchen counter and stabs Miguel, who dies instantly. Julia is charged with murder.

— What is the *actus reus* in Julia's crime?
— What is the consequence of the *actus reus*?
— Could the same consequence have been the result of different actions? Give examples.

Usually, certain circumstances must exist before an action is an offence. To illustrate, one type of assault is defined as follows:

> **244. A person commits an assault when**
> *(a)* without the consent of another person, he applies force intentionally to that other person, directly or indirectly.

The necessary circumstance here is that the force must be applied *without consent*. Therefore, if two students agree to a fistfight after school, probably neither can be charged with assault, since each has consented to the fight.

If you look at the definition of an offence in the *Criminal Code* and want to see what is required for *actus reus* in the offence, all three factors need to be considered: the action (or omission or state of being), the consequence, and the circumstances.

The Mental Element: *Mens Rea*

Mens rea refers to the mental state that must exist for criminal responsibility. Three different types of mental states can be required for *mens rea* in an offence: intent, recklessness, and knowledge.

Intent

In general, only those people who intended to cause the wrongful consequences of their actions are punished.

Farrell, while shopping in a crowded mall, accidently walks into Gilberti, another shopper. Gilberti falls to the ground, and is quite upset and embarrassed. She calls the police and claims that she has been assaulted.

— Refer to the *Criminal Code* section defining an assault. Do you think Farrell has committed an assault?
— What would be the *actus reus* in the offence?
— What would be the *mens rea* in the offence?

It is usually impossible to know for sure what a person intended in performing a certain action unless that person tells us. Therefore, the law allows a judge or jury to infer that people intend the natural consequences of their actions. In other words, in the example given above where Julia stabbed Miguel, a judge or jury can assume she meant to kill or at least seriously injure Miguel since death would be a natural consequence of being stabbed. It would be up to Julia to show that she had some other intention in mind, or that it was an accident.

Some offences require only **general intent** to cause the wrongful consequence. They are called "general intent crimes". For example, the offence of mischief is defined as follows:

> **387. (1) Every one commits mischief who wilfully,**
>   *(a)* **destroys or damages property...**

The only intent required for this offence is the intent to destroy property. If you accidentally start a fire while putting gas in your lawn mower, and the fire destroys your neighbour's garage, you have not committed the offence of mischief, since you did not have the intent to destroy property.

Other offences require an additional intent, **specific intent**. For a specific intent offence, two factors are necessary: the unlawful action must be intentional, and it must be committed with the intent to commit another illegal action. For example, one type of robbery is defined as assaulting a person "with intent to steal from him". The general intent here is the intention to assault, while the specific intent is the intention to steal. In other words, for this offence, the assault must be committed for the purpose of stealing.

You must look at the definition of a given offence to see whether it requires specific or general intent. Specific intent is usually indicated by words such as "with intent" or "for the purpose of". If these words are not used, the offence is probably a general intent crime.

—Read the following *Criminal Code* definition of kidnapping, which means "to take a person involuntarily from one place to another." What is the general intent required for this offence? the specific intent?

> **247. (1) Every one who kidnaps a person with intent...**
>   *(c)* **to hold him for ransom or to service against his will**
>   **is guilty of an indictable offence...**

—Would it be an offence under this section if Mario kidnapped his best friend, Sal, the night before Sal's wedding by taking him, against his will, to a bachelor party at Mario's cottage? What element is missing?

AN INTRODUCTION TO CRIMINAL LAW

Recklessness

For some offences, a person will be held criminally responsible if he or she acts recklessly.

Louise has been drinking steadily at a party. She knows she should not be driving but decides to take a chance. On her way home, she runs a stop sign and hits a pedestrian, who later dies.

—Is it likely that Louise intended to kill the pedestrian?
—Is it likely that Louise knew that by driving while drunk she might cause an accident and injure someone?
—Should she be held responsible for causing the pedestrian's death?

Usually we can say that people are being reckless when they can foresee the potential harmful consequences of the conduct but decide to take unjustifiable risks anyway. Louise can be charged under s.202 of the *Criminal Code*:

> 202. (1) Every one is criminally negligent who
> (a) in doing anything, or
> (b) in omitting to do anything that it is his duty to do,
> shows wanton or reckless disregard for the lives or safety of other persons.

Knowledge

Sometimes an offence requires knowledge of certain circumstances. For example:

> 312. (1) Every one commits an offence who has in his possession any property knowing that all or part of the property... was obtained by or derived directly or indirectly from
> (a) the commission in Canada of an offence...

This section is used for the offence of possession of stolen property. For someone to commit an offence under s.312, he or she must not only be in possession of the property, but also have knowledge that it was obtained through the commission of a crime.

Strict Liability and Absolute Liability

According to a recent Supreme Court of Canada decision, all "true criminal offences" require one of the types of *mens rea* we have just discussed. However, there are other offences under either provincial or federal law which impose liability without *mens rea*. These offences arise out of breaches of regulatory laws or laws passed for the protection of public health, welfare, or safety. Examples are traffic laws which regulate the use of the roads and laws prohibiting the sale of impure foods. There are over 20 000 federal offences of this type and, on the average, a similar number in each province.

These offences fall into two categories: those imposing **strict liability** and those imposing **absolute liability**. If the offence is one of strict liability, the prosecutor does not need to prove any form of *mens rea* to obtain a conviction, merely that the accused committed the *actus reus* in the offence. However, the accused can raise as a defence that he or she acted with due diligence, or in other words, without negligence. This means that the defendant's conduct must be that of a reasonable person in the same situation. If the accused can prove this defence, he or she will not be found guilty.

If the offence is one of absolute liability, the court will enter a conviction even though the accused has acted completely without fault. However, because of the general principle that punishment should not be inflicted without fault, a court will ordinarily presume that an offence which does not require *mens rea* is a strict liability one. Only when the statute is very clearly worded to indicate that absolute liability is intended will the court enter a conviction.

R. v. Chapin (1979) 7 C.R. (3d) 225 (S.C.C.)

Chapin was charged under the federal *Migratory Birds Convention Act* with hunting for game birds within a quarter-mile (about 400 m) of where bait was deposited. A conservation officer heard shots and went to investigate. As he approached the defendant, he observed a pile of grain about a foot (0.3 m) long and three inches (75 mm) wide. He testified that he was almost on top of it before he noticed it. Chapin was shooting from a blind about fifty yards (46 m) from the bait. She testified that she was unaware of the presence of the bait. Even when it was pointed out to her she did not know what it was.

The Crown argued that this was an absolute liability offence, while the defence argued that full *mens rea* was required. The Supreme Court of Canada held that the offence was one of strict liability and acquitted Chapin since she had acted reasonably. The court considered the following in reaching this conclusion:

1. The offence was not a "crime in the true sense", which would require *mens rea*. The purpose of the *Act* is to regulate and not to prohibit all hunting of migratory birds. It is legislation passed in the public interest to protect birds from indiscriminate slaughter.

2. There were a number of serious consequences which could arise out of a conviction, such as a maximum fine of $300 or six months' imprisonment, a mandatory prohibition from holding a hunting permit for one year, and the possibility of the defendant's having to forfeit the gun or other equipment used in violating the *Act*. These consequences made it unlikely that Parliament intended the offence to be one of absolute liability.

3. Hunting is a permitted sport. It would be unreasonable to require a hunter to search a circular area of a half-mile (0.8 km) diameter for the presence of illegally deposited bait before hunting.

Remember that whenever you want to know what kind of *actus reus* and *mens rea* an offence requires, or whether it is an offence of strict or absolute liability, it is important to read the definition of the offence carefully.

—Can you think of any reasons why absolute liability offences should be included in the law?

Attempts

Figure 4-4 An attempt to commit a crime is considered a criminal offence in itself.

R. v. Kosh (1964) 44 C.R. 185 (Sask. C.A.)

A police officer observed the accused and another man walking in a crouched position around a building one evening. The officer then saw one of the men lighting up the door of the building with a flashlight, and making motions with his other hand. After about two minutes, the men left the building. They were later arrested a short distance from the building.

Have these men committed an offence? A court said "Yes"; the men were found guilty of attempted break-and-enter. Section 24(1) of the *Criminal Code* states that

> **24. (1) Every one who, having an intent to commit an offence does or omits to do anything for the purpose of carrying out his intention is guilty of an attempt to commit the offence whether or not it was possible under the circumstances to commit the offence.**

To be charged with an attempted offence, the accused must have gone beyond mere preparation. The accused must have committed an action or omission directly connected with the offence.

A night watchman omits to lock a warehouse door in order to allow an easy entry for his accomplices who want to break into the warehouse that night. The plan to burglarize the warehouse is discovered by police. The watchman could be charged with attempted break-and-enter.

Parties to the Crime

It is not only the person who actually commits an offence who is responsible, but also anyone who has assisted that person, either before or during the commission of the offence. All of the persons who can be charged with the offence are called *parties to the offence*. The person who actually committed the *actus reus* and had the *mens rea* in the offence is also called the *principal actor*. Every party to the offence is subject to the same penalty regardless of the role played in the crime.

Aiding and Abetting

Section 21 of the *Criminal Code* provides that a person can become a party by **aiding and abetting** the principal actor. This means that the aider or abettor has intentionally either assisted or encouraged the principal actor.

A person can also be a party if he or she forms an *intention in common* with others to carry out an unlawful purpose (s.21(2)). If one of the others commits an offence to achieve the unlawful purpose, which was reasonably foreseeable, all will be parties to that offence.

Three people break into a house. While in the house, one of them stays at the front door as a look-out. The other two go into the bedroom to look for money and jewelry. They are surprised at the door to the bedroom by MacDuff, an elderly man who heard them come in. MacDuff decides to defend his house and tries to hit one of the intruders with a lamp. He is overpowered by two of the intruders, however, and is seriously injured.

All three of the people in the above example can be charged with assault as well as break-and-enter. They all had the common intention to break into the house, and it was reasonably foreseeable that someone could be home and could be injured during the break-in.

Counselling and Procuring

A person can also become a party to an offence by **counselling and procuring**. "Counselling" means advising or recommending that someone commit an offence, while "procuring" means getting someone to commit the offence.

Accessory after the Fact

An **accessory after the fact** is someone who helps the offender after the offence has been committed. This person is not a party to the offence, but can be charged under a separate section of the *Code* (s.23). This section makes it an offence for a person to "receive, comfort or assist" anyone that he or she knows has been a party to an offence to enable that party to escape. However, there is an exception made to s.23:

> 23. (2) No married person whose spouse has been a party to an offence is an accessory after the fact to that offence by receiving, comforting or assisting the spouse for the purpose of enabling the spouse to escape.

—Why has the law made an exception for persons who help their spouses to escape?
—Do you agree with s.23(2)?

Conspiracy

Ramona, Diane, and Frank plan to steal some stereo equipment from a store in their neighbourhood. At the last minute, they decide it is too risky and scrap their plan.

Have these three committed an offence? Yes, they have, for it is an offence to conspire, that is, to make an agreement to do an unlawful action. Whether or not the offence is ever carried out does not matter. You should note the key difference between an attempt and a **conspiracy**. In an attempt, a person actually does (or omits to do) something to commit the offence. The offence of conspiracy, on the other hand, is committed as soon as two or more people agree to perform an unlawful action.

—Look up s.423 of the *Criminal Code*. What are the specific types of conspiracy in this section? What are the penalties? Why should it be an offence to plan a crime? Do you think conspiracy charges are hard to prove? Can one person who plans a crime be charged with conspiracy?

The Presumption of Innocence and the Burden of Proof

There are two important principles of law concerning establishing the guilt of an accused.

The first principle is that *every person is presumed innocent until proven guilty*. Although we have inherited this principle from the English common law, it is now specifically stated in Canada's *Charter of Rights and Freedoms*.

> 11. Any person charged with an offence has the right...
>   (d) to be presumed innocent until proven guilty according to law in a fair and public hearing by an independent and impartial tribunal;

The second principle is that the prosecution in a criminal case must prove **beyond a reasonable doubt** that the accused committed the crime. The judge or jury hearing the case does not need to be absolutely convinced of the accused person's guilt. However, if either the judge or jury has a reasonable doubt as to the defendant's guilt, the accused must be acquitted. It is difficult to define what a reasonable doubt is. One judge defined it this way:

> "a reasonable doubt is that quality and kind of doubt which, when you are dealing with matters of importance in your own affairs, you allow to influence you one way or the other."

These two principles go hand in hand. They are the reason why the accused need not say anything to the police or even in court. At the trial, the prosecution must present its evidence first. At the end of the evidence, the Crown must have proven beyond a reasonable doubt that the accused committed the *actus reus* and had the necessary *mens rea* for the offence. Otherwise, the accused will be acquitted. Of course, if necessary, the accused may also choose to testify in order to raise a defence. If the accused does testify or present other evidence, it is only necessary to show that there is reasonable doubt as to whether the accused committed the offence. The accused does not need to prove his or her innocence. You should recall, however, that the prosecution can rely on the fact that people are usually presumed to intend the natural consequences of their actions. Usually, therefore, once the prosecution proves the *actus reus* in the offence, the accused must present some evidence that the action was not intentional, or raise a reasonable doubt in the mind of the judge or jury. If the accused can raise this doubt, the Crown will have failed to prove its case.

SUMMARIZING YOUR READING

1. Name the two main types of criminal law, and give an example of each.

2. Give a definition of crime.

3. Who suffers when crimes are committed? Explain.

4. What is the purpose of punishing offenders?

5. How can a victim of a crime seek compensation?

6. Do the actions which society prohibits ever change? Explain.

7. Which government, federal or provincial, has authority to make criminal law?

8. In what statute can you find most of our criminal law?

9. Explain what a provincial offence is. How is it similar to a criminal offence?

10. What are the two necessary elements of most crimes?

11. Does *actus reus* always require a physical act?

12. What three factors may be part of *actus reus*?

13. What are the three types of mental states which can be required for *mens rea* in an offence? Explain each one.

14. What is meant by "specific intent"?

15. Are there offences for which *mens rea* is not required? Explain.

16. What is the difference between strict liability and absolute liability?

17. If a person does not complete an offence, can a charge be laid? Explain.

18. Explain who, other than the principal actor, may be a party to an offence.

19. Are all parties to an offence subject to the same penalty?

20. What is an "accessory after the fact"?

21. Is it an offence to plan a crime with others if the crime is never carried out? Explain.

22. What does it mean to say that "every person is presumed innocent until proven guilty"?

23. Who has the burden of proof in a criminal trial?

24. Explain what it means to "prove a case beyond a reasonable doubt".

DISCUSSING KEY ISSUES

1. There are a few crimes, called "reverse onus" offences, which change the burden of proof in a criminal trial. For example, if you are found in possession of burglary tools, you will have to show that you had a lawful reason for having them. If you cannot, you can be convicted of possession of "house breaking instruments".

How do reverse onus offences change the principle that an accused is presumed innocent until proven guilty? Why do you think Parliament has created "reverse onus" offences? Do you think they are fair? Do you think the *Charter of Rights and Freedoms*, which guarantees the presumption of innocence, will affect the legality of these types of offences?

2. "To designate certain conduct as criminal in an attempt to control anti-social behaviour should be a last step...Men and women may have their lives, public and private, destroyed; families may be broken up; the state may be put to considerable expense; all these consequences are to be taken into account when determining whether a particular type of conduct is so obnoxious to social values that it is to be included in the catalogue of crimes."

From Report of the Canadian Committee on Corrections, *(Canada: Queen's Printer, 1969)*

Discuss the statement above. What do you think it means when it says "lives [are] destroyed, families broken"? What expenses does the state incur in making certain conduct criminal? For example, take a problem such as impaired driving. What means, besides criminal law, does society use to discourage drunk drivers? Come up with some rules for determining whether certain conduct should be considered a criminal offence.

PROJECTS AND ACTIVITIES

1. All provinces except Prince Edward Island have established Criminal Injury Compensation Funds. Research your province's fund by contacting the Ministry of the Attorney General. Who qualifies? What type of compensation is available? Make a report to the class or prepare a research paper.

2. During your study of criminal law, clip articles about crime from the newspaper and magazines. Can you identify what the offence is in each article? What is the *actus reus* in the offence? What *mens rea* is required? Is the offence a strict or absolute liability offence? Who are the parties to the offence?

RESOLVING CASES

R. v. St. Onge (1978) 21 A.R. 354 (Alta. Dist. Ct.)

St. Onge was a postal clerk who was accused of stealing from the post office. It was alleged that she had collected postage due money but then failed to affix the required stamps on the parcels.

The accounting system used by the post office credited each clerk with $400 every month. This credit was divided between stamps and cash. As St. Onge sold stamps, the amount of cash would increase and the stamp inventory would decrease. At the end of each month, an audit would be done and everything was supposed to balance to the $400 total. A deficit over a certain amount had to be paid by the clerk, while a surplus would be sent to Ottawa.

The Crown showed that St. Onge was collecting money from addressees who had been mailed packages with insufficient postage. The money would be put in the cash drawer. St. Onge was then supposed to affix a postage due stamp to the package, but she was not doing this. The Crown was able to show six incidents where this had happened. It was argued that these repeated incidents showed the intention to steal from the post office.

The accused argued that the failure to affix the stamps was due to carelessness and that she had not taken any money.

—What is the *actus reus* in this case? Has the Crown established it? Explain.
—Has the Crown proved the offence?

R. v. Roliff (1973) 11 C.C.C. (2d) 10 (Ont. C.A.)

The accused was charged under s.238(3) of the *Criminal Code*, which makes it an offence for a person whose licence is suspended to drive a motor vehicle. The Crown proved that the certificate of suspension had been issued by the Department of Transport and that the accused had been driving. The trial court convicted Roliff, who then appealed.

The appeal court held that the judge erred in not considering whether the evidence proved whether *mens rea* was present in the offence, and sent the case back for a new trial.

—What question did the judge fail to answer?
—What is the *mens rea* in this offence?

R. v. Sam Cosentino Ltd. (1966) 1.C.C.C. 79 (Ont. C.A.)

Section 19(a) of Ontario's *Construction Safety Act* states that

> 19. (a) "No person shall provide any machine, vehicle, tool or equipment, or any part thereof, for use by a person on a project under any rental, leasing or other arrangement if such machine, vehicle, tool, equipment or part is in an unsafe condition."

The accused rented a piece of heavy equipment known as a bantam back-hoe, which is used for digging trenches, to Johnson-Kiewit Subway Corp. The machine was defective. As a result of the defect, the bucket and the arm to which it was attached fell on a workman, who later died.

The accused was convicted of violating s.19a of the statute and fined $500, although it was clear that the defendant was unaware of the defect.

—Was any *mens rea* present on the part of the accused?
—Is this the type of offence for which *mens rea* may not be necessary? Explain.
—Should this be an absolute or a strict liability offence? Why?

R. v. Rodriguez [1978] 6 W.W.R. 667 (B.C.C.A.)

The accused was charged with trafficking in a narcotic (marijuana) because he had aided and abetted a person selling drugs. While at a beer parlour, the accused was approached by an undercover police officer named Barnard. The following conversation took place:

BARNARD: Hi, Chico. Do you have any stuff tonight?
ACCUSED: What do you want?
BARNARD: Some speed.
ACCUSED: I can get pot.
BARNARD: O.K.
ACCUSED: Come with me.

The accused then led the detective to another part of the same beer parlour, where the accused had a conversation with a third party, known to the detective only as "Mark". The detective did not overhear the conversation.

After this, Mark pulled out of his pants a clear plastic bag which contained marijuana. He handed the bag to the detective, whereupon the following conversation ensued in the presence of all three parties:

BARNARD: Is it pot?
MARK: Yeah.
BARNARD: Is it good?
MARK: Yeah.
BARNARD: Twenty dollars?
MARK: Yes.

At this point the detective paid $20 for the marijuana, and Mark said, "Smoke a joint now, if you like." The accused intervened to say, "It's good," and the detective said, "O.K."

—Do you think the accused should be found guilty?
—Has he assisted in the commission of an offence? In what way?

R. v. Soloway (1975) 28 C.C.C. (2d) 212 (Alta. C.A.)

The accused was charged with stealing a wallet from a Robert Barembruch. Barembruch had given a woman a ride home from a bar where they met. When they arrived at her home, there were several people there, including the accused, Soloway.

Barembruch fell asleep on the couch and woke up as he felt the woman taking his wallet out of his back pocket. To avoid a fight, he pretended to be sleeping. There was no money in the wallet, just identification papers. Barembruch heard the woman say that she was going to return the wallet. The accused then told her to keep it and that she could sell the I.D. for good money.

—Why has the accused been charged with theft?
—Should he be convicted?

5

Criminal Procedure: Before the Trial

Types of Offences
The Criminal Court System
Police Powers

Powers of Search
Procedures Following Arrest

Figure 5-1 Canadian law grants certain rights to persons under arrest.

A balance must be struck between the rights of citizens to go freely about their business and the need for the police and the courts to have the authority to enforce the law. Criminal procedure gives certain powers to the police and the courts, and, at the same time, gives certain rights and protections to those suspected of committing crimes. In short, the purpose of criminal procedure is to give us a method for acquitting the innocent and convicting the guilty.

This chapter will describe the criminal court system and some of the rules of procedure from the time the police have a suspect, until the trial.

Types of Offences

There are two main types of offences: **summary conviction offences**, which are the less serious, and **indictable offences**, which are the more serious crimes. As you will see, the nature of the offence determines which court will have jurisdiction to hear the case. You will also learn that whether the offence is a summary conviction offence or an indictable offence determines the powers of the police to arrest, the accused's right to be released before trial, and the kind of trial the accused receives.

There is also a third type of offence, called a **hybrid** or **dual procedure offence**. It may be tried as either a summary conviction or an indictable offence, depending on the circumstances of the case. It is the Crown attorney that decides how to treat the offence, before the trial of the accused starts. The Crown will consider such factors as the past record of the accused and the circumstances surrounding the commission of the crime, such as the amount of violence used, in making this decision. A hybrid offence is considered indictable unless the Crown chooses to treat it as a summary conviction offence.

Summary Conviction Offences	Hybrid Offences	Indictable Offences
Causing a disturbance in a public place	Criminal negligence in the operation of a motor vehicle	Kidnapping
Loitering on private property at night	Theft under $200	Break-and-enter with intent to commit an indictable offence
Being found in a betting or gaming house	Committing mischief by damaging public or private property	Robbery

Figure 5-2 Examples of the Types of Offences

The Criminal Court System

Figure 5-3 Canada's Criminal Court System

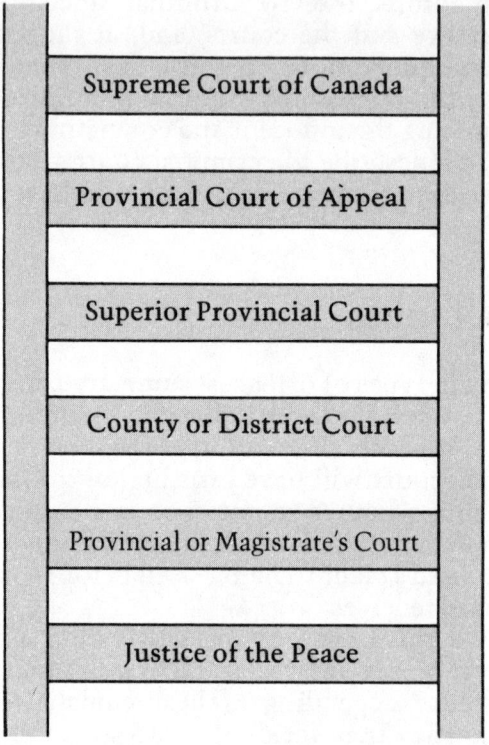

Since the provinces have the authority under Canada's Constitution to set up their own court systems, the courts vary slightly from province to province. However, as Figure 5-3 shows, in general you can think of a province's court structure as a ladder. Proceedings against an accused, who is called the **defendant** in court, start at the bottom and work up. On the first rung of the ladder, in provincial courts, are the Justices of the Peace. The police must go before a Justice of the Peace to obtain arrest and search warrants. Justices of the Peace also hold hearings to determine whether the accused should be released from custody before the trial, and can try summary conviction offences.

Magistrates or provincial court judges can perform any of the duties of a Justice of the Peace, and can try the less serious indictable offences, such as theft of property worth $200 or less.

The next rung of the ladder is occupied by the judges of the county or district courts, although some provinces, such as New Brunswick, Saskatchewan, and Alberta, do not have this level of court. These provinces have only a superior court. All but the most serious indictable offences, such as high treason or murder, can be tried in county or district courts. Trials may be held with or without a jury. In most provinces, these judges can also hear appeals from convictions for summary conviction offences.

Each province has a superior court, called either the province's Supreme Court or Court of Queen's Bench. The most serious indictable offences are tried in these courts. All trials in the superior courts must be before a judge and jury except in Alberta, where the defendant can choose to have a judge alone try the case.

—Make a court ladder for your province, using the correct names of the courts. You can contact the Attorney General's office for information about the courts in your province.

Police Powers

Once the police have a suspect whom they want to charge with a crime, they must decide how to bring the suspect before a court. There are three ways the police may compel a person to appear in court:

1. by giving the accused an **appearance notice**,
2. by going before a Justice of the Peace and having a **summons** issued, and
3. by **arresting** the accused.

Appearance Notice

An appearance notice is a written form which contains the name of the accused, the offence being charged, and the time and place the accused must appear in court. It can be used by the police as an alternative to arresting the person. The police officer will ask the accused to sign the form in duplicate. The accused is then given a copy.

Figure 5-4 Ways of Compelling an Accused to Appear in Court

Appearance Notice	Summons	Arrest
Copy given to accused by police at the scene of the offence. Names the offence; gives date, place and time that the accused must appear in court.	Police go to court to have Justice of the Peace issue summons which is served on the accused.	Usually reserved for serious crimes. With warrant—police go before Justice of the Peace to get warrant authorizing arrest of the accused. Without warrant—police can arrest without warrant in specific situations only.

Summons

A police officer may go before a Justice of the Peace and ask that a summons be issued and served on the accused. A summons is a court order directing the accused to appear in court at a certain time and place. The police officer must *lay an information* before the Justice; that is, the officer must "make out a case" against the accused. If the Justice of the Peace believes that there are reasonable grounds for suspecting that the accused committed the offence, a summons will be issued.

Note that when an appearance notice or a summons is used, the accused is not *detained* (arrested). The appearance notice or summons will simply tell the accused the charge, and when and where to appear in court. If the accused fails to appear as directed, the court can then issue a **bench warrant**, which will allow the police to make an arrest.

Arrest

There are some situations where the police will want to arrest an accused person rather than use a summons or an appearance notice. Arrests can be made with a **warrant** or, under some circumstances, without a warrant.

With a Warrant

A warrant, like a summons, is issued by a Justice of the Peace when the police lay an information. A warrant either names or describes the accused, briefly states the charge, and orders the police to arrest the accused and bring him or her to court.

Before issuing the warrant, the Justice must consider whether an arrest is *in the public interest*. If the Justice decides that an arrest is not necessary, a summons may be issued instead. In deciding whether it is in the public interest to issue the warrant, the Justice may consider such matters as the seriousness of the charge and the likelihood that the accused will show up for trial. A general principle guiding the Justice of the Peace's decision is that a warrant should not be used if a summons will work just as well.

Without a Warrant

There are several situations where the police can arrest a person without a warrant. Some of them are listed in section 450 (1) of the *Criminal Code*:

> 450. (1) A peace officer may arrest without a warrant
>   (a) a person who has committed an indictable offence or who, on reasonable and probable grounds, he believes has committed or is about to commit an indictable offence,
>   (b) a person whom he finds committing a criminal offence, or
>   (c) a person for whose arrest he has reasonable and probable grounds to believe that a warrant is in force within the territorial jurisdiction.

Notice an important difference between section 450 (1)(a) and (b): only (b) covers summary conviction offences.

—Read (a) and (b) again. What is the difference between a police officer's powers to arrest for indictable offences and for summary conviction offences?

As well, under s. 449 of the *Code*, the police can arrest without a warrant any person whom they believe has committed a criminal offence and is escaping from and being freshly pursued by persons who have authority to arrest that person.

There are two other situations in which the police may arrest without a warrant. Under s. 31 of the *Code*, a police officer who witnesses a breach of the peace may arrest any person whom the officer finds committing the breach of peace or who on reasonable and probable grounds the officer believes is about to join in or renew a breach of the peace. This section can be traced to the old common law that allowed anyone the right to arrest someone to prevent breaches of the peace. Unfortunately, the *Criminal Code* does not define "breaches of the peace". Case law seems to say that they involve situations of violence or danger to the person, such as a fistfight or an argument that may break into a fight. Some legal authorities say that s. 31 is generally intended to allow the police to intervene in crisis situations, for instance, when a large crowd becomes unruly.

Finally, the police, under s. 181(2) of the *Code*, can arrest without a warrant anyone keeping or found in a gaming house.

There are important limitations on these powers to arrest. If the offence is one of the less serious indictable offences listed in s. 483, such as theft under $200 or keeping a common gaming house, or a hybrid offence or a summary offence, the police cannot make an arrest without a warrant unless it is in the public interest. When a police officer is considering the public interest, the *Code* states that the officer must look at the need to

1. identify the person;
2. secure or preserve evidence of the offence; and
3. prevent the repetition or continuance of the offence.

After an arrest for one of the less serious indictable offences, the police must release the accused as soon as practicable. For example, if the only reason the accused is being held is to establish his or her identity, the accused should be released once this has been done.

If an arrest is not made, or if the accused is later released by the police, the accused may be given an appearance notice or the police may go to a Justice of the Peace to have a summons issued.

Other Persons with Authority to Arrest

Police officers are not the only people who are given authority to arrest. The above powers are also given to anyone considered a "peace officer". Section 2 of the *Criminal Code* defines "peace officer" as including a mayor, warden, reeve, sheriff, any officer or permanent employee of a prison, customs officer, and pilot while in command of an aircraft.

In addition, *anyone* may make an arrest under certain circumstances. The following list describes the circumstances that permit you, as a member of the public, to make an arrest.

1. If you find someone committing an indictable offence.
2. If you believe the person has committed any criminal offence and is being freshly pursued by persons with authority to make the arrest.
3. If you find someone committing an offence on property which you yourself own.
4. If you are requested by the police to assist in making an arrest.
5. If you detain someone to prevent or stop a breach of the peace for the purpose of turning the person over to a peace officer.

The Procedure for Making an Arrest

An arrest is made if a person is seized or touched for the purpose of detention. However, it is not always necessary to use physical force to arrest someone. If the person is told that an arrest is being made and why, and the person voluntarily goes with the officer, it is not necessary for the officer to touch the person to make the arrest valid. If actual physical force is used, only as much force as is necessary in the circumstances can be used.

- Saul was stopped by the police and told he was being arrested for impaired driving. He said "Oh no!" and ran off. Has Saul been arrested? Explain.
- Areta was accused by a store owner of shoplifting. The police asked her to go with them to the station. Has Areta been arrested? Why or why not?

The Rights and Obligations of an Arrested Person

Until a person is arrested, there is no obligation to go with the police to the station or, in general, to answer any questions. However, a good citizen may want to assist the police in the investigation of crimes. Even after a person has been arrested, the police do not have any authority to compel that person to answer questions. There is a right to remain silent, although you should be aware that the police do not have to inform suspects of this right. Any *voluntary* statement that a person does make to the police can be admitted as evidence against the person at trial. The Supreme Court of Canada has accepted the following test for determining whether a statement has been voluntary or not: Was the statement obtained "by fear of prejudice or the hope of advantage exercised or held out by a person in authority"? In other words, if a person makes a statement to a person in authority, such as a police officer, because the person has been threatened with punishment or promised leniency, the statement will not be considered voluntary.

You should also know that provincial laws *do* allow the police to stop a motor vehicle and require the driver to produce a driver's licence, vehicle registration, and proof of insurance. As well, the *Criminal Code* in s. 234.1 allows a police officer to require a driver of a motor vehicle to take a breathalyzer test where the officer reasonably suspects that the person is under the influence of alcohol.

Remember that although there is a right to remain silent, the police may arrest a person whom they plan to charge with an offence just to establish the person's identity. An arrest may be avoided by simply providing identification so that the police can give an appearance notice or have a summons issued.

The police can compel a person who has been arrested for an indictable offence to be fingerprinted and photographed. If the person is later found not guilty, the police do not have to destroy the fingerprints and photographs. They will remain part of the person's arrest record. The police may also ask a person to take part in an identification line-up, but there is no requirement to do so.

A person has a right to be informed promptly of the reasons for the arrest. This has long been a right at common law, and is stated in s. 29(2) of the *Criminal Code* and in the *Charter of Rights and*

Freedoms. If the person is arrested under a warrant, the *Criminal Code* provides that the accused may examine the warrant. These rights are subject to what is reasonable under the circumstances. So, for example, if a person is resisting arrest, the police do not have to immediately inform the person of the reasons for the arrest.

An accused has a right to retain and instruct counsel without delay. This right has long existed at common law and has been upheld by recent court decisions.

R. v. Ballegeer [1969] 3 C.C.C. 353 (Man. C.A.)

Ballegeer was charged with the theft of two Goodyear tires. The police obtained a signed confession and at his trial he pleaded guilty. He then appealed his conviction and asked for a new trial on the grounds that legal counsel had been actively denied to him. He claimed that the statement to the police was not voluntary and was given without legal advice. He said that he felt the signed statement compelled him to enter a guilty plea and that he now wished to plead not guilty. The facts which the police did not deny were as follows:

The police arrived at Ballegeer's place of employment and told him that he was being charged with break, enter, and theft. He asked to call his lawyer. The police refused his request even though there was a phone in the next room. While the police were talking with another employee, Ballegeer was able to slip into the next room and call his lawyer. Before he could get any advice, one of the police officers came in and demanded the phone. The lawyer asked to speak to his client but was refused. The lawyer then asked the police to relay his advice not to make a statement until he could speak to Ballegeer but the officer said that he would not do so.

The Court of Appeal allowed Ballegeer's appeal and directed that a new trial be held. In reaching his decision, the judge said "The facts surrounding this aspect of the case are disturbing to anyone who prizes the rights of individual liberty in a free society. Among these is assuredly the right, on being arrested or detained, to retain and instruct counsel without delay.... What the constable did was wrong and unjustifiable and his conduct cannot receive the sanction of the court."

—Why is the right to counsel so important?
—The judge also considered evidence that indicated that Ballegeer was not guilty and that his statement to the police was not voluntary. Do you think these factors affected his decision? Should they have?

Today, the right to retain and instruct counsel is guaranteed by the *Charter of Rights and Freedoms*. The *Charter* adds that the accused person must be informed of this right.

FRONT
CHARTER OF RIGHTS

I am arresting you for...(*ordinary language*).

It is my duty to inform you that you have the right to retain and instruct counsel without delay.

Do you understand?

BACK
POLICE WARNING

You need not say anything. You have nothing to hope from any promise or favour and nothing to fear from any threat. Anything you do say may be used as evidence.

Figure 5-5 The police usually inform an accused of his or her rights by reading a card like this one at the time of arrest. The exact wording varies from province to province, but the meaning is the same.

Finally, a person has a right under the *Charter* not to be *arbitrarily* (without just cause) detained or imprisoned. Although it is not clear yet how far the courts will go in interpreting this section, it at least means that a person has a right not to be illegally arrested.

R. v. Altseimer (1983) 38 O.R. 783 (C.A.)

The accused was convicted under s. 236 of the *Criminal Code* of driving with over 80 mg of alcohol in his blood. Altseimer's car was stopped by the police for a vehicle check under provincial legislation which allows police to stop cars at random to check for drunk drivers. The police detected alcohol on his breath and asked him to take a breathalyzer test. He "failed" the test and was subsequently charged and convicted.

On appeal, Altseimer claimed that he had been arbitrarily detained when he was stopped by the police for a vehicle check.

—**Do you agree?**
—**Do you think the police should be able to stop cars at random when there are no reasonable grounds for suspecting that an offence has been committed?**

Remedies for Illegal Arrest

What remedies are available to a person who feels that his or her rights have been violated? If a person has been arrested without a warrant and the arrest was not made on reasonable and probable grounds, the police can be sued under civil law for the tort of false imprisonment. In general, where an arrest is made under an invalid warrant, the arresting officer is protected if the officer did not know it was invalid. If excessive force is used in making the arrest, a criminal charge of assault may be laid or the officer can be sued under tort law for assault and battery.

Our legal system has long provided the right of *habeas corpus* to persons who have been illegally detained. The right of *habeas corpus* is the right of any person who has been detained to a hearing to determine whether the detention is legal, and to be released if the detention is illegal. This common law right is now specifically stated in the *Charter of Rights and Freedoms*:

> 10. Everyone has the right on arrest or detention...
> (c) to have the validity of the detention determined by way of *habeas corpus* and to be released if the detention is not lawful.

Habeas corpus cannot be used to challenge the substance of the charge; it is used only to challenge illegal procedures. For example, a person who is not informed of the charge or is denied the right to counsel could challenge the legality of the detention.

Another possible remedy provided by the *Charter* concerns the use of evidence obtained during an illegal detention. The *Charter* states

> 24. (2) Where, in proceedings under subsection (1), a court concludes that evidence was obtained in a manner that infringed or denied any rights or freedoms guaranteed by this *Charter*, the evidence shall be excluded if it is established that, having regard to all the circumstances, the admission of it in the proceedings would bring the administration of justice into disrepute.

So, for example, if an accused were denied counsel, a court could exclude any statements that the accused made to the police. Notice that this does not mean that *all* illegally obtained evidence will be excluded from the accused's trial. The court must decide that the violation of the accused's rights was so serious that admission of the evidence "would bring the administration of justice into disrepute."

—Recall the *Ballegeer* case. This *Charter* remedy did not exist when *Ballegeer* was decided. If the case were heard today, do you think the defendant could have had his signed statement excluded at his trial? What factors do you think the court would have considered in deciding whether its admission would bring the administration of justice into disrepute?

What about the right to resist an unlawful arrest? Although in theory this right exists, it may be very difficult to use. Remember, a police officer needs only reasonable and probable grounds to arrest for an indictable offence. So even if the accused did not commit the offence, the officer still may have grounds to make the arrest. If it is a summary conviction offence, the accused must actually be caught in the act. In this case, if the accused knows that he or she has not committed the offence, the accused may resist the arrest. However, not many people know offhand which offences are summary and which are indictable. Remember, too, that a hybrid offence is treated as indictable until the Crown elects to treat it as a summary conviction offence. Finally, many provincial statutes give the police authority to arrest people without a warrant, under certain circumstances. For example, a province's liquor control legislation may allow the police to arrest persons found intoxicated in a public place.

A person who resists a police officer making a legal arrest may be charged with the offences of resisting or assaulting a police officer "in the execution of his duty", both of which are very serious charges. Of course, if the arrest is found to be illegal, the accused has a complete defence to the charge. If a person feels that he or she is being illegally arrested, probably the best course of action is to submit to the arrest and rely on the other remedies the law provides.

Powers of Search

With a Warrant

In most situations, the police must obtain a **search warrant** to search a place. A search warrant is usually issued by a Justice of the Peace. Under s. 443 of the *Criminal Code*, the justice may issue a search warrant if satisfied by an information given by the officer under oath that there is in a building, receptacle, or place

> **443.** *(a)* **anything upon or in respect of which any offence against this Act has been or is suspected to have been committed,**

> (b) anything that there is reasonable ground to believe will afford evidence with respect to the commission of an offence against this Act, or
> (c) anything that there is reasonable ground to believe is intended to be used for the purpose of committing any offence against the person for which a person may be arrested without warrant.

— What do you think is meant by a building, receptacle, or place? Would these terms include cars? boats? backyards?
— What about searching a human body? If a bullet is embedded in a suspect's shoulder, should the police be able to force the suspect to undergo surgery to obtain the bullet?
— The police have a search warrant to enter Simone's house to look for stolen television sets. Can they break open a locked desk drawer? Would your answer be different if they were looking for illegal drugs?
— What if Simone refused to let them enter the house? Can the police use force to gain entry? If so, how much force?

The warrant must name the thing being sought. However, the police can seize other things which they believe to have been used for or obtained in the commission of the offence.

The *Code* provides in s. 444 that the search must be done during the day, unless the Justice authorizes a night search. Even the hours during which the search will take place must be listed on the warrant.

Figure 5-6 A Sample Search Warrant

FORM 5
Warrant to search (Section 443)

Canada,
Province of
(territorial division)
To the peace officers in the said *(territorial division)*:
    Whereas it appears on the oath of A.B., of   that there are reasonable grounds for believing that *(describe things to be searched for and offence in respect of which search is to be made)* are in at , hereinafter called the premises:
    This is, therefore, to authorize and require you between the hours of *(as the justice may direct)* to enter into the said premises and to search for the said things and to bring them before me or some other justice.
    Dated this   day of   A.D. at

....
A Justice of the Peace in and for

There are specific provisions in the *Code* which give police somewhat wider powers for searches involving certain offences related to "disorderly houses", gaming houses, bookmaking places, and bawdy houses.

—**Look up s. 181. What must a police officer do to obtain a search warrant for these offences? What additional powers does the police officer have?**
—**See also s. 353, 100, 101, 159, 160, 281.3 for other special provisions on searches.**

Search warrants may also be obtained under other federal statutes, such as the *Narcotic Control Act* and the *Food and Drugs Act*.

Without a Warrant

The police may search without a warrant any person whom they have arrested and any place under the arrested person's control, for example, the person's house or car.

The only other powers the police have to search without a warrant are for certain specific *Criminal Code* offences and certain offences under other federal statutes. The most important *Criminal Code* offence which gives special powers to the police is found in s. 99:

> **99. (1) Whenever a peace officer believes on reasonable and probable grounds that an offence is being committed or has been committed against any of the provisions of this Act, relating to prohibited weapons, restricted weapons, firearms or ammunition, he may search, without a warrant, a person or vehicle or place or premises other than a dwelling-house and may seize anything by means of or in relation to which he reasonably believes the offence is being committed or has been committed.**

Search Without a Warrant under the *Narcotic Control Act* and Other Statutes

The *Narcotic Control Act* is a federal statute which prohibits the use of certain drugs. Under this statute, the police can search without a warrant any place, other than a dwelling-house, and any person found in such a place, if they have reasonable grounds for believing that illegal narcotics are present. During the search, the police can also seize any other evidence of an offence. There are similar powers to search without a warrant under the *Food and Drugs Act*, the *Customs Act*, and the *Excise Act*.

— Why do you think the police are given broader powers to search under these *Acts*?

Remedies for Illegal Search

A person may go to court to ask that a search warrant be **quashed**, that is, ruled invalid. A Justice of the Peace who issued an invalid search warrant may be sued, although the Justice will usually be protected from civil action by order of the court that quashes the warrant.

Even though property has been seized illegally, a court may order that it be retained if it is evidence relevant to a crime. However, recall that s. 24 of the *Charter of Rights and Freedoms*, which was discussed in the section "Remedies for Illegal Arrest", prevents the admission of evidence that would bring the administration of justice into disrepute. This section may be used to keep out illegally obtained evidence at the accused's trial.

A person may resist a search which he or she believes is illegal, but the same risks are involved as in resisting arrest.

Figure 5-7 Do you feel that the police should have the right to make random searches?

Searches not policy

CALGARY (CP) — Policemen who conducted random searches of concert-goers at the Stampede Corral in Calgary last April overstepped their authority, a police spokesman says. "It has never been the policy of the police department to randomly search people," said Deputy Chief Ernie Reimer. "We have to have some grounds for that search." However, no reprimands have been issued over the incidents. A provincial court judge ruled last week such random searches are unconstitutional. The ruling is to be appealed.

R. v. Acker (1970) 9 C.R.N.S. 371 (N.S.C.A.)

The accused was charged with assaulting a police officer in the execution of his duty. The police observed Acker and a friend staggering along the highway. They stopped the cruiser alongside them and Acker and his friend immediately got in. Smelling liquor on the two men, the police decided to arrest them under a provincial statute making it an offence to be intoxicated in a public place. However, the police did not communicate this decision to the men, who were then taken to the police station. When the police attempted to search Acker, he resisted and assaulted one of the officers.

—Was Acker legally arrested? Explain.
—Was the search legal? Explain.
—What should be the outcome of this case?

Procedures Following Arrest

Judicial Interim Release

Before the *Bail Reform Act*, which was passed in the 1970s, only a Justice of the Peace could order the release of an arrested person. As a result, many people spent time in jail awaiting their trial. The purpose of the *Bail Reform Act* was to limit the number of people who were being detained before trial. Underlying the legislation is the principle that people should not be held before trial unless there is a clear reason for doing so.

—**Why should people be released, if at all possible, pending their trial?**

Two major changes introduced by the new legislation are

1. that the police have a duty not to arrest if certain types of offences are involved, unless it is in the public interest or they believe the accused will fail to appear for trial; and
2. that the police are now authorized to release an arrested person from custody in certain situations, if the reason for the arrest no longer exists. For example, the police may have had to arrest the person in order to establish his or her identity. Once this has been done, they can release the person and have a summons issued.

The new legislation no longer uses the term "bail" but refers instead to the **judicial interim release** of persons charged with crimes. By not using the term "bail", the *Bail Reform Act* emphasizes the fact that an accused person usually does not have to pay money (bail) before being released.

The *Bail Reform Act* also provides that if the police do decide to arrest a person, the arrest must be reviewed by the officer in charge of the lockup once the accused is brought to the station. This officer has the same duty to release the arrested person as the arresting officer, but his or her authority covers a greater number of offences. In addition, the officer in charge has the authority to make the accused sign a written **promise to appear** in court or enter a **recognizance** of up to $500. A recognizance is an agreement wherein the accused agrees to pay a certain amount of money only if he or she fails to appear in court for trial or any other required hearings.

Hearing before a Justice of the Peace

If the accused is not released by the police, the accused must be brought before a Justice of the Peace within twenty-four hours, or as soon as possible. For most offences, it is up to the Crown to *show cause* why the accused should not be released. For example, the Crown may show that the accused has failed to appear for court dates before. The Justice of the Peace is concerned with questions similar to those of the police: Will the accused show up for trial? Is it in the public interest to detain the accused? Is detention necessary for the protection or safety of the public? In deciding this last question, the Justice of the Peace is concerned with such factors as whether the accused will commit further crimes if released. "Public interest" has a broader meaning, including the need for the public to feel safe and secure and to believe justice is being done.

If the accused is released, the Justice of the Peace can impose any of the following terms:

1. Conditions, for example, not to associate with certain people, to remain in a certain area, or to deposit a passport.
2. Recognizances with or without **sureties**, who are people who will also sign the recognizance and therefore be responsible if the accused fails to appear.
3. A money deposit along with the recognizance.

If the offence is especially serious, for example, treason, hijacking, or murder, the hearing must be held before a superior court judge.

R. v. Thomson [1972] 7 C.C.C. (2d) 70 (B.C.S.C.)

The accused was charged in Vancouver with possession of marijuana for the purpose of trafficking. He had no previous record and was twenty-one years old. He had completed one year at university, and had recently been laid off by Ontario Hydro. He had been in Vancouver for about six weeks seeking employment when he was arrested. He had an apartment in Vancouver and a friend who was willing to act as a surety for him.

—Should Thomson be released before his trial? What factors would you consider in making this decision?
—If you released Thomson, what conditions would you impose on him?

If the offence is one listed in s. 457.5.1 of the *Criminal Code*, the onus to show cause shifts to the accused. In other words, the accused has the burden of convincing the court that he or she should not be detained before trial.

—Look up section 457.5.1 of the *Criminal Code*. In your opinion, why does the law "reverse the onus" for these offences?

SUMMARIZING YOUR READING

1. What is the purpose of the rules of criminal procedure?
2. In what way is the criminal court system like a ladder?
3. Describe the duties of a Justice of the Peace; a magistrate or provincial court judge; a county or district court; superior court.
4. What are the three types of offences?
5. Who decides how a hybrid offence should be treated? When is this decision made?
6. Explain the three ways in which the police can compel a person to appear in court.
7. Do the police always need a warrant to make an arrest?
8. What must a police officer do to obtain a warrant for arrest?
9. What must a Justice of the Peace consider before issuing an arrest warrant?
10. Does a Justice always issue an arrest warrant? Explain.
11. List all the situations in which a police officer can arrest someone without a warrant.
12. Explain the difference between a police officer's authority to arrest without warrant in the event of an indictable offence and of a summary conviction offence.
13. How does the *Code* define "peace officer"?
14. What authority do peace officers have to make arrests?
15. List the situations where anyone may make an arrest.
16. Explain what is necessary to make an arrest.
17. If you are arrested, do you have to answer police questions? Why might it be a good idea to at least identify yourself?
18. If the police stop you while you are driving a motor vehicle, what does the law require you to show them?
19. Do you have to take a breathalyzer test if you are asked to take one?

20. When can the police require a person to be fingerprinted and photographed? Can the police require a person to take part in an identification line-up?

21. Explain the rights of a person upon being arrested.

22. What remedies does a person who has been illegally arrested have?

23. Is it a good idea to resist if you think you are being illegally arrested? Explain.

24. Explain what the police must do to obtain a search warrant.

25. When can the police search without a warrant?

26. What remedies are there for illegal searches?

27. Why was the *Bail Reform Act* passed?

28. When an arrested person is taken to the police station, what must the officer in charge of the lock-up do?

29. What happens if the police do not release an arrested person? Explain fully.

30. What terms can a Justice of the Peace impose on a person being released from custody?

31. Are all hearings for interim release held before Justices of the Peace? Explain.

32. Does the accused ever have the onus of showing why he or she should not be detained? Explain.

DISCUSSING KEY ISSUES

1. What are some of the ways discussed in this chapter in which the law restricts the authority of the police? Discuss whether you think the police are too restricted or not restricted enough. Give examples from the chapter. For example, are police powers to search broad enough, or are they too broad? Why should law-abiding citizens be concerned about the extent of police authority?

2. A *writ of assistance* is a special type of search warrant issued only under the *Narcotic Control Act*, the *Food and Drugs Act*, the *Customs Act*, and the *Excise Act*. These warrants are issued by judges of the Federal Court of Canada, and are given to R.C.M.P. officers and other federal officers. A writ is given to a particular officer, rather than in connection with a specific offence. For example, an officer who holds a writ under the *Narcotic Control Act* can search any place, including a dwelling-place, if the officer

believes illegal narcotics are on the premises. The writ can be used as long as the officer is on the force or until the writ is cancelled.

Section 8 of the *Charter of Rights and Freedoms* provides a guarantee against unreasonable search and seizure. Do you think that the Court should continue to issue these warrants?

RESOLVING CASES

R. v. McKibbon (1973) 12 C.C.C. (2d) 66 (B.C.C.A.)

McKibbon was charged with assaulting a police officer with intent to resist lawful arrest.

A police officer saw McKibbon driving erratically and at a high rate of speed. He followed the car to a trailer park, where it stopped. As the officer was examining McKibbon's licence and car registration he noticed alcohol on McKibbon's breath and that McKibbon was unsteady on his feet. When McKibbon was asked to take a breathalyzer test, he ran. The officer caught up with him and a struggle took place. When McKibbon took the breathalyzer a short while later, he passed the test. Therefore, he was not charged with impaired driving but only with assaulting a police officer.

— **Impaired driving is an indictable offence. Did the officer have grounds to make a lawful arrest?**
— **Should McKibbon be convicted of the charge? Why or why not?**

R. v. James (1978) 7 C.R. (3d) 17 (Ont. C.C.)

The issue in this case was whether incriminating statements made by the defendant to the police should be admitted as evidence. That is, the question was whether the statements were made voluntarily.

As the defendant was entering Canada, customs officials found what they believed was an illegal drug in her suitcase. Two R.C.M.P. officers were called in to question her. She was given a standard police caution that she could remain silent and that anything she did say would be taken down and used as evidence. As the police were questioning James, they took down her answers. She refused to sign this statement.

James told the court that on two or three occasions, Officer Keddy told her to look into his eyes and tell him the truth. At one point, she said that he told her that if she would tell him the truth he would let her go and if she did not tell the truth, she would get a seven-year sentence. She also said that at this time, she had been up for almost twenty-four hours and at one point fell asleep and had to be awakened by the police. She told the court that this was her first trip to Canada and that she was anxious and frightened of Officer Keddy. She could not understand why she was being questioned if she had a right to remain silent.

—Should the statement be admitted? What rule should the court consider?

Re La Porte and the Queen (1972) 29 D.L.R. (3d) 651 (Que. Q.B.)

A Justice of the Peace issued a search warrant to allow a search of the body of Roger La Porte. La Porte had been arrested and in custody for several months when the police received information that he had been involved in a robbery about one-and-a-half years previously. During the robbery, gunfire had been exchanged. La Porte had scars on his neck resembling bullet wounds, and X-rays showed the presence of an object resembling a bullet in his neck. The warrant authorized the police to have qualified doctors extract the bullets.

To remove the bullet would require a general anaesthetic and would involve some risk to La Porte. La Porte refused to consent to the surgery and applied to the court to have the search warrant quashed.

—What factors should the court consider in deciding whether to quash the warrant?
—Does it matter whether the surgery would be of any benefit to La Porte? Does the degree of risk involved matter?
—Can a human body be considered a building, receptacle, or place?

R. v. Jaagusta [1974] 3 W.W.R. 766 (B.C. P.C.)

A police officer stopped a car driven by the defendant and told him that he was searching for drugs under the authority of the *Narcotic Control Act*. After searching the car, the officer attempted to search the defendant, who pushed him away. No drugs were found, but the defendant was charged with resisting a police officer in the execution of his duty. At the trial, the officer testified that he had no grounds at all for believing that the defendant had drugs in his car or on his person.

—Were the search of the car and the attempted search of the defendant legal? Explain.
—Was the defendant justified in resisting the search?
—What should be the outcome of this case?

R. v. Hynds (1982) 70 C.C.C. (2d) 186 (Alta. Q.B.)

The defendant asked the court to rule on the admissability of evidence obtained under a search warrant issued under the *Narcotic Control Act*. There were three errors in the search warrant. The name of the street where the house to be searched was located was misspelled "Habitant" rather than "Habitat". The address was typed in as 463, while the correct address was 465. The police officer making the search corrected this error in pen when he arrived at the house. The third mistake was that the narcotic being searched for was marijuana, not cocaine as indicated in the warrant.

The defendant argued that the search warrant was invalid, and that, therefore, his right under the *Charter* to be secure against unreasonable search and seizure had been violated. He asked that the court use its authority given under the *Charter* to exclude the evidence found during the search.

—**Were the rights of the defendant violated?**
—**Should the evidence be excluded? Explain.**

R. v. Dinardo (1981) 61 C.C.C. 52 (Ont. Cty. Ct.)

The defendant was charged with being an accessory to the offence of robbery and with having possession of property obtained by the commission of an indictable offence. The question before the court was whether two statements the defendant made to the police should be admitted as evidence.

Dinardo's lawyer had surrendered him to the police when Dinardo's parole was revoked. The lawyer told the police that his client did not want to be questioned without the presence of his lawyer. Dinardo's lawyer then left his name and phone number with the police, who assured him that he would be contacted before his client was questioned. A short while later, two police from the hold-up squad arrived and took Dinardo to another station, where he was questioned. At the end of the questioning, Dinardo gave a statement to the police. Apparently, the instructions of Dinardo's lawyer were not passed on to the hold-up squad police.

Dinardo's statements were voluntarily given. The only issue was whether the police had interfered with Dinardo's right to retain and instruct counsel.

—**Do you think the statements should be excluded? Explain.**

6

Criminal Procedure: The Trial

Starting the Trial Process
Rights of the Defendant at Trial
The Procedure for Trying Indictable Offences
The Procedure for Trying Summary Conviction Offences
Young Offenders

Figure 6-1 The early practice of not allowing jurors to eat, drink, or sleep was meant to encourage them to make speedy decisions.

The procedural rules which govern criminal trials today have not always been part of our judicial system. For example, basic procedural rights which we may take for granted today, such as the right to have a lawyer, to call defence witnesses, or even to testify on your own behalf, did not exist in earlier times. An accused in Canada did not even have the right to appeal a trial court's decision until 1923.

This chapter will look at some modern rules of procedure which determine the kind of trial a defendant receives.

Starting The Trial Process

The first step in any trial is the laying of an **information**, which is usually done by a police officer. However, private persons can lay informations and can even prosecute summary conviction offences, if the Crown refuses to do so. If the offence is indictable, a private person must have the permission of the Crown to prosecute.

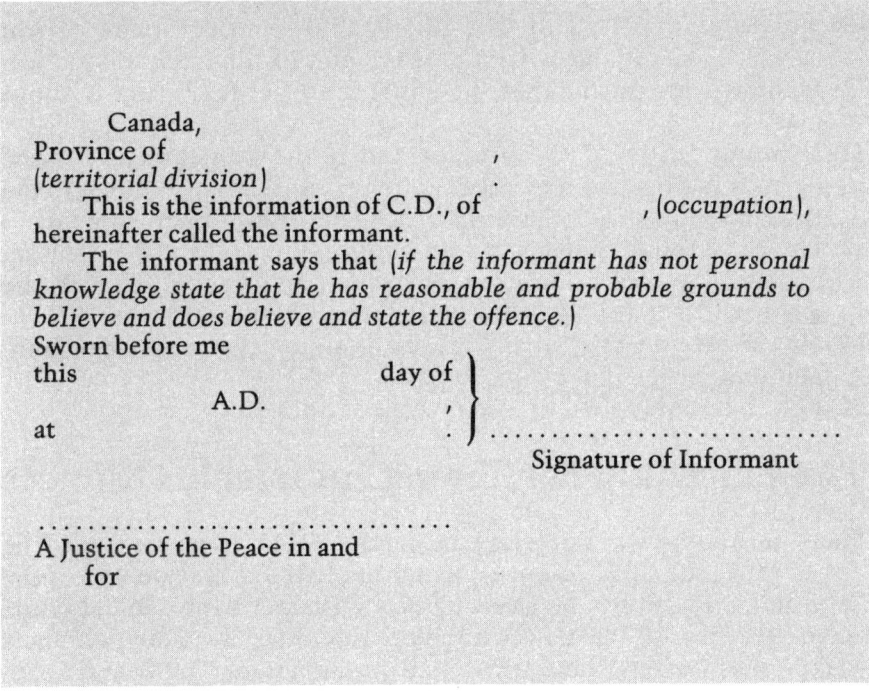

Figure 6-2 A Sample Information Form

The person who lays the information is called the **informant**. For summary conviction offences, the information must be laid within six months of the commission of the offence. There is no limitation period if the offence is indictable.

Rights Of The Defendant At Trial

Regardless of whether the trial is of an indictable or summary conviction offence, the defendant has certain rights. These rights either are part of the common law or are stated in the *Bill of Rights* or the *Charter of Rights and Freedoms*. They include the following rights:

1. To retain and instruct counsel and to be informed of this right.
2. To be informed without unreasonable delay of the specific offence being charged.
3. To be presumed innocent until proven guilty.
4. To be present at the trial and make a full defence.
5. To have the opportunity to prepare for trial.
6. To be tried within a reasonable time.
7. To a trial by jury if the offence is punishable by five or more years' imprisonment.
8. To an interpreter if necessary.
9. Not to be tried or punished again for the same offence.
10. Not to be deprived of life, liberty and security of the person except in accordance with the principles of fundamental justice. In short, this means that the court must act fairly and without bias.
11. If found guilty of the offence and if the punishment for the offence has been varied between the time of commission and the time of sentencing, to have the benefit of the lesser punishment.
12. Not to be found guilty of an act or omission, if at the time the act or omission was committed, it was not an offence. (That is, the right not to be found guilty under retroactive laws.)
13. Not to be subjected to any cruel and unusual treatment or punishment.
14. Not to be compelled to testify against oneself.

The Procedure For Trying Indictable Offences

There are several ways in which indictable offences can be tried. The less serious indictable offences, which are listed in section 483 of the *Criminal Code*, must be tried by a magistrate or provincial court judge. Section 483 offences include theft under $200 (which is usually shoplifting), fraud involving amounts under $200, and keeping a betting house.

The most serious indictable offences must be tried by a superior court judge and jury, except in Alberta, where the accused can elect to be tried by a judge alone. These offences are listed in s. 427 and include treason, murder, and bribery of a judge or a member of Parliament or provincial legislature.

For all other indictable offences, the defendant can choose how the offence will be tried from the following list of options:

1. trial by magistrate or provincial court judge
2. trial by county or district court judge alone (In the aforementioned situations, the Crown can insist that the trial be by jury if the offence carries a penalty of five or more years' imprisonment.)
3. trial by county or district court judge and jury
4. trial by superior court judge and jury (except in Alberta, where the defendant can choose to be tried by superior court judge alone)

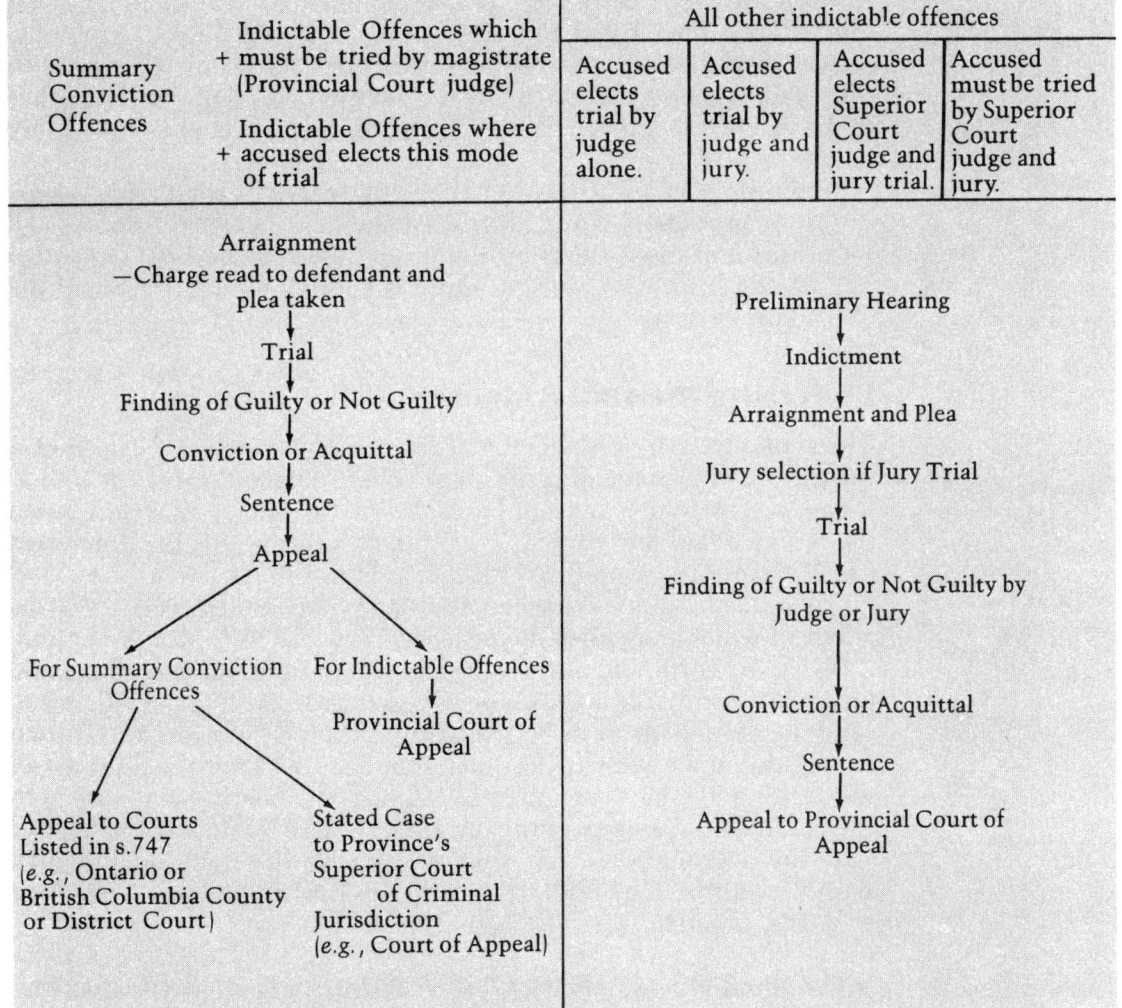

Figure 6-3 *Steps in the Criminal Trial Process. The procedure used is determined by the type of offence, and, in some situations, by the choice of the accused.*

CRIMINAL PROCEDURE — THE TRIAL 109

— Why do you think a defendant would choose a particular method of trial?
— What do you think are the advantages and disadvantages of a jury trial?

The Preliminary Hearing

If the trial of an indictable offence is not before a magistrate or provincial court judge, there must be a **preliminary hearing**, unless the defendant waives the right to one. The purpose of this hearing is to weed out weak cases and give the defendant a chance to see what kind of case the Crown has. The Crown does not need to prove the case beyond a reasonable doubt at this point. It is only necessary to show sufficient evidence to put the accused on trial. One court has said evidence is sufficient if it shows that the accused is probably guilty.

Preliminary hearings are held before Justices of the Peace, magistrates, or provincial court judges. At the hearing, each side can call witnesses and cross-examine the other side's witnesses. The judge will decide from this whether there is enough evidence to send the defendant to trial.

Preferring the Indictment

The actual trial of an indictable offence which is not to be tried by a magistrate or provincial court judge is begun by **preferring the indictment**. In all provinces except Nova Scotia, this means that the Crown prepares a **bill of indictment**, a written accusation that the defendant has committed a named offence. The bill is then *preferred* (presented) to the court when the defendant is *arraigned*, that is, when the charge against the accused is read and a plea is entered.

In Nova Scotia, the Crown prefers the indictment before a grand jury, whose only role is to decide whether there is enough evidence to send the defendant to trial. A hearing is then held where the Crown alone can call witnesses. The defendant does not have the right to call witnesses and is not even present. In fact, the hearing is not open to the public. If a majority of the jurors find there is enough evidence to send the defendant to trial, they will return the indictment signed with the words "true bill". If they do not find enough evidence for a trial, the indictment will be signed "no bill".

— The grand jury system used in Nova Scotia was originally used in every province and territory in Canada. Why do you think most places have stopped using grand juries?

Jury Trials

Each province has its own method for preparing a prospective list of jurors. In Ontario, for example, jury lists are compiled each year from lists of electors. A panel of jurors is selected from the jury list by a court official call the **sheriff** to be available for trials during a certain period of time. Each juror's name, address, and occupation is placed on a card. The court clerk then selects approximately twenty names at random as jurors for a particular trial.

Figure 6-4 A Juror being Sworn for Duty

—Check the legislation in your province governing jury selection. This statute is usually called the *Juries Act*. Who is eligible for jury duty? Who is ineligible? Why do you think this is so?
—If you know someone who has served as a juror, interview him or her. What were they paid for jury duty? What instruction were they given by the judge? What were their general impressions of the trial process?
—Serving on a jury can be an inconvenience. Why do you think it is an important duty for citizens to perform?

Once a defendant has elected a jury trial and has been arraigned, the jury will be selected from the names chosen by the court clerk. A jury is made up of twelve persons, except in the Yukon and the Northwest Territories where a full jury consists of six persons. The defendant and the Crown are allowed to question each juror. Each side can **challenge** a potential juror **for cause**, on the grounds that the juror is not impartial. For example, if the juror knows the accused, or is somehow connected with the case, it is likely that the juror's decision will be biased. When a juror is challenged, there is a trial on this issue. If it is proven that the juror is biased, he or she will be asked to step down from the jury.

The defendant and Crown also have a certain number of **peremptory challenges**. For these, there is no need to give a reason for wanting a particular juror to be rejected. The prospective juror can be rejected simply on the basis of appearance and the information contained on the card.

—Can you think of an example of when a lawyer might challenge a prospective juror peremptorily?

The seriousness of the offence determines the number of peremptory challenges allowed to the defendant. For example, for murder, the defence gets twenty challenges, while for an offence punishable by less than five years, the number is four. The Crown always has four peremptory challenges. In addition, the Crown has a right to ask up to forty-eight jurors to **stand aside**. A juror who is asked to stand aside goes to the end of the line of prospective jurors available for that trial. If the juror's name comes up again because of challenges and other stand-asides, the juror can be challenged but not asked to stand aside again.

The Trial

Regardless of which court hears the case, the stages of a trial are generally the same:

1. The defendant is arraigned.
2. Opening addresses may be made by the Crown and the defence.
3. The Crown calls its evidence.
4. The defence may ask that the case be dismissed for insufficient evidence to prove the offence or, if that does not pertain, the defence calls its evidence.
5. The Crown may call rebuttal evidence (evidence that contradicts the defendant's evidence). The defence may then call surrebuttal evidence.
6. Closing addresses may be made by the Crown and the defence.
7. In a jury trial, the judge charges the jury.

8. The jury retires to reach a verdict, or the judge makes a finding of guilty or not guilty.
9. The defendant is sentenced if found guilty, or acquitted if found not guilty.

The Arraignment

The defendant appears in court, where the charge is read. The defendant then enters a plea of guilty or not guilty. If a guilty plea is entered, the defendant will be sentenced. If a not guilty plea is entered, the trial continues.

Opening Addresses by the Crown and Defence

Each side may make an opening statement in which they outline their cases, including what evidence they will present for the judge or jury. The Crown makes the first address.

The Crown's Case

The Crown presents its case first by calling witnesses who will be **sworn in** before testifying. The Crown conducts an **examination-in-chief** of each witness. An important rule regarding questioning witnesses-in-chief is that they may not be asked **leading questions**, that is, questions which suggest their own answers. A question which can be answered by merely "yes" or "no" is probably a leading question.

Helga is being examined-in-chief by the Crown about a car accident she witnessed. The Crown says to her: "Did you see a blue Honda run a red light at the corner of Main and Gerrard at 8 p.m. on August 17, 1984?" The defence lawyer immediately objects to this question as leading the witness. The judge agrees and asks the Crown to rephrase the question. The Crown then asks this series of questions.

CROWN: Where were you at approximately 8 p.m. on August 17, 1984?
HELGA: Standing at the corner of Main and Gerrard.
CROWN: What did you observe?
HELGA: I saw a car run a red light and hit another car.
CROWN: Did you happen to notice the make or colour of the car which ran the light?
HELGA: Yes. It was a blue Honda.

There are many exceptions to this rule. For instance, it is acceptable to lead a witness on introductory matters that are not in dispute.

The Crown could say to Helga:

CROWN: Is your name Helga Svenson?
HELGA: Yes.
CROWN: Do you live at 109 W. 5th Avenue?
HELGA: Yes.

—Why do you think there is a rule against asking leading questions?

After the Crown examines a witness, the defence may cross-examine. Cross-examination has two main purposes. The first purpose is to weaken the other side's case. If the witness has made previous inconsistent statements, either in or out of court, the defence can challenge the witness on the inconsistency. The defence can also raise the issue of the credibility of the witness—whether the testimony of the witness is believable. If the defence could prove that Helga is colour blind, her testimony regarding the colour of the car and the traffic light would be considerably weakened. The character of the witness can also be attacked. If Helga has a criminal record or is biased because she is a friend of someone injured in the accident, this could be brought out in cross-examination.

The second purpose of cross-examination is to bring out new evidence favourable to the cross-examiner's case. The scope of cross-examination is very broad, so even if the Crown calls a witness to establish a minor fact, the defence can cross-examine on any issue in the case. There is no restriction on asking leading questions in cross-examination.

The Crown has a right to re-examine a witness after cross-examination, to clarify anything that came up in cross-examination. For instance, a witness might be asked to explain an apparently inconsistent statement. Generally, re-examination is limited to issues arising out of cross-examination. However, a judge may allow the Crown to insert new evidence which was left out during the examination-in-chief.

Motion For Dismissal by the Defence

Remember that the Crown must prove each element of the offence "beyond a reasonable doubt", while the defence does not need to say anything. For this reason, after the close of the Crown's case, the defence can make a motion asking that the judge dismiss the charges on the basis that the Crown has not proved its case.

The Defence's Case

If the judge refuses to dismiss the charge, which is the usual response, the defence will then call its evidence. The same steps will be followed: examination-in-chief, cross-examination, and re-examination.

Rebuttal Evidence

After the close of the defence's case, the trial judge may allow the Crown to present evidence which *rebuts* (contradicts) the defence's evidence. The defence may then be allowed to give evidence in *surrebuttal* to the Crown's *rebuttal* evidence.

The Rules of Evidence

The rules concerning how and what each side can present as evidence are quite complex. Some of these rules are stated in statutes such as the *Canada Evidence Act*; others have developed through case law. Although every rule has exceptions, the following discussion presents a few general principles of the law of evidence.

The first rule of evidence is that, to be admissible in court, evidence must be relevant to the **facts-in-issue**. The facts-in-issue are defined as follows:

1. Those facts which each side must prove to establish its case. For instance, the Crown must prove each element of the offence.
2. Collateral (secondary) facts such as the credibility of witnesses.

There are two types of evidence which can be used to prove facts-in-issue: **direct evidence** and **indirect** or **circumstantial evidence**.

Direct Evidence

This type of evidence consists of the testimony (oral evidence) of a witness that is given as proof of a fact. Let's go back to the case of Helga and the blue Honda. If Helga testified "I saw that the light was red when the Honda entered the intersection," she would be offering direct proof that the Honda ran a red light.

Direct evidence needs to be contrasted with **hearsay**. Hearsay is evidence given by a witness of what someone else said, wrote, or observed. If Helga testified that she did not actually notice the colour of the traffic light, but her mother, who was walking with her, told her it was red when the Honda entered the intersection, her evidence would be hearsay. This statement would not be admissible as proof that the light was red.

—**Why do you think hearsay is inadmissible?**

Indirect or Circumstantial Evidence

It is not always possible to have an eyewitness account of what happened when a crime has been committed. However, circumstances may be proved from which an inference can be drawn as to what happened.

Suppose that Helga was at home when the accident with the blue Honda occurred and that there were no other witnesses. The driver of the Honda did not remain at the scene and the driver of the other car died. However, blue paint chips from the scene of the accident, the fact that the owner of the Honda had the car repaired a few days after the accident, and the strange behaviour of the Honda owner the evening of the accident might all be circumstances or facts from which a judge or jury could infer that the Honda was the car involved in the accident.

In sum, circumstantial evidence is evidence of a fact from which the existence of a fact-in-issue can be drawn or inferred.

An important rule which was first stated in the English *Hodge* case is that, where the evidence against an accused consists only of circumstantial evidence, in order to find the defendant guilty, the judge or jury must be satisfied that the facts are inconsistent with any other rational conclusion than that the defendant is guilty.

R. v. *Hodge* (1838) 168 E.R. 1136 (Liverpool Summer Assizes)

A woman was robbed and murdered on her way home from the market. The accused, Hodge, knew her well and was seen near the spot where the murder was committed shortly before the murder occurred. However, four other people were also seen in the area at about the same time. The accused was seen a few hours after the murder burying something. It was dug up, and turned out to be money in about the amount of which the murdered woman was believed to have been robbed.

— Apply the rule discussed above. Would you find Hodge guilty or not guilty?
— Why do you think courts have adopted the rule in the *Hodge* case?

Material Objects and Documents as Evidence

The oral evidence of witnesses is not the only kind of evidence which can be admitted in court. Material objects or documents may be admitted if they are relevant to a fact-in-issue. However, it is important to note that material objects and documents, or **exhibits** as they are called in court, must be identified through the testimony of a witness. Assume, for instance, that the driver of the blue Honda was charged with impaired driving. An opened bottle of liquor found by the police under the driver's seat would be relevant circumstantial evidence that the driver had been drinking while driving. For the bottle to be admissible as an exhibit, it would have to be identified by the officer who found it.

Closing Addresses

Once the Crown and defence have each had an opportunity to present all the evidence pertaining to their cases, they may choose to make a **closing address** to the jury, or, if there is no jury, a **closing argument** to the judge.

If the defence has called no witnesses, the defence will give the first address; otherwise, the Crown will go first. In the addresses, each side will attempt to present its case in the most favourable light and will try to destroy the other side's case.

The Charge to the Jury

When a trial takes place before a judge and jury, it is the role of the jury to decide questions of fact, while the judge decides all questions of law. Examples of questions of fact would be: Is the defendant the person who committed the crime? Did the victim consent? Was the defendant so intoxicated that he or she could not form the specific intent of the crime? Questions of law concern such issues as whether or not certain evidence should be allowed, and the type of *mens rea* required for the offence.

In **charging the jury**, the judge reviews the evidence for the jury and tells them what law applies. For example, if the defendant has raised the defence of intoxication, the judge will first tell the jury whether, as a matter of law, that defence is available to the defendant, since it is available only for certain types of crimes. The judge will then review the evidence that indicates whether or not the defendant was in fact intoxicated when the crime was committed. The judge may also give an opinion of the facts, but it must be made clear that it is up to the jury to decide questions of fact.

In trials without a jury, the judge tries both fact and law.

Reaching a Verdict

After being charged, the jury retires to reach a verdict of guilty or not guilty. If there is no jury, the judge alone decides on the defendant's guilt or innocence. The defendant is then either convicted or acquitted. Trials before a jury require that the verdict be unanimous; that is, the jurors must *all* agree that the defendant is either guilty or not guilty. If the jurors cannot agree, a new trial will be ordered.

Sentencing the Defendant

If the defendant is convicted, the judge may order a **pre-sentence report** before passing sentence. Such a report is prepared by a probation officer, and discusses matters like the defendant's personal background, work record, and previous convictions. Usually, a recommendation regarding the sentence will be made in the report. At the sentencing hearing, the defendant can challenge any of the information in the report, and can also make submissions to the court regarding circumstances which may affect the sentence. For instance, the defendant might explain why the crime was committed, or what attempts he or she had made at rehabilitation since the crime was committed, such as attempts to control a drug or alcohol problem.

All of this information helps the judge decide what the proper sentence should be. In addition, the judge considers the seriousness of the offence—whether it was premeditated (planned); circumstances surrounding the offence such as whether violence was used; how common the crime is; and the usual sentence for this type of offence. Generally, the *Criminal Code* sets maximum terms of imprisonment for crimes. A judge can order any term of imprisonment up to the maximum. There are a few offences for which a minimum penalty is set. A person convicted of first degree murder must be sentenced to life imprisonment, which means twenty-five years of imprisonment without being eligible for **parole**, conditional release from prison before the entire term of imprisonment has been served. For those offences with a set minimum penalty, the judge must sentence the defendant to at least that penalty. If the sentence is for ninety days or less, the defendant may be allowed to serve the sentence intermittently. This means the defendant can serve the sentence on weekends, for instance. An intermittent sentence allows the convicted person an opportunity to continue working while serving the sentence.

If a defendant has been convicted of more than one offence, a sentence will be passed for each. Terms of imprisonment may be served **concurrently** (at the same time) or **consecutively** (one after the other). A judge can take into account the time spent in custody before and during the trial when determining a sentence.

The Prison System

If the term of imprisonment is less than two years, the convicted person will be sent to a provincial institution. Otherwise, the sentence will be served in a federal penitentiary. There are three types of federal penitentiaries—those with maximum, medium, and minimum security. The offender is first sent to a general reception area, where it will be decided in which type of institution the sentence should be served. Maximum security is intended for the most dangerous offenders, who need the most physical security: high walls, locked doors, and so forth. In medium security there is less supervision, while minimum security prisoners have a great deal of freedom within the institution.

It is not necessary for a prisoner to serve the entire term of imprisonment. Both provincial and federal prison systems allow prisoners to be paroled. A *parolee* (paroled prisoner) will have a parole supervisor to report to, whose job is to help the parolee readjust to living in society. If the parolee violates any of the conditions of parole, he or she may be returned to prison to serve the remainder of the sentence. Conditions of parole may include remaining within a certain geographical area, or refraining from certain activities.

Prisoners may also be granted *day parole*, which usually means they may leave the prison during the day, to attend school for example, but must return to the institution at night. Day parole can help prepare a prisoner for full parole. Prisoners may also be given *temporary absences* allowing them to remain away from the institution for up to several days with or without an escort for medical or humanitarian reasons.

Figure 6-5 Inside a Federal Penitentiary

The decision whether to grant parole is made by the twenty-six-member National Parole Board for federal offenders in both federal and provincial institutions, except where a province has its own Parole Board for inmates of provincial institutions. In most situations, a prisoner can apply for parole after serving one-third of the sentence or seven years, whichever is the lesser. However, it is up to the Parole Board to decide whether the inmate is ready for parole.

Inmates who are not paroled can also be released on **mandatory supervision** before their sentence expires. At the time the inmate enters prison, he or she is credited with a certain amount of "time off" (*statutory remission*) which can be lost for bad behaviour. Each month, the inmate can earn more time off for good behaviour (*earned remission*). Up to one-third of the inmate's sentence can be remitted through earned and statutory remission. Unlike parole, which is discretionary, inmates have a right to be released on mandatory supervision once they become entitled to it.

Other Sentencing Options

A judge has other options in sentencing besides imprisonment. The offender can be ordered to pay a fine, or to make **restitution** to the victim. A restitution order requires the offender to make a money payment to the victim as compensation for any harm suffered.

Community service orders, which require the offender to perform a certain number of hours of work in the community, are a recent type of sentence that some judges have been employing. A judge may give the convicted person a **suspended sentence** and place him or her on **probation**. An offender who has been placed on probation will have to report to a probation officer and must obey the terms set by the court. If the terms of the probation order are broken, the defendant will have to return to court where the judge may re-sentence the person. Terms of probation might include an order to report to the probation officer weekly, to continue a drug therapy program, or to continue working, for instance.

In some cases where a person has been found guilty, the judge may, instead of convicting the defendant, order a **discharge** either *absolutely* or *conditionally*. Discharges may be ordered for any offence except those for which the punishment may be fourteen years, imprisonment for life, or one in which a minimum term of imprisonment is set. A discharge may be ordered if the judge feels it is in the best interests of the accused and not contrary to the public interest. If the discharge is absolute, the defendant is deemed not to have been convicted. Therefore, if a job application asked whether the applicant has ever been convicted of a crime, the person could truthfully say "no". A conditional discharge places the defendant on probation for a certain period of time. If all goes well during the probation period, the discharge becomes absolute. However, a person receiving a discharge *does* have a criminal record, since the discharge is recorded in the same manner as any other court proceeding.

—**What do you think are some of the consequences of having a criminal record?**

The Purposes of Punishment

There are several reasons for punishing people who break the law. One of the oldest purposes of punishment is **retribution**, or vengeance. Even today, when an especially horrible crime is committed, there will be a cry from some quarters for an "eye for an eye, a tooth for a tooth". However, this is one of the least important purposes. Some courts have even rejected it outright as a purpose of punishment. In more recent years, **rehabilitation**, or reformation, has become the primary goal of punishment. The idea that criminals can be reformed into productive members of society has gained wide acceptance in this century.

Another purpose of punishment is **deterrence**. There are two kinds of deterrence—*general* and *specific*. By general deterrence we mean that the threat of punishment will discourage people from breaking the law. Specific deterrence means that a person who has been punished for breaking the law will be discouraged (and prevented while imprisoned) from breaking the law again.

People disagree about which of these purposes is the most important.

—**Which reason do you think is most important? How important are the other reasons?**
—**How do you think the various sentencing options available to a judge serve the purposes of punishment?**

Appeals Of Indictable Offences

The decision of the trial court can often be appealed to a higher court. Either the defendant or the Crown may appeal the conviction or acquittal, or the appropriateness of the sentence.

Sometimes there is an absolute right to appeal. At other times the right to appeal is discretionary; that is, the permission of the appeal court (or sometimes the trial court judge) must be granted before the appeal will be heard. Permission will be granted only for those cases which involve important or difficult issues.

Indictable offences are appealed to the provincial Court of Appeal, or, in Prince Edward Island, to the province's Supreme Court. There is a right to appeal only if the appeal concerns a question of law alone. If it concerns a question of mixed law and fact, the accused must have the permission of the Court of Appeal, or a certificate from the trial court judge stating that the case is a proper one for appeal.

There may also be a final appeal to the Supreme Court of Canada. There is a right to appeal to the Supreme Court of Canada on a question of law alone if at least one judge of the Court of Appeal of the province has dissented (disagreed) in giving the appeal judgement. Otherwise, the Supreme Court's permission is required for an appeal.

Usually, an appeal is "on the record" only: the appeal court makes its decision by considering the written record of what occurred during the trial. For example, the court may examine transcripts of what each witness said at the trial. It is very rare for an appeal court to hear new evidence from a witness.

—Why do you think appeal courts rarely hear new evidence? Under what circumstances do you think new evidence should be heard?

The purpose of an appeal is to decide whether an error was made during the trial. For example, the **appellant**, the person making the appeal, may argue that the trial judge made an error of law by allowing inadmissible evidence. Or the appellant may argue that an error of fact was made since there was insufficient evidence for a conviction.

Lawyers for the appellant and the **respondent**, the side opposing the appeal, submit written arguments setting out their positions. They may also make oral arguments before the appeal court, to give the court a chance to question each side. However, their arguments, both written and oral, concern only the error made at trial which will appear "on the record". The court will consider the arguments when examining the record.

If the appeal is allowed, the court may reverse the trial court's conviction or acquittal (unless the acquittal was based on the verdict of a jury), or order a new trial. If the appeal concerns the sentence, the court may alter the sentence.

—Why do you think an appeal court cannot substitute a guilty verdict for a person who has been found not guilty by a jury?

Obtaining a Pardon

A person who has a criminal record may apply to the National Parole

Board for a **pardon**. If it is granted, the person's records will be set apart and cannot be revealed without the consent of the Solicitor-General. An application for a pardon can be made only after a certain length of time has elapsed. Depending on the type of offence, this period is usually one to five years after the sentence has been served. The applicant will be investigated by the National Parole Board and if found to be of "good behaviour" will be given a pardon.

What effect does obtaining a pardon have on the convicted person? To begin with, you will notice that the records are not destroyed. They can be placed in the active file again if the person is convicted of another offence after the pardon has been granted, if the person lies on the application for the pardon, or if the person is of "bad behaviour". Unfortunately, "bad behaviour" is not defined in the legislation, so it is not clear what, in the opinion of the Parole Board, constitutes good or bad behaviour.

One of the chief disadvantages of having a criminal record is the effect it has on finding employment. For instance, if an employment application asks if you have a criminal record, you may not answer "No" even if you have a pardon. For this reason, the Canadian Human Rights Commission has recommended that companies amend their application forms to read: "Have you ever been convicted of an offence for which you have not been pardoned?"

Probably the chief advantage of obtaining a pardon is the personal satisfaction of knowing that although you have made a mistake, you have repaid your debt to society and have put the mistake in your past.

The Procedure for Trying Summary Conviction Offences

Summary conviction offences are usually tried by provincial court judges or magistrates. There are no jury trials in provincial or magistrate's court. The trial starts when the accused is arraigned. However, the accused does not need to be personally present for a summary trial as long as someone is there as his or her representative. If the defendant pleads guilty, the Crown must still at least summarize the facts of the case for the court. Usually, the defendant will then be convicted and sentenced.

When a not guilty plea is entered, the trial will follow basically the same stages as those of a trial of an indictable offence. After hearing all of the evidence, the judge will decide whether the defendant is guilty or not guilty and either convict the defendant or dismiss the information.

The penalties which the *Criminal Code* allows for summary conviction offences are fines of up to $500 and/or imprisonment for not more than six months. The judge may also order a conditional or absolute discharge.

Appeals of Summary Conviction Offences

There are two ways that a summary conviction offence can be appealed:

1. "on the record", or
2. by **stated case**

"On the record" is the usual way to appeal and involves basically the same procedure as discussed under appeals of indictable offences. This category of appeal is often heard in county or district courts. In an appeal "on the record", the defendant has a right to appeal either the conviction or the sentence. The Crown can appeal either the dismissal of the information or the sentence.

—Section 747 of the *Code* names the court of appeal for each province when the appeal is "on the record". What court hears this type of appeal in your province?

A stated case appeal involves a question of law only. The trial court judge states the question and sends it to the province's superior court of criminal jurisdiction. The name of this court for each province is listed in s. 2 of the *Criminal Code*. The appeal judge who hears the case will merely answer the question "yes" or "no" and send it back to the trial court, which can then alter its decision if necessary.

A further appeal to the province's Court of Appeal is possible only with leave (permission) of that court. The appeal must involve a question of law.

In some situations, a final appeal on a question of law may be made to the Supreme Court of Canada, but, again, the Court must give permission for the appeal.

Young Offenders

Although young people over a certain age are held responsible when they break the criminal law, a different procedure has been established to deal with them. This has not always been so. Before the twentieth century, children aged seven and over were tried in adult courts and could be placed in prisons with adults.

Then, in 1908, Parliament passed the *Juvenile Delinquents Act*, which set up a separate system for juveniles. Special courts, as well as separate places of custody, were part of the new system. The *Act* also set out a new approach to dealing with young offenders. Rather than treating juveniles as criminals, courts were to treat them as misdirected children requiring "help, guidance and proper supervision".

Times have again changed. The *Juvenile Delinquents Act* has been much criticized as being out of date. As a result, it has now been replaced by the *Young Offenders Act*. There is still a separate system for handling young offenders, but the philosophy of the new legislation has taken a different direction.

The *Young Offenders Act* still recognizes that young people may need guidance and supervision. However, there is a new emphasis on holding young people accountable for their law-breaking actions. Thus, the *Act* also recognizes that society has a right to be protected from law-breaking. In short, the *Young Offenders Act* treats young people more like responsible persons, but still not as fully mature adults.

One change that goes along with the new philosophy is the raising of the minimum age for criminal responsibility from seven to twelve. As well, the legislation provides for a uniform maximum age of seventeen for youth court jurisdiction. Under the *Juvenile Delinquents Act*, each province or territory could set its own maximum age as long as it fell between fifteen and seventeen. Therefore, the ages at which youths went to adult court varied across the country.

—Although the *Young Offenders Act* became law on April 2, 1984, it was decided that the section which provided for the uniform maximum age of seventeen would not come into effect until April 1, 1985. Why do you think the federal government delayed this section?
—Do you think it is a good idea to have one maximum age in Canada for sending young people to adult court? Explain.
—Some of the provinces opposed setting the maximum age for youth court at seventeen. Do you think this is too young, or too old?

Under the *Juvenile Delinquents Act*, a juvenile could be charged with delinquency for breaking any federal, provincial, or municipal law. This meant that a young person who broke a provincial law by being truant from school, for instance, could be treated the same as someone who committed break, enter, and theft. Many people felt this was unfair. Similarly, people thought it was unfair to handle municipal and provincial offenders under a criminal law statute. The federal government agreed with this criticism. As a result, the *Young Offenders Act* covers only the *Criminal Code* and other federal statutes. The provinces must enact their own legislation to deal with provincial offenders.

—Truancy has always been dealt with under the *Juvenile Delinquents Act*. Find out how your province is now handling truants.

In the past, it was not always clear whether young people had the same rights as adults who were charged with crimes. The *Young Offenders Act* has solved this problem by specifically stating the rights of young people. They include the following:

1. The right to a lawyer.
2. The same rights as adults to be released prior to trial.
3. The same right as adults to appeal the court's decision.
4. The right to be informed of their rights. (Why is this an especially important right?)
5. The same rights as adults to the due process of law and fair and equal treatment under the law. This includes those rights guaranteed in the *Charter of Rights* and the *Bill of Rights*.

Under the *Young Offenders Act*, court hearings are open to the public, unlike hearings under the *Juvenile Delinquents Act*. However, the media are still not allowed to use the names of young people in reporting cases.

In general, the trial of a young person resembles that of an adult. If the youth pleads not guilty, the Crown must prove each element of the offence. The young person can make any defence which would be available to an adult. If the young person pleads guilty or is found guilty, the court can impose several types of sentences, or *dispositions* as they are called in youth court, including the following:

1. An absolute discharge.
2. A fine of up to $1000.
3. Restitution of money or service to the victim.
4. A community service order requiring the youth to spend a certain number of hours providing a community service.
5. Detention in a hospital or similar place for treatment.
6. Probation for up to two years.
7. A custody order for up to two years unless the offence is one for which an adult could be sentenced to life imprisonment, or unless the youth is convicted of multiple charges. In these situations, the custody order can be for up to three years. Custody may be in an institution such as a training school or group home.

Under some circumstances, a young person may be tried in an adult court. If the youth has passed his or her fourteenth birthday, and is charged with a serious indictable offence such as murder or armed robbery, a judge may order the case to be sent to adult court. Before ordering the transfer, the judge must be of the opinion that, having regard to the interests of the youth, it is in the interest of society to try the young person in adult court. The *Young Offenders Act* sets out a list of factors for the court to consider in reaching such a decision. The most important factors include:

> 16. (2) *(a)* the seriousness of the alleged offence and the circumstances in which it was allegedly committed;
> *(b)* the age, maturity, character and background of the young person and any record or summary of previous findings of delinquency or guilt...
> *(d)* the availability of treatment or correctional resources....

Young Offenders and Criminal Records

The *Young Offenders Act* has clarified whether young people can be fingerprinted and photographed. It has established that they can, whenever an adult can be. In other words, if the youth is charged with an indictable offence, fingerprinting and photographing can take place. However, if no court proceedings are taken against the youth, or the charges are dismissed, or the youth is acquitted, the records must be destroyed.

If the young person is found guilty, all records, including court records, will be destroyed if the youth does not commit another offence within a certain period of time. The young person must have a clean record for two years after the sentence is complete for a summary conviction offence, five years for an indictable offence. While these records exist, they can be used for sentencing in adult or youth court.

SUMMARIZING YOUR READING

1. What is the first step in any trial?

2. List the rights of the defendant at trial.

3. Explain the ways in which indictable offences can be tried.

4. What is the purpose of a preliminary hearing?

5. Under what circumstances are preliminary hearings held?

6. What does "preferring an indictment" mean?

7. Explain the two types of jury challenges which the defence and Crown attorneys can make.

8. Explain the Crown's right to ask jurors to stand aside.
9. What happens when the defendant is arraigned?
10. Does the defence or the Crown present its case first? Explain.
11. What is examination-in-chief?
12. What is a leading question?
13. What are the two purposes of cross-examination?
14. When does re-examination take place?
15. What is the difference between direct evidence, hearsay, and circumstantial evidence?
16. Under what circumstances is a motion for dismissal made? Explain.
17. Explain what rebuttal and surrebuttal evidence are.
18. What does the judge do when charging the jury?
19. When a trial is before a jury, what is the jury's role? the judge's role? What is the role of the judge if there is no jury?
20. What is a pre-sentence report? When is it used?
21. Explain the sentencing powers of a judge for indictable offences.
22. Under what circumstances is a person who has been sentenced to a term of imprisonment sent to a provincial institution?
23. What is parole? day parole? Who decides whether and when a prisoner would be paroled?
24. Define "mandatory supervision". How does it differ from parole?
25. What are the purposes of punishment?
26. What are appeals "on the record" only?
27. Define "appellant" and "respondent".
28. What is the purpose of an appeal?
29. What can an appeal court do if the appeal is allowed?
30. Where are summary conviction offences tried?
31. What penalties does the *Criminal Code* allow for summary conviction offences?
32. What are the two ways in which summary conviction offences

can be appealed?

33. How were young people who committed crimes treated before the twentieth century?

34. When was the first *Act* dealing with juvenile offenders passed? What did it provide?

35. List some differences between the *Juvenile Delinquents Act* and the *Young Offenders Act*.

36. What dispositions can a judge make in the case of a young offender?

37. Can a young person ever be tried in an adult court? Explain.

38. When can a young person be fingerprinted and photographed?

39. What happens to the criminal records of a young person?

DISCUSSING KEY ISSUES

1. Although it can take many forms, plea-bargaining often takes place when a defendant agrees to plead guilty in exchange for a lesser charge, or the Crown's recommendation of a lighter sentence. It is unknown how frequently plea-bargaining takes place in Canada, but over 70% of all defendants plead guilty.
  (a) Why do you suppose plea-bargaining takes place?
  (b) What are the advantages for the defendant? for the Crown? for the court?
  (c) Can you think of some disadvantages of plea-bargaining?
  (d) Should the Crown be bound by its promises? For example, if the Crown promises to recommend a lighter sentence in exchange for a guilty plea, should the Crown be able to appeal the sentence later?
  (e) There are few controls on the methods used for plea-bargaining. Can you think of ways to make it fairer? Should judges be involved? Should the bargains be in writing? Should the defendant be required to have legal advice before striking a bargain?

2. Consider the role of the defence lawyer. Should a lawyer represent someone the lawyer believes or suspects is guilty? What if the accused wants to plead not guilty and the lawyer knows or suspects the accused is guilty?

3. In 1983, there were 11 132 men and 129 women in federal institutions, and thirty-seven penitentiaries for men and one for women in Canada. Why do you think there is such a difference between the number of men and women convicts in federal penitentiaries?

4. Comment on this statement describing the role of the Crown Attorney: "It cannot be overemphasized that the purpose of the criminal prosecution is not to obtain a conviction; it is to lay before a jury what the Crown considers to be credible evidence, relevant to what is alleged to be a crime...The role of the prosecutor excludes any notion of winning or losing; his function is a matter of public duty and which in civil life there can be none charged with greater responsibility." (R. v. Boucher (1954) 110 C.C.C.)

PROJECTS AND ACTIVITIES

1. Find out what kinds of correctional institutions are located in your province. Which are federal, which provincial? Are there any programs in your province providing alternatives to incarceration? Why might it be a good idea to find alternatives to prisons?

2. Every province has a system for providing legal assistance to persons accused of crimes who cannot afford to hire lawyers. Contact the Attorney-General's office in your province. Who qualifies for assistance? For what offences is assistance given?

RESOLVING CASES

R. v. Talbot [1966] 3 C.C.C. 28 (Que. Q.B.)

Talbot was charged with assault causing bodily harm. He was arrested, and appeared before a judge on March 3. He pleaded not guilty and his trial was set for March 6. He saw his lawyer on March 5. At court the next day, the lawyer asked for a postponement of the trial because he had only spoken to the defendant the day before. His request was denied. The lawyer then withdrew from the case. During the trial, Talbot asked for a lawyer to defend him. His request was refused. He was convicted of the offence and sentenced to six months' imprisonment.

Talbot appealed the trial court's decision and asked for a new trial.

—Has Talbot been denied a right to a fair trial? If so, in what way?
—Would Talbot's appeal be based on a question of law or fact?
—What do you think the appeal court's decision would be?

R. v. Sanchez-Pino (1973) 11 C.C.C. (2d) 53 (Ont. C.A.)

The defendant was charged with theft under $200. She was caught shoplifting merchandise worth about $78 from a department store. She was observed taking articles from the third floor women's department and also from the basement level. She did pay for two items of trivial value.

The defendant was twenty-five years old. She had come to Toronto from Chile as a graduate student on an exchange program at the University of Toronto. She was said to be a very good student who had worked with the Chilean government for three years on a program of examinations for teachers in Chile. If convicted, she would be deported, would lose her job and would not be able to continue in the program of visiting other universities throughout the world. Her lawyer asked that she be given an absolute discharge. The Crown opposed this on the grounds that shoplifting is a major problem in Toronto and that discharges should rarely be used, otherwise there would be no deterrent for this offence.

—Do you think the defendant should receive an absolute discharge? Explain your answer.

R. v. A. (1974) 26 C.C.C. (2d) 474 (Ont. H. Ct.)

The accused was found guilty of indecent assault. The victim was a female employee. A. had made several advances to her previously, but they had been rejected. On the evening of the assault, the victim was the last employee in the building. A. locked the door before she could leave and attacked her. She resisted and was able to escape, although she suffered bruises to various parts of her body and her clothing was damaged.

The accused was a forty-year-old businessman, married and living with his wife and two teenaged children. He had no other criminal record.

The judge considered the following factors in sentencing A.

(a) Imprisonment would likely ruin his business.
(b) For the accused, conviction alone was a substantial part of the punishment.
(c) Employers are in a position of trust and have a duty to protect their female employees.
(d) The victim of this kind of crime is often ashamed, embarrassed, and suffers in silence. Rarely will a women sue for damages in this kind of case.

—What sentence do you think would be appropriate? Give reasons to support your answer.

R. v. K. (1971) 5 C.C.C. (2d) 46 (B.C.S.C.)

The accused was charged on September 8, 1970 under the *Juvenile Delinquents Act* with committing the delinquencies of assaulting a police officer, obstructing a police officer in the execution of his duty, and causing a disturbance in a public place by fighting. The juvenile was in custody until September 14, 1970, when he was released on bail. The Crown applied to have the case transferred from juvenile to adult court. The application was refused on December 7, 1970 and the trial date was set for January 6, 1971. It was adjourned (postponed) on that date to February 1, 1971 at the Crown's request. On February 1, the Crown again asked for an adjournment because the Crown had failed to notify the accused's mother of the time and place of the trial, as required by law. The mother's presence as a Crown witness was also required to prove the age of the accused.

On both January 6 and February 1, the accused appeared for trial, along with his lawyer and seven defence witnesses. The judge refused to further adjourn the case and dismissed the charges for want of prosecution. On the same date, a second information was sworn out charging the accused with the same three offences that were in the first information. The accused was brought to court on the charges on February 11.

— Do you think the judge allowed the Crown to try to accused on February 11th?
— Have any rights of the accused been violated?
— Do you think it matters that the accused was a juvenile?

R. v. Dunn (1970) 9 C.R.N.S. 274 (B.C.S.C.)

The defendant was charged with failure to remain at the scene of an accident. The information alleged that the accident occurred "on or about the 16th day of March 1969".

Two Crown witnesses were asked to "tell what happened on the early morning of the 16th day of May, 1969." These witnesses then gave evidence which would have justified a conviction if the correct date had been used. No other witnesses identified the accused as the driver of the vehicle.

— What do you think the defence did when the Crown closed its case?
— Do you think the defence was successful?

7

Criminal Offences

Offences against the Public Order, Part II
Offences against the Administration of Law and Justice, Part III
Sexual Offences, Public Morals, and Disorderly Conduct, Part IV
Offences against the Person and Reputation, Part VI
Offences against the Rights of Property, Part VII
Wilful and Forbidden Acts in Respect of Certain Property, Part IX
Drug Offences

Figure 7-1

Every day as we read the newspapers or listen to the news on radio or television, we encounter reports like these dealing with crime. There is a tremendous variety of offences which are considered crimes. As you know, most crimes in Canada are listed in the *Criminal Code*, though there are a number of other federal statutes, such as the *Narcotic Control Act* and the *Food and Drugs Act*, which also deal with crimes. It would be impossible to discuss every criminal offence because of their number. Therefore, in this chapter we have attempted to select a variety to illustrate the range of criminal activities covered by the *Code*.

There are twenty-five parts to the *Criminal Code*. Parts II to X contain the definitions of and penalties for offences. This chapter will follow the order used in the *Code* in presenting the offences.

We will also look at some drug offences. These crimes are not in the *Code*, but in other federal statutes such as the *Narcotic Control Act* mentioned earlier.

Chapter 8 will discuss some of the defences available to a person accused of a crime. These will be general defences which can be used for most crimes. However, there are some defences that can be used only for specific crimes. The latter will be discussed in this chapter in connection with specific offences.

—Obtain a copy of the *Criminal Code*. Turn to the Table of Contents, paying particular attention to Parts II to X. Notice how the offences are organized under each part; for example, offences against the person are in Part IV, while property offences are in Part VII. In your notes, copy out the headings for Parts II to X, including two examples of crimes that fall under each heading.

Offences against the Public Order, Part II

This section of the *Code* includes such offences as treason, mutiny, and hijacking. They are offences which threaten state authority or public order.

Unlawful Assemblies and Riots

An organization called Citizens for a Nuclear-Free World organizes a number of demonstrations to take place in major cities across Canada on the last Saturday in July. In Edmonton, a very large crowd of anti-nuclear demonstrators turns out for the march to City Hall. A considerable number of people in favour of nuclear armament as a safeguard for world peace also turn out, and the heckling and jeering between the two groups begins to break into minor scuffles and skirmishes along the parade route. Some minor property damage to store windows occurs. The police become concerned that as the temperature rises on this hot summer day, so will tempers.

Two of the more commonly committed offences in Part II of the *Code* are unlawful assemblies and riots, which are defined in sections 64 and 65.

> 64. (1) An unlawful assembly is an assembly of three or more persons who, with intent to carry out any common purpose, assemble in such a manner or so conduct themselves when they are assembled as to cause persons in the neighbourhood of the assembly to fear, on reasonable grounds, that they
> *(a)* will disturb the peace tumultuously, or
> *(b)* will by that assembly needlessly and without reasonable cause provoke other persons to disturb the peace tumultuously.

—Can you name the elements of this offence?
—How many people are needed for an unlawful assembly?
—What specific intent is needed for this crime? Does the purpose need to be illegal?
—What is the *actus reus* required for this offence?

> 65. A riot is an unlawful assembly that has begun to disturb the peace tumultuously.

—How is a riot different from an unlawful assembly?

Notice that the disturbance must be *tumultuous*. Courts have held that this means more than just noisy. For example, one court has held that the disturbance must involve some element of actual or threatened violence or force.

Unlawful assembly is a summary conviction offence, while rioting is an indictable offence punishable by up to two years' imprisonment. The punishment for rioting can be much more severe, however. If, during a riot of twelve or more persons, a justice, mayor, sheriff, or lawful deputy of the mayor or sheriff reads to the assembly a proclamation commanding all persons to disperse, anyone who remains and is arrested may be liable to up to life imprisonment. This is often referred to as "reading the Riot Act".

Offences against the Administration of Law and Justice, Part III

These offences, as the heading suggests, involve threats to the legal system. Bribery of judicial officers, disobeying a court order, and perjury (lying under oath) are among the offences in this part of the *Code*, as is the following offence.

Obstructing a Public or Peace Officer

We have previously discussed, in the criminal procedure chapter, the offence of obstructing a peace officer in the execution of his or her duty (s.118). Recall that this offence may occur if a person resists an arrest or search. However, if the arrest or search is not legal, the officer is not acting in the execution of his or her duty, and no offence is committed.

There is a variety of ways in which peace officers can be obstructed. The following cases illustrate some of them.

> *R. v. Lawson* (1973) 22 C.R.N.S. 215 (Ont. Prov. Ct.)
> The defendant was found guilty of an attempt to obstruct a peace officer. He lied to the police about the whereabouts of a suspect whom the police were pursuing.
>
> *R. v. Jones and Hulier* (1975) 30 C.R.N.S. 127 (Y.T.)
> The defendants' dogs were picked up by an animal control officer. Jones and Hulier went to the animal shelter and released the dogs from the officer's truck over his objections. The court held that the animal control officer was a peace officer within s.2 of the *Code* (which defines "peace officer") and that the defendants had obstructed him while in the execution of his duty.
>
> *Knowlton v. The Queen* (1973) 21 C.R.N.S. 344 (S.C.C.)
> The police cordoned off an area in front of a hotel in Edmonton where Premier Kosygin of the U.S.S.R. would be staying. An assault had been attempted against him in Ottawa only a few days earlier. The defendant insisted on entering the area to take pictures of Kosygin. He was finally arrested and charged with obstructing police. The Supreme Court of Canada held that the police were executing their general duty to preserve the peace and prevent crimes and that the defendant had wilfully obstructed them.
>
> —Look up s.118 of the *Criminal Code*. What are the other ways in which the offence of obstruction can be committed?

Obstruction is a hybrid offence punishable either upon summary conviction or by indictment for up to two years' imprisonment.

Sexual Offences, Public Morals, and Disorderly Conduct, Part IV

This part contains offences which offend public morality, among them disorderly conduct, being nude in public, and performing indecent acts. It also contains certain sexual offences such as incest and sexual intercourse with a female under fourteen years of age. The offence of rape was previously in this part, but it has been redefined as sexual assault and is now found in Part VI, Offences Against the Person.

Obscene Materials

Certain novels are regularly banned by school boards across the country.

Toronto city council passed a by-law requiring all "adult magazines" to be kept on shelves of a specific height, in order to be out of the reach of young children.

In Vancouver, video outlets selling pornographic tapes were burned by arsonists as a statement against pornography.

These are just a few examples of the concern that Canadians have displayed, even to the point of violence, about the effects of pornography, or as the *Code* calls it, obscene materials.

> 159. (1) Every one commits an offence who
> (a) makes, publishes, distributes, circulates, or has in his possession for the purpose of publication, distribution or circulation any obscene written matter, picture, model, phonograph record or other thing whatsoever, or
> (b) makes, prints, publishes, distributes, sells or has in his possession for the purpose of publication, distribution or circulation, a crime comic.
> (2) Every one commits an offence who knowingly, without lawful justification or excuse,
> (a) sells, exposes to public view or has in his possession for such a purpose any obscene written matter, picture, model, phonograph record or other thing whatsoever,
> (b) publicly exhibits a disgusting object or an indecent show...

The most difficult element of this offence is proving that the material in question *is* obscene. Section 159(8) attempts to assist:

> 159. ...
> (8) For the purpose of this Act, any publication a dominant characteristic of which is the undue exploitation of sex or of sex and any one or more of the following subjects, namely crime, horror, cruelty and violence, shall be deemed to be obscene.

However, this definition, rather than giving a complete answer, only raises more questions: How is it decided what the "dominant characteristic" of a publication is? What is meant by "the undue exploitation of sex"?

Although this is a difficult and often unclear area of the law, the Supreme Court of Canada has given some guidance in the 1962 *Brodie* case which concerned whether the book *Lady Chatterley's Lover* by D.H. Lawrence was obscene. Four of the nine judges hearing the case said that to determine the dominant characteristic of the book, it must be read as a whole. Allegedly obscene passages or words should not be taken out of context. The purpose of the author also needs to be examined, to determine the book's artistic or literary merit. On the other hand, the Ontario Court of Appeal in a later case concerning a certain magazine, said that although the magazine as a whole must be considered, an obscene article or passage cannot be saved by surrounding it with non-obscene material.

—Is the later decision of the Ontario Court of Appeal inconsistent with *Brodie*?
—Can you reconcile the two court decisions?

In determining whether or not the material unduly exploited sex, the four judges in *Brodie* seemed to suggest two tests:

1. whether there is no more emphasis on the theme than is required in the serious treatment of the theme of the novel with honesty and uprightness;
2. whether the material offends community standards.

Although the four judges were not a majority, this last test seems to have been adopted by other courts as the most important in determining whether there is undue exploitation of sex. "Community standards" are taken to be those of contemporary Canadian society as a whole. Some courts have spoken of determining the *general average* of community thought and feeling on the issue.

—How should courts determine community standards? Should public opinion surveys be used as evidence? Should the opinions of writers and publishers be considered?

Section 159(3) sets out one defence that may be raised to a charge of obscenity:

> 159. ...
> (3) No person shall be convicted of an offence under this section if he establishes that the public good was served by the acts that are alleged to constitute the offence and that the acts alleged did not extend beyond what served the public good.

"For the public good" has been defined as meaning serving the needs of religion, morality, the administration of justice, science, literature, art, or other general purpose.

Section 159 is a hybrid offence punishable upon summary conviction or by indictment for up to two years' imprisonment.

Causing a Disturbance

Three students are turned away from a school dance because they have obviously been drinking. Angry that they cannot enter the dance, they begin to shout and curse outside the school. Neighbours who are disturbed by this noise call the police.

Figure 7-2 What offence are these students probably committing?

Notice that the person or persons causing the disturbance must be outside a dwelling house. A dwelling house is defined in s.2 of the *Code* as any part or whole of a building that is used as a temporary or permanent residence.

> **171.** (1) Every one who
>   *(a)* not being in a dwelling-house causes a disturbance in or near a public place
>   (i) by fighting, screaming, shouting, swearing, singing or using insulting or obscene language,
>   (ii) by being drunk, or
>   (iii) by impeding or molesting other persons...
>   is guilty of an offence punishable on summary conviction.

Offences against the Person and Reputation, Part VI

Offences in this part involve either violence to the physical being of the person ranging from assault to murder, or injury to the person's reputation through libel (the publication of material that damages a person's reputation). Driving offences such as driving while intoxicated are also included. Even though a driving offence may not cause actual physical injury, the potential for harming a person is great. Finally, there are several offences which prohibit hate propaganda, that is, advocating the killing of members of a certain group, or inciting hatred of a certain group.

Criminal Negligence

It is an offence to cause either death or injury to a person by criminal negligence. Criminal negligence is defined as follows:

> **202.** (1) Every one is criminally negligent who
>   *(a)* in doing anything, or
>   *(b)* in omitting to do anything that it is his duty to do,
>   shows wanton or reckless disregard for the lives or safety of other persons.
>
> (2) For the purposes of this section, "duty" means a duty imposed by law.

Two students returning from a party in the early hours of the morning decide to race their cars down Main Street. Just as they are approaching an intersection, a woman on her way home from her job at a local restaurant steps off the curb. She is seriously injured when one of the cars hits her.

— **Have the students in the above example been criminally negligent? Explain.**

Notice that no specific type of conduct is prohibited. Criminal negligence can occur through reckless driving, use of firearms, or any other conduct done in a dangerous manner, although the vast majority of these offences involve the misuse of automobiles. The conduct or *breach of duty* must show a reckless or wanton disregard for the lives or safety of others. One court has defined "wanton" as meaning undisciplined or ungoverned, while "reckless" means being careless about the consequences of actions. In practice, these terms are usually treated as if they mean the same thing. If you take an unjustifiable risk and either know or do not care about the consequences to others, your conduct can be called wanton or reckless.

This offence is one where a person may break the criminal law by *failing* to act. A breach of a legal duty may involve either a statute or common law. Consider the following case.

R. v. Popen (1981) 60 C.C.C. (2d) 232 (Ont. C.A.)

The defendant's wife had been found guilty of causing the death of their nineteen-month old daughter, Kim. Evidence showed that the child had been subject to severe physical abuse which finally led to her death. Although he was living with his wife and child, there was no evidence that Popen had ever participated in the abuse or had been present when it occurred. However, the Court of Appeal held that under the common law a parent has a duty to protect or remove a child from an environment where the child is subject to brutal treatment by the other parent or a third party.

— **What would the Crown have to show to prove that Mr. Popen was guilty of criminal negligence causing death?**

The maximum penalty for causing death through criminal negligence is life imprisonment; for causing injury, ten years.

Homicide

Homicide occurs when a person causes the death of another. Only *culpable* (blameworthy) homicide is criminal. Examples of *non-culpable* homicide would be a motorist accidently (and without criminal negligence) killing someone in a car accident, a police officer's killing someone in the course of duty, or a soldier's killing an enemy during wartime.

Figure 7-3 The Types of Homicide

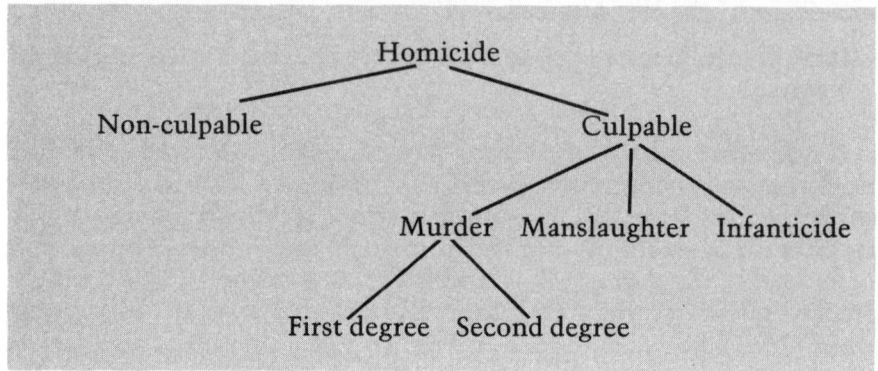

—**Look up s.205(5) of the *Criminal Code*. How does the *Code* define culpable homicide?**

There are three types of culpable homicide: murder, manslaughter, and **infanticide**.

"We've got the murder weapon and the motive ... now if we can just establish time-of-death."

Murder

Murder is the most serious form of culpable homicide. We tend to think of murder as being the intentional causing of death. However, this is only one of several ways murder can occur, although some form of specific intent is necessary. Other ways include the following:

1. Recklessly causing bodily harm you know is likely to cause death (s.212(a)(ii)).
2. Meaning to cause death to one person and accidently causing the death of another (s.212(b)).
3. Doing something for an unlawful object which you know is likely to cause death (s.212(c)).

The defendant in the following case was charged with murder under s.212(c).

R. v. Vasil (1981) 58 C.C.C. (2d) 97 (S.C.C.)

The defendant was charged with murder for causing the death of two children aged six and nine when he set fire to a house in which they were sleeping. Vasil had been living in the house with the children's mother, Gilchrist. Vasil and Gilchrist had not been getting along. On the night of the fire, they had gone to a party, leaving the children with a babysitter. They argued at the party and Gilchrist refused to leave with Vasil. He then drove to the house and took the babysitter home. He drove back to the house and found lighter fluid in the basement. Pouring the fluid on parts of the house and furniture, he started a fire. He then returned to the party and told Gilchrist that he was going to the police station. When she said, "You've done something to my children," he remained silent. At the police station, he confessed to setting the fire. When asked if there was anyone in the house, he said, "Yes, Lorna, six years, Allan, nine years." He said he set the fire because he was leaving Gilchrist and wanted to ruin some of the things around the house.

—Was Vasil properly charged under s.212(c)?
—What was his unlawful object?
—Should he have known that his conduct was likely to cause death?

Murder may also be charged where a person unintentionally and without recklessness causes the death of a person while committing certain serious offences such as hijacking, kidnapping, robbery, or breaking and entering. For example, if a person uses a weapon to commit the offence, even if the death is caused accidently, the person may be charged with murder, as in the following situation.

Fritz and Helmut were robbing a bank. While Fritz was pointing a gun at the bank employees, the bank manager tried to disarm him. As they wrestled, the gun went off, shooting and killing an employee of the bank.

— **Why do you think the law makes it murder to unintentionally and without recklessness cause death when committing certain crimes?**

Classes of Murder for Purposes of Punishment

Murder is classed in s.214 as either *first degree* or *second degree*. Murder is first degree in any of the following situations:

1. When it is planned and deliberate.
2. When the victim is a police officer, constable, or sheriff acting in the course of his or her duties, a prison guard or other prison employee, or any person working in the prison with the permission of the prison authorities (for example, social workers, doctors, or nurses).
3. When the death is caused during the commission of certain offences such as hijacking, kidnapping, or sexual assault.
4. When the defendant has been previously convicted of first or second degree murder.

If the murder does not fall within one of these situations, it is second degree murder. The maximum penalty for both first and second degree murder is life imprisonment. The difference is that a person convicted of first degree murder is ineligible for parole for twenty-five years, while a person convicted of second degree murder may be eligible after ten years in prison.

Manslaughter

If a culpable homicide is not murder, it is usually manslaughter (s.217), since the offence of infanticide is rare. Murder always requires specific intent, while manslaughter is a general intent crime. For example, a drunk driver who unintentionally kills a pedestrian would be charged with manslaughter rather than murder. Manslaughter often results when a person causes death by means of an unlawful action. In the example of the drunk driver who kills a pedestrian, the unlawful action is driving while impaired. Criminal negligence which causes death can also lead to a charge of manslaughter; that is, a person who has caused death by criminal negligence can be charged with manslaughter or with criminal negligence.

Murder Reduced to Manslaughter

A conviction for manslaughter may result when the charge is murder in two special situations.

1. If the defendant successfully raises the defence of intoxication.
2. If the defendant successfully raises the defence of provocation.

Intoxication

If it can be proven that the defendant was so intoxicated by drugs or alcohol as to be unable to form the specific intent necessary for murder, the defendant may be found guilty of manslaughter instead of murder. Recall the *Vasil* case. The defendant raised this defence since there was evidence that he had been drinking heavily that evening. The court held that it was a question of fact for the jury to decide whether he was so intoxicated that he did not realize that setting a fire in the house would be dangerous to the lives of the children.

Provocation

Another defence which may reduce murder to manslaughter is provocation. This defence can be used only when the offence charged is murder. It is contained in s.215 of the *Code*. Provocation is defined as "a wrongful act or insult that is of such a nature as to be sufficient to deprive an ordinary person of the power of self-control." An accused who raises this defence must show that the act was committed in "the heat of passion caused by sudden provocation". It is up to the jury to decide whether the act or insult was provocation and whether the accused lost self-control because of provocation.

The maximum penalty for manslaughter is life imprisonment.

Infanticide

> **216.** A female person commits infanticide when by a wilful act or omission she causes the death of her newly-born child, if at the time of the act or omission she is not fully recovered from the effects of giving birth to the child and by reason thereof or of the effect of lactation consequent on the birth of the child her mind is then disturbed.

As you can see, this offence can be charged only in very specific circumstances. It provides a lesser punishment (maximum penalty, five years' imprisonment) for what would otherwise be murder or manslaughter.

—Read s.216 carefully. List the circumstances that must exist for the offence of infanticide.

Offences Involving Motor Vehicles

Every province has legislation that regulates the use of streets and highways by motor vehicles, including any motorized vehicle such as a motorcycle or snowmobile. Such acts as speeding, running a red light or stop sign, and failing to yield are just a few of the types of provincial offences involving the use of motor vehicles. The *Criminal Code* also sets out several specific offences relating to the use of motor vehicles, some of them similar to provincial offences. However, in each case, the *Code* offence is more serious; in fact, serious enough to be considered a crime.

Figure 7-4 What are some of the offences which may be related to this type of accident?

Criminal Negligence in the Use of Motor Vehicles

This offence, found in s.233(1), is less serious than the offence of criminal negligence. The same test is used as for determining whether criminal negligence has occurred. However, if there has been no death or serious bodily harm as a result of the negligence, a charge under s.233 can be used. This offence is punishable upon summary conviction or upon indictment by up to five years' imprisonment.

Dangerous Driving

Dangerous driving (s.233(4)), is a less serious offence than criminal negligence in the use of a motor vehicle. The line between dangerous and criminally negligent driving may be difficult to draw, but the courts have said that dangerous driving does not involve reckless or wanton conduct. What is necessary is to look at the defendant's actual conduct and decide whether the lives and safety of others were endangered by that conduct and whether such danger "resulted from the driver's departure from the standard of care of a prudent driver", given all the circumstances.

Impaired Driving

It is an offence under s.234 for a person to drive or to have the care and control of a motor vehicle while impaired by alcohol or drugs. Since it is possible to have the care and control of a car without driving it, there are really two offences here. For example, if a police officer sees an intoxicated person getting into the driver's seat of a car and starting it, a charge of having care and control while impaired may be laid. If the officer waited until the person actually started driving, the charge would be driving while impaired.

The courts have been divided on whether an intention to drive is a necessary element of care and control. This issue was raised in the following case.

Ford v. The Queen (1982) 65 C.C.C. (2d) 392 (S.C.C.)

The defendant was charged with having care and control of a car while impaired. He had been at a party. Several times during the night, he had started the car because of cold weather; however, he arranged for someone else to drive home because he realized he was impaired.

The police found him behind the wheel of the car with the engine running. He had not traded places yet with the person who would be driving home.

The trial judge acquitted him, relying on s.237(1)(a) which states:

> **237.** (1) In any proceedings under section 234 or 236
>   *(a)* where it is proved that the accused occupied the seat ordinarily occupied by the driver of a motor vehicle, he shall be deemed to have the care and control of the vehicle unless he establishes that he did not enter or mount the vehicle for the purpose of setting it in motion;

The Court of Appeal for P.E.I. set aside the acquittal, saying that the purpose of s.237 was to assist the Crown but that even if the accused could prove that he did not intend to drive the car, the offence of care and control could be established other ways. The Court said: "Care and control may be exercised without [an intent to drive] where an accused performs some acts or series of acts involving use of the car, its fittings or equipment,...whereby the car may unintentionally be set in motion creating the danger the section is designed to prevent."

—The case was then appealed to the Supreme Court of Canada. What do you think the Supreme Court decided?

Proof of Impaired Driving

A court will look at all of the circumstances in deciding if a person was impaired. The defendant's performance on a breathalyzer is only one factor. Others are the ability to perform physical tests, general behaviour, the odour on the driver's breath, and the defendant's driving.

Penalties for Impaired Driving

Impaired driving is a summary conviction offence. As you know, the punishment for *Criminal Code* summary conviction offences is usually six months' imprisonment and/or a $500 fine. For some summary conviction offences such as impaired driving, however, different penalties are set out:

1. For a first offence, a fine of not more than $2000 and not less than $50 or imprisonment for six months or both.
2. For a second offence, imprisonment for not more than one year and not less than fourteen days.
3. For each subsequent offence, imprisonment for not more than two years and not less than three months.

—Why do you think the law requires a term of imprisonment after the first offence? Is this a good idea?

Driving with More than 80 mg of Alcohol in the Blood

> **236.** (1) Every one who drives a motor vehicle or has the care or control of a motor vehicle, whether it is in motion or not, having consumed alcohol in such a quantity that the proportion thereof in his blood exceeds 80 milligrams of alcohol in 100 millilitres of blood, is guilty of an indictable offence or an offence punishable on summary conviction...

The penalties for this offence are the same as for impaired driving.

—What are the differences between the offences of impaired driving and driving with more than 80 mg of alcohol in your blood?

Roadside Testing

Section 234.1 of the *Code* allows a peace officer who reasonably suspects that a driver or a person with care and control of a motor vehicle has consumed alcohol to demand that the person take a breathalyzer test.

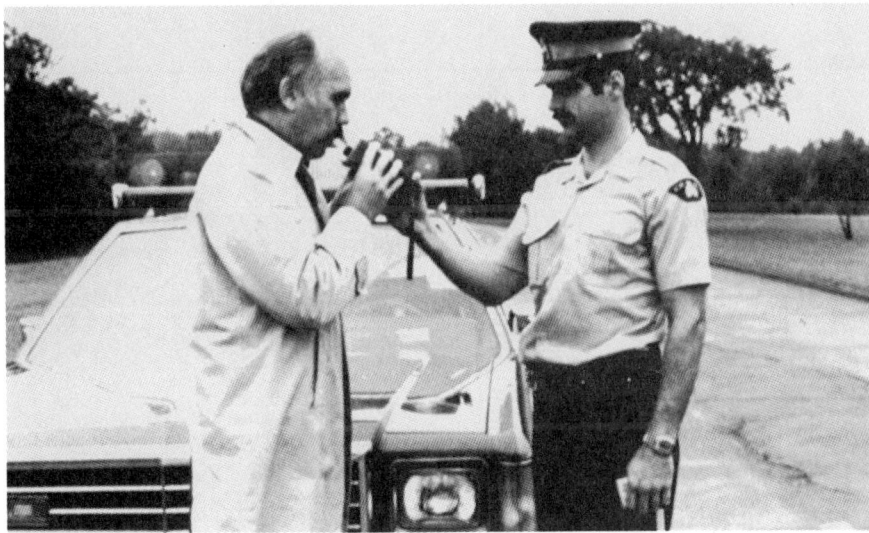

Figure 7-5 Taking a Breathalyzer Test

Section 235(1) allows a peace officer who on reasonable and probable grounds believes that a person is committing or has within the last two hours committed the offences of impaired driving or driving with over 80 mg of alcohol in the blood to demand that the driver take a breathalyzer test.

CRIMINAL OFFENCES 149

—What is the difference between these two sections? Section 234.1 is the newer one and has not yet been proclaimed in British Columbia or Québec. Why do you suppose Parliament enacted this section?
—Both sections make it a summary conviction offence to refuse to take the test unless the person has a reasonable excuse. Can you think of reasonable excuses for not taking the test?

Assault

The definition of assault is in s.244 of the *Code*. As you can see, it is possible to commit an assault without actually touching someone.

> 244. (1) A person commits an assault when
>   (a) without the consent of another person, he applies force intentionally to that person, directly or indirectly;
>   (b) he attempts or threatens, by an act or gesture, to apply force to another person, if he has, or causes that other person to believe upon reasonable grounds that he has, present ability to effect his purpose; or
>   (c) while openly wearing or carrying a weapon or an imitation thereof, he accosts or impedes another person or begs.

Figure 7-6 In which of these situations has an assault taken place?

An important element of the offence of assault is that the force must be applied *without the victim's consent*. There are many situations in which we permit others to touch or "apply force" to us. Examples are contact sports such as hockey or football, as well as dancing or even holding hands. Whether there has been consent can therefore be an important issue in a case. The *Code* assists somewhat by providing the following:

> **244. (3)** For the purposes of this section, no consent is obtained where the complainant submits or does not resist by reason of
> *(a)* the application of force to the complainant or to a person other than the complainant;
> *(b)* threats or fear of the application of force to the complainant or to a person other than the complainant;
> *(c)* fraud; or
> *(d)* the exercise of authority.

However, even where there is initial consent, assault may still take place if the force exceeds that to which it is reasonable to assume the victim consented. For example, there have been several cases where a hockey player has been injured in a fight during the game. Courts have held that hockey players do not consent to the use of excessive violence or force when playing the game. In addition, some courts have said that a person cannot consent to force which is likely to cause bodily harm.

Types of Assault for the Purposes of Punishment

There are three types of assault for the purposes of punishment:

1. Assault (s.245). This is the least serious offence. It is a hybrid offence punishable on summary conviction or on indictment by five years' imprisonment.
2. Assault with a weapon or causing bodily harm (s.245.1). This offence carries a maximum punishment of ten years in prison.
3. Aggravated assault (s.245.2). The maximum punishment for this offence is fourteen years in prison.

Aggravated assault is the most serious offence. It requires that the victim be wounded, disfigured, maimed, or have his or her life threatened by the assault.

It is also an offence under s.246 to assault a peace officer in the execution of his or her duty. This is a hybrid offence punishable on summary conviction or on indictment for up to five years in prison.

Sexual Assault

In 1982, the offence of rape was repealed and replaced with the offence of sexual assault. One of the purposes of the redefinition of the offence was to emphasize that the primary characteristic of this offence is that it involves physical violence against another person. Therefore, the definition of assault discussed earlier also applies to sexual assault. However, the Code does not define "sexual", so it will be up to the courts to decide whether an assault is sexual or not.

Unlike in the old offence of rape, the victim of sexual assault can be male or female, and a spouse can be charged with committing the offence.

Types of Sexual Assault

There are three types of sexual assault for the purposes of punishment:

1. Sexual assault under s.246.1. This is a hybrid offence punishable upon summary conviction or by indictment for up to ten years in prison.
2. Sexual assault under s.246.2(1) with use of a weapon or (2) by threatening bodily harm to a person other than the victim or (3) which causes bodily harm to the victim or (4) where the accused is a party to the offence with any other person. This type of sexual assault is an indictable offence punishable by up to fourteen years in prison.
3. Aggravated assault under s.246.3. This type of sexual assault which wounds, maims, disfigures, or endangers the life of the victim is punishable by life imprisonment.

Abortion

Section 251 of the *Criminal Code* prohibits abortion except where the operation is approved by a therapeutic abortion committee of a hospital. The grounds for approving the abortion are that a continuation of the pregnancy would endanger the life or health of the woman.

The various hospital committees across the country seem to interpret "life" and "health" differently. This has led to the criticism that the law is being applied unfairly. In addition, many hospitals do not have committees, which some say has led to further unequal treatment.

Despite the law, in the 1970s, Dr. Henry Morgentaler was acquitted three times by juries of performing abortions in his clinic, which was not considered a hospital and was therefore not authorized to perform the operation. One defence he used was the common law defence of *necessity*. Briefly, the defence of necessity is that it may be necessary to commit one wrong action to prevent the occurrence of a greater wrong. He argued that the abortion was necessary to save the woman's life or health and that it was impossible for her to obtain an abortion in a hospital.

In his first trial, the jury found him not guilty, but the Québec Court of Appeal overturned the acquittal (which was, at that time, legal), convicted him, and sentenced him to eighteen months in jail. The Supreme Court of Canada upheld the Court of Appeal's decision. He was then charged with performing another abortion. Again the jury found him not guilty. This time the Court of Appeal agreed with the jury verdict and dismissed the appeal. The Supreme Court of Canada refused to interfere with the appeal court's decision.

Meanwhile, there was so much public outrage over the fact that the Court of Appeal had overturned a jury verdict and ordered Morgentaler convicted that the federal justice minister ordered a new trial on the first charge. Again a jury found him not guilty. There were no further appeals, and Morgentaler was released from prison.

One consequence of the Morgentaler case was the enactment of s.613(4)(b) of the *Criminal Code*. This section prohibits a court of appeal from entering a conviction when a person has been acquitted by a jury. In this situation, the court may either dismiss the appeal or order a new trial.

— Why do you think people were so upset about the court's overturning the jury's verdict and convicting Morgentaler?
— Can you think of situations where necessity should be allowed as a defence against performing an illegal abortion?

Offences against the Rights of Property, Part VII

As the heading indicates, offences in this part concern interference with a person's property. The interference may consist of taking the property by theft or robbery, or obtaining property through an action like fraud.

Theft

Simply put, theft is knowingly taking something that belongs to another person. There are over twenty sections in the *Criminal Code* dealing with various types of theft. Section 283(1)(a) gives the basic definition of theft:

> **283.** (1) Every one commits theft who fraudulently and without colour of right takes, or fraudulently and without colour of right converts to his use or to the use of another person, anything whether animate or inanimate, with intent,
> *(a)* to deprive, temporarily or absolutely, the owner of it or a person who has a special property or interest in it, of the thing or of his property or interest in it,

Figure 7-7 What offence is occurring here?

Notice that theft occurs if the property is taken or converted permanently or temporarily. Property is taken temporarily if the thief does not intend to permanently deprive the owner of possession; that is, theft can be illegal borrowing. Conversion occurs when a person obtains property legally but then illegally keeps it. The defendant in the following case was charged with theft by conversion.

R. v. Johnson (1978) 42 C.C.C. (2d) 249 (Man. C.A.)

Johnson opened a bank account at a local branch of a national bank. By mistake, he was given an account number that had been previously assigned to a lawyer but which had not been used in over a year. The lawyer then made four deposits of $1500 apiece, which were credited to Johnson's account. When Johnson discovered the money, he immediately withdrew some of it and spent it on clothes and C.B. equipment.

—Apply the definition of theft in s.283. Why was Johnson charged with theft? Why theft by conversion? Should he be found guilty?

Important elements of the offence are that the taking or conversion be done *fraudulently* and without *colour of right*. "Fraudulent" indicates that the taking or conversion is done with criminal intent. On the other hand, if you take something under colour of right, it means that you believe that you have some legal right to the property. For example, if you honestly believe that a friend is giving you a book, while in fact the friend intended merely to loan you the book, the Crown would not be able to prove the essential element of the offence—that you kept the book without colour of right.

If the value of the property stolen is $200 or less, the offence of theft is hybrid. It is punishable either upon summary conviction or by indictment for up to two years' imprisonment. Theft of property worth over $200 is punishable by up to ten years' imprisonment.

Joyriding—A Special Type of Theft

> 295. Every one who, without the consent of the owner, takes a motor vehicle or vessel with intent to drive, use, navigate or operate it or cause it to be driven, used, navigated or operated is guilty of an offence punishable on summary conviction.

Since a car is usually worth more than $200, if it weren't for s.295 people who illegally "borrow" cars would be charged with the more serious indictable offence of theft. However, in most cases the police and the Crown can choose which offence should be charged. The length of time for which the car was taken and how far it was driven are circumstances they may consider in deciding which offence should be charged.

Robbery

> 302. Every one commits robbery who
> (a) steals, and for the purpose of extorting whatever is stolen or to prevent or overcome resistance to the stealing, uses violence or threats of violence to a person or property;
> (b) steals from any person, and at the time he steals or immediately before or immediately thereafter,

> wounds, beats, strikes or uses any personal violence to that person;
> *(c)* assaults any person with intent to steal from him; or
> *(d)* steals from any person while armed with an offensive weapon or imitation thereof.

R. v. Picard (1976) 39 C.C.C. (2d) 57 (Que. S.P.)

The accused was charged with robbery. He had snatched a purse from Vezina as she was strolling down the street. The evidence was that her purse was grabbed so quickly that she could offer no resistance. She was apparently not hit or pushed at the time her purse was taken.

—Has there been a robbery in this case?
—If there hasn't been a robbery, with what offence should the accused be charged?

The maximum penalty for robbery, which is an indictable offence, is life imprisonment.

Break-and-Enter

> 306. (1) Every one who
> *(a)* breaks and enters a place with intent to commit an indictable offence therein,
> *(b)* breaks and enters a place and commits an indictable offence therein, or
> *(c)* breaks out of a place after
>   (i) committing an indictable offence therein, or
>   (ii) entering the place with intent to commit an indictable offence therein,
> is guilty of an indictable offence and is liable
> *(d)* to imprisonment for life, if the offence is committed in relation to a dwelling-house, or
> *(e)* to imprisonment for fourteen years, if the offence is committed in relation to a place other than a dwelling-house.

—Why do you think the penalty for break-and-enter is greater if the place broken into is a dwelling-house?

Note that it is not enough to just break into a building. The purpose of breaking in must be to commit an indictable offence such as theft. Thus, if someone breaks into a cottage to seek shelter from a storm, break-and-enter has not taken place. However, s.306(2) puts the burden on the defendant to show that the purpose of breaking in was not to commit an indictable offence.

> 306. ...
>   (2) For the purposes of proceedings under this section, evidence that an accused
>   (a) broke and entered a place is, in the absence of any evidence to the contrary, proof that he broke and entered with intent to commit an indictable offence therein...

It is not necessary to actually break into a building. In other words, opening an unlocked door and walking in can also be break-and-enter because of s.308(b):

>   (b) a person shall be deemed to have broken and entered if
>   (i) he obtained entrance by a threat or artifice or by collusion with a person within, or
>   (ii) he entered without lawful justification or excuse, the proof of which lies upon him, by a permanent or temporary opening.

Possession of Property Obtained by Crime

> 312. (1) Every one commits an offence who has in his possession any property or thing or any proceeds of any property or thing knowing that all or part of the property or thing or of the proceeds was obtained by or derived directly or indirectly from
>   (a) the commission in Canada of an offence punishable by indictment; or
>   (b) an act or omission anywhere that, if it had occurred in Canada, would have constituted an offence punishable by indictment.

Figure 7-8 Is the prospective buyer taking a chance if he purchases the watch?

This offence is most commonly committed through the possession of stolen property. If someone sells or gives you property you have reason to believe was stolen, you may be charged with this offence. The doctrine of *recent possession* states that if someone is found in possession of *recently* stolen property and cannot give a reasonable explanation for possessing those goods, a judge or jury may convict the person. Without a reasonable explanation, possession of recently stolen property raises an *inference* (a logical conclusion) of guilt. However, if a person can give a reasonable explanation for having possession of the property, the burden then falls on the Crown to prove its case beyond a reasonable doubt.

If the goods are worth more than $200, the offence is indictable and punishable by up to ten years in prison. For goods worth less than $200, the offence is hybrid. It is punishable on summary conviction or on indictment for up to two years' imprisonment.

Wilful and Forbidden Acts in Respect of Certain Property, Part IX

This part contains offences involving destruction of or damage to property. Mischief, arson, and cruelty to animals are the types of conduct covered.

Mischief

> 387. (1) Every one commits mischief who wilfully
> (a) destroys or damages property,
> (b) renders property dangerous, useless, inoperative or ineffective,
> (c) obstructs, interrupts or interferes with the lawful use, enjoyment or operation of property, or
> (d) obstructs, interrupts or interferes with any person in the lawful use, enjoyment or operation of property.

Vandalism, the damaging of property, is just one way in which this offence can be committed. The following case illustrates another way the offence can be committed.

R. v. Biggin (1980) 55 C.C.C. (2d) 408 (Ont. C.A.)

The accused was charged under s.387(1)(d). Biggin was the president of the Union of Injured Workers. Union members led by Biggin held a demonstration in the lobby of the building where the Ministry of Labour has its offices. Travelers Insurance also had offices on the upper floors of the building. Biggin told the demonstrators that since the police would not allow them to go upstairs, the demonstrators should not allow anyone else upstairs. The demonstrators then linked arms and obstructed access to the elevators. Office workers for Travelers testified that they were prevented access to the elevators.

—Should Biggin be convicted? Explain.

Drug Offences

Offences concerning the use of drugs are not in the *Criminal Code*. The *Narcotic Control Act* deals with drugs considered narcotics, such as opium, heroin, methadone, cocaine, and cannabis (marijuana and hashish). Other drugs are handled under the *Food and Drugs Act*.

Narcotic Control Act

It is an offence under this *Act* to possess, traffic in, import, or export any of the drugs covered by the *Act*. In addition, it is an offence to cultivate the opium poppy or marijuana.

Possession

The *Narcotic Control Act* uses the *Criminal Code* definition of possession:

> 3. (4) For the purposes of this Act,
>   (a) a person has anything in possession when he has it in his personal possession or knowingly
>   (i) has it in the actual possession or custody of another person, or
>   (ii) has it in any place, whether or not that place belongs to or is occupied by him, for the use or benefit of himself or of another person; and
>   (b) where one of two or more persons, with the knowledge and consent of the rest, has anything in his custody or possession, it shall be deemed to be in the custody and possession of each and all of them.

Personal Possession

There are three things which the Crown must prove to show personal possession:

1. physical contact with the drug;
2. knowledge of what the substance is; and
3. control over the drug.

Apply these requirements to the following case.

Beaver v. The Queen (1957) 118 C.C.C. 129 (S.C.C.)

The accused was charged with possession of and trafficking in a narcotic. He sold a packet of morphine to an undercover police officer who was working under the name of Demeter. Beaver's defence was that he honestly believed that the packet contained milk sugar. Beaver testified that Montroy, a drug addict, had told him that Demeter had "double-crossed" him and that he wanted to "get even" with him. Demeter wanted drugs and Montroy proposed that he introduce Beaver to Demeter as someone who could sell him drugs. Instead of delivering drugs, however, Beaver would give him a packet of milk sugar. The price of the drugs would then be given to Montroy. Beaver agreed to this plan because he felt he owed Montroy a favour. On the day of the delivery, Beaver drove Demeter to a certain location, stopped, picked up a package, and gave it to Demeter, who paid the agreed price. The package turned out to contain morphine.

—Should Beaver be convicted of possession? Explain.

Constructive Possession

Possession under s.3(4)(a)(i) and (ii) is called *constructive* possession: the accused does not have to have had actual physical contact with the drug. Knowledge and control are the important elements of this offence. Consider the following case:

R. v. Senger (1955) 112 C.C.C. 351 (B.C. C.A.)

The accused was charged with illegal possession of drugs. Senger was in the room when another person was arrested for possession. The police observed Senger trying to twist something in his hand. The police grabbed his hand and took from it a ball of paper with three addresses on it. When asked what the addresses were, Senger said they were his girlfriends'. The police found that there were no women living at these addresses, but they found drugs hidden at each one.

—Should Senger be convicted? Did he have knowledge and control? Give your reasons.

Possession by More than One Person

The key element of proving possession under s.3(4)(b) is showing that a person had possession with the knowledge and consent of the defendant. Although the courts have not been consistent in their decisions, the most common view right now is that the accused must have had some control over the drug as well.

Marcia picks up Wayne in her car. On the way to a party, Marcia stops at another house to pick up some marijuana. Wayne knows what Marcia has picked up but says nothing. They continue to the party. On the way, the police, acting on a tip, stop them and search the car. The police find the marijuana.

—Examine s.3(4)(b) of the *Narcotic Control Act*. Can Wayne be jointly charged with Marcia for possession of the marijuana?

Trafficking

The *Narcotic Control Act* defines the term *traffic* as follows:

> 2. (a) to manufacture, sell, give, administer, transport, send, deliver or distribute, or
> (b) to offer to do anything mentioned in paragraph (a)...

The offence of trafficking is contained in s.4:

> **4. (1) No person shall traffic in a narcotic or any substance represented or held out by him to be a narcotic.**

—Reread the *Beaver* case. Could Beaver be convicted of trafficking?

It is also an offence to have possession for the purpose of trafficking. Courts may assume that a person has possession for trafficking if the person has possession of a large quantity of drugs. Notice that trafficking means more than selling drugs. Giving drugs to friends can also be trafficking.

The maximum penalty for trafficking, an indictable offence, is life imprisonment.

Importing and Exporting

This offence is considered so serious that a convicted person must be sentenced to at least seven years in prison, while the maximum penalty is life imprisonment. This is one of the few offences for which the law sets a minimum penalty. Bringing narcotics into Canada for personal use can be considered importing.

Cultivation of the Opium Poppy or Marijuana

Growing either of these plants is punishable by up to seven years' imprisonment.

Figure 7-9 It is a criminal offence to cultivate marijuana.

Food and Drugs Act

Under the *Food and Drugs Act*, certain drugs are classified as *controlled* (for example, amphetamines and barbiturates) while others are classified as *restricted* (L.S.D., mescaline, and peyote, among others). The controlled drugs include prescription drugs.

Controlled Drugs

It is an offence to traffic or have possession for the purpose of trafficking in a controlled drug. It is not, however, an offence to have possession of a controlled drug. The definition is narrower here than in the *Narcotic Control Act*:

> 33. ...
> "traffic" means to manufacture, sell, export from or import into Canada, transport or deliver, otherwise than under the authority of this Part or the regulations.

Notice that it is not an offence to *give* someone a controlled drug.

Trafficking in a controlled drug is a hybrid offence. Upon summary conviction, the maximum penalty is eighteen months' imprisonment. If the Crown proceeds by indictment, the maximum penalty is ten years' imprisonment.

Restricted Drugs

It is an offence to have possession of, traffic in, or have possession of a restricted drug for the purpose of trafficking. "Possession" is defined in the *Criminal Code*. The definition of "trafficking" is the same as for controlled drugs.

Possession of a restricted drug is a hybrid offence. Upon summary conviction, the penalties are as follows:

1. for a first conviction, a fine of $1000 or six months in prison, or both;
2. for subsequent convictions, a fine of $2000 or imprisonment for one year, or both.

If the Crown proceeds by indictment, the maximum penalties are a fine of $5000 or imprisonment for three years, or both.

Trafficking is a hybrid offence. It is punishable on summary conviction by imprisonment for eighteen months or on indictment by imprisonment for ten years.

SUMMARIZING YOUR READING

1. What parts of the *Criminal Code* contain offences?

2. What types of offences are contained in Part II of the *Code*?

3. What is the difference between an unlawful assembly and a riot? What are the similarities between the two offences?

4. What types of offences are contained in Part III of the *Code*?

5. Give three examples of the way in which the offence of obstructing a peace officer can be committed.

6. How does the law define obscenity? Consider the *Code* and case law.

7. What are the basic elements of the offence of causing a disturbance?

8. What types of offences are contained in Part IV of the *Code*?

9. Can a person be guilty of criminal negligence by not doing something? Explain.

10. How have the courts defined "wanton and reckless conduct"?

11. What is the difference between culpable and non-culpable homicide?

12. What are the three types of culpable homicide?

13. List the ways in which murder can be committed.

14. What is the difference between first and second degree murder?

15. Give three examples of situations in which the offence of manslaughter can be charged.

16. When may the offence of infanticide be charged?

17. What is the difference between criminal negligence in the use of a motor vehicle and dangerous driving?

18. What are the two offences covered by impaired driving? What is the difference between them?

19. What is the difference between the offences of impaired driving and driving with more than 80 mg of alcohol in your blood?

20. What are the two situations where a person can be required to take a breathalyzer test?

21. Give three examples of the way an assault can be committed.

22. Why is consent an important factor to consider in deciding whether an assault has been committed?

23. How is the offence of sexual assault defined?

24. When is abortion legal?

25. What types of offences are contained in Part VII?

26. Give two examples of the way theft can be committed.

27. Explain the terms "fraudulently" and "without colour of right" as used in connection with theft.

28. Explain the offence of joyriding.

29. What must be the purpose of breaking into a building for the offence of breaking and entering to be committed?

30. Can entering through an unlocked door be considered breaking and entering? Explain.

31. How is the offence of robbery different from theft?

32. Explain the doctrine of recent possession.

33. What types of offences are contained in Part IX?

34. Give two examples of how the offence of mischief can be committed.

35. What two federal statutes deal with drug offences? Give examples of the types of drugs covered by each of these *Acts*.

36. Explain the differences between personal possession, constructive possession, and possession by more than one person under the *Narcotic Control Act*.

37. How does the *Narcotic Control Act* define "traffic"?

38. How does the *Act* indicate the seriousness of the offences of importing and exporting?

39. What are the two classifications of drugs under the *Food and Drugs Act*?

40. What is the difference between trafficking under the *Narcotic Control Act* and under the *Food and Drugs Act*?

DISCUSSING KEY ISSUES

1. There has been much talk by the federal government about "decriminalizing" possession of marijuana. This would mean taking marijuana out of the *Narcotic Control Act* and putting it into

the *Food and Drugs Act*. What effect would doing this have? Would it be a good idea, in your opinion? Discuss.

2. Euthanasia, or "mercy killing", is not specifically mentioned in the *Criminal Code*, but it is a form of homicide. Are there any circumstances in which euthanasia could be justified? Discuss.

PROJECTS AND ACTIVITIES

1. During your study of this chapter, collect as many newspaper articles about crime as possible. Make a scrapbook. Label each article with the name of the crime that has been committed, the part of the *Criminal Code* under which this offence falls, and the section of the *Code* which describes the offence.

2. Are the penalties for drunk drivers sufficient? Find out the figures for highway deaths each year caused by drunk drivers. Consider s.234(2) of the *Criminal Code*, found below. This section may not yet be in force in your province. Find out whether it is. Do you think it will help?

> 234. (2) ...where an accused pleads guilty to or is found guilty of an offence under subsection (1) [impaired driving] the court before which he appears may, after hearing medical or other evidence, if it considers that the accused is in need of curative treatment in relation to his consumption of alcohol or drugs and that it would not be contrary to the public interest, instead of convicting the accused, by order direct that the accused be discharged upon conditions prescribed in a probation order, including a condition respecting his attendance for curative treatment in relation to his consumption of alcohol or drugs...

3. Write an essay on the conflict between freedom of speech and obscenity law. Should obscene material be prohibited, in your opinion? Is there any evidence that viewing or reading obscene material affects behaviour? Write you own version of a law for controlling obscene material, incorporating your own definition of "obscene".

4. Write a research paper on the federal gun control legislation. How does the *Criminal Code* control the use of guns? Do you think this is sufficient control or too much control? Try to include in your paper statistics concerning the frequency of gun-related crimes.

RESOLVING CASES

R. v. Lockhart et al. (1976) 15 N.S.R. (2d) 512 (C.A.)

Cecil Keddy was arrested for causing a disturbance. He and others had been drinking and swearing on a public street. He was arrested when the police arrived. Later that night, between twenty and thirty people, including the defendants, arrived at the jail. They were loudly swearing and demanding that Keddy be released. Police testified that people in the crowd yelled that if Keddy was not released, they would break him out. One defendant offered to fight with one of the officers. The police were worried about what the crowd might do, so they told the crowd that Keddy would be released within a half hour. The police eventually convinced the crowd to disperse. Keddy was released on an appearance notice a short time later.

About twenty minutes after his release, the crowd for no apparent reason returned and burst into the station, going down to the cells. By this time the R.C.M.P. had arrived, and the defendants were arrested and charged with rioting.

—At what point did the riot take place?
—What was the common purpose of the assembly?
—What made the disturbance tumultuous?

R. v. Delorme (1973) 15 C.C.C. (2d) 350 (Que. C.A.)

The accused, who operated a bookstore open to the general public, was charged with possession of an obscene book for the purposes of distributing. The book concerned a woman who submitted to various cruel and violent sexual acts. Three expert witnesses for the defence testified that the book had value as literature and as a psychological study. There was some suggestion that the book would be useful to students of literature or psychology. It had a plain cover with just the title which would not attract the general public. One witness, Dr. Manourier, a medical doctor and an expert in sexology, testified that it was a difficult book to read and not within everyone's grasp. The accused raised the defence of the public good.

—Would the defence succeed? Explain your answer.

R. v. Campbell (1980) 22 C.R. (3d) 219 (Alta. Q.B.)

The defendant was charged with causing a disturbance in a public place using insulting or obscene language. He was in the hallway and T.V. room of the Immaculata Hospital when the incident occurred.

The provincial court judge dismissed the charge on the grounds that the T.V. room and hallway were dwelling places. The Crown Attorney appealed.

—If you were the judge hearing the appeal, how would you decide this case?
—Can you think of arguments why a T.V. room or a patient's room should or should not be considered dwelling places?
—What about the administrative offices of a university which have been occupied overnight by students during a demonstration? Should the offices be considered dwelling places? Explain.

R. v. Stevens (1974) 26 C.R.N.S. 165 (N.S. C.A.)

The defendant was charged with the murder of one Reg Murphy. Stevens was described in a psychiatric report as being of dull-normal intelligence. This meant he was the type of person to act on impulse and whose judgement was somewhat impaired compared to that of the average person. Apparently, for two years before Murphy's death, Murphy had had an obsession to try to kill Stevens with his car. There were no reasons for his obsession, except that he seemed to dislike Stevens intensely. He had hit Stevens several times, the last time causing him to be hospitalized. While in the hospital, Stevens received a letter from the Nova Scotia Insurance Commission requesting information about the accident. After being released from hospital, Stevens went to Murphy's house to get information he thought he needed about Murphy's insurance. When Murphy saw who it was, he got his gun. Stevens tried to explain what he wanted but Murphy told Stevens to leave or he would "blow his head off".

Stevens returned to his home and "sat around for an hour or so". Then he got his gun and returned to Murphy's house. Stevens said his intention in taking the gun was to scare Murphy by firing at the house. When Murphy saw the gun he turned around and said "Oh geez old man, don't do that." Stevens thought Murphy was going for his gun so he fired, shooting him in the chest.

—Should Stevens be able to use the defence of provocation? Explain.

R. v. Dewitt and Sierens (1981) 62 C.C.C. (2d) 176 (Man. Prov. Ct.)

The accused were charged with taking stereo equipment worth over $6000 from the house of one Gariepy, a friend of theirs. They testified that they had warned their friend that his house could be easily broken into, especially since he often left his door unlocked. As a joke, they broke into his house when he was away one weekend and removed the stereo and other equipment. When Gariepy returned home, he immediately called the police. His friends were unable to contact him until the next day when they told him of their joke.

— Should the defendants be found guilty of theft? Was the taking done with deliberate intent?
— Would it make any difference how the victim would have felt if he had known the true facts at the time when the accuseds took the equipment?

R. v. Hart (1972) 21 C.R.N.S. 44 (B.C.C.A.)

The accused was convicted of having possession of a stolen colour T.V., a stereo tape deck, and a radio. He appealed his conviction to the Court of Appeal.

His evidence was that he purchased the T.V. from a man named Bill after talking with him in the early morning at an all-night café. He had met Bill and his friend Rod several other times in the early morning at the café; however, he did not know their last names or addresses.

Bill delivered the T.V., and after finding it in perfect working order and looking quite new, Hart paid $200 cash. He realized $200 was a low price, and, in fact, the T.V. was worth $590. He asked for a warranty and Bill assured him that he would bring it the next day. Bill did not do so, and when Hart saw him several days later, he again asked for a warranty. Bill put him off on this and then asked if he was interested in the other equipment. Hart was not interested in buying the other items, but was eventually convinced to loan Rod $50 and to take the equipment as security for the loan. After that, he never saw Bill or Rod again. Several days later, the police seized the goods and Hart was charged.

— In what situations should a person know goods are stolen?
— What do you think the decision of the Court of Appeal was? Give reasons for your answer.

8

An Introduction to Defences

The Incapacity of Young Children	Self-Defence
Insanity	Defence of Property
Automatism	Necessity
Intoxication	Mistake of Fact; Mistake of Law
Duress or Compulsion	Double Jeopardy

Figure 8-1

170 THE LAW, THE INDIVIDUAL, AND THE STATE

A person accused of committing a criminal offence will consider whether there are any defences which can be raised at the trial. First, the accused may merely deny committing the offence. To back up this denial, the accused may raise an **alibi** by saying that he or she was somewhere else when the crime was committed. This type of defence needs no further explanation. To obtain a conviction, the Crown must show that it was, in fact, the defendant who committed the *actus reus* and had *mens rea* in the offence.

Figure 8-2

This chapter will examine *general defences*, which justify or excuse conduct which would otherwise be criminal. Defences related to particular crimes have already been discussed in Chapter 7. Many general defences have been codified in the *Criminal Code*, while others are still part of the common law.

The Incapacity of Young Children

Before the twentieth century, under common law, children younger than the age of seven were considered incapable of having the maturity to understand the difference between right and wrong. Therefore, they were in law presumed unable to form *mens rea* to commit an offence. Between the ages of seven and fourteen, there was a *rebuttable presumption* that a child did not have the mental capacity to form *mens rea* in an offence. This meant that it was possible to rebut the presumption by showing that, in fact, the child *did* understand right from wrong. Obviously, the older the child, the easier it would be to prove that the child had the capacity to form the required intent for the offence.

As you have read, the federal government recently passed the *Young Offenders Act*. Therefore, the minimum age for criminal responsibility is now twelve. Provincial governments are wrestling with the task of deciding what to do with offenders under twelve. Most provinces are dealing with these young people under child welfare legislation.

—Do you agree with the raising of the age for criminal responsibility? What should happen to a child who breaks the law?

Although persons over twelve and under eighteen may be held responsible for their criminal actions, they are usually not prosecuted in adult courts, but in special youth courts, as Chapter 6 made clear.

Insanity

Another defence which concerns the accused's capacity to form *mens rea* for the offence is insanity.

R. v. Adamcik (1977) 33 C.C.C. (2d) 11 (B.C. Cty. Ct.)

The accused believed that he was a type of Robin Hood. He reported that he had many conversations with God, who directed his activities to help the poor. Adamcik escaped from the mental institution in which he was being treated, and went to Vancouver. While there, he saw a wooden crucifix for sale, displayed in what he thought was a blasphemous manner. Not having the money to buy the crucifix, he attempted to get a bank loan but was turned down. He then went to a friend's apartment and found a toy gun. He told his friend that God had told him to get the money from the bank so he could buy the crucifix and give it a proper home. His friend attempted to dissuade him, but he insisted that God would protect him. He then robbed the bank and went to the store. Instead of paying for the crucifix, he robbed the store of $102. He returned to his friend's apartment, where he was arrested by the police and charged with robbery.

The accused was found not guilty because he was insane at the time the offences were committed.

The defence of insanity is set out in the *Criminal Code*:

> **16. (1)** No person shall be convicted of an offence...while he was insane.
> **(2)** For the purposes of this section a person is insane when he is in a state of natural imbecility or has a disease of the mind to an extent that renders him incapable of appreciating the nature and quality of an act or omission or of knowing that an act or omission is wrong.

The defence of insanity is different from others in several important ways. First, the burden of proving the defence is on the accused (reverse onus). The accused must prove that, *on a balance of probabilities* (more likely than not), he or she was insane when the offence was committed. In other situations, you will recall, the accused need only raise a defence. It is up to the Crown to show that the accused committed the offence beyond a reasonable doubt. This burden of proof is on the accused because of s. 16.(4) which states: "Every one shall, until the contrary is proved, be presumed to be and to have been sane."

The second important difference is that a person found not guilty by reason of insanity is not released but instead is committed to a mental institution. The person is released from the mental institution only when authorities believe he or she is cured. Since this period of commitment may be longer than the prison sentence would be if a guilty verdict had been entered, the defence of insanity is used cautiously.

Third, insanity may be raised by the prosecution, with the permission of the judge. Before allowing the Crown to raise insanity, the judge must be convinced that the accused committed the offence. In these cases, the Crown must prove insanity on a balance of probabilities.

Whoever raises insanity must prove several things. The first is that the accused is in a state of natural imbecility or suffering from a disease of the mind. Natural imbecility refers to a state like mental retardation. Recently, the Supreme Court of Canada has said that

> "disease of the mind" embraces any illness, disorder or abnormal condition which impairs the human mind and its functioning, excluding however, self-induced states caused by alcohol or drugs, as well as transitory mental states...." (*R. v. Cooper* [1980] 1 S.C.R. 1149)

Personality disorders, schizophrenia, paranoia, and melancholia have all been considered diseases of the mind.

It is not enough to prove that the accused is suffering from natural imbecility or has a disease of the mind to succeed on an insanity defence, however. The accused's mental condition must have caused him or her either to be incapable of *appreciating* the nature and quality of the action, or to be incapable of knowing the action was wrong. "Appreciate" means more than just knowing what physical action, one is doing. For example, in the *Adamcik* case, the accused knew he was robbing a bank and store, but he did not appreciate the nature of the actions. That is, he thought he was acting on God's direction.

Delusions

In some situations, a person who is otherwise sane but who commits a crime while under a specific delusion may use the defence of insanity.

Figure 8-3 *A person who breaks the law while suffering a delusion may be able to use the defence of insanity.*

Fred and his neighbour have argued for years over who owns a strip of land between their houses. Recently, the arguments have become more intense. One night Fred thinks he hears his neighbour coming up his front steps. He believes the neighbour is carrying a gun. In fact, it is his daughter coming home from a date. Fred thinks he sees his neighbour pointing a gun at him. Fred takes his gun and shoots, seriously wounding his daughter.

— What is Fred's delusion?
— Should Fred be able to use the insanity defence?
— What if Fred, believing his neighbour was planning to kill him, went to his neighbour's house and shot him while he was eating his breakfast? Should Fred be able to use the insanity defence in this situation?

Section 16(3) of the *Criminal Code* states:

> **16. (3) A person who has specific delusions but is in other respects sane, shall not be acquitted on the ground of insanity unless the delusions caused him to believe in the existence of a state of things that if it existed would have justified his act or omission.**

In other words, a person may only use the insanity defence if the delusion would have justified the crime.

Automatism

The defence of automatism has developed through case law and so is not included in the *Criminal Code*. One case defined it as follows:

> Automatism is a term used to describe unconscious, involuntary behaviour; the state of a person who, though capable of action, is not conscious of what he is doing. It means an unconscious, involuntary act, where the mind does not go with what is being done. (*R. v. K.* (1971) 3. C.C.C. (2d) 84 at 84)

In other words, when the defence of automatism is raised, the defence is that the accused did not commit the *actus reus* of the offence. Actions committed while the actor is sleepwalking, or during an epileptic seizure, are types of "automatic behaviour".

Courts have distinguished between unconscious behaviour caused by internal factors or diseases of the mind and by external factors. If the unconscious behaviour is caused by an external factor such as a physical blow or the involuntary use of a drug, the accused can use automatism as a defence. If a disease of the mind is the cause of the behaviour, then the insanity defence must be used. The difference is important because, unlike a person who succeeds with the insanity defence, a person who successfully uses the automatism defence will be acquitted and released from custody.

Intoxication

Voluntary intoxication by either drugs or alcohol is not a defence in most situations. Of course, if the intoxication is so severe that it has caused a disease of the mind, insanity can be pleaded. However, intoxication *can* be used as a defence to certain offences. One example of using the defence of intoxication was given in the previous chapter, where it was explained how the defence can be used to reduce a charge of murder to manslaughter. Similarly, intoxication can be raised as a defence whenever a *specific intent* crime is charged to reduce the charge to a less serious offence. Recall that some offences require specific intent as a type of *mens rea*. The example used was a type of robbery which consists of assaulting someone with the intent to steal. It is possible for a person to be so intoxicated that he or she cannot form the specific intent to steal, though that person can still form the general intent to assault someone.

Figure 8-4 Intoxication cannot be used as a defence by a person who drinks to get the "courage" to commit the crime.

If the specific intent to steal is not proved in such a situation, an accused can still be found guilty of the general intent offence of assault. The assault is then called a *lesser included offence*; that is, it is necessary to prove the assault as part of the offence of robbery. Consider the following case:

R. v. George (1960) 34 C.R. 1 (S.C.C.)

The accused, who was charged with robbery, seriously assaulted an eighty-four-year-old man with his fists. According to the victim, the accused threatened to kill him if he did not give him some money. The accused told police that he had been drinking heavily all day. He said he remembered being in a house and hitting a man but did not remember anything else.

The trial court acquitted George of the robbery charge because of his intoxication. On appeal, the Supreme Court of Canada held that the judge should have considered whether the accused was guilty of assault, an included offence, and ordered a new trial.

Duress or Compulsion

Section 17 of the *Criminal Code* states:

> 17. A person who commits an offence under compulsion by threats of immediate death or grievous bodily harm from a person who is present when the offence is committed is excused for committing the offence if he believes that the threats will be carried out...but this section does not apply where the offence that is committed is high treason or treason, murder, piracy, attempted murder, sexual assault, sexual assault with a weapon, threats to a third party or causing bodily harm, aggravated sexual assault, forcible abduction, robbery, assault with a weapon or causing bodily harm, aggravated assault, unlawfully causing bodily harm, arson or an offence under sections 249–250.2 [abduction and detention of young persons].

R. v. Smith (1977) 40 C.R.N.S. 390 (B.C. Prov. Ct.)

The accused was charged with driving a motor vehicle while impaired. Testing done at the time she was charged indicated that she was legally impaired; however, she raised the defence of compulsion.

Smith had been out celebrating with her fellow workers and was expected home at 8 p.m. At midnight her husband went looking for her and found her in her parked car with a male person. Her husband jumped on her car hood and smashed the window with his fist. He pulled the male occupant out of the car and began fighting with him. In extreme fright, Smith started to drive her car to escape from her husband. He proceeded to chase her in his car and rammed her vehicle several times. The accused saw a police constable, stopped her car, and ran towards him. She testified that she had not intended to drive, but had to in order to escape being beaten.

The court observed that the husband was 6'4" (193 cm) tall, weighed 215 pounds (98 kg), and was very athletic, while his wife was a woman of slight build.

—Do you think Smith should be acquitted? Explain, referring to s. 17.

You will notice that s. 17 does not give a defence to someone who commits certain serious crimes. Thus, if Alphonso puts a gun to Basil's head and says "If you don't shoot Christopher, I will shoot you," and Basil then does shoot Christopher, Basil will not be able to use duress as a defence. It is said that a person in Basil's position ought to be willing to die rather than escape by the murder of an innocent person.

—What do you think of this statement?

What if the person acting under duress is not the principal actor but only a party to the offence, for example, the driver of a get-away car? The Supreme Court of Canada recently held that s. 17 applies only to the persons who actually commit the offence. Other parties to the crime can still use the common law defence of duress for any offence. Consider the following case:

Paquette v. The Queen (1976) 30 C.C.C. (2d) 417 (S.C.C.)

The accused, along with Simard and Clermont, was charged with murder. During a robbery of a Pop Shoppe in Ottawa, an innocent bystander was killed by a stray bullet fired by one of the robbers. The accused told the police that Clermont ordered him to drive to the store because he wanted to rob it. When he refused, Clermont pulled a gun and threatened to kill him. Simard was picked up later. The accused then drove Simard and Clermont to the store. He was threatened with revenge if he did not remain. He then drove around the block. After the robbery and murder, Clermont and Simard unsuccessfully attempted twice to get into the accused's car.

—Why was Paquette charged with murder?
—Should he be acquitted?
—Why should it make a difference whether the accused shot the gun or only drove the get-away car?

Self-Defence

Several sections in the *Criminal Code* deal with different situations in which a person may use force in self-defence. The general rule is stated in s.37:

> 37. (1) Every one is justified in using force to defend himself or any one under his protection from assault, if he uses no more force than is necessary to prevent the assault or the repetition of it.

Figure 8-5 *How does s. 37(1) apply to this situation? How can the teacher justify using force to restrain the student?*

The key idea here is that you can use only as much force as necessary to prevent the assault. Thus, if you shoot someone who has threatened you with a bare fist, you may find yourself charged with assault for using excessive force.

— Look up s.34 and 35 of the *Criminal Code*, which deal with self-defence when the assault is unprovoked, and when it is provoked. What is the difference between the two sections? Note that s.36 defines provocation for these two sections.

Defence of Property

The rules regarding defence of property are similar to those for self-defence. In general, an owner of property is justified in using as much force as necessary to prevent someone from taking it, trespassing on it, or in the case of a house, from breaking into it. As well, a trespasser to movable or real property who resists giving it up is deemed to have committed assault.

Necessity

In theory, the law recognizes the defence of necessity. Under this defence, a person is justified in breaking the law if by so doing the person avoids a greater harm or achieves a greater good than if the law were obeyed. Self-defence and duress are specific examples of situations of necessity wherein a person is justified in breaking the law. In addition, the Supreme Court of Canada has said that a general defence of necessity exists. Despite this statement, courts have been very reluctant to acquit a defendant on the grounds of necessity.

—Why do you think judges are reluctant to allow the defence of necessity?

Mistake of Fact; Mistake of Law

An honest mistake about a circumstance which leads a person to commit an offence may allow the person to use the defence of mistake of fact.

R. v. Woolridge (1979) 49 C.C.C. (2d) 300 (Sask. Prov. Ct.)

The accused was charged with bigamy, that is, going through a form of marriage while married to another. Woolridge had been told by his wife, who lived in Newfoundland, that she was getting a divorce. He was also told by a lawyer that he need not sign any papers for the divorce, and his wife's lawyer told him that the divorce was in process. Relatives later informed him that the divorce had been obtained. He then went through a ceremony to marry his second "wife"; however, the divorce was not in fact complete.

—What mistake has the accused made?
—Should he be acquitted?

You should know, however, that the general rule is that a mistake about whether an action is an offence is not an excuse, as the following section of the *Criminal Code* indicates:

> **19.** Ignorance of the law by a person who commits an offence is not an excuse for committing that offence.

—There are over 700 sections in the *Criminal Code*, in addition to other federal statutes containing criminal offences. Do you feel that it is fair that ignorance of the law is not a defence? What would result if it were a defence?

Double Jeopardy

A basic principle of criminal law is that a person cannot be placed in jeopardy twice for the same offence. In other words, a defence which can be raised is that the accused has been previously acquitted or convicted on the offence. This defence is stated in the *Criminal Code*, sections 535–538, and is now guaranteed by the *Charter of Rights and Freedoms*:

> 11. Any person charged with an offence has the right...
> (h) if finally acquitted of the offence, not to be tried for it again and, if finally found guilty and punished for the offence, not to be tried or punished for it again...

The technical name used for the defence is *autrefois acquit* (formerly acquitted) or *autrefois convict* (formerly convicted). The *Criminal Code* and case law have extended the use of this defence to situations beyond where the accused has been charged with exactly the same offence. For instance, a person cannot be charged with an included offence after being acquitted or convicted of the principal offence. Recall that an included offence is one which has the same basic ingredients as the principal offence. For example, one type of robbery is defined as "theft with the use of violence". Theft is thus an included offence of robbery. Similarly, possession of a prohibited drug is an included offence of the offence of possession for the purpose of trafficking. The defence of double jeopardy applies to included offences, because a defendant can be convicted of the offence charged or of any of the included offences.

Lucia is charged with murder for intentionally killing Roger by running over him with her car. The Crown fails to prove that the killing was intentional. However, the Crown does prove that Lucia was reckless. She is then convicted of manslaughter.

Manslaughter is an included offence of murder. Lucia has been convicted of manslaughter. The Crown could not then bring murder charges against her again for the killing of Roger, because Lucia could employ the defence of double jeopardy.

A very similar defence is that of *res judicata* (an adjudicated matter). The meaning of the defence is that once a matter has been decided by the courts, it cannot be raised again. This is a broader defence that applies to any fundamental issue that has previously been decided by a court. It has been used in cases where one action, such as a gun being shot, results in a single bullet killing two people. In such a situation, if a person is charged with causing one death and it is determined at the trial that the accused did not shoot the gun, the defendant can use the defence of *res judicata* if later charged with the killing of the second person. The court has already determined the fundamental issue that the defendant was not the person who shot the gun.

SUMMARIZING YOUR READING

1. Are all of the defences available to an accused stated in the *Criminal Code*? Explain.

2. At what age do young people become liable for their criminal actions?

3. How is the insanity defence different from other defences?

4. Explain the elements that must be proved for an insanity defence.

5. When can a person suffering from a delusion use the insanity defence?

6. Why is the *Criminal Code* section on delusions rarely used?

7. Does the defence of automatism negate the *mens rea* or *actus reus* in an offence? Explain.

8. Why would an accused prefer to use the defence of automatism over the insanity defence?

9. When can voluntary intoxication be used as a defence?

10. Define the defence of duress.

11. What are the limitations on the defence of duress under s.17 of the *Code*?

12. When can the common law defence of duress be used?

13. How much force can a person use in self-defence?

14. What is the rule regarding defence of property?

15. Explain the defence of necessity. Give an original example of when it might be used.

16. Explain the defence of mistake of fact.

17. What is the defence of double jeopardy?

DISCUSSING KEY ISSUES

Violence and Justice

1. Canadians who fear courts are placing too much dependence on psychiatrists to determine when dangerous persons should be indefinitely locked up can find some reason for their anxiety in recent comments made by Dr. Russell Fleming.

A director of the mental health centre at Penetanguishene, where many of Canada's criminally insane are kept, Fleming has confessed in a newspaper interview that he too worries about the role of his fellow psychiatrists.

The courts, says Fleming, "shouldn't ask us to get involved in this adversarial nonsense where a crown attorney shops around for a right-wing psychiatrist to say the man should go (to an institution), while defence shops around for a left-wing psychiatrist to say he shouldn't."

Fleming would prefer to see a system created by lawmakers that would designate a criminal a dangerous offender after repeated crimes, not on the basis of often-conflicting views by psychiatrists.

His conclusion is an acknowledgement that psychiatry is an imperfect science, and that too often psychiatrists are determining —rightly or wrongly—when society should be placed at risk.

It is one of the anomalies of Canada's system of justice that non-violent offenders are frequently and needlessly placed behind bars while hardened criminals, with records of violence, too often gain early release from custody. It would seem that the system's obligation to protect the public is being poorly balanced against the system's efforts to rehabilitate the offender.

Evidence of this is found in the way Canada handles cases against the criminally insane. Under the *Criminal Code*, "no person shall be convicted of an offence in respect of an act or omission on his part while he is insane." Persons found not guilty of a crime "by reason of insanity" are usually confined in an institution for the criminally insane, and released only when a panel of experts, empowered by the cabinet, feels it is safe.

Some American states have passed laws establishing minimum periods of confinement, regardless of improvement in the mental condition. Either the person is first found "guilty" of the crime and then tried on the insanity question, or is found "guilty, but insane." In each case, guilt is first acknowledged, followed by a conclusion which will lead to mental treatment. Many states, however, follow the Canadian practice.

In the opinion of American journalist John White, a specialist in science and parapsychology, guilt is guilt, regardless of the offender's mental condition at the time of the crime. Offenders should be required to serve a full sentence, "unless the preponderance of expert opinion feels that pardon or commutation is in order.

"At that point, compassion becomes proper—but not before. The legal system is intended to deliver justice, not compassion. Ignoring this crucial distinction has led to a shameful and dangerous situation in which admitted murderers are released into society without punishment and without even simple justice for the victim's survivors."

That situation has become common in Canada, where psychiatrists of varied opinion increasingly advise courts on matters which can expose the public to great risk. Their advice can be valuable, but it should not sway the courts from their basic obligations to protect the public against violent behaviour by hopeless psychopaths or ruthless, unrepentant criminals.

From The London Free Press, *Feb. 23, 1982*

(a) Do you agree with John White, who is quoted as saying that "guilt is guilt, regardless of the offender's mental condition"? Explain.

(b) Do you think people found not guilty because of insanity should be required to serve a minimum prison term regardless of their mental condition? Explain.

(c) Some legal writers think the defence of insanity should be abolished. Do you agree, or not? In your answer, consider whether you think the present defence is adequate or could be improved.

PROJECTS AND ACTIVITIES

1. Continue the clippings project you began with your study of criminal law. How many different defences are illustrated by the articles you have collected?

2. Check your province's law with regard to young offenders. How is it handling or planning to handle offenders under the age of twelve? Report your findings to the class.

RESOLVING CASES

R. v. Matson (1970) 1 C.C.C. (2d) 374 (B.C. C.A.)

The accused was charged with assault causing bodily harm. His car, which had been illegally parked, had been towed to a service station. Shortly after midnight, he went to the station and asked the owner, who lived in a house next to the station, if he could have the car. The owner said he would have to come back in the morning. The accused then asked if he could take some things from the car. The owner said "No." At that point, Matson ran to his car and tried to get his belongings. The owner ran up and put his arm around Matson's throat and asked him if he was going to leave. Matson said "Yes," and then attempted to pick up his property which he had dropped in the scuffle. The owner of the station grabbed his throat again and Matson bit him several times in the face, pushing him to the ground. The owner suffered a severe fractured skull.

—Should the accused be convicted?
—Was the owner justified in using force?
—What argument can be made on behalf of Matson?

R. v. Darquea and Martyn (1979) 47 C.C.C. (2d) 567

The accused were employees in a laboratory which was manufacturing methamphetamine, a controlled drug under the *Food and Drugs Act*. The laboratory was an illegal operation, and both men were charged with trafficking in drugs. Their defence was that they believed that the laboratory was licensed to produce the drug.

—What is the name of the defence they raised?
—Should they succeed? Explain.

R. v. Marky [1976] 6 W.W.R. 390 (Alta. C.A.)

The accused, a manager of a bar, was charged with assault causing bodily harm. He was attempting to eject an unruly male customer when the woman who was with the customer kicked him in the groin. Marky then grabbed a glass pitcher and struck the woman on the head, causing a cut needing 176 stitches.

—Why was the accused charged with assault?
—What defence can he use?
—Do you think he was convicted?

R. v. Bleta [1965] 1 C.C.C. 1 (S.C.C.)

The accused was charged with murder. He had been fighting with the deceased victim when he fell down, hitting his head on the pavement. The other man started to walk away. Bleta then got on his feet and fatally stabbed the victim. Witnesses said that the accused appeared dazed when he regained his feet. A psychiatrist testified that as a result of the fall, the accused had suffered a temporary brain injury which caused amnesia. After the blow to this head, Bleta was in the condition of a sleepwalker or an epileptic.

—What defence do you think Bleta used?
—Do you think he was successful?

R. v. King (1982) 38 O.R. 346 (C.A.)

The accused was charged with robbery. He had been drinking with the co-accused, P., from 12.30 p.m. until 5 p.m. When he told his friend he was getting tired, P. gave him what he called a "wake-up pill". After King told P. that he felt strange, P. told him that the pill was a "hit of acid". Then, following the instructions of P., the accused and P. robbed a store. King testified that "felt he was in a dream, standing there watching it happen." A drug expert testified that some of the effects of L.S.D. are that it distorts perception, expands consciousness, makes the taker feel removed from his body, and diminishes inhibitions and involves a loss of self-control and judgement.

—What defence or defences do you think the accused should raise?
—One issue was whether the drug was taken voluntarily or involuntarily. What effect should this have on the defence?
—Do you think the accused was convicted?

UNIT 2

The Law and Private Relationships

9 Human Rights
10 Private Wrongs: Torts
11 Civil Procedure and the Civil Courts
12 An Introduction to Contracts
13 Contracts: Capacity, Consent, and Legal Purpose
14 Completing the Contract

Human Rights

> Prejudice and Discrimination
> Human Rights Legislation
> The Complaint Process
> Affirmative Action—Cure and Prevention
> Human Rights Legislation and the *Charter of Rights and Freedoms*

The terms "human rights" and "civil rights" are sometimes confused. In Canada, as you learned in Chapter 3, "civil rights" are concerned with the individual's freedom from interference by the state. "Human rights", on the other hand, are concerned with the individual's right to freedom from discrimination by other individuals. In other words, civil rights laws are passed so that government cannot limit people's freedom without a good reason. Human rights laws are passed so that people cannot limit other people's opportunities without a good reason.

Does Canada really need human rights legislation?

Figure 9-1 Which type of right is being violated?

You take a friend, who is blind, out for lunch to celebrate her birthday. Your friend is not allowed into the restaurant because she has a seeing-eye dog with her.

The school cafeteria is a-buzz one lunch hour with a lot of new ethnic jokes. You see that one boy is noticeably upset by them. He is a member of the ethnic group referred to in the jokes.

While the examples above may not be dramatic violations of human rights, the shocking thing about such incidents is that they are a common feature of daily life. This is the reason why we need human rights legislation. Such legislation cannot stop all discrimination from occurring, but it can accomplish three things:

1. It can discourage people from discriminating again.
2. It can provide some compensation to people who have been discriminated against.
3. It lets people know that the majority of the population in our democratic society does not approve of discrimination.

Prejudice And Discrimination

When discussing human rights law, it is important to distinguish between **prejudice** and **discrimination**. These two terms are related, but only one is forbidden by law.

Tribunal to see if height rule for pilots unfair to women

By DOROTHY LIPOVENKO

The refusal of Air Canada to hire two women as pilots, because it says they are too short, will be heard before a Canadian Human Rights Commission tribunal.

Unable to reach a settlement with Air Canada after investigating the complaint of France Gravel and Lucie Chapdelaine, the federal commission announced yesterday it was appointing a tribunal to decide whether Air Canada's minimum height requirement for pilots discriminates against women.

Miss Gravel, 28, and Miss Chapdelaine, 26, were refused employment by Air Canada in December, 1978, and October, 1979, respectively, because they didn't meet the airline's minimum height standard for pilots of 5 feet, 6 inches.

However, a male pilot who is 5 feet 5¼ inches tall has been employed by Air Canada since 1966, the federal commission learned during its investigation of the case.

Miss Gravel, who is 5 feet, 5 inches tall, and Miss Chapdelaine, who stands 5 feet, 4 inches, were hired by Nordair earlier this year.

Brock Stewart, a spokesman for Air Canada, said the airline informed the commission last September that it "was quite prepared to consider an applicant of 5 feet, 2 inches, provided the safety of the aircraft would not be compromised" (based on an applicant's skill).

In their complaint, they said Air Canada discriminates against women because the required minimum height is not necessary for the safe operation of an aircraft. They argued that the requirement prevents more women than men from becoming pilots.

In its investigation, the commission found that several airlines, including CP Air, United Airlines, Nordair and Quebecair, have a hiring policy that considers a pilot's ability to reach control instruments more important than height.

Figure 9-2 Which of the two types of discrimination is this article discussing?

What is prejudice? A prejudice is an attitude we hold, sometimes even without knowing we hold it. It can be based on something we have been told by our family or other people we know. It can be a judgement we have made too quickly or without enough evidence to support it. It can be a belief based on ignorance or fear of the unknown. Whatever the source, prejudice against a particular group of people involves negative feelings about that group—perhaps dislike, or a belief that the group is in some way inferior. For example, a landlord who refuses to rent to young people because he or she feels that all young people are rowdy and irresponsible is prejudiced against young people.

There are two types of discrimination. The first type is related to prejudice: it is the process of acting on a prejudice. Practising this type of discrimination means that you let your prejudice about a group influence your actions toward an individual who is a member of that group. If an employer were to refuse to hire a member of a certain ethnic group or race because of that person's ethnicity or racial origin, the employer would be discriminating. Some legal writers call this type of discrimination *differential treatment*.

The second type of discrimination is called *disproportionate impact*. Disproportionate impact is more complicated than differential treatment, because people who inflict the former may not even realize what they are doing. Disproportionate impact discrimination involves placing an unnecessary barrier between a group of people and an opportunity. For example, suppose a restaurant owner makes it a personal rule to hire only employees who are blue-eyed and at least 180 cm tall. She hires six people. Not surprisingly, none of them is female, Oriental, Black, or Native Canadian.

Now, this restaurant owner may not have imposed the rule in order to avoid hiring women, Orientals, or members of other minority groups. She may just think that tall, blue-eyed people would look better in her establishment. But whether she wanted this result or not, she has placed a barrier (the rule) between women and minority group members, and a job opportunity. The rule has a disproportionate impact, because while *some* white male candidates will not get hired, virtually *no* women, Blacks, Orientals, or Native Canadians will be hired. The other important point is that the rule was not really necessary. The ability to do the job well is what counts.

To summarize, there are two ways in which you can discriminate:

1. by behaving more negatively towards a person than you would towards anyone else because that person is a member of a particular group (differential treatment); and
2. by imposing requirements or conditions which appear neutral but have the effect of excluding certain groups from an opportunity, or of making things more difficult for them (disproportionate impact).

No law can eliminate prejudice, because no law can stop people from believing whatever they like. Canadian human rights law forbids only discrimination, and discrimination in certain activities only, such as employment, accommodation, and public services. Furthermore, discrimination in these activities is forbidden for certain reasons only, such as race, creed, and sex. The activities and the reasons (or **grounds**) will be more fully discussed later in this chapter, as will exceptions to the law.

Does Canadian law forbid both types of discrimination? Recent court decisions have indicated that most Canadian human rights legislation forbids only differential treatment.

O'Malley v. Simpsons-Sears (1982) 38 O.R. (2d) 423 (C.A.)

O'Malley worked for Simpsons-Sears. In her job category she was required to work Friday nights and Saturdays. This arrangement was no longer satisfactory to O'Malley after she converted to the Seventh Day Adventist church, which considers Saturday to be the Sabbath. Simpsons-Sears was unwilling to allow her to simply take Saturdays off. Instead, they offered her a new working arrangement. The new arrangement did not require her to work on Saturdays, but also cut her hours almost in half. O'Malley was not willing to accept this cut in her salary. She therefore made a complaint of religious discrimination to the Ontario Human Rights Commission.

The Board of Inquiry which heard her case found that a rule that forced all employees in O'Malley's job category to work Saturdays created a disproportionate impact against Seventh Day Adventists and other religious groups with a Saturday Sabbath. However, the Board also stated that Simpsons-Sears could not be expected to close on Saturdays if many of its employees kept a Saturday Sabbath and that the Company had made an acceptable compromise offer. Simpsons-Sears had not breached the Human Rights Code.

The Court of Appeal upheld this decision and stated further that the Ontario Human Rights Code did not forbid disproportionate impact in any case.

The Ontario Human Rights Commission appealed this decision to the Supreme Court of Canada. The Supreme Court's decision could have an effect on the interpretation of human rights laws in other provinces as well, but it is safest to assume at this time that most Canadian human rights laws cover only differential impact. The only exception is Ontario's new *Human Rights Code*, which became law in June, 1982, and which specifically forbids the creation of disproportionate impact. Thus, if O'Malley's case were heard today in Ontario, she would win.

Human Rights Legislation

Jurisdiction

Whether a law can be passed by the federal government or a provincial legislature depends on the activities affected by that law, as you saw in Chapter 2. Human rights law in Canada affects four main activities:

1. employment
2. accommodation
3. the provision of services
4. discriminatory signs and notices on public display

Figure 9-3 The Four Areas Affected by Human Rights Legislation

While some human rights legislation deals with other activities, all of the statutes deal with at least these four. The four are all areas in which the provinces have the right to make laws, but the federal government can also legislate in these areas where federal employment, services, accommodation, or freedom of expression are affected. For this reason, all of the provinces and the federal government have their own human rights legislation, and the Northwest Territories and the Yukon have passed human rights **ordinances** (rules having the effect of legislation).

— If you worked for the Canadian National Railway and felt you had been the victim of discrimination, would your complaint be made under provincial or federal law? What if you worked in a grocery store?

HUMAN RIGHTS 195

Content of the Legislation

To get a clear view of human rights law, it is necessary to examine the activities affected, the prohibited grounds for discrimination, and the exceptions provided by the law.

Figure 9-4 Activities Affected by Human Rights Legislation

> The following activities are affected by most human rights legislation.
> Accommodation
> Employment
> Equal Pay
> Provision of goods
> Provision of Services and Facilities
> Membership in Unions, Professional Organizations
> Contracts
> Purchase/Sale of Real Estate
> Harassment
> Signs, Notices
> Employment Agencies; Advertising Applications
> Pension Plans and Funds

Activities Affected

Some Canadian legislation forbids discrimination in activities additional to the four main activities listed above. For example, British Columbia, Saskatchewan, Manitoba, New Brunswick, Nova Scotia, and Prince Edward Island specifically forbid discrimination in the sale of real estate.

The chart in Figure 9-4 shows most of the activities affected by human rights laws in Canada. As you look at the chart, keep in mind three important points about the activities shown.

First, an activity that is not specifically mentioned may be included in a general category. For example, Ontario does not specifically forbid discrimination in real estate sales, but it does forbid discrimination in contracts. Since every real estate sale involves a contract, these transactions are covered in the general category of contracts.

Second, although most of the law that affects human rights is included in human rights legislation, not all of it is. For instance, the law concerning equal pay for substantially similar work in Manitoba, Ontario, Nova Scotia, Saskatchewan, and the Yukon is not found in the human rights statutes of these provinces, but rather in their *Employment Standards* or *Labour Standards Acts*. In Newfoundland, the law about access to buildings for handicapped people is found in the *Building Accessibility Act*, rather than in the *Human Rights Act*.

Third, there are exceptions in every area, as you will see.

—**Human rights legislation is subject to change. Obtain a copy of your province's human rights legislation. What are the activities presently listed?**

Figure 9-5 Prohibited Grounds of Discrimination

> The following grounds of discrimination are prohibited by most human rights legislation.
>
> Race, Ancestry, Place of Origin, Colour, Ethnicity
> Citizenship
> Nationality
> Creed, Religion
> Sex
> Age—limited in some legislation to employment situations only
> Marital Status/Family Status
> Handicap—Physical and/or Mental
> —Limited in some legislation to employment situations only
> Record of Offences—Usually limited to employment situations
> Source of Income

Prohibited Grounds

All Canadian human rights legislation has identified certain grounds that are not considered acceptable reasons for discriminating. Like the activities discussed previously, some grounds appear in *all* Canadian human rights legislation, while others appear only in some human rights laws. In all Canadian jurisdictions, discrimination is forbidden on the grounds of race, colour, sex, religion or creed, marital status, and handicap (physical, mental, or both). However, only Ontario forbids discrimination because of citizenship, and only Saskatchewan, Manitoba, Ontario, and Québec forbid discrimination because of a person's being on welfare.

There are two main things to remember when you examine Figure 9-5. First, not all grounds of discrimination apply to every area of discrimination. For example, in the Ontario *Code* and in the federal *Human Rights Act*, discrimination on the grounds of record of offences is forbidden in employment situations only. Second, there are again exceptions that affect all grounds of discrimination.

It is also important to keep in mind that both the activity in which the discrimination has occurred and the grounds for the discrimination must be affected by the legislation. Consider the following case:

Blatt v. Catholic Children's Aid Society (1980) C.H.R.R. D/72 (Ontario Board of Inquiry)

Blatt complained to the Ontario Human Rights Commission, stating that he had been dismissed from his job because of his marital status. He had been fired after his employer, the Catholic Children's Aid Society, discovered that he was cohabiting with his fiancée.

The Board of Inquiry found that his dismissal was not based on his marital status but on a moral judgement about his living arrangement. Dismissal because of a moral judgement was not forbidden by the Code.

—What is your opinion of this decision?

Exceptions

The third important feature of Canadian human rights law is the fact that exceptions are included in the legislation. All Canadian human rights statutes have clauses stating that an action which might otherwise be called discriminatory will not be considered discriminatory under certain circumstances. For instance, the Ontario *Human Rights Code* states:

> 20. (2) The right under section 2 to equal treatment with respect to the occupancy of residential accommodation without discrimination because of sex is not infringed by discrimination on that ground where the occupancy of all the residential accommodation in the building, other than the accommodation, if any, of the owner or family of the owner, is restricted to persons who are of the same sex.

—What is the exception?
—Rewrite this section of the *Code* in your own words.
—Why do you think this exception was made?

While some exceptions are very specific, as in the example above, others are general. Most provinces and the federal government allow discrimination in some activities and on some grounds if the person who wants to limit the opportunity can prove that such a limitation is *bona fide* (in good faith, sincere) and reasonable. For example, in Ontario, an employer can discriminate on the grounds of age, sex, record of offences, and marital status, if any of these grounds is a reasonable and *bona fide* qualification because of the nature of the employment.

Niedzwiecki v. Beneficial Finance System (1981) **Ontario Human Rights Board of Inquiry (unreported)**

Mrs. Niedzwiecki applied for a managerial job with Beneficial Finance. The job involved travelling, and the person who interviewed Niedzwiecki turned down her application, telling her that married women were not willing to travel.

— Do you think this is a reasonable assumption? Why or why not?

The Board of Inquiry did not. It told Beneficial Finance that while it is reasonable to ask some employees to travel as part of their job, it is not reasonable to assume, without asking, that a married woman would not be willing to travel.

— Can you think of a job in which a requirement that a person be married (or single) is reasonable? To assist in your thinking, you might list the requirements of the job and ask yourself whether marital status is important in performing each requirement.
— If you think it is important, why do you think so?
— What exceptions are created by your province's human rights law?

Harassment and Reprisals

In addition to prohibiting certain types of discrimination in certain activities, human rights legislation prohibits two actions which a person can take against someone else: harassment and reprisals.

Harassment

Most of us have been harassed when we were small, by other children "picking" on us for one reason or another. **Harassment** becomes a serious issue in human rights law when a person repeatedly inflicts unwelcome, annoying, upsetting, or frightening behaviour on someone else because of such things as the victim's race, colour, sex, or handicap.

Ontario specifically forbids harassment in employment, accommodation, and certain other situations. In other jurisdictions, harassment is not specifically forbidden, but it is considered discrimination when it interferes with a person's right to do his or her job, to enjoy accommodation, or to take advantage of a public service or facility in peace.

Harassment can take the form of racial slurs, insults, unwanted physical contact, unwanted sexual advances, and other aggressive behaviour. Sometimes it is disguised as "just a joke", but if you have experienced it, you know that it hurts. It is a form of bullying and a misuse of power, whether it comes from your employer, landlord, or teacher, or a member of a majority group among your co-workers, co-tenants, or fellow students.

A student has a very bad speech impediment. She stutters when she is excited or nervous and she cannot pronounce the letter "r". The first time she answered a question in class, the class howled with laughter. At lunch break, someone behind her in line in the cafeteria imitated her stutter and everyone broke up again.

This behaviour has continued for several days. At first, she tried to laugh it off, but recently she has stopped answering questions in class.

—What effect has the behaviour of her classmates had on this student?
—Could this behaviour be considered harassment?
—On what grounds is it based?
—Would the student be able to complain successfully under any human rights law?
—Would your answer be different if these incidents had occurred at work?

Reprisals

An obvious problem in the enforcement of human rights legislation is that people are likely to be afraid to complain when they have to continue to deal with the person they have a complaint against. For example, a tenant may be afraid of being evicted by the landlord. An employee may be afraid of being fired.

This problem is acknowledged in all Canadian human rights legislation. In all jurisdictions, it is therefore illegal for anyone to take action against someone else because that person makes a complaint under the human rights law, or acts as a witness in a human rights complaint. In most jurisdictions, even threats of **reprisal** are forbidden and are reason for a complaint under the law.

The Complaint Process

Human Rights Commissions

Having a law "on the books" is one thing; enforcing it is another. To enforce the law, every province and the federal government have appointed a Human Rights Commission. The Northwest Territories and the Yukon are the sole exceptions. These Commissions vary in size from three to eleven members. Generally, the Commissioners are appointed by the Cabinet, and serve for a certain number of years.

The Commissioners' task is to administer the legislation. They direct a staff of employees in educating the public, promoting human rights, and investigating and attempting to settle complaints. If a complaint cannot be settled, most provincial human rights legislation provides that the Commission may report to the Minister responsible for the legislation, and recommend that a public hearing called a **Board of Inquiry** be held. Québec is the only exception to this rule; there, the complaint is heard in court.

What Happens When a Complaint is Made?

Paul applied for an after-school job as a waiter. The restaurant owner, Mr. Miller, told him, "I'm hiring only waitresses—sorry."

Paul decided that he had been discriminated against. He phoned his local office of the Human Rights Commission and made an appointment to come in to discuss his case. After Paul spoke with an officer at the Commission, Ms. Belyea, she filled out a complaint form, which Paul signed. (He is now called the *complainant*.) The officer then told him that she would look into the case and call him when she had done so.

Investigation

In some jurisdictions, there are time limits within which a complaint must be made. If there is no time limit, or if the complaint is made within the limit, the next step is investigation by the staff of the Commission. The staff member, who is often called an officer, will notify the *respondent* (the person against whom the complaint is made) and will interview that person to hear the other side of the story.

In Paul's case, four weeks after he made his complaint, Ms. Belyea telephoned. She told him that she had interviewed Mr. Miller. At first, Mr. Miller had said that he had a right to decide whom he was going to hire and whom he wasn't. However, she told him that while he had a right to insist on good workers, he could not insist that they be of any particular sex. Ms. Belyea advised Mr. Miller to get in touch with his lawyer and get the lawyer's opinion.

In most jurisdictions the law provides that the Commission officer can ask to see employment or tenancy records or hotel registers, for example, and can question employees, co-tenants, or customers.

Generally, the officer can investigate the complaint in much the same way as the police investigate a crime. For example, Ontario's *Human Rights Code* provides the following:

> 31. (3) A person authorized to investigate a complaint may
>   (a) enter any place, other than a place that is being used as a dwelling, at any reasonable time, for the purpose of investigating the complaint;
>   (b) request the production for inspection and examination of documents or things that are or may be relevant to the investigation;
>   (c) upon giving a receipt therefor, remove from a place documents produced in a response to a request under clause (b) for the purpose of making copies thereof or extracts therefrom and shall promptly return them to the person who produced or furnished them; and
>   (d) question a person on matters that are or may be relevant to the complaint subject to the person's right to have counsel or a personal representative present during such questioning and may exclude from the questioning any person who may be adverse in interest to the complainant.

—Compare these powers of the Commission officer investigating a human rights complaint to those of the police investigating a crime. Do you think it is a good idea to give these powers to Commission investigators? Discuss your reasons.

Conciliation and Settlement

All Canadian human rights law says that the Commission staff must try to settle complaints, rather than bring every one to a Board of Inquiry. Therefore, once the officer has investigated, there is usually a meeting between the complainant and the respondent. The officer tries to work out a settlement at this time. If a solution acceptable to everybody can be found, the complaint goes no further. For example, an employer might agree to let the complainant apply for the next available job. Usually a settlement is put in writing.

If one of the parties to the settlement later refuses to do what was agreed to, the other party can complain to the Commission. The complaint will then probably go to a Board of Inquiry or be enforced through the courts.

When Paul next heard from Ms. Belyea, she told him that after consulting with his lawyer, Mr. Miller had changed his mind. She asked whether Paul would like to come in to try to work out a settlement. Paul agreed to come.

—Why do you think the Commission places such an emphasis on trying to settle a case?

Ms. Belyea, Paul, and Mr. Miller met the same afternoon. Mr. Miller wasn't very happy, but he agreed to interview Paul for the job. The officer typed this agreement and everyone signed it. The next day, Paul got his interview and, since he was well-qualified, was offered the job.

—If a settlement had not been reached, what would have happened next?

The Board of Inquiry

A Board of Inquiry is a public hearing much like a court hearing, but more informal. The "judge" is, in most jurisdictions, a chairperson appointed by the government. At the hearing, the complainant and the respondent may be represented by lawyers, if they wish. The Human Rights Commission also has a lawyer.

As in a court hearing, each side gives evidence and cross-examines the other side. At the end of the hearing, a decision is made by the Board.

If the Board agrees that the law was broken in the case, it may make any of several different orders. Often the person who broke the law is ordered to make financial compensation to the person whose rights were denied. The Board may also make an order that especially fits the situation. For example, if a landlord refuses accommodation to a person on grounds forbidden by law, the Board may order the landlord to offer that person the next available apartment. An employer who has discriminated may be ordered to rehire an employee who was fired, or to offer the person who complained a fair chance at the next available job.

All legislation allows the decision of a Board of Inquiry to be appealed to the courts.

Affirmative Action—Cure and Prevention

When any group of people has been systematically discriminated against for centuries, it does not comes as a surprise that virtually no members of such a group tend to gain positions of power in society. Deliberate efforts to change this situation are referred to as **affirmative action**.

People who do not understand affirmative action often refer to it as "reverse discrimination", but this is a mistake. Hiring people simply because they belong to a minority group, regardless of qualifications, is not affirmative action.

What *is* affirmative action? Another way of defining it is to say that affirmative action is taking steps to change the effect of past discrimination. Affirmative action programs recognize that certain people have been denied work, education, and other opportunities because of discrimination, and try to help these people "catch up" to where they would have been if there had never been such discrimination.

The steps taken can include efforts to advertise jobs in such a way that minority groups will not be discouraged from applying; special training programs to help minority group members qualify for jobs; and preferential hiring practices in situations where two applicants, one of them a member of a minority group, have the same qualifications.

Affirmative action is not common in Canada, and with very few exceptions those programs which do exist are voluntary. The following are available in connection with affirmative action:

1. Exceptions in human rights legislation allowing people who want to initiate affirmative action programs to do so without being considered discriminatory.
2. A few provincial and federal government-initiated programs that give job training and sometimes special job opportunities to some groups that have been discriminated against in the past.

—Gusher Oil Company has just received a federal grant to help it drill for oil in northern Alberta. As a condition of the grant, the federal government has told Gusher that it must give special job training to Native people in the area.
Why do you think the government imposed this requirement?

Human Rights Legislation and the *Charter of Rights and Freedoms*

The *Canadian Charter of Rights and Freedoms*, part of the *Constitution Act, 1982*, contains a clause that takes effect on April 17, 1985. This clause is section 15, and reads as follows:

> 15. (1) Every individual is equal before and under the law and has the right to the equal protection and equal benefit of the law without discrimination and, in particular, without discrimination based on race, national or ethnic origin, colour, religion, sex, age or mental or physical disability.
> (2) Subsection (1) does not preclude any law, program or activity that has as its object the amelioration of conditions of disadvantaged individuals or groups including those that are disadvantaged because of race, national or ethnic origin, colour, religion, sex, age or mental or physical disability.

—In what ways do you think a person might be "disadvantaged because of race, national or ethnic origin, colour, religion, sex, age, or mental or physical disability"?

Will s. 15 be another way to enforce your rights when you are denied a job because of discrimination?—Probably not directly. The reason is that it is unlikely that people will be able to use the *Charter* in private, person-to-person disputes (although this issue has not yet been tested in the courts). Rather, the *Charter* provides a way to challenge the provincial or federal governments if any of them passes a discriminatory law.

Will human rights legislation be affected by the *Charter*? The answer is that it will, but only if someone wishes to argue that his or her equality rights are not being upheld by the legislation itself. For example, suppose that you are a person with a handicap. In many jurisdictions, there is an exception in human rights legislation that says that a physically handicapped person who is unable to obtain access to a building has not been discriminated against. It is this exception that you might wish to challenge in court under s. 15 of the *Charter*. You would argue that the provincial government, by including this exception to its human rights law, is denying you the equal protection or benefit of the law.

A person who has been affected by government action may also challenge that action under s. 15. For instance, a member of a majority group who has been denied a job or admission to an educational program because of a government affirmative action program may challenge the program through s. 15 of the *Charter*. However, you should note that s. 15(2), which specifically allows affirmative action programs, will probably make this challenge unsuccessful, unless the majority group member can show that the program was set up to benefit people who were not disadvantaged.

SUMMARIZING YOUR READING

1. What is the difference between civil rights and human rights? Give an example of each kind of right.

2. What three things can human rights legislation accomplish?

3. What is the difference between prejudice and discrimination? Which of them is forbidden by law?

4. Name the two types of discrimination. What is the difference between them? Given an example of your own for each.

5. Does Canadian human rights law forbid both types of discrimination? Explain.

6. Under what circumstances would a human rights complaint fall under federal jurisdiction?

7. What are the activities usually affected by human rights law? Provide an example of each.

8. What is the meaning of the term "grounds of discrimination"? Name some typical grounds.

9. What effect does an exception in human rights legislation have?

10. What is harassment?

11. If an employer fires an employee for giving evidence at a human rights Board of Inquiry hearing, is the employer breaking the law? What is this kind of action called?

12. Who is responsible for enforcing human rights laws?

13. What is a Board of Inquiry? When is one held?

14. What are the three phases of action taken when a complaint is received by the Human Rights Commission?

15. What can you do if a Board of Inquiry decides against you?

16. Does affirmative action mean that members of minority groups should be hired, whether or not they are qualified for the job in question? Explain.

17. Does the *Charter of Rights and Freedoms* deal with human rights? If so, in what way?

DISCUSSING KEY ISSUES

1. Do you think that laws against discrimination can change people's prejudices? Give reasons for your answer.

2. Why do you think there are exceptions in human rights legislation?

3. At one time or another, almost everyone has the experience of being laughed at by others; usually it is not a pleasant feeling. People often make racist or sexist jokes without really thinking about it. Do you think such jokes can be harmful? Explain.

4. Debate this statement:
"I have never discriminated against women. Why should I be denied a job because of an affirmative action program?"

5. "I'm not prejudiced—I'd hire a Native person, only my customers wouldn't feel comfortable."

Should employers be able to excuse their actions because the company's customers would be uncomfortable? Discuss.

PROJECTS AND ACTIVITIES

1. During your study of this unit on human rights, collect as many newspaper and magazine articles on the topic as you can find. As well, contact your provincial Human Rights Commission for pamphlets. Share them with the class, and create a bulletin board display.

2. Look up the United Nations *Convention on the Elimination of all Forms of Racism*. Compare it to the human rights legislation in your province.

3. You are the managing director of a small assessment clinic in which children are tested for learning disabilities. You need a secretary-receptionist who will type, file, answer the phone, and deal with some very worried and nervous parents and children. You are anxious not to discriminate in hiring. Write a job advertisement to put in the newspaper.

RESOLVING CASES

Surinder Anand is looking for his first apartment in the city in which he will be going to university. He sees an ad in the paper that says:

> 3 one-bedroom apartments.
> Responsible tenants; reasonable.
> Call Mr. Calvin at 112-1111.

Surinder clips out the ad and calls the number. Calvin says that all three apartments are still available, and Surinder says that he will be over that afternoon.

Surinder rings the bell marked "Superintendant—J.C. Calvin". The door opens and Mr. Calvin says, "Yes?" Surinder explains that he is looking for an apartment. Mr. Calvin looks at Surinder's turban with a strange expression on his face. Abruptly, he informs Surinder that the apartments are all taken and closes the door.

Surinder is a bit suspicious about that look on Mr. Calvin's face. He asks his friend, Brian, who is of Irish ancestry, to go to the apartment building and ask about an apartment. Brian goes, and Mr. Calvin shows him all three vacant apartments.

—Does it seem likely that Mr. Calvin has discriminated against Surinder?
—If so, what type of discrimination is this?
—What should Surinder do?
—Would the law that applies to this situation be federal or provincial?
—If this had happened in your province, what section of what Act would apply to Surinder's situation?

> Office space to rent; would suit businessman, professional—must be Canadian.

—What kind of tenant do you think this landlord is looking for?
—Do you think this ad would be considered discriminatory under your provincial legislation?

Thirteen-year-old Robbie Baker has cerebral palsy; his ability to walk and his speech are affected. One Saturday, his parents take him to a baseball game and then to a restaurant for lunch. The Bakers chat while reading the menu, then wait for someone to serve them. After about twenty minutes, a waitress comes over looking uncomfortable, and tells the Bakers, "Look, I'm sorry, but the manager says we can't serve you unless you can make your son be quiet. His voice is too loud; he'll disturb the other customers."

—What protection does your provincial statute provide for the handicapped? What kinds of handicap are protected?
—Whom would the Bakers complain about—the waitress, the manager, or both? To whom would they complain?
—What would the manager's defence be?
—Do you think the complaint would succeed?

Lila Petrakis negotiated a loan with a trust company in order to open a small business. When she arranged an appointment to sign the papers, she was told that she should bring her husband to co-sign the loan. "I thought my collateral was acceptable," she said. "Oh, it is," said the manager of the trust company, "but we like married women to have their husbands sign, as an added protection."

—What grounds of discrimination might apply here?
—What exceptions (if any) for this type of discrimination are provided in the law of your province?

Anna Marchese is a pioneer in the work force. At the age of thirty-five, she got a job as a coal miner, which meant that she could take home a much bigger paycheque to support her children. However, she had not been on the job long when one of her co-workers began to find excuses to get close to her. Then the touching and grabbing began. First, Anna tried to laugh it off. It did not work, so she told him to leave her alone. When he persisted, she reported him to her foreman.

The foreman said, "Look, lady, a mine shaft isn't a tea party, you know. You leave the guys alone and they'll leave you alone." After that the situation got worse. A number of her co-workers refused to speak to Anna, but made dirty jokes about her in her presence as if she weren't there. The man who initially bothered her kept making passes, which got increasingly rough. The last time she told him to leave her alone, he pushed her face down into a pile of mud and slag. This time Anna went to the boss. The boss had heard from the foreman about what was happening. He offered Anna a secretarial job in the office, which paid half of what she earned in the mines. He said, "Take the secretarial job or quit. I can't have all this trouble going on."

—What kinds of activities does this case illustrate?
—In your province, can Anna bring a complaint against her co-workers? against her employer?
—Does your provincial law provide an exception that might apply to the boss's position? Do you think that the boss could prove that the exception applies?

John is a waiter at Mrs. McNeil's restaurant. The provincial Human Rights Commission is investigating Mrs. McNeil's business practices, because of a complaint that she has denied service to people of certain ethnic origins. John was a witness to one denial of service, and he gave evidence to a Commission officer.

That afternoon, Mrs. McNeil fired John, saying that she needed to reduce the number of staff in the restaurant.

—Might Mrs. McNeil be breaking the law? Explain.

Harold Bator has been a firefighter for thirty-five years. He will be sixty in six months, but he is in excellent health, is very fit, and loves his work. Unfortunately, the collective agreement between his union and the city for which he works states that all firefighters must retire at age sixty.

Harold goes to his supervisor and explains that he doesn't want to retire until he is sixty-five. His supervisor says, "Look, I'd like to keep you on, but your union really fought for early retirement and you agreed to it when you started work here. Besides, Harold, you know we all slow down as we get older. What if you had a heart attack carrying someone out of a burning building?"

—Are there any exceptions to protection from discrimination on the basis of age in your province?
—Is retirement at age sixty for all firefighters a *bona fide* job requirement, in your opinion?

10

Private Wrongs: Torts

> Intentional Torts
> Negligence
> Strict Liability
> Additional Types of Torts
> Occupier's Liability

A young woman is walking through a park in the evening and is mugged. She manages to escape and the police eventually capture her attacker. However, as a result of the incident, the woman requires plastic surgery, misses a great deal of time from work, and becomes nervous about being alone.

—Has a crime been committed?
—What injuries or damage has she suffered that will not be compensated by convicting and imprisoning her attacker?

A young father arrives at his child's school, for a parent-teacher interview. When leaving the school, he slips on ice which had not been removed from the school stairs. He falls and breaks his leg.

—Has a crime been committed?
—Should the school have taken greater care to ensure that the premises were safe? Why?
—Should the school be responsible for the man's injuries?
—Should the man be compensated for his injuries?

You learned in Chapter 4 that criminal law concerns itself with offences against society as a whole. Our lawmakers have a duty to control certain kinds of behaviour in order to protect the community. They have therefore established criminal laws which impose a penalty on those who commit these offences. In the example of the attack above, the young woman is the victim of a crime. The police will act on behalf of society by arresting the alleged attacker, and the courts will determine innocence or guilt, imposing a penalty if there is a conviction. This process serves to protect society from future violence by this person and at the same time to impose a punishment for the crime. It usually does not provide compensation for the victim's expenses or suffering.

In response to this individual loss or suffering, it has been recognized that crimes are not the only kinds of offences which can be committed. As a result, the civil law has developed (primarily through case law) to allow individuals who have suffered injury, loss, or damage at the hands of others to seek compensation. In the attack scenario, the young woman's attacker, in addition to committing a crime, has committed a civil offence or wrong called a **tort**.

In the example with the young father, no crime has been committed. The wrong which the school board committed is not considered great enough to be a crime—an offence against society. However, the school board *is* responsible for ensuring that all school premises are safe. The failure to remove ice from the stairs of the school resulted in the man's broken leg. This carelessness on the part of the school board amounts to a tort. Both of these victims of torts are entitled to sue the person(s) responsible for their injuries; the court will decide whether a tort has occurred and what remedy is appropriate as compensation. Unlike in criminal law, where the wrongdoer repays society by being punished, in tort law, the **tortfeasor** (wrongdoer) must compensate the victim.

In a civil action, the person who has allegedly caused harm is known as the **defendant**, and the person who suffered the harm and is suing is called the **plaintiff**. The role of the court is to establish legal **liability** (responsibility) and to determine the appropriate remedy. The remedy could be financial compensation, called **damages**, or a court order, called an **injunction**, which orders the offender to cease a particular kind of harmful activity. The process involved in bringing a civil action, commonly called *suing*, will be discussed in detail in Chapter 11. This chapter will describe some of the most common torts for which an individual might resort to the courts. In general, three areas of tort law exist: intentional torts, negligence, and strict liability.

Intentional Torts

A certain amount of interference naturally occurs in day-to-day contact among people. For example, on a crowded bus, it is very likely that you will be bumped into, or have your toes stepped on. In situations such as these, you haven't really suffered any injury, and there is no intention on the part of your fellow passengers to cause you any harm. Therefore, no tort has been committed.

Figure 10-1 Has any tort been committed in this situation?

Intentional torts occur when the wrongdoer either intends to bring about a harmful result, or when he or she should realize that harm is virtually certain to result from a given action. Children, too, can be held responsible for their torts if they are old enough either to intend their actions or to understand that harm might result from their actions. Intentional torts may be classed under two main headings: interference with the person, and interference with property.

Interference with the Person

Assault and Battery

In tort law, an **assault** is a threat of bodily harm. The tort of assault occurs when someone threatens you in such a way that you reasonably believe and fear that that person has the ability and intention to immediately carry out the threat. **Battery** occurs when actual physical contact takes place. It is not necessary for physical harm to be caused. The courts have held that a kiss can be called a battery if it is unwanted and offensive to the person kissed.

Bruno and Jake have an argument in a tavern. Friends manage to separate the two before violence breaks out. Upon returning home, Bruno receives a call from Jake, who threatens to shoot him.
—**Is this an assault?**

Shortly thereafter, Jake knocks on Bruno's door.
—**Has an assault occurred now?**

Bruno opens the door to discover Jake standing on his front porch with a gun in his hand.
—**Is this an assault?**
—**Does it make any difference if the gun is not loaded?**
—**What if Bruno believes the gun to be a toy?**
—**At what point would the tort become a battery?**

Suppose, while driving along a highway, another driver cuts you off. You are angry at this careless driving and tailgate the car for several miles with your high beams on.
—**Do you think this would be considered an assault in tort law?**

False Imprisonment

Freedom is a concept and a state of being highly valued by our society. To be unlawfully denied the freedom to go about your business is to suffer a very grave civil wrong. The tort of **false imprisonment** involves the wrongful denial of this right to freedom of movement. For this tort to occur, you must be unlawfully confined against your will within fixed boundaries, or have to submit to having your liberty restricted by fear of physical force or damage to your reputation.

Chaytor et al.v. London, New York and Paris Association of Fashion Ltd. and Price **(1961) 30 D.L.R. (2d) 527 (Nfld. S.C.)**

Two employees of Bowring Brothers Ltd., a department store in St. John's, Newfoundland, entered a competitor's store to do some comparison shopping. They were spotted by Price, the manager of the competing store, who had the store detective detain them as "spies" while he called in the police to arrest them.

The Bowring employees accompanied the police because they felt compelled to do so and to avoid the embarrassment of a public scene in the store. They were held at the police station for about fifteen to twenty minutes and were then released without any charges being laid. They sued Price and his employer for false imprisonment.

—**Did the Bowring employees have an opportunity to leave the store?**
—**Were they falsely imprisoned, in your opinion?**

Intentional Infliction of Mental Suffering

A person who intentionally or recklessly says or does anything which causes someone else severe mental suffering is liable in tort for the resulting damage. The courts have, however, developed safeguards to protect against the making of frivolous claims of this nature. There must be a reasonable connection between the defendant's behaviour and the resulting mental suffering. The defendant's action or speech must be of a nature that would likely cause severe fright in a normal person, and the emotional distress must result in actual illness, not mere anguish.

Bielitski v. Obadiak (1922) 65 D.L.R. 627 (Sask. C.A.)

The defendant told a friend over the telephone that Steve Bielitski had hanged himself. This story was repeated a number of times and eventually reached Steve's mother. She believed the report to be true and suffered an extreme shock resulting in a physical illness which "incapacitated her for some time".

— Was the defendant's conduct in this case likely to cause severe shock in the ordinary person?
— Should the defendant have realized that the story might reach Mrs. Bielitski?
— Would it make a difference if the defendant claimed that this had just been a practical joke and that he had intended no harm to the plaintiff?
— Do you think Mrs. Bielitski was successful in her claim against Obadiak?
— Should the people who repeated the story have been held liable as well? Explain.

Invasion of Privacy

It is only recently that some courts have recognized the invasion of a person's privacy as a common law tort. However, three provinces, British Columbia, Manitoba, and Saskatchewan, have now passed legislation which protects a person's right to privacy from such interference as eavesdropping, electronic surveillance, and private investigation. Other provinces are currently considering legislation in this area. British Columbia's *Privacy Act* states:

> 1. (1) It is a tort, actionable without proof of damage, for a person, wilfully and without a claim of right, to violate the privacy of another.
>
>   (2) The nature and degree of privacy to which a person is entitled in a situation or in relation to a matter is that which is reasonable in the circumstances, due regard being given to the lawful interests of others.

- Why do you think provincial legislatures have passed or are considering passing legislation of this sort?
- The B.C. statute does not require "proof of damage". What other intentional torts discussed so far do not require actual harm? Why do you think this is so?
- What do you think "wilfully" means?
- What do you think "claim of right" means?
- Do you think that a husband who suspects his wife of having an affair would have the right to hire a private investigator to follow her? Would this be an invasion of his wife's right to privacy?

Interference with Property

Trespass to Land

The right of a landowner to enjoy his or her land without fear of interference by others is one of the oldest common law rights. Any entrance onto land without the consent of the owner is **trespass**. Under common law, a person owns, in theory, the air above his or her property and the earth below it to the centre of the earth. For instance, you are entitled to cut limbs from your neighbour's tree that overhang your property and interfere with your enjoyment of your land. Similarly, it would be a tort to drill down on a slant for oil below your neighbour's property. Governments have somewhat limited these common law rights, however. For example, the federal government has enacted legislation to allow the peaceful use of air space by airlines. The provincial governments have passed legislation claiming mineral rights, although a landowner is entitled to royalties and rent for the soil below his or her property and what it contains.

Suing for the tort of trespass is now uncommon, because the provinces have enacted trespass legislation such as Ontario's *Trespass to Property Act*, 1980. This legislation provides a more suitable remedy to the owner of land who has not suffered great harm but who wishes to rid his or her property of a trespasser. Instead of having to pursue the matter through the civil courts, the property owner can inform the police, who will lay charges against the trespasser. The property owner becomes a witness in a quasi-criminal matter, rather than bearing the expense of a civil action. The Ontario statute also provides for compensation to the landowner, up to a maximum of $1000.

- What is the name of the statute in your province which protects property owners from trespassers?
- Does it provide compensation to the property owner for damage suffered?

—Interview your school principal to determine how your province's trespass legislation is put to use in schools.

Trespass to Chattels

Chattels are any property other than land. Such things as clothes, jewellery, cars, and stereos are considered chattels. If you interfere with the chattels of another person without that person's consent, you have committed a tort. Interference can take a variety of forms. You can damage a chattel, as in scratching a car or breaking off its antenna. You can take the property of another, either permanently or for a limited period, as in joyriding (**detinue**). Finally you can dispose of someone's property, either through destruction or by selling it (**conversion**). All of these are ways of committing the tort of trespass to chattels.

—Suppose you are at a dance and mistakenly take someone else's coat at the end of the evening. Is this a tort?
—When you discover your mistake, you refuse to give up the coat to its rightful owner. Is this a tort?
—While the coat is in your possession, you damage it. Is this a tort? What if you lose the coat?

A relatively new type of case has appeared before the courts, involving the wrongful conversion of a person's "property rights" in the form of his or her name, pictorial image, and identity.

Heath v. Weist-Barron School of Television Canada Ltd. (1981) 34 O.R. (2d) 126 (H.C.J.)

Ian Heath, a six-year-old professional actor, took a course at Weist-Barron School of Television. The school later used Ian's photograph in advertisements for the school, against his express wishes.

Ian sued, and the School responded by asking the court to dismiss the claim on the grounds that there was no reasonable **cause of action**; in other words, that no tort had been committed. The court referred to an earlier case which held that a person has a right to the exclusive marketing of his or her name, image, and identity, and therefore refused to dismiss the plaintiff's claim.

Defences to Intentional Torts

A person charged with a criminal offence has certain defences available to the charge. Similarly, for a person being sued in tort, there are recognized defences which can be presented to the court as a denial of liability.

Consent

If a person freely consents to a certain action, even if that consent is only *implied*, he or she cannot later sue for any injury or loss suffered. For example, if you become involved in a fist-fight by choice, you may not later sue for the broken arm which results from the fight. Similarly, participants in contact sports are deemed to have consented to the usual bodily contact associated with that sport. Thus, a court would not compensate you for injuries suffered as the result of a stiff body check in a hockey game. However, it would award damages for head injuries resulting from an intentional attack with a hockey stick by another player, since the amount of force used has probably gone beyond your consent.

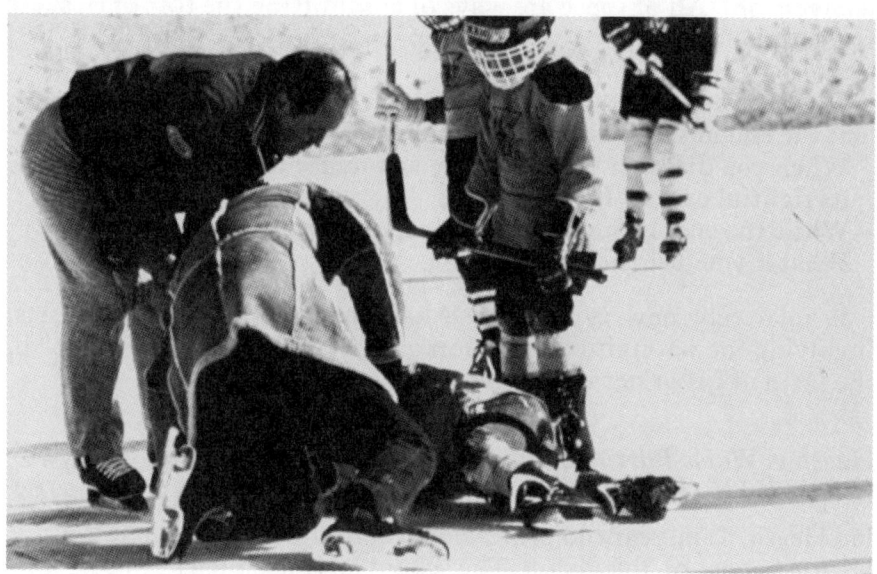

Figure 10-2 The law assumes that participants in certain sports have consented to normal bodily contact, but not to intentional violence.

Surgeons must be particularly careful about obtaining consent from their patients, or they will be liable in tort for battery. Courts have held that patients must be informed of the potential risks of operations generally, and of the particular operation to be performed specifically, or the patient's consent will not be considered valid. In addition, the common law provides that a patient must be mature enough to understand the nature of and the risks involved in the surgical procedure to be performed. The common law sets no specific age, but requires each situation to be judged individually. However, many provinces have statutes overriding the common law which set the minimum age at which a young person may consent to surgical procedures. For example, in Ontario, a patient must be at least sixteen years old to legally consent to hospital treatment.

Figure 10-3 Doctors must inform their patients of all the potential risks of a medical procedure, or they may be liable in tort for battery.

Halushka v. University of Saskatchewan (1965) 53 D.L.R. (3d) 436 (Sask. C.A.)

Halushka, a university student, consented to be a guinea pig to test a new anaesthetic. He was to be paid $50 for taking part in the experiment. The test was briefly explained to him, and he was told that it was perfectly safe. As well, he was required to sign a form releasing the doctors from liability.

During the test, a catheter was inserted into the vein of the plaintiff's arm and advanced towards the heart. The anaesthetic was then administered. The catheter was advanced through the heart chambers and out the pulmonary artery. Halushka suffered cardiac arrest at this point. His chest was cut open to allow manual heart massage to take place. His heart began to function again after a minute and a half of heart massage. When Halushka was eventually able to leave the hospital, he was given the $50 for participating in the experiment. Halushka sued the university hospital for battery.

— Did the university hospital sufficiently explain the risks involved in the experiment?
— Should the consent form which Halushka signed remove liability from the hospital?
— What do you think the court's decision was in this case?

Self-Defence and Defence of Third Party

Civil and criminal law both recognize your right to defend yourself from attack or from the threat of imminent attack. The force which you use in your own defence must be reasonable, given the circumstances. For example, drawing a knife to ward off an unarmed attack would likely be unreasonable. You are also entitled to use reasonable force in the defence of someone else who is under attack.

In a civil action, the onus is on the plaintiff to prove that a tort has been committed, and that he or she has suffered harm as a result. Once this has been done, the burden of proof shifts to the defendant to show that the force used in self-defence was reasonable.

Defence of Property

The principle of reasonable force also applies to the defence of property. A trespasser must first be asked to leave, unless the entry onto property has been violent. If this request is not complied with, the owner of property may use reasonable force to evict the trespasser.

Necessity

The defendant in a tort action can in certain circumstances use the defence of necessity. There are two kinds of necessity: *public* and *private*. In public necessity, the rights of the individual may be interfered with to protect the interests of the public. For example, a private house may be destroyed to prevent the spread of fire to the rest of the town. As unfair as this may seem, the defence here is complete, and the unfortunate owner of the destroyed house must bear the loss.

The defence of private necessity is much more limited. In using it, an individual seeks to protect private interests rather than those of the general public. The defence of private necessity may be used, for instance, in trespassing onto the land of another to protect one's own life, health, or property, provided that the harm caused is not disproportionate to the good intended. An example would occur if you were caught on a lake when a violent storm sprang up. You could then moor your boat to someone else's dock for the duration of the storm. The minor inconvenience that may result to the property owner is outweighed by the benefit of saving your life.

Legal Authority

In certain circumstances, statute law provides the authority for interfering with the rights of the individual. For example, the *Criminal Code* provides the authority for law enforcement officers to use as much force as is necessary to enforce the law. Therefore, a police officer acting on reasonable and probable grounds who arrests an innocent person would not be found liable in tort for false arrest or false imprisonment. As well, the officer would be justified in using force and would be held liable only if excessive force was used.

Teachers and parents are also authorized by the *Criminal Code* to use reasonable force in disciplining children; they may therefore claim this defence in civil actions. The authority for school boards to impose the strap as a punishment for misbehaviour comes from this section of the *Code*. Recently, however, public attitudes have been changing in this area, and many school boards have now abolished the strap. Likewise, parents who physically discipline their children must ensure that they do not use excessive force, or they could be found guilty of child abuse.

Negligence

In today's society, by far the bulk of tort actions coming before the courts are those involving **negligence**. The torts examined so far in this chapter have involved intentional conduct on the part of one person which results in harm to another. There are, however, many injuries which are not the result of any intent but rather arise out of negligence leading to loss or injury. Consider, for example, the number of car accidents which occur annually in Canada. Drivers of automobiles do not *intend* to be involved in accidents, yet even momentary negligence or carelessness in handling a vehicle can result in untold suffering, injury, and death to others. It must be noted, however, that not all accidents are the result of negligence.

What exactly, then, is negligence? A general definition is that it is a type of conduct which falls below the standard of conduct required by society, and which involves an unreasonable risk of harm to others.

James et al. v. River East Schools Division No.9 and Peniuk [1976] 2 W.W.R. 577 (Man. Q.B.)

Joni Lou James was an eighteen-year-old Grade 12 student when she was involved in an accident during a chemistry lab. Her teacher, Peniuk, had distributed written instructions to the class the day before the experiment so that students could review the information for homework. This written material was supplemented by oral instructions, and, the following day, by additional instructions written on the blackboard.

The experiment involved heating of nitric acid. During the experiment, students were expected to make a visual examination of the chemicals to determine when to begin applying heat. There was a danger of applying too much heat if the chemicals were not exactly ready. As well, the instructions warned that this acid had a tendency to spatter unless the heating process was conducted very carefully. The Grade 12 class had done some previous experiments with acids, but had no experience heating them. Eye goggles were available in the classroom, but students were not instructed to wear them. This particular experiment had been conducted many times before in the school without mishap and followed standard procedure.

The teacher was not immediately available to inspect the experiment, so the plaintiff and her partner continued the heating process according to the instructions. An explosion occurred which left the plaintiff with permanent facial scarring and injury to her tear ducts.

James and her father sued the chemistry teacher and the school board.

In a negligence action, a number of questions are placed before the court which must be answered in determining whether negligence has occurred. The answers to these questions are considered essential elements of proof in a negligence case.

1. Did the plaintiff have a legal responsibility or duty to the plaintiff to avoid inflicting harm?
2. Did the defendant's conduct fall below the standard of care required by society?
3. Was the defendant's conduct the cause of the plaintiff's loss or injury?
4. Did the plaintiff suffer real loss or injury?
5. Did the plaintiff contribute to his or her own loss or injury in any way?

Each question represents a principle of law relating to negligence. These principles are examined below. After considering them, apply the elements of proof to the *James* case and decide whether the courts would find the defendants liable.

Duty of Care

To whom do we owe a duty? What is our responsibility to our fellow human beings? The answer may come as a surprise. Unless a special relationship exists, as between parent and child, you are under no obligation to rescue a drowning person, for instance. Neither the criminal nor the civil law requires you to leave the dock or beach to help such an unfortunate. Should you voluntarily decide to attempt a rescue operation, you would then be under an obligation to exercise reasonable caution or care to avoid worsening the position of the swimmer or increasing the degree of harm.

—Why do you think the law does not require you to act when you see someone in danger and yet, if you do try to help, holds you liable for increasing the injuries suffered?
—Is it safer not to get involved?
—Is this a good law?

A distinguished judge, Lord Atkin, is responsible for establishing what is known as the "Neighbour Principle". He stated:

> The rule that you love your neighbour becomes in law you must not injure your neighbour; and the lawyer's question, Who is my neighbour? receives a restricted reply. *You must take reasonable care to avoid acts or omissions which you can reasonably foresee would be likely to injure your neighbour* (authors' italics). Who, then, in law, is my neighbour? The answer seems to be—persons who are so closely or directly affected by my act that I ought reasonably to have them in contemplation as being so affected when I am directing my mind to the acts or omissions which are called in question.
> [In Donoghue v. Stevenson [1932] A.C. 562 (House of Lords)]

To summarize, you owe a duty of care to anyone you should foresee may be harmed by your activities.

In addition to the "Neighbour Principle" of common law, many statutes impose a duty of care. For example, all provincial education Acts impose a duty on the principal to ensure that the school building and grounds are safe for staff and students and that adequate supervision of school property and activities is provided.

—Do teachers owe a duty of care to their students?
—What duty of care did Peniuk owe to Joni Lou James?

Standard of Care and the Reasonable Person

Once the court has established the existence of a legal duty of care, it must turn next to the question of the standard of that care. The test which is usually applied to the defendant's conduct is the test of the reasonable person. What would the reasonable person have done in this situation? Who is the reasonable person? One noted legal writer has described him or her as "the person on the Yonge Street subway" in Toronto. In other words, the reasonable person is the ordinary person of average intelligence and prudence to be found anywhere in Canada, who will weigh the risks involved in a certain type of conduct against the benefits, and who will exercise caution according to the degree of risk involved. This person will be able to foresee that there is greater risk involved when firing a gun than there is in hitting a tennis ball, and therefore will recognize that greater care must be exercised in the handling of a firearm to ensure the safety of others. The reasonable person reflects community standards of appropriate behaviour.

When determining whether a defendant's conduct lives up to the standard of care of the reasonable person, the court must take into consideration all of the circumstances. A child cannot be expected to foresee risk or danger in the same way as an adult; therefore, the standard applied must be reduced. A child must be judged according to the standard of other children of the same age, intelligence, and experience. On the other hand, professionals such as dentists and engineers may be required to exercise even greater care than the reasonable person, when acting within their professional capacity. For example, the standard of care expected of a passing motorist who stops to assist at the scene of an accident would be much less than that of a medical doctor who happens upon the accident and stops to offer aid.

Finally, the court will also look at the social benefit of the conduct as measured against the risk of harm. In many cases, the police have been absolved of liability when innocent bystanders have been injured as the result of police attempts to capture and arrest an escaping criminal. Similarly, a different standard of care may be applied when a fire engine speeds on its way to a fire and causes an accident than when an ordinary automobile accident occurs. The driver of the fire engine is not exempt from liability, but his or her conduct might be seen to be reasonable under the circumstances.

—Did Joni Lou James' teacher live up to the standard of care required of the reasonable person?
—What effect, if any, do compulsory education and attendance have on the standard of care of teachers and school boards?

Figure 10-4 and Figure 10-5 What duty of care is owed to the students in these situations? What standard of care?

Causation

It seems obvious that for a defendant to be liable in a negligence action, he or she must have been the cause of the plaintiff's harm. This element of negligence may be obvious but it is not always easy to establish. Consider the following case:

> *Mathews et al. v. MacLaren et al.* (1969) 4 D.L.R. (3d) 557 (Ont. H.C.)
>
> Mathews fell overboard from a cabin cruiser into the icy water of Lake Ontario in early May of 1966. Although no autopsy could be performed, it was believed that he suffered an immediate and fatal heart attack due to immersion in the frigid water. MacLaren, the owner of the boat, unsuccessfully attempted a rescue operation but did not follow standard rescue procedure. MacLaren, and all of his passengers, had been drinking all day. Mathews' body eventually slipped below the water and was not recovered. His family sued.
>
> —**Was MacLaren negligent? Did he cause the Mathews family's loss?**

The court found that, although MacLaren had not effected a suitable rescue operation, he had not caused Mathews' death. Mathews had fallen from the boat purely by accident, and his death was the result of the shock of contact with the frigid water. MacLaren had not contributed to his harm or worsened his situation by not being able to rescue the body.

The courts will frequently apply the "but for" test to questions of causation. That is, if the plaintiff's harm would not have resulted but for the defendant's negligence, the defendant will be held to be the cause of the harm.

The issue of foreseeability is also important in establishing causation. In general, the nature of the harm suffered must not be so *remote* or indirect that a reasonable person could not have foreseen its occurrence. The concept of an "Act of God" also enters here, in referring to accidents which are inevitable because they are completely unforeseeable and therefore beyond the control of the people involved. An example would occur when a car is struck by lightning and the driver loses control of it, injuring others. The lightning is an act of God, beyond the control of the driver, who cannot be held responsible for any harm caused.

—**Were Joni Lou's injuries foreseeable?**
—**Applying the "but for" rule, was Peniuk the cause of her injury?**

Generally, it is the plaintiff's duty to prove that the defendant caused the injury or loss. However, there are certain situations where it is assumed that negligence must have occurred, and the onus shifts to the defendant to show that negligent conduct has not taken place.

Saccardo v. City of Hamilton, et al. (1971) 2 O.R. 479 (H.C.)

A contractor was hired by the merchants' association in Hamilton to decorate hydro poles around the City for the Christmas season and to do repairs and maintenance of these decorations. During the month of November, there was considerable wind, which made repairs necessary; however, no general inspection system had been set up by the contractor. On a gusty day in early December, some decorations fell on the plaintiff, who suffered serious back injuries. In making a finding for the plaintiff, the judge said: "Things properly secured do not simply fall of their own weight in the absence of negligence or intervention by some third person."

In circumstances such as these, it is assumed that the "action speaks for itself", and to force the plaintiff to show exactly how the defendant caused the harm is to place too great a burden on the plaintiff.

—This principle of law is applied when a motor vehicle causes injury to a pedestrian. Why do you think this is so?

Real Loss or Injury

You have already seen that with some intentional torts, it is not necessary that real harm be caused. For example, in actions for assault, the mere fact of being threatened with harm is sufficient to allow the plaintiff to sue and be compensated. In negligence actions, this is not so. The plaintiff must be able to establish that real loss, harm, or injury has been suffered. Suppose you are driving your car through an intersection when an intoxicated motorist runs the red light and crashes his car into a telephone pole. You narrowly avoid collision with his vehicle; luckily, no other cars are in the intersection. You are understandably shaken and upset at the extreme recklessness of this driver. Can you sue for your fright and mental anguish? Although the drunken driver was certainly negligent in the operation of the vehicle and could be charged under provincial law or criminal law, there is no tort liability attached to the conduct because you suffered no real harm. You would not be able to sue successfully in this situation, unless you could show that you have suffered a subsequent psychiatric illness.

—Now that you have reviewed principles of law relating to negligence, how do you think the court ruled in the case of *James v. Peniuk*?

Defences to Negligence

If the plaintiff is unable to establish the defendant's negligence by proving that all four elements described above exist, then of course, the defendant is not liable. However, if duty of care, standard of care, causation, and damage are all established by the plaintiff, the defendant can employ either of the following defences to deny or reduce liability: **voluntary assumption of risk**, or **contributory negligence**.

Voluntary Assumption of Risk

To successfully employ the defence of voluntary assumption of risk, the defendant is required to show first, that the plaintiff clearly knew and appreciated the nature and degree of risk involved, and second, that he or she had voluntarily accepted this risk.

Mercer v. The Moler System of Barber Schools (1939) S.C. 29 (B.C.S.C.)

The plaintiff bought a home care product for bleaching hair. She bleached her normally dark hair to a shade of blonde. A short time later, she entered the defendant's hairdressing salon to have a permanent wave. The employee of the salon cautioned Mercer that her hair was already in a damaged condition owing to the bleaching and that the permanent wave would further damage her hair and that the ends would break off. When Mercer insisted that her hair be permed, the employee requested that she sign the following statement: "On this 5th day of December 1938 I take this permanent wave giving (*sic*) at the Moler Beauty parlour entirely at my own risk owing to its bleached condition." Mercer signed the statement.

When she returned home, she found not only that the ends of her hair broke off, but also that a great deal of her hair fell out. She sued the beauty parlour.

The court dismissed her action, stating that Mercer had deliberately taken the risk and had been warned of the consequences, and now must suffer the loss herself.

Contributory Negligence

Contributory negligence is not a complete defence. It can be used to reduce liability in situations where the plaintiff has not exercised the standard of care of a reasonable person in his or her own interest, and

Figure 10-6 Do you agree with the way in which the judge apportioned the damages? Do you think it is fair that the hotel had to pay more than its share because the other defendant's insurance could not cover the full amount?

therefore contributed to the harm suffered. A motorcyclist who does not wear a helmet or a construction worker who does not wear or use safety equipment may well contribute to any injuries received through the negligence of others. The blame attached to the defendant is reduced accordingly.

Treating contributory negligence in this manner is a relatively new development in negligence law. Under common law, contributory negligence was considered to be a complete bar to recovery of dam-

Served youth before crash, bar agrees to pay $1 million

BRIGHT, Ont. (CP) — A country hotel has agreed to pay almost $1-million for its part in a car accident that paralyzed an underaged drinker after he spent an evening in the tavern.

In a settlement that could have worrisome consequences for the hospitality industry, the Arlington House hotel has dropped an appeal of the damage award handed down by an Ontario Supreme Court jury two years after the 1980 accident.

Andreas Schmidt, 16 at the time of the accident, and Clayton Sharpe, then 18 and the driver of the car, were served three or four rounds of beer at the hotel before the accident.

Testimony indicated that Mr. Sharpe would have been noticeably impaired at the time he was served and that he registered a blood alcohol level almost twice the legal limit when his car left a country road and went into a ditch.

The jury held Mr. Schmidt 39 per cent responsible for his injuries because he wasn't wearing a seat belt and had accepted the risk of riding with Sharpe. Sharpe was held 55 per cent responsible and the hotel was held 15 per cent responsible.

The original award was set at $1.6-million and lowered to $1.15-million after deducting Mr. Schmidt's share of the blame. But since Mr. Sharpe had only $500,000 insurance, joint liability laws made the hotel responsible for the balance — almost $1 million.

A spokesman for the Hotel Association of Canada Inc. said the judgment could start a trend that would prove costly and worrisome for hoteliers.

Russell Cooper, association executive vice-president, said yesterday the award is one of the few million-dollar litigation judgments in Canadian history and represents the largest against a bar. The biggest previous award was less than $100,000, he said.

Since insurance premiums are a major part of a hotel's operating costs, the Arlington judgment could lead to others and force some bars out of business because of high payments, he said.

The settlement also comes at a time when groups leading the mounting campaign against drunk driving are demanding that bar keepers play a greater part in keeping drunk customers off the roads.

Mr. Schmidt's lawyer, Earl Cherniak of London, Ont., confirmed yesterday that a settlement had been reached with the hotel's insurance company and that his client will receive about $1.6-million including interest on the Supreme Court award made last year.

The award covers future costs and loss of income for the remainder of Mr. Schmidt's life as well as compensation to his family. He lives at home in nearby Drumbo, Ont.

He must use mechanical devices to eat and wash and is learning to write with his mouth.

Toronto lawyer Barry Percival, who represents the hotel's insurance company, confirmed that the appeal has been dropped. Details of the settlement will be filed with the Court of Appeal within the next week, Mr. Cherniak said.

Arlington House owner Jim Brady was unavailable for comment but Don Fonk, a barman at the hotel, said he and his fellow workers thought it was "not really fair" that the hotel had to make the settlement.

"You just can't catch everybody who is drinking underage," he said.

ages, no matter how minor the plaintiff's own fault had been. In many instances, this was clearly unjust. In the early twentieth century in Canada, only the province of Québec had the equitable principle of "common fault" as part of its Civil Code. In 1924, Ontario became the first common law province to recognize the value of this principle and to pass legislation to correct the injustices caused by the common law. The remaining provinces followed suit shortly thereafter. Today, the Ontario *Negligence Act* states:

> 4. In any action for damages that is founded upon the fault or negligence of the defendant, if fault or negligence is found on the part of the plaintiff that contributed to the damages, the court shall apportion the damages in proportion to the degree of fault or negligence found against the parties respectively.

Strict Liability

So far, you have read about torts in which the wrongdoer has either intentionally or negligently caused harm to another. There are some situations, however, where a person will be liable for damages even if he or she did not act intentionally or negligently. This liability exists because the nature of the activity itself involves such a high degree of risk.

Figure 10-7 A person who engages in legal but extremely dangerous activities will be held strictly liable for any harm or loss that occurs.

One situation in which courts will apply strict liability comes about when an occupier of land brings onto it something which, if it escapes, is likely to do mischief. This principle of law was established in the 1868 case of *Rylands v. Fletcher*, which concerned a situation where the defendants had built a water reservoir which collapsed and flooded the plaintiff's land.

Mihalchuk v. Ratke et al. (1966) 57 D.L.R. (2d) 269 (Sask. Q.B.)

Ratke hired a plane to spray his barley crops with a herbicide. A light wind caused the herbicide to drift onto the plaintiff's land, destroying his rapeseed crop, which was very sensitive to this type of herbicide. The court applied the rule in *Rylands v. Fletcher* and found the defendant liable.

Strict liability also applies to persons who keep animals. Owners of animals of a type known to be dangerous, such as lions, tigers, and snakes, will be strictly liable for any damage they cause. A person will also be liable for damages done by any animal of a type which is not usually dangerous, such as a dog or a cow, if the individual animal is known to be dangerous. Some provinces are passing legislation in this area to change the common law and apply stricter standards to the owners of domestic animals.

—Does your province rely on common law, or has it passed legislation setting out the liability of animal owners?

Vicarious Liability

In certain circumstances, a blameless person will be held responsible for the torts of another. The innocent person becomes jointly responsible with the wrongdoer for the harm done. This type of strict liability is called **vicarious liability**. For instance, the owner of a motor vehicle will be held vicariously liable if he or she lends the car and the other driver negligently injures someone. The defence available to the owner in denying liability is that the vehicle was operated without consent.

As well, an employer is vicariously liable for the tort of an employee, if the tort was committed in the course of the performance of duties associated with the employment. For example, a school board, as the employer, is held vicariously liable when a teacher who is teaching or supervising authorized school activities negligently injures a student. To deny liability, the employer must show that the employee was performing tasks outside the scope of his or her employment. Finally, parents can be found vicariously liable for the torts of their children if the parents have been negligent in the care and control of the children.

Additional Types of Torts

It is not possible to classify all types of torts under the three areas discussed so far: intentional torts, negligence, and strict liability. Some torts can be committed either intentionally or negligently and, in addition, sometimes without any fault if strict liability is imposed. Some areas of tort law are not concerned with a type of tort but rather deal with the liability of certain types of people, for instance, occupiers of land and manufacturers of consumer goods. The following discusses some of these other types of torts that cannot be easily classified.

Defamation

Defamation occurs when a person's reputation is wrongfully damaged. In general, there are two types of defamation: **slander**, which refers to oral statements or gestures, and **libel**, which refers to written statements. The common law and, in some instances, statute law, have expanded the definition of libel to include such modern methods of communication as cartoons, radio broadcasts, television programs, and films.

Monson v. Tussaud's (1894) 1 Q.B. 671

A wax statue of Monson, who had been acquitted of a charge of murder, was placed in Madame Tussaud's wax museum in London. The statue was placed near the statues of three criminals and next to the Chamber of Horrors.

—Was Monson being defamed?
—If so, would the defamation have been libel or slander?
—What harm or loss do you think he might have suffered?

In Alberta, Manitoba, New Brunswick, Nova Scotia and Prince Edward Island, statutes treat libel and slander alike. The plaintiff is not required to prove actual harm, such as loss of income. In the remaining provinces, the distinction between libel and slander is still made. In the event of libel, harm or loss is presumed to have occurred; in the event of slander, the plaintiff usually must show actual monetary loss, unless the slanderous statement refers to the person's ability to do his or her job, or to a criminal offence or disease.

—Why do you think proof of damage is required for slander but not for libel?
—Would it be less damaging to defame someone in a speech made to an audience of 300 than it would be to write a letter to a friend,

defaming the character of a mutual acquaintance? Does this help you to understand why some provinces have introduced statute law treating libel and slander the same way?

Defences to Defamation

The law must balance a person's right to protect his or her reputation against the right of others to freedom of speech. Therefore, several defences are available to the defendant in an action for libel or slander.

Justification

This defence is simply that the statement made is true. Justification is not a defence, however, if the defendant *mistakenly* believed the statement to be true.

Absolute Privilege

Statements made in Parliament, in provincial legislatures, during court proceedings, or between lawyers and their clients are protected by this defence, even if they are made maliciously. It is considered beneficial to society to allow persons in these situations to express their views openly and fully, without fear of legal action.

Qualified Privilege

A person making a statement without malice as part of public or private duties may raise this defence. An example of such a person would be a teacher who gives a reference on behalf of a student. The employer to whom the reference is given must be able to rely on the fact that it is an honest appraisal, not one made under fear of a lawsuit. Another example is shown in the following case:

> *McLoughlen v. Kutasy* (1979) 97 D.L.R. (3d) 620 (S.C.C.)
>
> A company doctor examined a job applicant and disqualified him in his report to the employer on the grounds of having a psychopathic personality. The doctor then successfully defended a libel action brought by the applicant. The court found that the doctor made the statement without malice and in the course of his duties.

Fair Comment

This defence is often used by newspapers and other media. A statement will not be considered defamatory if it is clearly an honest opinion about a matter of public importance. The comment must be based on facts, and be made without malice.

VanderZalm v. Times Publishers (1979) 96 D.L.R. (3d) 172 (B.C.C.A.)

VanderZalm, who was Minister of Human Resources in British Columbia, sued Times Publishers over a cartoon in which he was depicted as gleefully pulling wings from flies. Other flies without wings were shown moving on the table. VanderZalm claimed that the cartoon portrayed him as a "person who enjoys inflicting suffering on helpless persons".

VanderZalm was a controversial figure who, since being appointed Minister, had cut back on social assistance for community groups, the handicapped, and welfare recipients. The cartoonist testified that the cartoon was meant to criticize a statement of VanderZalm's in which he said that Indians were attracted to the bright lights of the city and that they should return to the reserves where there was more opportunity for them. The cartoonist claimed that the flies represented the Indians having their wings clipped so they could not fly or roam anymore.

—Would VanderZalm's suit be for libel or slander?
—Do you think a political cartoon could harm anyone's reputation?
—Does it make any difference that satire, parody, and caricature are usual in political cartoons?
—Does this cartoon go beyond fair comment? Who do you think should win this case?

Nuisance

A nuisance may arise from many sources: barking dogs, smoke from a factory, water and air pollution, persistent and harassing telephone calls. There are two classes of nuisance: private and public. Private nuisance refers to unreasonable interference with a property owner's use and enjoyment of his or her property. In deciding whether a private nuisance exists, the courts must balance your right to enjoy your land against the right of others to use their property as they wish. Consideration will be given to whether the defendant's use of land is appropriate for that area. For example, it is likely that a court would agree with the neighbours of a drummer in a rock band that a nuisance exists when the drummer practises in her townhouse basement. The results would be different if the drummer practised in a studio located among factories and warehouses. A court will also consider whether the defendant's activity is permanent or temporary.

"This is your last chance. Turn that stereo down."

Mr. and Mrs. Jelinek are renovating their house. The noise from the construction irritates Mrs. Jones, their seventy-year-old next-door neighbour.

Figure 10-8

- Can Mrs. Jones complain of a nuisance?
- Would it matter how long the construction is carried on? Or what time of day the work begins or ends? Or whether the house is on a busy city street, in a quiet suburb, or next to a car factory?
- What if Mrs. Jones has a heart condition which is aggravated by the noise?

A public nuisance, by contrast, interferes with the welfare or convenience of the general public. Blocking a public highway or polluting a lake or stream used by the general public are examples of public nuisances. Public nuisances are usually considered criminal or quasi-criminal offences, and not torts. They are usually prosecuted by the province's Attorney-General. Private individuals can sue for a public nuisance only if they can prove that their losses or injuries differ from those suffered by the general public. In one case, a real estate agent was able to collect damages when he was unable to show a property because of an obstruction on the highway.

Defences to Nuisance

Prescription

Prescription is a defence which a defendant may raise when sued for a nuisance that has existed without interruption for twenty years or more. In effect, the nuisance becomes legalized since no one has complained in so many years.

Legislative Authority

Another defence is **legislative authority**. For instance, railways and aircraft are allowed to operate by reason of statute law. Therefore, reasonable levels of noise and pollution associated with their operation are authorized by law. For this reason, people who live near railroad tracks cannot complain about the noise caused by passing trains.

Product Liability

A bottle of soft drink explodes. Kitchen cupboards fall off the walls of a new house. Brakes fail on a new car. These are just a few examples of situations in which consumers may be injured by faulty products.

Prior to the English case of *Donoghue v. Stevenson* in 1932, an injured person usually had no remedy unless there was a contract between the injured person and the manufacturer of the product. In *Donoghue*, a young woman became ill when she found a decomposed snail in a bottle of ginger beer which had been purchased for her. The court, using the neighbour principle discussed earlier, found that the manufacturer owed a duty of reasonable care to whoever it was that ultimately consumed the beer, even though there was no contract between the manufacturer and the consumer. Since this case, the area of product liability has rapidly expanded.

Not only manufacturers, but also wholesalers, retailers, repairers, or anyone else involved in the distribution of consumer goods may be found liable for negligence if a consumer is injured by defective goods. Liability may be based on improper design, manufacture, or repair, as well as on failure to warn, as in the example of a flammable chemical that does not have a warning written on its label.

Ives v. Clare Bros. Ltd. et al. (1971) 1 O.R. (H.C. J.)

The plaintiff, Ives, bought a gas furnace from a supplier, Merriman Sheet Metal & Heating Ltd. The furnace was manufactured by Clare Bros. and shipped assembled. It was installed by Merriman. The installation was checked by Twin City Gas, also named as a defendant.

Ives received gas and service from Twin City, who made three service calls to adjust the furnace. Twice there was gas leakage. Then, one day, Ives fell ill, and called in sick at work. He was found three days later, lying helpless in his living room, suffering from carbon monoxide poisoning. Upon investigation, it was discovered that four screws in this type of furnace tended to come loose, causing carbon monoxide to be produced. Clare Bros. were aware of the problem, but did not warn consumers.

—Who should be liable in this case—Clare Bros., Twin City, or both?

In general, negligence is required for liability. However, some provinces either already have or are considering passing legislation which would impose a higher standard of care on manufacturers and suppliers of consumer goods. For example, New Brunswick legislation makes suppliers of "consumer products" strictly liable for reasonably foreseeable losses or injuries caused by defects in design, material, or workmanship.

—Why should manufacturers be strictly liable for any harm their products cause consumers?
—Would it be better to make the consumer bear the loss if no negligence is proven?
—Do you think it would be difficult for a consumer to prove that a manufacturer was negligent?

Occupier's Liability

What duty, if any, should a person have to ensure that his or her property is safe for visitors? Should homeowners have a duty to keep their porch steps in good repair? Should a store owner have a duty to keep the entrance to the store free from ice in the winter? Should a cottage owner be allowed to set traps for trespassers? These are questions which the courts must answer when faced with cases involving occupier's liability.

Canadian courts have traditionally recognized three classes of visitors:

1. **invitees**, persons from whom the occupier receives or has the potential for receiving an economic benefit, such as customers in a store;
2. **licensees**, visitors such as social guests who have permission to be on the property but from whom no economic benefit is expected; and
3. **trespassers**, persons who enter the land without permission.

The type of duty owed by the occupier of the land to the visitor depends on the type of visitor.

The highest duty is owed to invitees, whom the occupier must protect from unusual dangers which he or she knows about or *should* know about. In other words, if a reasonable person should have realized that the danger existed, the occupier will be held liable.

The occupier of land owes a somewhat lesser duty to licensees: protecting them from concealed trap or dangers of which he or she is aware, such as falling tree limbs, or broken stairs.

Trespassers are owed the least care. The law requires that an occupier of land must not wilfully injure trespassers, by setting a trap for example, or recklessly disregard their safety.

Using these categories rigidly can lead to unfair results. For example, should the same duty of care be owed to a trespassing burglar and someone taking a short-cut across your lawn? The courts have developed techniques to avoid unfair results. Consider the following case:

Veinot v. Kerr-Addison Mines Ltd. (1975) 2 S.C.R. 311

Veinot, an experienced snowmobiler, was riding one night in an area frequently used by other snowmobilers. While travelling on what appeared to be a well-travelled public road, he ran into a metal pipe placed across the road and was severely injured. The plaintiff was in fact on the defendant's property. The pipe, which had been there for about twenty years, was used as a gate to prevent people from travelling on the road. The court found that, since the defendant knew that snowmobilers used this private road and had done nothing to prevent them from doing so, the plaintiff had implied permission to be there and should therefore be considered a licensee rather than a trespasser. The court also found that the pipe was a concealed danger of which the defendant was aware. The defendant was held liable for the plaintiff's injuries.

—Do you agree with the court's decision?
—In this case, the court found that the defendant could have easily made the pipe more obvious, by painting it for example. Should the amount of trouble incurred by the occupier to remove a danger matter?
—What if the defendant had been a cottage owner rather than a mining company? Should that make a difference?
—How could the defendant have prevented snowmobilers from trespassing?

If a trespasser is a child, courts have used the idea of *attractive nuisance* or *allurement*, saying that the child has been lured onto the property and therefore should be treated as a licensee, not a trespasser.

A child plays on a slag heap in a railway yard. He breaks through the crust, badly burning his foot.

—What other facts do you need to know to decide whether the railway is liable?
—Should it matter how old the child is?
—What responsibility should parents have to protect their children from harm?

The courts have also recently developed new categories of visitors in order to reach fairer decisions. For example, someone who pays to enter premises, like a movie patron, is considered a **contractual entrant**. The rules of ordinary negligence apply to this class of visitor. Alberta, Ontario, and British Columbia have gone even farther than the courts and have passed legislation which treats all visitors, except trespassers, alike. Alberta was the first province to do so, in s.5 of its *Occupier's Liability Act*.

> 5. An occupier of premises owes a duty to every visitor on his premises to take such care as in all the circumstances of the case is reasonable to see that the visitor will be reasonably safe in using the premises for the purposes for which he is invited or permitted by the occupier to be there or is permitted by law to be there.

—Why do you think the law is developing in this direction?

SUMMARIZING YOUR READING

1. Define the term "tort". How does tort law differ from criminal law?

2. Distinguish between the torts of assault and battery.

3. Is physical harm necessary before an assault and battery action can be brought before the courts? Explain.

4. In an action for false imprisonment, what must the plaintiff prove to the court?

5. What three restrictions are placed on a plaintiff suing for intentional infliction of mental suffering?

6. Do all provinces grant the right to sue for invasion of privacy? Explain.

7. Why have actions for the tort of trespass to land become uncommon?

8. Give three original examples of trespass to chattels.

9. What effect does "consent" have if a person is sued for an intentional tort?

10. Define "lawful authority" and give an example of this defence.

11. What test will the courts apply to a defence of self-defence? Give an example of a situation in which this defence may be used.

12. What is the distinction between an intentional tort and negligence?

13. Define each of the following: duty of care, standard of care, and causation.

14. Is loss or injury necessary for a negligence action to be brought? Explain.

15. What effect does the defence of contributory negligence have on a negligence action?

16. Give an original example of a situation in which the defence of voluntary assumption of risk could be successfully employed.

17. Define "strict liability". Why do you think this principle of law developed?

18. Name the two types of defamation, and give an original example of each.

19. Name and explain the four defences to defamation.

20. What is the difference between private and public nuisance?

21. Name the two defences a person can use if sued for a private nuisance.

22. Whom can a consumer sue if he or she is injured by a defective product? Explain.

23. What does an injured consumer probably have to prove?

24. What are the three classes of visitors that courts have traditionally recognized? What duty of care does the occupier owe to each?

25. How have provincial statutes changed the way in which the law treats visitors?

PROJECTS AND ACTIVITIES

1. Choose one of the following recent negligence actions. Research the case at a law library, and write a report outlining the facts of the case and the essential elements of proof of negligence as they apply to the case. Conclude your paper with your opinion of the court's decision.

Robson v. Chrysler Corporation of Canada Ltd.
(1962) 32 D.L.R. (2d) 49 (Alta. S.C.)

Stermer v. Lawson
(1980) 11 C.C.L.T. 76 (B.C.C.A.)

Reibl v. Hughes
(1981) 114 D.L.R. (3d) 1 (S.C.C.)

Young v. Burgoyne
(1981) 16 C.C.L.T. 100 (N.S.T.D.)

McMorran v. Dominion Stores Ltd.
(1977) 1 C.C.L.T. 259 (Ont. H.C.)

Moddejonge et al. v. Huron County Board of Education et al.
[1972] 2 O.R. 437 (Ont. H.C.)

2. As the introduction of this chapter pointed out, many torts are also crimes. It is extremely difficult to sue a wrongdoer who is behind bars or who lacks the financial resources to compensate the victim. For this reason, all provinces have introduced criminal injuries compensation funds. Research your province's fund, by contacting the Attorney-General's office. Who qualifies for compensation? What type of compensation is available? Make a report to the class or prepare a research paper on this topic.

RESOLVING CASES

Cachay v. Nemeth (1972) 28 D.L.R. (3d) 603 (Sask. Q.B.)

The plaintiff attempted to kiss the defendant's wife at a party. The defendant's karate blow broke the plaintiff's jaw and teeth.

—What tort has occurred?
—What defence might the defendant employ?
—What do you think was the outcome of this case?

Tillander et al. v. Gosselin (1967) 1 O.R. 203 (Ont. H.C.)

A three-year-old boy took the infant plaintiff out of her carriage and dragged her along the ground, causing severe injuries and brain damage. The parents of the baby girl sued the boy and his parents for battery on her behalf.

—Would the three-year-old defendant be held responsible in tort for battery?
—Would the adult defendants be liable for negligence?

Hayward v. F.W. Woolworth Co. Ltd. et al. (1979) 8 C.C.L.T. 157 (Nfld. S.C.)

The defendant employees of the F.W. Woolworth Co. believed that the plaintiff had shoplifted an $8 watch. When the plaintiff left the store, they restrained him, but they eventually released him when a sales slip was produced. The plaintiff sued for false imprisonment.

—Why did the defendants wait until the plaintiff left the store before approaching him?
—What powers of arrest do citizens have? (Refer to the *Criminal Code*, s.449.)
—Was the plaintiff falsely imprisoned? Explain.

Floyd et al. v. Bowers et al. (1980) 106 D.L.R. (3d) 702 (Ont. C.A.)

In June 1974, two thirteen-year-old boys were playing together at the Bowers' summer residence at Wasaga Beach. An argument arose between the two, and the defendant, Bowers, fired several shots from a pump-action pellet gun. One of these shots resulted in the loss of sight in one eye of the plaintiff.

The defendant's parents were visiting a neighbour at the time of the incident. The gun in question had been purchased by the defendant's father. Father and son had used the gun for target practice. The gun and ammunition were kept in an unlocked cupboard and the defendant knew of its location. Mr. Bowers had laid down a rule that the gun was not to be operated by the defendant except in the presence of his father, mother, or older brother.

—What tort did the defendant commit?
—Do you think that the defendant's parents should be held liable for their son's tort? What is the principle of law that applies to situations such as this?

Cherrey v. Steinke et al. (1979) 9 C.C.L.T. 276 (Man. Q.B.)

Cherrey and Steinke, along with a number of friends, spent an evening drinking in a hotel. Upon leaving the hotel, they purchased additional beer, drove to a farm, and continued drinking. Sometime later, they left the farm and drove back into town to another hotel. While parked near the hotel, the police made a spot check of the car and told the occupants not to drive.

At this point, the group of friends dispersed, except for Cherrey and Steinke. These two decided to drive to the home of a friend to continue the evening of drinking. While they were proceeding along the highway, a police car approached them. Steinke, the driver, made a U-turn and attempted to elude the police. The front tire blew out, and the car spun out of control and hit a telephone pole. Cherrey was seriously injured, and sued.

—As the driver of a motor vehicle, did Steinke have a duty of care to his passenger, Cherrey?
—Did he live up to the standard of care of a reasonable person?
—Was the defendant the cause of the plaintiff's injuries?
—Did Steinke have any defence in this case? Explain.

Jackson et al. v. Millar et al. (1976) 59 D.L.R. (3d) 246 (S.C.C.)

Sixteen-year-old Millar borrowed his father's car and along with two friends set out for the family cottage to go to an all-night drive-in theatre. The boys split the cost of the gasoline, and arrangements were made to stay overnight at the cottage if Millar was too tired to drive home.

The boys did sleep briefly during one of the features, and at about 6 a.m. set off for home. Millar was not an experienced driver, and had never before driven on a four-lane highway. The car did a 360 degree turn and then a further 180 degree turn. Jackson, who had been leaning slightly on the door, was flung from the car and was paralyzed from the waist down after the accident. Neither of the other two boys was injured. Jackson had not been wearing a seat-belt at the time of the accident, although evidence presented at the trial indicated that a working seat-belt was available and that the plaintiff was aware of this.

—Was the defendant negligent in his operation of the car?
—Would the defendant's father, as the owner of the car, be found vicariously liable?
—Is any defence available to the defendant(s)?

Sgro v. Verbeek (1980) 28 O.R. (2d) 712 (H.C.J.)

The plaintiff, a seven-year-old child, was bitten by the defendant's dog while petting it. The dog tended to run after strangers and bark at them, and was unused to small children. It had never before bitten anyone.

—Do you think the plaintiff won?
—What facts did the court consider?
—On what basis might the defendant have been liable?

Nor-Video Services Ltd. v. Ontario Hydro (1978) 4 C.C.L.T. 244 (Ont. H.C.)

The plaintiff cable television company sued Ontario Hydro for locating its electrical power installations in such a way as to interfere with the reception and transmission of television broadcast signals. Before the installation, Ontario Hydro had assured the plaintiff and the community that the new transformer would not affect reception and promised to correct any problems which might occur. The plaintiff sought damages to restore adequate reception.

—What area of tort law does this case illustrate?
—Should the defendant be responsible for compensating the plaintiff?
—Would it matter if other sites had been available, even if at greater cost?
—Does it matter whether the damage was reasonably foreseeable?
—Is the ability to watch television part of the reasonable enjoyment and use of land?

Brunski v. Dominion Stores Ltd. et al. (1982) 20 C.C.L.T. 14 (Ont. H.C.)

The plaintiff, Brunski, suffered injury to his right eye when an unopened 1.5 L bottle of Coca-Cola exploded as he was placing it in his refrigerator. This type of bottle was later withdrawn from the market because of similar accidents. Brunski sued Dominion Stores, where he had bought the Coke, Domglas, the manufacturer of the bottle, and Coca-Cola, the bottlers.

—On what grounds should Brunski sue?
—Explain who you think is responsible and why.

Rae and Rae v. T. Eaton Co. (Maritimes) Ltd. et al. (1961) 28 D.L.R. (2d) 522 (N.S.S.C.)

A mother handed her ten-year-old daughter a can of artificial snow to put in the garbage. Instead, the girl played with it by banging it on a concrete wall. The can exploded, and part of it went into the girl's eye. The label on the can said it was "Safe—Harmless—Easy to Use" but warned against puncturing it or storing it near heat. The plaintiffs sued the manufacturer, distributor, and retailer.

—What defence could the defendants raise? What do you think was the decision of the court?

Epp v. Ridgetop Builders Ltd. (1979) 7 C.C.L.T. 291 (Alta. S.C.)

Epp was a surveyor hired by the defendant to do some work at a building site. While working, Epp was injured when a wall collapsed. The wall was blown down by extremely high winds. At the trial, it was established that no-one else was working that day because of the wind. Epp testified that he realized the danger but decided to take a chance since the work would take only two or three minutes.

For this action, the plaintiff relied on the Alberta *Occupier's Liability Act*, quoted earlier in this chapter.

—Do you think he was successful?
—What other principles of tort law can be applied to this case?

Gertsen et al. v. Municipality of Metropolitan Toronto et al. (1973) 41 D.L.R. (3d) 646 (Ont. H.C.)

The municipalities of Metro Toronto and the Borough of York entered an agreement to use a ravine behind the Gertsens' house for a land-fill site. The land-fill consisted of household garbage mixed with earth. The buried garbage produced methane gas, which escaped to the neighbouring properties. Several years earlier, the gas had caused a fire in the garage of the house owned by the Gertsens at the time of this case. When the Gertsens purchased this house, they were informed of the problem but were told that it had been remedied and that the garage was safe to use.

One day, Gertsen entered the garage and turned on the ignition of his car. An explosion occurred, destroying the garage and car, and severely injuring Gertsen. The explosion was caused by the methane gas.

—**On what grounds should Gertsen sue the municipalities? Explain your answer.**

Saccone v. Orr (1981) 34 O.R. (2d) 317 (Ont. Cty. Ct.)

The defendant recorded a private telephone conversation with his friend, Saccone, without the latter's knowledge. Orr apparently made the recording in order to clear himself before City Council of an accusation made by a fellow councillor. Saccone learned of the existence of the tape and told Orr not to use it. However, Orr played the tape at the next council meeting and the whole matter was reported in the local paper, causing the plaintiff great embarassment. He brought an action against Orr.

—**Could the plaintiff sue for libel or for slander? Explain.**
—**Is there any other cause of action available to him? Explain.**
—**Should Saccone be compensated for his embarassment?**

11

Civil Procedure and the Civil Courts

> Young People and Civil Procedure
> Before Bringing an Action
> The Civil Courts
> Bringing a Civil Action
> Insurance against Civil Liability

One of the chief purposes of civil law is to settle disputes between people. For instance, two people may disagree about the meaning of a term in a contract they have entered into, or a person may claim that someone has committed a tort against him or her. When people cannot settle their disagreements themselves, a remedy is available—the person who believes that he or she has been wronged may bring a civil action or *lawsuit* against the person who has allegedly committed the wrong. Usually the victim of the wrong will ask the courts for compensation for the loss or harm which he or she claims to have suffered. The process of bringing the action or suing is known as **litigation**; the parties to the action are the **litigants**. More specifically, as you learned in Chapter 10, the person bringing the action is called the plaintiff, while the person being sued is known as the defendant. The settlement of private disputes by the courts is governed by the legal rules of civil procedure, which form the subject of this chapter.

Brad buys a stereo from Stereo Sound Inc. He uses the stereo for about a week; then a speaker stops working. The store refuses to replace the speaker, although there is a one-year guarantee on the system. The manager claims that Brad must have damaged the speaker, since it worked fine when tested at the store.

—If this dispute goes to court, who will probably be the plaintiff? the defendant?
—What kind of compensation would Brad claim?
—What would be your answers to the questions above if Brad had bought the stereo on time and refused to continue with his payments?

Young People and Civil Procedure

A child or young person may sue or be sued, but the court imposes some restrictions to protect the interests of all of the parties. The provinces are responsible for setting the age at which a young person can bring or defend an action in his or her own right (the age of majority). In Ontario, the age of majority is eighteen, while in British Columbia it is nineteen.

—What is the age in your province at which a young person can bring or defend a civil action?
—What other rights do young people gain when they attain the age of majority?

Young people under the age limit set by a province are called **infants** or **minors**, and must be represented in court by an adult. A minor who is suing someone must be represented by a **next friend**. Usually, the next friend is a parent, but any willing adult can fill this role. The next friend is responsible for ensuring that the minor's suit is not frivolous and that the minor plaintiff obeys the rules of procedure and orders of the court. If the plaintiff's suit is unsuccessful, the next friend will be responsible for paying **costs**, that is, both parties' expenses. Costs can include court fees such as those for filing documents, as well as legal fees.

It is not unusual for a young person to be named in a civil suit as the defendant. The court will appoint a **guardian** *ad litem* for a minor who is being sued to ensure that the minor's interests are protected. Again, the guardian *ad litem* can be a parent or any responsible adult. The guardian *ad litem* is not, however, responsible for costs if the infant defendant loses the action.

Similarly, a next friend or guardian *ad litem* must be appointed to protect the interests of the parties when a mentally incompetent person is involved in a civil action.

Before Bringing an Action

If you believe you have been the victim of a civil wrong of any kind, there are several matters to consider before beginning litigation.

Is It Worth Suing?

You may have heard the saying, "You can't get blood from a stone." When considering whether or not to sue, you would be well-advised to keep this statement in mind. Litigation can be time-consuming and very expensive. If the person whom you wish to sue does not have the resources to compensate you for your loss in the event that you win your suit, it might be a good idea not to begin an action. However, **judgements** (court orders) are valid in most provinces for ten years and are also renewable. It is possible that at a future date the person you believe responsible for the alleged wrong will be in better financial condition and able to compensate you. If you feel that this may be the situation, you would be wise to take civil action.

Do You Have a Cause of Action?

Your complaint must be one which, if proven true, provides a remedy in law. The complaint or reason for suing is known as the **cause of action**. The torts described in Chapter 10 and breaches of contract such as those in Chapter 13 could be causes of action. It is possible, however, to suffer some wrongs which are simply not actionable. For example, your hurt feelings over the careless gossip of a friend are not grounds for suing for slander. Or the driver of a car might negligently place you in a dangerous situation, but unless actual loss or injury is caused, you could not sue.

When Should You Sue?

The rules of civil procedure vary from province to province. You must therefore consider the *limitation periods* for beginning litigation, which are established by each province. In most provinces six years are allowed for bringing actions for debts such as those arising from contracts, loans, and rentals. However, it is necessary to begin an action against a medical doctor within one year of the cause of action. Victims of motor vehicle accidents must sue within two years of the accident. These are only a few examples of limitation periods. They are set out in a variety of provincial statutes, chief among them the provincial *Statute of Limitations*. The important point to remember is that if you wait too long to begin your suit, you will lose your right to seek compensation in the courts.

— Why do you think limitation periods for beginning an action exist?
— Why are there different periods for different types of actions?

The Civil Courts

Another important matter to consider when bringing a civil action is the appropriate court for the particular action. The jurisdiction or authority of courts is generally determined by three factors:

1. the subject matter of the case;
2. monetary limits on the amount of compensation claimed; and
3. territorial jurisdiction.

Two federal courts have jurisdiction over civil matters: the Federal Court and the Supreme Court of Canada. However, the administration of most of the courts in Canada falls under provincial jurisdiction. The names of the courts and the types of cases they hear therefore vary from province to province.

Courts under Provincial Jurisdiction

The vast majority of civil actions are tried (and appealed) in the courts which fall within provincial jurisdiction. There are generally three levels of courts within this framework; in addition, there are several special courts which deal with particular types of civil matters. The names of these courts will vary by province. Some provinces, such as Alberta, do not have all three levels of courts.

Small Claims Court

This is the lowest level of provincial court dealing with civil matters. Trials are by judge, justice, or magistrate alone.
These courts usually do not have jurisdiction to hear cases on such matters as defamation, false imprisonment, or disputes involving ownership of land.

Subject Matter	Typical actions include:
	• non-payment for services performed
	• settlement of minor damage claims (mostly for car accidents)
	• unpaid loans
	• rent disputes
	• consumer problems

Figure 11-1 Cases in Small Claims Court /(cont'd)

Figure 11-1 (cont'd)

Monetary Limits	From $250 in New Brunswick to $3000 in Metropolitan Toronto.
	Monetary limits are increased periodically to reflect inflation, or, as in the Toronto example, to ease the heavy case loads in the higher courts.
Territorial Considerations	Action should be brought in the court located nearest to where (a) the cause of action for which you are suing occurred; or (b) the defendant is living or carrying on business.

County or District Court

The County or District Courts form the middle tier of courts in most provinces. Trials can be either by judge or by judge and jury.

Figure 11-2 Cases in County or District Court

Subject Matter	Typical actions include: • property disputes • medical malpractice • motor vehicle accidents • division of assets of separating spouses • adoptions
Monetary Limits	Up to a high of $25 000 in British Columbia.
Territorial Considerations	The plaintiff can usually choose the county where the trial is to take place, except where the cause of action arose in a particular county and both parties reside in that same jurisdiction. Either part is entitled to ask for a change of venue.

Supreme Court

The Supreme Court of the province, as the name implies, is the highest level of court under provincial jurisdiction. Its trial division has jurisdiction to hear all civil matters, although, typically, because of the added expense of bringing an action in this court, only the most serious civil suits will be heard in it. Jury trials are available, but they rarely occur. The appeals division of the court is the last appeal stage for any civil action before it goes before the Supreme Court of Canada.

Figure 11-3 Cases in the Supreme Court of a Province

Subject Matter	Typical actions include: • motor vehicle accidents • medical malpractice • libel, slander, false arrest, malicious prosecution (usually jury trials) • breach of contract • bankruptcy • divorce • custody
Monetary Limits	No lower limit, but generally claims heard in this court are for amounts above the jurisdiction of the County Court.
Territorial Considerations	Similar to County Court procedure, above.

Special Courts

Two special courts usually found within provincial jurisdiction are the *Family Court* and *Surrogate* or *Probate Court*. The Family Court typically hears cases involving child welfare and applications for support of spouses and children. Some provinces have a Surrogate Court responsible for dealing with the estates of dead persons. It handles the *probating* of wills (proving their authenticity), appointment of administrators to handle the estates of people dying *intestate* (without a will), and any disputes concerning the division of assets under a will.

Courts under Federal Jurisdiction

Federal Court

The Federal Court hears civil matters involving suits brought by or against the Crown in the form of the federal government, its departments, agencies, and **Crown corporations** (corporations owned by the government). For example, if you were involved in a car accident caused by a Canadian Armed Forces jeep, you would bring your action in this court.

Supreme Court of Canada

The Supreme Court of Canada is an appeal court. In civil matters, there is no automatic right to appeal to the Supreme Court. The Court will grant permission for an appeal only if the case involves important principles of law or public policy. The great expense of bringing an appeal to this level of court substantially limits the number of civil appeals heard.

The appeal routes usually followed in civil matters are outlined in Figure 11-4, although there may be some provincial variations.

Figure 11-4 Routes of Appeal

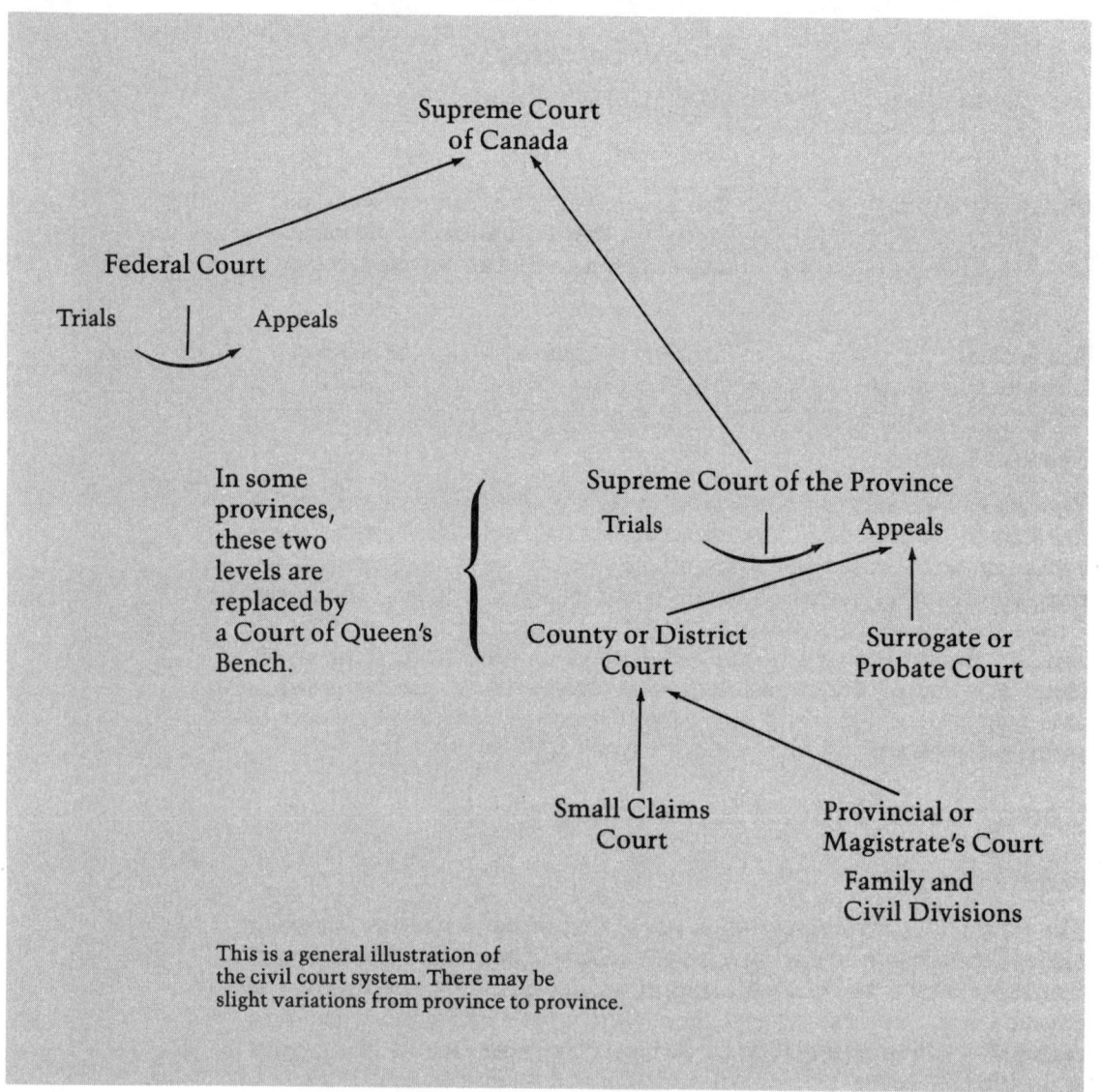

Bringing a Civil Action

The procedure involved in bringing a civil action depends largely on the nature and degree of harm the plaintiff claims to have suffered. If the plaintiff has a relatively small claim, a simplified, informal system (see Figure 11-5) exists to allow the case to be presented without a lawyer. For more complex civil matters or where the compensation claimed is greater, the plaintiff must bring the action in the higher courts. The procedure here is more complex and formal (see Figure 11-6), and a lawyer is probably necessary.

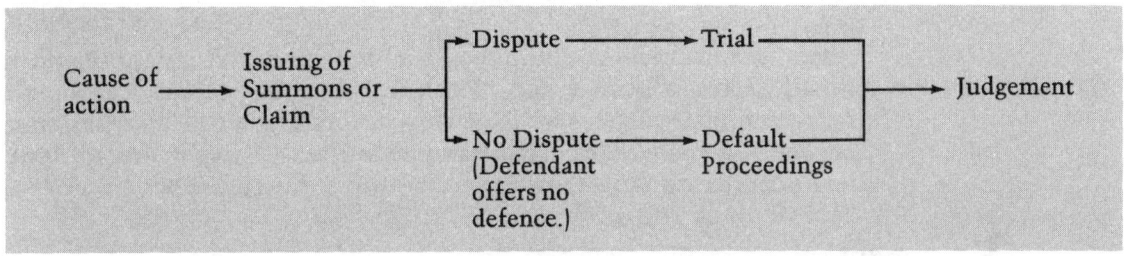

Figure 11-5 Procedure in Small Claims Court

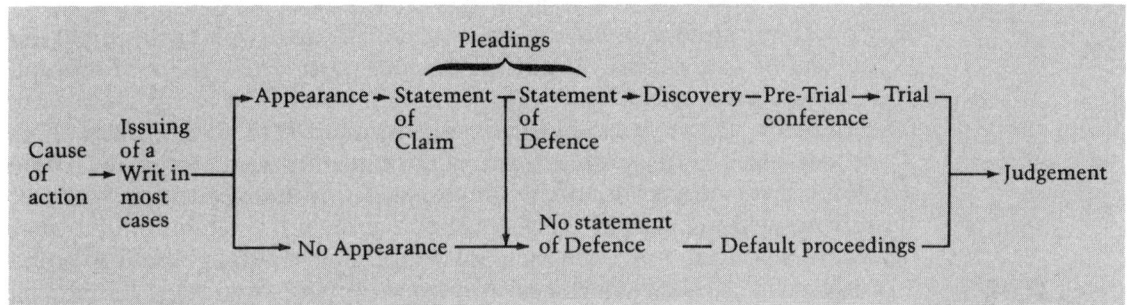

The remainder of this chapter will examine both the simplified procedure in Small Claims Court and, as comparison, the more formal procedure in the higher courts.

Figure 11-6 Procedure in County Court and in the Supreme Court of a Province

Civil Procedure in Small Claims Court

After months of searching, Ivan is unable to find a summer job. He decides to set up his own business and borrows some money from his father and the family van for this purpose. Ivan's business is to do painting, gardening, and other odd jobs for the residents of his community. One of these residents, Mrs. Blakemore, hears about Ivan's business and hires him to paint her living and dining rooms while she is away on a week's holiday. Ivan shows her the colour charts for the paint and receives a down payment to purchase the paint selected. Ivan and Mrs. Blakemore agree that the balance of the money owed will be $250 and that this will be paid when the job is completed. One week later, the job is finished and Mrs. Blakemore returns from vacation. She refuses to pay Ivan, however, claiming that the paint colour on the walls is not the colour she selected.

—Does Ivan have a cause of action?
—What harm or loss has he suffered?
—What is the probable limitation period for bringing this action? Is there any reason to delay bringing the action?
—Do you expect that Ivan might have difficulty winning this case?

Ivan's situation is an example of a civil dispute that might result in a Small Claims Court action for the collection of a debt. He should first attempt to reach a satisfactory settlement with his customer. However, if this is not possible and he wishes to sue, he must follow the procedure outlined in Figure 11-5 and detailed below.

The Summons or Claim

The first step in a small claims action is to notify both the court and the defendant of the intention to sue. Ivan must go to the Small Claims Court office. Here, the staff will assist him in filling out the necessary forms to begin the suit against Mrs. Blakemore. This process is begun with a legal document. In some provinces, the documents which begins the process is a **summons**, a notice that civil action is being taken. The summons is usually accompanied by a **claim**, a statement of the facts on which the action is based. In some provinces, to simplify the procedure, only one document (either the summons or the claim) is used. Whatever the individual provincial procedure, the purpose of these documents is essentially the same. They indicate to the court the names and addresses of the parties involved, and outline to the court and the defendant the nature of the claim being made. They also contain the plaintiff's view of the facts, including what happened, where it happened, who was involved, the harm suffered, and the compensation or remedy sought. In this case, Ivan would claim for recovery of the $250 agreed on as a balance by him and Mrs. Blakemore. The plaintiff will usually ask for costs in addition to compensation.

Ivan's summons or claim will be filed in the court office as a record of his intent to sue, and a copy will be served on the defendant. In some provinces, a court official, called a *bailiff*, is responsible for serving these documents; in others, doing this is the plaintiff's responsibility.

CLAIM FORM
FORMULAIRE DE DEMANDE

IN THE FIRST SMALL CLAIMS COURT OF THE JUDICIAL DISTRICT OF YORK REGION
DEVANT LA PREMIERE COUR DES PETITES CREANCES DU DISTRICT JUDICIAIRE DE YORK REGION

Between/Entre

Name/Nom: Ivan Pusnik — Plaintiff/Demandeur
Address/Adresse: 123 Main Street

Name/Nom: Phyllis Blakemore — Defendant/Défendeur
Address/Adresse: 456 King Street
Newmarket, Ontario

The Plaintiff claims from the Defendant(s) the sum of
Le demandeur réclame du (des) defendeur(s) la somme de $ 250.00
and costs for the action. Details below:
et les dépens. Détails ci-dessous:

Reason for Claim:
Motifs de la demande: I had an agreement with Mrs. Blakemore to paint her living and dining rooms for $325.00. This work was completed on August 15, 1985. Mrs. Blakemore refuses to pay the balance of $250 as agreed.

Dated at/Fait à Newmarket
this/ce 1st
day of/jour de September 1985

Signature: Ivan Pusnik

SM 004-2 (6/80)

Figure 11-7 *A Claim Form used by York Region Small Claims Court*

The Dispute

Once Mrs. Blakemore, the defendant, receives notice of Ivan's action against her, she has a limited period (usually ten days) to file with the court a document indicating her intent to defend the action. This document is usually called the **dispute**. If she does not respond within the time allowed, the plaintiff, Ivan, will win the case by default.

Mrs. Blakemore has an opportunity at this time to add a **counterclaim** or a **set-off** to the dispute. She may even add a third party to the proceedings, if she feels that someone else is to blame for the injuries the plaintiff claims to have suffered. A counterclaim must directly relate to the problem which caused the plaintiff's claim, while a set-off can be an unrelated debt which the defendant feels the plaintiff owes to him or to her.

—Do you think that Mrs. Blakemore might have either a counterclaim or set-off to Ivan's claim? Explain.

The Trial

The case will usually go to trial within two to four months of beginning the action, depending upon the caseload in the courts. This occurs only, of course, if the parties have not agreed to settle by this time. When the court sets a date for the trial, a *Notice of Trial* is sent to the parties. As mentioned, the simplified procedure of the Small Claims Court makes it unnecessary for either Ivan or Mrs. Blakemore to be represented by a lawyer. In most cases, the litigants can represent themselves. During the trial, both the plaintiff and the defendant take the stand and testify as to the facts of the case. They may call and examine any witnesses and present any relevant written documents as evidence. The rules for giving evidence in Small Claims Court are considerably relaxed, to aid the unrepresented parties in presenting their own cases.

After hearing all of the facts, the judge will make a decision, or judgement. The judgement is usually made at the time of trial, but if the facts of the case are complex, the judge may reserve giving the decision until a later time. If the judgement is in favour of the plaintiff, it will award appropriate compensation to the plaintiff and may include the plaintiff's costs.

Civil Procedure in the Higher Courts

The simplified procedure followed in Small Claims Court allows relatively swift and inexpensive settlement of private disputes. Unfortunately, many civil matters are much more complex than the example given in the case involving Ivan and Mrs. Blakemore; the harm suffered by individuals as the result of the actions of others can often be great. The following is an example of a more serious civil dispute, which would in all likelihood have to be resolved in the higher courts.

Figure 11-8 A more serious situation, such as this one, will likely go before a higher court.

Pina was riding her ten-speed bicycle to her summer job one sunny July morning. As she approached an intersection which did not require her to stop, a car driven by Mr. Ferdinand cut in front of her and made an unsignalled right-hand turn directly in her path. Unable to take any evasive action because of the lack of warning, Pina crashed into the car and was thrown from her bike. Her injuries included a broken arm and leg and assorted cuts and bruises. The bicycle was completely destroyed. Because of her injuries, Pina spent time in the hospital and was unable to return to her summer job. As a result, she was unable to save enough for her college tuition in September and had to borrow from her parents.

—Does Pina have a cause of action?
—Is it likely that Pina could bring this action by herself?
—What is the probable limitation period for bringing this action?
—Can you think of any reason why she might not wish to begin her action immediately?

Pina's accident is an example of a case that would likely go to the County Court level, due to the amount of harm she has suffered. She will likely require the assistance of a lawyer to help her prepare her case adequately for trial. The procedure which Pina must follow to bring her action is outlined in Figure 11-6 and detailed below.

The Writ of Summons and the Appearance

Most civil actions in County and Supreme Court begin with a **Writ of Summons**. (One exception to this rule is a divorce action, which begins with a **petition for divorce**). The Writ of Summons is a document served on the defendant (Mr. Ferdinand) to notify him that a civil action is being taken against him and that he has a limited period in which to respond (*enter an appearance*)if he wishes to defend the action. "Entering an appearance" does not mean, as it would imply, that Mr. Ferdinand must personally appear before the court. Rather, it is the term used to refer to the written response of the defendant. This document indicates that he will defend the action and names the lawyer who will be acting for him. As in a small claims action, failure to respond within the allowed time can lead to a default judgement against the defendant.

Pleadings

The next step in the civil action between Pina and Mr. Ferdinand is to exchange **pleadings**, detailed statements of facts called the **Statement of Claim** and the **Statement of Defence**

The purposes of the pleadings can be summarized as follows:

1. To give fair notice of the action to the parties. The defendant is entitled to know why a claim is being brought and the remedy being sought, and the plaintiff is entitled to know the nature of the defence being raised by the defendant.
2. To define precisely the question(s) or matter(s) in dispute between the parties.
3. To assist the court in its understanding of the dispute.
4. To serve as a record of the issues involved in the case, to prevent future litigation arising out of the same cause of action. For example, if for some reason Pina was unsuccessful in her action against Mr. Ferdinand, she could not at some future date bring this same case to court again. The pleadings serve as a record that this matter has already been litigated once.

The Discovery

The *discovery* is a pre-trial meeting of the parties before a special examiner. Counsel for each of the litigants can examine the other party under oath, and examine documents which will be presented as evidence at the trial. The pleadings are concerned with the facts of the case; the discovery is concerned with the proof of these facts. During the discovery, documents which will be presented in evidence must be produced for examination. As well, witnesses can be examined under oath and a transcript of their evidence prepared for use at the trial. Physical examination of a plaintiff whose claim is based on personal injury can be conducted by a doctor at this stage.

At any step in civil proceedings, it is possible for the parties to reach a settlement without having to go to trial. A frequent result of the discovery is that the parties agree to a settlement, once they have had this opportunity to examine the case of the other side. Even if settlement does not occur, however, the discovery process is useful because it allows the parties to better prepare their cases for trial. It lets them establish what facts, if any, are not in dispute, and examine the evidence which will be presented in court.

—In the civil action between Pina and Mr. Ferdinand, what witnesses might be called during discovery?
—What documents might be examined?
—What facts might be in dispute? undisputed?

The Pre-Trial Conference

In some provinces, including Alberta, British Columbia, Nova Scotia, and Ontario, a **pre-trial conference** may take place several weeks before the trial. This is a meeting between the lawyers for the litigants and a judge or other judicial officer. Once again, the parties seek to clarify and reduce the number of issues in dispute, with the aid of a judge who will often comment on the merits on the case. Pre-trial conferences were introduced to help ease the case load of the courts by helping the parties in civil actions reach settlement without having to go to trial. They have been very successful in doing so, or at least in reducing the amount of time for trying some cases.

—How do the litigants benefit by having their case settled out of court?

The Trial

The time between starting a civil action and having the case heard in the higher courts will usually be longer than for a small claims action. Higher court cases are more complex and difficult to prepare for trial, and the procedure for them is more complicated, as you have seen. Civil trials in the higher courts may be heard by a judge alone or by judge and jury. Certain types of civil wrongs, such as libel and false imprisonment, are almost always heard by a judge and jury. However, civil jury trials are not common in Canada; Ontario has by far the largest percentage of them.

Judges preferred, symposium told
Use of juries falling in civil cases

By MARINA STRAUSS

Judges generally make larger awards than juries in civil cases, according to Supreme Court chief justices in British Columbia and Ontario.

It appears that for this reason juries are not as common as they once were, says Chief Justice Gregory Evans of the Ontario Supreme Court trial division.

"I personally would not like to see the jury disappear in civil cases, because they bring a common sense approach to liability and damages," Chief Justice Evans told the second annual advocacy symposium in Toronto yesterday. The conference was organized by the Law Society of Upper Canada and the Canadian Bar Association-Ontario.

Chief Justice Allan McEachern of the Supreme Court of British Columbia said the "accumulated wisdom of most lawyers is clearly that most cases are better tried by a judge alone," which is a theory he adheres to.

While not calling for the abolition of juries, Chief Justice McEachern questioned whether juries should try complicated civil cases.

In personal injury trials, he said, judges are less likely to make a serious mistake than a jury, and some juries are afraid of the big numbers that judges have become accustomed to.

Chief Justice McEachern suggested that lawyers may not prefer juries because lawsuits tend to be so long, detailed and intensive.

But Mr. Justice Willard Estey of the Supreme Court of Canada predicted that juries will appear more frequently in complex, scientific trials and that people are better equipped to sit on juries because of the increased education, technology and communication in today's society.

Judge Estey also predicted that Ontario will not see huge awards by juries such as those made in the United States.

People are "too wary of get-rich-quick litigation because of a strong sense that jury members have, as members of the public, that they will in the final analysis pay those awards through higher insurance payments and higher taxes," Judge Estey said.

The jury system, Judge Estey said, will become more important as people become concerned about the increasing role that the state plays in their lives.

Chief Justice Evans said that advocates of retaining juries point to the apparent desire of the public to have their disputes disposed of by a jury of their peers.

Provincial legislatures soon will be addressing whether the cost and delay of using juries warrant continuation of the civil jury system, the Ontario Chief Justice said.

Figure 11-9 Summarize the points made by this article for and against the use of juries in civil cases. With which view do you agree?

Some of the reasons for the decline in the number of civil jury trials are as follows:

1. They take up to twice as long to present as civil actions before a judge alone and are therefore more expensive.
2. It frequently takes longer to bring a case to trial if a jury is to be called.
3. Jury verdicts are frequently appealed.

Each of the provinces sets the size of a civil jury. The decision of a civil jury, unlike that of jury in a criminal case, does not have to be unanimous. For example, in Ontario, where six jurors hear a civil action, only five must agree on the decision. Decisions in civil trials are made on a *balance of probabilities*, unlike in criminal matters, where guilt must be proven *beyond a reasonable doubt*. The burden is on the plaintiff to present enough evidence to support his or her claim, and to show that it is more likely than not that the defendant is liable.

—How many jurors does your province require for a civil trial?
—Why do you think the decision of a civil jury is not required to be unanimous?
—As a member of a jury hearing Pina's case against Mr. Ferdinand, would you find for the plaintiff on a "balance of probabilities"? Explain.

Judgement and Damages

In making a finding for the plaintiff, the judge or the jury must consider what harm has been suffered and what the appropriate remedy would be. You saw that in a situation such as Ivan's, the plaintiff would sue for recovery of a debt, whose amount is known. In other situations, such as those involving nuisance or trespass to land, the plaintiff might seek an **injunction** from the court. An injunction is a court order which directs the defendant to cease a certain type of behaviour or activity which is harmful to the plaintiff. In Pina's case, she would sue for **damages**.

"If we sue for half a million, there should be a couple of hundred in it for you."

Two main types of damages exist: special and general. *Special damages* include the plaintiff's out-of-pocket expenses such as medical expenses, loss of wages, and damage to property. *General damages* compensate the plaintiff for such things as pain and suffering and loss of enjoyment of life. *Punitive damages* are rare; they are assessed when the court wishes to impose a punishment on the defendant, whose actions have been particularly reprehensible. *Nominal damages* may be awarded when a legal right has been violated but no substantial harm has been suffered.

Enforcement

Once a plaintiff obtains a judgement in his or her favour, it is the plaintiff's responsibility to enforce the court order. The courts are not collection agencies. It is to be hoped that the defendant has the financial resources to pay the plaintiff promptly. If not, there are certain methods which can be employed. The most common are discussed below.

Garnishment

Garnishment is one method for a successful plaintiff to enforce the judgement. It allows the successful plaintiff to go to the court office and have a form issued which will direct an employer to deduct an amount from the wages of the defendant and direct this amount through the court to the plaintiff. The disadvantage for the plaintiff of this method is that a limit is set on the amount which can be deducted from wages, so that the defendant does not become destitute. Also, the plaintiff must repeat the garnishment procedure each time the unsuccessful defendant receives wages.

Writ of Execution

If the defendant owns real or personal property of value, the plaintiff can have the court issue a **Writ of Execution**. This document allows the sheriff to seize the personal assets of the defendant (with some exceptions) and sell them at public auction if the judgement is not paid within a certain time. This procedure is often called an **attachment of assets**. The Writ of Execution can also be registered against real property (land) owned by the defendant. This registration is called a **lien**; it prevents the defendant from selling, mortgaging, or dealing with the land in other ways until the Writ is removed. If the judgement is still not paid within a certain period, it is possible to force a sale of the property.

Judgement Summons

It is also possible to bring the defendant before a judge by way of a **Judgement Summons** to explain his or her financial position and the reason(s) for non-payment. The court may then order periodic payments until the judgement is satisfied.

Enforcement in Motor Vehicle Cases

A plaintiff who has received a judgement for injuries suffered in a motor vehicle accident may take a certified copy of the judgement to the Registrar of Motor Vehicles. This official is authorized to suspend the driver's licence of the defendant until payment is made.

Insurance against Civil Liability

— Suppose Pina is successful in obtaining a $7000 judgement against Mr. Ferdinand. Will Mr. Ferdinand be responsible for paying this amount out of his own savings?

Although automobile accidents are perhaps the most frequent cause of loss and injury today, people can be seriously injured by many other types of accidents as well. To protect themselves from liability for large amounts of damages, most people carry different types of insurance. Automobile insurance, for instance, is required by law in every province. Homeowners usually also have insurance, to protect themselves in the event that someone is injured on their property. Certain kinds of professionals, such as doctors and lawyers, must have insurance before they can practise.

Any type of insurance will have a monetary limit. If the victim's damages exceed the limit, the defendant must pay the remainder.

— Why do you think the provinces require automobile owners to have liability insurance?
— Do you think it is fair to make people buy insurance?
— What other kinds of liability insurance can you think of?

SUMMARIZING YOUR READING

1. What are two other terms which mean the same as "taking civil action"?

2. What are the parties to a civil action called?

3. What special protections does the court require when a minor or infant is party to a civil action?

4. What are "costs" in a civil action?

5. What is the importance of the saying, "You can't get blood from a stone"?

6. Define "cause of action". What would result if a plaintiff began a lawsuit without having a legally recognized cause of action?

7. What is the purpose of the summons and the claim in a small claims action?

8. What happens if a defendant does not dispute a claim?

9. Why are the rules of procedure relaxed in Small Claims Court?

10. What is the usual method for beginning a civil action in the higher courts?

11. What does "entering an appearance" mean?

12. What are "pleadings"? What purpose do they serve?

13. What purpose does the discovery serve? How does it achieve this purpose?

14. How does a pre-trial conference differ from the discovery?

15. What is the burden of proof on the plaintiff in a civil trial?

16. Distinguish between the two main types of damages.

17. Describe two of the methods available to the successful plaintiff to enforce a judgement.

18. What purpose does liability insurance serve?

DISCUSSING KEY ISSUES

1. Seventeen-year-old Judy was driving her car along Eglinton Avenue in Toronto on a rainy afternoon. As the diagram below illustrates, Eglinton at this point is six lanes wide, with parking along the curb lanes. Judy was driving at the speed limit. As she pulled into the right lane to pass a truck, Tony stepped out of his parked car without looking. Two fingers of Tony's left hand were severed when they became caught between his car door and Judy's vehicle. Tony was left-handed. He was thirty-five at the time of the accident, and married with two children. Before the accident, he was a carpenter, but afterwards he was unable to practise his craft.

(a) As a juror sitting for this case, what factors would you take into consideration when determining liability? Be specific. Refer

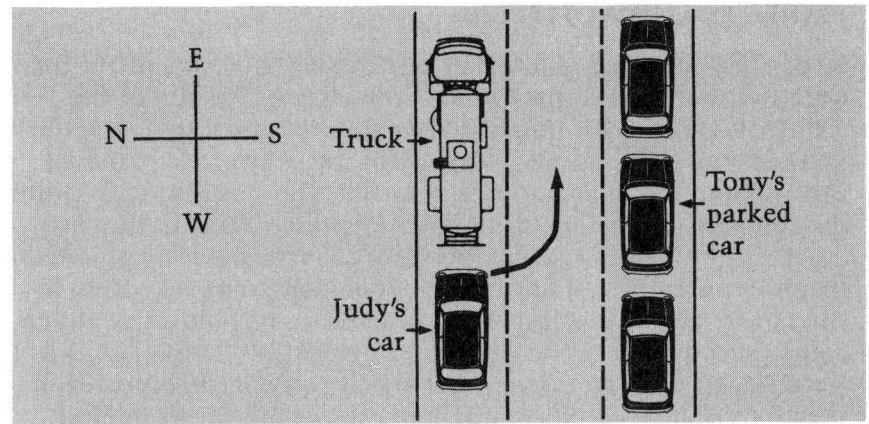

Figure 11-10

to the principles of negligence and the possible defences outlined in Chapter 10.

(b) If Judy is found liable, what factors would you consider when assessing the amount of damages? What kinds of damages would you award?

2. The courts try to put a money value on a plaintiff's pain and suffering, shortened life expectancy, loss of wages, loss of limbs, and other harm and losses. What happens if the victim of a car accident negligently caused dies instantly? In the past, the courts said that any tort action died with the victim, since there was no loss or harm in the ordinary sense. It was therefore said that it was better to kill your victim than to just injure him or her. The unfairness of this rule led to the passage in every province of statutes which allow the deceased's estate or the survivors to sue the wrongdoer for damages. There are usually two kinds of actions: (a) for the deceased's losses, such as funeral expenses; and (b) for the deceased's dependant's losses, such as loss of financial support.

(a) What damages should parents receive if their child is killed? Should it matter how old the child is at the time of death?

(b) A mother of two young children is struck and killed by a car while shopping. She was a full-time homemaker. What damages should her family recover?

(c) A woman undergoes a sterilization procedure. She becomes pregnant a few months later. Should she be able to sue the doctor (in what is known as a *wrongful life action*) who performed the operation? Would it make any difference if the child is born handicapped or with a hereditary disease?

(d) A man is injured and suffers continuous pain. He eventually commits suicide. Should his family be able to bring an action for wrongful death against the person responsible for the original injuries?

PROJECTS AND ACTIVITIES

1. (a) The Attorney-General of each province is responsible for the administration of the courts. Contact the Ministry of the Attorney-General for information about the court structure in your province, including the names of the courts, their areas of jurisdiction, and appeal routes. Prepare a chart outlining the information you have gathered, and make a presentation to the class.

(b) Contact the Small Claims Court in your area and obtain the forms required by a plaintiff and a defendant in a civil action in this court, as well as pamphlets available to the public describing court procedures.

(c) Locate as many newspaper articles as you can illustrating the kinds of civil actions brought in each of the courts of your province. Create a bulletin board display with all of the information you have gathered for this activity.

2. Name the court in your province which would likely hear each of the following actions:

   (a) a motor accident claim for $7000
   (b) an accident between a car and a Canada Post van
   (c) a deserted wife bringing an action against her husband for child support
   (d) a man suing his wife for divorce on the grounds of adultery
   (e) a person defaulting on a loan of $500 from a finance company
   (f) the defendant in an action for $40 000 wishing to appeal the jury's finding
   (g) a suit involving libel
   (h) a civil appeal from the provincial Supreme Court, appeal division
   (i) an employer that does not pay the required 4% vacation pay to a summer student, amounting to $60
   (j) an appeal from Small Claims Court

3. British Columbia is one of the provinces which has a "no-fault" system of car insurance. In this system, the insurer pays damages to whoever is injured, regardless of who was at fault in the accident. Research no-fault insurance schemes and write a report outlining their advantages and disadvantages.

12

An Introduction to Contracts

> Forms of Contracts
> Necessary Elements
> Offer and Acceptance
> Consideration

Every day, people make agreements with one another. Some of these are purely informal social agreements—promises to meet for a date, or to telephone a friend. Other agreements are more formal; these may be considered **contracts**. What is the difference between a social agreement and a contract? The main difference is that if you agree to do something in a contract, a court will *enforce* that agreement, while it will not enforce or in any way become involved with a purely social agreement.

You may be wondering how to go about making a contract. However, you have already done it many times, probably without even realizing it. A contract is made and carried out every time you buy something. A contract is also made when you rent something, like skis or rollerskates. In the latter situation, the contract you have made says that the rental company must let you use the equipment for some length of time and that you must pay them a certain amount and take reasonable care of the goods. If you have a summer job, the contract between you and your employer says that you will work specified hours and in exchange you will be paid a certain amount of money.

What, then, is a contract? A contract can be defined as an agreement between two or more people, which the law will enforce, to do or not do something. Contracts range from the very simple to the complex. A contract to buy a house can be extremely complicated and difficult to understand without the help of a lawyer. The contract that you make in buying a record or a chocolate bar is very simple. Whether simple or complex, however, all contracts contain certain basic elements. They are the subject of this chapter and the two chapters following.

Figure 12-1
Because contracts are generally binding at law, it is important to read them carefully before signing.

Forms of Contracts

Contracts fall into two main types: **contracts under seal** and **simple contracts**.

Contracts under Seal

Contracts under seal are also known as **specialty contracts**. A seal originally consisted of a large drop of sealing wax, into which the party making the contract would impress his or her family ring. The emblem on the ring identified the person and acted in place of a signature, showing that the person intended to be bound by the terms of the contract. This was the procedure for making important contracts centuries ago, when few people could read or write. The rest of the contract would be written out by a cleric (monk or priest), since the clergy were literate for the most part.

Today, a seal generally consists only of a small red sticker, or a dot printed on the contract, or even the word "Seal". The use of a seal is still required in some provinces for certain types of contracts such as sales of land and mortgages. Its presence indicates that the parties to the contract thought about it carefully and seriously, and intend to be bound by it.

Simple Contracts

A simple contract is any contract which is not under seal. It may be made orally or in writing, or it may be *implied* by conduct or performance. Oral, or **parol**, contracts may pose some problems. If such a contract is not carried out immediately, it may be very difficult to prove that a contract exists at all, unless there were witnesses. Even if the existence of the contract can be shown, the terms of the contract may become unclear over a period of time. Each party is relying on the honesty and the good memory of the other. For these reasons, it is always best to put longer-term contracts into written form.

You may be wondering how a contract can be implied by conduct or performance. Think of the following scenario: You go into a store, pick up a magazine, and place the correct amount of money on the counter. The clerk picks up the money and you walk out; neither of you has said a word. A contract has been made by performance. Nothing was spoken; nothing was written; but you and the clerk, by your actions, have formed a contract.

—Give examples of oral, written, and implied contracts.

Necessary Elements

In order for a contract to be valid, five elements must be present:

1. an offer and an acceptance
2. consideration
3. legal capacity of the parties
4. genuine consent
5. legal purpose

This chapter will examine the first two requirements; Chapter 13 will examine the other three.

Offer and Acceptance

As you are driving away in the car your mother lent you for this Saturday evening, you look at the gas gauge and see that the tank is almost empty. You pull into the nearest gas station. The attendant walks up to the car. "Ten dollars worth of unleaded regular, please," you say. "Okay," says the attendant. The two of you have just fulfilled one of the requirements for forming a contract: the making of an **offer**, and the acceptance of that offer. When you drove in to the station and asked for ten dollars worth of unleaded regular, you were making an offer to buy ten dollars worth of that fuel at the price posted on the pumps. An offer is a promise by one party (the **offeror**) to do something if the other party will agree to some specific condition or request. When the attendant said "Okay", your offer was accepted. Acceptance is the agreement by the other party (the **offeree**) to the condition or request specified in the offer.

Validity of the Offer

A valid offer has three essential elements:

1. It must be seriously intended.
2. It must contain definite terms.
3. It must be communicated.

Serious Intent

Suppose that you are in a group of people watching the swim team practise. Most of the observers are watching one particularly good athlete. The woman standing next to you turns and says, "I'd give my life savings if someone would teach me to swim like that." Being short of cash, you say, "I'll do it." Have you just made a contract? Does the woman have to pay you all her life savings for swimming lessons? Of course not. The offer was not made seriously. Although the woman probably *would* like to swim like the athlete, her "offer" was not serious—it was merely a figure of speech. Therefore, no valid offer was made.

Definite Terms

If a contract is for the sale of goods, the offer should generally include the price, a description of the goods, the delivery date, and any other critical piece of information. However, these terms do not always have to be stated specifically. When you go into a variety store and ask for a chocolate bar of a particular type, at least two things are assumed in your offer. It is assumed that delivery will take place immediately, and also that the price agreed upon is the "going" price for that particular bar. The fact that these two things are not expressed does not mean that they are not part of the offer, however.

Is it possible to make a contract and settle a major term, such as the price, later? The answer is usually "No", unless the contract itself specifies how the term is to be settled. For example, in the sale of a piece of land, it might be stated in the contract that the price will be determined by an independent appraisal. In general, if the parties do not agree on the price or on how it will be determined, there is no contract. Consider the following case:

Bowden and Bowden v. Shaw (1979) 34 N.S.R. (2d) 518 (N.S.S.C.)

The Bowdens asked the court to enforce a contract for the sale of a mobile home. When the plaintiffs had negotiated the purchase of the mobile home from the defendant all terms had been agreed to, with the exception of the price.

The court held that there was no contract which it could enforce. The court stated that it would not make a contract from indefinite terms for the parties. The contract would not be complete until the parties had agreed on the price.

Communication

Communication implies that the offer must be both sent by the offeror and received by the offeree. If an offer you send by mail gets lost, so that the offeror never receives it, the offer has not been communicated. If that same offer is delivered to the wrong person, who reads it, it still has not been communicated to the offeree. Again, no offer has been made.

Figure 12-2 Communication is one of the essential ingredients of a valid offer. What are the other two?

Say you have lost an expensive watch and have put a notice in the classified section of the newspaper offering a reward for its return. What would happen if a person found your watch and returned it to you without seeing the notice? Would you be legally required to give that person the reward? The answer is "No". An offer cannot be accepted before it has been communicated to the offeree. In this situation, the watch was returned before the offeree knew there was a reward for its return. It is impossible for a person to accept an offer of which he or she is unaware.

Advertisements

Figure 12-3

> CROSS COUNTRY SKI PACKAGE
>
> including
>
> SKIS
> BINDINGS
> POLES
> BOOTS
> For a limited time only
> $99.99

Is this advertisement an offer to sell a cross country ski package for $99.99 to the general public? According to contract law, it is not. Usually, an advertisement is considered to be an *invitation* to do business or to take offers, and not an offer. In other words, the advertisement above indicates that if a person comes into the store and offers $99.99 for the package, the store's workers will accept it. Nevertheless, under contract law, they do not have to accept this or any other offer. If they do not do so in this situation, however, they might be charged with misleading advertising under consumer protection legislation. Similarly, items on display in a store are invitations to do business. It is the buyer who makes an offer in taking the goods to the cashier. The case that decided whether the display of goods was an offer or not is the following:

Pharmaceutical Society of Great Britain v. Boots Cash Chemists (Southern) Ltd. (1952) All E.R. 456

Boots was charged with selling a drug in violation of a statute which required the sale of certain drugs to be supervised by a pharmacist. To comply with the statute, the store had a pharmacist stationed near the cash register. However, if the display was an offer, then the sale would take place when the customer accepted the offer by taking the drug off the shelf, and not when paying at the cash register.

The English Court of Appeal held that the sale was made when the customer took the goods to the register. The customer made an offer at that time. When the cashier entered the sale into the cash register, the offer was considered to be accepted.

—Do you agree with this rule of law?
—What would be the result if displays were considered offers?

Although the general rule is that advertisements are not offers, there are exceptions. Consider the following case:

Carlill v. Carbolic Smoke Ball Co. (1893) 1 Q.B. 256 (C.A.)

The Carbolic Smoke Ball Co. advertised in a newspaper that they would pay a reward of £100 to anyone who used their smoke balls three times a day for two weeks and then caught influenza. The money for the reward was deposited in a bank to show the company's serious intent, according to the advertisement.

Carlill did, in fact, catch influenza after using the smoke balls as directed. She wrote to the company to claim her reward. The company refused to pay, saying that the advertisement was simply an invitation to take offers and was not an offer itself. Carlill sued, arguing that she was accepting their offer by taking the smoke balls as directed.

The court found that, in this case, the offer of a reward constituted an intention to become involved in a legally binding contract; therefore, the advertisement was an offer. Carlill, by using the product as directed in the advertisement, was accepting that offer. Thus, a contract had been formed. The Carbolic Smoke Ball Co. was required to pay Carlill the £100 reward.

An advertisement, then, *can* be considered to be an offer, if it is worded in such a way that it appears to convey a seriously intended offer. Notice, too, that it is not necessary for an offer to be made to just one person to be valid. It is clear from the example of the reward for the lost watch and from the *Carlill* case that an offer can be made to the world at large.

Terminating the Offer

An offeror has the right to terminate an offer by **revoking** (withdrawing) it at any time before it is accepted. However, the offeree must have notice of the revocation. Notification may be direct; the offeror may simply notify the offeree that the offer has been withdrawn. Notification can also be indirect: it is considered valid even if the offeree hears from a third party that the offeror has sold the item in question to someone else.

Another way to terminate an offer is to let it lapse (come to an end). An offer lapses if it is rejected, or if the time specified in the offer for acceptance passes. If no particular time was specified, the offer lapses when a "reasonable" length of time passes, or if the offeror or offeree dies, becomes bankrupt, or is declared insane.

An offer is also terminated when a **counter-offer** is made by the offeree. In a counter-offer, the offeree makes a new offer instead of accepting the original one. Thus, the roles of the offeror and offeree are reversed.

—How do you think the courts decide what is a "reasonable" time for holding open an offer? Would the type of goods involved—perishable crops, stocks, real property in a stable real estate market—have any bearing on such a decision? Explain.

Validity of the Acceptance

Like an offer, an **acceptance** must meet certain requirements in order to be valid. The absence of a valid acceptance of an offer will prevent a contract from being formed. A valid acceptance can be broken down into two essential elements:

1. It requires a positive action, usually communication.
2. It must be unconditional.

Positive Action

You ask a friend whether you can rent his camping trailer so that you may go on a week's camping trip. He tells you that another friend has asked about renting the trailer, and he thinks it might be for the same week as you want it. You say that, if he can't rent it to you, he should let you know. Otherwise, you will pick up the trailer at the appropriate time. You hear nothing from him in the next while, so when you are ready for your trip, you go to his house to pick up the trailer. His sister tells you that he has just taken it on a two-week trip. You're disappointed. You thought you had a contract: that there had been an offer and an acceptance. In fact, there was no contract because, although there was a valid offer, no acceptance was communicated or indicated by an action. In general, acceptance cannot be by means of silence.

Some provinces have passed legislation to stress this concept. For example, Manitoba, British Columbia, and Prince Edward Island have made it illegal to distribute credit cards that were not requested. Saskatchewan and Ontario have legislation stating that anyone who receives unsolicited goods may treat them as gifts and use them without paying for them.

One exception to the rule that acceptance requires positive action occurs when the parties have agreed beforehand that silence means acceptance. One example is in the operation of book clubs. When a member is offered a new book and wishes to receive it by mail, he or she does nothing (acceptance by silence). Only if the member does not wish to receive the book must he or she do something—fill in the card offering the book with a refusal and send the refusal card back to the book club.

In some situations, an offer may be accepted by performance of an action. When it is implied by the offer that notice of such acceptance is not necessary, the acceptance need not be communicated. Think back to the case of *Carlill v. Carbolic Smoke Ball Co.* Carlill accepted the offer by using the smoke balls as directed.

Unconditional Acceptance

No changes in the offer may be made by a party who is going to accept it. The reason is simple. It is not possible to accept something which the offerer has not offered. As well, it is not possible to reject an offer and then to accept it at a later date. As mentioned earlier, once an offer is rejected, it is no longer in effect. However, an offeree may ask an offeror for explanations. For example, if you were going to buy a snowmobile, you might ask whether the price included the trailer attached to it. This is not asking for a change in the offer, but simply for a point of clarification.

JANE: I hear you want to sell your record collection. I'll give you $100 for it. (Offer)

GUNTHER: Are you kidding? It's worth a lot more than that. I could let you have it for $175 though. (A new offer, or counter-offer, is made.)

JANE: That's too much. I won't pay that much. (Counter-offer is rejected.) How about $125? (Another counter-offer is made.)

GUNTHER: You know you're getting a deal but okay. I'll take the $125. (Acceptance)

In the exchange above, there were a number of offers and counter-offers before there was finally an acceptance. The original offer of $100 was made by Jane. When Gunther made the counter-offer of $175, the original offer was automatically cancelled or revoked, and the new one was in effect. Jane then rejected Gunther's counter-offer. At this point no offer was in effect. Jane next made a counter-offer of $125, which Gunther accepted. At this time, only the offer of $125 could be accepted, because it was the only one that was in effect.

When Is A Contract Formed?

It is important for both the offeror and the offeree to know exactly when the contract is formed, because once it is, they are both bound by its terms. The general rule is that there is a contract as soon as the offeror receives a valid acceptance from the offeree. This rule works fine when the parties are dealing face to face. However, for situations where they are at some distance from each other and are using the mail or some other means of negotiating, the courts have developed certain exceptions to this rule. Why was this done? When parties deal face to face, both know immediately when the contract is formed. However, if the mail, for instance, is used, one party will necessarily be unaware of whether there is a contract while the acceptance is in the mail. Consider the following situation:

Alf sends a letter offering to sell his car to Berthe for $3000. He says: "Write to let me know if you want the car." A couple of days later, Cara hears that the car is on the market and offers Alf $3500 for it. The same day that Cara makes her offer, Berthe drops a letter in the mailbox accepting Alf's offer. Can Alf call Berthe to revoke his offer and then accept Cara's offer, or is he bound by Berthe's acceptance?

The question that arises here is, When is the contract made? When does the offeree make a valid acceptance? In this instance, does acceptance occur when Berthe puts her letter of acceptance in the mail? Or does acceptance occur only when Alf receives Berthe's letter?

In this situation, once Berthe has put her letter of acceptance in the mail, Alf cannot revoke his offer to her and sell his car to Cara. The rule is that if the offeror says that acceptance may be made by mail, the acceptance is valid when it is put in the mailbox. The same rule applies to the use of a telegram. That is, if the offeror says that acceptance may be made by telegram, the contract is formed when the acceptance is delivered to the telegraph office.

However, an offer might not specify how acceptance is to be made. In this event, the courts have said that in any situation where it seems reasonable to use mail for acceptance, acceptance will be valid when posted. For example, the fact that the offeror has mailed the offer implies that acceptance by mail is reasonable. This rule also applies to acceptance by telegram. However, if the offer states that acceptance should be made in a specific way, for example, by telephone, and the offeree mails or telegraphs the acceptance, the contract is not formed until the acceptance is actually received by the offeror.

It is also the offeror's option to state that acceptance will be valid only when received, or that it must be made a certain way. The offeree must then follow the directions of the offeror to make a valid acceptance.

Standard Form Contracts

The principles of offer and acceptance assume that there is some form of bargaining going on between the parties. Although this is true for some situations, such as the buying of a house, in most transactions the terms are set for specific goods on a "take it or leave it" basis. The *standard form contract* has been developed to suit the needs of modern business. In such a contract, all of the terms are on a pre-printed form which the consumer need only sign. The standard form contract is simply presented, and usually either accepted "as is" or rejected. It is useful for consumers to be aware that, even though by law some terms are not permitted in particular types of contracts, standard form contracts are often in favour of the seller. For example, such a contract may attempt to limit the liability of the seller if the product injures the consumer. Or a contract used by a hotel may state that it is not responsible for the lost or stolen property of its guests.

Suppose that you and your family have decided to go to the Bahamas for spring break. You decide to accompany your parents in picking up the airline tickets. On the way home in the car, you look at the tickets and notice that they have some small print on the back which seems to be the terms of the contract. You know that your parents have not even looked at the back of the tickets. Could they be bound by the contract? What if the back of the ticket says that there will be no refund if the parties cancel their reservation? The first thing to do in answering these questions is to check whether it was apparent that there was some form of contract on the back of the ticket. On the front of the ticket there will likely be a statement referring to the back, or just the words "See Back/*Au Verso*". Either would make it apparent that some part of the agreement was on the back.

The next thing to check is whether the contract was truly legible. Obviously, if the print was so small or so blurred that it could not be read by the average person, it would not be "communicated" in the true sense of the word.

Figure 12-4 A standard form contract must state clearly where the conditions of the contract are set out.

Would your parents, therefore, be bound by the conditions? The answer is "Yes", if the print was legible and the conditions of the back were apparent.

The general rule, then, is that the offeree is bound by the conditions of any contract which he or she freely enters. However, if the offeree did not read the contract and was not advised to read it, or if the offeree was not given reasonable notice of the terms, the courts might find that the contract is not binding.

Under some circumstances, even a standard form contract's terms may be changed before the offeree signs. Sometimes the offeree is concerned about some aspect of a contract. It may happen that a representative of the business will assure the offeree orally that the concern will be taken care of and the offeree has nothing to worry about. In fact, there may be something to worry about. A legal principle known as the **parol evidence rule** states that terms to which the parties have agreed but which have not been included in the contract cannot be used to add to or contradict the written contract. That is, oral terms, even those agreed to by both parties, are not legally binding. This rule applies equally to written terms which have not been included in the final contract. In summary, any addition to or deletion from a written contract must be included in the contract in writing, and must be signed by both parties. However, many businesses are unwilling to allow any changes to their standard form contracts.

Consideration

The second element necessary to the formation of a valid contract is **consideration**. In every contract, there must be something that makes the parties want to enter into an agreement, something that will benefit them both. The "price" or benefit is known as consideration.

Consideration can take many forms, but there are three main categories: money, goods and services, and forbearance. Money is likely the best known, as it is most common. Goods, material things like a car or a stereo, are also a common form of consideration. Services are non-material things such as travel on an airplane or admission to a theatre or the filling of a cavity in your tooth. Forbearance is the giving up of a right which you would normally have. Suppose that your friend Wanda owes you $50, to be paid by the end of the week. Near the end of the week, she comes to you and says that she will not be able to repay the money at that time. However, she proposes that, if you allow her to pay a week late, she will give you an additional $5. Is consideration present on both sides? There is—you are to receive an extra $5; Wanda is receiving the right to keep your money for an additional week (your forbearance).

As well, it is not necessary to receive consideration directly for a contract to be valid. For instance, you could pay a jeweller to make a necklace or a ring as a gift for a friend of yours. Although you would be giving consideration (payment), you would not be receiving any in return directly; your friend would be getting the piece of jewellery instead. Nevertheless, consideration exists on both sides.

Consider another situation. You offer to shovel the driveway of a neighbour who will be vacationing in Europe for two months. It is understood that you will not be paid. For the first month, you keep the driveway clear of snow. You realize, however, that you are not going to have enough time to do the work regularly because of your involvement in extramural activities at school. Your neighbour is very upset when he returns and finds his driveway blocked, and threatens to sue you. Does he have grounds for suing? The answer is "No". You agreed to do the work without receiving any payment (that is, *gratuitously*), and so have not been receiving any consideration. Thus, there is no contract. As you know, consideration must be given and received by both parties to a contract.

The single exception to the rule that consideration must be received by both parties occurs in contracts under seal. Such contracts are enforceable even if there is no consideration, since the use of the seal indicates that both parties thought seriously about the contract before entering it.

Consideration cannot be given for something a person is already legally bound to do. Suppose that, because you have not been doing very well in school, your father approaches your teacher, asking him to give you assistance during class. Your father tells the teacher that he would be pleased to take him on a fishing trip in return. The teacher agrees. Later, when the teacher asks about the trip, your father indicates that he has no intention of paying a teacher for doing the job he is supposed to do anyway. Can the teacher sue in order to get the trip? The answer is again "No". A teacher is legally required to teach his students, so you are entitled to all the benefit of his expertise and skill during class time.

Mme La Ferrière promises to give her granddaughter Marie $500 when Marie graduates from high school.

—Is this promise enforceable?
—What consideration is Mme La Ferrière receiving?
—How could Marie ensure that a court would enforce her grandmother's promise?

Partial Payment of a Debt

Your brother owes you $10, and you have agreed that he should pay it back in two weeks' time. At the end of the two weeks, he comes to you and says he has only $9 and asks you to accept what he has and let the other dollar go. You are feeling generous and agree. A week later you could use some money. Are you bound by your promise not to ask for the dollar? Can you collect the rest of the debt? The answer depends on which province you live in. In Québec, New Brunswick, Nova Scotia, Prince Edward Island, and Newfoundland, an agreement to clear a debt by paying less money will not be enforced by the courts. The agreement is invalid, according to the common law, because no new consideration has been given for the reduction of the debt. In these provinces, you can still collect the other dollar. The remaining provinces have passed legislation saying that if a partial payment of a debt is accepted as complete payment, there is no longer a debt. In these provinces, you could not collect the other dollar.

—Why do you think the common law has been changed by some provinces?
—Can you think of ways to avoid this rule?
—What if your brother gave you the $9 a week before it was due? Would you be receiving consideration then?

Adequacy of Consideration

While visiting a friend, you are shown a piece of old jewellery. Although the friend is not fond of it, you think it is pretty and decide that your mother would like it for a birthday present. You offer to buy it from your friend for $10, and she accepts. You do not have any money with you at the time, so you arrange to pay for it in a couple of days. You take the jewellery and go home. When you return to your friend's house with the payment, you are told that she wants a lot more money for it. Apparently, two or three months earlier, her mother had had the piece appraised, and learned that it was worth about $250. Will a court require you to pay the appraised value? The answer is "No". You have made a legal agreement, and even though the consideration (price) may not be adequate, the contract is still enforceable. The courts are not involved in making good deals for people or in protecting them from making bad deals. It is assumed that people agree only to contracts which they consider to be acceptable.

Bank of Nova Scotia v. MacLellan (1977) 78 DLR (3d) 1 (N.S.S.C.)

Mrs. MacLellan and her husband obtained a loan from the Bank of Nova Scotia for $5940. Both Mr. and Mrs. MacLellan signed the promissory note. Subsequently, the MacLellans were divorced. Not being able to pay the full amount of the loan remaining, Mrs.

MacLellan arranged with the bank to pay 25% of the remaining balance ($610). Mrs. MacLellan promised to help find her ex-husband, so that he could make the rest of the payment. The Bank later rejected the settlement, claiming that there was no new or additional consideration.

—Who was responsible for paying for the loan?
—Was there consideration for the agreement between Mrs. MacLellan and the bank? Explain.
—How does the adequacy of consideration affect the enforceability of an agreement?

Although consideration does not need to be adequate, it does need to have some value. Value means that it must be measurable in financial terms. Such things as love, friendship, and gratitude are not measureable in money, and so cannot be valid consideration. They are referred to by the odd term **good consideration**.

Promises of Gifts and Pledges

Telethons have become a common way to raise money for various charitable organizations. During telethons, frequent requests for pledges are made. Can a person who pledges some money be bound to pay? Usually, the courts hold that because there is no exchange of consideration, there can be no contract and the person cannot be required to pay. However, if the pledge is for a *specific* project such as the building of a new research laboratory, and the charity has started work on the project, a court may require the person to pay the pledge. The courts have said that the completion of the specific project is the "price" paid for the pledge. That is, the consideration received is knowing that the charity will be able to construct its building, do research, or whatever. If, however, the money pledged is to go into a general fund or is not used for the specific project it was pledged for, payment cannot be enforced. Of course, pledges made under seal are enforceable.

Past and Future Consideration

Suppose that, last summer at the cottage, your neighbours gave you the use of their boat on many occasions. It made your summer much more enjoyable, because your family does not own a boat. Since both cottages have been winterized, the families intend to use them during the winter. You tell your neighbours that, because they were so kind in lending you the boat during the summer, they may use your snowmobile during the winter at the cottage. It sounds good to them and they agree. However, during the winter, you decide to take the snowmobile home at the end of each weekend for safekeeping. Can your neighbours demand that you make your snowmobile available to them during the entire winter? They cannot—you are receiving no new consideration for the promise that you have made, so there can be no contract. You promised to make your snowmobile available out of gratitude for something that has been done in the past. **Past consideration** is not enforceable.

The Québec Nordiques want to trade one of their players. In discussions with the Vancouver Canucks, it is established that although Vancouver would like to have the player, they have no-one suitable whom they would wish to trade for him. They suggest that Québec can have their first draft choice in the next year. Québec agrees, and the Nordique becomes a Canuck.

The consideration that Vancouver receives in this situation is the player. The team receives it immediately. However, the Nordiques are to receive their consideration in the future. Such consideration is therefore referred to as **future consideration**. Future consideration *is* enforceable.

SUMMARIZING YOUR READING

1. Define "contract". How is a contract different from other agreements?

2. What is a contract "under seal"?

3. What forms may a simple contract take?

4. Explain what is meant by an implied contract. Give an original example.

5. Name two of the advantages of using a written contract instead of an oral one.

6. What are the five necessary elements that must be met if a contract is to be enforceable?

7. Who is the offeror? the offeree?

8. How does one determine whether an offer was seriously intended?

9. What is the effect of not deciding an essential term of a contract when the contract is made?

10. Must an offer be communicated? What are the two parts of communication?

11. Why is the method of communicating acceptance important?

12. What is the effect of the statement, "If I do not hear from you, I will assume you have accepted my offer"?

13. Why must an offer be accepted unconditionally?

14. What is the effect of a counter-offer?

15. List eight ways in which an offer can be terminated.

16. What may be the effect of not examining a standard form contract carefully? What factors will a court consider when deciding whether a consumer is bound by a standard form contract?

17. What legal rule applies to the effect of oral promises on a written agreement? Given this rule, how is it possible to make changes to any written agreement, including a standard form contract?

18. Define "consideration".

19. Why is consideration not a necessary element in a contract under seal?

20. What are the three main forms of consideration? Explain each.

21. Give an original example showing that something a person is legally bound to do cannot be given as consideration.

22. In your province, if a person accepts a lesser amount as full payment of a debt, is the debt considered fully cleared?

23. Why is good consideration not valid consideration?

24. Distinguish between past consideration and future consideration. Which is enforceable, and why?

PROJECTS AND ACTIVITIES

1. With another student, come to an agreement on the sale of something you own. Write the agreement in such a way that it includes the elements of a contract examined so far. Could an argument be made that the agreement is not enforceable? (If you and your partner disagree about the enforceability of the agreement, have another student listen to your arguments and decide who is right.) With your partner, determine the following:
    (a) What was the offer?
    (b) What, if any, were the counter-offers?
    (c) What was the acceptance?
    (d) What was the consideration for each party in the agreement?
    (e) Was the consideration on both sides valid?

2. Obtain a standard contract from a local business. Examine it carefully to discover the store's obligations and the customer's obligations. Make a list of all of these. Present them to the class for discussion. Take any questions the class might have to the business (or ask the owner/manager to come to class). Report to the class on the response of the business to the questions.

Evaluate the fairness of the contract. What might you want added? What would you like to see removed?

3. Look through magazines and newspapers in your library or at home to find articles dealing with contracts. These might involve the hiring of film stars or sports figures, sales, or many other matters. Photocopy or summarize these articles, and keep them in a file or a scrap book. Make arrangements with your teacher to report on them to the class. Once a week should be often enough. This project can continue until your study of contracts is complete.

4. Make a list of three or four contracts that you or members of your family have made recently.

   (a) Who made the offer? What was it? What was the acceptance?
   (b) What consideration did each party give?
   (c) In what form were the contracts (written, oral, or implied?)
   (d) Were any counter-offers made?

Bring your list to class for discussion.

5. A recent movement in Canada and the United States has been promoting the use of plain English, instead of legal terminology, in consumer contracts. Research this movement, paying special attention to the following:

   (a) The effect on consumers of having easily readable contracts.
   (b) The amount of acceptance by businesses.
   (c) How plain English contracts are interpreted by the courts.

RESOLVING CASES

Re Gibbons (1977) 22 Nfld. & P.E.I.R. 529 (Nfld. T.D.)

Gibbons, a builder, submitted a tender (an offer) to the Newfoundland Department of Forestry and Agriculture to construct a road for $80 300. The government required a deposit of 5% of the offer to be submitted with the offer. Gibbon's offer was accepted, but attached to the contract he was to sign was a memo. It said that in addition to the equipment Gibbon had offered to supply he would also have to supply any dump trucks the government engineer felt were necessary. Gibbons refused to go ahead with the altered contract and sued for the return of his deposit. The Department claimed that there was a valid contract, and since Gibbons would not perform, the government was entitled to keep the deposit.

—Was there a contract?
—What was the offer? the acceptance?

Friesen et al. v. Braun et al. (1950) 2 D.L.R. 250 (Man. K.B.)

Two brothers, the Friesens, entered into a contract with the Braun sisters to lease property on which the brothers operated a store. The lease also gave the Friesens the right to buy the property for a certain sum. However, the lease stated that the terms regarding how and when payment was to be made would be "discussed and decided upon by the parties at the time of the sale."

The brothers attempted to purchase the property, but the sisters refused to sell it to them. The Friesens sued for **specific performance** of the contract, that is, for a court order requiring the Brauns to live up to the terms of the contract and sell the property.

—Who do you think won this case? Explain your reasoning.

Tilden Rent-a-Car Co. v. Clendenning (1978) 83 D.L.R. (3d) 400 (Ont. C.A.)

Clendenning rented a car from Tilden. A clerk asked whether he wanted extra insurance coverage, and Clendenning indicated that he did. Without reading the contract he signed it. The contract included a statement that said that the customer acknowledged reading the contract. It also had a statement that said that, for the extra coverage that was purchased, the renter's liability was nil unless he was in violation of any provision of the agreement. On the back of the agreement was a condition stating that the customer must not operate the vehicle after consuming alcohol. Clendenning had been told when he had rented cars from Tilden before that the extra coverage meant a full non-deductible insurance.

After having had a very moderate amount of alcohol, Clendenning was involved in an accident. His ability to drive was found unaffected by the alcohol. Tilden sued for damages.

At trial, it was noted that Tilden advertised that a special feature of dealing with them was that a car could be rented speedily.

In a 2-1 decision, the Court of Appeal found for the defendant, Clendenning.

—What effect do you think Tilden's advertisement had on the outcome of the case?
—What general rule does court follow when a person signs a contract without reading it?
—Why do you think this general rule did not apply to this case? What might the clerk have done to make all of the provisions enforceable?
—If you had been the dissenting judge, what reasoning would you have applied to this case?

Dyck v. Manitoba Snowmobile Association [1981] 5 W.W.R. 97 (Man. Q.B.)

The plaintiff, Dyck, an experienced racer, took part in a snowmobile race at Beausejour, Manitoba. To register for the race, he read and signed an entry form which contained the following clause:

"INDEMNIFYING RELEASE"

"I have read the supplementary regulations issued for this event and agree to be bound by them. In consideration of acceptance of this entry or my being permitted to take part in this event, I AGREE TO SAVE HARMLESS AND KEEP INDEMNIFIED the M.S.A. and/or the M.S.A., its organizers, and their respective agents, officials, servants and representatives from and against all claims, actions, costs and expenses and demands in respect to death, injury, loss or damage to my person or property, howsoever caused, arising out of or in connection with my taking part in this event and not withstanding that the same may have been contributed to or occasioned by the negligence of the said bodies, or any of them, their agents, officials, servants or representatives. It is understood and agreed that this Agreement is to be binding on myself, my heirs, executors and assigns.

"IN WITNESS WHEREOF I/we have hereunder set my/our hand and seal this day of"

"'February 23, 1975'

"'[illegible]'   X _____ 'Ron Dyck'"
"(witness)

As Dyck was crossing the finish line, the official starter moved onto the track. Dyck's snowmobile hit the starter and then struck the track wall, seriously injuring Dyck.

Dyck sued the Association and the starter for damages for his injuries. He claimed that although he had read the form before this and other races, he did not know what it meant. He said that it was "mumbo jumbo" to him. He had never asked for an explanation of the clause.

—Should the exemption clause protect the Association? Give your judgement.

A.E. Hickman Company Limited v. Roses Aluminium Limited and Rose (1981) 36 Nfld. & P.E.I.R. 206 (Nfld. D.C.)

Roses Aluminium Company owed money to A.E. Hickman Company Limited, its supplier. Roses Aluminium was experiencing financial difficulties of which Hickman became aware. The credit manager of Hickman, Peckham, requested and received an interview with the owner of Roses Aluminium to discuss the probability of payment of the debt. Rose promised that he would personally guarantee that the debt would be paid if no court action was initiated against his company. He signed a statement to this effect. The arrangement was accepted by Peckham on behalf of Hickman.

When Rose did not pay as agreed in the interview, a suit was begun against him by Hickman. Rose applied to the court for a *motion of non-suit*. That is, he asked the court to dismiss the action because he had received no consideration in return for his promise; therefore, the agreement between him and Hickman was not enforceable.

—Was consideration extended by Hickman to Rose? Explain.
—Is the contract enforceable? Explain.

13

Contracts: Capacity, Consent, and Legal Purpose

Legal Capacity
Genuine Consent
Legal Purpose

Figure 13-1

Claire, sixteen, saved money from her summer job so that she could buy a stereo. She shopped carefully and found what she wanted. She offered to purchase the stereo and the clerk accepted. They agreed that Claire would pay a deposit at that time and the rest of the purchase price when the stereo would be delivered, two weeks later.

An offer, an acceptance, and consideration are all present in the above example; as you have learned, all of these are required for a valid contract. However, as Chapter 12 pointed out, there are other factors to consider as well in deciding whether a contract is valid:

1. The legal capacity or competence of the parties to make contracts.
2. Genuine consent from each party entering the contract.
3. Legal purpose of the contract.

This chapter discusses these elements of a valid contract.

Legal Capacity

By law, in some circumstances certain people do not have the legal capacity to make binding agreements, or have a limited capacity. We will examine three groups whose legal capacity is restricted: (a) minors or infants; (b) insane and intoxicated persons; and (c) corporations.

Minors

If you are a high school student, it is likely that you are a minor. As you read in Chapter 11, a person ceases to be a minor upon reaching the age of majority. Originally, this age was twenty-one across the country. Presently, the age of majority is nineteen in British Columbia, New Brunswick, Nova Scotia, and Newfoundland, and eighteen in the remaining provinces.

Voidable Contracts

Some contracts made by a minor are **voidable**. Such a contract is one that may be declared void at the option of one of the parties. In this case it is the minor who may carry out or ignore it; however, it is *not* voidable by the adult party. If the minor chooses to perform the contract, the adult is bound. If, on the other hand, the minor decides not to perform his or her obligations, the adult is not bound by the contract either. The law assumes that an adult does not require protection when making contracts, while a minor does.

There are two classes of voidable contracts, and the law treats them differently. The first class consists of contracts that have a permanent benefit and continuing obligations for the minor. The courts have decided that only agreements concerning land, the purchase of shares in a company, or the establishment of a partnership are in this class. These contracts are enforceable unless the minor **repudiates** (renounces) them before reaching the age of majority or within a reasonable time after reaching it. For example, suppose that when you are seventeen you decide to invest some money in stocks after studying the stock market in a business finance class. Since you are a minor, your obligation to pay for the stocks cannot be enforced. However, when you reach the age of majority, you will become responsible for the payments which are now due unless you declare, within a reasonable time, that you do not want to continue with the agreement.

The second class is made up of all other voidable contracts. This type of contract cannot be enforced against a minor and continues to be unenforceable unless the minor **ratifies** (approves) it within a reasonable time after reaching majority. Imagine that you, as a minor, buy a computer system and agree with the store that you will pay for it over the next year. One part of the system, a printer, is not in stock but is to be delivered later. Can the store require you to make payments on the system? It cannot, because, as a minor, the agreement is not enforceable against you. Suppose that, shortly afterwards, you reach your majority. Can the store then require you to make payments? The answer is "Maybe"; if you have ratified the agreement, you are treated like an adult and must pay. Ratification could be done in a number of ways: you could state that you intend to carry on with the agreement; you could make a further payment on the system; or you could accept delivery of some part of it, in this case, the printer. A court may decide that some other action on your part would ratify the contract but these are the most common. Some provinces have passed legislation stating very specifically how ratification must be made. Ontario, New Brunswick, Nova Scotia, Prince Edward Island, and Newfoundland require ratification to be in writing and signed by the minor. The *Infants Act* of British Columbia, on the other hand, states that ratification does not have any effect even when it is in writing.

—Why do you think some provinces require all ratifications of voidable contracts to be in writing?
—Why do you think British Columbia does not allow ratification of voidable contracts?

If you have not ratified the contract, you would not have to pay. However, it is unlikely that the law would permit you to simply keep the system: you would have to return it to the store. More will be said about this in the next section. As a result of this rule, businesses are often reluctant to make contracts with minors where large sums are involved. They often offer to make a contract with the parents instead, who, as adults, are bound by the agreement.

Avoidance of a Voidable Contract

If a minor decides not to carry out his or her obligations under a contract, that is, decides to *avoid* it, what happens? It depends on the degree to which the contract has been **executed** (carried out). If nothing of benefit has been received by either the minor or the adult, the contract is called **executory**. An executory contract can be cancelled by a minor, and the courts will treat it as if it never existed. Say you make an agreement with a shop to purchase a windsurfing board. The seller asks you to pick it up the next day and to make a down payment then. At this time, the contract is executory because neither party has received any benefit under it. You may change your mind about the purchase before returning to pick it up, and you will not be bound by the agreement.

Another possibility is that the contract has been *partially executed*. Partial execution would occur if you had received the item but had made no payments, or if you had made some payments but not all. In the first instance, you must return the item to the seller. The second situation is more complicated, and depends upon whether you received any benefit from your purchase. If you have received no benefit, that is, do not have the goods and you wish to cancel the contract, you are entitled to get back any payments you have made. If, however, you have received some benefit from the contract, you may cancel it, but you may not get back any payments. In addition, the seller can take back whatever has been given to you. The seller must accept, however, whatever portion of the goods are left, and in whatever condition. In the example of the windsurfing board above, assume that you have taken delivery of it and made a down payment. After using it for part of the summer, you decide to take it back to the store. The contract is partially executed, so you can return the windsurfer, and make no further payments. The store must accept it, no matter what condition it is in. However, you are not entitled to receive back any money which you have paid.

When a minor and an adult have fully carried out their respective parts of an agreement, the contract is said to be *fully executed*. The law in Canada is unclear as to whether a minor can avoid a fully executed contract. Consider the following two cases:

Fannon v. Dobranski [1970] 73 W.W.R. 371 (Alta. D.C.)

Fannon, a minor, paid $300 cash for a second-hand car. The car broke down after a few days and 112 km. The court held that Fannon could not get his money back because the contract was fully executed and he had received some benefit from it.

Bo Lassen v. Josiassen [1973] 4 W.W.R. 317 (Alta. D.C.)

Bo Lassen, a minor, purchased a used motorcycle for $130. He later decided that he did not want it and tried to return it. The motorcycle had not been used and was in the same condition as when he bought it. The court allowed him to get his money back if he returned the motorcycle.

—Can you see any difference in these cases?

The rule that some courts seem to be using is that if the minor can put the seller in exactly the same position as he or she was before the contract was made, by returning the goods unused and in pre-sale condition, the minor can avoid the contract and get a refund of any money paid.

Not all contracts are voidable by a minor. Some contracts are always **void**; others are always **valid**.

Void Contracts

If a minor enters into a contract that a court sees is clearly not in the minor's best interests, the court will declare that contract void. For example, if it is plain that a party with whom you have made a contract has taken advantage of you and that you have received little benefit compared to what you have given, a court will likely declare the contract void.

Valid Contracts

Two types of contracts are enforceable against a minor. The first class is made up of contracts of apprenticeship and employment, which are for the benefit of the minor. However, if the contract on the whole is not beneficial or takes advantage of the minor in some way, it is voidable at the minor's option. Provincial statutes such as the *Ontario Tradesman's Qualifications Act* set out the conditions under which apprenticeships must be operated so that the minor is to benefit from them.

The second and most common class of valid contracts is made up of contracts for **necessaries**. Since the law protects minors by making most contracts unenforceable by the other party, adults may be reluctant to become involved in business dealings with minors. This attitude can very definitely be to the disadvantage of young people. The law realizes this and, in response, allows contracts for necessaries to be enforceable against minors. In such a contract, the courts treat the minor much the same as an adult.

What are considered necessaries for minors? Necessaries are goods or services that are needed by a person at the time of purchase, and that are suitable to the person's *station in life* (social position). Necessaries include such things as housing, food, medical attention, clothing, and education.

Two boys go into a clothing store, each intending to buy a blue, hand-tailored blazer. The first boy comes from a wealthy family and goes to an old established private school whose uniform includes the wearing of such a blazer on many occasions. This boy has recently outgrown his old blazer. The second boy comes from a middle income family and goes to a public school near his home. He is becoming increasingly concerned about his appearance and would like to have the blazer for special occasions, although he has another jacket at home which fits him properly.

—Is the blazer a necessary to these boys?

The blazer is likely a necessary for the first boy but not for the second one. Only the first boy actually needs the jacket. The second boy already has a jacket; besides, it is questionable whether an expensive hand-tailored jacket is suitable to his station in life. What is a necessary to one person, then, may not be a necessary to another.

Figure 13-2
Whether an item of clothing is a necessary for a minor depends on the minor's station in life.

CONTRACTS: CAPACITY, CONSENT, AND LEGAL PURPOSE 293

Soon et al. v. Watson et al. (1962) 33 D.L.R. (2d) 428 (B.C.S.C.)

> The infant plaintiffs, Roy and Carole Soon, were married with one child. Carole Soon was expecting a second child. They were renting an apartment for $90 a month. Ray Soon's gross monthly income was approximately $210. They had saved $1300 to be used as a down payment on a house.
>
> The Soons negotiated the purchase of a house owned by the defendant, Watson. Shortly after signing the necessary documents of sale and taking possession of the house, the Soons became aware that "they just couldn't afford it." Their solicitor wrote to the defendant, Watson, indicating that "he had been instructed to rescind the...sale on the grounds of infancy." The keys to the house were returned to Watson and the house vacated. The Soons requested that the court rescind the contract.
>
> In deciding the case, the judge considered two main factors regarding the Soons' infancy. First, was the contract of benefit to the minors? He decided that given the facts that the couple had taken on the responsibility of marriage, that the additional cost of the house over the apartment was well compensated by the improved accommodation and investment value of the house, and that it was common for a young couple to use a large portion of their income on housing, the purchase was of benefit to the minors.
>
> He also decided that, since another child was expected, the purchase of a "modest home...(was) in their actual requirements." The house was, therefore, a necessary. The contract was enforced.

The law provides one exception to the enforcement of a contract for necessaries. If you buy a pair of jeans that you need for three times the normal price, would a court compel you to pay for them? When an adult contracts to buy something at a price much greater than what is usual, the adult is bound by the agreement. However, a minor can only be required to pay a fair market price for the purchase. A court would determine the fair market price on the basis of the normal price of such goods in that area.

Fraudulent Misrepresentation of Age

Fraudulent misrepresentation of age by a minor occurs when the minor lies about his or her age to get an adult to enter a contract. How does doing this affect the minor's responsibility to carry out the contract? Obviously, the adult entered into the contract thinking the minor was an adult and expecting to be able to ask a court to enforce the contract. Although fraud is involved, the minor cannot be forced to carry out the contract. However, the law will likely require the minor to return any goods received. In addition, the minor may be charged with fraud under the criminal law.

Parents' Liability

Parents are generally not responsible for the debts of their children. All provinces, however, require parents to be responsible for providing necessaries to their children under the age of sixteen. The *Criminal Code* contains this provision as well.

If you had bought goods previously on credit from a store and your parents had paid for them, the store could assume that your parents would pay again. Your parents would be responsible. Also, if your parents had told the store that you could buy goods and they would pay, a court would require them to pay. In both situations, you are acting on behalf of your parents or, in legal terms, as an agent of your parents. The subject of agency will be discussed in detail in Chapter 23.

Minors and Business

It should be clear by this time why companies are reluctant to do business with minors on anything but a cash basis. They are taking a large risk in giving a minor credit because, in most situations, there is no way in which they can force the minor to pay. For this reason, businesses usually try to make an adult responsible for a minor's debts. For instance, a store may require the promise of a parent to pay if the minor does not. A bank or credit union will require an adult to co-sign the promissory note for a loan taken by a minor. This gives them assurance of receiving payment if the minor fails to pay the debt.

Mentally Handicapped and Intoxicated Persons

People who are incapacitated by drugs or alcohol or who are mentally handicapped are treated in a way similar to minors. A person who is mentally handicapped or intoxicated by alcohol or drugs at the time of entering a contract is able to avoid the contract if

1. the person was not aware of entering the contract;
2. the other party was aware of the incapacitated person's condition.

The mentally handicapped or intoxicated person must repudiate the contract within a reasonable time after becoming sane or sober, or the right to avoid the contract will be lost. Also, if the person accepts a benefit from the contract after becoming sober, for example, delivery of goods ordered while drunk, the contract will be binding.

Intoxicated and mentally handicapped persons have the same contractual obligations for the purchase of necessaries as minors.

Corporations

Corporations are companies that have gone through a registration process, called **incorporation**, with a provincial government or the federal government. This process makes the company a legal "person". It is therefore capable of making contracts, borrowing money, and carrying on business in its own name rather than in the names of the owners (shareholders). The corporation's charter, the document stating its name, objects, and other required information, may limit the type of business which the corporation may become involved in, and therefore the types of contracts it may make.

If a corporation makes a contract outside of the authority set out in the charter, the contract may be void. At one time, when a corporation made a void contract, the courts applied the doctrine of *ultra vires* (Latin for "beyond the powers" or "beyond the authority") and found that the contract had no legal effect. This left the innocent party with no remedy. Today, all the provinces except Newfoundland and Nova Scotia have abolished the concept of *ultra vires*. For example, section 21(1) of the British Columbia *Companies Act* states:

> **21. (1) ...a company has the power and capacity of a natural person of full capacity.**

In most situations today, if a corporation makes a contract outside of its authority, the innocent party is protected. As well, the shareholders can sue the person(s) responsible for making the contract on behalf of the corporation.

Genuine Consent

As you will recall, a contract is defined as a promise or set of promises which the courts will enforce. These promises must be made voluntarily. This means you must be aware of the nature of the contract that you are entering into. Also, if you are forced into a contract, you certainly cannot be expected to carry it out. We are not talking here about the normal pressure of persuasion but a much stronger, perhaps even physical, force.

Freely entering into a contract whose nature is understood is called **genuine consent**. Four main conditions may prevent genuine consent. They are as follows:

1. misrepresentation
2. mistake
3. duress
4. undue influence

Misrepresentation

Innocent Misrepresentation

Imagine that you have saved quite a bit of money to buy your own horse. After looking for some time, you find one that you really like. You ask the owner about the present and past medical history of the horse. He tells you that the horse has never had a serious illness or defect, and that it is in perfect health now. Relying on this information, you buy the horse. After riding it for a few weeks, you find that the horse has a serious hip problem which hinders it from galloping. A veterinarian tells you that the defect is hereditary, so the horse has had it since birth, although it may only have shown up now. You take the horse back to the previous owner.

Has there been misrepresentation in the sale of the horse? The answer is "Yes". Misrepresentation is a false statement of a *material fact*. A material fact is one which induces a person to enter into a contract, and which may or may not become a term of the contract. What can you do in this situation? The answer depends upon whether the previous owner was aware of the defect in the horse, and whether the good health of the animal was a term of the contract.

If the owner was not aware of the defect, he misrepresented the facts *innocently* or *unknowingly*. This is referred to as **innocent misrepresentation**. In this situation, you may repudiate the contract and ask a court to order rescission of the contract, even if the good health of the horse was not a term of the agreement. If the court rescinds the contract, both you and the previous owner will return the consideration received. The intention of the law is to return both parties to the situation they were in before the contract was made. You may also be able to ask the court to award you compensation for any out-of-pocket expenses you incurred as a result of the contract, for example, the charge for renting a trailer to pick up the horse, and the bill from the vet who told you of the defect.

If the defect was discovered when the horse fell and had to be shot because it broke a leg, is there any way to rescind the contract with the previous owner? If the misrepresentation did not concern a term of the contract, there is not. Since you no longer have the horse to give back, the first owner cannot be returned to the situation he was in before the contract. However, if the misrepresentation does concern a term of the contract, you may be able to sue for damages for breach of the term instead.

To summarize, if the misrepresentation is innocent and does not concern a term of the contract, the only remedy you will have is rescission of the contract. This remedy is available only if both parties can be returned to the situation they were in before entering the contract.

Fraudulent Misrepresentation

If the person from whom you bought the horse was aware of the defect in the horse and purposely did not tell you about it when you asked, **fraudulent misrepresentation** has occurred. You have been induced into entering a contract by being told untrue information about a material fact. In this event, you have the right to repudiate the contract and sue for its rescission. If the misrepresentation is a term of the contract, you can ask for damages for the breach of the term. As well, you have an additional remedy not available to you if the misrepresentation is innocent—you can sue for the tort of deceit.

Graham et al. v. Legault et al. (1951) 3 D.L.R. 432 (B.C. S.C.)

Legault, knowing that Graham wanted to buy a house with an apartment suitable for renting, showed him a house which he owned and which had an apartment occupied by tenants. He did not, however, tell Graham that the apartment was unlawfully rented because the ceiling was too low, contrary to the building codes. No permit was obtained when the apartment was put in, and none would be granted now. Graham bought the house and, upon finding out about the illegal apartment, sued Legault for rescission and damages.

—What do you think Graham's lawyer would argue?
—What do you think would be the basis of the defence lawyer's argument?
—If you were the judge, how would the case be decided? State your reasoning.

Negligent Misrepresentation

There is yet another type of misrepresentation. *Negligent misrepresentation* occurs when a seller carelessly misrepresents a material fact about something that can injure or cause a loss to the buyer. Baldur has worked all summer to save for a car. One night, he sees an ad in the paper for a used car in his price range. He arranges to see the car, and goes for a test drive. The car handles fine, apart from a little wobbling of the steering wheel. The seller assures Baldur that it's always been like that and has been no problem. Baldur buys the car. Three weeks later, while he is driving down his street, the steering column gives way, and Baldur loses control of the car. He is slightly hurt, but fortunately he doesn't hit another car, and his car is barely scratched. If the seller should have known that the steering was about to go at any instant but carelessly told Baldur it was safe, negligent misrepresentation has occurred. Under these circumstances, Baldur can repudiate the contract and sue for rescission, and for damages for the tort of negligent misrepresentation. Of course, he would also be able to sue for breach of a term of the contract if the condition of the car was part of the agreement. In fact, in this situation it is probable that the contract would include a term stating that the car was in safe working condition.

When any of the types of misrepresentation occurs, the innocent party must repudiate the contract and seek rescission within a reasonable time after becoming aware of the misrepresentation. An undue delay may be considered by the courts as an acceptance of the contract despite the misrepresentation.

Contracts of Utmost Good Faith

In some circumstances, one party is required to reveal all the material facts which would influence the other party's decision to enter the contract, whether the first party is asked for the information or not. If all the material facts are not revealed, the contract may be avoided. A contract carrying such a requirement is called a contract of *utmost good faith*. One example is an insurance contract. If you are filling out an application form for insurance and give false information, or leave out some information that may affect your rate or whether you will get the policy, the policy may be avoided by the insurance company. If the false or missing information is discovered when you make a claim, the claim may not be paid.

Mistake

Suppose you want to buy a 35 mm camera. A salesperson points out all the features of what looks like the perfect camera for you. You decide to buy it for what seems to be a good price. A couple of days later, however, you discover that you could have bought the same camera at another shop for about $75 less. What a mistake! This may be of great concern to you, but it is of little concern to the law. The law will not try to make good deals for people. Therefore, this is not what the law means by mistake. The legal meaning of mistake can be understood by examining the three types: **common, mutual**, and **unilateral mistake**.

Common Mistake

Common mistake occurs when both the parties to an agreement make the same error. Say you agree to buy a jacket from the Athletic Association of your school. Later, you and the Association find out that the jackets were destroyed in a fire before you agreed to buy yours. Both you and the Association were unaware that the subject matter of the agreement did not exist at the time the contract was made. The agreement is, therefore, void.

Suppose that the jackets were not destroyed. The day after you order the jacket, you go to pick it up. A representative tells you that you are getting the only size 12 left. She shows you the tag. You had ordered a size 12, and the Association believed you were getting a size 12. However, when you put it on, you find that it must be a size 18. This is a fundamental error about the nature of the jacket. The contract is, therefore, voidable by either party.

Figure 13-3 Common mistake can occur when both parties to a contract are in error about the nature of an item.

To summarize, a common mistake about the existence of the goods makes the agreement void. A common mistake about the nature of the goods makes the agreement voidable by either party.

Mutual Mistake

Mutual mistake arises when both parties to an agreement make different errors. This error is often in the form of different interpretations of what has been said in making an offer and acceptance; often one party or both have been careless in interpreting what the agreement means. A court will not find the contract to be void. Rather, it will enforce what it considers to be the most reasonable interpretation of the facts of the case. On the other hand, if both interpretations are equally reasonable, the court may not enforce the contract at all, as the following case illustrates.

Angevaare v. McKay (1960) 25 D.L.R. (2d) 521 (Ont. C.C.)

McKay contracted with Angevaare to purchase a 1960 Mercedes Benz. The contract was arranged for by Angevaare's salesman, Van Der Meer. Both Angevaare and Van Der Meer had difficulty with the English language. As a result, McKay thought he was purchasing a special model Mercedes, whereas Angevaare and Van Der Meer believed they were selling the basic model. Angevaare sued McKay for specific performance of the agreement.

In deciding the case, the judge recognized that the vehicle Angevaare believed he was offering to sell was not the same vehicle McKay thought he was buying. "Or, in other words, the minds of the parties did not meet in one and the same intention." Therefore, there was no contract for the court to enforce.

Unilateral Mistake

Unilateral mistake is a mistake made by one party only. You may buy a bicycle that you think is of excellent quality because it is the type used in European road races. Later, you find that it is useless for your purposes. The contract cannot be avoided even though the seller may have realized your mistake, as long as no actual misrepresentations were made to you. The court will follow the principle of **caveat emptor**—"Let the buyer beware."

On the other hand, if you mistakenly believe that the seller has made the quality of the bicycle a term of the offer, and the seller knows of your error but does nothing to clear it up, you may have the contract declared void. You believe that you are accepting an offer that is actually different from that which the offeror offered.

In some cases, a person who has made a unilateral mistake about the nature of the contract he or she has signed may be able to avoid the contract by using the defence of **non est factum**, a Latin phrase meaning "It is not my deed." This defence developed when most people were illiterate and had to rely on someone else to read documents to them. If the illiterate person signed a document that was totally different from what he or she was told it was, the defence could be used. Today, *non est factum* is used more broadly. Even literate people may successfully use the defence, if they can show that trickery was used.

Royal Bank of Canada v. Gannon (1980) 42 N.S.R. (2d) 526 (N.S. S.C.)

The defendant, a sixty-one-year-old widow with a Grade 6 education, was asked by her son to guarantee a loan for his company. She understood from her son that the guarantee was for this present loan only. She signed the guarantee without reading it. The guarantee was, in fact, for "all debts or liabilities, present or future..." Gannon did not ask the bank's lawyer any questions about the document, nor did he explain anything to her.

The bank brought an action for enforcement of the guarantee. The defence argued that *non est factum* was applicable because the defendant did not understand the document and believed she was agreeing to something substantially different from what she was in fact signing.

The court, agreeing with the defence, dismissed the action. It said that, considering the defendant's lack of business expertise and her level of education, it was reasonable to believe that she thought she was agreeing to a contract that was substantially different from the one she signed.

There is another situation in which unilateral mistake can arise. Say you look at the written contract that you have just received in the mail—you cannot believe your good fortune. The contract is for the purchase of a personal computer that you know costs $2500, but the contract says $250. You quickly sign it and send it back to the company making the offer. Can you actually have the contract enforced at a price of $250? The courts say "No". This is a *palpable* (obvious) clerical error. It is a very different contract from what the computer store intended to offer, and is therefore not enforceable. If, however, the price on the contract was $2400, it would be enforceable, because it is not an obvious error. In principle, the law says that you cannot take advantage of an obvious clerical error.

Duress

Figure 13-4 Duress makes a contract voidable at the option of the victim.

In order for a contract to be enforceable, it must be entered into freely by all parties. Forcing a person into a contract by the use of violence, the threat of violence, or imprisonment is referred to as **duress**. The presence of duress makes the contract voidable by the victim.

In order to avoid a contract entered under duress, the victim must repudiate the contract soon after becoming free from the duress. If he or she does not, a court will consider the contract to be enforceable. Also, the victim must not do anything after becoming free from the duress to carry out his or her part of the contract. Doing so would be considered acceptance of the contract.

Undue Influence

More common than duress is **undue influence**. Undue influence is mental or emotional pressure by one party on another which robs the latter of free will. Not all pressure is considered undue influence, however. In many sales, some emotional or mental pressure is used by a salesperson. This is usually not seen as undue influence, but rather as a normal part of the selling process. There comes a point, however, when the pressure is no longer considered normal or fair. That point is determined by the degree of domination exercised and the amount of benefit received by the dominant party.

It is sometimes difficult to show the degree of domination in a situation, and therefore to prove the presence of undue influence. In some relationships, if undue influence is claimed and the dominant party has obtained an advantageous contract, a court will presume that it is present unless shown otherwise. In these relationships, one party has a special skill or knowledge which causes the other party to put trust in him or her. Parent and child, lawyer and client, doctor or nurse and patient, minister and parishioner are examples of this kind of relationship.

—What could a dominant party do to ensure that the weaker party would not later attempt to avoid the contract?

Legal Purpose

Even if all the other necessary elements of a contract are present, it will not be enforceable unless it has a legal purpose. Illegal contracts can be put into any of three categories:

1. those contrary to public policy
2. those contrary to common law
3. those prohibited by statute

Contracts Contrary to Public Policy

A contract that is contrary to public policy (the public interest) is unenforceable even if the contract does not violate any specific law. There are many types of contracts that may be unenforceable because of public policy. This section will look at some of the more common types.

Contracts in Restraint of Trade

Contracts in restraint of trade can take several forms, but the common factor is that they all attempt to limit competition in business.

Employer/Employee Relationships

An employer may put in an employment contract a clause stating that the employee agrees not to work for a competitor or to establish a competing business after the employment ends. Such a clause, called a *restrictive covenant*, may be against public policy, since it is an attempt by the employer to limit competition.

In some situations, however, the courts may enforce this type of clause. If the employee has trade or business secrets, a court would consider the restrictive covenant reasonable to protect the company's interests. For example, a chemist working for a cosmetic company would have the formulas for the company's products. In other words, although the courts look with great displeasure on attempts to restrict an employee's future work, a restrictive covenant will be enforced if it is a reasonable attempt to protect the employer's business. The key word here is "reasonable".

Restrictions on the Sale of a Business

When a person sells a business, the purchaser may want to put in the agreement of sale a term restricting the seller from starting a competing business. Usually such a term will state that the seller cannot start a competing business within a certain distance of the business being sold and for a certain period of time. Again, the courts will enforce this type of restrictive covenant only if it is reasonable. What is reasonable depends greatly on the circumstances. For example, a promise by a seller of a video equipment store in a large city never to set up a competing business anywhere in the city would likely be viewed as unreasonable and therefore unenforceable. On the other hand, if the seller was limited to not establishing a video store for one year within a four kilometre radius of the store being sold, the restriction would likely be valid.

Contracts in Restraint of Marriage

A court would not enforce an agreement never to marry, since it is seen by society as being in the public interest for people to marry and establish families. It is possible, however, for a partial restraint of marriage to be enforced by a court. A movie star or a model, for example, may be required not to marry during the term of his or her contract. He or she may appeal to a court on the basis that the restraint is unreasonable. If the court agrees that it is unreasonable, that clause will not be enforced.

— At one time, the R.C.M.P. had a five-year restraint of marriage clause in their contract. It has now been changed to two years. Why do you think this was done?
— Why do they have any restraint of marriage clause?

Contracts with Enemy Aliens

An **alien** is a person living in Canada who is not a Canadian citizen. Aliens have the same rights and responsibilities with regard to contracts as any citizen. An **enemy alien** is a person who has business interests or a residence in enemy territory during wartime. Generally, a contract with an enemy alien is considered to be against public policy and therefore void. In the few situations where such a contract is not seen as being against public policy, the agreement is interrupted during the conflict but may resume when peace returns.

Contracts Contrary to Common Law

A contract for the commission of a tort is contrary to the common law and is therefore unenforceable. For instance, if you agreed to pay someone to spread slanderous lies about another person, you could not be sued for non-payment. Similarly, a contract in which you agree to compensate the person who has agreed to spread the slander in the event that the person is sued and a court awards damages to the victim would not be enforceable, since it encourages the commission of a tort.

Contracts Prohibited by Statute

Many statutes, both federal and provincial, forbid the making of certain types of contracts. The following are only a few examples.

Betting and Wagering

Statutes in some provinces make contracts for betting unenforceable. There is no penalty for private persons who gamble, but the courts will not enforce the contract. Ontario's *Gaming Act* does, however, permit a loser to sue for recovery of a bet when $40 or more has been lost in one sitting and the action is brought within three months. However, it is illegal under the *Criminal Code* to run or be found in a gaming or betting house.

Contracts Made on Sunday

The federal *Lord's Day Act* states that contracts made on Sunday are illegal unless they are for necessaries or acts of mercy. The purpose of this law is to establish one day of rest for all Canadians. Sunday was originally selected to allow a predominantly Christian Canada to observe religious services.

Figure 13-5 The Lord's Day Act states that most contracts made on Sunday are illegal and therefore void.

In recent years, the powers of the *Lord's Day Act* have been given over to the provincial governments. Some provinces and even municipalities have passed their own laws governing the making of contracts and, therefore, the opening of places of business on Sunday. Ontario, for example, enacted the *Retail Business Holidays Act* in 1976. Manitoba passed a similar statute in 1977, and other provinces have followed suit. The purpose of these laws is to regulate the opening of large department stores and supermarkets, rather than all businesses. Usually, places of entertainment and tourist attractions have been permitted to remain open on Sunday. So have variety stores and drugstores, which are seen as dispensing necessaries.

Although these changes represent a major liberalization of the original concept of the *Lord's Day Act*, the *Act* is often interpreted differently from province to province.

At the time of writing, the federal *Lord's Day Act* and the various provincial statutes regulating the making of contracts on Sunday are being challenged in the courts as denying basic rights guaranteed by the *Charter of Rights and Freedoms*:

> 2. Everyone has the following fundamental freedoms:
>   (a) freedom of conscience and religion
> 15. (1) Every individual is equal before and under the law and has the right to the equal protection and equal benefit of the law without discrimination...based on... religion..."

Unconscionable Rates of Interest

Suppose that one day you go to a clothing store and pick out a new wardrobe costing several hundred dollars. You are going to put it on a bank credit card, but the clerk convinces you that the store's credit system is better. Later, when you receive the bill, you realize that the interest rate you must pay is 45% *per annum* (per year). You realize that this is very high and wonder whether you might have the contract set aside. You might, since many provinces have laws similar to Ontario's *Unconscionable Transactions Relief Act*. According to these Acts, it would be up to a court to decide whether the interest you have been charged is **unconscionable**; that is, unscrupulously excessive in the present marketplace. If the court found that the rate *was* unconscionable, it would either adjust the interest rate so that it was reasonable or it could set the contract aside.

In addition, how much interest you are charged must be made clear to you. This is the case for both loans and goods bought on credit. When you buy goods on credit, you are actually being given a loan for the amount of the goods. The lender must disclose the full cost of the loan in both dollars and rate of interest.

Contracts Whose Purpose is the Elimination of Competition

In addition to the contracts in restraint of trade which are unenforceable because they are against public policy, there are others which are illegal by statute. In the normal course of business, companies make many contracts among themselves. These contracts might be for the sale of their products, or they might be for cooperation in doing research and development or gathering statistics. These dealings are usually not seen as interfering with competition or trade and so are legal.

Other types of agreements that companies may make with each other are not looked upon so kindly by the law. Under the *Combines Investigation Act*, contracts between companies that are intended to eliminate competition are void. Companies may try to eliminate competition in many ways. They may contract to fix prices; that is, to set the prices that all parties to the contract will charge for specific goods. This practice, of course, eliminates price competition. They may also contract to standardize the quality of certain goods, thereby eliminating product competition. They may agree to restrict output, thereby forcing prices up. Or they may agree to work to keep others out of the market. All of these contracts are void by statute.

SUMMARIZING YOUR READING

1. Name three groups with restricted capacity to enter contracts.

2. Are contracts for non-necessaries that have permanent benefit binding on a minor? What must the minor do to avoid such a contract?

3. Are other contracts for non-necessaries binding on a minor? Will such a contract become binding when the minor reaches the age of majority?

4. How might a minor ratify a contract for non-necessaries that does not have a permanent benefit upon reaching majority?

5. Define the following: an executory contract; a partially executed contract; an executed contract. What effect does each have on a minor's contractual obligations?

6. Why does the law make contracts for necessaries enforceable against minors?

7. Describe a "necessary". What is meant by "station in life"?

8. What price can a minor be required to pay for necessaries?

9. Under what circumstances is an adult bound by a contract made with a minor? Why?

10. If a minor lies about his or her age in making a contract with an adult, is the adult bound by the contract? Explain.

11. Are parents generally responsible for the contracts made by their minor children? What are the exceptions to this rule?

12. If a person makes a contract while impaired by alcohol or drugs, what two things must be shown to prove incapacity?

13. Define "genuine consent". What four main conditions may prevent genuine consent?

14. Describe the three types of misrepresentation. What action might a court take in the event of each of these types?

15. What is common mistake? What is the effect of common mistake on a contract?

16. What is mutual mistake? What remedy will a court grant?

17. What is unilateral mistake? What action may be taken by the mistaken party?

18. What is the effect of a palpable clerical error?

19. Define "duress". What is the effect of duress on the enforceability of a contract?

20. Define "undue influence". What two things must be shown to prove the existence of undue influence?

21. What is the effect of undue influence on the enforceability of a contract?

22. What are some types of contracts that are considered contrary to public policy?

23. What is an alien? When may an alien not make binding contracts in Canada?

24. Can an employer prevent an employee from working for a competitor or establishing a competing business when the employment ends? Explain.

25. What types of clauses in a contract for the sale of a business may be considered illegal? What factors would a court consider in deciding whether the clause were valid?

26. Under what circumstances will a contract in restraint of marriage be enforced?

27. Is betting illegal? Explain.

28. Describe the circumstances under which an interest rate may be considered illegal by a court.

29. Name several methods by which companies might try to eliminate competition.

PROJECTS AND ACTIVITIES

1. Continue the scrapbook you began in Chapter 12.

2. Visit a local bank or credit union manager to find out how a minor could obtain a loan. Also ask how many loans are given to minors and what kinds of problems, if any, the institution has had with them. What would be the repercussions for a minor who did not repay a loan?

3. Obtain a copy of the federal *Lord's Day Act* and your province's legislation that deals with Sunday contracts. Examine both to determine exactly what is permissible. Evaluate the statutes to determine the following:
   (a) Do they reflect our modern lifestyle?
   (b) Should they, in your opinion?
   (c) Do they preserve our heritage and culture?
   (d) Should they, in your opinion?

Visit four or five businesses that are open on Sunday. Determine what goods and/or services they provide.

4. Generally, an employee has the right to work for a competitor after leaving his or her current employer. Examine the "trading" practices of professional sports to determine whether, in your opinion, this constitutes a restraint of trade and competition.

5. Native Canadians living on reservations are Crown wards and, as such, have limited capacity to enter certain contracts. Research and write a report explaining:
   (a) how the relationship between the Indian people and the Crown came about
   (b) in what way their capacity to contract is limited
   (c) whether there is any movement to change the status of Indians from being wards of the Crown
   (d) what effect the *Canadian Charter of Rights and Freedoms* may have on the special status of Native people

CASE DISCUSSION

Toronto Marlboro Major Junior "A" Hockey Club et al. v. Tonelli et al. (1977) 18 O.R. 21 (Ont. H.C.J.)

Tonelli, a minor aged seventeen, contracted to play amateur hockey for the Toronto Marlboro Hockey Club for three or, if the Club chose, four years. He was to receive minimal pay and, upon becoming a professional hockey player, was to pay to the Marlboros 20% of his first three years' salary. The Club could also trade him to another club or fire him at any time. When Tonelli reached eighteen, the age of majority in Ontario, he repudiated the agreement and signed a contract with the Houston Aeros of the World Hockey Association. The Marlboros sued Tonelli for breach of contract.

—What kind of contract did Tonelli enter? Was it void, voidable, or valid? Explain.
—What do you think the decision of the court was in this case?

Sherman v. American Insurance Co. (1937) 4 D.L.R. 732 (Ont. H.C.J.)

Sherman was attempting to recover losses from a fire in a house insured by American Insurance Co. In applying for the insurance, Sherman had not declared that there had been another fire in that house and that the insuring company had refused to renew the policy. American Insurance Co. refused to pay the claim; Sherman sued for payment.

—Was Sherman required by law to disclose this information even though it was not specifically asked for? Explain.
—Should the American Insurance Company be required to pay the claim? Why or why not?

Gaertner v. Fiesta Dance Studios Ltd. et al. (1973) 32 D.L.R. (2d) 599 (B.C. S.C.)

Gaertner, a thirty-one-year-old single woman, responded to an advertisement from the Fiesta Dance Studio for dance lessons. As time passed, she was convinced of her "great dancing ability" and was persuaded to sign additional contracts for dancing lessons. After she had signed a number of such contracts having a total value of $3933 and had taken many more lessons, one of her instructors told her that he was prepared to propose her as a member of the Gold Key Club. It was, according to him, a great honour. She would have to dance before a panel of three instructors who would evaluate her ability. At the same time, she would be filmed and the motion picture would be sent to New York to be evaluated. At the conclusion of the performance, the staff members rushed up to congratulate her. Champagne was opened and a cake appeared. Photographs were taken of the proceedings, and she was led off to the office of the manager where she was told that she had to sign up for $2573 worth of more lessons to bring her up to the standard required of a Gold Key member. Gaertner signed after making some objections.

Unknown to Gaertner, the whole scene was carried out without film in the movie camera. The procedure was a standing joke among the staff members. Gaertner asked the court for a return of the $6505 paid to the Fiesta Dance Studio Limited.

—Should Gaertner recover any or all of the money she paid to the Studio? On what grounds did you make your decision?

Regina v. Moffats Ltd. (1957) 7 D.L.R. (2d) 405 (Ont. C.A.)

Moffats, an appliance manufacturer, entered into a cooperative advertising scheme with some dealers. The scheme provided for Moffats to pay half of the dealers' advertising costs if the latter agreed to advertise Moffats' appliances at not less than a minimum retail price set by the manufacturer. Moffats argued that its motive in this action was merely to promote harmony among its dealers, rather than to encourage price fixing as such. Further, Moffats suggested that the scheme was only to advertise at a fixed price, not to sell at a fixed price.

The manufacturer was charged under the *Combines Investigation Act*, which reads in part:

> 34. (2) No dealer shall directly or indirectly by agreement, threat, promise or any other means whatsoever, require or induce or attempt to require or induce any other person to resell an article or commodity...
> (b) at a price not less than a minimum price specified by the dealer or established by agreement...

—What arguments would you make for the Crown?
—How do you think the defence would respond to the Crown's case?
—How should this case be decided, in your opinion?

Adams v. Canadian Cooperative Implements Ltd. (1979) 20 A.R. 532 (Alta. Q.B.)

The plaintiff farmer, Adams, purchased a used haystacker from a salesperson working for the defendants. The salesperson indicated that the stacker would work on the plaintiff's only tractor. The tractor had a 540 r.p.m. power take-off. However, the haystacker required a 1000 r.p.m. power take-off. The defendant believed that a conversion could be done to allow Adams' tractor to power the haystacker. It was subsequently discovered that such a conversion was not possible.

Adams sued for rescission of the contract on the grounds of innocent misrepresentation.

— Should Adams succeed in his suit? Explain.
— What factor in this case would have to be different if it were to be a successful suit for fraudulent misrepresentation?

Reliable Toy Company Ltd. and Reliable Plastics Co. Ltd. v. Collins [1950] 4 D.L.R. 499 (Ont. H.C.J.)

Collins was employed by Reliable as chief chemist in its chemical laboratory. A term of his employment contract was that he would not disclose any trade secrets or secret processes connected with the business. Upon his discharge, Collins earned a living as a consulting chemist and by promoting the sale of paint. The plaintiffs discovered that, in the course of this work, he was disclosing to certain of Reliable's competitors trade secrets that he had learned while an employee of Reliable.

Reliable sued Collins for damages and for an injunction to prevent further disclosure of the secrets.

— Given that Collins was no longer in the employ of Reliable, but that he was disclosing information learned while he was an employee, would you grant damages and an injunction to the plaintiffs? Give reasons for your decision.

Matériaux de Construction Castonquay Inc. v. Pelletier (1982) 38 N.B.R. (2d) 112 (N.B. Q.B.)

Matériaux de Construction Castonquay Inc. delivered goods to Pelletier at the cottage of a friend, Janice Scott. It was agreed between the parties that the cost of the goods would be paid in cash, no sales tax would be charged, no invoices or other documents would be prepared, and no record would be kept in the books of the plaintiff seller.

When the price of the goods was not paid by the defendant, the company sued.

— The judge declared that there was only one issue to be dealt with in this case. What is that issue?
— Was the agreement enforceable? Explain.

Taylor v. Armstrong (1979) 24 O.R. (2d) 614 (Ont. H.C.J.)

Taylor, a sixty-nine-year-old man, was substantially illiterate and relied upon others for all business transactions, including such minor things as writing cheques and paying bills. He seemed intimidated by any type of business transaction. He was separated from his second wife and was living with the defendant, Rita

Armstrong, at his residence. He relied upon Armstrong for all his business affairs.

Although they both had wills leaving all of their estates to each other, Armstrong convinced Taylor that they should make new wills. Taylor believed that the new wills were to be the same as the old wills, and agreed, to humour Armstrong. At the time of the signing, Taylor was required to sign two documents. He realized later that one was a will, and the other transferred part-ownership of his house to the defendant.

Taylor brought an action to set aside the transfer of part-ownership of property to the defendant. The action succeeded; two grounds for the decision were undue influence and *non est factum*.

—Explain how undue influence is a factor in this case.
—Explain how *non est factum* is a factor in this case.
—How might the defendant have acted differently to prevent these grounds from being available?

Murphy's Ltd. v. Fabricville Co. Inc. (1980) 117 D.L.R. (3d) 668 (N.S. S.C.)

After much negotiation and a number of offers and counter-offers, Fabricville entered into an agreement with Murphy's to lease commercial space. The cost of the lease was to be a base rate of $3.25 per square foot, plus extra costs. Realty taxes, one of the extra costs, had been part of the negotiations from the beginning but were not in the offer that Murphy's finally accepted by signing.

The court found that the parties had agreed orally that Fabricville would pay the realty taxes for the portion of the building it was leasing. However, the clause respecting taxes that actually appeared in the lease stated that Fabricville would be responsible for only a proportion of the increase in taxes after 1978.

The court also found that Fabricville was aware that Murphy was misinterpreting the tax clause. Murphy asked that the lease either be rescinded or rectified (altered to express the true intentions of the parties).

—What kind of mistake was made in this case?
—What argument could be made by the plaintiff?
—What argument could be made by the defendant?
—If you were the judge, how would you decide this case—what remedy would you grant? Give reasons for your decision.

Standard Construction Co. Ltd. v. Foundation Co. of Canada Ltd.
(1980) 28 N.B.R. (2d) 483 (N.B. Q.B.)

Foundation Co. of Canada Ltd. had a contract with the federal Department of Public Works to clear Dalhousie Island and construct a wharf, warehousing facilities, and other structures. Foundation had subcontracted some of the work to Standard Construction Co. Ltd. Standard was to clear the island and to use the rocks cleared to build a causeway.

One area of dispute was that, although both parties understood an item to refer to "rock facing—causeway", the contract read "rock fill—causeway". Neither party noticed the error when signing the contract.

—**How does the agreement differ from the written document?**
—**Should the contract as signed be enforceable? Why?**
—**What is the legal term for this type of error?**

14

Completing the Contract

Privity of Contract
Discharge of Contract
Breach of Contract

Remedies for Breach
The *Statute of Frauds*

Max and Jean have just entered a contract. Both parties have agreed to do certain things: Jean has agreed to paint Max's house, while Max has agreed to pay her for this service.

Figure 14-1

Although each of the parties in the above scenario has bargained in good faith, sometimes problems or questions can arise concerning the exact nature of each party's rights and obligations. This chapter will consider some of these issues by looking at questions such as these: Who has the right to enforce the terms of a contract? When can obligations be performed by someone who is not a party to the contract? What remedies are available when a contract is breached (broken)? What happens if performance becomes impossible?

Privity of Contract

The rule of **privity of contract** states that a contract cannot impose obligations or give benefits to anyone who is not a party to it. In other words, only the parties to the contract are bound by its terms. People who are not parties to the contract are called **third parties**, **third persons** or **strangers** to the contract.

Exceptions to the Rule of Privity of Contract

Third persons are often affected by a contract; therefore, the law allows exceptions to the rule of privity of contract to deal with such situations. Some of these exceptions are discussed below.

Insurance

Irmi Ebhardt is a lawyer. She and her husband have three children. To cover the family's loss of income if she dies, she has taken out life insurance. Her husband is the **beneficiary**, which means that if she dies the insurance will be paid to him.

Even though the contract of insurance is between Mrs. Ebhardt and the insurance company, Mr. Ebhardt can sue to have the company honour the agreement if his wife dies and the insurance company refuses to pay.

Every province has legislation that allows the beneficiary of an insurance policy to enforce its terms, even though this person is not a party to the contract.

Contracts Involving Land

The rule of privity of contract does not usually apply to contracts involving land (real property). For example, if rental property is sold, the tenant must continue to pay rent to the new landlord and the new landlord must carry out any of the former landlord's obligations.

Trusts

A **trust** is a contract in which *title* to (legal ownership of) property is given to one person, the **trustee**, on the understanding that it will be used for the benefit of a third party, the beneficiary. Even though the beneficiary is a stranger to the contract, he or she can enforce its terms if the trustee fails to perform as agreed.

One of the Ebhardts' children is mentally handicapped. They have a plan to set up a trust fund for this child to provide financial support after their deaths. The trustee will be a trust company. The company will receive a sum of money when both Ebhardts are deceased. The money will be invested, and the income will be used for the child's support. When the child dies, the trustee will divide the capital (the original sum of money) equally among all the surviving Ebhardt children.

Vicarious Performance

As you have seen, the privity of contract rule says that, with some exceptions, only the parties to a contract can enforce the terms of a contract. However, the party who signs the contract may not always be the person who actually performs the contract obligations.

The Fitzhughs hire an electrical contractor to wire the house they are building. It is quite possible that the contractor will not do the work personally, but will instead send an employee who is an electrician to do the work.

A situation where the person who actually performs the obligations of the contract is not a party to the contract is called **vicarious performance**. Unless personal performance by the party to the contract is a term of the contract, vicarious performance is an acceptable way of carrying out contractual obligations. This is not a true exception to the privity of contract rule, since the original party is still responsible for seeing that the contractual obligations are performed. Therefore, in the example, if the employee electrician fails to show up or does an inadequate job, the Fitzhughs would seek a remedy from the contractor, not the employee.

—Can you think of situations where personal performance would be a term in a contract?

Assignment

Assignment is the transfer of a party's rights under a contract to another party. Generally, only rights, not obligations, can be assigned without the consent of the other party. As Figure 14-2 shows, a person who assigns a right is called the **assignor**. The person who receives the right is called the **assignee**, while the person who must perform the obligation is the **promisor**.

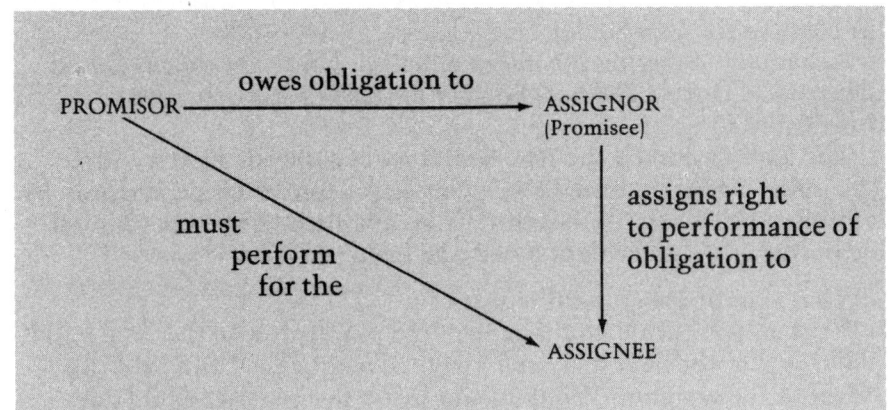

Figure 14-2 Assignment of Rights: The Relationship between Assignor, Assignee, and Promisor

A very common type of assignment involves **book debts**, money owed to a business by its customers. The business may assign the right to collect these debts to its own creditors to pay off its debts, or it may sell them to raise cash. The assignment of book debts is covered by specific legislation in every province.

There are two types of contractual assignment. The first occurs where the assignor transfers *all* rights under the contract. To be valid, the assignment must be of the complete right and in writing. As well, the promisor must receive notice in writing. This type of assignment, called a **statutory assignment**, is governed by statute in most provinces. Even where there is no provincial law, such assignments are still valid. The assignment is often of the right to collect a sum of money. Since the complete right is transferred, the assignor has no further interest in the contract. If the promisor fails to perform, it will be up to the assignee to seek a remedy against the promisor.

The other type of contractual assignment is called an **equitable assignment**, since in the past only courts of equity would recognize them. An assignment is equitable if only *part* of a right or debt is assigned, if the assignment is not in writing, or if the promisor is not given notice in writing of the assignment. However, the promisor must receive some type of notice for the assignment to be valid. The main difference between an equitable and a statutory assignment is that, in an equitable assignment, if the assignee wants to sue the promisor, the assignor must also be a party to the lawsuit.

An assignee of a contractual right may lose that right if notice of the assignment is not given to the promisor, as the following case illustrates.

Hazel v. Rahaman (1981) 32 O.R. (2d) 108 (Ont. H.C.J.)

Hazel was dismissed as an employee of Rahaman. Hazel sued for damages and costs for wrongful dismissal and was successful. In the suit, he had applied for and received assistance from the Legal Aid program of the Law Society of Upper Canada. He assigned the claim for costs to the Law Society.

Rahaman, in paying the judgement, paid both the damages and the costs to Hazel. The Law Society applied to have the costs transferred to it.

The application by the Law Society was set aside by the court. The judge stated that the Law Society, as assignee, could sue only by joining with Hazel, the assignor, as co-plaintiff. This was impossible in this case, as the debt owed had been satisfied.

— What type of assignment is this?
— What do you think would happen if a promisor who received valid notice that the debt had been assigned went ahead and paid the debt to the assignor? What do you think the assignee could do?
— What do you think a promisor should do upon receiving two separate notices that the same debt has been assigned to two different people?

An important rule regarding assignment is that the assignee cannot be in a better position than the assignor to enforce the contract. Thus, if the promisor could avoid the contract because it was entered under undue influence or because the goods the promisor received were defective, the assignee would not be able to enforce the contract. In other words, the assignee has only the same rights as the assignor in enforcing the contract.

Rights to a contract may also be assigned by *operation of the law* in two situations. First, when a person dies, the executor of the will, or the administrator if there is no will, is assigned all outstanding rights and obligations under the existing contracts of the deceased. The executor or administrator must pay all outstanding debts and other financial obligations of the deceased, and distribute the remaining assets of the estate according to the will.

Second, if a person goes into **bankruptcy**, a court will appoint a trustee to take charge of the bankrupt's property. The bankrupt's assets, including contractual rights and liabilities, are assigned to the trustee, who carries out the bankruptcy proceedings. The trustee **liquidates** (turns into cash) all assets of the bankrupt and pays the creditors as much as possible.

Discharge of Contract

At some time, all contracts come to an end. A contract which has ended is referred to as *discharged*. **Discharge** can be defined as the cancellation of the obligations under a contract, or the release of all parties from their obligations under a contract.

There are four usual ways in which a contract can be discharged:

1. performance
2. agreement
3. frustration
4. operation of the law

Another way is through breach of contract, which is a rather different method and will be dealt with separately.

Discharge by Performance

Discharge by performance occurs when both parties carry out all their obligations under a contract. The performance of obligations can take many forms, including the delivery of goods as in a sale, or the performance of a service as in a surgical operation.

If one party tries to carry out his or her part of the contract and, for some reason, the other party refuses to accept the performance, is the first party still obligated to perform? In most situations, the answer is "No". If an offer to perform is refused, the offer does not need to be made again. However, if one party offers to pay a debt and payment is refused, the debt will not be discharged, although no interest will have to be paid on it after the time the offer was refused.

It is interesting to note that for all debts in Canada, the creditor may require payment to be in Canadian legal tender. Only the following constitute legal tender: any amount of Bank of Canada notes (paper money); up to $10 in silver coins; up to $5 in nickel coins; and up to 25¢ in copper coins. Amounts over these do not have to be accepted in payment of a debt. Cheques, certified cheques, and money orders therefore do not have to be accepted, although they almost always are, in the normal course of modern business.

Discharge by Agreement

If both parties agree not to perform their respective duties under a contract, it is discharged by agreement. Such discharge can come about in any of three ways: by **waiver**, by **substituted agreement**, and through a clause of the contract that provides for its own dissolution under some circumstances.

Waiver

The parties have a contract that is in effect but which neither party wishes any longer to perform. They make an agreement to call off the original contract. Such an agreement is known as a waiver. If both parties have performed only part of their obligations, the consideration each receives is freedom from carrying out the remaining portion of the obligations. If, however, one party has performed all of his or her obligations, there is no consideration to give. Therefore, in order to make the agreement of waiver binding in such a situation, it should be made under seal.

Substituted Agreement

A substituted agreement can be achieved in any of three ways: **material alteration**, **accord and satisfaction**, and **novation**.

Material Alteration

Imagine that you have agreed to purchase a bedroom suite for your new apartment from a furniture store. Upon reflection, you realize that you cannot really afford the furniture. You decide to return to the store to ask for a change in your agreement: the purchase of a less expensive bedroom suite. The clerk tells you there is no problem; the less expensive suite can easily be substituted for your original choice. Have you made changes to an existing contract, or have you created a new one? Since the type of furniture and the price are major terms of the agreement, you have created a new one. Whenever the parties to a contract agree to a material alteration, the original agreement is discharged, and a new one is established.

Accord and Satisfaction

Lois has an agreement that is to last for four months with an exercise instructor. When the contract was made, the instructor was three months pregnant, but she believed that she could fulfill the agreement. After three months of classes, the instructor finds that she cannot continue with the heavy exercise. She decides to take some time preparing for her baby and looking after it before returning to her career. She offers to give Lois a refund of part of her fee and terminate the lessons. If Lois agrees, is the contract discharged? It is— if one party is unable to carry out the obligations under the contract, that person may offer to do something else, such as make a payment of money, to discharge the contract. This type of agreement is often in the form of an out-of-court settlement, and is referred to as accord and satisfaction.

As you can see, the purpose of material alteration is to form a new contract, while the purpose of accord and satisfaction is to discharge a contract.

Novation

After agreeing to make renovations to Steve's house, a carpenter realizes that he is overbooked and will be unable to carry out the contract. He discusses the problem with Steve and suggests that another carpenter, who will also do good work, might take on the job. Steve agrees. This process of releasing a party from a contract and substituting a new party is called novation. The original contract is dissolved, and a new one established. However, the terms of the new contract may be exactly the same as those of the original, as the following case illustrates.

Sheehy v. Edmonton World Hockey Enterprises Ltd. (1979) 105 D.L.R. (3d) 644 (Alta. Q.B.)

Sheehy entered into a contract to play hockey for the New England Whalers of the World Hockey Association in 1974 and did so until 1975. A clause of his contract read, "If Player is traded by the Club during the term of this contract, Club will pay Player Ten Thousand ($10 000.00) Dollars." When he was traded to the Edmonton Oilers in 1975, that sum was paid to Sheehy by the New England club.

Late in 1976, Sheehy was traded to the Birmingham Bulls, where he finished the 1975-76 season. In August of 1977, he demanded from Edmonton the $10 000.00 transfer fee. Edmonton's refusal led to this action.

In deciding the case, the judge determined that the contract which Sheehy held with the Edmonton Oilers contained exactly the same terms as that which had been held with the New England Whalers. The assignment of his contract from New England to Edmonton was by novation. Thus, Edmonton was responsible for paying the transfer fee to Sheehy upon his trade to Birmingham.

Contracts That Provide for their Own Dissolution

A contract may include a clause that releases one or both of the parties in certain situations. Usually, the situation is such that it would make it undesirable for the contract to continue.

Hilary, who lives in Québec, signed an employment contract with V & C Enterprises in British Columbia. The contract provided that Hilary would not start work until V & C found her housing that she considered acceptable.

If V & C does not find acceptable housing for Hilary, she will be released from her obligations under the contract. This type of clause, called a **condition precedent**, provides that some future event must take place before one party's obligations are established.

When José took his present job, he knew that he was replacing a sick employee who might not be able to return to work. A term in his contract provided that his employer might terminate his contract if the other employee recovered and wanted to return to work.

Such a term is called a **condition subsequent**. If the condition provided for actually happens, one party may choose to be released from his or her obligations under the contract.

If a contract of employment is for an indefinite period, it may contain a clause allowing either employee or employer to end the agreement, usually by notifying the other party. Such a clause is called an **option to terminate**.

Discharge by Frustration

Occasionally, a situation will arise where, through no fault of either party, it is impossible for the contract to be carried out, or where circumstances have changed so greatly that performance of the contract would be substantially different from the parties' original agreement. In such situations, the law will excuse a party for failure to carry out the contractual obligations. The contract is said to be discharged by frustration. If, for example, a rock group is to give a concert on a particular night and the lead guitarist becomes too sick to perform, the contract is discharged by frustration due to impossibility of performance.

Figure 14-3 A contract is discharged by frustration when performance is physically impossible.

Consider another situation, wherein a contractor agrees to build a sports stadium for a city for a set amount of money. However, a court orders work to be stopped, because of a dispute over the ownership of the land. After a number of appeals which take several years, the issue of who owns the land is finally settled. The city then insists that the contractor continue building the stadium for the price agreed to in the contract. However, the costs of materials and labour have increased considerably since the contract was made. The agreement may be discharged by frustration, because the performance of the contract would be very different from what was contained in the original document.

A contract will not be discharged by frustration if performance merely causes some hardship to one of the parties. That is a normal risk of making contracts. The agreement must be either impossible to carry out or substantially different from the original. Also, one party cannot deliberately make it impossible to carry out the contract. A musician, for instance, cannot sell his or her instrument and then claim impossibility of performance.

When a contract is frustrated, if neither party has carried out any part of his or her obligations, both are simply discharged from the agreement. However, in many situations, one party or both may have partially performed obligations. It might be quite unfair to simply discharge the parties from any further obligations. For instance, suppose you have made a deposit on a stereo and the store burns down before the stereo is delivered to you. You would probably be very unhappy if the store owner merely said "I cannot deliver the stereo because the contract has been frustrated. I have no further obligations to you." What about your deposit? Does the owner have to return it to you? To settle problems like this, the courts have, over the years, developed certain rules to apply when a partially performed contract is frustrated.

If one party has partially carried out the obligations under the contract by making a money payment, but has received no benefit under the contract, that person may retrieve any sum paid. In other words, a seller that has done work or spent money preparing goods to be delivered will still have to pay back any money received as a deposit if the contract is frustrated and the goods have not yet been delivered. On the other hand, if the seller has received a deposit and has delivered any portion of the goods, no matter how small, the seller is entitled to keep the entire deposit.

Thus, the rules developed by the courts provide an all or nothing solution. The buyer gets back either the entire deposit, or nothing. This solution is unfair to the seller who may have spent some money or time in preparing the goods for the buyer but who has not delivered anything at the time of the frustrating event. To remedy this injustice, the provinces of Prince Edward Island, New Brunswick, British Columbia, Ontario, Manitoba, Alberta, and Newfoundland have each passed a *Frustrated Contracts Act*. These *Acts* make the following provisions:

1. A party who has begun performance may keep as much of the deposit as is necessary to cover costs incurred up to the time of frustration.
2. If a deposit is due but not paid, the other party has a right to the sum necessary to pay costs incurred up to the time of frustration.
3. A court may award to the performer a reasonable amount of money for goods already delivered to the other party at the time of frustration.

Discharge by Operation of the Law

Bankruptcy

The process of declaring bankruptcy is governed by the federal *Bankruptcy Act*. As mentioned earlier in this chapter, declaring bankruptcy involves the liquidation of certain assets of the bankrupt person by a trustee. The bankrupt's debts are then paid proportionately, that is, in relation to the amount owed to each creditor. Even though the creditors will not be paid in full, by law, the bankrupt is discharged from any further obligations.

Limitation of Actions

If a person is owed money and the debtor refuses to pay, the creditor has the right to sue in a court of law to recover the money. However, every province has legislation that *bars* (prevents) a person from suing on a contract debt after a certain amount of time has passed. In the common law provinces, the limitation period is six years from the date on which the debt was due; in Québec, the period is five years.

Breach of Contract

Breach of contract is the breaking or violation of contractual obligations. Breach of the whole contract or of a material term of the contract, called a **condition**, will discharge the agreement. A condition is a term so basic and important that its breach would substantially change the nature of the contract. A non-material term is called a **warranty**. Breach of a warranty will not discharge the entire agreement, but it does entitle the injured party to damages.

Arnett v. Mohacsy (1981) 24 A.R. 414 (Alta. Q.B.)

Arnett responded to a newspaper ad in the Calgary Herald that was worded as follows:

> T-Bird: Exceptional. $2200.
> New motor, tires. 287-0972.

The ad had been placed by the defendant, Mohacsy.

Arnett and his wife went to look at the car. They inspected the car, including the motor, carefully, and took it for a test drive around the block. Mohacsy was not pushy about the sale. Arnett and his wife left for a short while to discuss the purchase. A decision was made to purchase the car. Arnett signed the bill of sale, paid the purchase price, and took delivery of the car.

Shortly afterwards, the engine seized and quit operating. It was determined at the trial that the engine was not, in fact, new.

— **Has Mohacsy breached the contract? Is the breach of a condition or of a warranty? Explain.**
— **To what remedy is the plaintiff entitled? Explain.**

Types of Breaches

Breach may occur in any of three ways:

1. express repudiation
2. rendering performance impossible
3. failure to perform

Express Repudiation

You have agreed to buy a car and have made a down payment on it. The person from whom you have bought it then tells you that she has changed her mind about selling the car. She has expressly repudiated the contract by stating outright that she does not intend to carry out her obligations. What can be done about this situation? You should notify the other party that you consider the contract breached and terminated, and that you reserve the right to sue for damages. The damages may include a return of the down payment you have made, the cost of renting a car until you find another one, and the costs of the lawsuit.

Rendering Performance Impossible

In the discussion of discharge by frustration, we mentioned that a musician who had an agreement to perform a concert could not sell his or her instrument and subsequently claim impossibility of performance. The musician, by so doing, would have breached the agreement. Generally, if a party to a contract does something that makes it impossible to carry out the contract, that party is considered to have breached it.

Failure to Perform

If one party fails to perform a contractual obligation, a breach has occurred, and the other party is freed from performing. An exception to this general rule is the doctrine of **substantial performance**. It states that, if one party has performed most, but not all, of his or her obligations, the other party cannot avoid performance. In other words, if one party has done everything except a minor part of the contract, the other party cannot refuse to perform. However, the other party can deduct the amount of money it takes to complete the contract.

Remember Max and Jean who entered a contract for Jean to paint Max's house? Jean has finished painting the house and has moved on to her next job. Max notices that Jean forgot to paint the front steps, although she was supposed to do so under their contract. Jean has breached the contract, but it is such a minor breach that Max would not be justified in refusing to pay her. He could, however, deduct from her payment the costs of buying paint for the steps and of hiring someone else to do the painting.

Figure 14-4 Breach of a minor part of a contract does not permit the party suffering the breach to avoid performance.

Remedies for Breach

In the event of a breach, four remedies are available to the injured party: damages, *quantum meruit*, specific performance, and injunction. The type of breach and the subject matter of the contract determine which remedy will apply.

Damages

Damages are *monies* (sums) paid by the breaching party for the purpose of putting the victim in the position he or she would have been in if the contract had been carried out. For example, a store that contracted with a manufacturer for the purchase of sportswear may sue for the extra cost of buying similar sportswear elsewhere in the event that the manufacturer fails to deliver the clothes.

The injured party in a breach of contract must attempt to *mitigate* damages, that is, to minimize losses. If he or she does not, a court will be reluctant to grant full damages for the loss.

A wholesale fruit and vegetable dealer has an agreement to sell a quantity of produce to a greengrocer. If the grocer expressly repudiates the contract, the dealer must attempt to resell the produce at the best possible price. The dealer cannot just let the produce rot and then sue for its value. The dealer's damages would be the difference between what the greengrocer would have paid, and the price the dealer obtained when the produce was resold.

The purpose of damages is to compensate the injured party, not to punish the breaching party. This explains why the victim of the breach can claim only actual losses. Sometimes, the precise amount of loss may be unclear. In such a situation, the amount will be estimated by the court. If the loss is minimal, a nominal award will be given by the court to the successful plaintiff to establish the validity of the claim.

Liquidated Damages

A contract may contain a term setting out the amount of damages to which each party will be entitled if the other party breaches the contract. Such a term is called a **liquidated damages clause**. A court will enforce the term if it believes that the parties have made a genuine attempt to estimate what their losses would be if the contract were breached. The court will do so even if the liquidated damages are much greater or less than the actual damages. If the court finds that the estimate of damages was not reasonable, but was intended to pressure one party into performing the contract, the court will not enforce the clause. In this case, the term is called a **penalty clause**.

—Why do you think courts will not enforce penalty clauses?

Payment of Damages

When a court awards damages to a plaintiff, the defendant may pay the award voluntarily. However, if the defendant (now called the *judgement debtor*) refuses to pay the plaintiff (the *judgement creditor*), the plaintiff must take further steps to obtain payment. The plaintiff may ask the sheriff of the county or district where the defendant lives to **levy execution** against the defendant's goods. The sheriff will then seize the defendant's property and sell it at auction. The proceeds will go to the plaintiff.

—Check your province's *Execution Act* or contact your local sheriff's office. Find out
  (a) what specific steps a judgement creditor must take to require the sheriff to levy execution;
  (b) what property is exempt from seizure.

Another step a judgement creditor may take is to obtain a **garnishee order**. This court order will be sent to the judgement debtor's employer. It will direct the employer to deduct part of the debtor's wages and give it over to the creditor.

Quantum Meruit

Paolo has made an agreement with an electrician to wire a new house that he is having built. The electrician has just started the work when Paolo breaches the contract by telling him that he has found someone else to do the work for less money. In such a case, the electrician has a right to *quantum meruit*. (*Quantum meruit* is a Latin phrase meaning "as much as it is worth".) This principle requires the offending party to pay a reasonable price for the work done until the time of breach.

If the electrician had completed most of the work, he would have relied instead on the doctrine of substantial performance. He could then have sued for the contract price, minus the cost of completing whatever minor work had not been done.

Specific Performance

Specific performance is a court order requiring the breaching party to carry out his or her obligations under the contract. The plaintiff must

Figure 14-5 *A court will not order specific performance if the contract requires personal service, since the court will not supervise the performance, and cannot decide whether performance is adequate.*

show the court that money damages are an inadequate remedy and that specific performance is the only proper compensation for the breach. A court will not order specific performance if it will require supervision by the court. Thus, a court will not order specific performance where the personal service of the party is required. For instance, it would not order a singer to give a concert or a football player to play football. Besides requiring court supervision, it would be too difficult for the court to decide whether the performance satisfied the contract.

Specific performance is often used in cases relating to the sale of land. Every piece of land is considered unique. Therefore, money damages are not usually an adequate remedy, since the money will not put the victim of breach in the same place he or she would have been if the contract had not been breached.

Injunction

In contrast to specific performance, which requires a person to act in a particular way, an injunction is a court order restraining a person from acting in a particular way. An injunction is usually granted when an ongoing breach must be stopped. If a tenant has been using a building in a way other than that allowed by the lease, the court may grant an injunction that will order the tenant to discontinue using the premises in the offending way.

Hi-Fi Express Inc. v. Walsa Ltd. et al. (1981) 61 C.P.R. (2d) 71 (Ont. H.C.J.)

Hi-Fi Express had rented commercial space from Walsa Ltd. in a Metropolitan Toronto shopping plaza; the lease commenced in 1977. A clause in the lease provided that "the lessor...will not rent any other premises in the shopping centre...to be used as a retail stereo store or business and that it will not permit direct or indirect competition with the lessee's business." In 1981, Walsa entered into an agreement to rent space in the same plaza to Fairview Electronics Limited. The space was to be used to carry on a video equipment sales and rental business. Hi-Fi Express applied to the court for an injunction.

Hi-Fi Express argued that, when the original lease had been signed, very few stereo shops were also involved in the sale and rental of video equipment. However, since that time, the practice had become common. It contended that the agreement between Walsa and Fairview would violate its agreement with Walsa in view of the fact that it had entered the video business as well as continuing the stereo business.

The court agreed with the plaintiff and granted the injunction restraining Walsa from entering the agreement with Fairview until the lease with Hi-Fi Express terminated.

The *Statute of Frauds*

Alice Beecham and her daughter Elizabeth had been searching for a house to buy. One Saturday, while driving home from shopping, they saw a house with a "For Sale" sign in front of it. They stopped and talked to the owners, the Pateks, who were selling the house themselves, without a real estate agent. The Beechams liked the house immediately on touring it. Alice Beecham thereupon offered the Pateks a price several thousand dollars less than the asking price. After a brief discussion, the Pateks accepted it. Then the Pateks and Alice Beecham sat down and worked out the other major terms of the contract. Afterwards, they all shook hands.

When Alice Beecham called the Pateks the next day, she was dismayed to find that they did not intend to go through with the sale. It turned out that, after the Beechams had gone home, the Pateks had decided that the offer was too low. The Pateks called their lawyer, who told them that they were not bound by the agreement.

Why is it that the Pateks were not bound to the contract? Since proving the terms of an oral contract could be very difficult, every province has legislation stating that certain types of oral contracts are not enforceable in court. This does not mean that the contract is not valid, but it does mean that a court will not help the parties to enforce it.

The first legislation that dealt with this issue was the English *Statute of Frauds*, passed in 1677. The types of contracts it required to be in writing were as follows:

1. Any contract that is to take more than one year for both parties to carry out.
2. Any contract that deals with the sale of land or the acquisition of an interest in land such as mineral rights, a mortgage, or a lease.
3. Any promise to pay the debt, default, or miscarriage of another person (that is, to be a guarantor for a debtor).
4. Any promise of a gift on the condition that a marriage take place.
5. Any promise by an executor or administrator to pay the debts of a deceased person out of his or her own funds.

Each province's legislation requires some or all of these types of contracts to be in writing in order to be enforceable.

—**Obtain a copy of the *Statute of Frauds* for your province. What kinds of contracts does it say must be in writing?**

Does the written agreement have to be in a formal document, or may it be in a less structured format? The following case looks at this question.

Ditlove et al. v. Davis Industries 1979 Sask. Q.B. (unreported)

Ditlove sued Davis Industries Ltd. in connection with a contract involving the sale of the defendant's steelmaking operations in Regina and Saskatoon. Since the contract was within the *Statute of Frauds*, the court had to decide whether the agreement was in writing. Ditlove claimed that the agreement was shown by (a) a memo signed by the president of the company, who personally controlled its affairs; (b) a letter from the company's accountant to Ditlove reviewing the terms of the memo; and (c) a letter from Ditlove's lawyers to the president of the company setting out the terms of the agreement. The company claimed that these letters and memos did not satisfy the requirements of the *Statute of Frauds*.

The court decided that the letters and memos were sufficiently specific to indicate that an agreement had taken place.

It is clear from this that the contract does not need to be contained in one document. However, the written record of the agreement must contain all of the essential terms of the agreement and must be signed by the party denying the existence of the contract.

Part Performance of Contracts Regarding Land

One exception to the *Statute of Frauds* provides that an oral contract regarding land may become enforceable if one party begins to perform his or her obligations and the contract meets certain requirements:

1. The action or part performance must clearly indicate the existence of the contract.
2. Part performance must have been done by the plaintiff, who will suffer loss if the contract is not enforced.

Starlite Variety Stores Ltd. v. Cloverlawn Investments Ltd. et al. (1978) 92 D.L.R. (3d) 270 (Ont. H.C.J.)

Cloverlawn was in the business of building shopping plazas and renting space in them. Cloverlawn orally negotiated an agreement with Starlite, the operator of a chain of small variety stores, under which Starlite would rent commercial space from Cloverlawn for a convenience store. An offer to lease was drawn up but was never signed.

During the time of construction, Starlite requested certain changes in the storefront and in the location of electrical conduits. The defendant made these changes, and others that were later requested. Also at this time, Starlite ordered signs and shelving for the store at a cost of over $5000.

Subsequently, Cloverlawn had discussions with Mac's Convenience Stores Limited for the lease of the same commercial space at a higher rent. When a lease was signed with Mac's, Starlite brought an action for specific performance of its agreement with Cloverlawn.

—Does the *Statute of Frauds* apply to this case? Why?
—Should the doctrine of part performance apply to this case? Explain your reasoning.
—What do you think the outcome of this case was?

The Sale of Goods

Originally, the English *Statute of Frauds* required any purchase of goods with a value of £10 or more to be in writing. In 1893, that provision was transferred to the English *Sale of Goods Act*. Today, every province except British Columbia has a similar provision in its *Sale of Goods Act*. The amount of the purchase varies among the *Acts* from $30 to $50.

Contracts covered by these *Acts* are enforceable without evidence in writing if any of the following conditions is present:

1. The buyer has done something that would recognize the existence of a contract, and has received the goods.
2. The buyer has offered part payment to the seller, who has accepted it.

3. The buyer has given the seller something of value "in earnest". Something of value given in earnest is not part payment for the goods; rather, it is a token, to be held by the seller to show that the buyer is serious about the agreement. It will eventually be returned to the buyer.

SUMMARIZING YOUR READING

1. Explain the rule of privity of contract.

2. Who is a "stranger" to a contract? By what other names is a stranger known?

3. Are contracts for life insurance exempt from the rule of privity of contract? Explain.

4. Describe a situation concerning land in which the rule of privity of contract does not apply.

5. Describe how trusts are affected by the rule of privity of contract.

6. What is vicarious performance? Under what conditions is it acceptable?

7. Define "assignment".

8. Briefly describe the roles of the promisor; the assignor; and the assignee.

9. In what situation can an assignee alone sue a promisor?

10. How can a statutory assignment be made enforceable in court?

11. In an action involving a partial assignment, who must be parties to the action?

12. Can an assignee receive better rights than the assignor had in the original contract? Explain.

13. Describe two situations in which rights under a contract may be assigned by operation of the law.

14. Define "discharge". Name the ways in which a contract may be discharged.

15. Briefly describe "discharge by performance". What is the effect of one party's refusal to accept an attempt by the other party to perform obligations under the contract?

16. What constitutes "legal tender"?

17. Describe briefly "discharge by agreement".

18. What is the effect of a waiver agreement? When should such a contract be under seal?

19. What is the effect of a material alteration on a contract?

20. What is the difference between material alteration and accord and satisfaction?

21. What causes novation to occur? What is the effect of novation?

22. How might a contract provide for its own dissolution?

23. Differentiate between condition precedent and condition subsequent.

24. What is an option to terminate?

25. Name the two situations that will lead to discharge by frustration.

26. What is the result of a frustrated contract if neither party has carried out any part of his or her obligations?

27. What are the major provisions of the *Frustrated Contracts Acts*?

28. How is a bankrupt discharged from contractual obligations by operation of the law?

29. Define "breach".

30. Name and briefly describe the three ways in which breach may occur.

31. What is the doctrine of substantial performance?

32. What is the purpose of damages as a remedy for breach? What obligation is placed upon the injured party? What are two ways in which a judgement for damages may be enforced?

33. In what situation does *quantum meruit* apply?

34. What is the difference between specific performance and an injunction?

35. Name the five types of contracts that must be in writing to be enforceable, according to the *Statute of Frauds*.

36. What three conditions must be present in order to make part performance applicable in contracts regarding land?

37. When may contracts for the sale of goods be enforceable without evidence in writing?

PROJECTS AND ACTIVITIES

1. Find out from three car dealerships whether they assign their rights under financing agreements. To whom are rights assigned? Why does the dealership assign them? What effect, if any, does the assignment have on the warranty of the vehicle?

2. From the students' association of your school, obtain a contract made with a band to play a school dance. Does it contain provisions for discharge of the agreement? Why are these provisions included? Are there other conditions that might discharge the contract? What other provisions for discharge might a band want in a contract?

3. Obtain a contract for a car rental. Examine it, classifying each term as a condition or warranty. Why do you consider each condition important enough to the agreement to discharge the whole contract if breached?

4. Complete the scrapbook begun in Chapter 12. Look through each of the articles and identify the concepts discussed in this unit on contract law. You will be looking for the following:
   (a) intent to create legal relationships
   (b) simple contracts and contracts under seal
   (c) offer and acceptance
   (d) consideration
   (e) legal capacity
   (f) freely consenting parties
   (g) illegal contracts
   (h) privity of contract
   (i) assignment
   (j) discharge
   (k) breach
   (l) applications of the *Statute of Frauds*

5. Research the process of declaring personal bankruptcy, paying particular attention to the assignment of rights and obligations under various contracts, and the discharge of those contracts upon the completion of bankruptcy proceedings.

RESOLVING CASES

Marquis Holdings Ltd. v. Parsons (1982) 37 Nfld. & P.E.I.R. 345 (Nfld. D.C.)

Parsons was a commercial tenant in a building owned by the plaintiff. Parsons had for some time tried to have Marquis fix the furnace and a serious leak in the roof. He finally stopped paying the rent of $600 a month and, while one month in arrears in the rent, moved out. Marquis then changed the locks and attempted unsuccessfully to rent the premises for twice as much as Parsons had paid ($1200 per month). Marquis also sued for the rent in arrears when Parsons moved out, and for the total rent due under the remainder of the lease.

—Has Marquis made a reasonable attempt to mitigate its damages?
—If you were the judge, what damages would you allow?

Tanu et al. v. Ray et al. (1981) 20 R.P.R. 22 (B.C. S.C.)

Mr. and Mrs. Tanu entered an agreement with Mr. and Mrs. Ray to purchase the Rays' house. The Rays later regretted signing the contract and refused to go through with the deal. The Tanus brought an action for specific performance of the contract. Their evidence was that the house was closer to a school and to Mr. Tanu's place of work than their current house, and that there were no other equivalent houses in the neighbourhood in the same price range.

—Is this a case where specific performance is an appropriate remedy?
—Would damages be inadequate? Explain your reasoning.

Graham v. Voth Bros. Const. (1974) Ltd. and Powell River Shopping Plaza Ltd. [1982] 6 W.W.R. 365 (B.C. C.C.)

Graham had a contract with Voth Bros. to haul away earth that was being removed from a site. Graham had subcontracted a major portion of the work to other operators. When the job was completed, Voth Bros. contended that many of the trucks had not been fully loaded and demanded that Graham reduce his billing before any payment would be made. Because Graham had to pay his subcontractors, failure to receive the money from Voth Bros. would certainly have put him into bankruptcy. Therefore, he accepted the demands of Voth Bros. and issued invoices for lower amounts. Voth Bros. paid these invoices. Graham then brought an action for the recovery of the balance of the original invoices.

During the trial, the court found that Voth's claims that the trucks were not fully loaded were unfounded. The court also found that Voth knew that by not making any payment to Graham, even though it was clear that he was entitled to payment, Graham would be forced into bankruptcy.

—The defendants put forth the defence of accord and satisfaction. How would you deal with this defence as counsel for the plaintiff?
—What do you think was the decision in this case?

Day v. Roach (1981) 29 B.C.L.R. 107 (B.C.S.C.)

Roach agreed to sell Day a townhouse in Victoria for $59 900. There was to be a $1000 down payment, and a mortgage of $49 500. The balance, $9400, was to be deposited in Roach's lawyer's trust account on January 26, 1981 and paid to the seller on January 30, 1981. The balance was, in fact, deposited in trust on January 28, 1981.

Roach, not wanting to continue with the sale, took advantage of the late deposit; he refused it and the completion of the sale. Day sought specific performance of the agreement.

—Is the time when the deposit was put in the trust account a condition, a warranty, or neither? Explain.
—Should specific performance be ordered? Explain.

Freeland v. Freeland (1982) 19 A.L.R. (2d) 180 (Alta. Q.B.)

David Freeland obtained land for homesteading in 1967. His father Wilbur and brother Donald worked the land. David left the area in 1969. In 1972, Donald obtained more land for homesteading in David's name. (He believed he could not get it in his own name.) Donald did all the work on this portion of the land, and made all payments.

When a dispute arose in the family as to who owned the second piece of land, an oral arrangement was made as follows: Donald would have the northwest quarter section, David would have the southeast quarter section, David and Wilbur would jointly have the northeast quarter, and Donald and Wilbur could farm the eastern half section for ten years without payment to David.

David subsequently refused to carry out the agreement. Donald asked the court to enforce the agreement.

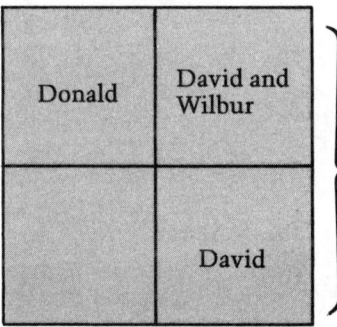

Figure 14-6

—Should the *Statute of Frauds* be invoked in this case? Explain.
—Should the agreement be enforceable as it stands? Explain.

UNIT 3

The Law and the Family

15 Forming the Family Unit
16 Children and Their Parents
17 Ending the Relationship
18 Wills and Inheritance

15

Forming the Family Unit

Engagement
Creating a Valid Marriage
After the Wedding

Cohabiting Couples
Domestic Contracts

Marriage is the traditional first step in the creation of a new family unit. It is likely that most people who marry are not primarily concerned with the legal aspects of marriage. Rather, they may well think more about what the relationship will mean to them personally on a day-to-day basis. There will be emotional and social, as well as financial, changes. Individuals respond to all of these changes in different ways. However, the law defines marriage in a very precise way. It is therefore useful to know about the effects of the legal aspects of marriage.

Legally, marriage involves a change in status. When the status of unmarried people changes to that of husband and wife, or **spouses**, a whole new set of rights and responsibilities that did not exist between them before is created. These rights and obligations are imposed by the state and enforced by the courts. This chapter examines the requirements for a valid marriage, and the legal rights and duties that accompany marriage.

—This chapter will be examining the legal effects of marriage. What are some of the emotional, social, and financial aspects of getting married?

Engagement

The legal rights and responsibilities of engaged people can, in fact, be established even before the wedding. When two people become engaged to be married, they have entered a contract to marry. Suppose that an intended bride decides that she cannot go through with the wedding, and breaks her engagement.

Figure 15-1

—Could the intended groom force her to carry out her engagement to marry him?
—Would she have to return her engagement ring?
—What should be done with all of the wedding presents?

Some engaged couples never do take marriage vows, for a variety of reasons. The engagement can be broken by mutual consent. However, when two people agree to marry, but legal marriage does not take place because of the fault of one of them, a **breach of promise** has occurred. Breach of promise is the wrongful breaking of the contract to marry. Many such cases have come before the courts. The principles of these cases can be summarized as follows. First, the courts will not order a marriage to take place. Forcing people to marry is clearly against the public interest.

Next, gifts given by the engaged couple to one another in contemplation of the marriage are considered to be *conditional* gifts. Therefore, if the engagement is broken by mutual agreement, all gifts given in contemplation of the marriage must be returned. For example, an engagement ring is given in contemplation of the marriage, but a birthday gift is not, and therefore does not have to be returned. However, the person who wrongfully breaks the engagement cannot demand the return of gifts, like the engagement ring, which were given "conditional" on the marriage taking place. Gifts given by others to the engaged couple are also considered to be conditional and must be returned if the wedding does not take place, no matter what the reason.

Finally, the person responsible for the decision not to marry may be required to compensate the intended spouse for harm suffered. Damages may be awarded by the court when an engagement is wrongfully broken, just as in other breach of contract actions. For instance, general damages have been awarded for such "losses" as injury to the feelings of the jilted party; the loss of potential social position; and the loss of the opportunity to be supported. Special damages have been awarded for such items as wedding expenses, the cost of the wedding dress and trousseau, and the loss of income when a job is given up because of the expected marriage.

Baxter v. Lear (1976) 23 R.F.L. 342 (Man. Q.B.)

In April of 1971, the defendant, Lear, gave Baxter an engagement ring. The wedding date was set for April, 1973, because Lear was an R.C.M.P. cadet and could not marry for two years. When Lear was transferred to a new city, Baxter gave up her job and moved to be near him. She was accompanied by her child from another relationship, and the three began living together as a family. Subsequently, the plaintiff made a wedding dress and purchased wedding invitations, but the marriage was postponed when Lear was transferred to Ottawa.

After this move, the defendant broke the engagement, but he invited Baxter and her child to visit Ottawa to discuss the situation. As a result of this trip, the engagement was revived, but some time later, Lear again broke the engagement against the wishes of his intended bride. Baxter sued and was awarded special damages of $1611.60 for the loss of income due to the first move, the trip to Ottawa, the wedding dress, and the invitations. She also received general damages of $1000 for her injured feelings, embarrassment and emotional disturbance, and the loss of the opportunity to have a father for her child.

—What is your opinion of this decision?
—What purpose do you think the engagement period should serve?
—Should a person be penalized because he or she feels incapable of taking the important step of marriage?
—Why do you think the right to sue for breach of promise originally existed?
—Does the breach of promise action still make sense today?

Some provinces are abolishing the breach of promise action. Ontario, for example, has revised its *Marriage Act* so that the common law right to sue for breach of promise to marry no longer exists.

Creating A Valid Marriage

In every marriage ceremony, the bride and groom exchange promises, but making marriage vows is not all that is necessary for creating a valid, legal marriage. You may remember from your study of Canada's Constitution that both the federal and provincial governments have authority over marriage. The federal government has jurisdiction over marriage and divorce. This means that it has authority over the *essential requirements* for a valid marriage. Most of these essential requirements are found in the common law.

The provincial governments have the authority under the Constitution to pass laws for the solemnization of marriage. That is, the rules which must be followed for a marriage ceremony to be legally conducted fall within the jurisdiction of the province. These rules are called the *formal requirements* of marriage. Each of the provincial governments has passed a *Marriage Act* outlining these formal requirements.

The Essential Requirements of Marriage

Sir J.P. Wilde, a famous nineteenth century British judge, defined marriage as "a voluntary union for life of one man to one woman to the exclusion of all others." As brief as it is, this definition actually includes three of the essential requirements.

Man and Woman

First, marriage must be between a man and a woman. Although there have been cases of homosexual couples applying for licences to marry, or going through a wedding ceremony, the law does not recognize the existence of a marriage between people of the same sex. The law regarding marriage has developed from **canon law** (church law). The church has always considered children to be an essential part of marriage. For this reason, marriage must of necessity be between a man and a woman.

In addition, the bride and groom must be capable of **consummating** the marriage (having sexual intercourse). The inability to have sexual intercourse on the part of either is called *impotence* by the law. It does not matter whether the cause of impotence is physical or psychological, but if it is incurable and it existed at the time the marriage was performed, the marriage may be declared invalid. However, sterility, the incapacity to have children, does not affect the status of the marriage.

Consent

The second aspect of Sir Wilde's definition is that the man and woman must voluntarily consent to the marriage. A person who consents to marry out of fear or because of severe pressure from others has not voluntarily consented to the marriage. In these situations, consent has been obtained under duress and is therefore not valid.

A mistake as to the nature of the ceremony or the identity of the person one is marrying may invalidate the marriage, because of the lack of true consent. Consider the following case:

Jiwani (Samji) v. Samji (1980) 11 R.F.L. (2d) 188 (B.C.S.C.)

The twenty-two-year-old plaintiff, Jiwani, asked the courts to declare her marriage invalid. Originally from Uganda, she had resided in Canada for seven years. She spoke English quite well.

Marriage customs in Uganda involved two ceremonies: the betrothal (engagement) ceremony, and the marriage (wedding) ceremony. The plaintiff's parents pressed her to marry the defendant, and in August, 1977 she went through a civil marriage ceremony in the office of the marriage registrar. One week later, in her parents' home, a betrothal ceremony according to Ugandan custom took place. At this time, the plaintiff told her friends that the marriage would likely not take place for a year. The plaintiff's parents pressured her to have the wedding ceremony performed right away, and when she refused, the defendant told her that they were already married.

In her evidence, Jiwani told the court that she thought the civil ceremony which took place in August, 1977 was for the purpose of obtaining government permission to marry. The marriage had never been consummated. In her distress at the news that she was already married to the defendant, the plaintiff went to her doctor, who sent her to a lawyer. The judge found that, because Jiwani did not understand the nature of the ceremony she had gone through with the defendant, she could not be said to have voluntarily consented. The marriage was declared invalid.

—**What evidence do you think the judge took into consideration in declaring this marriage to be invalid?**

Freedom to Marry

If, as Sir Wilde said, marriage is between one man and one woman, to the exclusion of all others, it follows that the parties must not be married to anyone else. This is the third essential requirement. In Canada, a person must be single, widowed, or legally divorced before being able to marry. A person who marries when he or she is not free to do so can be charged with the crime of **bigamy**. The second marriage will be void. As well, the person's first spouse will have grounds for divorce.

An unusual situation occurs when a spouse disappears in circumstances where the other spouse suspects he or she might be dead. It is possible in this event to apply to the courts after a certain period (usually seven years) for a Declaration of Presumption of Death. If it is granted, the spouse who obtained it is free to remarry. However, if the first spouse should turn up alive, the second marriage is void. Without any intention, bigamy has occurred. An unintentional bigamist would not be prosecuted under criminal law, however. Although, as you can imagine, cases such as this are rare, England has solved the problem by changing the law. In England, when a spouse is declared by the courts to be presumed dead, the marriage is also dissolved. Future marriages of the "surviving" spouse are therefore protected.

Mental Competence

The fourth essential requirement is that people who marry must be mentally competent to understand what marriage actually is, as well as the rights and responsibilities which are created by it. Certain mental illnesses can invalidate a marriage; so can drug or alcohol intoxication, as this Alberta case shows.

Meilen v. Andersson (1977) 6 A.R. 427 (Alta. S.C.)

The plaintiff, Meilen, who normally resided in Alberta, was living for a period of time in Los Angeles, California. There he met the defendant and a man named Tom McGowan. The evidence presented to the court was that Andersson and McGowan were involved in a cult. They tricked the plaintiff into taking narcotics, which he was not in the habit of doing. The plaintiff was kept in a drugged condition for six weeks, during which time he married Andersson in Las Vegas. He finally escaped from the cult after a threat was made against his life.

Meilen asked the court for a declaration that his marriage was void because he did not have the mental capacity at the time the ceremony was performed to consent to the marriage. The court held the marriage to be void.

Age

It is necessary to be of a sufficient age in order to marry. At common law, this age is twelve for girls and fourteen for boys. Provincial legislation, however, has amended the common law rule by setting higher minimum ages. This change reflects the legislators' feeling that it is not in the public interest to allow children to marry.

Consanguinity and Affinity

The final requirement for creating a valid marriage which falls under the federal government's jurisdiction concerns the family relationship. The relationships between the man and the woman. Before marriage, intended spouses cannot be too closely related by blood or by marriage to one another. Certain relationships are within what is known as a prohibited degree of **consanguinity**, or blood relationship. Some relationships created by marriage are within a prohibited

Figure 15-2 Prohibited Degrees of Affinity and Consanguinity

SCHEDULE A
(Section 24)

Degrees of affinity and consanguinity which, under the statues in that behalf, bar the lawful solemnization of marriage.

A man may not marry his
1. Grandmother.
2. Grandfather's wife.
3. Wife's grandmother.
4. Aunt.
5. Wife's aunt.
6. Mother.
7. Step mother.
8. Wife's mother.
9. Daughter.
10. Wife's daughter.
11. Son's wife.
12. Sister.
13. Granddaughter.
14. Grandson's wife.
15. Wife's granddaughter.
16. Niece.
17. Nephew's wife.

A woman may not marry her
1. Grandfather.
2. Grandmother's husband.
3. Husband's grandfather.
4. Uncle.
5. Husband's uncle.
6. Father.
7. Step father.
8. Husband's father.
9. Son.
10. Husband's son.
11. Daughter's husband.
12. Brother.
13. Grandson.
14. Granddaughter's husband.
15. Husband's grandson.
16. Nephew.
17. Niece's husband.

The relationships set forth in this table include all such relationships, whether by the whole or half blood, and whether legitimate or illegitimate.

Statutes of Manitoba 1982-83-84, c.57—Cap. M50

degree of **affinity**, or family relationship. The relationships which are too close to allow the formation of a valid marriage come to us from the common law. As well, many of the provinces have included within their *Marriage Acts* a list similar to that found in Figure 15-2.

—**What reason do you think there is for not allowing marriages to take place when people are within a prohibited degree of consanguinity? within a prohibited degree of affinity?**
—**The lists in Figure 15-2 have remained largely unchanged since they were introduced in England in 1563. Can you identify any areas where you think change should occur?**

The Formal Requirements of Marriage

As you have read, the *Marriage Act* of each province outlines the formal requirements for creating a valid marriage.

Certain of the formal requirements vary from province to province. For example, Alberta's *Marriage Act* requires a couple to have blood tests taken before the wedding can occur. This is not so in all provinces. However, there are three formal requirements that are common to all the provinces.

Licence or Banns

The first formal requirement is that before a wedding takes place, it is necessary to obtain a marriage licence. In some provinces, the *publication of banns* may take the place of a marriage licence. This involves the announcement, during a church service, of the intention of two people to marry. The announcement must be read a certain number of times, as set out in the statute. Then the marriage ceremony may take place. In Ontario, the banns must be read on three successive weeks; the wedding can take place five days after the final banns are read. The purpose of publishing the banns is to allow anyone who knows a reason why the couple should not marry to come forward. However, a person who is divorced must obtain a licence before marrying. The licence will not be issued until proof of divorce is presented.

It is the responsibility of the official granting the licence (or publishing the banns) to ensure that the parties can legally marry. The statute prohibits issuing a licence to people who are too closely related, who are already married, or who are under age, for example.

Ceremony

The second formal requirement is that a marriage ceremony of some kind must take place. The ceremony must be performed by a person

I'll try. © Chronicle Features.

authorized by the statute. Civil marriage ceremonies can be performed by judges and Justices of the Peace. Religious ceremonies can be performed by religious leaders—ministers, priests, and rabbis, among others. It is necessary to have two witnesses to a marriage; they are responsible for signing the Marriage Register, a book kept by the official performing the ceremony. A record is kept of all marriages which occur within each province.

Age

The final formal requirement relates to the age of the bride and groom. As you have seen, the federal government uses the common law ages for marriage—twelve for girls, and fourteen for boys. However, the provinces have instead set their own minimum ages for marriage. A marriage licence will not be issued, and no banns will be published, if the parties are under age.

Although there is some provincial variation, in general, it is necessary for a person to be at least eighteen before being able to marry without parental consent. Between the ages of sixteen and eighteen, therefore, parental consent is required; however, the courts will sometimes dispense with this requirement if they feel that the parents are being unreasonable in their refusal to consent.

A person under the age of sixteen generally cannot marry. Exceptions are made where a girl is pregnant, or is the mother of a living child. In Ontario, however, a marriage may not take place under any circumstances if one of the parties is under sixteen years of age.

—Why do you think the provinces have legislated in this area, despite the existing federal law?
—Why do you think Ontario has further restricted the age at which young people may marry?

Re Gruell and Leonard (1976) 23 R.F.L. 370 (Sask. D. C.)

Shauna Leonard and Brian Gruell applied to the courts because Leonard's parents refused to give their consent to her marriage. Leonard was seventeen years old and attending Grade 12 while working part time when this application was heard. She had left home nine months before following a dispute with her parents and had been living with Gruell ever since that time.

Gruell was twenty-one years old. He had completed Grade 12 and had a scholarship to attend university, but he had postponed his education indefinitely and was working full-time. He owned a car and a house trailer in which the couple lived, and had savings.

The couple had tried to gain Leonard's parents' consent to their marriage but had been unsuccessful. The Leonards felt that there was no reason for their daughter to rush into marriage at her age, and that the chances of survival of a teenage marriage were slim.

—If you were the judge hearing this application, what factors would you consider important in reaching your decision?
—What would your decision be? Why?
—Obtain a copy of the *Marriage Act* for your province. What formal requirements does it establish with respect to the following?

(a) licences and/or banns
(b) people authorized to perform marriage ceremonies
(c) the age required for marriage with or without consent
(d) waiting period (the required time between issuing of the licence or the reading of the banns, and the marriage ceremony)

Invalid Marriages

Invalid marriages fall into two categories: either void *ab initio* or voidable. A marriage which is void *ab initio* is one which, in the eyes of the law, never existed. This is so even though a marriage ceremony has taken place and the couple has begun living together. Failure to meet such essential requirements as being legally free to marry or being mentally competent are examples of grounds which render a marriage void *ab initio*. If a marriage is void *ab initio*, there is no legal necessity for the couple to apply to court for a declaration that the marriage does not exist. The "spouses" are already legally free to marry other partners.

A voidable marriage is one wherein a defect exists, such as impotence, which can make the marriage invalid. During a legal process called **annulment**, a court will examine the defect in the marriage. If the defect is considered significant, the court will grant a declaration of nullity. Once it is granted, a voidable marriage ceases to exist, and, in fact, is retroactively declared never to have existed. However, before the declaration is granted, the marriage is legally valid.

It is not always easy to determine whether a marriage is void *ab initio* or voidable. The common law is often unclear, and, in many cases, the provincial *Marriage Acts* do little to clear up the matter. Legal advice can be helpful. However, often the answer to the question "Is this marriage void *ab initio* or voidable?" is not known until a court rules on the matter.

After the Wedding

As we said at the start of this chapter, marriage involves a change in status for the partners. It also carries various rights and duties. Once the bride and groom enter their new home and begin life together as husband and wife, they will begin to discover what their new status, and their rights and responsibilities, involve.

Society's definition of the rights and responsibilities of marriage has been changing over the years, and it is likely to continue to evolve. Sir William Blackstone, an eighteenth century legal author, commented on the status of husbands and wives as follows:

> "By marriage, the husband and wife are one in law; that is, the very being or legal existence of the woman is suspended during the marriage, or at least is incorporated and consolidated into that of the husband."
> *(Commentaries, Book I)*

This statement meant that, at common law, a woman lost most of her legal rights when she married. She could no longer contract in her own name; she could not sue or be sued without her husband being joined as a party to the action; and she could not hold property. Although women have never been required by law to take their husband's name, doing so is a tradition symbolizing the joining of the woman's legal personality into her husband's.

While women lost many of the rights they had while single, men had new obligations placed upon them by law when they married. Husbands were responsible for the support of their wives and children. This responsibility to support a spouse was not placed on wives.

Times have changed, and statute law has remedied many of the injustices of the common law, bringing men and women onto a more equal footing in marriage. Section 1 of Alberta's *Married Women's Act* illustrates some of these changes:

> (1) Subject to this Act, a married woman
> - *(a)* is capable of acquiring, holding and disposing of any property,
> - *(b)* is capable of making herself and being made liable in respect of a tort, contract, debt or obligation,
> - *(c)* is capable, without her husband being joined as a party, of suing and being sued, either in contract, including a contract made between her and her husband, or in tort, or otherwise, and
> - *(d)* is subject to the law relating to bankruptcy and to enforcement of judgements and orders,
>
> in all respects as if she were an unmarried woman.

All the provinces now have similar legislation which recognizes the legal rights of married women.

The Rights and Responsibilities of Spouses Today

What rights and obligations are imposed on spouses by the law today? The three most important rights of a married couple relate to support, property, and custody of children.

Support

The *Criminal Code* places a major responsibility on spouses:

> 197. (1) Everyone is under a legal duty
> - *(b)* as a married person, to provide necessaries of life to his spouse;

(Note that "he" in the *Criminal Code* refers to both male and female.)

— What are "necessaries of life"?
— Do you think that failure to live up to this duty should be a criminal offence? Why or why not?
— The wording of this section was changed in the 1970s from "as a husband" to "as a married person". Why do you think this change was made?

Common law and some provincial statutes allow a married person to pledge his or her spouse's credit for the purchase of necessities. Although this right exists, it is not commonly exercised in today's society. The reason is partly that merchants are unwilling to extend this kind of credit, and also that a spouse's obligation to support can be enforced through the courts.

Some provincial statutes have placed an obligation on both spouses to be responsible for their own support and the support of their partner. For example, Ontario's *Family Law Reform Act* states:

> 15. Every spouse has an obligation to provide support for himself or herself and for the other spouse, in accordance with need, to the extent that he or she is capable of doing so.

—How does this statute change the traditional relationship of husband and wife?
—Does your province have a law which places this obligation on both spouses? In your opinion, should it? Why?

Property

Legally speaking, the chief advantage of marriage is tied to property matters. A married person has the legal right to inherit from his or her spouse's estate, whether or not there is a will. Each spouse also has the right to share in the other's property, particularly the property obtained after the wedding, if the marriage should break down and end in separation or divorce. The rights relating to property will be described in greater detail in Chapter 17.

Custody

In recent years, the most important consideration in any custody dispute has become the best interests of the child. Still, the existence of a valid marriage gives both spouses custody and access rights to their children which often do not exist for unmarried couples who have children. These matters will be expanded upon in Chapter 16.

Cohabiting Couples

Two people living together as husband and wife who are not married are involved in what is called a **common law marriage** or common law relationship. Although the law has never prevented men and women from living together without being legally married, it is only in recent years that such relationships have gained social and legal recognition in Canada.

Living together can in some situations result in real hardship for one of the spouses if the relationship ends or if one of the spouses dies. For this reason, the law has introduced some changes to protect the parties involved. The law still does not, however, recognize these relationships as valid marriages, no matter how long they have existed. Therefore, it does not provide all of the same rights and protections as it grants to married people.

The criminal law treats cohabiting couples as though they were not involved in any familial relationship. Under the rules of evidence, a married person generally cannot be forced to testify against his or her spouse. This is not true for cohabiting spouses. As well, a violent domestic dispute between married people will be heard in the Family Court, which may try to take a remedial course. The same kind of dispute between people living together would be heard in Provincial Court instead, using criminal procedure.

The two most important rights enjoyed by married people, the right to share in each other's property after marriage breakdown or death, and the right to be supported, are often not legally extended to common law partners. However, some federal and provincial laws have granted limited rights to cohabiting couples. Federal statutes recognize the rights of cohabiting spouses under the Canada Pension Plan, the *Family Allowance Act*, and the *Unemployment Insurance Act*. Provincial statutes such as *Workers' Compensation*, *Criminal Injuries Compensation*, family maintenance legislation, and provincial health care plans also establish certain legal rights for people who are living together in "relationships of some permanence". These statutes require cohabiting spouses to live together for a specified length of time before their rights are recognized by the law. In some cases, the period of cohabitation required to qualify for these rights is reduced when there is a child of the relationship. For instance, in Ontario, dependent cohabiting spouses have a right to be supported if they meet the cohabitation requirements outlined in the *Family Law Reform Act*:

> **14. In this Part**
> *(b)* **"spouse" means a spouse as defined in section 1, and in addition includes,**
> **(i) either of a man and woman not being married to each other who have cohabited,**
> **(1) continuously for a period of not less than five years, or**

> (2) in a relationship of some permanence where there is a child born of whom they are the natural parents, and have so cohabited within the preceding year,...

—Why do you think that there are time limits before common law spouses gain any legal rights?
—Why is this time limit reduced when there is a child of the relationship?

Federal and provincial laws each establish different time requirements. In British Columbia, partners who live together as husband and wife for two years have the same responsibility to support themselves and each other as spouses who are legally married. In Alberta, on the other hand, cohabiting spouses do not have a right to support no matter how long they have lived together.

—How does the British Columbia law differ from the Ontario law quoted above?
—In your opinion, which is the better law? Why?
—What rights do cohabiting spouses in your province have with regard to support?

Although in most provinces common law spouses have gained some rights regarding support upon the breakdown of their relationship, they do not have a right to share each other's property. It is important to note that while the married state automatically confers property rights, the state of living together does not do so. This matter will be discussed more thoroughly in Chapter 17.

Domestic Contracts

Domestic contracts are a recent development in family law. Couples can enter into such agreements at any point in a relationship. At one time, certain of these contracts were not enforceable at common law. For instance, a contract between spouses which stated how the property would be divided in the event that the marriage did not succeed was unenforceable. It was considered against public policy to make a contract which contemplated a finite duration for a marriage. Today, however, provincial family law recognizes domestic contracts made before marriage, during marriage, or in the event of marriage breakdown.

A **marriage contract** is an agreement between two people who are about to be married or who are already married. It sets out the terms and conditions which will govern the relationship, according to the wishes of the couple.

Two people who are living together in a common law relationship may enter into a contract called a **cohabitation agreement**. In it, the couple makes arrangements concerning the support of themselves and each other, the care and support of children, and the sharing of property and each other's estates. The contract thus covers the areas where cohabiting spouses usually have few or no legal rights.

A **separation agreement** is a contract made between married spouses when their marriage breaks up. It provides for support, division of family property, and custody of children, among other matters. This is the type of domestic contract which has existed for the longest time. Separation agreements will be discussed in greater detail in Chapter 17.

Marriage contracts and cohabitation agreements can include anything the spouses wish, as long as both agree on the contents. The list of items shown in Figure 15-3 is not exhaustive, but it does outline some of the basic terms which such a document might include.

Figure 15-3 The Contents of a Domestic Contract

Financial Matters	Will both spouses work? Who will pay for household expenses? How much money will the spouses try to save, and for what purpose(s)?
Household Arrangements	Who is responsible for housework? How much time will each spouse have for hobbies, friendships, vacations? Who may join the household? Relatives? Pets?
Property	Where will the spouses live? Who owns what during the relationship? In the event of separation? In the event of death?
Children	Who is responsible for family planning and birth control? Should there be children? How many? Who is responsible for child care? What moral and religious training should the children have? Who is responsible for discipline?
Change	Should the contract be reviewed from time to time? How can the agreement be changed? How will disagreements be resolved?

—**Can you think of any other areas which you might wish to include in a domestic contract?**

Domestic contracts must be signed and witnessed before they are valid. Some provinces, such as Alberta, require that the parties have independent legal advice before signing a domestic contract, to ensure that both are well aware of their legal rights before signing.

A person who decides to enter into any type of domestic agreement with his or her spouse cannot expect the courts to enforce all of the terms of the contract. For example, the courts will not order a spouse to do the dishes or take out the garbage, as agreed in the contract. Promises such as this are not enforceable; the courts will not become involved with such minor matters.

Agreements which are considered by the courts to be against public policy will also not be enforced. For instance, it would be against public policy for spouses to agree not to have any children; the courts would not help enforce this term of a contract. Also, though spouses can include a term concerning the custody of their children in the event of separation, the courts will always apply the test of what is "in the best interests of the child". For this reason, they may not enforce this term of the contract. In fact, some provinces prohibit spouses from dealing with the issue of custody of their children in any contract other than a separation agreement.

It is important to note that the home in which a married couple lives is given particular protection by law. For this reason, it is not possible for a spouse to give up in a marriage contract his or her rights to possession of what is called the *matrimonial home*.

While separation agreements have been common for many years, the newer forms of domestic contracts are still used infrequently. They are, however, an interesting innovation which provide couples with an opportunity to reach their own agreement about the rights and obligations created by their relationship.

—What advantages are there to drawing up a domestic agreement?
—What disadvantages are there to such an agreement?
—What particular protections might a person involved in a common law relationship wish to include in a domestic contract?

SUMMARIZING YOUR READING

1. What does the statement, "Legally, marriage involves a change in status" mean?

2. What is breach of promise?

3. What compensation is available in an action for breach of promise, in those provinces which allow this action?

4. Why are some provinces abolishing the breach of promise action?

5. Name and describe the essential requirements for a valid marriage.

6. Name and describe the formal requirements for a valid marriage.

7. What is annulment? What is the distinction between a marriage which is void *ab initio* and one which is voidable?

8. At common law, when a man and a woman married, they were considered to become one person. What effect did this have on the legal rights of married women?

9. To what three major areas do the legal rights of a married couple relate? Briefly describe these areas.

10. Define "common law marriage".

11. In what ways does criminal law treat cohabiting couples differently from married couples?

12. What rights of married spouses does the law not extend to cohabiting spouses?

13. Why has the law changed to recognize the rights of cohabiting spouses in some situations?

14. Give two examples of statutes which recognize common law relationships.

15. What restriction do these laws usually place on the rights of common law spouses?

16. What three types of domestic contracts are recognized by law? Who may enter into these agreements?

17. Give several examples of terms which could be included in a domestic contract.

18. Give two examples of terms in a domestic contract which would likely not be enforced by the courts.

DISCUSSING KEY ISSUES

1. "Marriage is much too easy to enter and far too difficult to get out of."
    (a) In your opinion, is marriage too easy to enter?
    (b) What problems are created if marriage is too easy to enter?
    (c) What changes could you propose to make people more seriously consider whether to marry?
    (d) Do you think that these suggestions might help to reduce the number of broken marriages?

2. In the 1960s, anthropologist Margaret Mead suggested that marriage should have two separate steps:

(i) Individual marriage would be the trial step, wherein a man and a woman would live together for as long as they agreed to without making any permanent commitment to one another.

(ii) Parental marriage would begin when a child was conceived. At this time, the couple would enter into a legal contract which would bind the parties until the child or children reached adulthood.

   (a) What is your opinion of this suggestion?
   (b) What advantages and disadvantages do you see in it?

3. State whether or not there is a defect in each of the following marriages. If there is, state whether it is a formal or an essential requirement which is lacking.

   (a) Jim, nineteen, was dating a sixteen-year-old girl, who became pregnant. Her parents told Jim that he must marry their daughter or they would bring criminal charges against him. Jim was afraid that they would carry out their threat so he married his girlfriend, even though he did not feel ready for marriage.

   (b) A man and a transsexual marry. (A transsexual is a person who has had an operation to change his or her external genitalia and hormonal balance to that of the opposite sex.)

   (c) A woman remarries after her husband was declared missing in action and presumed dead in wartime. Two years after her marriage, she has news that her first spouse is still alive.

   (d) Two seventeen-year-olds elope and get married because their parents are trying to break up their relationship. They give their ages as eighteen when they apply for the licence.

   (e) Ingrid and David meet and marry after a two-week courtship. A month after the wedding, Ingrid, a very religious person, discovers that David has been married before and is divorced. Ingrid is shocked by this news and wants to have her marriage to David annulled.

   (f) Angelina and Domenic decide to write their own wedding ceremony, and to get married in a park on a hill-top. They invite a friend to officiate at their wedding and to hear their vows to one another.

   (g) Gerry and Alka, who have both been under treatment in a mental institution, run away from the institution and get married.

   (h) A woman who is not capable of having children gets married. Her husband, who wants to have a large family, is very upset when he learns of her inability and seeks to have the marriage annulled.

   (i) A man who knows he is incapable of having sexual intercourse gets married. He does not tell his wife about the problem until after the ceremony.

4. Jack and Louise have been married for five years. On their fifth anniversary, they decide to draw up a marriage contract. The following clauses are taken from their agreement:

(iii) The parties agree that in the event of a marriage breakdown, the wife shall retain custody of the children.

(vi) The parties agree that the husband is the sole owner of a cottage property inherited from his parents.

(viii) The parties feel that household duties are a joint responsibility of the husband and wife and agree to share these tasks equally.

(x) The parties agree that, until all children of the marriage are old enough to attend school, the wife shall remain at home with the children, and will not seek employment. The husband is solely responsible for the support of the family during this period.

    (a) Which of the above clauses would a court likely enforce? Explain.

    (b) Which of the above clauses are probably unenforceable? Explain.

    (c) Can you think of any reason to include an unenforceable clause in a marriage contract?

PROJECTS AND ACTIVITIES

1. Investigate the marriage customs and traditions of any three religions. In what ways are they similar? How do they differ? How do these religious ceremonies compare to a civil marriage ceremony? Report your findings to the class.

RESOLVING CASES

Iliopoulos v. Getas (1981) 32 O.R. (2d) 636 (Ont. C.C.)

Iliopoulos and Getas met in October, 1978 and became engaged a month later. The plaintiff, Iliopoulos, gave Getas a gold coin on a chain when they announced their intention to marry to her parents. He later gave her a one-carat diamond engagement ring as well. For Christmas he gave her a gold cross with a diamond on a chain.

Because of problems which developed in the relationship, Iliopoulos eventually broke the engagement, although Getas made several attempts to save the relationship. She even brought in her father and uncle as mediators. The plaintiff sued for the return of the gifts listed above, valued at $8000. He also sued for the value of a sheepskin coat, a three-piece-suit, and several sweaters. He had left these clothes at the defendant's house, and, when the engagement was broken, she instructed her mother to throw them out.

- By law, does Getas have to return the first engagement gift? the engagement ring? the Christmas gift?
- Should the plaintiff be able to receive compensation for his clothing which Getas disposed of?
- Would Getas be able to sue for breach of promise in this Ontario case?

Parihar v. Bhatti (1981) 17 R.F.L. (2d) 289 (B.C.S.C.)

The twenty-four-year-old plaintiff was born in Fiji and moved to Canada in 1975. She met the defendant in 1978 through her sister. A few days after this meeting, the plaintiff's family arranged a marriage for her with the defendant, without her participation in the discussion. She subsequently told her family that she did not wish to marry. Nevertheless, a marriage ceremony did take place. The plaintiff did not participate in the wedding festivities. She signed the registration of marriage, then left her parent's home and took her own apartment. The marriage was never consummated. The plaintiff asked the court to declare her marriage to the defendant void.

- What argument do you think the plaintiff used when asking the court for an annulment of her marriage?
- What factors would you take into consideration if you were the judge hearing this case?
- Is there any reason for maintaining this marriage?
- What decision would you, as judge, reach?

Truong v. Malia (1977) 25 R.F.L. 256 (Ont. H.C.)

The plaintiff was a Vietnamese woman living in Canada as a landed immigrant since 1973. In 1975, she returned to her native country to teach and was trapped in Vietnam as the South Vietnamese government collapsed. In order to avoid the great physical risks of remaining in the country, the plaintiff went through a form of marriage with an American citizen. There was no intent to live as husband and wife, and the marriage was not consummated. The plaintiff was allowed to leave Vietnam after the marriage. She returned to Canada and sought an annulment.

- On what grounds would the plaintiff seek to have her marriage annulled?
- Should this marriage be declared void?

Iantsis v. Papatheodorou (1971) 1 O.R. 245 (C.A.)

The plaintiff asked for a declaration that her marriage was void because the defendant, a native of Greece, had falsely tricked her into marriage in order to gain the appropriate status to apply for Canadian citizenship. The parties had never cohabited. The court held that the marriage was valid and quoted the following statement from a previous similar case:

> "No marriage shall be held void merely upon proof that it had been contracted upon false representations, and that but for such contrivances, consent never would have been obtained. Unless the party imposed upon has been deceived as to the person, and thus has given no consent at all, there is no degree of deception which can avail to set aside a contract of marriage knowingly made."
>
> *(Swift v. Kelly* (1835) 3 Knapp 257 at p. 293, 12 E.R. 648*)*

—**What purpose is served in upholding the validity of this marriage?**
—**What options might be available to the plaintiff to end the marriage?**
—**What similarities and differences are there between this case and the *Truong* case, above?**

Alspector v. Alspector [1957] O.R. 454 (C.A.)

Mr. Alspector, an elderly widower, married the plaintiff in a marriage ceremony performed according to the requirements of the Jewish faith. Mr. Alspector was aware that a marriage licence was required, but because he intended to leave Canada soon after his marriage to live in Israel, he did not comply with this requirement. Mrs. Alspector was not aware of the omission. The couple did not leave Canada after all, and resided together as husband and wife for seven years. When Mr. Alspector became ill after this time, he was hospitalized. Upon release from the hospital he was taken to his daughter's home.

Mrs. Alspector then received a letter from a lawyer representing the Alspector family. The letter addressed her by her previous married name. It asked her to move from her home, because the family, acting on Mr. Alspector's behalf, wished to sell the house. Realizing that the validity of her marriage was being questioned, Mrs. Alspector applied to the courts.

—**What is the defect in this marriage?**
—**Do you think it would make this marriage invalid?**
—**What factors would you take into consideration when making a decision in this case?**

16

Children and Their Parents

The Legal Rights of Children   Adoption
The Legal Rights of Parents

Figure 16-1

Freuchet, *Pierre and Suzanne, are delighted to announce the birth of their son, Alain, on October 28. Proud grandparents are M. and Mme J. Freuchet, and Mme G. Girard.*

As you have learned, when a man and a woman marry, they take on a new legal status: that of husband and wife. When they have a child together, their status changes again—to that of parents. Once again, this change in legal status brings with it a new set of rights and obligations.

Society respects and safeguards the privacy of the family, especially in its all-important task of raising children. However, society does expect parents to meet certain minimum standards of care. These standards are set out in a variety of provincial statutes, some of which will be examined in this chapter. The minimum standards of care established by law can be considered as being the rights of children, and, conversely, the obligations of parents. When parents fail to meet their obligations, the law can step in to protect the child. In some circumstances, criminal law will punish the parent for such failure.

The Legal Rights of Children

In many societies, past and present, children sometimes received a standard of care quite different from that prescribed in our modern society. In ancient Rome, for instance, fathers had absolute power of life and death over their children, though it was very seldom exerted. Like Rome, most cultures saw children as being their parents' property. In many parts of the world, when food was scarce, the weakest members of society—children and old people—were abandoned to die so that others could live. Child slavery still exists in certain parts of the world. And, in industrializing nations during the nineteenth century, young children worked in factories, mines, and fields under the same arduous conditions as adults—often for up to twelve or fourteen hours a day.

In Canada, the late nineteenth century saw a change in our attitude towards children. Legislation was passed restricting child labour in certain occupations, such as mining and factory work. This legislation considerably improved the lot of many children who had previously laboured long and hard for minimal pay.

Figure 16-2 Young Mineworkers, early 1900s

At about the same time, universal public education for children was becoming a desirable and accepted concept. As well, legislation was passed recognizing the right of children to be treated differently from adults in criminal proceedings.

Another important legal change was that the courts were beginning to recognize that they had jurisdiction to look into the best interests of the child. Children were no longer considered the property of their parents. They were seen to have a legal status and certain rights recognized by the courts, and to be entitled to some minimum standard of care. This chapter will examine four important legal rights of children:

1. the right to financial support
2. the right to an education
3. the right to live with their parents and siblings (brothers and/or sisters)
4. the right to protection from physical or emotional harm or neglect

Financial Support

Every province has legislation establishing the right of a child to be supported by his or her parents. For example, Ontario's *Family Law Reform Act* states:

> 16. (1) Every parent has an obligation, to the extent the parent is capable of doing so, to provide support, in accordance with need, for his or her child who is unmarried and is under the age of 18 years.
> (2) the obligation under subsection 1 does not extend to a child, who being of the age of 16 years or over, has withdrawn from parental control.

As was pointed out earlier, the law sets only a minimum standard. The ability of the parent to provide support determines the level of support the child is entitled to. In other words, a child is not guaranteed any particular level. Also, like the Ontario *Act* quoted above, each provincial statute defines "child" for the purpose of support by setting an age limit.

Re Haskell and Letourneau (1980) 25 O.R. (2d) 139 (C.C.)

When the parents of Scott Haskell separated, custody was awarded to the father. Mr. Haskell remarried, but Scott did not get along very well with his step-mother. At the end of a summer vacation spent with his mother, Scott's father refused to allow him to return to his home.

Scott began living with his mother, who had also remarried. Scott's step-father had a severe drinking problem which eventually made it impossible for sixteen-year-old Scott to remain in the home. He moved out and began living with another family while he continued going to school. He sued both parents for support.

— Under s.16 of the Ontario *Family Law Reform Act*, is Scott entitled to support from his father? his mother?
— What effect should the fact that Scott moved out of his mother's home have on his right to support?
— If the court decided to award support to Scott, what other important factor would the court have to consider?

The *Criminal Code* imposes the following obligation on parents:

> **197. (1) Every one is under a legal duty**
>   *(a)* **as a parent, foster parent, guardian or head of a family, to provide necessaries of life for a child under the age of 16 years.**

— What do you think "necessaries of life" would include?
— What would be the result of parents' failure to live up to this legal duty?
— Does this section of the *Criminal Code* establish an enforceable right of children? Explain.

In general, the right of children to be supported is not affected by the marital status of the parents. If the parents are not married, however, it may be necessary for the mother to take the *putative* (alleged) father to court to prove the paternity of her child before the court will order the father to support his child. (The identity of the mother of a child is very seldom in dispute). A court action to prove paternity is called an **affiliation proceeding**. **Forensic medicine** (medical science as applied to the law) has developed new tests which have an accuracy rate of over ninety percent in establishing whether a man is the biological father of a child. Such tests were used in the following case.

Dollighan v. Dollighan (1978) 3 R.F.L. (2d) 210 (Ont. C.C.)

The Dollighans separated in October, 1973. The husband learned of his wife's pregnancy in April, 1974, and denied that he could be the father of the child. After the birth of the baby, the wife sued for child support.

The little girl looked strikingly like Mr. Dollighan, and her blood group and type were compatible with the putative father's. The court ordered Mr. Dollighan to pay child support. He appealed.

New forensic tests were made on the blood serum and cells of the putative father and the little girl. The tests showed that Mr. Dollighan could not be the father of the child. The court reversed the support order.

Children born outside of marriage in provinces that follow the common law are called **illegitimate**. In these provinces, illegitimate children have no right to inherit from their father unless they are specifically mentioned in his will. Some statute law extends the common law practice of discriminating against children born out of wedlock. For example, in Nova Scotia, the *Children of Unmarried Parents Act* states that the estate of the father of a child born out of wedlock must continue to support the illegitimate child if an Affiliation Order has been made by the court. However, a judge may change this order if continuing to support the illegitimate child would harm the financial position of the deceased's wife and legitimate children. An illegitimate child naturally has the usual right to inherit from his or her mother.

Some provinces such as Ontario, Prince Edward Island, and New Brunswick have passed legislation to remove entirely the distinction made in law between legitimate and illegitimate children.

—Children have no say in the circumstances of their birth, yet some provinces "penalize" illegitimate children by reducing their legal rights. Is this just, in your opinion?

Education

The concept of the right to universal public education for children, established in this century, was the first major recognition of the child as an individual with basic legal rights that should not be denied. The right to be educated is therefore a very important right.

Certain criticisms of this right can be made, however. Chief among them is that while children do have the right to go to school, this is not necessarily the same thing as the right to an education. Children with special needs, such as those with physical and mental handicaps, have often been denied the right to an education. School boards *can* provide special education programs for these exceptional children, but in many cases such programs are simply not available. Saskatchewan school boards are unique in that they have been providing special education programs since the early 1970s. The other provinces are just now beginning to look at this area of children's rights. Ontario has recently amended its *Education Act* to require every child of school age to be enrolled in school. The *Act* also requires the Boards of Education to provide special programs to meet the needs of

Figure 16-3 *A fundamental right of children is to live with their families.*

children who have "behavioural, intellectual (including the intellectually gifted), physical, or multiple exceptionalities".

Children have not only the right to an education, but also the obligation to go to school. Each province has an *Education Act* making school attendance compulsory, with only a few exceptions. Parents in their turn have a responsibility to make sure that their school age children do attend school.

—Obtain a copy of the *Education Act* for your province. What age requirements are attached to compulsory education?
—Which children, if any, can be exempted from compulsory attendance?

Living with Parents and Siblings

Children have a right to live with their parents and siblings. This right should not be easily interfered with by the state. Only in situations where the parents fail to live up to the minimum standard of care expected of them is the state authorized to overrule this right to family autonomy and to step in to protect children by taking them away from their parents or placing the family under supervision.

Protection from Harm or Neglect

Provincial child welfare legislation outlines the situations which justify interference with the family in the event of physical or emotional harm to a child. You should become familiar with your own provincial statute, but in general all provincial legislation defines a child in need of protection in terms similar to those in New Brunswick's *Child and Family Services and Family Relations Act*:

> 31. (1) The security or development of a child may be in danger when
>   - (a) the child is without adequate care, supervision or control;
>   - (b) the child is living in unfit or improper circumstances;
>   - (c) the child is in the care of a person who is unable or unwilling to provide adequate care, supervision or control of the child;
>   - (d) the child is in the care of a person whose conduct endangers the life, health or emotional well-being of the child;
>   - (e) the child is physically or sexually abused, physically or emotionally neglected, sexually exploited or in danger of such treatment;
>   - (f) the child is living in a situation where there is severe domestic violence;
>   - (g) the child is in the care of a person who neglects or refuses to provide or obtain proper medical, surgical or other remedial care or treatment necessary for the health or well-being of the child or refuses to permit such care or treatment to be supplied to the child;
>   - (h) the child is beyond the control of the person caring for him;
>   - (i) the child by his behaviour, condition, environment or association, is likely to injure himself or others;
>   - (j) the child is in the care of a person who does not have a right to custody of the child, without the consent of a person having such right;
>   - (k) the child is in the care of a person who neglects or refuses to ensure that the child attends school; or
>   - (l) the child has committed an offence.
>
> (2) Where the Minister receives a report or information about any situation that causes him to suspect that the security or development of a child may be in danger, he shall investigate and shall take such steps as he considers necessary to protect the child.

Some of these definitions of a child in need of protection may seem rather vague. For example, what exactly is an "unfit" place for a child to live? What is "emotional neglect"? Although case law has helped to define these terms, some provinces feel that the law must be more precise in order to avoid unnecessary interference with the family. Ontario, for example, is in the process of revising its *Child Welfare Act*. The Ministry of Community and Social Services, which is responsible for drafting new legislation, has recently recommended that "...the present definition of a child in need of protection be replaced by grounds that are more precise, objective, and that focus on serious harm or risk of such harm to the child."

In most provinces, the task of investigating parents who fail to live up to the required standard of care in raising their children is the responsibility of a government department or ministry. In British Columbia, for example, the Ministry of Human Resources has this task. However, in Manitoba, Nova Scotia, and Ontario, the task falls to organizations called Children's Aid Societies. Although they are not part of the government itself, these organizations are funded by the government and regulated by statute law.

Child welfare laws in many provinces require people to report all suspected cases of child abuse or neglect to the ministry or agency responsible for child protection, as this section of Alberta's *Child Welfare Act* illustrates:

> 35. (1) A person who has reasonable and probable grounds to believe and believes that a child has been abandoned, deserted, physically ill-treated or is in need of protection shall forthwith report the grounds of his belief to the Director or to a child welfare worker of the Department.
>
> (3) Any person who fails to comply with subsection (1), in addition to any civil liability, is guilty of an offence and liable to a fine of not more than $500 and in default of payment to imprisonment for a term not exceeding 6 months or to both fine and imprisonment.

You may be wondering what happens when a report of suspected abuse or neglect is received. The first step is always to investigate the report. While the main purpose of child welfare law is to protect the child, the ministry or agency is also concerned with attempting to help parents, so that the child will not have to be removed from the family. Family counselling and supervision of the family by a social worker are ways of protecting the child and at the same time helping the family to stay together.

It is probably understandable, even obvious, that children should be removed (at least temporarily) from violent homes. Nonetheless, it should also be noted that many studies indicate that children often suffer psychological harm when they are removed from their families, no matter what the home situation is like. It is necessary, therefore, for the law to make sure that two important factors are taken into consideration and balanced in any decision to interfere with the family:

1. the right of children to live with their parents and siblings, and
2. the right of children to be protected from harm or neglect.

In other words, child welfare agencies and courts must seek to solve the family problem in the way which will be least harmful to the child.

Figure 16-4 Do you agree or disagree with the opinion set out in this article?

Change urged in Family Act

SASKATOON (CP) — It is too easy for social workers to take children from their families under Saskatchewan's Family Services Act, says a report prepared by two legal aid staff members in Prince Albert.

The act should be changed to permit the Social Services Department to apprehend a child only as a last resort, says the report.

The report recommends the department be required to prove "beyond reasonable doubt" that a child is in need of protection instead of — as now — requiring parents to prove their fitness to have their child in their home once the youngster has been apprehended.

If the family situation is so bad that a child is in immediate danger, however, the Children's Aid Society or the ministry responsible can take the child out of the home. If this is done, a court hearing must be held within a certain number of days. The period varies from province to province. If, after hearing all of the evidence, the court decides that the child is in need of the protection of the law, the court has several options available. Again, these will vary slightly by province. For example, in Ontario, any of the following orders can be made:

1. The child is to remain in the family, but a social worker is to supervise the family for up to twelve months.
2. The child is made a temporary ward of the Children's Aid Society and is placed in a foster home, group home, or residential treatment centre. The parents can be given visiting rights if this kind of wardship order is made. Eventually, if the home situation improves, the child will be returned to the family.

3. In the most serious cases, the child is made a permanent ward of the Crown. The parents permanently lose custody of the child, who will be placed in a foster home, or adopted. The parents do, however, have the right to a review of this order if the child has not yet been adopted.

A child who is the subject of a protection hearing has the right to be represented by a lawyer. This is another example of the new rights gained by children in the 1970s.

As an additional protective measure, many provinces have set up child abuse registers in which are kept the names of people who are suspected of or convicted of abusing children. This information is confidential. The registers are designed to help child protection agencies investigating a possible child abuse situation to get a more complete history of an alleged abuser.

The Legal Rights of Parents

As you read at the start of this chapter, until quite recently children were considered their parents' property, and had few identifiable rights. During the present century in particular, this situation has changed dramatically. Parents have not lost all rights with respect to their children, however. Most of the rights of parents in dealing with their children arise from the fact that parents have legal custody and guardianship rights.

Custody and Guardianship

The most basic right of parents is to have the physical care and control of their children. The right to the care and control of a child is referred to in law as **custody and guardianship**, although the term most commonly used is "custody".

Custody gives the parent the right to make many decisions affecting the life of the child:

1. determining the religion of the child
2. consenting to medical attention for the child, where the child's consent is insufficient
3. consenting to the marriage of a child who is a minor, but old enough under provincial law to marry
4. managing the child's property
5. consenting to the adoption of the child
6. receiving notice of a legal action against the child
7. disciplining the child

This last right of parents, to discipline their children, is actually included in the *Criminal Code*:

> **43.** Every schoolteacher, parent or person standing in the place of a parent is justified in using force by way of correction toward a pupil or child, as the case may be, who is under his care, if the force does not exceed what is reasonable under the circumstances.

The key words in this section are, "what is reasonable under the circumstances". Unreasonable force in disciplining a child could result in child protection proceedings against the parent, as you learned earlier in this chapter.

Custody in a Broken Marriage

When married parents are living together, they share custody and guardianship rights. However, when they separate or get divorced, the issue of custody must be decided either by an agreement between the parents or by the courts.

In such a situation, if the parents can mutually agree upon a custody arrangement, then the courts usually will not interfere. However, if they cannot agree, a custody hearing will take place in the courts.

The Role of the Courts

The adversarial system used in our courts all too often results in parents fighting over their child as a prize to be won in the battle, forgetting that the child's best interests should be the important issue. It is therefore one of the functions of the court to keep this issue foremost in mind when making custody decisions.

—What factors do you think a judge would look at in deciding what is in the best interests of a child?

Parents fighting over child custody often have difficulty remembering that what they consider a bad spouse does not necessarily make a bad parent. Until recently, the courts seemed to have the same problem. Thus, the conduct of a spouse might be used to deny child custody to that person. However, in the 1970s, several decisions of the Supreme Court of Canada seemed to indicate that conduct should be considered as a factor only if it directly relates to that person's ability to be a parent; in other words, if it relates to what is in the best interests of the child.

K. v. K. (1976) 23 R.F.L. 58 (Alta. Prov. Ct.)

The husband and wife in this case separated because of the wife's homosexual relationship. Both the father and the mother applied to the court for custody of their seven-year-old daughter.

The mother was at this time living in a homosexual relationship. A psychiatrist testified that the mother and daughter had a very loving and close relationship. He further indicated that there was no reason to believe that the mother's living arrangements would result in the child's growing up with a homosexual preference, especially since the mother was not militant or active in the gay movement and she and her partner were very careful about their conduct in front of the child.

The father also had a loving relationship with his daughter. He admitted to using marijuana and hashish from time to time, but not in the presence of his child.

The judge stated that the mother's homosexuality was only one factor to be considered, and was no more a bar to her getting custody of her daughter than the father's use of drugs. Applying the best interests of the child test, the judge awarded custody to the mother, with reasonable access (visiting rights) granted to the father.

—When would a parent's sexual preference be relevant to the interests of the child, in your opinion?

Decisions affecting the custody of children are never final; a case can be brought back to court if evidence indicates that the best interests of the child are no longer being met.

There are three basic kinds of custody awards, which will be examined below. In addition, it is possible for the courts to award custody to someone other than the parents in certain situations.

Sole Custody

One parent has the physical care of the child and the right to make all decisions affecting the child. The other parent may have visiting rights.

Split Custody

One parent has the day-to-day physical care of the child, while the other parent has the right to make the decisions affecting the child. This is a very uncommon type of custody award.

Joint Custody

This is the most recent development in child custody. In it, the parents share both decision-making and day-to-day care. The child lives with one parent for a certain period, and then with the other parent, in turn. It is only parents who are capable of cooperating in caring for their child despite their own personal differences who are awarded joint custody. It is not, therefore, awarded very frequently, but can be agreed to by the parents in a separation agreement.

Custody to Other Persons

Custody does not have to be awarded to a parent. If neither parent is considered fit to have custody, the court can grant it to other people, either relatives or non-relatives. This is made clear by such statutes as Ontario's *The Children's Law Reform Amendment Act*:

> 21. A parent of a child or any other person may apply to a court for an order respecting custody of or access to the child or determining any aspect of the incidents of custody of the child.

Custody of Children Born out of Wedlock

The rights of parents to custody of their children can be affected by the lack of a legal marriage. In particular, the unmarried father loses his right to the custody of his child in those provinces which have not abolished the concept of illegitimacy. For example, Alberta's *Domestic Relations Act* states that

> 39. ...the mother of an illegitimate infant is the sole guardian of the illegitimate infant.

Section 39 means that the mother of the child is the only parent entitled to make any decisions affecting the welfare of the child. This can include the right to place the child for adoption. The father might be required by the court to support the child, but he has no legal right to custody unless he can prove to the satisfaction of the court that the mother is unable to provide adequate care for the child.

Re Staples (1972) 6 R.F.L. 279 (B.C.S.C.)

Alma Burgie, the mother of a child born out of wedlock, brought this action in order to obtain a Writ of *Habeas Corpus*, a legal document which would allow her to regain custody of her son from the father, Leon Staples.

Burgie and Staples had lived together for at least six years and had never married. Both admitted that Staples was the father of the child. After their separation, the boy visited his father for a holiday, but he was not returned to his mother at the end of the vacation.

By the time the court heard this matter, Staples had moved to another province and had married. The court was favourably impressed with the home environment the father would be able to provide for the child. In addition, Staples alleged that the child's mother was a heavy drinker, but presented no evidence to support his statement.

The court ordered that the child be returned to his mother, stating that "The law is clear that the mother of an illegitimate child is ...entitled to its custody unless serious concern for the welfare of the child requires that she be denied custody."

—What is your opinion of this decision?
—Would your opinion be different if the parents had never lived together with the child as a family?

Ontario is one of the provinces that has recently passed legislation (the *Children's Law Reform Act*) abolishing the concept of the illegitimacy of children.

> 1. (1) Subject to subsection (2), for all purposes of the law of Ontario a person is the child of his or her natural parents and his or her status as their child is independent of whether the child is born within or outside marriage.
> (2) When a child has been adopted, the child is the child of his or her adopting parents as if they were the natural parents.

This section not only improves the rights of children born out of wedlock, but also gives their fathers and mothers equal rights to custody.

Vessey v. Coyle et al. (1982) 25 R.F.L. (2d) 80 (P.E.I.S.C.)

Barry Vessey and Dale Coyle were the natural parents of a child, Sherry Lynn, born out of wedlock. They lived together with the child for about six months and then separated. Coyle took the child and returned to her parents' home. Eight days later, she notified Vessey that she was transferring custody of Sherry Lynn to her brother and sister-in-law for the purpose of adoption. Vessey sued for custody of his daughter.

> Prince Edward Island, where this case was heard, has abolished the concept of illegitimacy.
> —Would the child's mother alone have the right to place Sherry Lynn for adoption under the P.E.I. law?
> —How would you decide this case, and what factors would you take into consideration?

The Effect of Annulment on Children

At common law, children born to parents whose marriage was void *ab initio* or whose marriage was voidable and subsequently annulled were considered to be illegitimate. You have learned that this would affect certain of the children's rights, as well as the courts' decision about which parent would have custody of the child, in those provinces which have not abolished the concept of illegitimacy. However, some of these provinces have passed or amended statute law in order to ensure that the status of children will not be affected by annulment. Consider, for instance, the following section of Nova Scotia's *Children of Unmarried Parents Act*:

> 35A. The child of a void marriage, whether born before or after commencement of this Section, shall be deemed to be the legitimate child of his mother and father if the mother and father have at any time celebrated a marriage in accordance with the laws of the place in which the marriage was celebrated and if either the mother or father or both believed that the marriage was valid.

In these situations, custody of children is decided on the basis of what is in the children's best interests.

Adoption

Adoption is a process which creates a legal parent-child relationship between people who are not naturally parent and child. When this relationship is created, the legal rights and responsibilities of the natural (biological) parents are ended.

Each province has legislation which deals with the following issues:

1. Who may be adopted?
2. Who may adopt?
3. Who may arrange adoptions—government departments, Children's Aid Societies, doctors, lawyers, clergymen?

4. How are adoption hearings to be held? Who must attend? Who must be given notice? Who gives consent to the adoption? What happens at a hearing?
5. Assessment of the adoptive parents: How suitable are they? How is this decided?

—Obtain government pamphlets dealing with adoption, and answer as many of the above questions as you can for your province.

All adoption orders must be approved by a court. In making an adoption order, the court must consider two things in particular:

1. Is the adoption in the child's best interests? To determine this, courts will apply a similar test to that used when deciding custody.
2. Whose consent is necessary for the adoption, and when is consent not required?

Consent

In general, the consent of both parents is required before a child can be adopted. This is not so in those provinces which give no rights to unmarried fathers. It also does not hold true if the parents have lost custody of the child through abuse or neglect.

Consent must be both voluntary and informed. That is, the parent or parents must realize that adoption will put an end to all parental rights and responsibilities with respect to the child. For this reason, most provinces have set a period after a child's birth during which the mother cannot consent to its adoption. For example, in the Northwest Territories, this period is four days; in Ontario, seven days; and in Prince Edward Island, fourteen days. The period is intended to allow the mother to recover from the effects of giving birth and to consider the importance of her decision.

Children over a certain age will also be asked to consent to their adoption. In Ontario, this age is seven years; in Québec, ten years; and in Alberta, fourteen years. However, the court may in some situations decide that the child's consent is not necessary.

—In your opinion, is a young child able to determine what is in his or her best interests?
—Do you think a child of seven is able to understand the nature and importance of adoption proceedings?
—At what age do you personally think that such comprehension becomes possible?

Most provinces now have a limitation period during which a parent may withdraw consent for adoption. In Ontario, for instance, a parent is given twenty-one days. After this, consent can be withdrawn only if, given all of the circumstances, it is in the child's best interests. The limitation period was intended to correct a tendency on the part of the courts to return children to their natural parent(s) even after the children had lived for a considerable time with their adoptive parents. At one time, the courts placed much emphasis on the right of the parent to have custody of the child. As you know, they have now shifted away from the parent's rights to what is in the best interests of the child.

Rights of the Adopted Child

In recent years, much media attention has been given to the right of the adopted child to know who his or her biological parents are. Some provinces, including Ontario, have set up a Voluntary Disclosure Register where adopted children eighteen years of age and over may register their desire to contact their biological parents. If the parents also register, contact between them can be arranged. Not all provinces have this system, however. For instance, s.94 of Manitoba's *Child Welfare Act* states that the true identity of an adopted child will be revealed only in the "case of strong and compelling reasons."

—Should adopted children have the right to know their biological parents?
—Should they have the right to know other information about their background, for example, other siblings, inherited diseases, nationality?
—Should biological parents who place their children for adoption have a right to anonymity?
—Does the Voluntary Disclosure Registry system seem to be a suitable solution to this conflict of rights?
—What should the rights of adoptive parents be? For instance, should they be able to prevent their adopted children from learning about their biological parents?

SUMMARIZING YOUR READING

1. Identify the four basic legal rights of children discussed in this chapter.

2. How does a child's right to support under provincial law differ from the provisions in s.197 of the *Criminal Code*?

3. Is a child's right to support affected by the marital status of the parents?

4. Explain the meaning of the term "illegitimate".

5. What is an affiliation proceeding? When does such a procedure take place?

6. What is special education? Is it a right of all children in Canada?

7. What is "compulsory education"?

8. Describe three situations in which a child might need the protection of the law.

9. What orders might a court that declares a child to be in need of protection make?

10. What is a child abuse register? What is its purpose?

11. List some decisions affecting a child that may be made by a parent who has custody of that child.

12. What test is applied by the courts when making a decision about custody?

13. When does the conduct of a spouse affect his or her right to child custody?

14. Are custody orders final? Explain.

15. Describe three types of custody orders.

16. How are custody rights affected by marital status?

17. What is adoption?

18. Who must consent to an adoption?

19. Can consent to an adoption ever be withdrawn? Explain.

20. Why have some provinces introduced legislation to limit a parent's right to withdraw consent for the adoption of a child?

DISCUSSING KEY ISSUES

1. In 1979, the Year of the Child, Sweden passed legislation making it illegal for parents to spank their children. What do you think of this law? What limits should be placed on parents' rights to discipline their children?

2. How should child abusers be treated? Should they be prosecuted by the criminal justice system and punished, or should they be treated as people who have social and psychological problems requiring treatment by trained professionals?

3. Native Canadian children who have been taken into custody by child welfare authorities have frequently been placed in foster homes outside the Native Canadian community. As well, they are

often adopted by non-Native families. This has become a very sensitive issue in many northern communities.

(a) Should a Native child have the right to be placed with a family who will be able to maintain the child's ties with his or her cultural roots?

(b) What problems might be created for a child who is placed outside the Native Canadian community?

(c) Should children be placed only in homes where their religious, ethnic, or racial backgrounds can be preserved?

4. Children have successfully sued their parents for physical injuries resulting from beatings, incest, and auto accidents. However, there have not been any Canadian cases where children have successfully sued for emotional or psychological scarring as the result of "mal-parenting".

(a) Should children be able to sue their parents for emotional or psychological abuse? Discuss.

(b) What problems would this ability create, in your opinion?

5. When do the rights of children begin? The Ontario *Family Law Reform Act* states:

> **67. No person shall be disentitled from recovering damages in respect of injuries incurred for the reason only that the injuries were incurred before his birth.**

(a) Do you think this section would allow the child of an alcoholic or drug-addicted mother to sue for any deformities caused by the mother's addiction?

(b) Is the unborn child of an alcoholic or drug-addicted mother a child in need of protection?

(c) Should the authorities responsible for child welfare be able to step in to protect an unborn child? In what ways might they do so?

6. A three-year-old child is brought into the hospital suffering from burns to sixty percent of her body. She is in critical condition, and doctors advise an immediate transfusion. The child's parents are Jehovah's Witnesses and refuse consent for the transfusion. Child welfare authorities apply for an emergency hearing requesting the court to grant temporary custody of the child to the Children's Aid Society so that it may give consent for the transfusion. The parents object to this transfer of custody as a violation of their religious beliefs.

(a) In your opinion, should the state have the right to overrule a parent's religious beliefs?

(b) If so, in what situations?

PROJECTS AND ACTIVITIES

1. What obligations are placed on parents by the criminal law? Obtain a copy of the *Criminal Code* and research the sections which apply to parents and their children. Report your findings to the class.

2. Children have many rights other than those discussed in this chapter. Once a child reaches the age of majority, he or she usually has full legal rights or capacity as an adult, but some rights are attained even before this time. In your province, at what age does a child or young person have the following legal rights?
    (a) to quit school
    (b) to work
    (c) to consent to medical care
    (d) to have legal counsel
    (e) to enter into a contract
    (f) to marry without parental consent
    (g) to sue or to be sued
    (h) to get a driver's licence
    (i) to vote
    (j) to purchase alcoholic beverages
    (k) to be treated as a young offender
    (l) to be treated as an adult within the criminal justice system
    (m) to become engaged
    (n) to make a will
    (o) to witness a will
    (p) to testify under oath in court

3. Obtain copies of the appropriate statutes in your province and any government publications dealing with legislation affecting children. Try to determine the rights of children in the following areas:
    (a) *Financial Support*
    (i) What is the name of the statute in your province which outlines the obligation of parents to support their children?
    (ii) What is the age limit for support set by the statute?
    (iii) What stand does the law in your province take regarding the rights of children born outside of marriage?
    (b) *Education*
    (i) Does your province require school boards to provide special education programs for exceptional children?
    (ii) Should the school boards do so, or should this be the financial responsibility of the parents, as it has been in the past? What is your opinion?
    (c) *Autonomy of the Family and Protection from Harm*
    (i) What is the definition of a child in need of protection in

your province? How does your provincial statute compare to the section of New Brunswick's *Child and Family Services and Family Relations Act*, quoted in this chapter?

(ii) Does your provincial statute place an obligation on people to report suspected child abuse or neglect?

(d) *Custody and Guardianship*

(i) What are the rights of the father of a child born out of wedlock in your province?

(ii) Is this situation fair, in your opinion? If not, what changes would you recommend?

RESOLVING CASES

Children's Aid Society of Winnipeg v. M. and S. (1980) 13 R.F.L. (2d) 65 (Man.C.A.)

The Children's Aid Society applied for permanent custody of two children. Their mother was twenty-two years old and unmarried. She had a history of alcoholism and promiscuous relationships with men. Evidence given at the trial indicated that during the period of investigation, the mother had lived with six different men. On two occasions she was arrested for being drunk in the street and was sent to a detoxification unit. On at least three occasions, she left her children with babysitters for "long periods of time", without making suitable arrangements for their care. Even after the children were taken into custody by the C.A.S., she did not contact the Society promptly about her children.

The mother testified that she would stop drinking only if her children were returned to her.

— Has the mother in this case lived up to the minimum standard the law requires of parents?
— As the judge hearing this case, what test would you apply in making your decision?
— What evidence would be particularly important in your decision?
— Should the mother be deprived permanently of the custody of her children, in your opinion? If not, what other options might you consider?

Benoit v. Benoit (1972) R.F.L. 180 (Ont. Prov. Ct.)

Mr. and Mrs. Benoit were Roman Catholics and their children were raised in this faith. When the Benoits separated, the mother was awarded custody and the father, reasonable access. After the separation, the father became a Jehovah's Witness. On his visits to the children, the father began discussing religion with them, and he gave them books to read about his new faith.

The mother testified that these discussions left her children upset and confused and that she found them difficult to control after their father's visits. She applied to the court to have Mr. Benoit's access to his children stopped.

—Which parent had the right to decide the children's religion?
—Should Mr. Benoit have the right to discuss religion with his children?
—Should Mr. Benoit have an absolute right to visit his children?
—As the judge hearing this application, what would you decide?

Wong v. Graham (1980) 13 R.F.L. (2d) 139 (Man. Prov. Judges Ct.)

The unmarried parties to this action lived together for two-and-a-half years. They had one child. Both parents applied for her custody when the relationship broke down.

In his judgement, the judge made the following statement: "We have then a two-year-old girl whose parents both apply for her custody. I should say that I believe that both applications are *bona fide* (in good faith, sincere)...Had Jennifer been a legitimate child, I think that my decision would have been more difficult." Custody was awarded to the mother, with access awarded to the father.

—On what basis was custody of Jennifer awarded to her mother?
—At the time of the trial, Jennifer was two years old. If she had been born within wedlock, do you think her mother would still have been awarded custody? Why?

Re Adoption No. 71-09-013131 (1973) 9 R.F.L. 196 (B.C.S.C.)

A marriage took place between a sixteen-year-old girl and an eighteen-year-old boy. Nine weeks later, a child was born. The marriage lasted for only four-and-a-half months. The child lived with the paternal grandparents after the separation. The mother was anxious for a reconciliation with her husband. She consented to the adoption of her child by the paternal grandparents after the child's father and his parents pressured her to do so. The mother believed after discussion with her in-laws and her husband's grandfather that a reconciliation was possible in the future and that the child would be returned at that time. However, the husband had no interest in a reconciliation. The mother applied to the courts to revoke her consent to the adoption.

—What argument would the mother present to the courts to support her request for withdrawing the consent to the adoption?
—Should her application be granted, in your opinion? Explain.

Erhart v. Bowers (1980) 13 R.F.L. (2d) 209 (B.C.S.C.)

The mother of a two-year-old boy applied to the courts to withdraw her consent for adoption. The mother and father of this child were unmarried. They led a nomadic lifestyle. At the time of the child's birth, he was given up for adoption because the father did not wish to have a child interfering with their lifestyle. Four days later they changed their minds, and the child was returned.

Less than a year later, the child was again placed for adoption and began living with a couple with a stable home life. The consents for adoption were signed. A short time later, the boy's biological parents separated, and the mother applied to the court to revoke her consent.

When the case came up before the courts the following year, the mother had become an active church member and was attempting to stabilize her life.

—Would it be in the child's best interests to allow the mother to withdraw her consent to the adoption?
—What weight should the court attach to the mother's change in lifestyle?
—What do you think was the decision of the court?

17

Ending the Relationship

> Separation Agreements
> Separation and Provincial Legislation
> Divorce
> **Annulment**
> Ending the Common Law Relationship
> Violence in the Family

"For better, for worse
For richer, for poorer
In sickness and in health
'Til death do us part."

Many brides and grooms have exchanged this promise or one similar during their wedding ceremony. Marriage is intended to last forever. However, statistics tell us that approximately forty percent of Canadian marriages do not last forever. For many reasons, the spouses who made vows on their wedding day are unable to keep their promises, and the relationship breaks down.

—**What do you think are some of the major causes of marital breakdown?**

Domestic relationships can be ended in a variety of ways. Married couples can separate and live apart, or can end the relationship by annulment or divorce. Cohabiting couples can simply begin living apart. No matter how simple or complex the process of ending the relationship, it is always emotionally painful for the women, men, and children involved. Difficult decisions must be made during the process concerning the custody of children, financial support, and the division of property.

Chapter 16 looked at the position of children caught in the breakdown of the parental relationship. This chapter will focus on the procedures used by the spouses to end the domestic relationship. Both federal and provincial laws apply when marriages end. You learned earlier that the Constitution gives the federal government jurisdiction over marriage and divorce. Thus, it is responsible for establishing the grounds for divorce. The provincial governments are responsible under the Constitution for property and civil rights. The rules for the division of the property accumulated by spouses during their relationship therefore fall under provincial law, as do the rules for awarding support.

"We had a trial separation, but she found me."

Separation Agreements

Entering into a separation agreement is the most common way for spouses to settle their affairs when the marriage breaks down. Separation agreements are domestic contracts between spouses who have agreed to live separate and apart. The agreement can include any terms agreeable to the separating husband and wife. It will usually cover at least the following matters:

1. the division of the spouses' property
2. the custody and support of their children
3. the support of one of the spouses

Separation agreements are usually drawn up by a lawyer. Some provinces require both spouses to obtain independent legal advice before entering into the contract. While this is not necessary in all provinces, it is certainly a good idea, because once the separation agreement is signed and witnessed, it becomes binding and enforceable. Only in very limited circumstances will a court set aside any part or all of a separation agreement. For instance, the separating couple can agree on the custody of their children, but the court will set aside this term of the agreement if it is not in the children's best interests. Also, an agreement will likely not be upheld by the court if either of the parties was unduly pressured to sign it. Provincial legislation can set out other situations where a court may set aside a separation agreement. Ontario's *Family Law Reform Act*, for example, lists the following three situations in section 18(4):

> (4) *(a)* where the provision for support or the waiver of the right to support results in circumstances that are unconscionable;
> *(b)* where the provision for support is to a spouse who qualifies for an allowance for support out of public money; or
> *(c)* where there has been default in the payment of support under the contract or agreement.

—Explain each of the above statements in your own words.

The Value of Separation Agreements

Although the process of ending a marriage is rarely painless, entering into a separation agreement is a way to avoid the bitterness (and expense) of lengthy court battles. It is always better for the spouses to be able to reach an agreement that best suits their particular circumstances than to have a court impose a settlement on them.

Additionally, once the agreement is in effect, there is an income tax advantage to the couple. The spouse paying support is allowed to deduct these payments from his or her income when preparing a tax return. The receiving spouse must claim the payments as income. Since this spouse is usually in a lower tax bracket, the overall taxes paid are lower, putting more money into the hands of the family. This is an important consideration, because the process of separating and setting up two households in the place of one is generally very expensive.

Separation and Provincial Legislation

Often spouses cannot reach an agreement about how to settle their affairs when the marriage is over. If a separation agreement cannot be reached, the couple has no choice but to apply to the courts to settle the issues of custody, support, and property division. Custody was examined in Chapter 16. We will now look at the various provincial laws affecting property and support. This is an area of law which underwent dramatic change in the 1970s.

Property Rights Before Law Reform

In 1975, the Supreme Court of Canada heard the case of Irene Murdoch, an Albertan whose marriage had ended after twenty-five years. Mrs. Murdoch had applied to the courts for a share of the property she and her husband had accumulated during their marriage. At the time the *Murdoch* case was heard by the Supreme Court, the system of law which applied to the property rights of spouses in all of the common law provinces was the **separation of property** system. In general, under this system property was owned by the person who bought it, inherited it, or received it as a gift. The system of separation of property created many hardships for wives in families which followed the traditional pattern of husband as breadwinner and wife as homemaker and mother. Because the husband was usually the one with the money to make purchases, all property acquired and used by the family belonged to him, unless it was specifically registered in the names of both him and his wife. If the couple separated, the wife often owned nothing.

When the Supreme Court of Canada delivered its decision on the *Murdoch* case, it became obvious to many Canadians that family law reform was needed. See whether you agree once you have read this case.

Murdoch v. Murdoch [1975] 1 S.C.R. 423

The Murdochs married in 1943 and separated in 1968. Mrs. Murdoch began a court action claiming a one-half interest in the house, land, and other assets owned by her husband on the grounds that they were equal partners in running their ranch, and that her labour throughout their marriage entitled her to a share.

All of the lands involved in her claim were registered in her husband's name. The money used to purchase them came from Mr. Murdoch's bank account and the proceeds from the sale of previous land owned by him. Mrs. Murdoch had made a small financial contribution to the purchase of the first piece of property, and later an additional $4000 came from her bank account. Her husband claimed at the trial that this sum was in fact a loan from his mother-in-law. In addition, Mrs. Murdoch purchased furniture and appliances for the household. During the marriage, Mrs. Murdoch performed the tasks of a wife and mother, but she also did "haying, raking, swathing, mowing, driving trucks and tractors and teams, quieting horses, taking cattle back and forth to the reserve, dehorning, vaccinating, branding, anything that was to be done." Mr. Murdoch gave evidence that his wife did "just about what an ordinary rancher's wife does. Most of them can do most anything."

The trial judge dismissed Mrs Murdoch's claim, stating that he found no intention of partnership, that he believed the $4000 contribution was a loan from Mrs. Murdoch's mother, and that her contribution of labour was that of any ranch wife. The majority judgement of the Supreme Court of Canada upheld this decision on appeal. Mrs. Murdoch lost her case.

In his **dissent judgement** (minority opinion) given on appeal, Supreme Court Justice Bora Laskin stated that Mrs. Murdoch had "contributed considerable physical labour to the building up of assets claimed by the husband as his own and had also made a modest financial contribution to their acquisitions." He would have allowed her a share based on the doctrine of **constructive trust**. Constructive trust is an equitable principle of law which would allow Mrs. Murdoch's claim, because to deny it would unjustly enrich her husband who had benefitted by her contributions over a period of twenty-five years.

— Why was it important to the decision that all lands were registered in Mr. Murdoch's name?
— At common law, Mrs. Murdoch was entitled to a share of the property only if she could show that she had made a substantial contribution of money or labour. The trial judge and the majority of the Supreme Court felt that her contributions were minimal. Do you agree?
— Should marriage be considered an economic partnership, in your opinion?
— Should a contribution by a spouse to child care and household management be recognized financially if the marriage breaks down?
— Why do you think this case brought a loud outcry for law reform from across the country?

By the time Mrs. Murdoch lost her final appeal before the Supreme Court of Canada, many provincial law reform commissions were hard at work recommending changes in the laws relating to property and the family. The Ontario Law Reform Commission, for instance, had published a report which outlined the following need:

"to evaluate the adequacy of those laws in view of changed economic and social conditions pertaining to the family, to state the basic principles required for a modern code of family law...and to suggest remedial legislation to establish such a code." (Ontario Law Reform Commission *Report of Family Law*, Part II, Marriage.)

—Can you identify any of the social and economic changes of the 1960s and 1970s of which the Commission was speaking?

Provincial Family Property Legislation

How did the provinces respond to this need for change? The nine common law provinces have passed statutes roughly similar, although certainly not identical. The following section from Saskatchewan's *Matrimonial Property Act* illustrates the basic principle upon which these statutes operate:

> 20. The purpose of this Act, and in particular of this part, is to recognize that child care, household management and financial provision are the joint and mutual responsibilities of spouses and that inherent in the marital relationship there is joint contribution, whether financial or otherwise, by the spouses to the assumption of these responsibilities that entitles each spouse to an equal distribution of the matrimonial property, subject to the exceptions, exemptions and equitable considerations mentioned in this Act.

—To what extent does Saskatchewan's *Marital Property Act* seem to recognize marriage as a partnership?
—If the marriage breaks down, how is the matrimonial property to be divided?
—What kinds of property do you think are "matrimonial property"?

Each of the provincial statutes includes a statement which recognizes the contributions of both spouses to a marriage by setting out a basic right to a division of family property (usually on the basis of equal sharing). However, each of the statutes defines family property in a different way. Also, each establishes different reasons for varying

"How did things go down at the old divorce court?"

the equal division of the property. For example, the **family assets** (family property) which Ontario spouses are entitled to share equally are defined in the following way:

> (3) *(b)* **"family assets" means a matrimonial home as determined under Part III and property owned by one or both spouses and ordinarily used or enjoyed by both spouses or one or more of their children while the spouses are residing together for shelter or transportation or for household, education, recreational, social or aesthetic purposes...**

—What do you think "ordinarily used" means?
—Which of the following do you think would be defined as a "family asset" under Ontario law?

(a) a savings account in the wife's name only, which she used for her own purposes
(b) the same savings account, but this time used to pay household expenses and pay for family vacations
(c) a collection of Persian rugs kept by the husband in glass cases to display to other collectors
(d) a camper, boat, and trailer purchased by the husband and used by the family for camping trips
(e) an expensive painting owned by the husband's company but hanging in the matrimonial home

The Ontario *Family Law Reform Act* does not, as a general rule, grant spouses a share of property which is defined as a non-family asset. Such property would usually be business assets. In order to

ENDING THE RELATIONSHIP 393

qualify for any share of this type of property, a spouse has to show that he or she has made a real contribution, as outlined in s.8 of the *Family Law Reform Act*:

> 8. Where one spouse or former spouse has contributed work, money or money's worth in respect of the acquisition, management, maintenance, operation or improvement of property, other than family assets, in which the other has or had an interest, upon application, the court may by order,
>   (a) direct the payment of an amount in compensation therefor; or
>   (b) award a share of the interest of the other spouse or former spouse in the property appropriate to the contribution,
> and the court shall determine and assess the contribution without regard to the relationship of husband and wife or the fact that the acts constituting the contribution are those of a reasonable spouse of that sex in the circumstances.

Other jurisdictions have given a broader definition to the kinds of property which spouses are entitled to share upon marriage breakdown, or have indicated in the provincial legislation a more favourable attitude towards the sharing of business assets. The *Matrimonial Property Act* of Newfoundland outlines as one of the purposes of the *Act*:

> (3) (d) [to] provide for judicial discretion in sharing business assets built up by a spouse during marriage.

Québec reformed its Civil Code in 1970 and introduced a family property system called a **partnership of acquests**. Under the partnership of acquests, there are two categories of property: private property and acquests. The Civil Code defines private property in a restricted list which includes all property owned by the spouses before marriage; inheritances; and property intended solely for personal use (for instance, clothing). All other property is an acquest.

In Québec, when a marriage breaks down, or one of the spouses dies, the acquests (all property obtained during the marriage, except as outlined above) are to be equitably divided by a court. This property would include business assets. The partnership of acquests applies to all spouses who do not specifically opt out of the system by means of a domestic contract.

—Obtain a copy of the statute which deals with family property in your province. What kinds of property are spouses entitled to share when the marriage breaks down?
—Does your provincial statute differ significantly from the Ontario law quoted above?
—If so, why do you think it is different?

Unequal Sharing

The provincial family property statutes allow the courts some discretion in awarding an unequal division of property in certain situations. Some of the statutes outline a list of circumstances the court might consider. What factors do you think a court should take into consideration? The following two cases might help you in answering the question.

Sweetman v. Sweetman (1981) 7 A.C.W.S. (2d) 91

At the time of the marriage, the husband was seventy-four, the wife, sixty-three. The wife owned the matrimonial home and its contents and had purchased them about twenty years before the marriage took place. The marriage lasted twenty-one months.

—How would you divide the assets of these spouses?
—What factors would you take into consideration?

Weir v. Weir (1979) 23 O.R. (2d) 765 (Ont. H.C.J.)

The Weirs separated after more than fourteen years of marriage. Before her marriage, Mrs. Weir had worked, but her husband requested that she quit her job. He had a very successful law practice and was concerned about seeming to be unable to support his wife. In addition, his attitude was "You run the house, I'll run the business." Mrs. Weir took over all household and child-rearing duties during her marriage, leaving her husband free to pursue his career and business interests.

When the Weirs separated, the family assets included a house worth $137 000 and a cottage worth $55 000. The husband had business assets valued at $237 000. The court awarded Mrs. Weir the matrimonial home and half of the proceeds of the sale of the cottage. She also received maintenance for herself and support for her children.

—What factors do you think the judge took into consideration in making this division of the Weirs' assets?
—Would your division have been the same as the judge's?

Provincial Support Legislation

Another area of provincial law reform in the 1970s relates to the support obligations of spouses. Before reform, only husbands could be ordered by the courts to provide support. Wives did not have this obligation, even when they were clearly in a better financial position than their husbands. The provincial statutes have remedied this unjust situation and, at the same time, have imposed an obligation on spouses to be responsible for their own support where possible. When awarding support, the courts will consider two main factors: need, and the ability to pay.

Dieter v. Dieter (1982) 37 O.R. (2d) 296 (Ont. C.A.)

The spouses were married for twenty-five years before the forty-nine-year-old husband left the wife. The wife was fifty-four years old and suffering from ill-health at this time. She had not been in the work force since her marriage. The husband stated his earnings at $25 600 a year.

At the trial, the wife was awarded sixty percent of the family assets and $500 per month for two years as support. The wife appealed and the husband cross-appealed.

On appeal, it was discovered that the husband was in fact earning $31 253 a year and that he had a pension plan and a Registered Retirement Savings Plan which would benefit him in the future. The Court of Appeal upheld the division of the family assets but felt that it was unreasonable to expect that the wife would be able to support herself in two years' time. The Court increased the support payment to $800 per month and removed the two-year limit.

—Do you agree with this decision? Why or why not?

Until these recent reforms, a spouse would lose the right to be supported by engaging in certain conduct. For instance, a single act of adultery used to disentitle a wife from any financial support. Conduct no longer disentitles a spouse from support. However, if the conduct is very serious, it can be taken into consideration when the court is determining the appropriate amount of support, as shown by this section from New Brunswick's *Child and Family Services and Family Relations Act*:

> **115. (6) In determining the amount, if any, of support in relation to need, the court shall consider all the circumstances of the parties including,**
> *(t)* the conduct of the parties, where such conduct unrea-

> sonably precipitates, prolongs or aggravates the need for support or unreasonably affects the ability to pay support.

—What factors does your provincial statute outline to guide a judge in awarding support?
—What effect, if any, does conduct have on an award of support in your provincial legislation?

Divorce

Provincial property legislation is not the only area of family law to undergo major change in recent years. The federal law relating to divorce changed considerably during the late 1960s. In 1984, there were plans to alter it radically.

Prior to the reform of the *Divorce Act* in 1968, Canadian husbands could divorce their wives on only one ground—adultery. If adultery could not be proven, no divorce could be granted, no matter how unsuccessful the marriage. Wives could obtain a divorce if they could prove that their husbands had committed any of the following matrimonial faults: **adultery**, rape, **sodomy**, **bestiality**, or **desertion**. The law at this time did not take into consideration the fact that marriages can break down for many other reasons, not all of which are the "fault" of either spouse.

The *Divorce Act*, 1968

The reformed *Divorce Act* allowed many more grounds for divorce. Section 3 set out the fault grounds for divorce, called *matrimonial offences*. Section 4 recognized, for the first time in Canada, that marital breakdown should also be grounds for a divorce. In all, the new *Act* set out ten grounds for legally ending a marriage.

Matrimonial Offences

The following grounds are set out in s.3 as fault grounds, or matrimonial offences:

1. adultery
2. an assault involving sexual intercourse; bestiality, sodomy, or homosexual acts
3. bigamy
4. mental cruelty
5. physical cruelty

The vast majority of divorce actions based on matrimonial offences involve the grounds of adultery or cruelty. The remaining fault grounds represent less than one percent of all divorce actions.

Permanent Marital Breakdown

The following grounds were accepted by the 1968 statute as evidence that a marriage had permanently broken down:

1. Imprisonment for lengthy periods:
   (a) for a total of three years in the five years before the divorce action is begun;
   (b) for two years when the sentence is for ten or more years and the imprisoned spouse has no more right to appeal.
2. Gross addiction to alcohol or drugs for a period of at least three years, where there is no reasonable hope for a cure in the near future.
3. Non-consummation of the marriage for a period of at least one year. This means that the marriage has never been consummated because of illness, inability, or refusal, and one year has passed since the wedding ceremony.
4. Disappearance for at least three years, when the whereabouts of the spouse are unknown and an effort has been made to locate the spouse.
5. Separation for a period of three years, or five years if the petitioner is the spouse who has deserted the marriage.

The most common marriage breakdown ground used is the three-year separation. Although the spouses must be living separate and apart, the courts have granted divorces in cases where the spouses both resided in the matrimonial home but lived completely separate lives. Spouses are allowed one reconciliation attempt lasting for no more than ninety days. If the period of reconciliation is of greater duration, but the spouses separate once more, the three-year waiting period for starting divorce proceedings must begin again.

The New Divorce Reform

In early 1984, the government introduced Bill C-10, new draft legislation to once again reform the divorce laws. This draft legislation was in response to the Law Reform Commission of Canada's recommendation that divorce law be simplified and the adversarial nature of the divorce process be reduced. Bill C-10 is intended to repeal sections 3 and 4 of the 1968 statute and to replace them with the following:

3. (1) Subject to section 5, a petition for divorce may be presented to court by
   (a) a husband or wife, or
   (b) a husband and wife, if permitted by any rules of court or regulations made under section 19 to present the petition jointly,

   on the ground that there has been a breakdown of their marriage.

   (2) On a petition for divorce, a breakdown of a marriage is established if, and only if,
   (a) the husband and wife assert, in the manner prescribed by any rules of court or regulations made under section 19, that the marriage has broken down; or
   (b) the husband and wife have lived separate and apart for a period of one year or more that immediately precedes, includes or immediately follows the date of presentation of the petition.

   (3) On a petition for divorce, no decree of divorce shall be granted before the expiration of one year after the date of presentation of the petition unless the condition specified in paragraph (2)(b) is fulfilled.

   (4) For the purposes of paragraph (2)(b),
   (a) a husband and wife shall be deemed to have lived separate for any period for which they have lived apart if, for that period, either of them had the intention to live separate and apart from the other; and
   (b) a period during which the husband and wife have been living separate and apart shall not be considered to have been interrupted or terminated
      (i) by reason only that either spouse has become incapable of forming or having an intention to continue to live so separate and apart or of continuing to live so separate and apart of the spouse's own volition, if it appears to the court that the separation would probably have continued if the spouse had not become so incapable, or
      (ii) by reason only that there has been a resumption of cohabitation by the spouses during a single period of, or during periods amounting in the aggregate to, not more than ninety days with reconciliation as its primary purpose.

Breakdown sole basis

New law will speed and simplify divorce

By JEFF SALLOT
Globe and Mail Reporter

OTTAWA — Marriage breakdown would become the sole basis for divorce under new federal legislation that would generally speed and simplify divorce proceedings and for the first time would allow grandparents a chance to claim custody of children.

Justice Minister Mark MacGuigan introduced so-called no-fault amendments to the Divorce Act yesterday that would eliminate the requirement for one spouse to accuse the other of marital misconduct, such as adultery or cruelty, or for the spouses to sit out a three-year separation to end a marriage legally.

In uncontested cases, the spouses could obtain divorce one year after filing court papers stating that they believed their marriage was beyond redemption. More than 90 per cent of all divorces now are uncontested.

Under Ottawa's proposals, divorce could also be granted if the parties said they already had been separated for one year.

The bill, which Mr. MacGuigan said he hopes will become law by summer, would allow spouses to end failed marriages without even having to make an appearance before a judge in court.

Because of dual jurisdiction in divorce law, however, this process would require the approval of the particular province. Mr. MacGuigan said he has received indications from most provincial governments that they would welcome this reform as a way to cut the backlog of cases clogging the courts.

At first glance the package of divorce law reforms looked good to Svend Robinson, justice critic for the New Democratic Party. Conservative critic Allan Lawrence said his party would have to study the bill in caucus next Wednesday before any endorsement could be given.

Mr. MacGuigan said one of his greatest concerns was the interests of children of broken homes.

For one thing, he said, the accusatory proceedings that the present law requires to prove grounds for divorce often poison the atmosphere when the important questions of child custody and support arise.

The reforms, the Justice Minister said, should eliminate the need for a child to have to go into a courtroom and testify that he saw "daddy beating mommy" for the mother to prove cruelty. Such cases are traumatic for children but sometimes legally necessary under the present law.

The amendments also would permit grandparents – or anyone else having an interest in the welfare of the children, including neighbors to step in between feuding parents and apply for custody. The judge would still determine the custody question on the basis of what appears best for the child.

Judges could also grant visiting rights to grandparents or any other person to whom the child has an emotional bond.

Anticipating the criticism of Catholic clergy and others concerned that divorce law reform will weaken the role of family life in society, Mr. MacGuigan said his amendments only make it easier for men and women to end the legal bonds that tie them together long after love has died.

The changes should not increase divorce rates, he said, because "governments don't make social reality, except maybe around the edges."

The purpose of the amendments, the first rewriting of divorce laws since 1968, is to "relieve a great deal of human misery...while at the same time preserving the institution of marriage."

The bill imposes a duty on lawyers to advise clients of the availability of conciliation and mediation services.

Most divorce proceedings now cost between $700 and $1,000. Mr. MacGuigan said his proposed streamlining of proceedings should cut legal bills by one-third to one-half.

The amendments also will make it easier for courts to enforce support and maintenance payments by requiring a security deposit. And they will allow courts to take into account the prospects that an unpaid homemaker might be able to find paid employment after divorce.

In assessing maintenance payments, courts would no longer look at misconduct by a spouse or who is at fault. The pertinent factors would be simply the economic conditions and circumstances of the parties.

Mr. MacGuigan said the bill would give courts the power to apportion child-support payments on the basis of the relative abilities of the parents to pay "in light of the financial resources and needs of both parents and children."

The minister also said he hoped that the money provinces save in legal aid costs as a result of the divorce law reforms would be plowed back into conciliation services.

Figure 17-1 What is your opinion of the new legislation which would make marital breakdown the sole basis for divorce?

Note that the new legislation would create a single ground for divorce—marriage breakdown. Under it, a divorce decree would be granted in either of the following circumstances:

1. one year after the divorce petition if the couple had separated immediately before beginning divorce proceedings, or
2. if the couple has completed a one-year period of separation.

The procedural details of petitioning for divorce will also be simplified if the new legislation passes. Much of the adversarial nature of present divorce proceedings will be eliminated, since "fault-finding" will no longer be a requirement for divorce.

If Bill C-10 (or a revision of it) passes and becomes law, divorce in this country will have changed very significantly. As you have seen, the process prior to 1968 relied on a very few fault grounds, and was very difficult. The 1968 reform provided additional grounds, making divorce more accessible to many couples whose marriages were no longer workable. As well, it introduced the concept of marriage breakdown. The proposed reform would simplify divorce still further by eliminating fault and creating the single ground of marriage breakdown.

The Divorce Process

The legal document which begins the divorce process is called a **petition for divorce**. The spouse bringing the action is the **petitioner**. The spouse being sued for divorce is the **respondent**.

Over ninety percent of all divorce actions under the 1968 statute have been undefended. That is, the spouses themselves settled such issues as custody and support, either by making a separation agreement or by applying to the courts under provincial legislation. The divorce action was necessary simply to formalize the end of the marriage and leave the spouses free to remarry if they wished.

In divorces such as these, the process is fairly simple. The petition is served on the respondent, and a trial date is set. Generally, only the petitioner appears at the trial, which often takes just a few moments.

If the divorce is defended or *contested*, the spouses have not been able to settle all of the issues relating to the breakdown of the family unit. Usually, numerous pre-trial hearings occur before the trial in an attempt to settle or reduce these matters. Eventually, the case will go to trial, and usually, both parties appear. This is a much more time-consuming and expensive process than for the undefended divorce.

It is not yet clear what amendments will be made to the divorce process when the new legislation passes, but the draft legislation proposes simplifying the procedure to reduce the expense and bitterness caused by lengthy trials. The process may in fact be taken out of the courts altogether in divorce proceedings where all issues other than the actual termination of the marriage have been resolved.

When the court grants the divorce, a legal document which officially ends the marriage is issued. This document is called the **decree nisi**. Usually, the petitioner must wait ninety days after the decree nisi is issued before applying for the final divorce decree, the **decree absolute**. However, the final decree can be issued at the time of the trial at the discretion of the judge. The former spouses are not free to remarry until the decree absolute is issued and the divorce is final.

—Why is there a ninety-day waiting period before the final divorce decree is granted?
—Under what circumstances might a judge waive the waiting period?

Annulment

As you may recall, annulment is the legal process used to end a marriage and declare that it never existed. Marriages can be invalid because they fail to meet the requirements set out in federal or provincial law.

Since 1968, when the federal government reformed the *Divorce Act*, making it easier to get a divorce, annulments have become much less common. However, the procedure is still available for spouses who, for personal or religious reasons, do not wish to end their marriage by divorce and who qualify for an annulment. In addition, spouses who cannot divorce because their marriage was never valid in the first place can have the marriage annulled.

A couple involved in a marriage which is void *ab initio* need not go through a formal annulment procedure. However, because this area of law is controversial and often difficult to understand, most people do apply to the court for a formal declaration, called a decree of nullity, that the marriage is not valid. The decree of nullity must be issued for a marriage which is voidable because it fails to meet the requirements of a valid marriage. After the granting of the decree, the legal status of the former spouses reverts back to that of single people.

You may wonder why the law makes a distinction between void *ab initio* and voidable marriages. Consider the following questions, keeping in mind that a voidable marriage legally exists until a decree of nullity is issued, and then it is as if the marriage never existed; a marriage which is void *ab initio* never has existed.

—What do you think will happen if the husband in a marriage which was void *ab initio* because of a former marriage dies, and his will

states that his estate will be divided equally between his "wife" and the children of his first marriage? Who can inherit? Would your answer be different if the marriage was voidable but had not been annulled?
— The wife in a void *ab initio* marriage is arrested and charged with a criminal offence. The Crown prosecutor feels that her "husband" has information relating to the case and wishes to subpoena him to testify against his "wife". Remember that spouses usually cannot be forced to testify against one another. Can the Crown compel the "husband" to testify? Would your answer be different if the marriage was voidable but had not been annulled?

Provincial Property and Support Legislation in the Event of Annulment

Provincial law sets out the rights of spouses to divide their property and to claim support when the marriage breaks down. Although the rights of spouses vary from province to province, a person whose marriage is void *ab initio* or is voidable still qualifies as a "spouse" under provincial property legislation. For example, Newfoundland's *Matrimonial Property Act* includes the following definition:

> 1. *(e)* "Spouse" means either of a man and woman who
>   (i) are married to each other
>   (ii) are married to each other by a marriage that is voidable and has not been voided by a judgment nullity, or
>   (iii) have gone through a form of marriage with each other, in good faith, that is void and are cohabiting or have cohabited within the preceding year.

Ending the Common Law Relationship

As you have seen, ending a marriage can be a very complex and time-consuming legal procedure. In comparison, a relationship between cohabiting, or common law, spouses can be ended very simply. Although these relationships are as emotionally difficult to end as marriage, legally, all the spouses need to do is separate and live apart. If they are single people, they are free to begin new relationships or to get married at any time.

If the cohabiting spouses have had a child together, the breakup of the relationship can become legally more complex. They may have to go to court if they are not able to agree on custody or on the amount of support required for the child.

In all provinces, except Alberta, cohabiting spouses are entitled to seek support. As you learned in Chapter 15, the various provincial statutes usually require that the spouses cohabit for a specified period before this support obligation exists. For example, in Ontario cohabiting spouses must have lived together for five years or have had a child before becoming eligible for support; in Nova Scotia, one year of cohabitation creates support obligations.

The major difference between married and unmarried spouses when the relationship ends is in the area of the division of property. The common law relationship does not give cohabiting spouses the right to share in the property obtained while they lived together. The common law principle of separation of property which applied to married couples until the legal reforms of the late 1960s and the 1970s still applies to cohabiting spouses. To be entitled to a share of the property, a cohabiting spouse must prove one of the following:

1. ownership
2. financial contribution to the purchase of the property
3. work or money's worth contribution to the property
4. evidence of an intention of the parties to share the property

The evidence of an intention to share takes the form of a **trust**: although one spouse has legal title to the property, that person holds a share of the property *in trust* for the benefit of the other spouse. Trusts can take a variety of forms, from written agreements to unstated but implied intentions.

Pettkus v. Becker [1980] 2 S.C.R. 834 (S.C.C.)

Rosa Becker, thirty, met Lothar Pettkus, twenty-five, in 1955. Shortly after meeting, Pettkus moved in with Becker. The couple never did marry, although Pettkus introduced Becker to others as his wife and he did eventually claim her as a dependant spouse on his income tax return.

From 1955 to 1960, both parties were working. Becker paid all living expenses, allowing her common law spouse to save $13 000 by 1960. This money was used to purchase property and a beekeeping business, which were placed in Pettkus' name. For the next fourteen years, the spouses worked together in the business.

In 1974, after nineteen years together, Becker permanently separated from Pettkus, claiming physical abuse. She sued for an interest in the property, which by this time was valued at $300 000.

At trial, she was awarded $1500 plus forty beehives minus the bees. The trial judge discounted her claim, stating that he found no intention between the parties to share. He further stated that she had paid the household expenses in the first five years "in the hope of seducing a younger defendant into marriage."

The Ontario Court of Appeal disagreed with the trial judge on the basis that he had vastly underrated Becker's contribution to the relationship and the business.

In the final appeal, the Supreme Court of Canada applied the doctrine of constructive trust and upheld the Ontario Court of Appeal's award to Becker of a one-half interest in Pettkus' property. In applying this principle, which is intended to prevent the unjust enrichment of a person, Mr. Justice Dickson stated that Pettkus "had the benefit of nineteen years of unpaid labour, while Miss Becker has received little or nothing in return."

—Constructive trust is the principle which the Supreme Court of Canada just five years earlier, refused to apply in the case of a married couple, the Murdochs. Can you offer any explanation for this dramatic turnabout?

The result of the *Pettkus v. Becker* case seems very similar to the rights of married spouses. However, it should be kept in mind that, as a married spouse, Becker would automatically have had a one-half interest in the matrimonial home and furnishings, the car, and other family assets. This would not necessarily have been true of the non-family, business assets. As you know, in many provinces, even a married spouse must show a contribution of work, money, or money's worth to the accumulation of business assets. It was Becker's contribution over a very lengthy period which resulted in the award of a one-half interest in all the property. Like a married spouse, a cohabiting spouse who could not prove a significant contribution, or a person in a short-term common law relationship, would most likely not receive a half-share of the other spouse's property.

Violence in the Family

Recently a great deal of media attention has been focused on a serious problem taking place behind closed doors in Canadian homes: domestic violence. It can take many forms: child abuse (discussed in Chapter 16); physical and verbal abuse of the elderly; and violence between spouses, which most commonly takes the form of *wife-battering*.

In 1982, a federal government Parliamentary Committee on Health, Welfare and Social Affairs reported, "We have found that wife-battering is not a matter of slaps and flying crockery. Battered women are choked, kicked, bitten, punched, subjected to sexual assault, threatened and assailed with weapons." What remedies are available to the victim of violence in the family?

Criminal law provides two possible remedies for the victim: a **peace bond**, and the laying of criminal charges.

Figure 17-2 In 1983, the Criminal Code *sections relating to assault were amended. The amendment allows police to lay assault charges against battering spouses, even if the police have not witnessed the assault. Why is this change in the law so important for victims of domestic violence?*

A peace bond is a written promise or recognizance to keep the peace. A battered woman can lay an information before a Justice of the Peace under s.745 of the *Criminal Code* if she feels that her spouse will cause her injury. The Justice can then require the spouse to sign a peace bond. Failure to live up to the terms of this written promise can result in a fine or jail term.

It is also possible to lay criminal charges for assault. It is usually up to the victim to do this by laying an information before a Justice of the Peace, because the police have traditionally been reluctant to bring criminal charges when violence has occurred between family members. It is not common for someone who is charged with such an offence to be arrested. Usually a summons to appear in court will be issued to the alleged offender.

Both of the above remedies suffer from the same problem: these procedures can take quite a long time, and the victim of the abuse may have nowhere else to go in the interim except back to the home in which the violence occurred.

Police instructed to press charges for wife assault

By BRIAN GORY
Special to The Globe and Mail

WINNIPEG — Manitoba husbands who attack their wives have been warned they will be charged with a criminal offence, even if their wives refuse to press charges.

Attorney-General Roland Mr. Penner said yesterday that he has instructed police forces throughout the province to lay charges of common assault, assault causing bodily harm or sexual assault if they find evidence while investigating domestic disputes.

"We think the wife is in a very dependent position and in a threatening position and that unless there is early interference by authorities, it could lead to serious on-going wife battering, and we want to do everything possible to stop that," Mr. Penner said. "If the wife says 'I just don't want to press charges,' charges will still be laid."

Previously, at least in common assault cases, even when wives wanted to lay charges, they were advised that they had to launch their own private prosecutions without police assistance.

If the wife's testimony is the only evidence, however, the Crown may be forced to drop the charge at a later time, Mr. Penner said. However, he feels that just the procedure involved in laying the charge and having a husband appear in court will act as a deterrent.

Reaction has been swift to the announcement. Caroline Garlich, a residential worker at Osborne House, a home for battered women, said, "we've had police here all day to take charges."

And Sharon Sawatsky, the co-ordinator of sexual assault programs at a community health clinic, Klinic, welcomed the Attorney-General's tough stand. By laying a charge, even though a wife refuses to do so, law enforcement people are "making a statement to the woman that it's not her fault," she said. "It's important for her to know that. Often, society leaves the impression that she is somehow responsible for the assault perpetrated against her."

The change in Manitoba policy was based on the experience of law enforcement officials in London, Ont., who adopted a similar plan for Middlesex County two years ago. Ontario figures show that, before the tougher Crown stance, only 3 per cent of assault cases resulted in court action; now the rate is 88 per cent.

Crown Attorney Michael Martin said the policy appears to be successful. He said few husbands become repeat offenders after their first run-in with the law. Judges have meted out sentences of 30 days to three months in jail in some cases.

Provincial statutes such as the *Family Law Reform Act* of both Ontario and Prince Edward Island provide a spouse with two other possible ways to deal with domestic violence: a **restraining order**, and exclusive possession of the matrimonial home. For example, the Ontario *Family Law Reform Act* states:

> 34. Upon application, a court may make an order restraining the spouse of the applicant from molesting, annoying or harassing the applicant or children in the lawful custody of the applicant and may require the spouse of the applicant to enter into such recognizance as the court considers appropriate.
> 45. (1) [The court on application may] by order
>   *(a)* direct that one spouse be given exclusive possession of a matrimonial home or part thereof for life or for such lesser period as the court directs...

It should be pointed out that while s.34 applies to both married and cohabiting couples, s.45 applies to legally married spouses only. A victim of abuse in a common law relationship would have to begin trespass proceedings and obtain an injunction forbidding the abusive spouse from entering the home. This can be a more lengthy and complicated process.

While these remedies can help to protect a victim from any further violence, they don't offer any help in deciding what the future of the marital or cohabiting relationship is to be. Counselling agencies are available to help the spouses maintain the relationship without having to resort to violence. However, it is probably inevitable that the victimized spouse will consider ending the relationship through separation or divorce.

SUMMARIZING YOUR READING

1. What is a separation agreement? What will it usually include?

2. Will a separation agreement ever be disregarded by a court? Explain.

3. Why is the *Murdoch* case so significant in family law?

4. Explain the separation of property system.

5. What basic right of spouses do the new provincial property laws establish? How does this differ from the situation prior to reform?

6. List five factors a court should consider when dividing family property.

7. What reform of the provincial support legislation took place in the 1970s?

8. What two main factors will a court consider when awarding spousal support?

9. What effect can spousal conduct have on the awarding of support in your province?

10. What were the grounds available for divorce before the 1968 reform?

11. Name the two categories of grounds established by the 1968 *Divorce Act*.

12. What are the two most common fault grounds for divorce?

13. What is the most common marital breakdown ground?

14. Briefly summarize the most recent reform proposal for divorce.

15. What does it mean to say that a divorce action is "undefended"?

16. After a divorce action, when is the marriage officially ended?

17. What is the difference between a marriage which is void *ab initio* and a marriage which is voidable?

18. What is a decree of nullity?

19. Are common law spouses entitled to support?

20. What system of law usually applies to the division of property between cohabiting spouses?

21. What must a common law spouse who wishes a share in property prove to a court to establish the claim?

22. What remedies does the criminal law provide for victims of domestic abuse?

23. What remedies do provincial statutes provide for battered women?

DISCUSSING KEY ISSUES

1. Divorce law in Canada is moving away from a system based on fault to a no-fault system. Discuss the advantages and disadvantages of this dramatic change in the law.

2. In your opinion, should cohabiting spouses have the same rights as married spouses when they separate? Explain your answer.

PROJECTS AND ACTIVITIES

1. Obtain a copy of your province's statute on matrimonial property. Prepare a chart which outlines the following:
   (a) When may spouses apply for a division of property?
   (b) What property can be divided?
   (c) What property will be excluded?
   (d) What factors will be considered by the court when dividing property?

2. The eight-year-long marriage of Gene and Rachel Jastrow is breaking up. They have two children: Helen, five, and Daniel, six-and-a-half. Both children are in school full-time.

   Gene earns $28 500 per year. His wife works part-time and earns $10 900. They bought a house two years ago which is valued at $90 000. The mortgage is approximately $55 000, and the house carries for about $800 per month, excluding taxes and utilities. They also own a three-year-old Oldsmobile and a new Honda Civic.

   The house has three bedrooms, kitchen, living/dining room, all comfortably furnished. The family has a colour TV, stereo system, washer/dryer, refrigerator, stove, and dishwasher.

   Each of the spouses has hobby and sports equipment. The Jastrows have only one debt besides their mortgage payment: a $5000 bank loan used to purchase the Honda for Rachel. The spouses cosigned the loan.

   Prepare a separation agreement for the couple, taking into consideration the provisions of your provincial statute and what is fair and reasonable for the Jastrows. Remember that a separation agreement is intended to resolve disputes between spouses—not cause them.

   You will have to consider at least the following factors:
   (a) custody and support of children
   (b) where the spouses will live
   (c) division of property
   (d) debts
   (e) support of spouses

   In addition, do a rough budget for this couple to ensure that they will be able to live within the terms of your agreement.

3. The enforcement of court orders for support of spouses and children has become a major problem. Contact the government department responsible for family law and the Family Court.

Research the various methods available to a spouse to enforce a court order for support. Report your findings to the class.

4. What facilities, if any, are available for battered women and their children in the area where you live? Report your findings to the class.

RESOLVING CASES

Powolny v. Powolny (1982) 26 R.F.L. (2d) 250 (Ont. H.C.J.)

The husband and wife met in Poland where the wife (aged forty-six) had been a nurse for twenty-five years. Upon assurances of a good life in Canada, she married him and came to live in Ontario where the husband (aged sixty) carried on a farming operation. In leaving Poland, she gave up a secure job, pension benefits, and ownership of an apartment.

The marriage lasted for only three years; the wife petitioned for support and a division of assets. The family assets were valued at $35 000. In addition, the husband had the farming operations as a non-family asset.

The wife was enrolled in English classes at the time of the trial, to obtain fluency in the language.

—What factors would you take into consideration when dividing the assets of these spouses?
—How would you divide the assets?
—Is the wife entitled to support? Explain your reasoning.

Mundinger v. Mundinger (1969) 3 D.L.R. (3d) 338 (Ont. C.A.)

The Mundingers were married in 1939 and separated in 1965. Mrs. Mundinger claimed that her husband's conduct towards her had often been cruel throughout the years of their marriage. She was particularly distressed by her husband's adulterous relationship with an employee in his company. This relationship began in 1953 and continued throughout the remaining years of the marriage.

Mrs. Mundinger claimed that her husband's conduct caused her to have a nervous breakdown. She even attempted suicide and was hospitalized intermittently from April, 1965 to May, 1968. While she was in hospital, her husband presented her with a separation agreement. In this agreement she was to receive a lump sum of $5000, and in return was to give up all right to support and sign over her half-interest (valued at $30 000) in their home and farm. She refused to sign, and consulted a lawyer who wrote to the husband suggesting the basis for a settlement.

The husband next presented a very similar version of the agreement to his wife; however, the $5000 was increased to $10 000. His wife was at this time under a psychiatrist's care and was taking tranquilizers. She signed the second separation agreement in June, 1965.

In her evidence at the trial, Mrs. Mundinger testified that her husband had threatened her and had also supplied her with liberal amounts of brandy prior to her signing of the agreement.

— In your opinion, should the terms of this separation agreement be set aside? What facts do you consider important in making your decision?

D. v. D. (1980) 13 R.F.L. (2d) 279 (Man. C.A.)

The parties were married for twenty-nine years, and had six children who were all adults at the time of the trial. The husband deserted the wife in 1979 and began living with a considerably younger woman.

At the trial there were two issues in dispute. First, the wife wished to remain in the matrimonial home, for which she had a strong sentimental attachment, while the husband wished it sold. Second, the wife asked for maintenance from the husband.

The matrimonial home was registered in the names of both spouses (joint tenancy). The home was valued at approximately $80 000. Both husband and wife were employees of the government. The wife was earning $26 562 and had reached a plateau in her earning power. The husband, on the other hand, was earning $45 522, with very good chances for continued advancement.

— What reasons might the wife put forward to support her request for sole possession of the matrimonial home?
— On what basis would the husband oppose this argument?
— What do you think was the decision of the court concerning the matrimonial home?
— Is the wife entitled to maintenance, in your opinion? Why or why not? If so, how much would you award?
— Would the husband's conduct in deserting his wife have any bearing on her right to support?

Coles v. Ferguson (1980) 13 R.F.L. (2d) 193 (Alta. C.A.)

The parties began living together in 1972. At that time, the woman was a widow with two children. She owned a home valued at $23 000 (subject to a mortgage) and was living on welfare. The man began supporting her, her two children, and eventually a third child, who was born to the couple. The common law wife, Coles, worked on a part-time basis during the relationship. Both spouses contributed to a joint bank account.

When the third child was born, the couple decided that an addition on the house was necessary. Ferguson worked approximately 400 hours on the building of this addition and contributed $31 415, of which some came from his savings and some from loans he took in his own name.

Coles' attitude began to change toward Ferguson around the time the renovations were completed. She eventually had him evicted from the home. Ferguson brought an action for an interest in the home. At the time of the trial the home was valued at $83 000. Without the renovations, the home would have been worth $53 000.

—Do cohabiting spouses have a right to share in property?
—On what basis would Coles oppose Ferguson's claim to an interest in the house?
—What evidence would Ferguson put forward to support his claim?
—What principle of law relates to this case?
—What do you think was the decision of the court?

18

Wills and Inheritance

The Law of Wills	The Law of Intestacy
Provision for Dependants	Executors and Administrators

"Aaaaaaaa! . . . It's George! He's taking it with him!"

In times past, many civilizations made a practice of burying property with a dead person. The idea behind this practice was to provide for the dead person in the afterlife. However, there was almost always property left behind, and, for millennia, rules about the disposal of this property have been a part of every society's legal system. In Canada, it is the provinces that have jurisdiction to make law affecting a person's property upon his or her death.

The property which a person owns at death is called the **estate**. It includes any property owned by the deceased outright, and any other *property interest*, such as a mortgage, that the deceased may have.

The phrase "owns at death" is important, since some of the property which a person holds during life may not be owned by that person at death. For example, if property is held jointly (that is, if it is *joint property*) there is a *rule of survivorship* which says that when one joint owner dies, the other gets the property.

Janet and Neil are joint owners of a house. If one of them dies before the other, the survivor will become the sole owner of the house. In other words, if Janet dies first, her interest in the house will not be part of her estate. It will not be property she "owns at death".

The phrase "property interest" is also important. Suppose Janet and Neil owned the house, not jointly, but as **tenants in common**. A tenant in common owns only a part of the property. Janet, therefore, can leave her half-interest in the house to whomever she wishes. In this case, her half-share of the house will be part of her estate when she dies.

Figure 18-1

The law that deals with the distribution of a person's estate has three basic purposes:

1. To set up a manner of disposing of the estate in accordance with the deceased's wishes. Each province has a statute which contains the rules for making a valid will. These rules and the procedure form the *law of wills*.
2. To ensure that people who had a right to depend on the deceased receive fair treatment. Provisions for **dependant's relief** are also included in provincial statutes.
3. To set up rules for distributing the estate when the dead person has not made a will. This is called the *law of intestacy*.

The court that deals with most questions involving estates, such as probate of a will, or the appointment of administrators, is called Surrogate Court. The more complicated questions, those concerned with the interpretation of wills, are taken to the Supreme Court or Court of Queen's Bench of the province.

The Law of Wills

In death as in life, the law imposes very few limitations on what people may do with their property. However, there are legal rules concerning what makes a will valid, that is, legally effective. As you read through the rules set out below, you will see that most of them are aimed at preventing problems that could arise simply because the person who made the will cannot be there to explain what he or she intended. The person making the will is called the **testator**. (The feminine form of this word is **testatrix**. This book will use the form "testator" when referring generally to a maker of a will.)

Making a Valid Will

Since the law that governs the validity of wills is provincial, it varies from province to province. However, there are some basic rules that apply across Canada. These rules concern the following matters:

1. the requirement that a will must be in writing
2. the minimum age for making a valid will
3. the need for mental competence
4. freedom from undue influence
5. the requirement that the will must be signed and witnessed

Writing

The will must be written in longhand, or typed. There is no such thing as a valid oral will, not even one made by tape recording.

Age

A testator must be of the age of majority. In some provinces this age is eighteen; in others, nineteen. Most provinces make some exceptions to the age rule, however. For example, it is usually possible for a married person to make a valid will at any age. Some provinces allow a parent of any age to make a will for the benefit of his or her child. Also, actively serving members of the Armed Forces or the Merchant Marines can make valid wills even if they are below the age of majority.

—Why should a minor not be able to make a will?
—Why do you think the law makes exceptions to this rule?

Mental Competence

The law of wills states that a person who is not mentally competent cannot make a valid will. A lawyer who drafts a will for someone has a duty to ascertain that the person appears to be mentally competent.

If an interested person, such as a member of the family, can prove in court that the testator was insane, senile, or intoxicated by drugs or alcohol at the time the will was made, a court will declare the will invalid. However, there has to be good evidence before the court will find that the testator was not of sound mind. If someone makes an unusual will, mental competence is a factor which the court will consider. Generally, though, it takes more than a strange term in a will to make a court conclude that the testator was mentally incompetent, but it is still wise for a person wishing to write an unusual will to take precautions. In this situation, a lawyer will advise the testator to include an explanation. For example, it might look odd if elderly Mr. Battaglia were to leave all his money to the Society for the Prevention of Cruelty to Animals (S.P.C.A.) instead of to his children. But what if Mr. Battaglia included an explanation mentioning that he had been interested in the S.P.C.A. for years and that, since he had bought houses for all of his children, he felt he had done enough for them? It would be unlikely that Mr. Battaglia's children could prove he was mentally incompetent on this evidence alone.

—What factors might a court consider in determining whether a testator is mentally competent?

Undue Influence

A will is supposed to represent the wishes of the deceased. If someone talks, bribes, bullies, or nags the testator into signing something that does not really represent what the testator wants, the will may be found invalid by a court because of undue influence. Of course, this will not happen unless someone later applies to court to have the will declared invalid. As with mental competence, there has to be good evidence that the testator was unduly influenced before a court will declare a will invalid.

Mr. Plaut, who is old and sick, wants to finish his life in the rooming-house where he has lived for forty years. Mrs. Craig, his landlady, hints that unless she has "something to look forward to" in his will, she will evict him. Mr. Plaut agrees to leave her $10 000.
   After his death, Mr. Plaut's next-of-kin apply to court to have the will invalidated, saying that Mrs. Craig applied undue influence.

Mrs. Lee lives in the same rooming-house as Mr. Plaut did. She is eighty and cannot walk very well. She is befriended by Beverley, a student who lives in the house. Beverley runs Mrs. Lee's errands and spends time visiting with her every so often. After Mrs. Lee dies, Beverley finds that Mrs. Lee has left her $10 000. Mrs. Lee's next-of-kin apply to court to have the will declared invalid, saying that Beverley used undue influence.

— In the first situation, the next-of-kin may be successful. In the second, the will would likely be found valid. Why do you think these results would occur?

Signature and Witnesses

A will must be signed at the end by the testator, or by someone whom the testator asks to sign in his or her place. If another person signs, it must be done in the testator's presence and in the presence of the witnesses.
   There is also a requirement, with some exceptions that will be discussed below, that the testator must have at least two people witness his or her signature. To witness the will properly, these people must watch the testator sign, and sign the will themselves in the testator's presence.

— What do you think is the reason for requiring wills to be witnessed in most situations, and to be signed in every situation?

   The witnesses to a will do not have to read it. They merely watch the testator sign, and then sign themselves. They should, however, be capable of understanding what they are doing. Also, they should know the testator well enough to know that the testator is signing his or her own name to the will. Most lawyers advise that witnesses be over the age of majority.

Most provincial laws have a provision that a gift made by will to a witness to the will, or to the husband or wife of a witness, is invalid. In some provinces, such as Ontario, a witness who has been left a gift may apply to court to have the gift declared valid. Usually, the person must prove that there was no undue influence on the testator, or that there were at least two other witnesses who did not receive gifts under the will. However, the best idea is not to ask **beneficiaries** to witness a will. Beneficiaries are the people to whom the testator leaves gifts in the will.

Mrs. Geroli was very ill when she made her will. She signed the will alone in her hospital room, and then later asked her daughter to take the will out to be signed by her doctor and a friend.

—Was the will validly witnessed? Explain.

As mentioned earlier in this chapter, the purpose of the law of wills is to set up a manner of disposing of a deceased's estate according to his or her own wishes. The common law recognized early on that a person might sometimes be unable or unwilling to find witnesses. Therefore, there are exceptions to the requirement for witnesses in making a valid will. Most provinces allow a will made without witnesses to be considered valid in either or both of the following circumstances:

1. If the testator is actively serving as a member of the Armed Forces or is a Merchant Marine on a voyage.
2. If the testator is making a **holograph will**, that is, a will entirely in the testator's own handwriting and signed by the testator.

—Why do you think these exceptions were made?
—In what situations would they be necessary?

The Contents of a Will

There is no law requiring a testator to use any particular phrases in the will. A will is valid as long as the rules about writing, age, mental competence, freedom from undue influence, signature, and witnesses (unless exceptions apply) are kept. The words used are the choice of the testator.

However, it is a good idea for a testator to remember the purpose of a will when writing one. A will is a list of instructions about what the testator wants done with his or her property. A will should be dated, because the last will made is the one that counts. It should appoint an **executor (executrix)**, whose role it is to gather the testator's estate together, pay the testator's debts and expenses, and pay the **legacies** (the gifts made in a will) to the beneficiaries. If the testator does not make his or her wishes clear and reasonable, or doesn't dispose of all his or her property, the executor will have to go to court for assistance in interpreting the will.

Clarity and Reasonableness

Since clarity in a will is very important, it is probably a good idea to have a lawyer give advice in its preparation or draw it up. For example, a will might say that the testator wishes to leave his or her estate to his or her children. Is it clear whether this is intended to include any adopted children or children born out of wedlock? A testator who wants all his or her wishes carried out should leave clear instructions.

In addition, if an executor is left with instructions that are illegal, impossible to carry out, or seriously unreasonable, the executor or one of the beneficiaries may apply to a court for help. A court may instruct the executor to ignore the testator's wish.

Uncle Fred left $1000 to Sigi to be paid "as soon as Sigi beats up that pesky policeman who gave me a traffic ticket in 1960." In this situation a court would tell Uncle Fred's executor to pay Sigi the money without making sure that he had done as he was asked, since assaulting a police officer is illegal.

Frida, who was very absent-minded, left one grand piano to two sisters who lived at opposite ends of the country. If Frida's executor asked a court for instructions, the court would probably order the piano sold and the proceeds divided between the two sisters, because the instruction in the will was impossible to carry out.

Lin was left $100 000 in his mother's will "on the condition that he never marry". Lin can have both the money and the freedom to marry. You should remember, though, that it is only when a request in a will is truly unreasonable that a court would allow it to be ignored.

The Residue

Another point on which an executor may need legal advice is how to deal with the **residue** of the deceased's estate. The residue is any property left over after specific gifts have been given.

A will does not take effect until the testator dies, which may be a long time after the will is written. The amount of property in the estate at the time of death may be greater than at the time the will was written. The testator may not have updated the will to include the property acquired after the making of the will. It can also happen that the testator simply did not specifically mention all property owned. What happens to this residue?

There are two ways to deal with the residue. The first is to put a clause covering it into the will.

When Anna made her will in 1980, she had a house, a car, a piano, and $5000 in a bank account. She left the house and its contents to her niece "together with the residue of my estate". She left the car to her nephew, and $3000 to a friend. When Anna died, the bank account contained $10 000. The executor paid Anna's bills, debts, and taxes, and gave the car to the nephew and $3000 to the friend. All of the rest of Anna's property, including the extra money in the account, went to Anna's niece.

—What do you think would happen if Anna's property at the time of her death was less than what was mentioned in her will?

If no clause disposing of residue is included in the will, the executor must apply to a court. The court will decide who will receive the unnamed parts of the estate.

Making a Valid Change

It is important to remember that a valid change to a will can be made only by the same rules as those which govern the making of a will. That is, the change must be written; it must be signed or initialled and witnessed (unless your province allows holographs); and so forth.

The best way to make a change is to write out a separate document, called a **codicil**, in the same way as the will, and attach it to the will, or to make a new will.

Making a Valid Revocation

Revocation is an action by a testator that puts an end to a will. In most provinces, a will is considered to have been revoked in any of the following circumstances:

1. If the testator intentionally destroys it.
2. If the testator makes a new will.
3. If the testator marries, unless the will states that the testator is planning to marry and names the future spouse.

In connection with the last point above, some provincial laws say that the surviving spouse can choose not to have the will revoked even if the will was written before the marriage. For example, section 16 of Ontario's *Succession Law Reform Act* states:

> 16. A will is revoked by the marriage of the testator except where...the spouse of the testator elects to take under the will, by an instrument in writing signed by the spouse and filed within one year after the testator's death in the office of the Surrogate Clerk for Ontario...

Re Witham [1938] 3 D.L.R. 142 (N.S.S.C.)

The testator did sewing for a living. After her death, it was found that her will had been torn, but that she had sewed it together again. The court had to decide what Witham's intention had been.

—Would a court think that she had revoked the will? Why or why not?

Provision for Dependants

There is no law in Canada that requires a testator to leave property to anyone in particular. However, in most provinces the law protects dependants, those people whom the deceased had a legal duty to support, from being left without provision. The legislation specifies those who can apply to court as dependants, and gives them the right to claim an allowance out of the deceased's estate. Some examples of dependants in provincial law are spouses, parents, and children. In most provinces, common law spouses and children born out of wedlock cannot qualify as dependants. Ontario and a few others are exceptions to this rule.

—Do you think it is fair for common law spouses and children born out of wedlock to be excluded as dependants?

Recently, family law has been revised to more accurately reflect society's views of the rights and obligations of spouses. Nevertheless, the law of wills still lags behind the times where dependants are concerned, as the article in Figure 18-2 (overleaf) illustrates.

—What is the law concerning those who can qualify as dependants in your province?

A dependant must make a claim for support within a specified time. The court must then decide whether the person qualifies as a dependant according to the law, and what, if anything, he or she should receive from the estate.

In some provinces, such as British Columbia and Nova Scotia, a

Figure 18-2 What is your opinion of the proposal set out in this article? Which do you think is more important—a person's right to dispose of property according to his or her wishes, or a spouse's right to support?

Widows denied assets won by divorcees

TORONTO (CP) — Wives and husbands are better off financially to divorce than to stick it out to the bitter end in an unhappy marriage, a Toronto lawyer says.

Linda Silver Dranoff said in an interview nothing has been done to better the financial situation of widows and widowers who are disinherited by their mates.

The Family Law Reform Act of Ontario, enacted in 1978, ruled men and women must share family assets when a marriage ends in divorce. But it doesn't protect a woman who remains in a marriage with a man who isn't prepared to share the fruits of their labors with his wife.

The act limits benefits to situations of marriage breakdown; it does not apply upon death.

"Most cases of disinherited spouses do not go to court because lawyers would tell them that they have no right to ownership of family assets held in the other spouse's name unless they are mentioned in the will or are destitute," says Dranoff.

Some have tried

- "A few hardy souls have pressed their cases forward anyway and were not given ownership of the other spouse's property. The most they got was a small lump sum or a modest amount of monthly support if they needed it."

She cited three cases:

- An 82-year-old widow was left $1 by her husband, whose estate was valued at $71,459.16. She was on a government pension of $390.98 a month and had $6,000 to her name. The estate was ordered to pay her $50 a month.

- A widow aged 64 made a claim against her husband's estate of $195,000 and got $15,000. She was earning $13,000 a year as a part-time sales clerk and also did the laundry and scrubbed the floors of her husband's barber shop in addition to running the household. If she had been divorced, she probably would have received $95,000.

- A 73-year-old widower claiming against his wife's $118,000 estate had a $300 monthly pension. The court gave him $45,000, but a court appeal decision took the award away, saying the trial judge should not have taken away the share of the woman's children by giving it to her widower. It was a second marriage that lasted 14 years.

"If the attorney general cannot give a good reason why the legislation should remain the way it is...then the law must be changed to give widows and widowers the same rights to share in property accumulated during a marriage as a divorced or separated person gets," Dranoff said. "If a woman stays with her husband to the end in an unhappy marriage and is disinherited, she goes to court to plead as a beggar for what's rightfully hers."

person can apply as a dependant only when the deceased person has left a will. If the person dies without a will, the dependant person cannot claim support.

In other provinces, Ontario among them, an application by a dependant for support can be made whether or not the deceased person left a will.

George and Martha were married for fifty years. They were not getting along very well in George's last years, and when George died, Martha found that the will left her only their house. The rest of George's $200 000 estate was left to their children. Martha is unable to work, is seventy-two years old, and has no other source of income.

— If Martha applies to court for support from George's estate, do you think the court will give her an allowance from the estate? Why or why not?
— What if she and George had not been legally married? On what would her right to support depend in this situation?
— Suppose Martha was George's sister and faithful housekeeper, not his wife. Does your province allow her to apply as a dependant?

"Therefore, I leave everything to my trusted lawyer."

The Appointment of Guardians

People usually appoint guardians for their dependant children (and, in some situations, for other dependants) in their wills. Doing so is a good idea, and a well-chosen guardian will usually be accepted by the family and by the court. However, if the court feels that the person chosen is in any way inappropriate, it will appoint someone else instead. The person appointed may have volunteered for the task of guardian. Or the court may appoint someone of its own choosing. In the appointment of a guardian, the court's first concern is what is in the best interests of the children.

A person who has been appointed guardian in a will does not have to accept the responsibility. Therefore, it is a good idea for a testator to find out whether the person being appointed is willing to act as guardian.

The Law of Intestacy
Dying Intestate

What happens if a person dies without making a will? All provinces have legislation that sets out the rules that apply when a person dies *intestate*. The basic rule is that the husband or wife gets the first share of the property, up to a certain amount. In Ontario, the amount is $75 000; in Manitoba, $50 000, for instance. In most provinces, if there is more than that amount in the estate, the surviving spouse and the children share it equally. If there is no surviving spouse, the children share everything equally. If there is no surviving spouse or child, all the property goes to the deceased's parents. If there are no parents, the deceased's brothers and sisters share all the property, and so on.

There are two major disadvantages to dying without making a will. The first is that the relevant provincial law of intestacy may not bring about the kind of property distribution the deceased had in mind. There are rigid rules about who may inherit and what share they may receive. For example, no province allows anyone other than a blood relative or a legally married spouse to inherit from a person who dies intestate. This means that common law spouses, friends, and the deceased's favourite charity are excluded. A common law spouse in Ontario may apply for support as a dependant, but may not receive as much as the deceased person would have left him or her in a will. Another rule is that blood relatives in a similar class of relationship, such as all of the deceased's children, or all of the nieces and nephews, receive equal shares if they get a share at all, regardless of whether their needs are equal. Most provincial laws exclude children born out of wedlock from inheriting from their natural father's estate if they are not included in a will. Illegitimate children can inherit from their mother just like children born of a marriage, however.

If a person dies intestate and has no spouse or blood relatives, the deceased's estate goes to the province.

The second major disadvantage of intestacy is that it usually takes longer to distribute the estate of a person who dies without a will. This is because a person who wishes to deal with the estate must apply to court to be appointed **administrator (administratrix)** of that estate. If no one applies, then the court will appoint someone to act as administrator. An administrator carries out much the same tasks as an executor. More will be said about this later in the chapter.

Common Disasters

When two people (especially spouses) die at the same time, or when it is impossible to find out who died first, problems can arise about how to distribute their property. This is so whether or not they had wills. The people most often affected by this situation are the relatives of spouses.

Alberto and Rosa, who are married and childless, die in a car crash. It is impossible to tell who died first. Both have wills leaving all of their property to each other. Rosa's will says that if Alberto dies before she does, her property is to go to her parents. Alberto's will leaves all of his property to his parents if Rosa dies before him.

Here is the problem: If we assume that Alberto died first, all of his property would become Rosa's before she died. Therefore, all property owned by the couple would go to Rosa's parents, with nothing left over for Alberto's parents. If we assume that Rosa died first, Alberto's parents would be the only ones who inherit.

In many cases of common disaster, it is impossible to determine who died first. Therefore, a rule developed under common law. Unless the order of death could be proven, the people were assumed to have died at precisely the same time. This meant that, if there were no wills, the property of each would go to his or her next-of-kin. If there was a will (or wills), though, the situation could be more complicated, and often was. For this reason, many provinces enacted legislation stating that, unless the order of death could be proven, the older person would be assumed to have died first. That would put whatever property was involved into the estate of the younger person, to be distributed to his or her beneficiaries or next-of-kin.

Recently, some provinces, such as Ontario and Manitoba, have changed the law again. In these provinces, the legislation says that, unless the order of death can be proven, each person is assumed to have survived the other, as illustrated by s. 61 of Ontario's *Succession Law Reform Act*:

> 61. (1) Where two or more persons die at the same time or in circumstances rendering it uncertain which of them survived the other or others, the property of each person, or any property of which he is competent to dispose, shall be disposed of as if he had survived the other or others.
> (2) Unless a contrary intention appears, where two or more persons hold legal or equitable title to property as joint tenants, or with respect to a joint account, with each other, and all of them die at the same time or in circumstances rendering it uncertain which of them survived the other or others, each person shall be deemed, for the purposes of subsection 1, to have held as tenant in common with the other or with each of the others in that property.
> (3) Where a will contains a provision for a substitute personal representative operative if an executor designated in the will,
>   *(a)* dies before the testator;
>   *(b)* dies at the same time as the testator; or
>   *(c)* dies in circumstances rendering it uncertain which of them survived the other,
> and the designated executor dies at the same time as the testator or in circumstances rendering it uncertain which of them survived the other, then, for the purpose of probate, the case for which the will provides shall be deemed to have occurred.

Of course, the problem of survivorship can be avoided completely if people provide for a common disaster situation in their wills. This is why many couples leave their property to each other on condition that the inheriting spouse survives the other by a certain period, such as thirty days. They then include instructions about how their property should be distributed if the other spouse does not survive.

Executors and Administrators

When a person dies, someone is needed to tidy up the deceased's financial affairs and distribute his or her property. You read earlier that if the one who fulfills these tasks is appointed by the testator, he or she is called an executor or executrix. If the person is appointed by a court, he or she is called an administrator or administratrix. Executors and administrators are often called **trustees** because they must act on behalf of and in the best interests of other people—the deceased and the beneficiaries.

The main difference between an executor and an administrator is the source of their authority to act. Their duties are usually the same: to collect the property; pay debts, expenses, and taxes; and distribute what is left of the estate to the beneficiaries.

The Appointment of an Executor

Almost anyone can be appointed as an executor by the person making the will. The only conditions are that the person must be of the age of majority, and of sound mind. The testator does not have to have the future executor's consent. However, it makes sense to be sure that the person chosen as executor is not going to refuse the responsibility when the time comes. It is also a good idea to appoint an alternative executor, in case the first person is unable or unwilling to act.

Unlike a witness to the signing of a will, an executor can receive a gift in the will.

The executor has the right to follow the instructions in the will as soon as the testator is dead. However, most executors first apply to court for **Letters Probate**, a document which states that the will is valid and which confirms the appointment of the executor. The probate document proves to people, such as the manager of a bank where the deceased had an account, that the executor has the right to collect the deceased's property.

The Appointment of an Administrator

If someone dies intestate, or if the executor(s) named in the will is (are) unable or unwilling to act, the relatives of the deceased must apply to court to have an administrator appointed. Usually the court will appoint a close relative who will fulfill the necessary tasks. Often the administrator will be required to post a bond (give security) of a certain amount of money. If the estate is mishandled, the court will reimburse the heirs out of the bond money. If no problems arise, the bond is returned to the administrator after the estate is distributed and the administration is complete.

The powers and duties of an executor and an administrator are very similar, but there are some differences, as set out in Figure 18-3 (overleaf).

Figure 18-3 A Comparison of the Powers and Duties of an Executor and an Administrator

EXECUTOR	ADMINISTRATOR
Burial: With money from the estate, pay reasonable expenses for funeral and/or burial.	Same as for Executor.
Examination of Will: Notify beneficiaries. Take care of immediate needs of family. Take care of property. Start following instructions in will.	No will to examine unless it is a situation in which the named executor was unable or unwilling to act, or the administrator is dealing with property that was not disposed of in the will.
Collect and make a list of all property.	Same as for executor.
Advertise for creditors: the executor must pay the debts of the deceased person.	Same as for executor. Advertise for relatives; that is, find blood relatives who might be entitled to property.
Deal with dependants' applications for support (if any).	Same as for executor.
Distribute the property according to the terms of the will.	Distribute the property according to provincial law of intestacy.

SUMMARIZING YOUR READING

1. Is the law that deals with wills and estates provincial or federal?

2. Give some examples of property that may form a deceased's estate.

3. Give an example of property that is not included in an estate. Why is it not included?

4. What is the purpose of the law of wills?

5. Is it possible for someone to make a will by recording his or her wishes with a tape recorder?

6. Is a will valid if the testator was forced to sign it?

7. What does it mean to say that a will has been properly witnessed?

8. Does a witness have to know what is in the will?

9. Can the testator leave a gift in the will to a witness? to the spouse of a witness? to the executor?

10. Are there any special words which must be used in making a will?

11. What are the important points to include in a will?

12. What is the residue of an estate?

13. What should a person who wishes to change a term of his or her will do?

14. A will is usually considered to have been revoked in any of three circumstances. What are they?

15. Can the guardianship of children arranged in a will be changed after the parents die?

16. Can a common law spouse inherit when his or her spouse dies intestate?

17. Can anyone but blood relatives inherit when a person dies intestate?

18. If someone who was financially dependant on a deceased is left out of that person's will, what should the dependant person consider?

19. What is the difference between an executor and an administrator?

20. What are the major duties of an executor? of an administrator?

DISCUSSING KEY ISSUES

1. As noted earlier in this chapter, the law in Canada does not say how a testator must leave his or her property, or to whom. If spouses are not getting along, for example, one spouse can leave the other much less by will than the law would require if they had divorced. Do you think this is fair? What rules (if any) should there be about support by will for family members, and why?

PROJECTS AND ACTIVITIES

1. Printed will forms are available from stationery stores. Obtain a copy of one of these forms and prepare a will for yourself. To whom would you like to give your stereo or radio, record or tape collection, schoolring, favourite sweater, and so on? Have two class-mates witness your signature. Test your will for clarity by having your executor explain how he or she would carry out your wishes.

2. Read the statute that contains the law concerning wills and estates in your province. Find the answers to the following questions and write a brief report or report your findings to the class.

(a) If a child is born to unmarried parents, can that child inherit from his or her father if the father dies intestate?

(b) Who can apply for support from a deceased's estate?

(c) How old must a person be to make a valid will? Are there any exceptions?

(d) Are holograph wills legally valid in your province?

RESOLVING CASES

Re Worrell [1970] 1 O.R. 184 (Ont. Cty. Ct.)

Worrell's will was challenged in court by a relative who said it was invalid. The will left almost the entire estate to Barfoot, a nephew of Worrell, and to Barfoot's family.

At trial, the lawyer who had drafted the will testified about the facts surrounding the making of the will. These were the facts. First, the lawyer drafted the will according to instructions written by Barfoot and signed by Worrell. Second, the lawyer never met Worrell. He knew only that Worrell was eighty-two years old and living in a home for the aged. Finally, the lawyer handed the will to Barfoot, who said that he would see that the will was signed and witnessed.

— What questions arise because of the way in which the will was made?
— Did the relative have reason to challenge the will's validity?

Re Fairfoul (1973) 41 D.L.R. (3d) 152 (B.C.S.C.)

Fairfoul made a will. In it he left money to his son, on the condition that his son divorce his wife.

— If the son wanted to stay married, could he still get his inheritance? Explain.

Re Terrio Estate: Weir v. Beers et al. (1979) 24 N.B.R. (2d) 627 (N.B. Q.B.)

Terrio, who was very old when she died, left a holograph will. Her family applied to court for help in interpreting the will, as they were having trouble in understanding what her wishes had been.

The will looked like this:

"this is my last will & testament revoaking all others

Jan. 22, 1976

Maudie this is for you, if I should pass away which I must do befor to long as I am very old and I am sick. Please sell this house as it is to much bother for you to keep, it will bring a good price in the next few years. I want you to give Verna Penny and Roberta 1 thousion and also give David John 1 thusion tanya and Robert each 5 hundred each the morgage has to be paid that is about 3 thusion I want 4 thusion left for Sheryl to be put in a trust fund for her when she is 19 or 20 years old

Old Gran Weir Terrio   over

I want to help get Bob a head stone

---

this is if she goes thereu school here is 3 thusion morgage on this place 5 and 8 & should get 16 thusion for it try to get one thusion for you and after every thing is paid up there should be a few Dollars to put in a trust fund for Sheryl

    Mrs. Mary Weir
      Terrio

PS if I pass out quick, Just devide what is left between you and Sheryl."

Close relatives of the deceased included the following:
Maude Weir, her daughter-in-law;
Verna Beers, Penny Kottaris, and Roberta Landry, her granddaughters;
John and Tanya Kottaris, Penny's children and the deceased's great-grandchildren;
Robert Landry, Roberta's son and the deceased's great-grandson.
"Bob" refers to the testator's deceased son, Robert John Weir.
"Sheryl" refers to Verna Beers' daughter, Cheryl.

The court had to decide who was to be the executor, and what gifts had been made and how they were to be paid to the beneficiaries.

—**What do you think the court decided?**

Re Kindl (1983) 39 O.R. (2d) 219 (Ont. H.C.J.)

The deceased, Dr. Kindl, left a will (dated December, 1980) which provided that the residue of his estate be left to "my wife". If she predeceased him, his parents became the beneficiaries of the will. In September, 1981, Mrs. Kindl petitioned for divorce on the grounds of adultery. A decree nisi was issued in June, 1982. Four days later, Dr. Kindl died. His will had not been changed and a decree absolute had not been issued. Dr. Kindl's parents applied to have a decree absolute issued, ending their son's marriage. The court held that only the petitioner or respondent could apply for the final divorce decree.

—**Was Mrs. Kindl still the wife of the deceased at the time of his death?**
—**Should she be able to inherit?**

Re Davies and Davies (1979) 27 O.R. (2d) 98 (Ont. Surr. Ct.)

Mr. and Mrs. Davies married when in their early sixties. It was a second marriage for both of them, and Mrs. Davies had an adult son from her first marriage.

When the Davies married, Mr. Davies sold his home and moved into his wife's home. During the marriage, Mr. Davies paid all the living expenses of the couple.

Both Mr. and Mrs. Davies made wills during the marriage. When Mrs. Davies died at the age of seventy-eight, it was discovered that she had left all her property to her son.

Mr. Davies applied to court, not for money for his support, but for the right to stay in his wife's house for the rest of his life. He applied under Ontario's *Succession Law Reform Act* as a dependant of his deceased wife.

Section 64(d) of the *Succession Law Reform Act* defines a dependant as

> (i) the spouse or common law spouse of the deceased,
> (ii) a parent of the deceased,
> (iii) a child of the deceased, or
> (iv) a brother or sister of the deceased, to whom the deceased was providing support or was under a legal obligation to provide support immediately before his death.

The *Act* contains a provision that allows a court to make an order for the support of a dependant out of a deceased person's estate:

> 65. (1) Where a deceased, whether testate or intestate, has not made adequate provision for the proper support of his dependants or any of them, the court, on application, may order that such provision as it considers adequate be made out of the estate of the deceased for the proper support of the dependants or any of them.

The court first had to decide whether Mr. Davies was a dependant of his deceased wife. It then had to decide whether the right to live in the house could be defined as "support".

The court considered two matters. The first was that a married couple had an obligation, under Ontario's *Family Law Reform Act*, to support one another. The second was a definition of "support", taken from the *Shorter Oxford English Dictionary*. The definition included the following: "...to provide for the maintenance of; to supply with the necessaries of life; to assist by one's presence or attitude."

The court also considered four other factors. First, Mr. Davies was capable of providing maintenance for himself but was not capable of purchasing a home similar to the two-bedroom home in which he lived. If he were to use all of his capital to purchase a similar home, he would not be capable of maintaining himself in that home. Second, Mr. Davies was seventy-two years of age. Third, his needs included living in the neighbourhood where he had lived for the past ten years, close to his friends and acquaintances and in familiar surroundings. Finally, he would never be able to find paid employment.

—Why did the court need to decide whether Mr. Davies was a "dependant" and whether the right to live in a house could be considered "support"?
—Do you think the court found Mr. Davies to be a dependant?
—Do you think Mr. Davies obtained the right to live in the house? Explain.
—Why do you think the court considered the personal information about Mr. Davies?

UNIT 4

The Law and the Marketplace

19 Consumer Law
20 The Law of Bailment
21 The Law of Real Property
22 Landlord and Tenant Law

19

CONSUMER LAW

> The Sources of Consumer Law
> Consumer Problems and Legal Remedies
> The Prevention of Consumer Problems
> Buying on Credit

—What can you do

(a) when you have bought a "lemon"?
(b) when you have "signed on the dotted line" for something you don't need and cannot afford?
(c) when the product does not do what the manufacturer promised?

Questions like these involving the sale of goods are the concern of consumer law. The law that affects sales in Canada is a wide and varied area. It involves the common law, the law of contracts, and many statutes, both federal and provincial.

This chapter will discuss only consumer sales. A **consumer** is a person who is buying goods or services or both, for personal or family use, not for business purposes.

The Sources of Consumer Law

Where can the consumer find out what his or her rights are when a problem in the purchase of goods or services arises? The following steps provide a guideline, referring the consumer to all three sources of consumer law—the common law, statute law, and the law of contracts.

1. The consumer should look at the provincial or, in some cases, federal statutes. These laws are usually meant to cover particular situations such as door-to-door sales, sales of particular types of products, buying on the installment plan, and so forth. Sometimes these laws set up agencies to handle particular problems.
2. The consumer should consider the contract of sale. In some situations, the written or oral terms of a contract will decide any problem that may arise. In other situations, the legislation will overrule the contract.
3. The consumer should refer to the common law. If no written or oral contract term and no statute deals with the problem, there may be a common law rule that applies to the situation.

The *Sale of Goods Act*

Earlier in the history of Great Britain and Europe, there was not much need for special protection for consumers. Society was largely agricultural. People produced most of the food and goods they needed. The items they could not make were often traded or bartered for, rather than bought with money. Much of the selling and trading was done in open-air public markets. Sellers and buyers were usually acquainted with one another. Anyone selling bad merchandise therefore ran the risk of public disapproval in a small, closed community.

This state of affairs changed rapidly as industry and mass-production of goods appeared on the scene. Towns grew out of villages, cities out of towns. Soon money transactions replaced barter almost entirely. In the larger communities, consumer sales became private as stores replaced public markets. The increasing complexity of economic systems made it necessary to clarify the rules developed by the courts for governing sales. A statute was finally passed in England in 1893 that codified all the common law rules that had grown up in connection with sales of goods. The British *Sale of Goods Act* set out standards for both sellers and buyers.

Today, all provinces in Canada have a *Sale of Goods Act*. These *Acts*, although not identical, do in general follow the English statute.

The *Sale of Goods Act* of each province contains certain broad, general rules that cover certain situations in which problems may arise. For instance, the *Acts* require certain contracts for the sale of

Figure 19-1 Early Consumer Protection—The Seller's Reputation in the Community

goods to be in writing in order to be enforceable, as Chapter 14 explained. When they were drafted, the *Acts* were intended to list the common law rules of sales. Some of the more important rules contained in the *Acts* concern **conditions** and warranties. Though you have already met these terms in the chapters on contracts, it will be useful to redefine them here.

Conditions and Warranties

A condition, according to the law of contract, is a term so important to a contract that the contract is almost meaningless if the term is broken. If a condition is breached by the seller, the buyer can usually get back any money paid for the item. The seller cannot require the buyer to take a repaired product or an exchange, although the buyer may agree to do so. The buyer can insist on an immediate refund, plus any expenses.

Trini bought a car. The first time she drove it, the motor fused, never to run again, through no fault of Trini's. Since an essential element of a car is its ability to be driven, the car dealer breached a condition of the sale. Trini successfully sued for a refund of her money and for the cost of having the car towed.

A warranty is also a term of a contract of sale; however, it is less important than a condition. If a warranty is broken, the buyer can only sue for damages. He or she cannot insist on getting a refund or on exchanging the product. Possible damages include the cost of repairing the merchandise.

Morris bought a pair of skis that were advertised as never needing waxing. After the first season of use, the skis were not running smoothly—they needed wax.
   The skis are not useless just because they need waxing after a season of use. Therefore, it is likely that a court would not consider the "no-wax" promise to be a condition. Instead, it would consider it to be a warranty. Rather than getting a refund, Morris would receive some money damages.

   The provincial *Sale of Goods Acts* have two main functions: to set out the remedies that are available when a condition or warranty has been breached, and to set out when a condition or warranty must be considered to have been *implied*.

Implied Conditions and Warranties

An implied condition or warranty is one that is imposed on a sale by law. It does not matter whether it is stated or written by the seller. In other words, the *Sale of Goods Acts* impose some "ground rules" on the contract of sale. Implied conditions and warranties always apply *unless* the buyer and seller agree that they do not apply.
   What types of implied conditions and warranties are set out in the *Sale of Goods Acts*? The first condition is that the seller has a right to sell the goods. Therefore, a buyer who discovers that someone else actually owned the goods has a right to his or her money back from the seller.
   A second common implied condition is that the goods being sold are new and unused. If not, the seller must reveal this fact to the buyer. Another is that when a buyer purchasing goods relies upon a description (as in ordering goods from a catalogue), the goods must be identical to that description.
   An example of an implied warranty is that the buyer is to enjoy undisturbed possession of the goods. As long as a buyer meets payments (thereby fulfilling the buyer's part of the contract), he or she should not be bothered by the seller or anyone associated with the seller.

Problems with the *Sale of Goods Acts*

The *Sale of Goods Acts* are useful legislation, but there are four major problems that arise when people try to use them to resolve modern consumer situations.

The first problem is that the *Acts* do not deal with many aspects of the marketplace today. For instance, they do not cover services. Nor do they provide protection against false or misleading advertising.

The second problem is that the *Acts* are often unclear about the remedies available to a buyer. Remedies are dependent upon whether it is a condition or a warranty that has been breached. Sometimes, though, it is not easy to tell what is a condition and what is a warranty. Additionally, even if a contract states that a term is a condition or a warranty, the *Sale of Goods Acts* might state that, under certain circumstances, a breach of condition may be treated as a breach of warranty or *vice versa*.

For example, section 12(2) of Ontario's *Sale of Goods Act* deals with condition and warranties this way:

> 12. (2) Whether a stipulation in a contract of sale is a condition the breach of which may give rise to a right to treat the contract as repudiated or a warranty the breach of which may give rise to a claim for damages but not to a right to reject the goods and treat the contract as repudiated depends in each case on the construction of the contract, and a stipulation may be a condition, though called a warranty in the contract.

Section 12(2) states that the "construction of the contract" must be considered. This means that the buyer's rights will be decided, to a great extent, according to how a judge might interpret the wording of the individual's contract. Two people who have the same problem might therefore have different remedies depending on what their written or oral contracts say.

You have bought a canoe that is advertised as being able to take white water conditions. You take it on several lake trips and experience no problems. Then you shoot some rapids. The canoe strikes a rock and springs a leak.

—Refer to s. 12(2) of Ontario's *Sale of Goods Act*. What would you have to consider in deciding what remedy you would be likely to get?

The third major problem with the *Sale of Goods Acts* is that they were written before merchandising became as complicated as it is today. Here is an example. Section 15 of Ontario's *Act* imposes an implied condition that goods bought for a particular purpose must be fit for that purpose. However, the condition applies only in certain circumstances. For one, the goods must be the type of goods that it is "in the course of the seller's business" to sell. The buyer must also "expressly or by implication make known to the seller" the purpose for which the merchandise is intended to be used. Furthermore, brand-name or patented merchandise is not included in the merchandise to which this section of the law applies. Section 15(1) runs as follows:

> 15. (1) Where the buyer, expressly or by implication, makes known to the seller the particular purpose for which the goods are required so as to show that the buyer relies on the seller's skill or judgement, and the goods are of a description that it is in the course of the seller's business to supply (whether he is the manufacturer or not), there is an implied condition that the goods will be reasonably fit for such purpose, but in the case of a contract for the sale of a specified article under its patent or other trade name there is no implied condition as to its fitness for any particular purpose.

—Do you think that the average buyer making a purchase would know whether s. 15(1) applied to that purchase?

Yachetti et al. v. John Duff and Sons Ltd. et al. [1943] 1 D.L.R. 194 (Ont. Cty. Ct.)

Yachetti bought some pork sausages for her family's dinner. She browned the sausages in a frying pan, then covered them with a lid and left them to simmer for an hour and a half.

The family ate the sausages. Yachetti subsequently became ill with trichinosis, a parasitic disease which can result from eating pork which is not completely cooked. The Yachettis sued the seller for breach of an implied warranty under the *Sale of Goods Act*, that meat be reasonably fit for the purpose for which it was sold, and of reasonable quality.

The seller gave evidence that fresh pork could be considered completely safe to eat only after it had been cooked to 131 degrees Farenheit (about 55°C), and that thorough cooking was normal before pork was consumed. On cross-examination, Yachetti stated that she may have tasted the sausages during the first half-hour of cooking.

The judge therefore decided that Yachetti had eaten some sausage before it was completely cooked. He noted that under the *Sale of Goods Act*, the seller was not liable for breach of implied warranty when the buyer used a product in other than the normal way, unless the buyer informed the seller that the product would be used in an abnormal way. The judge concluded that, since eating pork before it had been sufficiently cooked was not a normal use, the seller was not liable for the harm to Yachetti.

> If Yachetti had thought to explain to the seller that she had a habit of tasting as she cooked, and the seller had not warned her not to do this, she may have had a remedy under s.15(1).
>
> —**Do you think Yachetti thought she was dealing with the pork in an unusual way?**

The fourth difficulty with the *Sale of Goods Acts* in most provinces is that they do not apply if there is a contract term that deals with the problem that arises. It is therefore possible for a seller to write out a contract of sale that cuts the consumer off from much of the protection offered by the *Sale of Goods Acts*. Thus, it is always wise for the consumer to read a contract of sale. A contract may state, for instance, that there are no conditions or warranties attached to the sale. So, if the goods fall apart the next day, the buyer may have no remedy at law. The consumer who is ignorant, unwise, or desperate enough to agree to such terms might well be in real trouble if problems with the product arise.

—**In your experience, do most consumers read their contracts of sale?**

Because of the consumer problems that have arisen in connection with the *Sale of Goods Acts*, all provinces and, for some circumstances, the federal government, have enacted special consumer laws. These laws make sure that consumers have more protection than the *Sale of Goods Acts* provide. The protection generally extends to contracts for services as well as for goods.

Consumer Problems and Legal Remedies

It is in the following areas that problems most often arise in consumer sales: (a) defective products; (b) high pressure sales by door-to-door sellers; (c) false or misleading advertising or sales practices; and (d) unconscionable transactions. All of these problem areas are discussed in turn below.

Defective Products

As you have read, the *Sale of Goods Acts* are often not very precise about whether a problem is a breach of a condition or of a warranty. Therefore, they do not make it clear what remedy is available to the consumer who buys a "lemon". Moreover, the terms of a sales contract may deny the consumer any protection which the *Sale of Goods Acts* might have provided. To resolve these difficulties, some provinces have passed legislation to improve consumer protection.

HERMAN

"Solid as a rock and light as a feather."

British Columbia has amended its *Sale of Goods Act* to provide that a contract of sale to a consumer may not take away the conditions and warranties offered by the *Sale of Goods Act*. Manitoba, the Northwest Territories, Nova Scotia, and Ontario have *Consumer Protection Acts* that do the same. Saskatchewan's *Consumer Products Warranties Act* and New Brunswick's *Consumer Products Warranty and Liability Act* not only ensure that the conditions and warranties under their *Sale of Goods Acts* apply, but also provide sections that tell the consumer quite clearly what remedy is available in given situations. The Saskatchewan *Act*, at s. 20, serves as a good example. The *Act* lists certain warranties that must be honoured by the seller. When any of them is broken, s. 20(1)(i) sets out a remedy:

> **20. (1)** *(i)* [T]he party in breach shall, within a reasonable period of time, make good the breach free of charge to the consumer but, where the breach has not been remedied within such reasonable period of time, the consumer shall be entitled to have the breach remedied elsewhere and to recover from the party in breach all reasonable costs incurred in having the breach remedied...

—In your province's consumer legislation find the following:
  (a) the section that provides for conditions and warranties; and
  (b) the section that provides for consumer remedies.

—Are these sections clear and easy to understand? If they are, explain what protection is provided. If not, what questions does the legislation raise?

High-pressure Door-to-Door Sales

Adam signed a contract to buy a set of encyclopedias. The door-to-door sales agent was very persuasive. Ten minutes after the sales agent left, Adam was wishing he hadn't signed the contract. He didn't really like the first volume, and the rest of the set would cost more than he could afford.

A consumer can get into real difficulties by agreeing in a weak moment to buy something expensive. This frequently happens when the consumer buys at home or at someone else's home rather than in a store. Some provinces have recognized this problem. Ontario and British Columbia have *Consumer Protection Acts*, and New Brunswick has a *Direct Sellers Act*, all of which allow a consumer to change his or her mind, cancel the contract, and get a full refund within a certain "cooling-off" period after the sale. Generally, this type of *Act* applies under the following circumstances:

1. If the consumer has agreed to buy something over a certain value.
2. If the consumer has not paid in full (that is, if the contract is executory).
3. If the sale was made somewhere other than the seller's business premises.

—Check whether your province has a law that protects consumers in door-to-door sales. If it does, read the law and answer these questions:
   (a) Is there a money limit on the sale? If so, what is the limit?
   (b) How many days does the consumer have to change his or her mind?
   (c) What must the consumer do to let the seller know that the contract is cancelled?

False or Misleading Advertising or Sales Practices

A local department store advertised towels on sale at a "one-time-only, 50% reduction!" Elena bought some towels. The next day she went into another store displaying the same towels, at the same price as she had paid. There was no "sale" sign, and the store clerk there told Elena that the price was the regular price for the towels.

Figure 19-2
Which part of section 2(a) of the Ontario Business Practices Act *deals with this situation?*

Mme Marchant, who lives alone, is very old and is sometimes forgetful. In October, she had a chimney sweeping company clean the chimney of her house. In late November, forgetting that the work had recently been done, she called Nifty Cleaners Company to examine the chimney. The Nifty representative told Marchant that the chimney was very dirty, and charged her fifty dollars to clean it.

These situations are examples of deceptive, that is, false or misleading, advertising or sales practices. While consumers can expect a certain amount of sales enthusiasm, there is a difference between a vague claim such as "This car is the greatest ever!" and a claim that the consumer might rely on, such as "This car gets 5.5 L per 100 km in highway driving!"

Many provinces, among them Alberta, British Columbia, Ontario, and Prince Edward Island, have laws that forbid deceptive sales practices. Section 2(a) of the *Ontario Business Practices Act*, for instance, forbids the making of the following types of representations (statements) to a consumer:

> 2. *(a)* (i) a representation that the goods or services have sponsorship, approval, performance characteristics, accessories, uses, ingredients, benefits or quantities they do not have,

CONSUMER LAW 445

(ii) a representation that the person who is to supply the goods or services has sponsorship, approval, status, affiliation or connection he does not have,

(iii) a representation that the goods are of a particular standard, quality, grade, style or model, if they are not,

(iv) a representation that the goods are new, or unused, if they are not, or are reconditioned or reclaimed, provided that the reasonable use of goods to enable the seller to service, prepare, test and deliver the goods for the purposes of sale shall not be deemed to make the goods used for the purposes of this sub-clause,

(v) a representation that the goods have been used to an extent that is materially different from the fact,

(vi) a representation that the goods or services are available for a reason that does not exist,

(vii) a representation that the goods or services have been supplied in accordance with a previous representation, if they have not,

(viii) a representation that the goods or services or any part thereof are available to the consumer when the person making the representation knows or ought to know they will not be supplied,

(ix) a representation that a service, part, replacement or repair is needed, if it is not,

(x) a representation that a specific price advantage exists, if it does not,

(xi) a representation that misrepresents the authority of a salesperson, representative, employee or agent to negotiate the final terms of the proposed transaction,

(xii) a representation that the proposed transaction involves or does not involve rights, remedies or obligations if the representation is false or misleading,

(xiii) a representation using exaggeration, innuendo or ambiguity as to a material fact or failing to state a material fact if such use or failure deceives or tends to deceive,

(xiv) a representation that misrepresents the purpose or intent of any solicitation of or any communication with a consumer...

If a consumer is deceived in any of these ways by a seller, Ontario's *Business Practices Act* offers three remedies. The consumer can

1. sue for a refund;
2. charge the seller with a provincial offence; and/or
3. report the seller to the Ontario Ministry of Consumer and Commercial Relations. The Ministry may order the seller to obey the law.

Figure 19-3 Do you feel that the judgement described in this article was a fair one? Why or why not?

Example needed, judge says
'Sale' costs owner $30,000

A Toronto clothing retailer has been fined $30,000 for running a continuous sale for a year. The judge commented that the rising frequency of misleading advertising prompted him to make an example of the accused.

The Young Manufacturers Inc. and owner Michael Goldgrub pleaded guilty to five counts of misleading advertising after running continuous sales in stores between September, 1980, and September, 1981. The firm also operates Toronto Leather Fashions and a number of Woolskins stores.

Provincial Court Judge Milton Cadsby commented in his judgment: "It seems to me that with increasing frequency this kind of case is coming before the courts, and very large corporations are involved, corporations which have a good reputation in the business community.

"...when the practice of appearing to be running a sale, when in fact a sale is not being run, becomes such a common thing in business in Canada, the small retailer has to get, I guess you could say, into the swim. He has to go along with what seems to be a prevailing business practice."

He said he could understand the problems a small retailer would have in competing with large companies "carrying on with a business practice of this type."

However, he said, it annoyed him that small retailers were committing similar advertising offences every day "right here in College Park (where the Provincial Court is located).

"Therefore, an example has to be made of those convicted. It is a business practice which must be stopped, or the public can never feel they have an opportunity to purchase goods at a genuine bargain price."

He said in setting the fine he was taking "into account the previous conviction of the corporation relating to this kind of business practice."

The federal government has also passed legislation concerning some deceptive sales practices. The federal legislation imposes criminal penalties for such practices. The *Combines Investigation Act* forbids false or misleading advertising, either oral or written, for instance. This includes advertising "sales" of goods that are not truly at discount prices (as in our example above), and selling a product above its advertised price.

Figure 19-4 Do you feel that the judgement described in this article was a fair one? Why or why not?

Health food ads net $20,000 fine

Loblaws Ltd. has been fined $20,000 in Provincial Court for false advertising. The conviction came after signs were posted in four North York Loblaws stores in May, 1982, which asked Why Pay Health Store Prices? A federal Department of Consumer and Corporate Affairs investigator noted prices of eight Loblaws health food items including trail mix, sesame sticks, roasted mixed nuts and toasted corn and compared them with the same items in 44 Toronto area health food stores. The survey found that Loblaws prices were on average almost 50 cents higher on each item.

CONSUMER LAW   447

The *Combines Investigation Act* also deals with some particular unfair practices. A common one is known as "double-ticketing". If a product has two price tickets, the store must sell it at the lower price. Not to do so is double-ticketing, and is illegal. Another such practice is called "bait-and-switch" selling. It occurs when the seller offers a product at an extremely low price (the bait), without having a reasonable stock of the product on hand. The seller quickly runs out of the sale item and pressures the consumer into considering a higher-priced model (the switch). Bait-and-switch is also a criminal offence under the *Combines Investigation Act*.

The consumer who has experienced any of these types of dishonest sales practices can report the problem to the Director of Investigation and Research under the *Combines Investigation Act* at the Federal Department of Consumer and Corporate Affairs. The Director's investigation of the complaint may lead to the laying of charges against the seller.

Unconscionable Transactions

Billy McCarthy is developmentally handicapped. He is employed at a sheltered workshop at a very low rate of pay. A fast-talking salesperson convinces McCarthy to sign a monthly-payment contract on a colour television. McCarthy does not understand when he signs that the payments will amount to all of his monthly income.

At common law, a grossly unfair deal involving an aged, ill, illiterate, or otherwise disadvantaged consumer was called an **unconscionable transaction**. This type of practice is now specifically forbidden by legislation in many provinces. For example, s.2(b) of Ontario's *Business Practices Act* says that a sale may be considered unconscionable when the seller knows or ought to know any of the following facts:

> 2. (b) (i) that the consumer is not reasonably able to protect his interests because of his physical infirmity, ignorance, illiteracy, inability to understand the language of an agreement or similar factors,
> (ii) that the price grossly exceeds the price at which similar goods or services are readily available to like consumers,
> (iii) that the consumer is unable to receive a substantial benefit from the subject-matter of the consumer representation,

> (iv) that there is no reasonable probability of payment of the obligation in full by the consumer,
> (v) that the proposed transaction is excessively one-sided in favour of someone other than the consumer,
> (vi) that the terms or conditions of the proposed transaction are so adverse to the consumer as to be inequitable,
> (vii) that the person is making a misleading statement of opinion on which the consumer is likely to rely to his detriment,
> (viii) that the person is subjecting the consumer to undue pressure to enter into the transaction...

—Which of these facts, if any, apply to Billy McCarthy's situation?
—Does your province have legislation that protects against unconscionable transactions? What kind of protection is offered?

The Prevention of Consumer Problems

While it is useful to have the right to sue to obtain a refund when a problem arises in connection with unfair selling, most consumers would agree that it is even better not to have the difficulty in the first place. However, no law can prevent problems from arising. There will always be those who don't know or don't care about the law. Still, legislation does exist which was designed to help prevent consumer problems in some important areas:

1. controlling certain types of sales
2. preventing or controlling the sale of certain products
3. making manufacturers responsible for the quality of their products
4. group actions by consumers

These areas will be examined individually below.

Controlling Certain Types of Sales

A number of provinces and the federal government have enacted laws that control the ways in which sales can be conducted.

Door-to-Door Sales

In Ontario and New Brunswick, among others, door-to-door sellers must be registered or licenced with a provincial agency. This makes it somewhat easier to monitor their activities.

Pyramid Sales

Pyramid selling is a marketing scheme in which one person convinces another person to sell a product. The second person is also encouraged to recruit new people in turn to sell the product and work "under" him or her. The problem with the scheme arises because people are required to buy the stock in order to sell it, and if the pyramid works, there will soon be more salespeople than customers in any given location.

Figure 19-5
Pyramid Selling:
How It Works

Pyramid sales schemes are forbidden by the federal *Combines Investigation Act*, unless a province decides to allow them. Several provinces, for example, Ontario, Alberta, British Columbia, and Saskatchewan, permit pyramid selling, and control the sales schemes through registration.

Referral Sales

The *Combines Investigation Act* also forbids **referral sales** and makes them a criminal offence. In this type of sale, the seller offers the buyer a discount or a return of part of the sale price if the buyer will help attract more customers.

Whizzo Cleaning Supplies called on Jonas and persuaded him to buy a floor polisher and accessories for his house. The Whizzo representative told Jonas that if he named three of his friends and they could be persuaded to buy Whizzo equipment, Whizzo would refund half the cost of Jonas' purchase.

Preventing or Controlling the Sale of Certain Products

Have you ever wondered why you can legally buy prescription drugs from a pharmacist only? The reason is that there are both federal and provincial laws regulating the sale of this type of product, and others.

The federal government has passed four major laws concerning the sale of particular products. The *Hazardous Products Act* lists two classes of dangerous products. The products on one list are banned completely; it is illegal to sell them. An example of this kind of hazardous product is ceramics containing more than a certain amount of lead in the glaze.

> **Caution**: Keep out of reach of children. In case of eye contact, flush thoroughly with water. If swallowed, drink large quantities of water. Call physician immediately.

Figure 19-6 An example of the type of warning label which must be affixed to certain products on the second list of the Hazardous Products Act

The products contained in the second list can be sold, subject to certain regulations. Children's car seats, for example, can be sold only if they meet certain construction requirements and carry detailed labels with instructions for proper use, the manufacturer's name, and the model number.

The *Food and Drugs Act* creates rules for the sale, labelling, advertising, and packaging of certain listed drugs, such as amphetamines and barbiturates. It also regulates the content and sanitary standards of food, cosmetics, and health devices.

The *Narcotic Control Act* contains lists of drugs that are classified as narcotics. The *Act* makes it a criminal offence to manufacture, sell, give away, or even possess certain drugs, such as marijuana and codeine, except under the conditions set out in the law.

The *Motor Vehicle Safety Act* sets out car safety standards. The *Act* also requires car manufacturers to give notice to purchasers of any defects that become apparent after the cars are sold. From time to time you will hear that an automobile manufacturer is recalling a certain model of car manufactured in a particular year to check all the cars for a defect which has been discovered.

In addition, the provinces all have laws and regulations concerning the quality or condition of certain products offered for sale, from food to cars.

Attorney General of Canada v. Labatt Breweries of Canada Ltd.
(1979) 104 D.L.R. 646 (Fed. C.A.)

Regulations under the federal *Food and Drugs Act* prescribe standards for both beer and light beer. Beer must contain not less than 2.6 percent alcohol and not more than 5.5 percent alcohol. Light beer must contain not less than 1.2 percent and not more than 2.5 percent alcohol.

Section 6 of the *Food and Drugs Act* deals with advertising. It states:

> 6. Where a standard has been prescribed for a food, no person shall label, package, sell or advertise any article in such a manner that it is likely to be mistaken for such food, unless the article complies with the prescribed standard.

Labatt's Limited put a new brand of beer on the market. The label and the carton stated that this beer contained four percent alcohol. The beer was called "Special Lite".

The Attorney-General of Canada prosecuted Labatt's Limited under s. 6 of the *Food and Drugs Act*.

— Did "Special Lite" have the alcohol content of beer or light beer, under the *Food and Drugs Act* regulations?
— What do you think the court's decision was in this case? Give reasons for your answer.
— Contact your provincial ministry in charge of consumer affairs to identify any statutes that concern a particular product. List as many examples of this type of legislation as you can, and the particular products that the legislation deals with.

Manufacturer Responsibility

Until now, we have discussed only consumer remedies against the seller. What about remedies against the manufacturer?

The *Sale of Goods Acts* and consumer legislation are based on contracts between the buyer and the seller. Since the manufacturer is in most cases not the seller, the manufacturer is not considered a *party* to the contract. The manufacturer therefore usually cannot be sued for breach of contract.

There is one situation, however, in which a manufacturer *can* be considered a party to the contract: when the consumer has relied on an *express warranty* by the manufacturer. An express warranty is a written or published promise of quality.

Murray v. Sperry Rand (1979) 96 D.L.R. (3d) 113 (Ont. H.C.J.)

Murray, a farmer, bought a harvester manufactured by Sperry Rand from a farm machinery dealer. He bought the harvester because he had read about its many performance-features in a brochure published by the manufacturer.

When Murray had used the harvester for a few days, he realized that the machine was not performing at anywhere near the level promised in the brochure. Murray sued not the dealer, but the manufacturer.

The Ontario High Court relied on sales law as it had developed in English courts. The court looked at the brochure published by Sperry Rand, and decided that the manufacturer had, in effect, promised Murray, "If you buy this harvester, we guarantee that it will perform up to this standard." Since Murray had bought the harvester relying on the brochure, the court held that Sperry Rand must pay damages for failure to live up to its side of the bargain.

The *Sperry Rand* decision is helpful in deciding cases where a consumer has relied on a manufacturer's express warranty when buying the product. Often, though, there is no warranty, or the consumer has not relied on the warranty in deciding to buy the product. Is there any other situation in which the manufacturer may be liable for a defective product?

In certain situations, a consumer may sue the manufacturer successfully in tort. Usually, the manufacturer can be sued successfully only if the following are true:

1. the defective product caused personal injury or property damage, **and**
2. the consumer can prove negligence in the manufacture of the product.

Chapter 10 examined how a manufacturer's liability (product liability) to consumers for negligence developed in case law. However, the most successful method of making a manufacturer responsible to the consumer in the same way as a seller is through legislation. Saskatchewan, New Brunswick, and Québec, for example, have consumer legislation that imposes the same responsibilities on the manufacturer as on the seller. Other provinces provide this protection only in specific situations. For instance, Alberta, Manitoba, and Prince Edward Island have passed laws about sales of farm machinery or implements. The relevant *Acts* provide that, if there is a defect in farm machinery, the farmer can sue both seller and manufacturer for repairs or replacements.

—Does your province give the consumer a right to sue the manufacturer for repair, replacement, or refund where defective goods are concerned?
—Do you think manufacturers would be more careful if they knew they could always be sued in this way?

Group Actions by Consumers

When a large group of consumers bands together in seeking a remedy, the consequences for the manufacturer are often much more serious than the consequences of one person's lawsuit. The financial penalty for the manufacturer is larger, and there is often much publicity involved. Group actions also have the advantage for consumers of saving time, trouble, and money for the individual consumer. This fact may encourage consumers to seek a remedy. Consumer group actions are often an effective deterrent to careless manufacturing, unfair sales practices, and other problems.

Group action is possible in some provinces and very difficult in others. There are two ways for a group of consumers to sue. One is the **substituted action**. It occurs when the Director who administers a business practice statute sues on behalf of a group of consumers. The provinces which allow this kind of lawsuit include Alberta, British Columbia, and Saskatchewan. In a substituted action, the Director shoulders the expense and trouble of suing, but there is no guarantee that the Director will take on a given consumer case.

The other type of consumer group action is the **class action**. In a class action, one consumer sues on behalf of all others who have the same problem. Among the very few provinces that allow this type of action are Québec and British Columbia. Some provinces, such as Ontario, where the law makes bringing a class action very difficult, are considering passing legislation to make it easier.

—Think of or try to find examples of situations where large numbers of consumers had or have a complaint against a manufacturer.
—Do you think group legal action by consumers might discourage a manufacturer from producing a defective product? Why or why not?

Buying on Credit

In general there are three ways in which consumers can purchase goods when they cannot pay the full price immediately: taking out a loan, using a credit card, or paying by installments through a conditional sales contract. All three types of credit have problems associated with them. Some provinces have reacted to certain of these problems by enacting legislation.

The Cost of a Consumer Loan

In any type of consumer loan, including installment-payment plans and credit card accounts that are not paid in full, the cost of borrowing can add up to a lot of money. Many people find it difficult to assess the real cost of a loan; therefore, they "sign on the dotted line" without realizing what they are getting into. In response to this problem, most provinces have legislation which requires a lender to give the consumer/borrower a clear statement of the cost of borrowing. Section 24 of Ontario's *Consumer Protection Act* shows the type of statement required:

> 24. Except as provided in section 25, every lender shall furnish to the borrower, before giving the credit, a clear statement in writing showing,
>   (a) the sum,
>   (i) expressed as one sum in dollars and cents, actually received in cash by the borrower, plus insurance or official fees, if any, actually paid by the lender, or
>   (ii) where the lender is a seller, being the amount of the cash price of the goods or services, including any insurance or official fees;
>   (b) where the lender is a seller, the sums, if any, actually paid as a down payment or credited in respect of a trade-in, or paid or credited for any other reasons;
>   (c) where the lender is a seller, the amount by which the sum stated under subclause (a)(ii) exceeds the sum stated under clause (b);
>   (d) the cost of borrowing expressed as one sum in dollars and cents;
>   (e) the percentage that the cost of borrowing bears to the sum stated,
>   (i) under subclause (a)(i), where the lender is not a seller, or
>   (ii) under clause (c), where the lender is a seller, expressed as an annual rate applied to the unpaid balance thereof from time to time, calculated and expressed in the manner prescribed by the regulations;
>   (f) the amount, if any, charged for insurance;
>   (g) the amount, if any, charged for official fees; and
>   (h) the basis upon which additional charges are to be made in the event of default.

—Does your province have legislation that requires the lender to disclose the cost of a consumer loan? What information must be given?

Defective Goods and Credit Card Purchases

Cathy bought a rug from Fly-by-Night Carpets. She paid with a credit card. She was unable to pay off the full account in the first month, so she paid part of the amount owing. After only seven weeks, Cathy was already beginning to see bare patches in the pile, despite the fact that the rug experienced only ordinary wear and tear. The rug had worn out before she had even finished paying for it.

Does the consumer have any protection when using a credit card to buy goods which turn out be to be defective? The answer depends on the type of credit card used. If Cathy bought from a store using that store's credit card, her rights are the same as they would have been if she had paid cash. Here, the store is the seller as well as the issuer of the credit card. The consumer's obligation to pay will depend on whether the seller has met its obligations under the provincial *Sale of Goods Act* and consumer legislation.

But what if Cathy had used a credit card issued by a bank or another financial institution? Here, the issuer of the credit card is not the seller. Does Cathy have to pay the credit account in full and rely on asking the seller for her money back? Financial institutions that issue credit cards maintain that all they are doing is lending money to the consumer. Most credit card contracts have a clause stating that any disputes about a sale must be settled between the consumer and the seller.

The law is not clear on the question of whether a credit card issuer that is not the seller is affected by a seller's breach of responsibilities. To date, there has been no legislation and no major court case dealing with the problem. Therefore, it is useful to keep in mind when purchasing with a credit card that the credit card contract usually stresses that any dispute is between buyer and seller only—you have to pay your credit card bill.

—If you discover a flaw in merchandise right after you buy it, most reputable stores will allow it to be returned within a few days. If you return an item bought with a credit card, what do you need to get from the store?

Conditional Sales

Sometimes, consumers buy "on the installment plan". The legal term for this kind of transaction is a **conditional sale** In a conditional sale, the buyer signs a contract which states that a down payment has been made, and that the rest of the purchase price is owed to the seller. The important point to remember about a conditional sale is that while the buyer has possession and use of the goods, the seller legally has title to them (owns them) until the full purchase price has been paid.

The fact that the seller still owns the goods gives the seller a very strong position if the buyer does not make payments on time. Often, conditional sales contracts state that, if the buyer does not pay on time, the seller can *repossess* (take back) the goods, and keep all the payments made by the consumer until that time.

All provinces have legislation affecting conditional sales. Some provinces, such as Saskatchewan, Alberta, and Nova Scotia, have *Conditional Sales Acts*. Other provinces, like Ontario and Manitoba, deal more generally with conditional sales, through consumer legislation. Such legislation usually concerns the form of the contract, registration of the contract, and repossession.

The usual rules about the form of a conditional sales contract are that it must be in writing, describe the goods, set out all of the terms and conditions, identify the buyer and seller, and be signed by the buyer.

Problems with Conditional Sales and Some Legal Solutions

Most provinces have recognized a major problem with conditional sales contracts—that a buyer might sell the unpaid-for goods to a third party who does not know that title to the goods is really held by another party. If this happens, either the new buyer or the original seller suffers a loss. Most provinces have dealt with this problem by creating registries, government offices where conditional sales contracts may be registered within a certain time limit set by law. Any seller that registers a contract within this time is protected, because every third party buyer has a duty to check the register before buying goods. If the new buyer fails to check the registry, and the original seller repossesses the goods, the new buyer is out of luck. The third party buyer in this situation has no right to keep the goods. His or her only remedy is to sue the person from whom he or she bought the goods for a refund.

Repossession under a conditional sales contract is also an area where some provinces have seen a need for legislation. The seller in a conditional sales contract has both a common law and a contractual right to take back goods if payments are not made. This right exists because the seller still owns the goods. However, the seller cannot legally use force to repossess. Some provincial legislation provides that the seller must notify the buyer of an impending repossession. In Saskatchewan and Alberta, the legislation states that the seller cannot repossess certain types of property, such as farm implements and mobile homes. Ontario, Nova Scotia, and New Brunswick provide that when the buyer has paid two-thirds or more of the purchase price, the seller cannot repossess.

Most provincial law dealing with conditional sales provides that a seller that repossesses must keep the goods for a certain period, to allow the buyer a chance to pay the amount due on the contract price and get the goods back.

—There are a number of other rules set out by provincial law for conditional sales. Why do you think this type of sale is the subject of so much legislation?

Credit Reporting Agencies

Before giving a consumer a store credit card or allowing payment by installments, most sellers want certain information about the consumer. The information has to do with whether the customer will be reliable in paying bills or installments on time. To get this information, sellers turn to credit reporting agencies, which exist in every province. They are private businesses that collect information about people. For a price, the agency will report the desired information to the seller.

A problem arises in that the information collected by a credit reporting agency is sometimes false or misleading. Acting on such information, a seller may refuse a consumer credit, despite the fact that the consumer is a perfectly reliable credit risk. To try to prevent this difficulty, all provinces have legislation controlling credit reporting agencies. Usually, an agency cannot operate without a licence. The law also specifies who may see a credit file—usually information can be given only to employers, insurance companies, landlords, and credit-granters such as stores and banks. Anyone who asks for a credit report must inform the person about whom the report will be made. That person has the right to know the name and address of the agency that made the report, and the contents of the report. The agency also has a duty to tell any person who asks whether it has a file on that person, and if so, what the file contains. If the file contains wrong information, the person asking can correct the information.

—Check whether your province has a *Consumer Reporting Act* or similar legislation. What kind of protection does it give the consumer? What can a consumer do if a credit reporting agency has incorrect personal information?

—What kind of information do credit agencies collect? How do they get access to this information?

Enforcing Payment of Bills

If a consumer does not pay bills on time, a seller may use a number of methods to try to obtain payment. A common remedy is for the seller to sue the consumer, win a court order requiring the consumer to pay, and then pay a public official such as a sheriff to enforce the court order. The sheriff may legally take away and sell the consumer's personal property to pay the debt. If the consumer owns real estate, the court order may be registered against the title of the real property. The consumer will not be able to sell or mortgage the real estate without paying off the debt.

Collection Agencies

While having property sold by a sheriff is never pleasant, the sheriff's methods are often far more polite than those of **collection agencies**.

A collection agency is a private business which a seller may hire to collect a bill. Often the seller uses a collection agency instead of going to court to try to force the consumer to pay. Usually the agency charges the seller a percentage of the debt owed by the consumer.

Collection agencies have sometimes gone beyond the bounds of reasonable behaviour in dealing with consumers in debt. Harassment by agencies can reach the point where criminal charges could be laid, but usually agencies stop just short of committing a criminal offence.

For this reason, most provinces have passed laws that attempt to control collection agencies. Some provinces, such as Ontario and Alberta, have general legislation that says only that collection agencies must be registered, and that people may complain to a specific

Figure 19-7

Pay up or else!

public official if a collection agency behaves badly. Other provinces, such as British Columbia, New Brunswick, Saskatchewan, Québec, and Manitoba, go farther. Their legislation forbids certain activities specifically. The *Collection Agencies Act* of New Brunswick is typical of this type of specific law. Section 13 of the *Act* states:

> 13. (1) No collection agency shall
>   (a) collect or attempt to collect for a person for whom it acts any moneys in addition to the amount owing by the debtor;
>   (b) make any charge against a person for whom it acts in addition to those contained in the form of agreement or in the information pertaining to fees filed with the Minister;
>   (c) send any telegram or make any telephone call for which the charges are payable by the addressee or the person to whom the call is made, to a debtor for the purpose of demanding payment of a debt; this includes the collect calls for so-called tracing purposes, whether completed or not;
>   (d) include the spouses of debtors in Court actions and other attempts in the collection of outstanding accounts when it is clear that only one party is liable for the debt;
>   (e) use any signature on a letter or form of letter or the imprinted name or signature of any employee that is not employed by the collection agency; and that in talking with debtors, the proprietor, partners or employees must use the only name that is rightfully their own;
>   (f) conduct enquiries
>   (i) through persons other than the debtor for the purpose of demanding payment of a debt, or
>   (ii) at the place of employment of the debtor for any purpose in relation to the debtor, except with his approval;
>   and
>   (g) use threatening, intimidating or coercive language; cite loss of employment, loss of community ranking or sufferance of embarassment; or, by the timing of personal or phone contacts to irregular hours, intrude upon the privacy of the home and the family of the debtor, the regular hours being from 9 in the forenoon to 9 in the afternoon of the same day.

—Do you think it would be a good idea for your provincial government to forbid the operation of collection agencies altogether? Give reasons for your answer.

SUMMARIZING YOUR READING

1. What are the three main sources of consumer law?

2. What is the difference between a condition and a warranty?

3. What are the two main functions of provincial *Sale of Goods Acts*?

4. What does it mean to say that the *Sale of Goods Acts* set out when a certain condition or warranty is "implied"?

5. Name four problem areas in which a *Sale of Goods Act* may fail to meet the needs of consumers.

6. Which area of legislation forbids false advertising—provincial, federal, or both?

7. Give two examples of misleading sales practices.

8. What is double-ticketing?

9. Describe a consumer transaction that could be called "unconscionable".

10. Name and describe three sales techniques that are forbidden or controlled by law in Canada.

11. Name two types of products that can be sold only according to certain rules set out in legislation.

12. What is an "express warranty" by a manufacturer? Why is this an important concept in sales contracts?

13. If no express warranty is given, can a consumer sue the manufacturer when a product is defective? If so, what two facts must the consumer prove?

14. Explain the terms "substituted action" and "class action".

15. What two elements make a conditional sale different from any other kind of sale?

16. A seller in a conditional sale can repossess under certain circumstances. What factors may affect the seller's right to repossess? Why does the seller have the right to repossess?

17. What is a credit reporting agency?

18. Who may see a person's credit agency file?

19. What is a collection agency?

DISCUSSING KEY ISSUES

1. Before consumer legislation was passed, it was the responsibility of the buyer to make sure that he or she did not buy bad merchandise. This responsibility was called the *caveat emptor* rule. A buyer had very few remedies against a seller. This situation has changed to some extent. Given the material in this chapter, do you think that today's consumers are overprotected, or underprotected? Discuss and give reasons for your answer.

2. (a) You have bought a defective product for personal or family use. The seller refuses to refund your money. You want to find out whether you can get your money back by suing in Small Claims Court. Should you look at your province's *Sale of Goods Act*? Is this *Act* likely to be your only source of assistance? Explain.

   (b) You have
   (i) bought a broom from a door-to-door sales agent. You paid the full price at the time.
   (ii) signed a contract at your home for a set of encyclopedias. You have received the first volume. You will pay for the others as you receive them—20 volumes at $20 each.

Suppose that your province has a law that deals with door-to-door sales. Which of these contracts are you likely to be able to cancel? Give reasons for your answer.

   (c) The sales agent who sold Emily a car said two things that Emily remembered. He said, "This is a really great car!" and "This car will get 6 L per 100 km under most conditions." When Emily began driving the car, she found that neither claim was true. Which false claim is forbidden by law in most provinces? Why is it forbidden?

   (d) Jean wanted to buy a can of soup on which there were two different price tickets. The check-out clerk said, "That's not on sale any more; you'll have to pay the higher price." What is this practice called? What law forbids this practice?

   (e) A collection agency starts harassing you about a bill that you forgot to pay. Is there any law that might help you?

PROJECTS AND ACTIVITIES

1. Contact the Ministry or Department in your province that is responsible for consumer affairs. Obtain copies of pamphlets and posters about your provincial consumer legislation. Create a bulletin board display. Also, clip as many articles about consumer problems from newspapers and magazines as you can find during your study of this topic. Add them to your display.

2. You have been hired to promote the sale of Kleeno Toothpaste. Write a television advertisement that you think will increase sales, but keep the ad strictly legal. Omit anything that you think would breach any Canadian consumer legislation.

3. Do some research into the safety standards set by legislation dealing with either children's toys and clothing, or automobiles. What is the legislation that covers these areas of concern? Is it federal or provincial? What standards does the legislation set? Prepare a written report, or report your findings to the class.

RESOLVING CASES
Gagnon v. Geneau (1951) 1 D.L.R. 516 (N.B. S.C.)

Gagnon asked Geneau, a cattle dealer, to find him a milk cow. Geneau sold Gagnon a cow which Geneau had carefully inspected. Gagnon thought the cow looked all right; however, he soon found that it did not produce milk. He sued to get his money back, under the *Sale of Goods Act*. He relied on s. 14(1), which states:

> **14. (1)** Where the buyer, expressly or by implication, makes known to the seller the particular purpose for which the goods are required, so as to show that the buyer relies on the seller's skill or judgement, and the goods are of a description which it is in the course of the seller's business to supply (whether he be the manufacturer or not), there is an implied condition that the goods shall be reasonably fit for such purpose....

—What would make Gagnon rely on Geneau's skill or judgement?
—Could Gagnon prove that he had told Geneau the purpose for which he wanted the cow?
—Do you think a court would give Gagnon his money back?

Carr v. G. & B. Auto Mart Ltd. (1978) 89 D.L.R. (3d) 59 (Man. Q.B.)

In 1976, Carr read a newspaper advertisement for a 1972 Chevelle with 26 000 miles (41 600 km) on the odometer. He went to G. & B. Auto Mart and inspected the car advertised. He was told that it had sat unused for two-and-a-half years, and that he could have it for $2262.50. G. & B. Auto Mart told Carr all they knew about the car—it was clean, had low mileage, and had been in a minor accident, and the trunk did not open. Carr agreed to buy the vehicle. On the purchase agreement, G. & B. Auto wrote "As is—No warranty". The dealer also gave Carr an "Unsafe Motor Vehicle Dealer's Certificate", but all the spaces where the specific unsafe features of the car should have been marked in were left blank.

From the start, the Chevelle did not run properly. It had transmission problems, and used large quantities of oil. G. & B. agreed to pay half the cost of a new transmission, but even with a new transmission, the problems continued. Finally, Carr learned two things from a mechanic who looked at the car. The first was that the accident mentioned by G. & B. had not been minor. The second was that the 1972 Chevelle's engine had been replaced with an engine from a 1970 car of another make.

Carr sued to get his money back. He relied mainly on Manitoba's *Consumer Protection Act*, s. 58(1)(e) and (f):

> 58. (1) Not withstanding any agreement to the contrary, the following conditions or warranties on the part of the seller are implied in every retail sale of goods and in every retail hire-purchase of goods:
> (e) A condition that the goods are of merchantable quality, except for such defects as are described.
> (f) A condition that the goods correspond with the description under which they are sold.

—Do you consider that Carr received what he was promised by G. & B.?
—Did G. & B. Auto breach a condition of the contract under the *Consumer Protection Act*, in your opinion?
—Would the fact that the purchase agreement was marked "As is—No warranty" make any difference in the decision of the court?

Frisken v. Holiday Chevrolet-Oldsmobile Ltd. (1976) 72 D.L.R. (3d) 288 (Man. C.A.)

Frisken bought a used car from Holiday. The car did not run properly; it kept stalling because of a broken wire between the battery and the coil. After seven days of trying to drive the car, Frisken had it towed back to Holiday and demanded his money back. Holiday protested that Frisken must allow them a reasonable opportunity to make the car fit for service, but Frisken refused, and sued under Manitoba's *Consumer Protection Act*. The court agreed that a condition of sale had been breached by Holiday.

— Did Holiday have a right to try to fix the car?

Stubbe v. P.F. Collier and Son Ltd. (1977) 74 D.L.R. (3d) 605 (B.C. S.C.)

P.F. Collier and Son Ltd. sold encyclopedias door-to-door. The company, in training its sales agents, required them to memorize a sales pitch and to use the same words with every customer. One part of the sales routine was the "door opener", which was designed to get the sales agent into the customer's home. The "door opener" was a series of questions designed to give the customer the impression that the representative was conducting a survey about a television ad campaign.

When the Collier representatives called at Stubbe's home, they used the technique they had been taught. After the sales pitch, Stubbe, who was president of a local branch of the Consumer's Association of Canada, told them that he thought their sales practice was in breach of the British Columbia *Trade Practices Act*. Stubbe won the confidence of the Collier representatives, and he convinced them to give him copies of the Collier training material.

Stubbe brought an action under the *Trade Practices Act*, requesting the court to order Collier to stop the following practices:

1. The "door-opener" described above.

2. A false suggestion that the consumer was "qualified" for a special lower price.

3. A suggestion that the price of the encyclopedias was insignificant by comparing payments with the cost of cigarettes, without immediately revealing the true total price.

4. A suggestion that the encyclopedia was a new edition when, in fact, it was a revised edition.

Section 2 of the *Trade Practices Act* defines "deceptive practices" as follows:

> **2. (1) for the purposes of this Act, a deceptive act or practice includes**
> *(a)* **any oral, written, visual, descriptive, or other representation, including non-disclosure; or**
> *(b)* **any conduct**
> **having the capability, tendency, or effect of deceiving or misleading a person.**
> **(2) A deceptive act or practice by a supplier in relation to a consumer transaction may occur before, during, or after the consumer transaction.**

— In your opinion, are the four practices listed above deceptive? Explain your answer.
— What do you think was the court's decision in this case? Explain your reasoning.

R. v. Bristol-Meyers of Canada Ltd. (1979) 48 C.C.C. (2d) 384 (Ont. Cty. Ct.)

Bristol-Meyers had a broadcast advertisement for Fleecy Fabric Softener. The advertisement claimed that "Fleecy in the rinse softens right through the wash for three times more softness than any dryer product..." The *Combines Investigation Act*, s. 36(1), states:

> 36. (1) No person shall, for the purpose of promoting, directly or indirectly, the supply or use of a product for the purpose of promoting, directly or indirectly, any business interest, by any means whatever,
> (b) make a representation to the public in the form of a statement, warranty or guarantee of the performance, efficacy or length of life of a product that is not based on an adequate and proper test thereof, the proof of which lies upon the person making the representation.

— What kind of evidence would a court consider when deciding whether or not Bristol-Meyers was breaching this section of the Act?
— What do you think the court decided?

R. v. Ens [1980] 1 W.W.R. 639 (Sask. D.C.)

The *Collection Agents Act* of Saskatchewan contains the following provision in s. 29:

> 29. (1) No collection agent or collector shall,
> (g) make telephone calls or personal calls of such nature or with such frequency as to constitute harassment of the debtor, his spouse, or any member of his family...
> (j) give, or threaten to give, by implication, inference or statement, directly or indirectly, to the person who employs a debtor, his spouse or any member of his

> family information that may adversely affect the employment or employment opportunities of the debtor, his spouse or any member of his family.

Ens was a collection agent working on a case. Over two days, he made six telephone calls to a consumer who owed a debt Ens was trying to collect. Ens made no calls at night or at meal times. However, in the course of the six calls, Ens shouted on several occasions, and threatened to go to the consumer's employer, to his bank manager, and to a "bankruptcy board" that did not exist. Ens also threatened to start court proceedings.

A court action was in fact started, but in the meantime, the consumer laid a charge against Ens under the *Collection Agents Act*.

—What facts would the Crown rely on to prove that Ens had harassed the consumer?
—What arguments would you make if you were defending Ens?
—What do you think the decision of the court was in this case? Explain.

20

The Law of Bailment

> Creating a Bailment
> Taking Care of Bailed Property
> The Common Law Rules
> Legislation and Bailment
> Contracts and Bailment

Joe borrowed a record from Mario. Paula offered to look after Zubieda's kitten while Zubieda was away. Ying left a coat to be dry-cleaned. Alison parked her car in a downtown lot. Irving sent a birthday present to his uncle Fred, using the services of Speedy Courier Ltd.

All of these people are affected by the law of bailment. The law of bailment covers several types of transactions that involve **personal property**; that is, any type of property other than land. All of these transactions have two elements in common. First, someone takes possession or control of someone else's personal property. Second, the possession or control is temporary. The factor that distinguishes a bailment from a gift or a sale is therefore that the person who gets possession of the property is only expected to possess it for a limited time, not to become the owner. The property must be returned, or dealt with as the owner requests.

The person who owns the property and gives it to someone else temporarily is called the **bailor**. The person who possesses and controls the property temporarily is called the **bailee**. When someone temporarily takes control of someone else's property, a **bailment** is created.

Using two of the examples above, we can identify the bailor and the bailee. When Joe borrows a record from Mario, Joe is the bailee; Mario is the bailor. When Irving sends a birthday present to Uncle Fred, Irving is the bailor; Speedy Courier Ltd. is the bailee.

—In the rest of the examples given above, decide who is the bailor and the bailee.

Creating a Bailment

For a bailment to exist, the bailor must deliver personal property to, or leave the property with, the bailee. The bailee must in turn consent to taking control of the property. The bailee's consent can be in words or in writing, or be understood from his or her actions.

Harold v. Saskatchewan Wheat Pool (1980) 6 S.R. 297 (Sask. D. C.)

Harold, a cattle farmer, delivered eleven cattle to a stockyard controlled by Saskatchewan Wheat Pool to be sold. At the time of delivery, Harold found the cattle pen unattended, but he delivered the cattle anyway. Since no one was there, Harold did not receive a receipt.

Some time later, Harold was paid by the stockyard for the ten cattle it had sold. When Harold asked what happened to the eleventh steer the stockyard replied that it had received only ten cattle.

Harold sued, claiming that the stockyard had been the bailee of his cattle and had been negligent in losing one of them.

—What is necessary to create a bailment?
—Do you think the court found that a bailment had been created? Give a reason for your answer.

Taking Care of Bailed Property

What kind of responsibility does a bailee take on when taking possession of someone else's property? What happens if loss or damage occurs?

The degree of responsibility will depend on three factors: (a) the terms of the contract between bailor and bailee; (b) any legislation that may apply to the situation; and (c) common law rules. The common law provides the ground rules of bailment. These common law rules apply unless a contract between the bailor and bailee, or legislation, or both, change the situation. In other words, if neither a contract nor legislation covers the actual problem that has occurred, the common law rules apply. Therefore, in deciding whether a bailee is liable for damage to bailed property, there are certain questions to ask:

1. Is there a contract (oral or written) between the bailor and bailee? If so, does the contract set out who has the responsibility in this situation?
2. Whether or not there is a contract term that deals with liability, there may be legislation that covers bailments in the particular situation. What does it say? Does it apply despite what the contract may say?
3. If neither the contract nor the legislation covers the situation, what are the common law rules?

This chapter will look at these three areas. We will examine the common law rules first, because they form the basis of the law of bailment. Then we will look at how a contract or legislation can change the situation.

The Common Law Rules

The general rule under common law is that a bailee has to take "reasonable" care of bailed property. Furthermore, there is a difference between court actions involving bailments and other court actions. When a bailor sues a bailee for damaging bailed goods, once the existence of a bailment is proved the bailee (defendant) has the burden of showing that he or she was *not* responsible for the damage. In other civil actions, the plaintiff has the burden of proving who caused the damage.

The degree of care that the bailee must take under common law varies according to the type of bailment. There are two main types of bailment: **bailment for reward** (that is, for money or some other reward), and **gratuitous bailment** (bailment without charge). Different standards of care apply to the two types.

Gratuitous Bailment

A gratuitous bailment usually involves a favour to someone. The general rule of common law for this type of bailment is that when the bailee takes care of the bailor's property without charge or reward, the bailor usually can't expect more than an ordinary standard of care.

If both bailor and bailee benefit from the bailment, the bailee is expected to take the same degree of care that a reasonable person would take in the care and control of his or her own property.

Figure 20-1

—Who benefits from this bailment? What is the benefit received?
—What standard of care must Anne take?

This ordinary standard of care changes somewhat if only one of the bailor and the bailee benefits from the bailment. If the bailee is the only one who benefits, he or she is not liable for ordinary wear and tear, but is liable for even slight negligence. If the bailee uses the property in any other way than the purpose for which it was borrowed, or lends it to someone else, the bailee is liable for any damage to the property caused by that unplanned use. On the other hand, if the bailor is the only one who benefits from the bailment, the bailee is liable only for gross negligence, or if the instructions of the bailor were not followed.

Katya borrows a silk scarf from Renata.

— Who benefits from this bailment, the bailor or the bailee?
— If it rains while Katya is out wearing the scarf, and the colours run, would Katya be liable for the damage? Explain.
— If Katya left the scarf lying on a chair and her puppy playfully chewed it to rags, would she be liable? Explain.

Lise asks George to take care of her canary while she is on vacation. George tells Lise he doesn't know anything about canaries, but she says—"Oh, it's easy. Just give him some food and water once a day." George agrees to look after the canary.

— Who benefits from this bailment, bailor or bailee?
— George carefully feeds and gives water to the canary, but he leaves a window open on a cold day and the canary dies of pneumonia. Is George liable? Explain.
— What if George decides that he wants to have a vacation too? He puts a cup of seed and a cup of water on the floor of the cage and goes away for two weeks. When he comes back, the canary is dead. Is George liable? If so, why? If not, why not?

MacIntyre v. Clark Motors (P.E.I.) Ltd. (1976) 13 Nfld. & P.E.I.R. 108 (P.E.I.S.C.)

A representative of Clark Motors visited Mr. and Mrs. MacIntyre at home with a 1968 car for sale. The salesman said he would like to interest the MacIntyres in trading in their 1966 car for the 1968 model. The salesman suggested that the MacIntyres drive the '68 model for a while, to decide whether or not they wanted it. The salesman drove away in the MacIntyre's car, leaving them with the '68 model.

While Mr. MacIntyre was test-driving the '68 car, he drove it off the road and the car was badly damaged. MacIntyre asked for the return of his own car, but Clark Motors refused, saying there had been a sale, and that the '68 model car belonged to MacIntyre. MacIntyre sued to get his car back.

— What would the court consider in deciding whether a sale or a bailment had occurred?
— If there was a bailment, who benefitted from the bailment, the bailor, the bailee, or both? State the standard of care that would apply in each situation.
— If the court found that a bailment had occurred, would Clark Motors have to prove that MacIntyre had breached the standard of care expected of him, or would MacIntyre have to prove that he had not breached this standard?
— Is a gratuitous bailment likely to involve an agreement that says

- who is liable if the property is damaged? Explain.
- Make up an example of a situation in which there is a gratuitous bailment agreement with a term that deals with liability.

Bailment for Reward

A bailment for reward is usually a business transaction that benefits both bailor and bailee. For this reason, the bailor and bailee often agree by contract about who will bear any losses that occur. There is sometimes also legislation covering the situation. However, there are still situations where bailor and bailee have to rely on common law rules.

June owns a van. She agrees to transport Magda's furniture to her new home outside of town for $50. Since June is a careful businessperson, she tells Magda in advance that the van is not padded inside and that she will not be responsible if the furniture gets scratched. Magda says "Okay, I'll take the risk." On the way to Magda's new home, the van gets hit by lightning and a fire starts in the back of the van. By the time it is put out, much of the furniture is ruined.

- Do Magda and June have a contract? If so, does it deal with the problem that has come up?
- What two areas of law must June and Magda consider in deciding who bears the loss of the furniture?

The common law rules about bailment for reward vary according to the type of bailment. As in most bailments, if the bailor sues, it is up to the bailee to prove that the required standard of care has been maintained.

Storing Property

A party that promises to store something for another party may be in the storage business, or may store property as part of some other business. The bailee that stores property must do the following:

1. Provide a type of storage that is appropriate for the property stored. For example, a warehouse that stored frozen food in a hot area would be liable for damage to the food.
2. Take reasonable care of the property.

Facelle Co. v. Jaybee Warehousing (1978) 22 N.B.R. (2d) 56 (N.B.S.C.)

Facelle Co. arranged to store a shipment of paper towels, facial tissues, and other paper products in a warehouse owned by Jaybee.

The paper products were stored partly on racks and partly on the floor. Because of an abnormally mild winter and heavy rain, the city sewer system was overloaded. Water from the sewer backed up onto the floor of the warehouse, and a number of cartons on the floor were soaked. Facelle sued Jaybee.

—What standard of care did Jaybee have to maintain? What might the court consider when deciding whether that standard had been upheld?
—Did Facelle have to prove that Jaybee had been negligent?

Figure 20-2

Repair Work

People often leave property with someone who is going to do repairs or clean the property. The bailee that repairs or cleans property must do the following:

1. Do the work agreed upon with the reasonable care and skill called for in the circumstances.
2. Take reasonable care of the property.

***Short v. Deer Lake Sales and Service Ltd.* (1962) 47 M.P.R. 374 (Nfld. Q.B.)**

Short brought his car to Deer Lake Sales and Service Ltd. for repairs. Soon after the car was left at the garage, it caught fire and was ruined. Short sued. The court found that the mechanic at Deer Lake

Ltd. had caused the fire when he used a welding torch to make a repair, and sparks from the torch caught in the upholstery.

—What standard of care applies in this situation?
—What might the court consider in deciding liability?
—What did the bailor have to prove? What did the bailee have to prove?

Renting Property

When personal property is rented, both the bailor and the bailee have specific responsibilities at common law. The bailor must take reasonable care to ensure that the property is fit for the use for which it is intended. If the property has a defect of which the bailor is aware or should be aware, the bailor is liable for any loss or damage caused by the defect. The bailor is liable even when the defect was not easy to see, if the bailee can prove that the bailor was negligent in not discovering the defect.

Arrow Transfer Co. Ltd. v. Fleetwood Logging Co. Ltd. (1961) 30 D.L.R. (2d) 631 (B.C.C.A.)

Fleetwood Ltd. rented a heavy crane from Arrow Ltd. The contract of rental specifically said that the equipment would be "in good condition and working order". However, while the crane was being operated it broke, due to a hidden flaw in the metal. Arrow sued Fleetwood for the damage to the crane, but its action was unsuccessful.

—What would Fleetwood argue in defending the case?
—Since the defect was a hidden one, under what circumstances would Arrow be liable for the damage?
—Why was Arrow's action against Fleetwood unsuccessful? Explain.

The bailee of rented property must take reasonable care of the property. The bailee is responsible for any damage or loss caused by negligence. This is true no matter who is using the property. For example, if you rent a lawnmower and lend it to your brother, who damages it, you are held liable, not your brother. However, the bailee is not responsible for damage caused by ordinary wear and tear.

Townsend Air Services Ltd. v. Hansen (1975) 7 O.R. (2d) 41 (Ont. Cty. Ct.)

Hansen rented a small airplane from Townsend Air Services. He had a pilot's licence which allowed him to fly during the day only. Hansen made a verbal agreement with Townsend that he would return between 4:00 and 4:30 p.m., since the sun was due to set at

5:30 p.m. At 4:00, Hansen called Townsend to say that he would be delayed. By 5:00 there was a storm and the sky was dark. At 7:30 p.m. Townsend received a call from Hansen, who reported that he had crash-landed and completely wrecked the plane. Townsend later sued.

—What standard of care applies to Hansen?
—Who has to prove that Hansen was or was not negligent?
—What facts would the court consider in deciding whether Hansen was negligent?

Holding Property as a Pledge or Pawn

A person who borrows money is often asked to leave some personal property with the lender as security for the debt. This property is referred to as a *pledge*. The lender's "security" lies in the fact that the lender may sell the property if the debt is not repaid. However, if the property, when sold, brings more than the amount of the unpaid debt, the lender must give the excess to the borrower.

A *pawn* is similar to a pledge, but the term is used only when property is pledged to a licenced pawnbroker.

Anyone who holds pledged or pawned property is responsible for taking reasonable care of that property and is liable for any loss or damage due to negligence.

Transporting Property

A person or company that transports personal property for payment is called a carrier. There are two types of carriers: **private carriers** and **common carriers**. Each type has slightly different responsibilities as a bailee.

A private carrier is a person or company that sometimes transports goods for other parties, often in the course of another business. For example, say that Luigi runs a fruit and vegetable store. He occasionally delivers orders for customers at the end of the day, if they live close enough to his store. He charges for this service, but Luigi would be considered only a private carrier. He can choose to offer or refuse this service, and acting as a carrier is not his primary business. If anything happened to the customers' orders, Luigi would be liable if he had not taken reasonable care in the delivery.

A common carrier, on the other hand, is a person or company whose primary business is the transporting of personal property. For example, Speedy Movers Ltd., which is in the business of moving furniture, is a common carrier. At common law, Speedy Ltd. cannot refuse to ship furniture for anyone who offers to pay the right price, as long as Speedy has a suitable truck available.

A common carrier such as Speedy Movers Ltd. has a higher level of responsibility for the goods being transported than a private carrier. The rule is that, whether or not Speedy is negligent, the company is liable for any loss or damage to the goods during the course of the trip. This is true unless the loss or damage is caused by any of the following:

1. An *act of God*, a term referring to a natural catastrophe such as a hurricane, flood, or volcanic eruption.
2. An action by an enemy of Canada, such as bombing during wartime.
3. Inherent defects in the property being transported. If a defect in the goods is responsible for the damage, the common carrier is not liable. For example, a common carrier would not be responsible for rot in a shipment of apples if the rot had begun before the apples were loaded.

Can a common carrier limit its responsibility? The answer is "Yes, but never completely". The common law in Canada allows a common carrier to limit its responsibility by contract in most situations. However, because of the high degree of responsibility that a common carrier has at common law, a court will be very strict in interpreting the contract.

The courts observe two major rules in dealing with common carriers' contracts. The first is that if the contract is not clear, the benefit of the doubt is given to the owner of the goods. That is, unless the contract clearly covers the problem that has arisen, it is assumed that the common carrier is responsible for any loss or damage.

Figure 20-3 A railway company is an example of a common carrier.

Tuffy Insulated Trucks Inc. runs a common carrier service. Tuffy's standard contract contains this clause:

> "Tuffy Insulated Trucks Inc. will not be liable for damage caused by weather conditions."

Marisa sent several crates of oranges to a friend, using Tuffy Trucks' delivery service. Unfortunately, all the usual insulated trucks were in service, so the manager of the company sent Marisa's oranges in a non-insulated truck rented from a car rental company. There was a bad snowstorm that day, and the oranges froze on the way and were spoiled. When Marisa sued, Tuffy's manager argued that their clause about the weather conditions should protect the company. However, the judge interpreted the contract strictly. Tuffy was in the business of carrying goods in insulated trucks and it must live up to its promise if it wanted to benefit by that clause in its contract. Since Tuffy had not supplied an insulated truck, it could not rely on the contract to protect it from liability.

The second rule used by the courts in interpreting common carriers' contracts is that common carriers cannot limit their liability for negligence.

Speedy Movers Ltd., the common carrier mentioned earlier, has a clause in its standard contract that says:

> "All goods transported at owner's risk."

On one delivery, some of Speedy's employees played a game of "catch" inside the van with some of the boxes. Several small lamps contained in the boxes were broken. The owner of the lamps sued.

—Would the clause in the contract protect Speedy Movers Ltd.? Explain.

Legislation and Bailment

Legislation can replace the common law rules affecting bailment. Legislation can also add new elements to a bailment, such as special rules affecting the bailee's right to be paid for services rendered.

The federal Parliament and the provincial legislatures all may make laws that affect bailment, since a bailment may involve a federal area of jurisdiction (such as interprovincial shipments) or a provincial area (such as property). An example of provincial laws that limit the liability of a bailee is the *Innkeepers' Acts* enacted by many provinces.

At common law, the position of an innkeeper (someone who runs a hotel or motel) was similar to that of a common carrier—that is, the innkeeper had to accept any fit and orderly person as a guest, if space was available. Like a common carrier, an innkeeper was strictly liable for goods brought into the hotel by a guest, unless the innkeeper could prove that the loss or damage was caused by the guest's own negligence.

An innkeeper no longer has this kind of strict duty, because of the various *Innkeepers' Acts*. Some *Acts* simply impose a flat monetary limit to liability, except in special circumstances. For example, s.4 of Ontario's *Innkeepers' Act* states:

> 4. (1) No innkeeper is liable to make good to any guest of his any loss of or injury to goods brought to his inn, not being a horse or other live animal, or any gear appertaining thereto, or a carriage, to a greater amount than the sum of $40 except,
>   (a) where the goods have been stolen, lost or injured through the wilful act, default, or neglect of the innkeeper or a servant in his employ;
>   (b) where the goods have been deposited expressly for safe custody with the innkeeper.
> (2) In case of such deposit, it is lawful for the innkeeper if he thinks fit, to require, as a condition of his liability, that the goods shall be deposited in a box or other receptacle, fastened and sealed by the person depositing the goods.

Other provinces have similar laws with different money limits.

—Does your province have an *Innkeepers' Act*? If so, how does it limit the liability of a hotel or motel for guests' property?

As we said earlier, legislation may sometimes grant special rights to a bailee. For example, a statute may give a bailee a **lien** on the bailor's property. A lien is the right to keep property until a certain fee is paid, as, for example, when a watch is left for repair. A statute may also give the right to sell the property if the debt is not paid. The Ontario *Innkeepers' Act* grants this type of right in s.2:

> 2. (1) An innkeeper, boarding-house keeper or lodging-house keeper has a lien on the goods of his guest, boarder or lodger for the value or price of any food or accommodation furnished to him or on his account.

> (2) In addition to all other remedies provided by law, he has the right, in case the same remains unpaid for three months, to sell by public auction the goods of the guest, boarder or lodger, on giving one week's notice of the intended sale by advertisement in a newspaper published in the municipality in which the inn, boarding house or lodging house is situate or, in case there is no newspaper published in the municipality, in a newspaper published nearest to the inn, boarding house or lodging house.
> (3) The advertisement shall state the name of the guest, boarder or lodger, the amount of his indebtedness, the time and place of sale, and the name of the auctioneer, and shall give a description of the goods to be sold.
> (4) The innkeeper, boarding-house keeper or lodging-house keeper may apply the proceeds of the sale in payment of the amount due to him and the costs of the advertising and sale, and shall pay over the surplus, if any, to the person entitled thereto on application being made by him therefor.

A statute can also control the extent to which a bailee can limit liability by contract. For example, the federal *Railway Act* allows a railway to limit its liability by contract, but the railway must get the approval of the Railway Commission before doing so.

Another example is seen in provincial legislation such as Ontario's *Public Commercial Vehicles Act*. That *Act* provides that the Ontario government may make regulations that apply to carriers' contracts, no matter what the contract may say. The regulation that deals with livestock carriers provides an example. The following is one of the rules that govern livestock carriers' contracts under the *Act*:

> *Consignor's Risk*
>
> Where it is a term or condition that the goods are carried at the risk of the consignor or owner, the condition covers only such risks as are necessarily incidental to transportation and does not relieve the carrier from liability for any loss, damage, injury or delay that may result from any negligence or omission of the carrier, its agents or employees, and the burden of proving the absence of negligence or omission is on the carrier.

—Explain this rule in your own words.

Contracts and Bailment

Often, bailees try to limit the liability that the common law imposes. They can usually succeed in doing so if they can prove that the bailor agreed to the limited liability by accepting the terms of a contract.

Appleton et. al v. Ritchie Taxi et al. [1942] O.R. 466 (Ont. C.A.)

Appleton wanted to park his car at the Ritchie Taxi parking lot, so he drove up to the booth at the lot. The attendant told Appleton to leave the keys in the car so that the car could be moved if necessary. Appleton agreed, and the attendant wrote Appleton's licence number on a ticket and handed the ticket to him. Appleton put the ticket in his pocket without reading it.

When Appleton returned to the lot, his car and the items in it had been stolen. Appleton sued. In court, Ritchie Taxi pointed out that the back of the ticket that Appleton had received displayed these words:

> Parking Conditions
>
> The management is not responsible for damage or loss by fire, theft, collision or otherwise to the car or its contents.
>
> No attendant has authority to accept responsibility.

Ritchie argued that this term on the ticket was part of the contract between the company and Appleton.

The Ontario Court of Appeal considered that, in the circumstances, Ritchie had been negligent. Then it went on to decide whether the ticket limited Ritchie's liability. The court decided that there was no reason why Appleton should have looked at the ticket, since he had probably considered it as merely a receipt for his car. The court also noted that Ritchie had not taken any steps to bring the words on the ticket to Appleton's attention. For this reason, the court decided that Ritchie could not rely on the ticket to limit its liability.

Contracts can also be used to add to the bailee's rights. For example, a dry cleaning business might include a clause like the one in Figure 20-4 (overleaf) in its contracts with customers.

Figure 20-4 Under what circumstances could the drycleaner rely on this clause?

> Eezee—Klean Dry Cleaners
> 5091 10th St. N.E.
> Calgary, Alberta
>
> **#A12167**
>
> Articles left for over 6 months will be sold to defray storage costs.

As the case above shows, the courts apply the same rule to bailment contracts as they do to standard form contracts (discussed in Chapter 12). If the term limiting the bailee's liability is not brought to the bailor's attention, a court will likely find that the term is not enforceable.

SUMMARIZING YOUR READING

1. What distinguishes a bailment from a gift or sale?

2. Who is the bailor in a bailment? Who is the bailee? Give an example of a bailment, naming each party.

3. Can a term in a contract replace a common law rule of bailment?

4. Can legislation replace a common law rule of bailment?

5. Does a bailor who sues for damage to bailed property usually have to prove that the bailee was negligent? What does the bailee have to prove?

6. Define "gratuitous bailment". Give an example.

7. Give an example of a gratuitous bailment in which both bailor and bailee benefit.

8. If both bailor and bailee benefit from a gratuitous bailment, what standard of care must the bailee meet?

9. Give an example of a gratuitous bailment in which only the bailee benefits. In this situation, what standard of care must the bailee meet? In what circumstances would that person be liable for loss or damage?

10. Give an example of a gratuitous bailment in which only the bailor benefits. In this situation, what standard of care must the bailee meet? In what circumstances would that person be liable for loss or damage?

11. What is a bailment for reward? Give an example.

12. Can a contract change the common law rules of bailment for reward? Provide an example of a situation in which common law rules apply despite the fact that a contract was made.

13. Explain the common law responsibility of a bailee who is (a) storing property; (b) repairing property.

14. Explain when the bailor who rents property might be responsible at common law for loss or damage.

15. Explain when the bailee who rents property will be responsible at common law for loss or damage.

16. If you rent a lawnmower that breaks when you use it because it is old and worn out, are you responsible for repair or replacement at common law?

17. What is the standard of care for a private carrier at common law?

18. What is the standard of care for a common carrier at common law?

19. Give an example in which the bailee's common law liability is limited by statute. What does the statute do?

20. What is a lien?

21. How can a bailee for reward limit common law liability without the help of a statute?

22. Can a bailee limit liability through contract if the bailor has not seen the contract?

PROJECTS AND ACTIVITIES

1. Collect as many of the following as possible: parking lot receipts; tickets for drycleaning, pawnshops, repair services, courier services, car rentals, etc.

Do these bailees attempt to limit their liability to the bailor? Summarize your findings and report to the class.

RESOLVING CASES

Albert et al. v. Breau (1977) 19 N.B.R. (2d) 476 (N.B. S.C.)

Albert and Savoie each brought a truck to Breau's service station for repairs. Breau did some repairs on Albert's truck, but had no time to do anything with Savoie's truck at the time it was brought in. Savoie asked Breau if he could use some of Breau's tools and do the repair himself. Breau consented and Savoie used the tools.

Partway through the evening, a fire started in the service station. Both Albert's and Savoie's vehicles were damaged. Both sued Breau for negligence. One of the first questions to come up at the trial was whether Breau was a bailee for reward in respect of both the vehicles.

—What facts does a court consider in deciding whether a bailment has occurred in any situation?
—What facts would Albert point to in order to establish that Breau was the bailee of his vehicle?
—What facts would Savoie point to in order to establish bailment?
—What do you think the court decided in each case?

Hubbard v. Sisters of St. Joseph [1943] O.W.N. 703 (Ont. C.A.)

Hubbard was employed as a dietician at a hospital. When she began her employment, she was told to hang her coat and hat in a room on the first floor. Unlike the nearby nurses' coatroom, this room had no lockers, and thefts were fairly common. In fact, Hubbard's hat and gloves were stolen on one occasion. She complained about the loss, but nothing was done. Some time later, her fur coat was stolen. Hubbard sued the nuns who ran the hospital.

—What type of bailment was created in this case?
—The court considered the question of who benefitted from this bailment. Why was this issue important?
—List the reasons that counsel for Hubbard would put forward in saying that it was the Sisters of St. Joseph who benefitted from the bailment.
—List the reasons that counsel for the Sisters would put forward in saying that it was Hubbard who benefitted from the bailment.
—What do you think was the outcome of this case?

Beverage Sales Ltd. v. Canadian National Railway Co. and Woodward's Ltd. (1974) 7 Nfld. & P.E.I.R. 84 (Nfld. S.C.)

Beverage Sales Ltd. sold some crates of bottled beer to a purchaser. The C.N.R. delivered the beer to Goose Bay in November. Woodward's Ltd., a carrier firm, was then supposed to pick up the beer from the C.N.R. dock and deliver it to the purchaser's warehouse.

When the C.N.R. delivered the beer to Goose Bay, Woodward's trucks were all busy. Woodward's stored the beer in an unheated warehouse until some trucks were free. The beer froze and was spoiled before it was delivered. Beverage Sales sued both the C.N.R. and Woodward's.

—Identify the bailees in this situation.
—What type of carrier is the C.N.R.? Woodward's?
—What responsibility did each of the bailees have in transporting the goods?
—Do you think the court considered the C.N.R. responsible for the damage? What about Woodward's? Explain.

Chaing v. Heppner et al. (1978) 6 B.C.L.R. 76 (B.C. C. C.)

Chaing took an extremely valuable gold and diamond watch to Heppner Credit Jewellers for repair. Heppner accepted the watch. During the next eight or nine months, Chaing dropped in at least eight times to inquire as to whether the watch was ready. Each time, Heppner said it was not, and on one occasion, he told Chaing that some of the parts had been lost. He told Chaing that he had ordered replacement parts from Switzerland.

Most of the time he had the watch, Heppner kept it in a safe, along with other valuable jewellery. However, when the watch was finally ready to be repaired, Heppner's assistant left it out on a workbench covered by glass overnight. That night, the store burned down, and the watch was destroyed. Chaing sued.

—What type of bailment existed here?
—What standard of care is the bailee in this type of situation expected to maintain?
—Did Chaing have to prove that Heppner was negligent, or did Heppner have to prove that he was not negligent?
—What do you think the court decided in this case? Why?

Manitoba Public Insurance Corp. v. Midway Chrysler Plymouth [1978] 1 W.W.R. 722

A car insured by Manitoba Public Insurance was left for repairs with Midway. A Midway employee left the car in a fenced and locked parking lot, but forgot to remove the keys. During the night a car thief drove the car through the locked metal gate. The car was recovered, but was damaged. The insurance company sued.

— If you were Midway's lawyer, what would you have to prove? List the facts that you would use to back up your argument.
— Do you feel Midway was liable? Why?

Smith and Sons Ltd. v. Silverman **[1961] O.R. 648 (Ont. C.A.)**

Smith's car was left in Silverman's parking lot. The attendant asked the person who left the car (Sussman) to leave the keys so the car could be moved. The attendant then handed Sussman a ticket on which was printed in large letters:

> We are not responsible for theft or damage of car or contents however caused.

Sussman did not look at the ticket. When he returned, he found that the car had been damaged. The car's owner, Smith, sued.

At the trial, Silverman argued that not only did the ticket contain words that limited his liability, but the parking lot also displayed four lighted signs, each about 0.8 m by 1.0 m in size. Each sign carried the same message as the ticket.

The court held that, while ordinarily Silverman would have been found negligent for damaging the car, he had made special efforts to bring the limiting conditions of the contract to customers' attention. Any reasonably observant person could have noticed the signs. Therefore, Silverman could rely on the signs to limit his liability. The Ontario Court of Appeal agreed with the trial court's decision.

— Compare this case to *Appleton et al. v. Ritchie Taxi et al.*, discussed earlier in this chapter.
— Why do you think the court decided that there was a valid contract limiting liability in one of these cases, but not in the other?

Marine Construction Ltd. v. Metro Engineering and Construction **(1978) 20 Nfld. & P.E.I.R. 504 (Nfld. S.C.)**

Metro Engineering leased a barge from Marine Construction. Metro soon decided that the barge was not needed, but did not return it to Marine. During the lease, the barge was lost at sea due to a unusually severe storm. Marine Construction sued for the full value of the barge.

At trial, the court noted that at common law, a bailee must return the property if the bailor requests its return. There is an exception to this common law rule when the property has been lost or destroyed for a reason that is not the fault of the bailee. However, the court also noted that Metro had signed a leasing contract. The contract contained the following clauses:

6. MAINTENANCE, OPERATION AND REPAIRS:

The Lessee shall not remove, alter, disfigure or cover up any numbering, lettering or insignia displayed upon the Equipment, and shall see that the Equipment is not subjected to careless or needlessly rough usage, and shall, at the Lessee's own expense, maintain and ultimately return to the Lessor the Equipment and its appurtenances, together with any tools and accessories pertaining thereto, the whole in good repair and running order, fair wear and tear excepted.

8. DAMAGE TO EQUIPMENT

The Lessee shall indemnify the Lessor against all loss and damage to the Equipment during the rental period and the appraisal of any such loss or damage shall be based on the value stated in the Details of Equipment. Any shortage or damage claimed by either party must be made known in writing to the other party within thirty days after receipt by claimant of the Equipment otherwise any such claim shall be extinguished.

— Metro was relying on an exception to a common law rule. Can a contract overrule the common law?
— Do you think the court went on to consider whether or not Metro had been negligent? Explain.

21

The Law of Real Property

> The Meaning of Real Property
> Ownership and Title to Real Property
> Concurrent Ownership
> Other Interests in Land
> Protecting Interest in Land—Registration Systems
> Restrictions on the Use of Property
> Transferring Title to Land

The purchase of a home is one of the most important and costly investments most people ever make. Although people generally have a lawyer assist them when buying or selling a house, it is very useful to be familiar with some of the rules governing the use of land.

This chapter will look at some of the rules concerning the ways in which land can be owned, the rights and obligations of ownership, and the methods of transferring property.

Although property is a matter of provincial jurisdiction, the fundamental laws relating to property are similar throughout Canada.

Figure 21-1

The Meaning of Real Property

There are two types of property: personal and real. As you have seen, personal property is any property other than land, that is, such moveable property as cars, clothes, stereos, and jewellery. **Real property** is land and everything attached to it. Such items as buildings (and the things attached to buildings) and trees and other plants are called **fixtures**. In the purchase of a piece of land, unless the buyer and the seller agree otherwise, the buyer is also purchasing all of the fixtures attached to the land.

Just what exactly does the owner of real property have? It has been said that property ownership includes the land to the centre of the earth and the space above the land "to the heavens". In fact, although the owner may own land to as far below the surface as can be reached, today, ownership of airspace is restricted to what is necessary for the ordinary use and enjoyment of land.

Condominiums are a practical application of the principle that the airspace above the land can be owned. Condominiums are living units which often look much like apartments. However, each unit is owned separately rather than rented. A condominium building will also have some property such as a club house or children's play area, as well as hallways that are owned in common by all of the residents. Condominiums are possible because the airspace above the land can, by law, be divided horizontally.

Figure 21-2 *Buying a condominium is becoming an increasingly popular form of home ownership.*

Similarly, since ownership includes everything under the surface of the land, property owners can sell or lease the right to mine for minerals under their land.

Ownership of and Title to Real Property

Strictly speaking, no one except the Crown owns land in Canada. This is a continuation of a practice which started when William, the Duke of Normandy, conquered England. After the conquest, William claimed all of the land for himself as King. He then gave grants of land to his most important officers in exchange for their services. However, these grants did not give them ownership. William could take back the land if the officers failed to perform their obligations. It was only gradually that people holding grants of land from the Crown received the rights or interests we today consider to be part of ownership, such as the right to sell land or pass it on by will.

Although owners of land no longer have any obligations to the Crown, Canada inherited the remnants of this system as part of our common law heritage. You may be familiar with the term **Crown lands**. These are lands that have never been granted to anyone. In

490 THE LAW AND THE MARKETPLACE

addition, some Crown grants expressly reserve certain rights, such as oil and minerals rights, to the Crown.

In summary, all land in Canada belongs, at least in theory, to the Crown. This is why if a person dies intestate and without heirs, any land that person owned *escheats* (reverts) to the Crown. As a result, although we commonly speak of "ownership" of land, it is really more accurate to speak of a person's "interest in land".

Another reason for using the term "interest" rather than "ownership" is that it is possible to have many different types of rights or interests in land. An interest can be very broad; it can include the right to live on the land indefinitely, or be restricted, as in the right of a tenant to occupy the land until the lease expires.

Estates

The most important types of interests in land are called **estates**. These interests include the right to possess the property. Today, there are two main types of estates: **fee simple estates** and **life estates**.

Fee Simple Estates

A fee simple estate is, in practical terms, what is normally considered ownership. Another way of referring to the owner of a fee simple estate is to say that the person has **title** to the property. A person who has a clear title to property can live on the property indefinitely as well as sell it, rent it, *mortgage* it, or give it away. In other words, the fee simple estate is the largest "bundle of rights" that it is possible to have in a piece of property.

Life Estates

A life estate interest in land is similar to a fee simple estate in that the holder possesses the land. However, the interest lasts only as long as the holder lives. Life estates are often given in wills. For instance, one spouse may give the other a life estate in the family cottage, the property then to go to the couple's children in fee simple after the surviving spouse's death. The spouse who has the life estate can use the property but cannot make any substantial changes to it without the consent of the children. However, it would be possible for the children, who have what is called a *future interest* in the cottage, to join with the spouse who has the life estate and sell the fee simple estate in the property. Thus, it is possible to divide a fee simple estate in such a way that several people hold interests in the same piece of land.

Concurrent Ownership

More than one person can be the owner of the same interest in land. The two ways in which this can happen are called **joint tenancy** and **tenancy in common**. As well, every province has special rules regarding the rights of spouses in each other's property, as you read in Chapter 17.

Tenancy in Common

Unless they agree otherwise, tenants in common hold property equally. This means that they are entitled to an equal share of any profits from the land. Each tenant is also entitled to use all of the property, unless they agree to divide the land into separate lots. A tenant in common may sell his or her interest or pass it to heirs upon death.

Joint Tenants

The main difference between tenancy in common and joint tenancy is the **right of survivorship** available in the latter. When a joint tenant dies, that person's interest automatically goes to the other joint tenants: this is the right of survivorship. A joint tenancy can be destroyed or severed in various ways. For instance, if a joint tenant sells his or her interest, the interest turns into a tenancy in common. However, if there are two or more joint tenants, they still remain joint tenants to each other, but are tenants in common to the new owner.

Other Interests in Land

There are several other kinds of interests in land, which are not considered estates. The most important are those created by **easements** and **restrictive covenants.**

Easements

The Ceratos own a farm that has a lake on part of the property. They decide to sell lakefront lots for a housing development. On one of the lots, they reserve a **right of way** which will allow their family to get to the lake.

An easement is a right to or interest in land that a landowner has over another person's property. Rights of way are common types of easements. Unlike the holder of a fee simple or life estate, the holder of an easement does not have the right to possess the property. Rather, the holder of an easement has a right to a specific use of the land. The holder of a right of way therefore can cross another person's land in order to reach his or her own property.

Other types of easements are the right to string wires over land, or to bury telephone cables below ground, or to let the branches of a tree on one's land overhang a neighbour's property.

Easements attach to the land. That is, once they are created, they are transferred to new owners of the property. In other words, if the Ceratos sell their farm, the new owner will be able to use the right of way to the lake.

Easements may be created by *reservation* or by *express grant*. In the **deed**, the document which transferred Mr. Cerato's land to the new owners, there was a paragraph describing the right of way and reserving its use to the Ceratos. This is an easement by reservation. An easement created by express grant is likely to be in a separate document in which one landowner gives the right to another landowner.

In some parts of Canada, easements can also be created by **prescription**. In this situation, there has been open use of an easement for twenty years without interruption, although it has never been formally created by means of a document. Easements by prescription can be created only in the eastern provinces and the parts of southern Ontario and Manitoba where the Registry Act system is used. This system will be discussed shortly.

Instead of putting the easement in the deed, the Cerato family continues to use a path to the lake that runs across Mr. and Mrs. Mung's property. The Mungs do not object to this use. After seven years, they sell the house to the Zolkowskis. Fifteen years later, the Zolkowskis argue with one of the Ceratos' daughters and decide to block the family's access to the lake.

It is too late for the Zolkowskis to take this action. The twenty years started to run when the property was sold to the Mungs. When the Zolkowskis purchased the property, only thirteen years remained before the easement by prescription became attached to the land.

Restrictive Covenants

The Ceratos are concerned that the lakefront lots which they are selling to the developer be used for residential and not commercial purposes. What can they do to ensure this?

When the land is transferred to the developer, the Ceratos can put a term in the deed restricting the use of the property to residential purposes only. Restrictive covenants limit the use of land for the benefit of nearby landowners. For instance, they may allow only certain types of buildings to be put on the land by specifying minimum floor space, or number of floors, or type of building material to be used. Restrictive covenants must be negative. In other words, they must state what *cannot* be done with land. Like easements, restrictive covenants attach to the land and bind future owners.

—Why is it important that easements and restrictive covenants attach to the land? Would future owners be bound if an easement or covenant were made by contract between the two present owners? Explain.

Protecting Interests in Land—Registration Systems

It may not be obvious who has the title to a piece of property and whether that title is of the complete fee simple type or whether others hold interest in the land. When a person is considering purchasing someone's interest in land, the purchaser will want to know what exactly the interest consists of. Does the vendor (seller) of real property have clear title, or is a mortgage outstanding? Is the property subject to easements or restrictive covenants? As well, the holder of an interest in land will want to protect it from the claims of others. For these reasons, interests in land are always registered. Registration protects both the holders of property interests and future purchasers.

There are two systems used in Canada to register interests in land: the Registry Act system and the Land Titles system.

The Registry Act System

The Registry Act system is the older of the two. It is used in Nova Scotia, Newfoundland, Prince Edward Island, New Brunswick, most of southern Ontario, and parts of Manitoba. There is usually a land registry office for each county or district, where interests in land must be registered.

A person who has an interest in land must file a document with the registry office. The person filing receives a copy on which is stamped the date of registration; the original is kept by the office. Once a document is filed, a note which briefly describes it is made in a volume called an **abstract book**. Each piece of property has its own page or pages listing all the registered documents affecting the property. The documents themselves are filed separately, however, and it is necessary to examine each of them if someone wishes to determine who has interests in the property.

The Land Titles System

This system is also known as the *Torrens system* after the Australian military officer who invented it. As in the Registry Act system, each county or district has an office where documents are registered. Under the Land Titles system, when a document is filed by a person with an interest in the land, an employee of the land titles office brings the title of the property up to date in a volume called a **register**. Unlike an abstract book, the register itself shows who the registered owner is and what other interests are presently registered against the land. Thus there is no need to examine the documents if someone wishes to find out about a piece of land; all the relevant information is contained in one location in the register.

Adverse Possession

Despite registration systems, it is possible to get title to land in a way similar to obtaining an easement by prescription. You may have heard of the phrase "squatter's rights". Squatters are people who live on land which they do not own, without the consent of the owners. This type of occupation, called **adverse possession** (that is, possession adverse to the interests of the true owners), may result in the squatters gaining the legal right to remain on the property. If squatters treat the land as their own openly and continuously for a certain period, they may extinguish or end the rights of the landowners, in their own favour. The key point is that the squatters must treat the land as their own. Thus, occupying land with the consent of the owner could not be considered adverse possession. On the other hand, paying taxes or putting up a building on land without the consent of the owner would be acts of ownership on the part of a squatter.

Provinces which allow squatter's rights have statutes that set out the limitation period for establishing title by adverse possession. For example, in Ontario the period is ten years, while in Nova Scotia it is twenty years. In general, adverse possession exists only for land under the Registry Act system.

Hall et al. v. Springall et al. (1979) 9 R.P.R. 61 (Ont. Cty. Ct.)

Lot 61 and the house on it were purchased in 1945 by the plaintiff's parents. At that time, there was a cement driveway for lot 61 abutting lot 62. To enter or exit the car from the driver's side, it was necessary to walk on lot 62. The owners of lot 62 never complained about this use of their property. In 1960, the plaintiffs, who were the current owners of lot 61, put in an asphalt driveway with the permission of their neighbours. This driveway encroached on lot 62 by 1.1 feet (about 0.35 m) at the street and 1.9 feet (about 0.6 m) at the rear of the lot.

In 1961, lot 62 was sold. The new owners never complained about the encroachment or the fact that part of lot 62 was used when people entered or exited from the driver's side of the car.

In 1973, the defendants became the owners of lot 62. They demanded that the plaintiffs remove part of the driveway encroaching on their property. In 1975 and 1976, the defendants wrote to the plaintiffs reminding them of the encroachment and stating that they did not intend to lose the property by adverse possession. Finally, in 1978, the defendants erected a fence approximately 1 foot (0.3 m) south of the lot line, cutting off part of the driveway. The plaintiffs sued for a declaration of adverse possession or, alternatively, for acknowledgement of an easement.

—Should the plaintiffs be claiming title by adverse possession, an easement, or both? Explain your answer.
—When did the time start running for an easement? for adverse possession?
—Who should win this case, in your opinion?

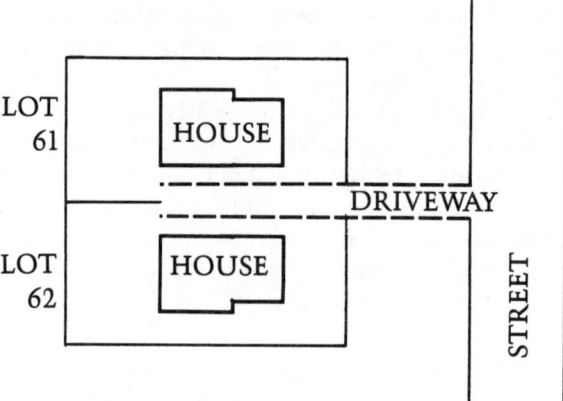

Figure 21-3

Restrictions on the Use of Property

The tort of nuisance in connection with the use of land was discussed in Chapter 10 of this text. You will recall that landowners who foul the air with noxious odours or disturb their neighbours' peace with unreasonable noises can be sued. The common law restricts the use of property in other ways as well. For instance, adjoining property owners are entitled to have their land supported by each other's land.

Figure 21-4 Property owners have the right to the support of the adjoining land.

A landowner whose property has water, such as a river or stream, running through it has the right to reasonable use of the water. However, if the water is navigable, the public has the right to travel on it. Also, every downstream owner of land has a corresponding right to the water in its unaltered state as regards both volume and quality. The upstream landowner's use of the water is therefore restricted to uses which do not interfere with the downstream owners' rights. The upstream owner cannot build a dam, for instance.

Zoning

Today, perhaps the greatest restriction on the use of land consists of the many municipal zoning by-laws and other forms of legislation which control the use of property to protect the rights of landowners. Property may be zoned for industrial, commercial, or residential use. Building codes will set out the standards that must be maintained when a building is being erected. Every homeowner should know that building permits must be obtained before structural changes are made to a house.

Provincial legislation such as Ontario's *Planning Act* controls the development of subdivisions. The *Act* states that a plan of subdivision must be approved by the Ministry of Housing, which will consult with the concerned municipality before building can be undertaken. Typically, subdivision plans will require the developer to provide services such as streets and sewers. The developer may also be required to donate a certain percentage of the land to the public to be used as parkland.

—Why do you think there is so much land-use control? Do you think it is necessary?
—Check the zoning by-laws in the area where you live. What restrictions do they impose?

The ultimate limitation on the rights of property owners to the use of their land is the federal and provincial governments' right to **expropriation** of property. All provinces and the federal government have legislation which allows them to take property without the owner's consent. This property is then generally used for a public purpose such as the construction of roads or a public building like a school. When property is expropriated, the statutes provide that the owners are entitled to compensation for their property.

—Check your province's *Expropriation Act*. What can you do if you object to your property being expropriated? To what kind of compensation are you entitled?

Transferring Title to Land

There are several ways in which a landowner can give property to someone else. It is possible to make a gift of land, or to transfer land in a will. If a landowner dies intestate, the land will be transferred to his or her spouse or family, as set out in statute law. If the deceased is a joint tenant, the land will go automatically to the other joint tenant(s). However, the most common way of transferring an interest in land is by sale.

After Francine and Jim had been married several years, they had saved enough money to purchase their first home. Franco and Adelia were ready to retire and put up their house for sale. Francine and Jim saw the house and decided it was the one they wanted.

Scenes similar to this one are repeated thousands of times every year in Canada. Because transactions involving real property are very important to most people and are sometimes complex, the services of a lawyer are usually obtained. However, it is useful for everyone to be generally familiar with the stages in the purchase and sale of a house. The steps involved are as follows:

1. entering the listing agreement
2. making the offer to purchase
3. arranging financing
4. searching the title
5. closing the transaction

The Listing Agreement

Franco and Adelia Eremef may try to sell their house themselves. However, if they are like most people, they will enter a contract with a real estate agent to sell the house for them. Such a contract is known as a **listing agreement**. The agreement will name a price and the terms of the sale and will have an expiry date. It will also set out the **commission** (fee) to which the real estate agent is entitled as payment for selling the house.

A listing agreement can be either *exclusive* or a *multiple listing*. If it is exclusive, only the agent who enters the agreement can offer the house for sale. In a multiple listing, any member of the local real estate board can try to sell the house. Multiple listings usually involve a higher commission for the agent who sells the house.

The Offer to Purchase

When Francine and Jim decide that they would like to buy the Eremefs' house, they will draft an **offer to purchase**, also known as an *Agreement of Purchase and Sale*. The real estate agent who is selling the house may assist them in drafting this document, or Francine and Jim could have their lawyer do it for them. Recall from your earlier study of contracts that the *Statute of Frauds* requires contracts concerning land to be in writing. It is not possible to make a valid verbal offer to purchase or sell land.

The offer to purchase names the price which the purchasers are willing to pay for the property. This price may or may not be the listing price. The offer also includes any representations made by the *vendor* (seller). For example, if the house has a basement apartment, there may be a representation that the apartment can be rented legally without violating any municipal by-law. If the Eremefs are offering to sell their appliances with the house, this too will be indicated in the offer to purchase. On the other hand, if there is some fixture that the vendors do not want sold with the house, the offer must say so.

It is not always easy to tell whether or not something is a fixture. Built-in shelving, bathroom cabinets, and chandeliers are all types of fixtures. But what about hanging mirrors, smoke alarms, and portable backyard sheds? If the parties cannot agree and the dispute goes to court, a judge will consider the degree to which the object is annexed (attached) to the house, and whether it is annexed for the benefit of the house. For example, if a dining room mirror has been attached to the wall in such a way that to remove it would damage the wall, it is likely that a court would consider it a fixture.

Franco and Adelia have a treasured antique chandelier hanging in their dining room. They do not wish to sell it with the house and have informed their real estate agent of this. The listing agreement specifically states that the house does not include the chandelier. When Francine and Jim are drawing up the offer to purchase, a term excluding the chandelier from the sale will be included.

The offer also contains a description of the property. Usually a street address and the dimensions of the lot are given. Rights of way and other easements must also be described in the offer.

If the purchasers have a house that they are trying to sell, they may make their offer conditional upon the sale of their own house. In other words, if the purchasers' house is not sold within a certain period of time, their offer to purchase is cancelled. This type of offer is called a **conditional offer**: it is not firm until a certain condition is fulfilled. Usually there will be a time limit within which the condition must be met. If it is not met, then the offer is cancelled.

There are other types of conditions which a purchaser may put in an offer. For instance, if someone is buying a house with plans to renovate it, the offer could be made conditional upon obtaining a building permit. Or an offer to purchase an older house could be conditional upon a building inspection which certifies that the house does not have any major structural faults. A vendor would, of course, prefer an unconditional offer, since there is always the chance that some condition will not be fulfilled and the sale will not go ahead.

Jim and Francine, with the assistance of the real estate agent, prepare their offer, which is for a few thousand dollars less than the Eremefs' asking price. A deposit is put down with the offer. The offer gives the Eremefs forty-eight hours to accept. After that time, the offer lapses.

If the Eremefs accept by signing the offer, a binding contract is created between the parties. The contract will state how many days there are until the deal closes; that is, how many days before the actual ownership of the house is transferred. In this example the transaction is to close in thirty days. This gives Francine and Jim time to arrange financing and to search the title of the property.

Arranging Financing

One of the most important terms of the offer concerns the method of payment. Jim and Francine plan to use their savings, about $10 000, as a down payment on the house. The rest of the purchase price will have to be borrowed. Few people pay cash for their homes; most need some assistance in financing the purchase of a house, which usually involves obtaining a **mortgage**. There are several methods of doing this.

The purchasers may offer to *assume* (take over) the vendor's mortgage, making up the balance of the purchase price in cash or by obtaining a second mortgage on the property. Alternatively, the vendor may agree to *take back* a mortgage. That is, the vendor loans a certain percentage of the purchase price to the purchasers in the form of a mortgage. If the mortgage is to be obtained from a bank or other financial institution, the offer may be conditional upon the purchaser being able to get a mortgage. It could happen that, because of the condition of the house or the purchaser's financial circumstances, the financial institution might refuse to take the risk of granting a mortgage. In a situation like this, the purchasers would want to be released from the offer since they could not afford the purchase. Thus, placing this condition in an offer is very important.

What exactly is a mortgage? Very simply, a mortgage is a loan given by a **mortgagee** to a **mortgagor** for the purchase of real property. In legal terms, it is more complicated than this. Under the registry system, it is the mortgagee that obtains legal title to the property, as security for the loan. The mortgagor has the right to possession and use of the property, and the right to *equitable title*, that is, the right to obtain the legal title once the loan is paid off. Under the Land Titles system, legal title does not pass to the mortgagee, but a **charge**, or interest, in the mortgagee's name is registered against the property until the loan is paid off.

It is possible to have more than one mortgage. In fact, second mortgages are quite common. If the purchasers still do not have enough money to purchase the house after obtaining a first mortgage, they apply for a second mortgage. The main difference is that a second mortgage loan will cost the purchasers more than the first; that is, the interest charged on the loan will be higher.

If the purchasers fail to make their mortgage payments, the mortgagees have a right to sell the house or take other action to get their money. If this happens, the first mortgagee will be paid off first.

Another way of financing the purchase of a house is by entering an agreement of sale or installment agreement with the vendor. Such agreements are more common in the western provinces than in the east. The purchasers may make payments to the vendor that are similar to rent. When a certain amount of the total price has been paid, the purchaser receives title to the property.

Cost of Financing

Figure 21-5 Certain banks and credit unions are now permitting home owners to pay off their mortgages more quickly through prepayments.

Although mortgages are commonly given for five-year terms or less, payments are usually *amortized* over twenty- or twenty-five-year periods. In other words, monthly payments of principal and interest are based on a twenty- or twenty-five-year schedule. At the end of each term of the mortgage, most people renew the mortgage for a further term, although it is possible to pay it off completely. Few people realize just how much money in interest charges a mortgage costs over twenty to twenty-five years. For example, a $50 000 mortgage at twelve percent interest would cost $216 200 over twenty years of payments of $540.50 a month. Prepayment schemes such as the one described in the following article are a means whereby mortgagors can save large amounts of money.

B of M allows faster mortgage repayment

By MARTIN MITTELSTAEDT

In a bid to win new mortgage business, the Bank of Montreal is allowing home owners to increase their monthly payments, an action that could cut years from the life of these loans and reduce by thousands of dollars the amount paid in interest.

The change, the first of its type in the banking industry, is sure to increase the already fierce competition for mortgages in Canada and cause other lenders to publicize the advantages of their early payment schemes.

"We've done some market research and consumers tell us they want more flexibility in their mortgage arrangements and they want to become debt-free faster," said Thomas Alton, president of the bank's mortgage subsidiary.

Under terms of the new plan, home owners can raise monthly payments by up to 10 per cent once a year for a fee of $25. If the higher rate becomes too difficult, they can go back to the previous level for another $25 charge.

This change is being combined with a plan the bank introduced last year, which allows extra payments of up to 10 per cent against the original value of a loan once a year without a penalty.

Although principal prepayment schemes are common, Mr. Alton said the right to raise the amount paid monthly is a first. "Nobody in Canada that I'm aware of allows this," he said in a telephone interview.

Most financial institutions let home owners make a prepayment once a year on the anniversary date of the loan. Some still levy a charge for this privilege, however.

Other mortgage lenders and bankers were not impressed by the changes announced yesterday because different early payment options at other institutions also have the effect of shortening payback periods.

"I can't get terribly excited about this one," said one rival banker, who also said the biggest difference in the Bank of Montreal scheme is that it allows increased payments at any time during the year, rather than just the renewal date of the loan.

When borrowers start taking advantage of Bank of Montreal changes, Mr. Alton said he expects a higher rate of mortgage repayments, but the volume of new business will more than compensate for any declines in its loan totals.

Using a typical $50,000 mortgage paid over 25 years (interest of 12 per cent and monthly payments $516), the savings for home owners could be enormous under the scheme, according to bank figures.

For example, if monthly payments are increased 10 per cent a year, the maximum allowed, the mortgage would be paid off in just less than 9½ years, saving $65,300 in interest. With payments up 5 per cent a year, the mortgage's life would be 12¼ years and the savings $53,791.

And if a 10 per cent prepayment on the principal was made at the end of the first year, the loan would be paid off in 17 years, with interest savings of $44,741.

Searching the Title

After the offer has been accepted, the purchaser, or more usually, the purchaser's lawyer will *search the title* to the property. A title search involves going to the registry office or land titles office where the documents affecting the property are registered to check the vendor's title to the land.

—**Imagine what would happen if you decided to buy a house and then, after paying the purchase price, discovered that the person you had been dealing with was a tenant and not the owner.**

By searching the title, the purchaser can find out who the legal, or registered, owner of the land is, and what interests such as easements, restrictive covenants, or liens exist against the land. One type of lien the purchaser or the lawyer will look for is called a **mechanic's lien**.

Shortly before the Eremefs put their house up for sale, they discovered a leak in their attic. They were told by a contractor that they needed a new roof. They entered an agreement with the contractor to replace the roof.
   In the middle of the job, the contractor went bankrupt while owing back wages to the three workers who had been shingling the roof.

Every province has a *Mechanic's Lien Act* to protect those people who provide goods or services for the improvement of real property. In the Eremefs' case, both the contractor and the workers have a right to a lien against the Eremefs' property if they are unpaid. To protect workers against contractors who go bankrupt or otherwise refuse to pay them, the legislation provides that the party receiving the goods or services must hold back a certain percentage, usually between fifteen and twenty percent, of the money due to the contractor. The money is held back for a certain period after the job is finished. For instance, in Ontario the hold-back period is thirty-seven days, while in British Columbia it is thirty-one days, and in Nova Scotia, forty-five days. If no lien is registered by this time, the money can be released, since the right to register a lien ceases to exist.

The contract the Eremefs entered with the contractor stated that the cost of the work would be $7000, half to be paid when work commenced and half when the work was completed. To protect themselves from mechanic's liens, the Eremefs held back fifteen percent, or $525 of the first payment of $3500. When they learned that the contractor was bankrupt, they paid this money into court. The court then supervised distribution of the $525 to the workers. If the Eremefs had not held back the $525, the workers could have had a lien against their property. If the Eremefs did not then pay the lienholders the amount of the *hold-back*, they could be sued and their property could be sold to satisfy the claim.

Searching under the Registry Act and Land Titles Systems

Searching the title under the Registry Act system is often a long and complex task. Using the notes in the abstract book, it is possible to trace back all previous owners of the property to the original Crown grant. It is not usually necessary to go back that far, however. Provincial statutes provide that it is only necessary to search back over a certain period, usually forty years, to establish the state of the title. Any interest which is not re-registered within that time is considered to be extinguished.

A purchaser or lawyer searching the title at the registry office first examines the abstract book and makes a list of all the documents affecting the property. Then the lawyer asks to see the documents, and examines them to find out how or whether any of them affects the vendor's title. Each deed for the past forty years is examined to ascertain whether any easements were given. The description of the property is checked to make sure that the present owner has the right to sell what is being offered for sale. These are only two examples of the many things to check for.

Searching title under the Land Titles system is much less complex. Because the title to land is updated each time a new document is registered, the purchaser's lawyer need only find the page in the register that describes the property being searched. The register shows who the registered owner is, and what interests, if any, are presently registered against the land. In this system, the government guarantees that the information in the register is correct. Therefore, if a mistake is made, the government will be liable for any losses.

Objections to Title

If the lawyer for the purchaser finds no problems with the title, the deal can proceed to closing. If there *are* objections to the title, the vendor's lawyer is notified, and is expected to clear the title before the closing can proceed. For instance, a new survey of the property may be required to determine exactly where the lot lines are. If the property is much different from that described in the offer, the price may be adjusted. If there is a substantial difference between the property described by the vendor and the actual property, the purchaser may be entitled to rescind the offer.

The lawyer's work is not complete after the visit to the registry or land titles office. The lawyer also has to go to the local tax office to make sure that all taxes owing have been paid, and to the sheriff's office to ensure that there are no **executions** against the property. An execution can be registered against the property of a person who has not paid the damages owing to the successful plaintiff in a civil action. The execution prevents the person from mortgaging or selling the property.

Closing the Transaction

Francine and Jim were able to obtain a mortgage from their local credit union. A search of the title by their lawyer did not turn up any problems. On the day that the sale is to be closed, their lawyer will make a last-minute check to see whether any new interests have been registered against the property, and will meet the Eremefs' lawyer at the land titles or registry office to close the transaction.

Usually, the lawyer for the vendors prepares the deed. Then the lawyers for both the vendors and the purchasers meet at the land titles or registry office to complete the transaction and register the deed immediately.

—Why is it so important to register the deed as soon as possible?

Figure 21-6 A Statement of Adjustments

Statement of Adjustments as of November 30, 1985 Bertrand sale to Cochrane 139 Waverly Road, Calgary		
Sale Price		$60 000.00
Deposit	$2 000.00	
Insurance: Purchaser to arrange own insurance		
Utilities: Meter to be read on closing—no adjustment		
Municipal Taxes for 1985 are: $560.59 paid up to December 31, 1985. Vendor's portion $512.98		
Credit Vendor:		47.61
Fuel Oil: 800 L		139.40
Balance due on closing by certified cheque payable to Messrs. Jenson & Devlin as per direction	58 187.01	
	$60 187.01	$60 187.01
E. & O. E.		

At the closing, among the documents the lawyer for the purchasers receives are the deed and a **statement of adjustments**. The statement of adjustments shows exactly how much is owing to the vendor, including such things as payment for heating oil in the oil tank (if any), and prepaid insurance or property taxes. In exchange for a certified cheque for the balance owing to the vendor, the purchasers' lawyer receives the keys to the house on behalf of the new property owners.

SUMMARIZING YOUR READING

1. Name the two types of property. Explain the difference between them.

2. What does a landowner own besides the surface of the land?

3. Give an example of dividing land horizontally.

4. Give three examples of fixtures.

5. Does anyone really own land in Canada? Explain.

6. What does it mean to say that a person has title to land?

7. Define the following terms: fee simple estate; life estate; easement; restrictive covenant.

8. What are the two types of concurrent ownership? What is the main difference between them?

9. What are the two methods used for registering interests in land? Discuss the differences between the two.

10. Explain how a person can get title to land by adverse possession. Does it matter whether the land is under the Registry Act or the Land Titles system?

11. Explain the rights of a landowner whose property has water running through it.

12. What kind of restrictions are there on land use today?

13. What is expropriation?

14. What are some of the ways to transfer land to someone else? What is the most common way?

15. What is a listing agreement? What is the difference between a multiple listing and an exclusive listing?

16. What is an offer to purchase? What terms will an offer contain? What usually accompanies an offer?

17. How can one determine whether an object is a fixture?

18. Define the following terms: mortgagee; mortgagor; mortgage.

19. What is the purpose of searching the title to property?

20. What may happen if an owner does not register an interest held against land?

21. What types of interests may be registered against the title to property? What is a mechanic's lien?

22. Where else should the purchaser look to check the title to property besides the registry office and the land titles office?

PROJECTS AND ACTIVITIES

1. Contact a real estate agent. Obtain a copy of a listing agreement and an offer to purchase. Make a list of the terms used in these documents. With the assistance of the agent, where required, define the terms.

2. Some provinces have New Home Warranty Plans. If any defects turn up in a new house within a certain period, the builder guarantees to repair the defect. If for some reason the builder does not honour the guarantee, the homeowner can collect from a government fund into which the builder must pay. Find out whether your province has such a plan by contacting the ministry responsible for housing. What protection does the plan provide for the owner of a new house? If your province does not have such a plan at this time, is one being considered for the future?

3. Property rights have not been entrenched in the *Charter of Rights and Freedoms*. Prepare a research paper on the movement to entrench these important rights.

4. Go to the land titles or registry office closest to your school. Try to find out the history of the property on which your school is built. What was there before the school? Who were the previous owners of the land? When was the Crown grant made? Report your findings to the class.

CASE DISCUSSION

Mastermet Cobalt Mines Ltd. v. Canadaka Mines Ltd. (1978) 5 R.P.R. 169 (Ont. C.A.)

In 1936, the owner of 104 acres of mining lands severed the ownership of the surface from the ownership of the mining rights. The issue in this case was whether it was the plaintiff (appellant) owners of the surface rights or the defendant (respondent) leasers of the mining rights that owned the tailings found on the property. ("Tailings" is the term used to refer to a powdered residue from the processing of silver ore.)

The tailings had been deposited on the surface of the land for many years and eventually formed a new surface to a depth of 5.9 feet (about 1.8 m). Until recently, they had been considered waste material. However, new technology and the high price of silver made it economically feasible to process the tailings to recover the silver they contained.

The judges hearing the case considered the *Mining Act*, which gives the following definitions:

> 16. The verb "mine" and the word "mining"...include any mode or method of working whereby the earth or any rock, stratum, stone or mineral-bearing substance may be disturbed, removed, washed, sifted, leached, roasted...or dealt with for the purpose of obtaining any mineral therefrom, whether it has been previously disturbed or not...
> 19. "Mining rights" means the ores, mines and minerals on or under any land where they are or have been dealt with separately from the surface...
> 27. "Surface rights" means every right in land other than the mining rights.

—Who should win this case, in your opinion? Explain your answer in detail.

Arbitus Park Estates Ltd. v. Fuller et al. (1976) 2 R.P.R. 126 (B.C. S.C.)

The defendants, a retired couple, purchased a lot upon which to build a home. Unknown to them, the lot was subject to a registered building scheme. A building scheme exists where several pieces of land, usually a subdivision, are all mutually subject to restrictive covenants. In this case, the restrictive covenant read as follows:

> ...The Purchaser/Grantee hereby covenants and agrees with respect to lots one (1) to one hundred and seventy-five (175) inclusive that no construction or erection or installation of a dwelling, detached garage, boathouse, mobile home or commercial building shall commence on any lot until the plans and specifications for such construction or erection have been approved in writing by the Vendor/Grantor.

By the time the defendants discovered that plans had to be approved by the directors of Arbitus Estates, their house and detached garage were about three-quarters finished. However, they did attempt to seek the approval of Arbitus. The house plans were approved, but not the plans for the garage. Although they knew their garage plans had not been approved, the defendants finished building it.

The plaintiffs then applied to the court for a mandatory injunction, which would order the defendants to tear down the garage.

In reaching its decision, the court considered that the defendants had spent $10 000 on the garage, and that they had brought the building to the attention of the plaintiffs. The only objection to the building given in court was that it was too close to the side lot line. The covenant was registered, so the defendants were deemed to have had notice of it.

—Do you think the court should grant the mandatory injunction?
—Would damages be a fairer remedy, in your opinion?

Kragh-Hansen et al. v. Kin-Com Construction and Developments Ltd. et al. (1979) 13 R.P.R. 22 (B.C. S.C.)

The plaintiffs, Kragh-Hansen, brought an action against the defendants for misrepresentation. The plaintiffs had purchased an apartment building which was being used as a four-plex by Kin-Com Construction, which had also built it. The real estate agent who had assisted at the sale, James Woods, was also a defendant.

The offer of purchase stated that two of the apartments were illegal, but the plaintiffs were assured orally by Woods that it would be a simple matter to get a licence for the apartments from the municipality. Woods was given this information by Mocnik, the head of Kin-Com.

After the deal was closed, Kragh-Hansen learned that they would be unable to get a licence, and were ordered by the municipality to cease using the units as dwellings.

—Do you think the plaintiffs succeeded in their action? Explain your answer.
—If the plaintiffs did succeed, how do you think the court determined their damages?

Leading Investments Ltd. v. New Forest Investments (1981) 20 R.P.R. 6 (Ont. C.A.)

The appellant, Leading Investments, entered a standard form listing agreement with the respondent, New Forest, to sell a piece of property. The agreement included the following terms:

"I agree to pay a commission of 5% of the sale price on any sale or exchange howsoever effected during the currency of this authority. It is understood and agreed that the said commission is to be paid on the date set for completion of the sale, if the said listing Broker or his sub-agents procure a valid offer on the terms and conditions set out in this listing agreement or on such other terms and conditions as I may accept..."

Liebig, on behalf of the respondent, presented Miller, on behalf of the appellant, with an offer to purchase which contained the following terms:

I agree to pay the Agent a commission of 5% of the sale price for having procured this Offer, said commission to be deducted from the deposit [paid by the purchaser] on the date set for completion of sale and I irrevocably instruct my Solicitor to pay direct to the said Agent, any unpaid balance of commission from the proceeds of the sale...

Miller apparently did not understand the meaning of these terms, and signed the offer without legal advice. The transaction did not close because the purchaser was not able to complete the deal. The respondent then refused to give back the deposit which the purchaser had forfeited to the appellant. The appellant sued for the deposit plus interest, while the respondent counterclaimed for its commission plus interest.

The trial judge ruled that where there was a conflict, the terms of the offer to purchase superseded the listing agreement. The judge held that the respondent was entitled to the commission. The vendors appealed this decision.

— Which document do you think best represented the terms of the parties' agreement? Is it logical that the appellant would change the terms to its disadvantage?
— Should the reasonable expectations of the parties about the agreement make any difference? What do you think the common practice among real estate agents and vendors is for paying the commission? Should the court consider this?

22

Landlord and Tenant Law

> Lease and Tenancy
> Residential *versus* Commercial Tenants
> The Sources of Landlord-Tenant Law
> The Rights and Responsibilities of Residential Landlords and Tenants
> Terminating the Lease
> Rent Review Law and Rent Control

Are you planing to move away from home at some time, perhaps after finishing school? Are you wealthy enough to buy your own home right away? If the answer to the first question is "Yes", and the answer to the second question is "No", you will need to know about the legal rights and responsibilities of landlords and tenants.

The rules governing the relationship between landlords and tenants are among the oldest elements of any legal system, because shelter is a necessity of life. In most social systems, some people have owned land, while other people have paid to live or work on it.

You have seen that in Canada, jurisdiction over the law that affects property is provincial. All the provinces have passed landlord and tenant legislation. While the legislation is not the same in every respect, certain similarities are evident in the laws of all provinces.

This chapter will examine the general rules of landlord and tenant law, with occasional references to differences between various provincial laws.

Lease and Tenancy

A *landlord* is a person who has agreed to let someone else, the *tenant*, occupy all or part of a piece of the landlord's property. A landlord has legal rights and responsibilities because of his or her position as landlord. In some situations, a person who does not own the premises, such as a property manager, may have the legal rights and responsibilities of a landlord.

The landlord-tenant relationship is created by agreement. The landlord agrees to allow the tenant to occupy all or part of the property. The tenant agrees to occupy the property, and usually agrees to pay *rent* in some form. A contract called a *lease* is thus created between the landlord and the tenant. The lease may be oral or written. However, remember that the *Statute of Frauds* in each province applies to these contracts. So, in Ontario, for example, any lease for more than three years must be in writing to comply with the *Statute of Frauds*.

There are three main points that must be agreed upon if a landlord-tenant relationship is to be created. These elements of the agreement make the agreement a valid lease. They constitute the difference between becoming a tenant and being invited as a guest.

Figure 22-1 Two Valid Ways of Entering a Lease

Definition of the Premises

First, it must be reasonably clear just what is being rented. Is it a room? the first floor of a house? a whole house? an apartment? If the latter, then which apartment? If either the tenant or the landlord is not sure whether a certain part of the premises is included, he or she may apply to court for a decision, but there must be a general agreement about the premises. For example, if Wei Lan agrees to rent an upper duplex, but is not sure whether the outside stairs are for her use only, the agreement is still clear enough to create a landlord-tenant relationship. She may have to go to court, though, to find out whether she has exclusive use of the stairs.

Rent

A definite rent must be agreed upon, if rent is expected. A landlord does not have to charge rent to create a landlord-tenant relationship, but, if rent is charged, it must be clear what it is to be. Rent is usually paid in money, but it may also be in other forms, such as work. Apartment caretakers and superintendents often pay their rent in work.

Exclusive Possession

The landlord must agree in the lease to give the tenant exclusive possession of the rented premises. Not even the landlord can enter the premises unless the tenant consents, or unless special conditions apply, as in an emergency.

Residential *versus* Commercial Tenants

A person who rents a home is known as a residential tenant. Someone who rents a place to work—a studio, a shop, an office—is a commercial tenant. In both of these types of tenancies, all three elements of a valid lease must be present: definite premises, a definite rent, and exclusive possession for the tenant. However, there are some important differences between the rights of commercial and residential tenants.

To put it simply, in most provinces, commercial tenants have fewer guaranteed rights than residential tenants. This situation exists because residential tenants often have rights written into the law that apply regardless of the agreement between landlord and tenant. For commercial tenants, on the other hand, all conditions must be in the lease. Common law and statute law grant very few rights to commercial tenants. It is therefore very important for a commercial tenant to try to arrange a favourable lease, because the lease is the major source of that tenant's rights.

Since most of the rights of commercial tenants are to be found in the individual leases, and the terms of the leases vary according to what the commercial landlord and tenant agree to, the rest of this chapter will concentrate on residential tenancies.

—Why do you think the law gives residential tenants more protection than commercial tenants?

The Sources of Landlord-Tenant Law

There are three sources of tenants' rights and responsibilities: the common law (except in Québec), statute law, and tenants' written or oral leases.

Common Law

Certain common law rules affect landlords and tenants. These rules apply unless they have been replaced by legislation or, in some cases, unless the parties have agreed by contract (the lease) that they will not apply.

Statute Law

As mentioned above, legislation may replace common law rules. For example, at common law there was no limit on the amount of money that a landlord could require as a security deposit. This sum could be used to cover any damage the residential tenant might do, or to cover unpaid rent. However, various provinces have legislation that limits the landlord in a residential tenancy to a maximum of one month's rent as a security deposit.

While a landlord and tenant can often replace common law rules with terms in a lease, this is usually not possible with statute law. For instance, no matter what the lease may say, an Ontario residential tenant does not have to pay more than one month's rent as a security deposit, because the right not to pay more is guaranteed by statute.

Leases

You have just learned that agreements in a lease can replace the common law, but usually cannot replace statute law. The following illustrates the way in which the lease, statute law, and common law apply to a landlord-tenant problem.

Melina Sklavos was looking for an apartment. She found a one-bedroom flat at a price she could afford, but she commented to the landlord that it looked pretty shabby, since the paint was peeling off most of the walls and there were some deep scratches on the floor. The landlord said, "Oh, don't worry about that—I will paint all the walls and repolish the floors before you move in." Melina said that, on that condition, she would like to rent the place. She asked whether she should sign a lease, but the landlord said "I don't use leases—just leave your deposit. I'll give you a receipt, and the place is yours on the first of May."

On the first of May, Melina moved in. She found that the promised painting and polishing had not been done. Furthermore, the stove did not work, the toilet was broken, and there was a hole in the bathtub.

—**What can Melina do?**

At common law, Melina would have had no recourse—there was no common law rule saying that a landlord had to provide a place that was fit to live in. But remember that both a lease and legislation can alter the common law.

Figure 22-2 Leases and legislation both make it necessary for landlords to provide premises that are fit to live in.

Melina's agreement with the landlord did not mention the really serious problems with the apartment, since she did not know about them. However, almost all provinces in Canada have statutes establishing the basic minimum standards which must be met for residential premises to be considered fit to live in. The landlord must obey these standards, and have the stove, toilet, and bathtub repaired. In addition, Melina's oral lease contained a condition about painting and floor polishing. Although this goes beyond the minimum standards, Melina can force her landlord to make these more minor repairs as well. She can apply to court for an order requiring her landlord to get the appliances and fixtures repaired, and she can sue for breach of her oral lease.

The Rights and Responsibilities of Residential Landlords and Tenants

There are certain general rights and responsibilities that residential landlords and tenants have everywhere in Canada. If these rights are denied or these responsibilities ignored, the injured party has the right to go to court for help. The court may award damages for loss of money, order the landlord or tenant to carry out his or her duties, lower the rent, declare that a tenant may "break" the lease, or order the tenant to give up the premises to the landlord. This last remedy is called an **order for possession**, more commonly referred to as **eviction**. The court's order will depend on the type and seriousness of the problem.

The following sections discuss the major rights and responsibilities of landlords and tenants. Though details vary by provinces, the general rules are similar, as we have said. These rules usually apply regardless of what the lease may say.

Freedom from Discrimination

All provinces have human rights laws that forbid landlords to discriminate in choosing tenants or in the terms of the tenancy. These rights were described in detail in Chapter 9. The following case illustrates this form of legislative protection:

Gurman v. Greenleaf Meadows Investment Ltd. (1982) 3 C.H.R.R. D/808 (Board of Inquiry under Manitoba Human Rights Act)

Two sisters and their brother, all in their twenties, decided to share an apartment. They answered an ad and went to see the superintendent, Adams. Susan Gurman introduced herself and said, "This is my sister and brother, Jennifer and Kenneth." Adams said, "I'm sorry, we don't rent to single people." Susan replied, "We're all working." However, Adams continued to refuse. Susan said "That doesn't make sense." Adams then asked Jennifer, "Are you and Kenneth married?"

—Why do you think Adams did not want to rent the apartment to the Gurmans?
—The Manitoba *Human Rights Act*, section 4, states:

> 4. (1) No person, directly or indirectly, alone or with another, by himself or by the interposition of another, shall
>   (a) deny to any person or any member of his family, the right to occupancy of any commercial unit or any housing accommodation; or
>   (b) discriminate against any person or any member of his family with respect to any term or condition of occupancy of any commercial unit or housing accommodation, unless reasonable cause exists for the denial discrimination.
> (2) For the purpose of subsection (1), the race, nationality, religion, colour, sex, age, marital status, physical or mental handicap, family status, ethnic or national origin, or the source of income of a person does not constitute reasonable cause.

—Based on s.4, was Adams' refusal reasonable?
—What would you decide if you were the judge in this case? What remedy would you grant?

Payment of Rent

Rent must be paid in full and on time. The general rule is that the tenant is responsible for getting the rent to the landlord, but this rule can be altered by agreement or by practice. For example, the landlord may regularly arrive to collect the rent.

Under the common law, if a tenant failed to pay the rent, a landlord was allowed to take and sell enough of the tenant's belongings to pay the rent. This was called the landlord's right to **distrain**. Almost all provinces now have legislation saying that a residential landlord cannot distrain, although the landlord in a commercial tenancy can still do so.

The statutory provision that ends distraint for residential tenancies in Ontario is in Part 4 of the *Landlord and Tenant Act*, which deals with residential tenancies. Section 86(1) states:

> **86. (1) No landlord shall distrain for default in the payment of rent whether a right of distress has heretofore existed by statute, the common law or contract.**

—Why do you think a landlord may distrain the property of a commercial tenant, but not that of a residential tenant?

Cottam v. Smith [1947] O.W.N. 880 (Ont. C.A.)

Smith had been a tenant in the same place for ten years. Her rent was due on the first of the month, but for years Smith paid at any time during the first part of the month, and the landlord took no action. After ten years, a new landlord bought the premises. This landlord came to the premises to collect the rent any time between the first and fifteenth of each month. Smith offered to deliver the rent to the landlord, but the landlord left the arrangement as it was.

After three years of this arrangement, the landlord suddenly sued for eviction when the rent had not been paid by the sixteenth of the month. The landlord claimed that the rent was fifteen days late.

—Is it the tenant's responsibility to deliver the rent cheque, ordinarily?
—Was it Smith's responsibility in this case? Explain.

Security Deposits

You have seen that the landlord of residential premises is allowed to collect a security deposit at the beginning of a tenancy. In Ontario, the security deposit may only be used by the landlord against the last month's rent; it is "security" that the last month's rent will be paid. In other provinces, such as Alberta, the security deposit may be applied to pay for repairing any damage caused by the tenant, as well as to unpaid rent. Most provinces require the landlord to give notice to the tenant if he or she wants to keep the security deposit or any part of it for any reason. If the tenant does not consent to the landlord's keeping the money, both may go to court or to a tribunal that deals with landlord-tenant problems to settle the issue. The court or tribunal can make an order about how the money is to be used, or order the landlord to refund all or part of it.

Most provinces impose a limit on how much money a landlord may require as a security deposit. In Ontario and Alberta, it is up to one month's rent. In most other provinces it is much less. For example, in Nova Scotia the limit is half of one month's rent. In all provinces, the landlord must pay the tenant interest on the deposit. In provinces other than Ontario, if the landlord is not going to try to keep any part of the security deposit, it must be returned to the tenant within a certain time, usually ten or fifteen days after the tenant vacates the premises. In Ontario, the security deposit is simply applied to the last month's rent. If the rent has gone up since the tenancy started, the tenant must send the landlord enough money to make up the difference.

When Angelina moved into her Calgary apartment three years ago, her landlord asked for a security deposit. After two years and nine months in her apartment, Angelina gave her landlord notice that she intended to leave at the end of the year. When she left, she expected to receive her security deposit, but her landlord told her that he was keeping it to repaint the apartment to repair the damage she had caused. Since Angelina lived in Alberta, the landlord had a right to use all or part of the security deposit for repairs, but Angelina felt that she had done no damage to the apartment. She applied to court to get her security deposit back.

Alberta's *Landlord and Tenant Act* has this to say about Angelina's situation:

> 39. (2) If a landlord fails to return all or part of a security deposit to a tenant in accordance with subsection (1), then, whether or not a statement of account was delivered to the tenant, the tenant may commence an action in court to recover the whole of the deposit or that part of the deposit to which the tenant claims to be entitled.
>
> (3) In proceedings taken under subsection (2), the court
> (a) shall determine the amounts, if any, that the landlord is entitled to deduct from the security deposit in accordance with the conditions agreed to by the tenant, and
> (b) if the deductions so determined are less than the amount of the deposit, shall give judgement in favour of the tenant for the balance.
>
> (4) No deduction may be made from a tenant's security deposit for normal wear and tear to residential premises during the period of his tenancy.

—When Angelina applied to the court for a return of her security deposit, what did the court have to consider?

Winston lives in Sarnia, Ontario. His landlord asked for one month's rent as a security deposit when he moved into the apartment. When Winston wanted to leave, he gave his landlord three months' notice. When the final month came around, he sent his landlord a cheque for the difference between his security deposit and his present rent. That cheque plus the security deposit took care of the last month's rent. However, when Winston moved, his landlord claimed that Winston had damaged the apartment. The landlord would have to sue Winston in Small Claims Court if Winston did not agree that he caused damage.

—Compare Angelina's case with Winston's. Who has to sue in each?
—If your landlord accused you of damaging your apartment, would you rather be governed by Ontario law or Alberta law? Why?
—Can a residential landlord in your province demand a security deposit? If so, how much can it be? Can the landlord keep the security deposit to apply to the cost of repairs after a tenant leaves?

Quiet Enjoyment

The right to **quiet enjoyment** is a common law right which also appears in most provincial legislation. Quiet enjoyment does not mean a right to absolute silence in the premises, but rather a right to freedom from serious interference with the tenant's use and enjoyment of his or her part of it. Quiet enjoyment is not quite the same as a landlord's duty to keep the premises fit to live in, which will be discussed later. It is possible to use and enjoy an apartment even though it needs repairs. Also, there are situations in which a tenant can lose quiet enjoyment, despite the fact that the rented home is in good repair.

Most provincial legislation states that a tenant who does not have quiet enjoyment may sue the landlord for a decrease in rent, or may apply to the court for permission to break the lease and leave.

Frederic v. Perpetual Investments Ltd. (1968) 2 D.L.R. (3d) 50 (Ont. H.C.J.)

Frederic leased an unfurnished apartment from Perpetual Investments Ltd. Shortly after she moved in she began to suffer headaches, coughing, and dizziness. She discovered that one of the rooms below her apartment was a garage storage room, and that carbon monoxide was leaking into her apartment. She sued Perpetual for breach of the obligation to allow the tenant quiet enjoyment of the premises.

—What do you think the court decided?

Right to Privacy

Although the landlord owns the rented residential premises, the law in most provinces makes it clear that, until the landlord gets an eviction order from the court, the rented premises are the tenant's private quarters. The landlord may enter only under certain circumstances, and usually only after written notice is given to the tenant at least twenty-four hours before entry. The circumstances under which a landlord may enter are as follows:

1. When the tenant consents.
2. When there is an emergency such as a fire or burst pipe.
3. When the tenant has notified the landlord that he or she is leaving, and the landlord wants to show the premises to a new tenant. In Ontario the landlord does not have the right to show the premises to a new tenant, unless the tenant who is living there has consented to it.

Often, the right to enter is included in a lease. A landlord can be charged under provincial law with trespass for entering without the right to do so.

Despite the tenant's right to privacy, generally the tenant may not change the lock or add a lock without giving the landlord a key. Nor may the landlord alter the locks without giving the tenant a key, since doing so would amount to an illegal eviction.

—Does your province's legislation have rules about changing the locks on rented premises? Does it mention security devices?

Fitness of Accommodation

It was mentioned earlier that, under the common law, a landlord could collect the rent even if the residential premises were not fit to live in. In almost all provinces, this rule has been changed by legislation stating that the landlord does have a duty to repair in most cases. All the basic elements of a living space—electricity, major appliances that go with the premises, heating, plastered walls, weatherproofing, sanitary facilities, and pest control—must be maintained by the landlord. Repairs involving these items must be paid for by the landlord, unless the damage was carelessly or deliberately caused by the tenant or the tenant's family or friends.

If a landlord fails to make necessary repairs, a tenant may apply to a court for an order requiring the landlord to do the repairs, for a decrease in rent, or for an end to the tenancy. The tenant should first inform the landlord of the need for repairs and give the landlord a chance to do them.

Cleanliness and ordinary housekeeping chores are the tenant's responsibility. If the tenant insists on being such a bad housekeeper that a health hazard is created, a court will usually grant the landlord an eviction order.

> *Levin v. Active Builders Ltd.* [1973] 6 W.W.R. 279 40 D.L.R. (3d) 299 (Man. C.A.)
>
> Levin's landlord, Active Builders Ltd., had not quite completed construction on the apartment building when Levin moved in. There were still some holes in the outside walls where service pipes were being installed. Unfortunately, some mice got into the building through the holes. The mice caused damage to Levin's furniture. Levin sued his landlord for the cost of the repairs.
>
> —Is Levin or the landlord responsible for mouse control? Why?
> —In this case, Levin depended on a section of Manitoba's *Landlord and Tenant Act* which requires a landlord to keep the premises fit for habitation. If Manitoba had no such legislation, would there be a common law right which Levin could have relied on?

Notice Before a Rent Increase

All provinces require the landlord to give the tenant written notice of any plan to raise the rent. Usually the tenant must be informed at least three months before the rent increase is to take effect.

Jack's landlord, Schmidt, plans to raise the rent next month. She informed Jack of this plan today. Jack can ignore this and go on paying the rent he has been paying, since Schmidt's notice was not in writing, and she did not give Jack enough advance warning.

—How much notice must a residential tenant in your province receive before the landlord may raise the rent?
—Must the notice be in writing?
—How often can the landlord raise the rent?

Assignment and Subletting

Assignment and **subletting** are both methods of giving all or part of residential premises to a new tenant. The difference between them is that if a tenant sublets, he or she either remains in the accommodation or intends to return. If the tenant assigns the lease, he or she is planning to leave for good.

Ilona was renting a three-bedroom apartment. She decided to let Hélène rent one of the bedrooms. Ilona was subletting the bedroom to Hélène.

Françoise is going away for the summer, but doesn't want to give up her apartment. She sublets the apartment from June to September, returning at the end of September.

Wolfram lives in Toronto but is planning to move permanently to Vancouver. His lease does not expire until December, but he wants to move in August. He assigns his lease to Gunnar.

Under common law, the original tenant remains responsible for the rent until the lease has expired, whether the premises are sublet or assigned. It is best, therefore, for the original tenant to try to have the landlord and the new tenant make their own tenancy agreement if the original tenant does not want to return. This way, the original tenant does not have the worry about being liable for rent or repairs after leaving.

What if the landlord does not want the original tenant to assign or sublet? Most provincial legislation says that the landlord cannot unreasonably refuse permission to do either. This means that if the original tenant finds a suitable, reliable person to take over the apartment, the landlord must consent.

Sometimes the landlord charges a fee to assign or sublet. Some provincial laws state that the landlord cannot charge more than the reasonable expenses incurred in subletting. "Reasonable expenses" could include the fee for advertising the vacancy in a newspaper, or the cost of cleaning the apartment.

Figure 22-3

— Give one other example of reasonable expenses a landlord might have in an apartment-subletting situation.
— Does your provincial law allow the landlord to charge a fee for subletting?

Terminating the Lease

A landlord and tenant usually agree that the premises are to be rented for a specific period—a year, for example. What happens when the lease ends? The answer depends on whether the tenant wants the lease to end, or not.

A tenant who wishes to leave can do so at the end of the lease. The tenant must give the landlord notice of the intent to leave. The notice period varies from province to province, and may depend on the length of the lease.

What if the tenant does not want to leave? In provinces other than Ontario, the tenant must leave at the end of the lease if the landlord wants the tenant to go. In some provinces, such as Alberta, the landlord has to give the tenant notice to leave. Once proper notice is given, the tenant must move.

Suppose the tenant is coming to the end of the lease, but the landlord has not given notice to leave. In this situation, the tenant may decide to rely on a common law rule about the creation of a **periodic tenancy**. A periodic tenancy is one that renews the rights of landlord and tenant for specific lengths of time called *terms*. A term can be a week, a month, a year, or longer. The tenant can create a periodic tenancy by paying rent at regular intervals. For example, if the tenant continues to pay rent monthly after the lease period ends, a monthly periodic tenancy is established. As long as the landlord accepts the rent, the tenant remains a tenant through the next term. The tenant can stay until the landlord stops accepting the rent. Depending on the province, the landlord may have to give notice of the end of the periodic tenancy before he or she can make the tenant leave.

When Richard rented his Edmonton apartment, he signed a lease for a year. In the lease, Richard agreed to pay rent monthly. Toward the end of the year, Richard realized that his landlord had not given ninety days notice that the tenancy was to end. He liked his apartment and did not want to move, so, on the day that would have been the last day of the tenancy, he mailed the landlord another month's rent. The landlord cashed the cheque.

Richard now has a periodic, month-to-month tenancy. He can continue the tenancy as long as the landlord accepts his rent cheques. If the landlord wants to end this tenancy, he must give

Richard the amount of notice provided for monthly tenancies in Alberta. In the meantime, Richard can continue with the rights and responsibilities of a tenant.

Security of Tenure

The discussion above describes what happens when a tenant does not wish to leave at the end of an agreed period of tenancy anywhere in Canada, except Ontario. The situation in Ontario is different because residential tenants in this province have a very important right—**security of tenure**. This right comes into use when the tenant wishes to stay in the rented premises, and the landlord wants to evict the tenant.

Under security of tenure, Ontario's *Landlord and Tenant Act* limits the landlord's right to evict the tenant to certain specified situations. Unless one of the reasons listed in the legislation applies to the situation, the tenant can stay on in the rented home, paying rent at the same intervals as in the original lease. A periodic tenancy is thus created.

Security of tenure exists regardless of what the lease, oral or written, states. Unless the landlord can convince an Ontario court that one of the reasons for eviction provided by law applies to the case, the tenant can stay.

An Ontario tenant can be forced to leave for any of the following reasons:

1. The landlord needs the unit for him- or herself, his or her spouse, child, parent, or spouse's parent. If the tenant has a lease or has agreed to rent for a particular period (a year, for example), the tenant cannot be made to leave before the end of the agreement.
2. The landlord requires possession for demolition, conversion to another use, or extensive repairs and renovations. (The repairs and renovations must be so extensive that they require a building permit.)
3. The tenant has failed to pay the rent and does not pay within fourteen days of receiving notice.
4. The tenant is continually late with the rent.
5. The tenant or the tenant's guests wilfully or negligently cause damage to the premises or surrounding areas. The landlord must give the tenant seven days to repair the damage. If nothing has been done after seven days, the landlord can go to court for an eviction order.
6. The tenant permits or carries on an illegal activity or business in the premises.
7. The tenant or the tenant's guests seriously interfere with the reasonable enjoyment and use of the premises by the landlord or

other tenants (for example, by giving wild parties or harassing other tenants). The tenant must be given seven days to change this behaviour.
8. The tenant or the tenant's guests seriously interfere with the safety and rights of other tenants (for example, by owning so many pets that they pose a health hazard or by assaulting other tenants). The tenant must be given seven days notice to change the situation.
9. The premises are so overcrowded that health and safety standards are violated. The tenant has seven days to correct the situation.
10. The tenancy was part of an employment agreement and the job is terminated.
11. The tenancy was part of an agreement to buy a condominium and the deal falls through.

Unless one of these reasons exist, an Ontario tenant cannot be evicted, no matter what the original lease stated about the length of tenancy.

During the time of writing of this text, British Columbia had security of tenure; however, the government introduced new legislation removing this security. In the rest of Canada, the tenant's right to stay in the rented premises depends on his or her agreement with the landlord. Tenants in provinces other than Ontario often prefer to have a written lease, since it is good evidence of how long the landlord has agreed to let them stay. By contrast, tenants in Ontario do not need a written lease for this purpose. Not having one may be an advantage, since written leases often contain clauses tailored for the landlord's benefit only.

—An Ontario landlord clearly cannot evict a tenant just because he or she feels like doing so. Why do you think the Ontario law protects tenants in this way?

Kay v. Parkway Forest Developments (1982) 25 O.R. (2d) 329 (Ont. Div. Ct.)

When Kay and her child moved into a Toronto area townhouse, her landlord warned her that she'd have to get rid of her cat—the lease said "No Pets". However, after a while Kay noticed that several of her neighbours in the townhouse project had dogs, and nobody seemed to be very worried about the "No Pets" rule. Kay bought her child a dog named Buddy.

Buddy was well-behaved and quiet, and Kay kept him in the house or in the fenced back yard. However, the landlord found out about Buddy, and started a court action to evict Kay.

The landlord succeeded at trial, but Kay won her case when she appealed. The Divisional Court of Ontario firmly stated that no matter what a residential lease might say, under Ontario law a tenant could be evicted only for the reasons given under the *Landlord and Tenant Act*. The *Act* did not include ownership of a pet among those reasons.

—Look at the list of reasons for which a landlord can evict in Ontario. Which of these reasons *might* apply because a tenant keeps a pet?
—Did Kay breach a contract (her lease) by having a pet? If so, would the landlord have any remedy?
—What if Kay lived in an "Adults Only" building and became pregnant? Could her landlord evict her?

Rent Review Law and Rent Control

Several Canadian provinces, for example, Ontario, Newfoundland, and Québec, have rent review legislation. This legislation imposes some limits on a landlord's ability to raise the rent of certain residential premises.

Most provincial landlord-tenant law states that rent may not be raised on a residential unit more than once a year. That means once per year per unit, *not* once per year per tenant. Furthermore, as mentioned previously, the landlord always has to give notice of a rent increase (usually ninety days).

Rent legislation has three functions. It

1. identifies the type of residential accommodation that the law will affect;
2. sets a limit on the yearly increase in rent; and
3. provides for an agency to review applications for rental increase.

Ontario's rent review law, for example, identifies certain types of accommodation according to the amount of rent charged and the date at which the accommodation became rental premises. Most types of residential accommodation in Ontario that were available for rent before 1976 are covered by the legislation, as long as the rent is below $750 per month. In rental accommodation covered by the Ontario rent review law, a landlord cannot legally raise the rent by more than six percent without a rent review hearing. If the landlord does raise the rent over this amount, the tenant can simply refuse to pay more than a six percent increase, and can wait for the landlord to apply for a hearing.

Sandra lives in a one-bedroom Ottawa apartment that her landlord has rented since January 1, 1976. The rent is less than $750 per month, so Sandra's landlord may not increase the rent by more than six percent without a rent review hearing and permission from a Residential Tenancy Commission.

Steven's parents pay more than $750 monthly rent on their house. Steven's parents' landlord is not bound by Ontario rent review law.

Rent review law does change from time to time. It is therefore important to look at the legislation if you wish to know the law in this area.

—Does your province have rent review legislation?
—Why do you think some provinces have passed this kind of legislation?
—If your province does have rent review, what types of rental properties are affected?
—Which properties are excluded? Why do you think this is so?

SUMMARIZING YOUR READING

1. Is tenancy law provincial or federal?

2. What three essential elements make a tenancy agreement different from an invitation to spend the weekend as a guest? Explain each element.

3. Must a lease be in writing?

4. Who is a residential tenant? a commercial tenant?

5. Why does a lease affect the rights of a commercial tenant more than those of a residential tenant?

6. Name the three major sources of landlord and tenant law.

7. Is landlord and tenant law affected by human rights legislation?

8. What is the effect of a late rental payment?

9. Who is responsible for ensuring that the landlord receives the rent?

10. What is a security deposit?

11. Is the right to "quiet enjoyment" the right to complete silence in the rented premises? Explain.

12. The landlord owns the premises, so he or she can come to inspect them at any time.—Right or wrong? Explain.

13. Can the tenant/landlord change the lock on the rented premises without giving the landlord/tenant a key? Explain.

14. Who is responsible for repairs—the landlord or the tenant? Explain.

15. A landlord told her tenant that she wanted a ten percent increase in next month's rent cheque. Is this a valid notice of rent increase? Explain.

16. What is the difference between assignment and subletting?

17. What alternatives does a tenant who doesn't live in Ontario and who wants to stay in the rented premises past the end of the lease have?

18. Explain the term "security of tenure".

19. What must an Ontario landlord who wants to evict a tenant consider?

20. What three functions does rent review law have?

DISCUSSING KEY ISSUES

1. Landlords once had the upper hand over their tenants; however, over the years, tenants have gradually received more protection from statute law. What evidence can you find in this chapter which supports this statement? Why do you think this change has occurred?

2. Recently, the Ontario government appointed a commission to discuss rent review legislation. Representatives for landlords stated that residential landlords should make profits equal to those made in high-risk investments such as oil and gas.
   Not everyone agrees with this point of view. Some people think that, as an essential service, residential rental and its business profits should be controlled by law in the same way that medical services and food production are. Which view do you agree with? Give reasons to support your answer.

3. It has become quite common, especially in urban areas, for landlords to designate certain properties as "Adults Only". It is therefore becoming increasingly difficult for families to find suitable rental accommodation. What is your opinion of this practice? Should landlords be able to restrict their tenants in this way?

PROJECTS AND ACTIVITIES

1. Obtain copies of two residential lease agreements. What do they say about exclusive possession? Do they mention quiet enjoyment? repairs and maintenance? subletting rights? Would statute law in your province override any of the terms?

RESOLVING CASES

Albert v. Pelletier (1976) 66 D.L.R. (3d) 536 (N.B. S.C.)

Albert rented an apartment in a small apartment building owned by Pelletier. The apartment could be reached only by a stairway going up the outside of the building and ending in a porch outside Albert's apartment. The steps and porch were old and rather shaky, and Albert asked Pelletier to repair them, but he did not do so. One evening Albert and a guest were standing on the porch and leaning on the railing. The railing collapsed. Both fell and were injured. Albert sued her landlord.

Because of the law of New Brunswick in this area, the verdict in the case partly depended on whether the stairs would be considered part of the rented premises.

—What factors do you think the court considered in coming to its decision?
—How would you rule in this case? Why?

Pajelle Investments Ltd. v. Herbold (1975) 62 D.L.R. (3d) 749 (S.C.C.)

Herbold and her daughter were attracted to an apartment building run by Pajelle Investments Ltd., partly because it advertised a swimming pool and sauna for tenants and air conditioning in the apartments. Some time after the Herbolds moved in, Pajelle Ltd. stopped supplying air conditioning, and closed the pool and sauna "due to mechanical breakdown too expensive to repair".

Herbold sued successfully. Pajelle finally appealed the case to the Supreme Court of Canada.

—Does a landlord have to live up to what was advertised? Give reasons for your answer.
—What do you think the Supreme Court decided in this case?

Balageorge v. McCulloch et al. [1977] 4 W.W.R. 195 (Man. Q.B.)

McCulloch caused a fire in his apartment by careless smoking. His landlady sued for the cost of the repairs.

—What do you think the court decided? What influenced the decision?

Parkes et al. v. Howard Johnson Restaurants Ltd. [1970] 74 W.W.R. 225 (B.C. S.C.)

The landlord wanted to get rid of his tenant, so he decided to make things unpleasant. He removed the doors that led to part of the tenant's premises, cut off the heat, interfered with the elevator service to the tenant's premises, and cut down the tenant's electrical supply.

—What common law right of the tenant might help him in this situation?

Re Quann and Pajelle Investments Ltd. (1975) 7 O.R. (2d) 769 (Ont. Cty. Ct.)

A number of tenants who lived in the same highrise apartment building took their landlord, Pajelle Investments, to court to try to force it to make repairs. There was no question that repairs were needed. The buzzer and intercom system to the apartments did not work; there were no locks on some main doors to the outside; there were problems with the swimming pool; and the air conditioning system was out of order. A number of orders to repair the unfit premises had been issued by the City of Toronto.

In arguing before the court, the landlord noted the following facts in its defence. First, several of the tenants thought the building was all right and did not mind living there. As well, some of the tenants who applied to court had known about the problems when they moved into the building. Finally, some of the damage was caused by tenants' children. (The landlord had provided the children with no place to play. The children therefore played in the halls, lobbies, and laundry rooms.)

—Do you think that any of these arguments would make a difference in the decision of the court?

UNIT 5

The Law and the Workplace

23 Employment Relationships and the Law
24 Collective Bargaining

23

Employment Relationships and the Law

> The Employment Contract
> Individual Bargaining and Employment Relationships
> Employer and Employee
> Principal and Agent
> Independent Contractor and Client

Most Canadians spend forty to fifty years of their lives working eight hours a day, five days a week, to make a living. It is obvious that our role as an employee or an employer is very important in our lives. Therefore, it is useful to know as much as possible about the legal rights and responsibilities involved in the employment relationship.

The Employment Contract

The employment relationship is formed by a contract between two parties. One party, the *employee*, promises to perform a service (work), and the other party, the *employer*, agrees to pay for that service. As in any other contract, all of the basic elements must exist for the employment contract to be valid.

The employment contract generally does not have to be in writing, and, in fact, most often it is oral and quite informal. However, the *Statute of Frauds* requires any contract which will take longer than one year to complete to be in writing. This requirement naturally applies to employment contracts which are for a definite term of longer than a year. But what happens when the oral or written employment contract does not specify how long the employment relationship will last? Although the answer to this question varies according to the type of employment relationship, in general, the common law presumes that the contract exists indefinitely. It is ended when either of the parties gives **notice** of an intention to end the relationship, or when one party ends the relationship for a justified reason, such as breach of the terms of the contract. Thus, under this general rule, if the contract does not state that it will continue for more than one year, the law assumes that it might not last for a year and therefore need not be in writing to be enforceable.

In most situations, the parties are free to fashion the terms of their agreement or contract to suit themselves. Common law and statute law generally apply to employment relationships only when the oral or written agreement does not specifically provide for a certain situation. However, as you will soon see, statute law increasingly sets out minimum standards relating to wages, hours of work, and vacations, among other factors of the relationship of employer and employee.

Figure 23-1
Employment contracts are generally oral and informal.

There are two main ways of establishing an employment contract: through individual bargaining, or through **collective bargaining**. Collective bargaining occurs when a **union** is formed to represent individual members in bargaining for the *collective agreement* (employment contract). The law governing collective bargaining forms the subject of Chapter 24. This chapter will examine individual bargaining.

Individual Bargaining and Employment Relationships

There are three employment relationships which can result from individual bargaining:

1. the employer and employee relationship
2. the principal and agent relationship
3. the independent contractor and client relationship

It is important to be able to distinguish among these, because the rights and obligations of the parties involved in each relationship are different.

Employer and Employee

This employment relationship is known in legal terms as the *law of master and servant*. However, this somewhat outdated terminology is generally replaced with the more familiar terms "employer and employee". The employer-employee relationship is probably the most common type of employment relationship, and is the focus of this chapter.

Who is an employee? The answer might seem obvious, but many court battles have been fought over this very question. At common law, the issue is one of control; that is, how much control does the employer have over the employee? There are four main factors which generally characterize an employer-employee relationship:

1. The employer has the power to select employees.
2. The employer pays wages or some form of remuneration to the employee.
3. The employer determines what work is to be done and has the right to control the method of doing the work.
4. The employer has the right to discipline or dismiss the employee for misconduct.

Statute law often defines "employee" in much more limited terms. The answer to the question "Who is an employee?" often becomes a matter of interpreting the definition provided by a given statute to see whether the individual worker is entitled to the rights or protection provided by the law. The following case illustrates this situation.

Yellow Cab Ltd. v. Board of Industrial Relations, Sadownik, Dunbeck, Alberta Union of Provincial Employees, Yellow Cab Drivers' Association (1981) 24 A.R. 275 (S.C.C.)

Sadownik and Dunbeck were drivers for Yellow Cab Ltd. They brought a complaint against the company claiming that it was interfering with their right under the *Labour Act* to organize a local of the Alberta Union of Public Employees.

The issue in this case was whether Sadownik and Dunbeck were "employees" under the *Labour Act*. If not, they were not entitled to form a union.

The company owned the cabs, provided licence plates and insurance, and provided maintenance on the cars. The drivers rented the cars on a daily or weekly basis, and purchased gas from the company. The drivers' income came directly from passengers.

The *Labour Act* provided the following definitions:

> "employee" means a person employed to do work who is in receipt of wages, and
> "wages" includes any salary, pay, overtime pay, and any other remuneration for work or services, however computed, but does not include tips and other gratuities.

— In your opinion, would Sadownik and Dunbeck be employees under the common law definition given earlier?
— Three decisions in the Alberta courts ruled that the drivers were employees. Given the facts of this case and the definitions in the *Labour Act*, why do you think these decisions were reached?
— The Supreme Court of Canada overturned the Alberta courts' decisions. Sadownik and Dunbeck were not employees and were therefore not entitled to form a union. On what basis do you think the Supreme Court reached this decision?

In addition to defining "employee" for the purposes of the particular statute, statute law often specifically excludes some employees from the protections outlined in the law. For example, Alberta's *Employment Standards Act* sets a limit on the number of hours an employee can be required to work daily and weekly, and requires the employer to pay overtime for any hours over this number. However, the *Act* exempts the following workers from this protection:

> 22. (1) Section 21 does not apply to an employee entirely in
>   (a) a supervisory capacity,
>   (b) a managerial capacity, or
>   (c) a capacity concerning matters of a confidential nature,
> and whose duties do not, other than in an incidental way, consist of work similar to that performed by other employees who are not so employed.

—Why do you think the *Act* has exempted these employees?

Common Law and the Employer-Employee Relationship

Increasingly, the workplace is being regulated by statute law to provide a better balance between the bargaining positions of the employer and the employee. However, this is not to say that the common law has no effect on this type of employment relationship. Although the following are not the only areas in which the common law has an influence, we will examine three situations where the unwritten law is important to the workplace and to the employment contract:

1. the employee's obligations to the employer
2. the common law action for wrongful dismissal
3. the employer's liability for the employee's torts

Employee's Obligations

The employment contract obliges the employee to perform the work for which he or she was hired. The common law says that this means that the employee must be competent and must exercise due care in carrying out the tasks related to the employment. It does not mean that an employee is never entitled to make a mistake, but repeated incompetence or carelessness would almost certainly be a breach of the employee's contract and would justify dismissal.

Included in the obligation to perform work is the duty to be present for work and to be punctual. Repeated absenteeism, even when the employee is seriously ill and cannot report for work, is therefore a breach of the contract. Conduct of this kind might provide the employer with **just cause** to terminate the employment relationship.

Figure 23-2 *Punctuality is one of the employee's obligations to the employer.*

Other forms of conduct on the part of the employee may also be viewed by the employer (and by the courts) as a failure on the part of the employee to live up to his or her common law obligations. The conduct might be illegal, immoral, or simply undesirable. Stealing from the employer would be an example of the first; drunkenness would fall into the third category. In some employment situations, living in a common law relationship might qualify as immoral conduct justifying dismissal. For instance, a teacher working for a religious affiliated school board might be dismissed for such conduct.

Conduct which justifies dismissal is often a matter for the courts to decide, and, as you can imagine, the courts' decision usually reflects the values of society at the time and place the case is heard. What was considered immoral or undesirable 100 years ago may be perfectly acceptable today.

Finally, the employee owes a duty of loyal, faithful service to the employer. An employee who actively competes with the employer, for example, is not a loyal, faithful "servant".

William R. Barnes Co. Ltd. v. MacKenzie (1973) 34 D.L.R. (3d) 463 (Ont. H.C.J.)

The plaintiff was a construction and building materials supply company. The defendant, MacKenzie, was employed as a division manager for the company. Unknown to the plaintiff, the defendant also owned a rival business, B. & W. Construction.

MacKenzie was sued by his employer because of a number of business transactions which caused loss to the plaintiff company. One example was that MacKenzie sold a kind of gravel to his own company at $22/ton and then immediately resold it to a customer of Barnes Co. Ltd. at $27/ton, undercutting the quote he had given on behalf of the plaintiff company by $2/ton. There were a number of incidents such as this in the plaintiff's Statement of Claim against the defendant.

The court, in awarding judgement for the plaintiff, summarized the law in this area as follows:

"There is a duty on the part of a servant to serve his master faithfully...In the absence of a written contract of employment such a term is implied into the contract of employment. The extent of the obligation varies, of course, with the class of the employee. The defendant in this case was in a position of special confidence. He was the manager of a division of the plaintiff and had considerable authority. The plaintiff was entitled to the undivided attention of the defendant to the plaintiff's business and, in my view, the defendant was in serious breach of his duty."

Wrongful Dismissal

As you have just seen, when an employee has not lived up to the obligations imposed by the employment contract or by common law (where there is no express agreement), the employer is often justified in ending the employment. If the employer wishes to end the employment contract but does not have just cause, he or she is obliged to give a reasonable amount of advance notice to the employee that the employment will terminate on a certain date. The employer may give pay instead of notice. A written employment contract can set down the required period of notice. Moreover, statute law provides a minimum period of notice for "employees" as defined by the Act. However, it is the common law action for wrongful dismissal that often brings the most satisfactory results to the employee who has been terminated without cause. The reason is that the courts often interpret "reasonable" notice much more generously than does statute law.

Warren v. Super Drug Markets Ltd. (1966) 54 D.L.R. (2d) 183 (Sask. Q.B.)

The plaintiff, a pharmacist, was employed by the defendant company for five years as a manager of one of its stores. At the time of hiring, there was no stipulation that the employment contract was to end on any particular date. Warren was dismissed from his employment by the President of the company; he then sued for wrongful dismissal.

The defendant claimed the following:

"the plaintiff misconducted himself, particulars of which are as follows:

1. He absented himself from his employment on the 26th day of June, 1964, without permission or any notice to the defendant.
2. He failed to place and keep the said store in the immediate charge and under the personal superintendence and *bona fide* management and conduct of a licenced pharmaceutical chemist on each Saturday and Sunday during the period of his employment."

The plaintiff's evidence showed that he had left the store three hours early on June 26, to begin his annual vacation, leaving the store under the supervision of a qualified pharmacist. He felt this was justified, since the July 1st statutory holiday fell within his vacation period but he was not taking an extra day for it. On the second point, Warren testified that an undergraduate pharmacist was in the store on weekends and that a qualified pharmacist was "on call" to give advice by telephone. This situation was known to the Operations Manager for the company, although apparently not to the President.

—How can employment contracts for indefinite periods be terminated?
—In your opinion, was Warren in breach of his obligations to his employer? Explain.
—Was there just cause for his dismissal?
—Should Warren be entitled to compensation? Explain.
—If so, what factors would you take into consideration in assessing damages?

The compensation sought in a wrongful dismissal action is money damages. The courts will not order a wrongfully dismissed employee to be reinstated.

Employer's Liability for Employee Torts

Luba Subasic is employed by a courier company. Her employer has supplied her with a van which she uses during business hours. Luba is involved in an accident one day while she is driving. She is at fault in the accident and cause $800 damage to the other vehicle.

—Who do you think should be liable for the damage in each of the following situations—Luba or her employer?

Figure 23-3

(a) The accident occurs on the weekend when Luba is returning from a ski trip. She is driving the van with her employer's permission because her own car is in for repairs.
(b) The accident occurs while Luba is making a delivery during regular business hours using the company van.
(c) The accident occurs when Luba decides to visit a friend during her lunch hour. Luba is aware that driving the van for this purpose is against company policy.

As you may recall from your study of torts, the law of vicarious liability applies to the employer-employee relationship when third parties suffer damage as a result of the employee's tort. The test which is often applied is whether the employee was acting in the course of his or her employment. The employer is liable not only for actions that were directly authorized, but also for the way in which the employee has performed the action. For example, Luba's employer authorized her to drive the van in making deliveries and is jointly responsible for her while she is driving if a third party suffers loss or harm. Clearly, the company has not authorized Luba to be a negligent driver, but if this is in fact the way she has carried out her employment, the employer is vicariously liable.

The liability of the employer is not unlimited, however. If the employee was not acting within the scope of the employment, but was off on a "frolic of his or her own", then the employer is not liable.

Statute Law and the Workplace

Very few employees can actually bargain on an individual basis with the employer. Famous athletes or musicians or highly skilled professionals or executives have the power to bargain effectively. With most people, however, the employer presents the terms of the employment contract and the person either takes it or leaves it. Thus, the worker has traditionally been very much at the mercy of the employer. It is for this reason that governments have stepped in over the years to legislate minimum standards and protections for employees.

Both the federal and the provincial governments have passed legislation affecting the workplace. While most employees fall within provincial jurisdiction, some employees are governed by the *Canada Labour Code*, a federal statute. Employees in areas under federal jurisdiction such as the airline and rail industries, banks, telecommunications, interprovincial trucking, and Crown corporations all fall under the scope of the *Canada Labour Code*. The reason for this is the division of powers granted under the Constitution.

In general, all provinces and the federal government have legislated minimum standards of protection for employees in the following areas:

1. minimum age for employment
2. minimum wage
3. maximum hours of work and overtime pay
4. holidays and vacation pay
5. equal pay
6. maternity leave
7. notice of termination
8. health and safety legislation and Workers' Compensation
9. human rights

Minimum Age

Each province has legislation which limits the employment of young people. Child welfare legislation prohibits children from being employed in certain jobs. In Ontario, children under the age of sixteen cannot be employed on the streets after 9 p.m.—as flower sellers, for instance. Provincial education Acts generally require that young people (usually up to the age of sixteen) must be in full-time attendance at school. In addition, employment legislation restricts the hiring of young people below a certain age in particular occupations, such as construction, where there is a threat to the health or safety of the young person.

—At what age can young people in your province leave school to seek full-time employment?
—At what age can a young person in your province work in
  (a) a service industry?
  (b) manufacturing?
  (c) construction?

Minimum Wage

Every Canadian province sets a minimum wage for all employees who are covered by the provisions of labour or employment standards legislation. Employees who are entitled to be paid minimum wage cannot agree to work for less, and it is an offence for the employer to pay less. In most jurisdictions, there is more than one minimum wage. Ontario, for example, has a general minimum rate, a learner rate, a construction rate, a student rate, as well as several other standards for specific occupations.

—What is the minimum wage for a seventeen-year-old employed full-time in your province as a cashier at a food chain?
—Is the rate different if that person works only part-time?

"I reviewed your salary, as you requested. We're paying you too much!"

Maximum Hours of Work and Overtime Pay

The maximum number of hours that an employee can be required to work per day or per week varies across the country. Both the federal government and the provinces have legislation on this matter. The *Canada Labour Code* sets forty-eight hours per week as the limit beyond which overtime must be paid, while Ontario's limit is forty-four hours. British Columbia's *Employment Standards Act* sets the standard work day at eight hours. An employee who works more than eight hours, up to a maximum of eleven hours per day, must be paid one-and-a-half times the regular rate for the overtime hours.

The legislation usually sets out daily or weekly rest periods and meal breaks as well. For example, Ontario's *Employment Standards Act* states:

> 22. Every employer shall provide eating periods of at least one-half hour, or such shorter period as is approved by the Director, at such intervals as will result in no employee working longer than five consecutive hours without an eating period.

Figure 23-4 Providing time for rest periods is one of the employer's obligations to the employee.

Alberta's labour standards legislation provides the following minimum protection:

> 28. An employer shall allow his employees at least
>   (a) 24 consecutive hours of rest each week,
>   (b) 48 consecutive hours of rest in each period of 14 consecutive days,
>   (c) 72 consecutive hours of rest in each period of 21 consecutive days, or
>   (d) 96 consecutive hours of rest in each period of 28 consecutive days.

—What does your provincial legislation say about hours of work, overtime pay, and rest periods?

Holidays and Vacation Pay

Employees covered by provincial employment or labour standards legislation or the *Canada Labour Code* are entitled to take a certain number of holidays (called statutory holidays) with pay, or to be paid at a premium rate of pay if they work on the holiday. The number of these paid holidays and their actual dates vary from province to province. Workers in British Columbia, for instance, are entitled to the following statutory holidays: New Year's Day, Good Friday, Victoria Day, Canada Day, British Columbia Day, Labour Day, Thanksgiving, Remembrance Day, and Christmas.

In 1944, Ontario became the first province to pass legislation giving all employees covered by the legislation a compulsory annual vacation with pay. By 1970, all jurisdictions had similar legislation. The length of the vacation varies, depending upon which federal or provincial law covers the employee. It is usually based on the length of time the employee has worked for the employer. The qualifying employee usually receives full salary for the vacation period, but in any event, the statutes provide a minimum amount of pay. In New

Brunswick, the employee must receive no less than four percent of his or her annual income as vacation pay. An employee whose employment is terminated before qualifying for paid vacation must also be paid this minimum rate of vacation pay for the entire period worked.

—What statutory holidays is an employee who qualifies under the statute in your province entitled to? what length of vacation? what amount of vacation pay?

Equal Pay

The requirement that men and women be given equal pay for substantially similar work can be found in either the human rights statutes or in the employment standards Acts of each province.

Re Leisure World Nursing Homes Ltd. and Director of Employment Standards et al. (1980) 29 O.R. (2d) 144 (Div. Ct.)

Leisure World employed both nurse's aides, who were all women, and orderlies, who were all men. The jobs performed by these employees were very similar, yet the orderlies were paid more than the nurse's aides. This was found to be contrary to the provisions of the Ontario *Employment Standards Act*. The company was required to pay the nurse's aides the same rate of pay in the future, plus a sum of money to compensate them for the lower pay received in the past.

Provincial legislation guaranteeing equal pay applies only when the jobs in question are substantially similar. The *Canadian Human Rights Act*, however, provides additional protection for employees who fall under federal jurisdiction. Employers must pay these employees equal wages for work of equal value. This requires an employer to rank the skills needed and responsibilities involved in the work, as well as the value to the employer of the work, and then to pay men and women the same wages according to this ranking.

—Which do you feel is more just—equal pay for equal work, or equal pay for work of equal value?
—The provinces frequently argue that legislating equal pay for work of equal value would be too difficult and expensive for employers. What is your opinion of this argument?

Maternity Leave

A female employee is allowed to take time off without pay in order to

Figure 23-5 *As increasing numbers of women enter the work force, issues such as equal pay for work of equal value and granting maternity leave are being covered by legislation.*

give birth to a child. In most jurisdictions, she is allowed seventeen weeks away from her job on maternity leave; she cannot be dismissed while on this leave. If she returns within the allowed time, she must be reinstated in her previous position or a comparable one. She may also be eligible to collect benefits from Unemployment Insurance during her leave.

—In your opinion, should fathers be allowed to take paternity leave?
—Should people be allowed to take unpaid leave similar to maternity leave when they adopt a child?
—Should the inconvenience to an employer be taken into consideration in any or all of these situations?

Notice of Termination

Statute law provides standards for minimum amounts of notice which employers are required to give when terminating the employment contract without cause. The amount of notice required varies considerably from province to province. In Ontario the *Employment Standards Act* sets out the following notice periods:

> **40. (1)** No employer shall terminate the employment of an employee who has been employed for three months or more unless he gives,
> - (a) one week's notice in writing to the employee if his period of employment is less than two years;
> - (b) two weeks' notice in writing to the employee if his period of employment is two years or more but less than five years;
> - (c) four weeks' notice in writing to the employee if his period of employment is five years or more but less than ten years; and
> - (d) eight weeks' notice in writing to the employee if his period of employment is ten years or more,
>
> and such notice has expired.

You should recall, however, that the common law often provides a better remedy for the employee who has been unjustly dismissed. In one Alberta case in the early 1970s, a fifty-five-year-old woman who had worked in the laundry of a hospital for nine years and who had over forty years of experience received twenty-six weeks' wages instead of notice when the court found that she had been unjustly dismissed.

—Since the common law seems to provide a more generous remedy to the employee who has been dismissed without cause, why do you think statute law has been passed in this area at all?

Health and Safety Legislation and Workers' Compensation

At common law, the employer had an obligation to provide a safe place of work, a safe system of work, and competent co-workers. However, it was sometimes difficult for the employee who was injured on the job to prove that the employer was negligent and responsible for the accident, and so to receive damages from the courts. Workers' Compensation funds were set up by the provinces early in this century to help resolve the problem. Workers' Compensation is similar to a no-fault insurance plan. Only employers, not employees, are required to contribute to the fund. When an employee is injured on the job, no matter what the cause of the injury, the fund will pay for medical expenses, long-term disability, and, in some instances, retraining if the employee is unable to return to his or her previous employment.

The introduction of a scheme of Workers' Compensation can generally be seen as a step forward for employees. However, it should be pointed out that for some employees, the loss of the right to sue an employer for damages creates a hardship. If an employee has been seriously injured by an employer's negligence, the compensation under Workers' Compensation can be substantially less than the amount a court might award.

The number of claims made after the introduction of Workers Compensation schemes indicated that certain workplaces were very hazardous. The provinces eventually responded to this situation by passing industrial and construction safety legislation to set standards for the workplace which employers had to meet. In recent years, this legislation has been extended; now it is not just the factory and construction site that must be safe for workers, but also the office, the store, and the school, among others.

The legislation covers not only those hazards caused by, for instance, unsafe equipment, but also such dangers as environmental pollution. Special safety precautions must be taken in a work environment where employees are required to work with hazardous materials such as chemicals emitting toxic fumes. Occupational health and safety legislation also provides that a worker may refuse to work in certain situations until a health and safety committee can investigate, as New Brunswick's *Occupational Health and Safety Act* indicates:

> 8. (3) An employee may refuse to do any act at his place of employment where he has reasonable grounds for believing that the act is unusually dangerous to his health or safety.
>
> 8. (3.1) Any employee who is concerned that an act may be unusually dangerous to his health or safety shall refer the concern to his superior, and, in the event the concern is not resolved to his satisfaction, to a safety committee established pursuant to regulation or, where a safety committee has not been established, to an officer.
>
> 8. (3.2) No employee shall be disciplined by reason of the fact alone that he has refused to act if his refusal to act is authorized by subsection (3) and he complies with subsection (3.1).

The employee, of course, always has a responsibility to follow safety instructions and exercise due care with respect to fellow employees.

Human Rights

Human rights legislation is dealt with in detail in Chapter 9; however, it is worthwhile to briefly re-examine it, and to summarize the effects of this legislation on the workplace in particular.

Figure 23-6 Many provincial Human Rights Commissions have developed employment application forms which are non-discriminatory.

Sample Job Application Form

This is a condensed version of an approved job application form used by an equal opportunity employer.

APPLICATION FOR EMPLOYMENT

Date: _____ Position applied for: _____

PERSONAL INFORMATION

Name: _____
        Surname   Middle Name   First Name

Address: _____
         Street & No.   City/Town   Province   Postal Code

Phone: _____
        Home   Business

Are you legally permitted to work in Canada? Yes/No _____

EDUCATION

Date	Institution	Course	Degree/Dip/Cert
_____	_____	_____	_____
_____	_____	_____	_____
_____	_____	_____	_____

EMPLOYMENT (Begin with the most recent)

1. Employer: _____
   Address: _____
   Name of Supervisor: _____ Phone: _____
   Position held: _____
   Duties: _____
   Date of employment: From: _____ To: _____
   Reason for leaving: _____

2. Employer: _____

REFERENCES   (NAME 2 business or work associates. Recent graduates may name teachers or professors)

1. _____ Years acquainted: ____ Phone: _____
2. _____ Years acquainted: ____ Phone: _____

ADDITIONAL INFORMATION
_____
_____

I certify that the statements made by me in this application are true and complete. I understand and agree that a false statement may disqualify me from employment, or result in dismissal.

_____   _____
Signature   Date

Human rights laws have an effect on the following areas of employment:

1. hiring practices, including job applications, job interviews, employment agencies
2. promotions and conditions of employment
3. membership in unions and professional associations
4. in some provinces, equal pay for equal work

Employees or candidates for employment may not be discriminated against for any of the forbidden grounds outlined in the legislation. You will remember that the following grounds are included in all human rights legislation in Canada: race, place of origin, religion, colour, age, sex, and marital status. Some provinces include additional protections. Ontario is one of the jurisdictions that forbids discrimination on the basis of an employee's record of offences. British Columbia employers cannot refuse to hire a person on the basis of the applicant's political beliefs.

—Provide an example of how an employer might discriminate in each of the areas of employment listed above.

Special Federal Employment Protection

Canada Pension Plan

Most employees, except those in the province of Québec, are entitled to an earnings-related pension under the Canada Pension Plan when they retire or become disabled. Employees in Québec have very similar protection under the Québec Pension Plan. The Canada Pension Plan is a federal government fund into which both employees and employers pay premiums based on income, up to a maximum amount. Some classifications of employees are exempt from these pension plans. For example, workers in agriculture, horticulture, fishing, hunting, trapping, forestry, logging, and lumbering who work less than twenty-five days a year or who make less than $250 a year are not included.

Unemployment Insurance

The federal government has established the Unemployment Insurance Commission to assist individuals who find themselves out of work. It is the right of an unemployed worker to collect unemployment insurance, provided that he or she qualifies. In order to qualify, the person must have been working in insurable employment and paying premiums from each paycheque for a certain length of time, specified in the regulations of the *Unemployment Insurance Act*.

The *Act* defines insurable employment as

> 3. (1) *(a)* employment in Canada by one or more employers, under any express or implied contract of service or apprenticeship, written or oral, whether the earnings of the employed person are received from the employer or some other person or whether the earnings are calculated by time or by piece, or partly by time and partly by piece, or otherwise.

Unemployed workers who qualify for benefits collect a percentage of their previous earnings for a specific length of time. This period varies according to such factors as the length of time the person has worked; the geographical area in which the claimant lives; the time of the year; and the type of work experience of the claimant.

The unemployed worker who receives unemployment insurance benefits must (a) be available for work; (b) be actively searching for work; (c) report all earnings from employment on reporting cards; and (d) report to a Canada Employment Centre as directed. Failure in any of these areas could result in the cancellation of unemployment insurance benefits.

As mentioned at the beginning of this chapter, there are two other main types of employment relationships besides that of employer-employee. The rest of this chapter will examine these relationships, principal-agent and independent contractor-client, comparing and contrasting them with the employer-employee relationship.

Principal and Agent

Assume that your parents decide that the family has outgrown your present house. They put it up for sale with a real estate company and sign a listing agreement, offering the house for sale at a price of $149 000 for sixty days. The real estate agent, Agnes Melnichuk, assures your parents that she will do her best to find a purchaser for your house. In the meantime, your parents begin looking for a new house that will meet the family's needs at a price they can afford.

When your parents put their home up for sale, they entered into a relationship of agency. The **agent** is the real estate brokerage company, and Agnes Melnichuk is a *sub-agent* of the company. The agent is authorized by the **principals**, your parents, to represent them in transactions with other people, or, in legal terms, *third parties*.

In the case of an agency relationship involving real estate, the agent is only authorized to find a purchaser for the property offered for sale. In many other agency relationships, however, the agent is authorized to enter into contracts with third parties for the principal. These contracts are binding on the principal, provided that they would have been valid contracts if the principal had entered into them directly. In other words, a principal who is legally competent to enter into contracts may authorize an agent to make contracts on his or her behalf, and will be bound by these agreements.

Agency relationships can be established in a variety of ways, discussed below.

Agency by Express Agreement

An agent by express agreement derives the authority to act from an agreement with the principal. This agreement can be in writing, but does not have to be. You may have heard the term **power of attorney**. Let's assume that your parents both have to leave town on business while your house is being offered for sale. In order not to miss an opportunity to sell the house, they sign an agreement called a power of attorney with your uncle. This document allows your uncle to act as your parents' agent should an offer to purchase be presented while they are away. Your parents (the principals) might authorize your uncle (the agent) to accept any offers over $139 000, for instance. They will be bound by a contract to sell the house entered into by your uncle on their behalf. In addition, your uncle is bound by the terms of the agreement with your parents and cannot go beyond the authority granted to him. For example, if he accepted an offer to purchase the house for $130 000, your parents would not be bound by this contract, because they had not authorized it.

Some employees can also be agents. A buyer in a large department store is an employee of the store, but is also authorized as an agent to make contracts to purchase merchandise for the store. The store is bound by these contracts, provided that the agent has not overstepped his or her authority.

Agency by Estoppel

Agency relationships can also be created by a legal principle called **estoppel**. Say you go to a stereo equipment store, purchase an expensive tape deck, and charge it on your parents' credit card. Your parents have agreed that you may have the tape deck as a birthday and graduation gift. Your parents, naturally, pay the bill when it arrives. Several weeks later, you again take the credit card and purchase some additional equipment from the same store. This time, your parents have not authorized your purchase and they have no desire to pay the bill. However, having once paid your bill and not having notified the store that they would not pay in the future, they are *estopped* (prevented) from denying liability for the contract with the stereo store. They must pay the second bill. (They will undoubtedly have a great deal to say to you about the matter, however!)

Agency by Ratification

What if your second purchase of stereo equipment was made on a time payment plan instead? You expect that your parents will pay, and pledge their credit at the store. You have not been authorized by your parents to make the purchase and therefore cannot be considered their agent. However, if your parents do make some of the time payments in order to help you out and keep you out of trouble, they have ratified the contract and have become liable for it. To summarize, agency by ratification occurs when a person acts as the agent of another person without authority, and the resulting contract is not repudiated immediately by the proposed principal.

Agency by Necessity

The agency relationship can also be created by necessity. Suppose that you agree to dog-sit for a friend while she is on vacation. Unfortunately, the dog becomes very ill. Fearing it might die, you take it to a veterinarian for treatment. Your friend will be responsible for paying the vet bills when she returns, because you became her agent by necessity. This kind of agency relationship is limited to situations of real necessity or emergency, however.

—List three other examples of principal and agent relationships.
—In each case, is the agent authorized to make the contract for the principal, or simply to bring together the parties so that a contract can be made?
—Identify the kind of agency relationship which exists in each of your examples.

Independent Contractor and Client

Let's return to your parents' attempts to sell your home. The search for a new house in your neighbourhood at an affordable price is very discouraging. In addition, no suitable offers to purchase are received for your house. The listing agreement with the real estate company expires.

Your parents conclude that it would be a better idea to expand your present house by adding a large extension with a family room, two new bedrooms, and another bathroom. They hire an architect to design the extension, and then a general contractor. Alf Brady, the contractor, will be responsible for hiring and supervising the various tradespeople (carpenters, plumbers, electricians, among others) who will be working on the house for the next few months. The general contractor signs a contract with your parents setting out his responsibilities and the fee for the job.

When your parents hired Alf to supervise the construction of the extension, they entered into an employment relationship with an independent contractor. Although the contractor has been hired by your parents, he is actually in business for himself. There are usually four factors at common law which can be applied to test whether a person is an independent contractor, as opposed to an employee:

1. Independent contractors control their own work.
2. They own or supply their own tools.
3. They have a chance of making a profit.
4. They have a risk of loss.

However, the courts have taken factors other than these four into consideration, and indeed have ruled that not all four need exist to establish an independent contractor-client relationship. The court will also examine the degree of control that the person doing the hiring has over the person hired.

The contractor in our example is ultimately responsible to your parents for ensuring that the addition is satisfactory. He, not your parents, is responsible for supervising the work and the workers. The tools required are supplied by the contractor or by the tradespeople (subcontractors) he hires to work on the house. Generally, the contractor sets a price for the total job and pays the subcontractors directly. If he has correctly priced the job and efficiently supervised the tradespeople, the contractor should make a profit on the job. However, there is always the risk of loss if he has not done so.

—Contrast the four factors which determine whether a person is an independent contractor with the earlier common law test of the employer-employee relationship.
—How does the independent contractor differ from an agent?

Figure 23-7 summarizes the three employment relationships we have discussed, and sets out the liability in tort of employees, agents, and independent contractors.

	Definition	Liability for Tort
Employer and Employee	Employer controls the work to be done by the employee and the method by which it is to be done.	Employer is liable if the employee was acting in the course of his or her employment.
Principal and Agent	Agent is authorized by the principal to act for him or her. The agent does not act under the direct control of the principal, but cannot exceed the authority given.	Principal is liable for the wrongs of the agent committed in the course of the employment (agency).
Independent Contractor	Contracts to perform a service for the employer, but uses his or her own methods. Is not subject to the control of the employer, except as to the final quality of the work. Has a chance of profit and a risk of loss.	An independent contractor is responsible for his or her own torts except where the employer is aware that the work or the method is likely to cause harm and allows that work to continue.

Figure 23-7 Comparison of the Three Employment Relationships

SUMMARIZING YOUR READING

1. In the employment contract, what is the consideration given by each party?

2. Does an employment contract have to be in writing? Explain.

3. How can the employment contract be terminated?

4. What are the two main ways of arriving at an employment contract?

5. Why is the question "Who is an employee" an important one?

6. What four factors identify an employer-employee relationship at common law?

7. What are three common law obligations placed on an employee?

8. Provide three original examples of conduct which might give an employer just cause to terminate the employment contract.

9. What is wrongful dismissal?

10. What is notice? Does it always have to be given to an employee?

11. What is vicarious liability?

12. In what situation will an employer be held vicariously liable for the employee's torts?

13. Under what circumstances is the employee solely responsible for his or her own torts?

14. Why have so many statutes been passed to regulate the workplace?

15. What types of employees fall under the jurisdiction of federal legislation?

16. What were the employer's common law obligations with respect to safety in the workplace?

17. Why was it necessary for the provinces to set up a system of Workers' Compensation?

18. What important right have workers gained under health and safety legislation?

19. What rights do employees have under the Canada Pension Plan?

20. What rights do employees have under the *Unemployment Insurance Act*?

21. How does the principal and agent relationship differ from the employer-employee relationship?

22. What four factors distinguish the independent contractor from the employee?

PROJECTS AND ACTIVITIES

1. Obtain five sample application forms used by employers in your community. Examine them carefully. Do they seem free of questions which might be considered discriminatory? Fill out at least one of these forms.

    Compare these application forms to the sample form found earlier in this chapter which has the approval of the Alberta Human Rights Commission, or to the approved form in your own province.

2. Contact a Canada Employment Centre to obtain specific details of how to apply and qualify for unemployment insurance. For how long may you collect benefits? How is the amount of the benefits determined? Report your findings to the class.

RESOLVING CASES

Poirier v. Kovats, Doing Business under the Name and Style of North Shore Aluminum Co. (1976) 14 N.B.R. (2d) 262 (N.B. S.C.)

The plaintiff, Poirier, claimed that he was entitled to vacation pay as an employee under the *Vacation Pay Act*. He worked as a salesman for the North Shore Aluminum Co. and received commission on his sales only. He was not assigned a sales territory by the defendant company. No hours of work were set, there was no quota to meet, and the plaintiff provided his own transportation.

The New Brunswick *Vacation Pay Act* stated:

> 1. *(a)* "earnings" means the pay received or receivable by an employee for work done by him for an employer.

"Employee" was defined as follows:
"Employee" means a person employed for remuneration or a wage but does not include a person who is employed
 (i) 24 hours or less a week,
 (ii) in domestic service or agriculture, or
 (iii) by the Crown.

The *Act* required four percent of the employee's earnings to be paid for vacation pay.

— Would Poirier be considered an employee at common law? What facts would you use to support your answer?
— Would Poirier qualify as an employee under the definition contained in the statute?
— What do you think the court decided?

Price v. Simpsons-Sears (1977) 6 A.R. 96 (Alta. S.C.)

The plaintiff had been employed by Simpson-Sears for fourteen years, six years of which he was a divisional manager. He had a good employment record until the incident which brought about his dismissal.

Price sold a suit to Egan Badel, the manager of the sporting goods department. The suit was priced at $145 but the plaintiff marked it down to $79.99 and then deducted a further $12 to reflect Badel's staff discount. Price did not record the sale in the markdown book, which was usual store procedure. The suit was sent to the tailoring department for alterations with the name "Paul Jones" on the tailoring tag.

When this sale came to the attention of Simpson-Sears' management, Price was dismissed from his employment. He sued for wrongful dismissal.

At the trial, the plaintiff testified that the false name on the tailoring tag was to speed the alteration process, which frequently took longer for staff. He said that the suit was due to go on sale shortly after the sale to Badel anyway, and that while it was his usual practice to record sales in the markdown book, he could not remember doing so in this case.

—Was Price in breach of his employment contract, in your opinion?
—Do you think the company was justified in terminating the plaintiff's employment? Explain your reasoning.
—What do you think the court decided in this case?

Strilchic v. Lalonde et al. (1973) 32 D.L.R. (3d) 613 (Man. C.A.)

Koons and Lalonde were employed as drivers of the defendant taxi company. Lalonde was off duty on the particular evening in question and had been partying with two women in a hotel. When the three left the hotel, they found a cab which was driven by Koons. Koons already had a passenger, but it was agreed that the three would get in anyway. Koons delivered his passenger to his destination and then radioed the dispatcher that he was returning and that he was available to pick up new fares. He did not notify the dispatcher of Lalonde and his companions' presence, which was against company policy. Koons was intending to drop off Lalonde at his apartment and then radio his location to the dispatcher again.

On the way back, Lalonde insisted on driving. He was involved in an accident, which injured Strilchic. Koons and Lalonde were found liable by the courts, but on appeal the issue that had to be decided was whether the taxi company should be held vicariously liable for the tort of its employees.

—Was Koons acting in the course of his employment? Explain.
—Should the defendant taxi company be held vicariously liable?

Longdo v. McCarthy and Gordie's Auto Sales Ltd. (1980) 28 N.B.R. (2d) 56 (N.B. Q.B.)

The plaintiff, Longdo, owned a van which he wanted to sell. He left the van with Gordie's Auto Sales Ltd., owned by the defendant, McCarthy, to be sold for a ten percent commission. On the instructions of the manager, the van was moved from one used car lot to another by Lavigne, an employee of the defendant company. Lavigne had been drinking and negligently caused an accident with an ambulance.

The owner and passengers of the ambulance successfully sued Longdo and Lavigne. Longdo paid the judgement and then brought an action against McCarthy and Gordie's Auto Ltd. for the tort of the employee, Lavigne. Longdo's claim for damages included the damage to the van and the amount of the judgement he had paid to the accident victims.

—On what principles of law would the ambulance owner and passengers sue Longdo and Lavigne?
—On what basis would Longdo then bring suit against Lavigne's employer?
—What test would the court apply to Lavigne's conduct when determining the liability of his employer?
—What do you think was the decision of the court?

Bone v. Hamilton Tiger Cats (1979) **Ontario Human Rights Commission Board of Inquiry**

Jamie Bone was an excellent quarterback at the University of Western Ontario. He was invited to try out for the Hamilton Tiger Cats, but he was informed at training camp that the Ti-Cats did not hire Canadian quarterbacks. The main reason for this practice was a policy of the Canadian Football League called the "designated import rule", which allowed a team to hire an additional imported player to fill the role of quarterback.

Jamie Bone was dropped from training camp after several weeks. He had had very little opportunity to display his talents because the coach was preoccupied with assessing the American candidates. Jamie brought a complaint to the Ontario Rights Commission.

—Upon what ground of discrimination would Jamie Bone base his complaint?
—In your opinion, did the designated import rule of the C.F.L. discriminate against Canadian quarterbacks? Explain.

24

Collective Bargaining

The Development of Collective Bargaining
The Collective Bargaining Cycle

*Figure 24-1
Belonging to a union and participating in a legal strike are rights of most Canadians.*

It is almost impossible to read the newspaper without finding a headline about a labour dispute in which workers are threatening to **strike**, or are already on strike, or are being threatened with a **lock-out** by their employer. A strike is a refusal by employees to work. Its purpose is to put pressure on an employer to settle a labour dispute. Legally, the right to strike is restricted to employees in a **union**. What exactly is a union, and why has the law provided a weapon as powerful as a strike to unions?

The Development of Collective Bargaining

A union is an organization of employees who work together for a common purpose, such as improving wages or working conditions. Today, roughly 3 500 000 Canadians, or thirty-one percent of the labour force, belong to unions. However, it was not all that long ago that labour unions were considered criminal conspiracies to prevent or limit fair competition in the marketplace. Employees who attempted to unionize could be jailed for their activities. This situation changed when the criminal law was codified in 1892. The *Criminal Code* did not classify unions as criminal conspiracies. Gradually, unions have gained greater legal recognition and bargaining power, to the point where today most workers enjoy the following right, as stated in Newfoundland's *Labour Relations Act*:

> **5. (1) Every employee has the right to be a member of a trade union and to participate in its activities.**

As you read in Chapter 23, the individual employee generally lacks the power to bargain effectively with the employer. When the Industrial Revolution substantially changed the workplace, the power of the employer increased tremendously. During much of the nineteenth century, workers in factories and mines worked incredibly long hours in unsafe and unhealthy conditions for poor pay.

Workers found that banding together to bargain with the employer about wages and working conditions could be much more effective in improving their situation than bargaining individually. Thus, collective bargaining was born. Small craft unions in which the employees shared a common skill, such as carpentry, were the first unions. Now, this type of union exists alongside such huge industrial unions as the United Steel Workers of America. The latter type include all of the employees working in a particular industry, no matter what the skills of the individual worker. Though unions may vary in size or type, they have a common purpose: to bargain with the employer as a collective unit. In other words, the union becomes the agent for all of the individual members and is authorized to bargain for the employment contract, called the **collective agreement**. The contract becomes binding on all of the members, once they *ratify* (approve) it by taking a vote.

The Collective Bargaining Cycle

This chapter will examine the five stages that make up the collective bargaining process or cycle:

1. Organization. Employees with a common interest or purpose decide to work together in an organized fashion.
2. Certification. The union *(bargaining agent)* must be recognized by the government before it can legally bargain for its members.
3. Negotiation. The bargaining process, whose purpose is to arrive at the collective agreement, begins between the union and the employer.
4. Stalemate Resolution. A procedure is set out in provincial and federal legislation which must be followed when the union and the employer cannot arrive at a collective agreement through negotiation. This process begins with the aid of a third party *(conciliator)* and can end with a strike or lock-out.
5. Contract Administration. Once the collective agreement is reached, the administration and interpretation of the contract begin. When the term of the contract expires, the process begins again with negotiation.

Organization

There are many reasons why individual employees might wish to join or form a union, but it is probably safe to say that the most important reason is to increase their bargaining power. When the employees in a particular workplace decide to unionize, they have two basic choices: they can find an existing union which can represent their interests and apply for **certification** (recognition by government) as a **local** (branch) of the parent union; or they can create an independent union by drafting a constitution, electing officers, enlisting members, and applying for certification. The only practical difference between these two choices is that when applying to a parent union, it is not necessary to draft a constitution for the organization. Rather, the constitution of the parent union is adopted by the local. This chapter will examine the process involved when employees choose to form a new union.

Before we can examine this process, we must first ask, "Who can unionize?" Most employees in Canada fall under provincial legislation, while some employees, such as those working in banks or for airlines, fall under federal jurisdiction. All of the provinces and the federal government have passed legislation which sets out the right of employees to unionize and places some limitations on this right for certain classes of employees. For example, the *Trade Union Act* in Saskatchewan defines "employees" who have the right to unionize in the following way:

> (2) *(f)* "employee" means:
> (i) any person in the employ of an employer except any person whose primary responsibility is to actually exercise authority and actually perform functions that are of a managerial character, or any person who is regularly acting in a confidential capacity in respect of the industrial relations of his employer...

—Why do you think the law exempts these employees from the right to unionize?

Once it is established that a group of employees has a right to unionize, the first step is to draft a constitution for the union. The constitution includes such things as the name of the organization; its purpose; the procedure for electing union officers who will represent the **bargaining unit** (all the members); the duties of the officers; the frequency of meetings; and the amount of membership fees or dues. Once the constitution has been drafted, the union begins its membership drive. A sufficient number of employees must become members of the union before the next phase of the collective bargaining cycle can begin.

Certification

The federal government and all the provinces have set up agencies, usually called Labour Relations Boards, to deal with many aspects of the employer-employee relationship. Each Labour Relations Board (L.R.B.) is responsible for recognizing a union as the bargaining agent for a group of employees who have organized. While it is possible for an employer to recognize a union voluntarily, this does not commonly happen. Usually, the union must sign up a certain percentage of the employees before the union can obtain certification.

Each province's labour statute and the Canada *Labour Code* set out the circumstances under which a union may apply for certification, and when certification will be granted. For example, the Ontario *Labour Relations Act* provides rules based on the following situations:

1. Automatic certification of the union if fifty-five percent of the employees are members.
2. Rejection of the certification application if less than forty-five percent of the employees are members.
3. Conducting a representation vote if between forty-five and fifty-five percent of employees are members; certification is granted if a majority vote in favour of the union.

—How do the rules set out in your provincial labour relations statute compare?

In most jurisdictions, a vote of the employees may not be necessary even when the union cannot show the required percentage of members among the employees, if the employer has engaged in **unfair labour practices**. In these circumstances, certification may be allowed because the employer's activities have made it difficult for the Labour Relations Board to determine the exact number of employees wishing to unionize. The following case illustrates such a situation.

United Steel Workers of America and Radio Shack and Groups of Employees [1979] 2 Can. L.R.B.R. 281

The United Steel Workers of America applied for certification of the employees of Radio Shack at the company's Barrie, Ontario location. According to the Ontario *Labour Relations Act*, two bargaining units were necessary—one for full-time employees, one for part-time employees. The union could show evidence to the Labour Relations Board that more than fifty-five percent of the full-time employees had become members of the union. Certification was granted. However, the membership among the part-time staff was only sufficient for the Board to order a representation vote to be taken. The Steelworkers asked that the vote be dropped and certification granted because of Radio Shack's unfair labour practices.

The union gave evidence of the following activities of the employer:

1. Two employees were fired because of their union organizing activity. This was illegal, and the Labour Relations Board ordered that they be reinstated. However, Radio Shack did not reinstate one of them in his previous position. He was given a less desirable job and was isolated from other employees, both by location and by the time allowed for lunch and break periods.

2. The company posted a notice that union organization during working hours was forbidden. This was legal within the *Act*, but then Radio Shack allowed an anti-union petition to be circulated during working hours.
3. A foreman of the company said to several members of the bargaining unit that "if the union gets in, the company will pack up and move west." This foreman also stated that a scheduled seven percent wage increase would not be paid if the union got in.
4. Radio Shack management supplied between twenty and thirty of the 170 employees with red T-shirts carrying the slogan "I'm a company fink" on the front and "and proud of it" on the back.

Certification of the bargaining unit of part-time employees was granted. The Board stated that "it is unlikely that the true wishes of the part-time employees would likely be ascertained by the taking of a secret ballot vote in this case."

—Give at least three reasons why an employer would wish to block the formation of a union.
—Should an employer be allowed to do anything to discourage unionization, in your opinion?

It should be pointed out that it is also possible for a union to engage in unfair labour practices. For instance, it is illegal in all jurisdictions for an uncertified union to organize a strike to force the employer to recognize the union as the bargaining agent for the employees.

Negotiation

Once the union has been certified, it will give notice to management (the employer) that it wishes to begin negotiating the first collective agreement. The union has by this time elected representatives to negotiate for the bargaining unit. A draft proposal for a collective agreement is then presented to management. Management likewise makes a proposal as to what it considers to be a basis for settlement. Then the bargaining begins.

Figure 24-2 Negotiation begins with the exchange of proposals between union and management.

The union's proposal can be simple or quite complex, but in most cases it will include many or all of the items discussed below. During the bargaining process, both union and management have a legal duty to **bargain in good faith**. This duty includes meeting to negotiate, discussing the proposals put forth, and having a serious intent to arrive at a collective agreement.

Wages

This part of the proposal would normally include hourly rates on salary scales, overtime rates, and holiday rates. In the 1970s, cost of living allowances (COLA clauses) became important parts of collective agreements to protect employees from the effects of inflation.

Fringe Benefits

These might include vacation pay, sick leave, paid lunch or break periods, medical and dental insurance, and pension plans.

Seniority Systems

Unions usually wish to include a system in the collective agreement recognizing an employee's length of service, especially for the purposes of pay increases and promotion. At the very least, the union usually wishes to ensure that any necessary layoffs will be on the basis of seniority; those employees with the least seniority are to be laid off first.

Union Shop Agreement

Many unions wish to reach a *union shop* agreement with management. In a union shop, all employees hired by the company, except those in managerial positions, must become members of the union.

Grievance Procedure

A system must be agreed to whereby union and employer can settle disputes about the interpretation of the contract or a violation of the contract.

—Try to obtain a copy of a collective agreement of a union in your area. What provisions, if any, does the agreement make for each of the items outlined above? What additional items are included, if any?

Other Provisions

The union can also attempt to bargain for any other provision which is important to the bargaining unit. During the 1970s, the workplace was changing dramatically because of technological advances. Many unions began to actively bargain to protect members from any harmful effects of this rapid technological change. Some unions were successful in obtaining this protection. In addition, the Canada *Labour Code* was amended to require employers under federal jurisdiction to give advance notice of technological changes to a union. Several provinces have followed suit. For instance, Saskatchewan's *Trade Union Act* provides that:

> **43. (2) An employer whose employees are represented by a trade union and who proposes to effect a technological change that is likely to affect the terms, conditions or tenure of employment of a significant number of such employees shall give notice of the technological change to the trade union and to the minister at least ninety days prior to the date on which the technological change is to be effected.**

Figure 24-3 What other possible methods might unions use to cope with the introduction of new technology?

—What does the phrase "terms, conditions or tenure of employment" mean?

Technology kills jobs, union says

New micro-processor technology has eliminated two jobs for every job created in technology-related administrative occupations in the federal Government in a six-year period, a union policy paper says.

The paper says the worst is still to come. Clerical occupations will be hardest-hit with the introduction of integrated office systems which file and retrieve information electronically.

The document on technological change and office automation, prepared by the Public Service Alliance of Canada, says that between December, 1974, and December, 1980, positions in the technology-related occupations of data processor, office composing equipment operator, mailing service equipment operator and microphotography equipment operator increased by 2,014.

But during the same period, the traditional occupations of typist, stenographer, communicator, bookkeeping equipment operator, calculating equipment operator and duplicating equipment operator decreased by 4,500.

The paper states that an alternative to a reduced labor force is better redistribution of the available work by reducing hours and giving more paid leave.

The union says the new technology can have an adverse impact on its membership if introduced as a labor-saving device or without regard to employee needs.

The paper says that those who discount the unemployment effects on the premise that the new jobs will be as numerous as those they eliminate are indulging in wishful thinking.

Delegates to the union's convention called for protection in collective agreements against the impact of technological change, including a requirement of six months' notice in advance of its introduction.

Unions in Saskatchewan which receive this notice from the employer can then give notice to begin collective bargaining for the purpose of revising the agreement as it relates to terms, conditions, or tenure of employment.

—What possible harmful effects might technological change have on members of a bargaining unit?
—Why would some jurisdictions pass legislation in this area?

Stalemate Resolution

More than half of the collective agreements in Canada are agreed to at the bargaining table. However, statute law sets out the procedure to be followed when negotiations to reach a collective agreement break down. While legislation varies across the country, generally, the procedure to end a stalemate or breakdown in the bargaining process involves the following stages, illustrated in Figure 24-4: **conciliation** (or **mediation**), **arbitration**, and strike and/or lockout. They are discussed in turn below.

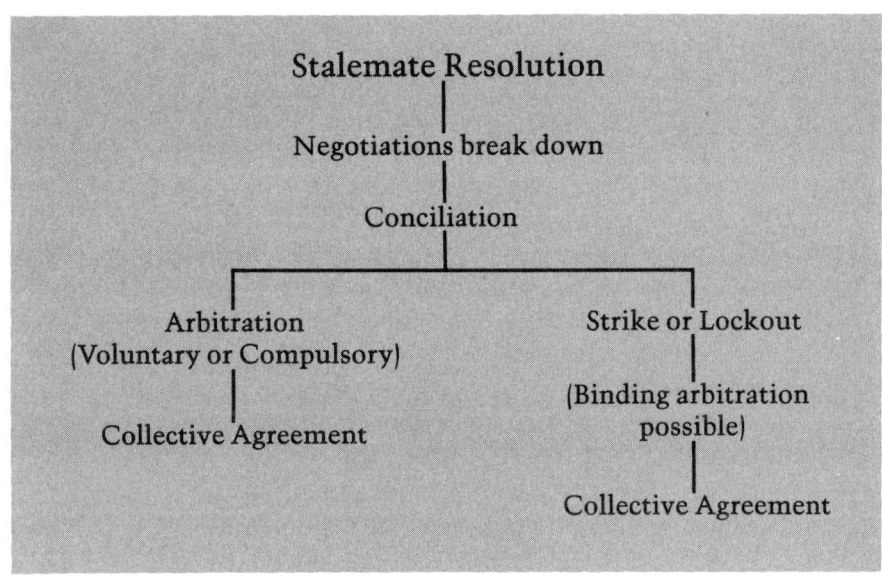

Figure 24-4 The Ways of Resolving a Labour Dispute

Conciliation

This process involves a neutral third party appointed by the government who meets with the representatives of both union and management to attempt to resolve the stalemate. Conciliation must take place before a union is in a position to call a strike vote.

The *conciliator* can become actively involved by suggesting possibilities for settlement, or can simply encourage the parties to continue meeting and negotiating. You should note, however, that a conciliator has no power to impose a settlement on the parties.

The conciliator must report to the Minister of Labour within a set time limit, which varies from province to province, if the conciliator is unable to help the parties arrive at a collective agreement. The Minister has the power to appoint a conciliation board to continue the process of trying to reach a contract, but does not always use this power. The union cannot take a strike vote, and a work stoppage cannot legally take place, until a certain number of days after the conciliator or conciliation board reports failure to the Minister, or until a certain number of days after the Minister decides a conciliation board should not be appointed. The time period between this report and the beginning of a legal strike or lockout varies from jurisdiction to jurisdiction. In Ontario, for instance, the period is seventeen days. In Prince Edward Island, the bargaining unit may strike and the employer may lock out the employees when attempts to reach an agreement have failed and either of the following situations exists:

> 40. (3) *(a)* A conciliation officer appointed by the Minister has been unable to bring about an agreement between the parties, and fourteen days have elapsed from the date on which the report of the conciliation officer was filed with the Minister and conciliation board or mediator has not been appointed under section 26 or section 33; or
> *(b)* a conciliation board or mediator has been appointed and has been unable to bring about an agreement between the parties and seven days have elapsed from the date on which the report of the conciliation board or mediator was filed with the minister.

—How does this compare to your province's legislation?

Mediation

In some provinces, a third party called a *mediator* might try to resolve the stalement after conciliation has failed. The conciliator is usually a government official, whereas the mediator is a private individual agreed to by both the union and management. The mediator's role is the same as the conciliator's. Mediation is simply one more attempt to reach an agreement before resorting to a strike.

Arbitration

Arbitration is a process wherein a third party has the power to impose a settlement on the union and the employer. Arbitration can be voluntarily agreed to by the parties. If this is so, they usually also agree to the selection and appointment of the arbitrator.

In some situations, arbitration is compulsory, and the arbitrator is appointed by the government. Compulsory arbitration is imposed on those employees who have the right to bargain collectively, but who do not have the right to strike. Public servants often fall into this category, as do other employees whose jobs are said to be **essential services**—for example, police, hospital workers, and firefighters. Arbitration can also be imposed upon striking workers who are legislated back to work by the government because the strike is seriously interfering with the public.

Remember, the decision of an arbitrator is binding whether the arbitration process was entered voluntarily or was compulsory.

Strikes and Lockouts

For many people, "unions" and "strikes" are almost synonymous terms. You have probably heard people complaining about a particular strike because it caused them inconvenience or hardship. For example, when postal workers go on strike, private individuals and businesses are greatly inconvenienced. Indeed, strikes are extremely costly for the employees and employers involved, as well as for the economy as a whole.

Canada has quite a high rate of work stoppages. Why, then, were strikes ever legalized? A work stoppage is the ultimate bargaining tool with which workers can try to force the employer to bargain. This tool is often the only effective means of balancing the power of the employer and the employees. It is a legal right which was slowly and painfully gained by the labour movement. Strikes are legal only when the following conditions have been met:

1. The bargaining agent has been recognized.
2. No collective agreement is in force.
3. The conciliation process has taken place.
4. The bargaining unit has authorized the strike by a vote.

A strike that occurs during the course of a collective agreement or before the union is in a legal position to strike is illegal. It is called a **wildcat strike**. The courts, or the Labour Relations Boards in some areas, can issue injunctions to stop an illegal strike. Companies affected by an illegal work stoppage can sue the union for damages.

Weins Contracting Ltd. et al. v. MacMillan Bloedel (Alberni) Ltd. et al. (1974) 40 DLR (3d) 593 (B.C.S.C.)

The plaintiffs were independent contractors who had a contract with the defendant company to cut timber. MacMillan Bloedel's unionized employees (members of the defendant union) were concerned about the company's contract with the plaintiff. The union therefore passed a policy requiring all independent contractors working for MacMillan Bloedel to sign an agreement to abide by all conditions and agreements established between the union and MacMillan Bloedel. The plaintiffs refused to sign.

At a meeting between union and management officials, MacMillan Bloedel was advised that, unless the independent contractors signed, several work crews might not report for work. Subsequently, three work crews failed to report and at a union meeting it was unanimously agreed that the membership would not return to work.

Because of the union's activities, MacMillan Bloedel suspended the contracts of the plaintiffs, who were then out of work from February 15 to March 2. The plaintiffs sued the company and the union for damages and for an injunction to prevent the union from continuing or repeating the strike action.

The court granted the injunction and ordered the union to pay damages because of the illegal strike. MacMillan Bloedel was not found liable for damages because its action was prompted by a labour disturbance. As well, its contract with the plaintiff allowed it to suspend the contract at any time.

When a union is in a legal position to strike, the employer is also in a legal position to lock out the employees. A lockout is exactly what its name implies. The employer simply locks its doors to prevent the employees from reporting for work. The purpose is the same as that of a strike—to put pressure on the other side to negotiate a settlement.

The Rights of Employees During a Strike

First, an employee involved in a legal strike has the right to return to his or her job when the strike is over. In 1934, the right to peacefully **picket** the employer's place of business during a legal strike was won. The picket line is useful in allowing striking workers to communicate information to other members and to acquaint the public with the reasons for the work stoppage.

—**Why is the right to picket an important one for unions to have won?**

Striking employees can also attempt to organize a **boycott** of the employer's products, by gaining the support of other unions and the general public for their cause. A successful boycott puts greater pressure on the employer to settle.

Employees on strike do not have a right to collect unemployment insurance, but unions often have strike funds for workers.

The Rights of Employers During a Strike

Most jurisdictions allow the employer to hire other workers during a strike. These workers are often called "strikebreakers" or "scab labour" by striking employees.

—Should this practice be allowed, in your opinion?

Employers also have the right to be free of the threat of violence or property damage during a strike. Injunctions can be issued to stop picketing if this threat exists.

Contract Administration

Eventually, a collective agreement is reached and the final phase in the bargaining cycle begins—administration of the contract. As mentioned earlier, this stage might involve disputes over the interpretation of a clause in the agreement, or over a perceived violation of the contract. No matter what the source of the conflict, the collective agreement will contain a **grievance** procedure for resolving such disputes. The following situation details how the grievance procedure can work.

Olga has worked for Excel Electric Company for eight years and is a union member. During her years with the company, she has worked her way up to shift supervisor. The company decides to begin manufacturing a new high-tech product line and advertises for a supervisor for this new department. This position will pay more than Olga's current job, and Olga is fascinated by the field of high technology. In fact, she has been taking night courses at her local community college. She feels that, on the basis of her seniority with the company, her skills, and her work record, she should receive this promotion. She is confident that with some on-the-job training, she could fill this position effectively.

The collective agreement between Olga's union and the company contains the following clause:

> "When any vacancy occurs within the bargaining unit, it shall be filled on the basis of seniority, providing the senior employee is reasonably qualified to perform the duties of that position."

The company instead hires Irene, a graduate of a technical college with two years' experience in a related industry. Olga is shocked to learn that she didn't get the promotion, and wonders whether she can grieve her employer's decision.

Although the exact grievance procedure is determined by the terms of each collective agreement, in general, the process will be similar to that described below.

Olga first talks to her union **steward**. A steward is elected by the union membership to represent the union and individual employees in discussions with management. If the steward feels that a violation of the contract has occurred, the formal grievance can begin. Olga outlines the nature of her grievance in writing. She states the facts as she sees them, the section of the contract which has been violated, and the remedy or solution she is seeking. Both she and the steward sign the grievance, and it is presented to Olga's supervisor.

It is possible for the grievance to be settled at this point, but since the hiring of staff was wholly a decision made at a higher management level, Olga's grievance is likely to have to go further. At this point, Olga and representatives of her union might meet with a management committee to try to resolve the dispute.

—What arguments do you think the union would make on Olga's behalf at this meeting?
—What arguments would the company likely make to support its hiring of Irene?

If the parties are unable to resolve the grievance, an arbitration hearing might have to be held. In an arbitration hearing, both sides in the dispute have an opportunity to present their case, very much as they would in court. The difference is that the parties get to choose who the "judge"—the arbitrator—will be.

If Olga is successful in her grievance, she will receive the promotion and Irene will not join the company, at least not in this position as manager of the new department.

The Right to Fair Representation

It should be pointed out that a union has an obligation under labour legislation to fairly represent the members of the bargaining unit. If the union acts in a manner which is arbitrary, discriminatory, or in bad faith in representing one or more of its members, the employee(s) might have a grievance against the union. This type of grievance should be taken to the Labour Relations Board, the agency responsible for administering labour legislation. If the grievance cannot be settled by an officer of the Board, an arbitration hearing is held.

Under the Ontario *Labour Relations Act*, the Board may make one or more of the following orders if it finds that the union has not fairly represented its member(s):

1. direct that the actions complained of cease;
2. direct that the actions complained of be remedied;
3. direct that an employee be reinstated;
4. award damages.

We have now followed through the complete bargaining process. When the term for the collective agreement is almost over, the union will give notice to management that it wishes to begin negotiating a new collective agreement. The collective bargaining cycle begins again at this point.

SUMMARIZING YOUR READING

1. What is a union?
2. Define "collective agreement".
3. What reasons can you give supporting the need for unions in the workplace?
4. What two choices are open to employees who wish to unionize?
5. Define "certification".
6. Do all employees have the right to unionize? Explain.
7. What information should the constitution of a union contain?
8. To whom does a union apply for certification in your province? Will a union be certified in every situation? Explain.
9. Give an example of an unfair labour practice. What effect do unfair labour practices have on the certification process?
10. Briefly outline the negotiation process.
11. Explain the meaning of the phrase "bargaining in good faith".
12. Distinguish between the terms "conciliation" and "arbitration".
13. What does the term "essential service" mean?
14. When is a union in a legal position to strike?
15. What is a wildcat strike?
16. What is the purpose of an injunction?

17. When can a company lock out its employees? Why would it do so?

18. What obligation does a union owe to its members?

DISCUSSING KEY ISSUES

1. Make a list of ten different occupations. Beside each, indicate whether you feel each is an essential service. Should employees in these occupations have the right to strike? Share your list with your classmates and be prepared to discuss your reasoning.

2. Debate the following resolution, or write an editorial: Resolved that the police (doctors, nurses, teachers, whatever you wish to insert) should not have the right to strike.

3. What effect should the profits of a company have on the wages of its employees? How do you decide what is a fair wage?

PROJECTS AND ACTIVITIES

1. If there is a local or national labour dispute taking place while you study this chapter, collect newspaper articles about the dispute and write a brief report outlining the reasons for it, how long it has been going on, and the steps being taken to resolve the dispute.

2. Does the Student Council or Student Union at your school have a constitution? If so, obtain a copy of this constitution. What is the name of your student organization? What is its purpose, according to the constitution? How are the officers elected, and what are their duties and responsibilities? What, if any, duties do the members have? (For instance, are there membership fees? What rights do these fees give to the members?)

If your student organization does not have a written constitution, write one.

In what ways is a student council different from a trade union?

3. Contact the Canadian Union of Public Employees (C.U.P.E.) or a large industrial union such as the United Steelworkers of America to discover the process for establishing a local of the parent union. Report your findings to the class.

4. Write a research paper on the Canadian Labour Congress. Answer such questions as these: What is it? What is its role in the labour movement? When was it organized?

5. Write a research paper on the farm labour movement. Why has this area of employment traditionally been excluded from unionization? Why is there a movement to unionize?

RESOLVING CASES

United Steelworkers of America v. Homeware Industries et al.
(1981) 81 C.L.L.C. 546 (Q.L.R.B.)

The union applied for certification without a representation vote, claiming that the employer's conduct made it impossible for the true wishes of the employees about the union membership to be determined. The union could show support of forty-five percent of the employees. In the absence of unfair labour practices on the employer's part, the union could be certified only after a representation vote wherein a majority of the employees favoured union membership.

The unfair labour practice claimed by the union occurred as follows. When the company became aware of the union organization drive, and on the request of two employees, the company suggested that an employee committee be established to deal with problems in the workplace and to try to reach satisfactory settlements. The union claimed that this sudden desire to form an employee committee was simply to draw support away from the union.

— Why did the union have to prove that the company had engaged in unfair labour practices?
— If the Labour Relations Board did find that the company had engaged in unfair labour practices, what could it rule?
— Do you think that Homeware Industries was guilty of unfair labour practices? Explain.
— Do you think the union was granted certification? Explain.

Service Employees' International Union, Local 183 v. K-Mart Canada Ltd. (1981) 81 C.L.L.C. 16 084 (O.L.R.B.)

The Service Employees' International Union applied to the Ontario Labour Relations Board for certification without a representation vote, and accompanied the application with a complaint of unfair labour practices against the employer, K-Mart Canada Ltd.

Two employees of the store, Kelly O'Connor and Beverly Clark, decided to explore the possibility of unionizing the store. They approached S.E.I.U. and subsequently began a union membership drive among their fellow employees. As soon as the store learned of their activities, O'Connor and Clark were placed under the constant surveillance of management trainees while at work. Except during lunch hours, the two women were never out of the sight of the trainees, were not allowed to take phone calls, and were accompanied to and from the washroom. This situation continued for about three weeks. While many employees had shown initial interest in the union, it ceased as the surveillance continued and the two women were isolated from their fellow employees.

At the same time, the company began a campaign to actively discourage the employees from joining the union. Each employee was exposed to at least five meetings during regular working hours at which store management spoke against union membership. An anti-union petition was then circulated by three employees.

A university student who had been hired as a part-time store detective was fired shortly after having a conversation with management in which he voiced support of the union. He was rehired almost immediately on the advice of the store's lawyer, however.

The union never did manage to sign a majority of the employees as members. They had signed thirty-four of the eighty-five employees—about forty-two percent.

—Do you think K-Mart engaged in unfair labour practices? Explain.
—Were these practices significant enough in your opinion to deprive the employees of their rights to freely choose union membership?
—Do you think the union was granted certification? Explain.
—Why do you think labour law allows a union to be certified without a representation vote when there have been unfair labour practices on the part of the employer?

Vancouver Museums and Planetarium Association v. Vancouver Municipal and Regional Employees' Union et al. (1981) 81 C.L.L.C. 218 (B.C.C.A.)

The Museums Association applied to the courts for an injunction prohibiting picketing of its premises, and for damages for the following:

1. trespass
2. inducing breaches of contracts or interfering with contractual relations
3. conspiracy to injure the plaintiff in its business
4. obstruction
5. intimidation
6. watching and besetting

The plaintiff claimed that, on two weekends when between thirty and fifty picketers were on the picket lines, complaints were received from patrons of obscene and abusive language, of picketers recording the licence plate numbers of cars passing through the picket line, and of photographs of patrons being taken. No-one was actually prevented from entering the museum, however.

— During a legal strike, what rights do employees have?
— What rights does the employer have?
— Should the union be responsible for economic loss suffered by the plaintiff because of picketing? In what circumstances? Explain.
— What do you think was the decision of the court?

District of Coquitlam v. District of Coquitlam Fire Fighters Union, Local 1782 (1981) 81 C.L.L.C. 452 (B.C.L.R.B.)

Captain John Gibson is a firefighter. At the time this complaint was heard, he not only occupied the most senior position within the bargaining unit, but was also the president of his union local. In a written report on his performance, Gibson's superior officer indicated that his chances for promotion were reduced because, in his position as the local president, he had taken stands against some policies of his employer.

The union brought a complaint stating that the employer's comments amounted to discrimination on the basis of union activity and intimidation designed to make Gibson limit or cease his union activities. The Union claimed that these were violations of the British Columbia *Labour Code*.

This matter was taken directly to the Labour Relations Board, without the usual grievance procedure. The reason for doing so was that the performance review of Captain Gibson was not prepared as the result of a term of the collective agreement. It could not, therefore be arbitrated.

The employer claimed that the remarks were "fair comment" — the honest opinion of a superior made while evaluating Captain Gibson's performance.

— Do you feel that Gibson's superior discriminated against him on the basis of his union activities? Discuss. If you do find discrimination, suggest an appropriate remedy.

The Canadian Union of Public Employees, Local 870 v. The Perley Hospital (1981) 81 C.L.L.C. 763 (O.L.R.B.)

The employees, mostly nursing staff, of the Perley Hospital staged an unlawful strike. Hospital workers under *The Hospital Labour Disputes Arbitration Act* perform an essential service and therefore do not have the right to strike. A stalemate at the bargaining table must be resolved by binding arbitration instead of a strike.

After the strike, the hospital dismissed the president and vice-president of the union local. It also disciplined other union executive members and members of the local who had participated in the strike by imposing suspensions ranging from one to ten days.

In addition, the Hospital did not recall thirty-eight of its employees, most of whom were nurse's aides holding the most junior positions in the bargaining unit.

The Union claimed that this was an unlawful lockout designed to "discourage the employees from normal lawful union activity."

The Hospital claimed that it was taking advantage of the unlawful strike to upgrade the quality of its nursing staff. The Hospital replaced the nurse's aides with thirty-eight new employees who were either registered nurses or registered nurse's aides.

—What is an essential service? What right do workers in an essential service lose?
—What is arbitration?
—When can an employer lawfully lock out members of the bargaining unit?
—Do you think the Hospital was engaged in an unlawful lockout? Explain.

Cameron and Teamsters Local Union 213 and Shuswap O'Kanagan Dairy Industries Co-operatives Association [1982] 2 Can. L.R.B.R. 215 (B.C.)

Margaret Cameron, a member of the Teamsters Union, worked for the Shuswap O'Kanagan Dairy Industries Co-op Association (called Noca) for eighteen years, at its butter packaging plant in Salmon Arm, British Columbia. In 1978, Noca began transferring its butter operation to its Vernon, B.C. plant, leaving only a small staff in Salmon Arm to run the cheesemaking operation. Cameron, who was sixty-two at the time, was laid off by Noca. She launched a grievance claiming that, first, she had been dismissed contrary to the collective agreement because employees junior to her continued to work at the Salmon Arm plant, and second, she was entitled to severance pay.

In discussions with union representatives about the possibility of "bumping out" a junior employee, Cameron was told that the work in the cheesemaking operation was physically very demanding and that she would be replacing a male employee if she did exercise her right. Cameron provided a medical certificate to her employer indicating her physical ability to work.

The union then proceeded to reach a settlement with Noca for severance pay for Cameron, but did not pursue her right to "bump". Cameron brought a grievance against her union, claiming that it had violated s. 7(1) of the British Columbia *Labour Code:*

> **7. (1)** A trade union or council of trade unions shall not act in a manner that is arbitrary, discriminatory or in bad faith in representing any of the employees in an appropriate bargaining unit...

At the hearing, union representatives claimed that they did not know whether Cameron would be able to perform the work and that the only way to have determined this would have been to throw an elderly woman "to the wolves" by putting her on a shift. They also stated that, if she had been incapable of performing the work, the union was afraid it would reduce her chances of getting a fair severance settlement.

— Do you think that the union acted in an arbitrary manner? in a discriminatory manner? in bad faith? Refer specifically to relevant facts in the case.
— Do you think that the Labour Relations Board found that the union had breached its duty of fair representation of its members? Explain. If so, suggest an appropriate remedy.

Glossary

absolute or **conditional discharge** A court order whereby a person convicted of a crime is deemed not to have been convicted. If the discharge is conditional, the person must successfully serve a period of probation before the order becomes absolute.

absolute liability In criminal law, a type of offence which does not require *mens rea*. If *actus reus* is proved, there is no defence.

abstract book Under the Registry Act system, the book in which interests in land are recorded.

acceptance Agreement to the conditions or requests specified in an offer.

access The right of the non-custodial parent to visit his or her child.

accessory after the fact A person who helps the offender after an offence has been committed.

accomplice A person who is a party to a crime.

accord and satisfaction Discharge of a contract, where one party agrees to accept something else when the other party cannot perform the original agreement.

Act A law passed by a government; a statute.

actus reus Latin for "guilty action"; the physical element of a crime.

administrative law The decisions of government agencies and boards and the law which regulates them.

administrator A person who is appointed by the court to administer a deceased person's estate when there is no will.

adoption A process creating a legal parent-child relationship between people who did not previously share that relationship.

adultery Voluntary sexual intercourse between a married person and someone other than that person's spouse.

adversarial system (or **process**) The system of trial in which each side presents its version of the facts and the law for impartial consideration before a judge or judge and jury.

adverse possession Occupation of land which is adverse to the true owner's interest and which may eventually extinguish the rights of the true owner.

affiliation proceeding A court hearing to try to establish the paternity of a child for the purpose of awarding support.

affinity A relationship created by marriage.

affirmative action An attempt to make up for the effects of past discrimination.

agent One who acts on behalf of another.

aiding and abetting Assisting or encouraging the principal party to a crime.

alibi A defence raised by a person accused of a crime that he or she was somewhere else when the crime was committed.

alien A person living in Canada who is not a Canadian citizen.

annulment The process of making a marriage legally void, as though the marriage never existed.

appearance The action of coming into court or into the record of a proceeding.

appearance notice A written form given to the accused by the police which tells the accused the offence being charged and when the accused must appear in court.

appellant A party who appeals the judgement of a court to a higher court.

appellate court A court which has the power to review decisions of lower courts.

arbitration A process for settling disputes between union and employer through a third party whose decision is final and binding.

arraignment The stage of the criminal proceeding when the charge is read to the accused and a plea is entered.

arrest The detention, with or without a warrant, of a person accused of committing a crime.

assault In tort law, the threat of bodily harm; in criminal law, the threat of actual physical contact without consent.

assignee The party to whom contractual rights are transferred.

assignment The transfer of a right under a contract to another person.

assignor A person who transfers his or her rights under a contract to another person.

attachment of assets Taking property into the custody of the law.

autrefois acquit, autrefois convict The defence of double jeopardy, where an accused claims that he or she has been previously acquitted or convicted of the offence charged.

bailee A person who controls someone else's property temporarily.

bailment The process of taking temporary possession of the property of someone else.

bailment for reward A bailment in which the bailee is paid by the bailor.

bailor A person who gives his or her property to someone else temporarily.

balance of probabilities The burden of proof in a civil case; the plaintiff must prove that it is more likely than not that the facts are as he or she claims.

bankruptcy A process by which the assets of a debtor who can no longer meet his or her obligations are divided among the creditors.

bargain in good faith An obligation placed on employer and union to seriously negotiate.

bargaining agent A trade union which acts on behalf of employees either in collective bargaining or as a party to a collective agreement with an employer.

bargaining unit All employees for whom a union is authorized to bargain.

battery In tort law, physical contact without consent.

bench warrant A warrant for arrest issued by a judge; for example, if an accused fails to appear for trial.

beneficiary A person who receives benefit from a trust or a will.

bestiality Sexual intercourse with an animal.

beyond a reasonable doubt The burden of proof on the prosecution in a criminal trial. The accused is presumed innocent until it is proved beyond a reasonable doubt that the accused committed the crime.

bigamy Marrying a person while still legally married to someone else.

bill A proposed piece of legislation.

bill of indictment A written accusation prepared by the Crown Attorney and presented to the court when the defendant is arraigned.

binding Enforceable at law.

Board of Inquiry A hearing held by an administrative tribunal.

bona fide Latin for "in good faith"; sincere and honest.

book debts The money owed to a business by its customers.

boycott General refusal to deal with an employer.

breach The breaking of contractual obligations.

breach of promise Breaking a promise to marry.

by-law A rule passed by a municipal government.

canon law Rules applied by church authorities.

case law The decisions of courts; judge-made law.

cause of action The incident which gives rise to a lawsuit.

caveat emptor Latin for "let the buyer beware"; a legal principle.

certification Official recognition by a labour relations board of a union as the bargaining agent for a group of employees.

challenge for cause A challenge of a potential juror by either side on the grounds that the juror is not impartial.

charge A term used under the Land Titles system: a registered interest against a piece of real property.

charging the jury A review made by the judge for the jury after each side in a trial has presented its case.

chattels A type of personal property; any kind of property other than land and choses in action. Same as "chose in possession".

child abuse Mental, physical, or sexual mistreatment of a child.

chose in action Intangible personal property which has value only because a court will if necessary enforce the right to it; for instance, a right under a contract.

chose in possession Personal property which is tangible and can be possessed. Same as "chattels".

circumstantial (indirect) evidence Evidence from which the existence of a fact-in-issue can be inferred.

civil law Another term for private law, the law of governing the relationship between individuals.

civil law system The legal system of Québec and most of Europe, which is based on a code, as opposed to common law.

civil marriage ceremony A non-religious ceremony before a judge or Justice of the Peace.

civil rights Individual rights guaranteed by law which cannot be interfered with by the government.

claim A legal document setting out the plaintiff's case against the defendant; same as a Statement of Claim, but at a lower court level.

class action A lawsuit in which one person sues on behalf of a group.

closing address Closing statements which the Crown and defence may make to the jury summarizing their cases.

closing argument Closing statements by the Crown and defence to the judge when there is no jury.

codicil An addition to a will.

codify To place all the law on a topic into one statute or code.

cohabitation agreement A contract between common law spouses.

collection agency A private business hired to collect money owed to the hirer.

collective agreement The employment contract between an employee and the members of a union.

collective bargaining Labour negotiations between management and a union representing the individual employees.

commission The fee to which a real estate agent is entitled upon selling a house, usually a percentage of the sale price.

common carrier A person or company that is in the business of transporting personal property.

common law marriage An agreement wherein a man and woman live together as husband and wife without a formal marriage ceremony.

common law system (1) The legal system of Canada's federal government and all provinces except Québec; (2) law originally developed from case law.

common mistake Occurs when both parties to an agreement make the same mistake.

community service order An order by a judge requiring a person convicted of a crime to do volunteer work for the community as part of the sentence.

conciliation The process by which a third party attempts to assist an employer and a trade union in arriving at a collective agreement.

concurrently Sentences imposed upon a convicted person which run at the same time.

condition A material or very important term of a contract.

conditional discharge See absolute or conditional discharge.

conditional offer An offer which is not firm until a certain condition is fulfilled.

conditional sale An agreement in which a purchaser pays for something he or she has bought by means of installment payments.

condition precedent A term in a contract stating that some future event must take place before one party's obligations are established.

condition subsequent A term of a contract which states that if a certain event occurs, one party will be released from his or her obligations.

conflict of interest Occurs when a party who has a responsibility to be impartial and unbiased has a personal interest in the outcome of a situation.

consanguinity A blood relationship.

consecutively Sentences imposed upon a convicted person which run one after another.

consideration The thing of value which each party to a contract receives from the other.

conspiracy An agreement to perform an unlawful action.

constitution The body of laws which establishes the political and legal foundations of a nation.

constructive trust An equitable principle to prevent the unjust enrichment of one party at the expense of another.

consumer A person who buys goods or services or both for personal or family use.

consummate To complete a marriage by sexual intercourse.

contract An agreement to do or not to do something between two or more people which the law will enforce.

contract under seal A contract which is in writing and under seal. Also known as "specialty contract".

contractual entrant A person who pays money to enter land.

contributory negligence A partial defence to negligence, that the plaintiff contributed to the harm through his or her own negligence.

conversion The tort of disposing of another's property by destroying or selling it.

costs The expenses involved in a lawsuit.

counselling and procuring Advising or getting someone to commit a crime.

counterclaim In a civil action, a legal claim which the defendant may also have against the plaintiff.

counter-offer An offer made in response to another offer.

criminal procedure The rules by which substantive criminal law is enforced.

(the) Crown In a criminal case, the prosecutor.

Crown corporation A corporation owned by the government.

Crown lands The lands in Canada that have never been granted to anyone by the Crown.

custody and guardianship Having the legal authority to care for a minor (infant).

damages Money awarded by a court to compensate a person for a wrong suffered.

decree absolute The final divorce decree, which completely severs the marriage bonds.

decree nisi The initial divorce decree, granted at trial.

deed The document by which ownership of land is transferred.

defamation Injury to the reputation of another by libel or slander.

defendant The party sued in a civil trial; the accused in a criminal action.

dependant's relief A law which allows dependants to seek financial support.

desertion The willful abandonment of an obligation or duty; a ground for divorce.

deterrence In criminal law, a purpose of punishment: to discourage specific criminals from breaking the law again and to generally deter the public from breaking the law.

detinue A tort wherein a person obtains property lawfully but then unlawfully retains possession of it for a certain period.

direct evidence Evidence of a witness given as proof of a fact.

discharge To cancel the obligations under a contract; to release the parties from their obligations. In a trial for an indictable offence, dismissal of the defendant by the judge without punitive sentence.

discrimination An action based on prejudice; usually involves differential treatment or the inflicting of disproportionate impact on a particular group.

disposition The decision of the court in a case involving a young person charged with committing a crime.

dispute A legal document in which the defendant answers the plaintiff's claim.

dissent judgement In an appeal, the minority opinion of the court.

distrain To seize a tenant's possessions in order to sell them to compensate the landlord for rent owed.

discovery A pre-trial process to disclose evidence to be presented during the trial.

domestic contract A contract between married, separated, or common law spouses.

due process of law A principle of justice expressed in the *Canadian Bill of Rights* that no person can be deprived of life, liberty, security of the person, or enjoyment of property except in accordance with the law.

duress The use of violence, threat of violence, or imprisonment to make a person do or say something against his or her will.

easement A type of interest in land which allows a landowner certain non-possessory rights over another person's property; for example, a right of way.

enemy alien A person living in Canada whose residence or business interests are located in enemy territory during wartime.

equitable assignment A type of contractual assignment where only some of the rights under the contract are assigned.

equity A body of law in which decisions are based on what is fair or just, not on a strict application of the law; administration of law by the spirit, not the letter, of the law.

essential services Certain areas of employment which are designated as necessary; employees in these areas do not have the right to strike.

estate The interest which a person has in real or personal property.

estoppel A restriction which prevents a person from denying or admitting something because of former actions.

eviction A process in which a landlord goes to court to obtain an order requiring a tenant to leave the rented premises.

examination-in-chief The questioning of its own witnesses by one side in a court action.

exclusive possession The right to occupy premises without having to share the premises with anyone.

executed In a contract, carried out.

execution A claim registered against the property of a person who has not paid the damages owing to the successful plaintiff in a civil action.

executor The person appointed in a will to carry out the terms of the will.

executory A contract where neither party has performed his or her obligations as yet.

exhibits Material objects and documents used as evidence during a trial.

expropriation The taking over of private land by government for the public good.

facts-in-issue The facts which must be proved to establish the case, as well as collateral facts, such as the credibility of a witness.

false imprisonment Unlawful physical restraint or detention.

family assets A term used in some provincial property statutes to refer to the property acquired by spouses and used for family purposes.

federal system A two-level system of government.

fee simple estate The largest parcel of rights which a person can have in land.

fixtures The objects attached to land, such as trees, buildings, and the things attached to buildings.

forbearance The giving up of a right; a type of consideration.

forensic medicine Any medical knowledge applied to the purposes of the law.

fraudulent misrepresentation A false statement of a material fact given knowingly or intentionally to induce a person to enter a contract.

fundamental (natural) justice The legal principle that everyone has the right to be heard and to be treated impartially and without bias; must be followed in legal proceedings.

future consideration Consideration to be received sometime in the future.

garnishee order An order sent to a judgement debtor's employer ordering the employer to set aside a certain amount of the debtor's wages to be applied against the judgement.

garnishment The setting aside by a judgement debtor's employer of a certain amount of the debtor's wages to be applied to the judgement.

general intent A type of *mens rea* required for some

crimes; the intent to perform a wrongful action.

genuine consent Freely entering into a contract whose nature is understood.

good consideration Those things that cannot be measured in money. Not valid consideration.

gratuitous bailment Occurs when a bailee takes charge of the bailor's property without charge or reward.

grievance A formal complaint made by an employee, the union, or management when it is believed that the collective agreement has not been followed.

grounds A term used in many areas of law; generally means "reasons".

guardian *ad litem* A person who represents a minor who is being sued.

habeas corpus The right of every person who has been detained or arrested to have a court hearing to determine whether the detention is legal.

harassment Unwelcome, annoying, upsetting, or frightening behaviour.

hearsay Evidence of a witness of what someone else said or wrote.

holograph will A handwritten will that has not been witnessed.

homicide Causing the death of another human being.

human rights The right of the individual to be protected from discrimination.

human rights legislation Provincial and federal legislation that protects people from certain types of discrimination.

hybrid (dual procedure) offences Crimes which the Crown may choose to try as either summary conviction offences or as indictable offences.

illegitimate Born out of wedlock.

impartiality Lack of bias.

included offence An offence which has the same basic elements as the principal offence, the offence being charged.

incorporation The creation of a legal body or person; done through registration with the federal or a provincial government.

indictable offences The most serious crimes.

infant A person who has not reached the legal age of majority; a minor.

infanticide In criminal law, the unlawful killing of an infant by its mother soon after its birth.

informant A person who lays an information.

information An accusation sworn before a judge or Justice of the Peace.

injunction A court order directing a person to cease a certain type of behaviour or activity.

innocent misrepresentation A false statement of a material fact given innocently or unknowingly.

insurable interest An interest in property or a person's life that would result in a financial loss for the insured if the property or life were damaged or destroyed.

intestacy Dying without making a will (intestate).

invitee An entrant to land from whom the occupier receives or has the potential for receiving an economic benefit.

joint tenancy Joint ownership of land; carries the right of survivorship.

judgement An order of a court.

Judgement Summons A court order commanding a debtor to appear before the court to explain why a judgement has not been satisfied.

judicial Pertaining to the administration of justice.

judicial authority Authority exercised by judges in court.

judicial interim release The pre-trial release of persons accused of crimes.

jurisdiction The extent of authority to act.

just cause Good reason.

lapse To no longer be in effect.

leading questions Questions which suggest the answer, i.e., can be answered by "Yes" or "No".

lease A contract between landlord and tenant concerning the renting of real property.

legacy A gift made by will.

legislation Statute law; law made by a government.

legislative authority Authority given by statute.

legislature A body of elected representatives who make our laws.

Letters Probate A court document which states that a will is valid, and confirms the appointment of the executor.

levy execution To seize the property of a judgement debtor and sell it to pay off a judgement; done by a sheriff.

liability Legal responsibility for a wrongful action.

libel Written statements, radio and television programs, and movies which harm a person's reputation.

licensee An entrant to land from whom the owner derives no economic benefit; for example, a visitor or guest.

lien A legal claim upon real or personal property to satisfy a debt.

life estate An interest in real property which ends when the holder dies; that is, an interest wherein the property cannot be transferred by will or intestacy.

liquidate To turn assets into cash.

liquidated damages clause A contract clause which sets out the amount of damages to which each party is entitled if the other party breaches the contract.

litigants The parties involved in a civil action: the plaintiff and the defendant.

listing agreement A contract which gives the terms of the sale made with a real estate agent by homeowners who wish to sell their property.

litigation The process of suing; a lawsuit.

local A basic unit of union organization, also called a branch.

lock-out The closing of a place of employment by management, done to compel employees to agree to conditions of employment.

majority opinion In an appeal, the decision by the majority of the judges on the panel.

mandatory supervision The release of an inmate before the full sentence is served because of time off for good behaviour.

marriage contract A contract between a husband and wife outlining their agreement about how certain aspects of their marriage will be conducted.

master and servant The employer-employee relationship.

material alteration A change of a major term in a contract; discharges the contract and creates a new one.

material fact A fact which induces a person to enter a contract.

mechanic's lien A type of interest registered against property by a person who has provided goods or services for property and has not been paid.

mediation A process to resolve a labour dispute through the appointment of a neutral third party.

mediator A person appointed by labour relations officials to assist employer and union in the bargaining process.

mens rea Latin for "guilty mind"; the mental element of a crime.

minor A person who has not reached the legal age of majority; an infant.

misrepresentation False statement of a material fact.

money's worth Physical labour, goods, or improvements to property.

mortgage A loan which the mortgagee gives to the mortgagor; secured by the mortgagee's receiving legal title to but not possession of the property.

mortgagee A party that gives loans secured by title to property.

mortgagor A party that receives a loan which is secured by title to property.

motion for dismissal A motion made by the defence at the close of the Crown's case in a criminal trial asking that the charges be dismissed for lack of evidence.

mutual mistake Occurs when the parties to an agreement each make a different mistake.

necessary A good or service supplied to a minor which is needed at the time of purchase and is suitable to the minor's station in life.

negligence Conduct which falls below the standard of behaviour required by society and which involves an unreasonable risk of harm to others.

next friend A person who represents a minor who is suing.

non est factum Latin for "It is not my deed"; a defence used to avoid a contract when the person has signed something totally different from what he or she thought it was.

notice A written statement of intent.

novation The substitution of a party to a contract with the consent of the parties.

null and void Having no legal effect.

offer A promise by one party to do something if the other party will agree to some specific condition or request.

offeree A party to whom an offer is made.

offeror A party that makes an offer.

offer to purchase Agreement of purchase and sale; document containing the terms of the offer, drafted by the parties who wish to purchase a house.

option to terminate A term in a contract of indefinite length stating that one party or both can end the contract at will.

order for possession A court order allowing a landlord to enter rented premises and exclude the tenant.

ordinance A rule established by a governing body; similar to legislation.

pardon A process of forgiving the crime of a convicted person and setting aside his or her record.

parol Oral.

parol evidence rule An oral or written term agreed to by parties which will not be allowed to add to or to contradict the agreement once the contract is formalized.

parole The conditional release of an inmate before the full prison term has been served.

partnership of acquests The family property system used in Québec under the Civil Code.

past consideration A benefit received by a person before he or she has promised to do something; not valid because not bargained for.

patriated Brought to one's own country, as in the patriation of the Canadian Constitution.

peace bond A written promise to a court to keep the peace.

penalty clause A term in a contract which entitles one

party to a certain sum of money if the other party fails to perform, where the sum is not a reasonable estimate of the injured party's damages but is punitive.

peremptory challenge The rejection of a potential juror without cause; each side in a criminal trial has a certain number of peremptory challenges.

periodic tenancy A tenancy in which the rights of landlord and tenant are renewed for specific lengths of time called "terms".

personal property All property other than land: chattels and choses in action.

petition for divorce The legal document commencing the proceedings to end a marriage by divorce.

petitioner The plaintiff in divorce proceedings.

picket Striking workers who are posted at a place of business to publicize a labour dispute.

plaintiff The party that sues.

pleadings The documents filed with the court which set out the positions taken by the parties to a lawsuit.

power of attorney A legal document authorizing a person to act on behalf of another.

precedent A rule established in a judicial decision, to be followed in similar cases.

preferring (presenting) the indictment The method of beginning the trial of an indictable offence which will not be tried by a magistrate or Provincial Court judge.

prejudice An assumption or fixed idea about a group—usually negative; an untested judgement.

preliminary hearing A pre-trial hearing for an indictable offence which is not going to be tried before a magistrate or Provincial Court judge; used to weed out the weak cases and give the defendant a chance to see the Crown's case.

prescription A right which one person may gain to another's property through use over a period of time.

pre-sentence report A report prepared by a probation officer before the sentencing.

pre-trial conference A meeting of the parties before a judge to clarify the issues in dispute prior to trial.

principal A person for whom another is an agent.

private carrier A person or company that sometimes transports goods.

private law The law governing the relationships between individuals; also called "civil law".

privity of contract The rule that a contract imposes obligations on or gives benefits to the parties to the contract only.

probate To establish the validity of a will.

probation The process whereby a convicted person may have a sentence of imprisonment suspended and instead be released, on the condition that he or she must be of good behaviour and must fulfill all other conditions set by the judge.

procedural equality One definition of equality before the law; means that the law is applied equally to all the people it affects even though the law itself may not treat people equally.

procedural law The law which sets out the methods whereby rights and obligations can be enforced.

promisee In contract law, the person who transfers a right under contract. Same as assignor.

promise to appear A form signed by an arrested person before release by the police in which the accused promises to appear in court.

promisor The person who must perform when a contractual right is assigned.

property interest An element of the legal ownership of something; for example, possession, control, right to use, right to destroy.

public law The law governing the relationship between government and individuals and among branches and levels of government.

pyramid selling A marketing scheme wherein the sellers are encouraged to recruit others to work under them. If the pyramid works, there are soon more salespeople than customers in any one location.

quantum meruit A legal remedy which requires a person to pay a reasonable price for goods or services rendered.

quash To rule invalid.

quasi-criminal offence An offence against certain provincial laws, the penalty for which resembles that for committing a crime.

quasi-judicial bodies Administrative boards and agencies which make decisions affecting individuals.

quiet enjoyment A tenant's right to freedom from any serious interference with the use and enjoyment of rented property.

ratify To approve or confirm.

real property Land and everything attached to it.

recognizance Generally, a signed statement or promise made to a judge or Justice of the Peace to keep the peace and abide by any conditions set out in the order; in criminal law, the accused agrees to pay a certain amount of money if he or she fails to appear for the stated court date.

referral sale A type of sale in which the seller offers the buyer a discount if the buyer will help to attract more customers.

register Under the Land Titles system, the book in which interests in land are recorded.

regulation An addition to a

statute, dealing with details that may change over time.

rehabilitation The process of reforming a person.

repeal To cancel a statute.

reports Volumes in which judges' court decisions (case law) are recorded.

reprisal A form of revenge; an action taken against a person because of something that person has said or done.

repudiate To reject, renounce.

rescind In contract law, to cancel; to return the parties to their positions before the contract was made.

residual power The federal government's authority to make laws in areas not specifically assigned to the jurisdiction of the provinces.

residue (of an estate) Property not specifically mentioned as a gift in a will.

res judicata Latin for "a matter adjudicated"; that is, once an issue has been determined by a court, it cannot be raised again. A broader defence than *autrefois acquit* or *autrefois convict*.

respondent (1) The party in a criminal or civil case who opposes the appeal; (2) the defendant in a divorce action.

restitution order In a criminal case, an order by the judge requiring the convicted person to repay the victim of the crime for the damage which has been done.

restraining order A court order requiring a person not to annoy or harass his or her spouse and/or children.

restrictive covenant (1) An agreement not to do something; (2) an agreement which restricts the use of land, as in allowing its use for residential purposes only.

retribution Vengeance.

revoke To cancel, annul, take back.

right of survivorship The right of a surviving joint tenant to the property owned in joint tenancy.

right of way A legal interest in property that gives a person the right to pass through another's piece of property to get to his or her own property; a type of easement.

rule of law The legal principle that society is governed by law that applies equally to all.

rule of precedent The following by judges of legal principles or decisions established in previous similar court cases; same as *stare decisis*.

search warrant A document usually issued by a Justice of the Peace, authorizing the police to search a building, receptacle, or place.

security deposit An amount of money left by a tenant with the landlord to cover any damage caused by the tenant to the premises or to cover the last month's rent.

security of tenure A tenant's right to stay in the rented premises unless the landlord has a specific legal reason to remove the tenant.

separation agreement A contract settling their affairs between a husband and wife who have agreed to live apart.

separation of property (system) An ownership system under which property is owned by the person who bought it, inherited it, or received it as a gift.

set-off A claim by a defendant in a civil action that the plaintiff owes him or her a sum of money for a debt unrelated to the cause of action.

sheriff An officer of the court who has the power to enforce court orders.

simple contract A contract not under seal.

slander Oral statements or actions which harm another's reputation.

sodomy Anal sexual intercourse.

specialty contract A contract which is in writing and under seal. Generally called a "contract under seal".

specific intent A type of *mens rea* required for some criminal offences; the intent to commit an unlawful action for another unlawful purpose; for instance, assault with intent to steal is a type of robbery.

specific performance A remedy in equity in which the court orders one party to do something.

spouse (1) A husband or wife; (2) a man or woman living in a common law relationship.

stand aside The right of the Crown to ask up to forty-eight jurors to go to the end of the line of the jurors eligible for a trial.

stare decisis Latin for "to stand by former decisions"; the following of legal principles or precedents established in previous court decisions.

stated case A summary conviction appeal involving a question of law only.

statement of adjustments The statement presented at the closing of a real estate sale; shows how much the purchaser owes the vendor.

Statement of Claim See claim.

Statement of Defence In a civil action, the defendant's response and defence to a Statement of Claim.

statute (law) Legislation, law passed by any legislative body; an Act.

statutory assignment A type of contractual assignment wherein all of the rights under the contract are assigned.

steward A union official to whom individual employees can turn for information and assistance in matters pertaining to the collective agreement.

strict liability In criminal law, a type of offence for which no *mens rea* is required. If *actus reus* is established, the only defence

GLOSSARY 589

is that the defendant acted with due diligence (without negligence).

strike A work stoppage by union members to enforce their contract demands.

stranger (to a contract) Any person not a party to a contract. Also called "third party", "third person".

subletting The passing on of an apartment by its tenant to another tenant for some limited period.

substantial performance The legal principle that, if one party has performed most but not all of his or her contractual obligations, the other party cannot avoid performance.

substantive criminal law The law which prohibits certain actions, defines defences, and sets out penalties.

substantive rules The law which states the rights and obligations of individuals.

substituted action A lawsuit in which the Director who administers a business practice sues on behalf of a group of consumers.

substituted agreement A means of discharging a contract; can be achieved in three ways: material alteration, accord and satisfaction, and novation.

summary conviction offences The less serious crimes.

summons An order to appear in court, issued by a Justice of the Peace.

surety A person who signs a recognizance for an accused; will be held responsible if the accused fails to appear for a court date.

suspended sentence Occurs when a judge who has sentenced a person to a term of imprisonment places the convicted person on probation instead. If the person violates probation, the term of imprisonment may have to be served.

sworn in The state of a witness who has, before testifying, taken an oath to the effect that the evidence to be given is true.

tenancy in common Joint ownership of land that does not have the right of survivorship; a tenant in common may pass on property by will or intestacy.

testator/testatrix A male/female person who makes a will.

third party (third person) Any person not a party to a contract. Also called "stranger to the contract".

title Ownership.

tort A civil offence or private wrong.

tortfeasor A person who commits a tort.

trespass (1) An unlawful entry onto another's property; (2) unlawful interference with another's chattels or real property.

trespasser A person who enters onto land without consent.

trust Occurs where one party holds an interest in property for the benefit of another.

trustee A person who holds property for the benefit of another, and who must act on behalf of that other person.

ultra vires Latin for "beyond the powers"; used to refer to actions which are beyond the authority of a government.

unconscionable Extremely unfair, unscrupulously excessive in the given situation.

unconscionable transaction A business exchange in which a person is taken advantage of in a very unfair way.

undue influence Personal pressure exerted to induce another person to do something; for instance, enter a contract, make a will.

unfair labour practices Certain illegal activities of an employer or union members.

unilateral mistake A mistake made by one party to an agreement.

union An organization whose purpose is to represent and negotiate for the employees of a particular company or industry.

valid Legal, properly constructed or carried out.

vendor A person who is selling property; usually used for real property.

venue Place of trial.

vicarious liability Responsibility of one person for the action of another.

vicarious performance Occurs where a party to a contract has someone else actually perform the obligations but the party is still responsible for proper performance.

void Of no legal effect; not legally valid.

void *ab initio* Latin for void "from the beginning"; not legally valid from the start.

voidable A contract that may be declared void at the option of one or both parties.

voluntary assumption of risk The legal principle that no harm is done to one who consents; a defence to negligence that the plaintiff voluntarily accepted the risk.

waiver An agreement by the parties to call off all or part of a contract.

ward A minor (infant) placed in the charge of a guardian or a court either temporarily or permanently.

warrant for arrest A court order, usually issued by a Justice of the Peace, ordering the police to bring an accused to court.

warranty A non-material term of a contract; less important than a condition.

water rights The right of a landowner to the reasonable use of water that runs through his or her own land.

wildcat strike An illegal strike action.

witness To watch; also refers to a person who has been present and has observed a certain event.

Writ of Execution A court order authorizing a sheriff to seize and auction off the assets of an unsuccessful defendant in a civil action.

Writ of Summons The document which usually initiates a civil action.

Index

A

Abortion, 152-53
Abstract book, 494
Absolute liability, 72-74
Acceptance, contract, 269-70
  validity of, 274-75
    positive action, 274-75
    unconditional acceptance, 275
Accessory after the fact, 76
Actus reus, 69-70
Administrative law, 7
Adoption, 378-80
  child, rights of, 380
  consent, 379-80
Adversarial system, 15
Adverse possession, 495
Affiliation proceeding, 367
Affirmative action, 203-204
Agreement of Purchase and Sale—See Offer to Purchase
Aiding and abetting, 75-76
Allurement, 238
Annulment, 352, 402-3
  effect on children, 378
  provincial property and support legislation, 403
Anti-discrimination—See discrimination
Appeals
  indictable offences, 121-22
  summary conviction offences, 124
Appearance notice, 87
Arraignment, 110, 113
Arrest, 88
  illegal, remedies for, 93-95
    evidence illegally obtained, 94
    habeas corpus, 94
    right to resist, 95
  by persons other than police, 90
  procedure for making, 90-91
  following, 99-100
  warrant, 88-89
Arrested person, rights and obligations, 91-93
Assault, 150-51
Assault and battery, 213-14
Assignment, 318-19
Attachment of assets—See Writ of Execution
Attempted offences, 74-75
Automatism, 175

B

Bail—See Judicial interim release
Bailiff, 254
Bailment, 469
  common law rules, 470-78

contracts and, 481-82
creating, 469
gratuitous, 470-72
legislation and, 478-80
property
  holding as pledge or pawn, 476
  renting, 475-76
  storing, 475-76
  transporting, 476-77
  repair work, 474-75
  for reward, 473
Bail Reform Act, 99
Balance of probabilities, 260-61
Bankruptcy, 320
Bench warrant, 88
Beyond a reasonable doubt, 77-78
Bill of Rights, 10, 13
  civil rights and freedoms, 44-46
Bills
  passing, 32-36
  private members, 32
  public, 32
  Royal Assent, 34
  taxation, 34
Board of Inquiry, 203
Book debts, 319
Breach of contract, 326-28
  express repudiation, 327
  failure to perform, 328
  part performance, 333-34
  remedies for, 329-32
  rendering performance impossible, 327-28
  sale of goods, 334-35
Breach of the peace, 89
Breach of promise, 343
Break-and-enter, 156-57
Breathalyzer tests, 91
By-laws, 27
  criminal law, 68

C

Canada Act, 25
Canada Elections Act, 50
Canada Pension Plan, 551
Canadian Charter of Rights and Freedoms, 5, 25
  civil rights and freedoms, 43-44
  enforcement, 59
  equality rights section, 36
  general matters, 59-60
  habeas corpus, 94
  illegally obtained evidence, 94
  limitations, 46-47
  other rights not denied by, 60

  override clause, 44
Canon law, 22
Capital punishment—See Death penalty
Case law, 23
  statutes, interpreting, 37
Cause of action, 248
Certification, 563, 564-65
Charter of Rights and Freedoms—See *Canadian Charter of Rights and Freedoms*
Chattels, 217
Child abuse, 369-73
Children
  illegitimate, 368
  legal rights, 365
    education, 368-69
    financial support, 366-68
    living with parents and siblings, 369
    protection from harm or neglect, 369-73
Circumstantial evidence—See Evidence, indirect
Civil actions—See also Civil procedure
  before bringing, 248
  bringing, 253
  courts, 249-52
  damages, 262
  judgement, 261
  limitation periods, 248
Civil freedom—See Freedoms
Civil law—See also Private law
  system, 18-19
  and common law compared, 23-24
  general principles as source of, 23
Civil liability
  insurance against, 263
Civil procedure
  higher courts, 256-63
  Small Claims Court, 253-56
  young people and, 247
Civil rights, 43—See also Human rights; Rights
Charter of Rights and Freedoms, 47
  democratic rights, 50-51
  enforcement, 59
  equality rights, 53-56
  fundamental freedoms, 48-49
  legal rights, 52-53
  minority language education rights, 58-59

592 INDEX

mobility rights, 51
official languages rights, 56-58
sources of, 43-46
Claim, statement of, 254, 258
Class action, 454
Closing address, 117
Closing argument—See Closing address
Cohabitation, 354-56
Collective bargaining, 536
  certification, 564-65
  cycle, 563
  organization, 563-64
  contract administration, 573-74
  development of, 562-63
  negotiation, 566-69
    fringe benefits, 567
    grievance procedure, 567
    seniority systems, 567
    union shop agreement, 567
    wages, 567
  stalemate resolution, 569-73
    arbitration, 571
    conciliation, 569-70
    mediation, 570
    strikes and lockouts, 571-73
Common law, 22, 23
  and civil law compared, 23-24
  precedents, 20
  system, 19-21
Community service orders, 120
Compensation for crime, 66
Compulsion—See Duress
Computer crime, 67
Condition
  consumer law, 438-39
  implied, 439
  precedent, 324
  subsequent, 324
Conditional sales, 456-57
  problems and legal remedies, 457-58
Conflict of interest, 14
Conscience and religion, freedom of, 48
Consent, 218
Conspiracy, 77
Constitution
  defined, 25
  patriation, 25
Constitutional law, defined, 5
Consumer(s)
  credit, buying on, 454
  law, sources of, 437
  loan, cost of, 455
Consumer protection
  controlling certain sales, 449-50
  defective goods and credit card purchases, 456
  defective products, 442

false or misleading advertising or sales practices, 444-48
group actions, 454
high pressure door-to-door sales, 444
manufacturer responsibility, 452
preventing sale of certain products, 451-52
unconscionable transactions, 448
Contract(s)
  breach of—See Breach of contract
  consideration, 278-82
  contrary to common law, 305
  corporations, 296
  defined, 268
  forms, 268
  necessary elements, 269
  parol, 269
  simple, 269
  under seal, 268
  discharge of—See Discharge of contracts
  domestic—See Domestic contracts
  duress, 302-303
  to eliminate competition, 307-308
  employment—See Employment contract
  with enemy aliens, 305
  executory, 291
  forbidden by statute, 305-306
    betting and wagering, 305-306
    made on Sunday, 306-307
  genuine consent, 296-303
  interest, unconscionable rates of, 307
  law, defined, 4-5
  legal capacity, 289-96
  legal purpose, 303-308
  liquidated damages clause, 329-30
  mentally handicapped and intoxicated persons, 295
  minors, 289-95
  misrepresentation, 297-99
    fraudulent, 298
    innocent, 297
    negligent, 298-99
    utmost good faith, 299
  mistake, 299-302
    common, 299-300
    mutual, 300
    unilateral, 301-302
  necessaries, for, 293
  offer and acceptance, 269-75
  partial execution, 291
  penalty clause, 330

Privity of—See Privity of contract
public policy, contrary to, 304
in restraint of marriage, 305
in restraint of trade, 304
restrictive covenant, 304
undue influence, 303
valid, 292
void, 292
voidable, 289-92
  avoidance of, 291-92
when formed, 276-78
Contractual entrant, 238
Contributory negligence—See Negligence
Coroner's court, 39
Counselling and procuring, 76
Counter-claim, 256
Courts, 38-39
  civil, 249-52
    federal jurisdiction, 251-52
    porovincial jurisdiction, 249-51
  superior, in provinces, 87
  system, criminal, 86
Courts of Chancery—See Courts of Equity
Courts of Equity, 21
Credit
  bills, enforcing payment of, 459
Credit...cont'd
  collection agencies, 459-60
  reporting agencies, 458
Crime(s)
  defined, 65-66
  basic elements of, 69
  parties to the offence, 75-76
  principal actor, 75
  attempted offences, 74-75
  general intent, 71
  intention in common, 76
Criminal
  court system, 86-87
  negligence, 72, 140-41
Criminal Code
  arrest without warrant, 88-89
  enforcement, 67
  when passed, 68
Criminal law
  defined, 5
  jurisdiction, 67-68
Criminal offences
  abortion, 152-53
  against the administration of law and justice, 136
  assault, 150-52
  against the person and reputation, 140-46
  against property rights, 153-58
  against the public order, 134-35

sexual, public morals, and disorderly conduct, 137-40
wilful and forbidden acts in respect of certain property, 158-59
Criminal procedure
arrests, 90-95
following, 99-100
criminal court system, 86-87
defined, 65
hearing before Justice of the Peace, 100
offences, types of, 85
police powers, 87-90
powers of search, 95-98
Crown Attorney, 66
Crown lands, 490-91
Custody
children born out of wedlock, 376-78
joint, 376
parents' rights, 373-74
broken marriage, 374-76
to other persons, 376
spouses rights, 354
Customs Act, search without a warrant, 97

D
Damages, 212, 261-62
breach of contract, 329
liquidated, 329-30
payment of, 330
general, 262
special, 262
Dangerous driving, 147
Day parole, 119
Death penalty, abolition of, 12
Defamation, 231
defences to, 232-33
Defence(s)
automatism, 175
delusions, 174-75
double jeopardy, 181-82
duress or compulsion, 177-79
insanity, 172-74
intoxication, 176-77
mistake of fact; of law, 180
necessity, 180
of property, 179
self-defence, 179
statement of, 258
of third party, 219-20
young children, incapacity of, 171-172
Defendant, 86
civil action, 212
rights at trial, 108
sentencing, 118-19
Delusions, 174-75

Discharge, 120
Discharge of contract, 321-26
by agreement, 321-24
contracts providing for their own dissolution, 323-24
substituted agreement, 322-23
waiver, 322
by frustration, 324-26
by operation of the law, 326
bankruptcy, 326
limitation of actions, 326
by performance, 321
Discovery, 258-59
Discrimination, 191-94
equality rights, 53-56
prohibited grounds of
Bill of Rights, 54
Charter of Rights and Freedoms, 53
rental accommodation, 516
Dispute, 256
Disturbance, causing, 139-40
Divorce, 397
law, reform, 398-401
permanent marital breakdown, 398
petition for, 258, 401
Divorce Act, 1968, 397-98
Domestic contracts, 356-58
cohabitation agreement, 357
marriage contract, 356
separation agreement, 357
Double jeopardy, 181-82
Driving with more than 80 mg of alcohol in the blood, 149-50
Drug offences, 159-63
importing and exporting, 162
possession, 160
constructive, 161
by more than one person, 161
personal, 160
restricted drugs, 163
trafficking, 161-62
Dual procedure offence—See Hybrid offence
Due process of law, 10
Duress, 177-79

E
Earned remission, 120
Ecclesiastical law—See Canon law
Employee, obligations, 538-40
Employer liability for employee torts, 541-42
Employer-employee relationship, 536-37
common law and, 538
independent contractor and client, 554-55
principal and agent, 552-54

statute law and the workplace, 542-43
wrongful dismissal, 540-41
Employment
equal pay, 546
holidays and vacation pay, 545-46
human rights, 551
maternity leave, 546-47
maximum hours of work; overtime pay, 544-45
minimum age, 543
minimum wage, 543-44
notice of termination, 547-48
occupational health and safety, 548-49
protection, federal, 551-52
workers' compensation, 548-49
Employment contract, 534-36
Engagement, 343-45
Equality
before the law, 54-56
procedural, 56
Equity, law of, 21-22
Estates, 491
fee simple, 491
life, 491
Euthanasia, 17
Evidence
direct, 115
indirect, 116
rebuttal, 115
rules of, 115
surrebuttal, 115
illegally obtained, 94
material objects and documents as, 116
Excise Act, search without a warrant, 97
Exhibits, 117
Express grant, easements, 493
Expression, freedom of, 49

F
Facts-in-issue, 115
Fair comment, 233
False imprisonment, 214
Family
assets, 393
court, 251
law, defined, 5
violence, in, 405-7
Federal Court, 38, 251
Federal government
jurisdiction of, 25-26
residual power, 26
Fingerprints, taking, 91
Food and Drugs Act, 163
controlled drugs, 163
restricted drugs, 163

594 INDEX

search without a warrant, 97
Freedoms
    civil, 43
        sources of, 43-46
    fundamental, 48-49
        conscience and religion, 48
        expression, 49
        peaceful assembly, 49
Fundamental justice, 12
    right to be heard, 12-13

G
Garnishment, 262
Governor-General, 28
Guardian *ad litem*, 247

H
Habeas corpus, 94
Hearsay, 115
Homicide, 141-42
House of Commons, 30-31
Human Rights—See also Civil
    rights; Rights
    defined, 43
    employment, 551
Human Rights Commissions,
    200-201
    complaint, 201
    conciliation and settlement,
        202-203
    investigation, 201-202
Human rights legislation, 200-203
    activities affected, 196-97
    and *Charter of Rights and Freedoms*, 204-205
    defined, 5
    exceptions, 198-99
    harassment, 199-200
    jurisdiction, 194-95
    prohibited grounds, 197
    reprisals, 200
Hybrid offence, 85

I
Identification line-up, 91
Illegal arrest—See Arrest
Impaired driving, 147
    penalties for, 148
    proof of, 148
Indictable offence(s), 85
    appeals of, 121-22
    jury trials, 111-12
    preliminary hearing, 110
    procedure for trying, 108-109
    trial, 112-19
Indictment, bill of, 110
    preferring, 110
Individual bargaining, 536
Infants, 247
Information, laying, 88

Injunction, 212
    breach of contract, 331-32
Innoncence, presumption of, 77
Insanity as defence, 172-74
Intent, 70
    general, 71
    specific, 71
Intentional infliction of mental
    suffering, 214-15
Intestacy, 424-26
Intoxication as defence, 176-77
Invasion of privacy, 215-16

J
Joyriding, 155
Judges, Provincial Court, 86
Judgement, 248
    civil actions, 261-62
        enforcement, 262-63
    summons, 263
Judicial interim release, 99
Judiciary, independence of, 14-15
Jurisdiction
    criminal law, 67-68
    penitentiaries, 68
    prisons, 68
    reformatories, 68
Jurors, challenging, 112
Jury
    charge to, 117
    trial—See trial
Justices of the Peace, 86, 95
Justinian's Code, 19

K
Kidnapping, 71

L
Labour law, 5
Landlord(s)
    defined, 512
    residential, rights and responsibilities, 516
        discrimination, 516
        distrain, right to, 517
        security deposits, 518-19
        when tenant can be evicted,
            525
Landlord and tenant law, 512-13
    exclusive possession, 513
    premises defined, 513
    rent, 513
    sources of, 514-16
        common law, 514
        leases, 514-15
        statute law, 514
Law
    acceptance of, 8-9
    change, procedure for, 12
    classes of, 6-8

    private, 7
    procedural, 87
    public, 7
    substantive, 7
    defined, 6
    due process of, 10
    equal application of, 11
    functions of, 3-6
    government by, 10-11
    impartiality, 14
    Rule of, 8
Lawmaking
    Parliament, supremacy of, 45-46
    process, 25-37
        federal system, 25
        judicial, 37-38
        jurisdiction, 25-27
        parliamentary system, 27-31
        statutes, passing, 32-36
Lease(s), 514-16
    terminating, 523-24
Legal authority as defence, 220,
    235
Letters Probate, 427
Liability, 212
Litigants, 246
Litigation, 246

M
Magistrates, 86
Mandatory supervision, 120
Manslaughter, 144-45
    murder reduced to, 145
Marriage
    common law, 354-56
        ending, 403-5
        domestic contracts, 356-58
    essential requirements, 345-49
        age, 348
        consanguinity and affinity,
            348-49
        consent, 346
        consummation, 345
        freedom to marry, 347
        mental competence, 347
    formal requirements, 349-51
        age, 350
        ceremony, 349-50
        licence or banns, 349
Marriage cont'd
    invalid, 351-52
    spouses rights and responsibilities, 353-54
Master and servant—See
    Employer-employee relationship
Matrimonial
    home, 358
    offences, 397
Mechanic's lien, 503
Mens rea, 70-72

intent, 70
knowledge, 72
recklessness, 72
Mercantile law, 22
Minority rights—See Civil rights; Discrimination
Minors, 247
   contracts, legal capacity, 289-95
Mischief, 159
   defined, 71
Mortgage
   obtaining, 501
   cost of, 502
Motor vehicle
   criminal negligence, 147
   judgement enforcement, 263
Municipal governments, jurisdiction, 27
Murder, 143
   classes of, 144

N
Napoleonic Code, 19
Narcotic Control Act, 68, 159
   search without a warrant, 97-98
National Parole Board, 120, 122
Natural justice—See Fundamental justice
Negligence, 221-29
   causation, 225-26
   contributory, 227-29
   duty of care, 222-23
   defences to, 227
   real loss or injury, 226
   standard of care and the reasonable person, 223-24
Next friend, 247
Non-family assets, 393
Nuisance, 233-35
   defences to, 235-36

O
Obscene materials, 137-38
Occupier's liability, 237
   allurement, 238
   contractual entrant, 238
Offences, types of, 85
Offer, contract(s), 269-70
   advertisements, 272-73
   counter-offer, 274
   terminating, 273
   validity of, 270-71
Offer to Purchase, land transfer, 499
Opposition, Her Majesty's Loyal, 30

P
Pardon, obtaining, 122-23
Parents, custody rights, 373-74

Parliament, supremacy of, 45-46
Parliamentary system, 27-31
Parol contracts, 269
Parol evidence rule, 278
Parole, 119
Partnership of acquests, 394
Peace bond, 405
Peace officer, 90
   obstructing, 136
Peaceful assembly, freedom of, 49
Penitentiaries, 68
Pleadings, 258
Police
   force, provincial responsibility to maintain, 67
   powers of
      breathalyzer tests, 91
      fingerprints, 91
      identification line-up, 91
      photographs, 91
      search, 95-98
      vehicle, stopping, 91
Pornography and censorship, 137-39
Possession of property obtained by crime, 157-58
Precedents, 20
Prejudice, 191-94
Prescription, 235
   easements, 493
Pre-sentence report, 118
Pre-trial conference, 259
Principal and agent, 552-54
Prisons, 68
Prison system, 119-21
Private law, 7
Privilege
   absolute, 232
   qualified, 232
Privity of contract, 317-20
   exceptions, 317
      assignments, 318
      contracts involving land, 317
      insurance, 317
      trusts, 318
      vicarious performance, 318
Probate Court—See Surrogate Court
Probation, 120
Probation officer, 118
Procedural law, 7-8
Proclamation, statutes, 34
Product liability, 235-36
Promise to appear, 99
Property
   bailed, caring for, 469-70
   defence of, 179, 220
   law, 7
   family
      provincial legislation, 392-97
      unequal sharing, 395

   personal, 468
   real—See Real property
   restrictions on the use of, 496-98
   rights, spouses, 354
   title to, 491
Provincial courts, 38-39
Provincial government, jurisdiction, 26
Public law, 7
Public officer, obstructing, 136
Public servants, 30
Punishment, purposes of, 121
   deterrence, 121
   rehabilitation, 121
   retribution, 121

Q
Quantum meruit, 330
Quasi-criminal offences, 68
Quasi-judicial bodies, 12
Quebec civil law, 18-19

R
Real property
   defined, 489-90
   easements, 492-93
   estates—See Estates
   Joint tenants, 492
   ownership and title of, 490-91
   registration systems, 494-96
   restrictive covenants, 493-94
   tenancy in common, 492
   transferring title, 498-506
      adjustments, statement of, 506
      closing transaction, 505-6
      financing, arranging, 501-2
      listing agreement, 499
      offer to purchase, 499-500
      searching title, 503-5
Recent possession, 158
Recognizance, entering, 99
Reformatories, 68
Registry Act system, 494
   title searching, 504
Regulations, statutes, 36-37
Rent review law, 526-27
Reservation, easements, 493
Residual power, 26
Res judicata, 181
Restitution, 121
Rights—See also Civil Rights: Human Rights
   of accused to retain and instruct counsel, 92-93
   of arrested persons, 91-93
   of defendant at trial, 108
   defined, 43
   not to be detained without just cause, 93

limits on, 46-47
prompt information of reasons for arrest, 91-92
to remain silent after arrest, 91
young offenders, 126
Riots, 134-35
Risk, voluntary assumption of, 227
Robbery, 155-56
Royal Assent, 28, 34
Rule of law, 8
Rule of precedent—See *Stare decisis*

S
Sale of Goods Act, 437-38, 440-42
Search(es), 95-98
when carried out, 96
illegal, remedies for, 98
warrant
with, 95-97
without, 97-98
Security deposits, rent, 518-19
Security of the person, 13-14
Self-defence, 179, 219-20
Senate, 28, 30
Sentencing, 118-20 See also Punishment
community service orders, 120
discharge, 120
probation, 120
restitution, 120
suspended sentence, 120
young offenders, 126
Separation
agreements, 388-90
value of, 389-90
property rights before law reform, 390
Set-off—See counter-claim
Sexual assault, 152
Sheriff, 111
Simple contracts, 269
necessary elements, 269
Small Claims Court, 249-50
Specialty contracts—See Contracts under seal
Specific performance, 21, 330-31
Spouses
rights and responsibilities, 353-54
custody, 354
property, 354
support, 353
Stare decisis, 20, 21, 37
Statute, 6
coming into force, 34

law, 23
passing, 32-36
proclamation, 34
regulations, 36-37
Royal Assent, 28
Statutory remission, 120
Strict liability, 72-74, 229-30
Strikes, 571-73
employee's rights, 572-73
employer's rights, 573
wildcat, 571
Substantive law, 7
Substituted agreement, 322-23
Summary conviction offence, 85, 124
Summons, 88, 254
Writ of, 258
Support, 353
children, 366-68
provincial legislation, 396-97
Supreme Court, 38, 250-51
of Canada, 252
Surrogate Court, 39, 251
Suspended sentence, 120

T
Tax law, defined, 5
Temporary absences, 119
Tenancy, periodic, 523-24
Tenants
accommodation, fitness of, 521
assignment and subletting, 522
notice before a rent increase, 521-22
privacy, right to, 520
rent, payment of, 517
residential vs. commercial, 513-14
security of tenure, 524-26
Theft, 153-54
Title
objections to, 504-5
searching, 503
transferring, 498-506
Tort law, 7
Tort(s)
defamation, 231, 232-33
intentional, 213-17
defences to, 217-21
interference with the person, 213-16
interference with property, 216-17
negligence, 221-29
nuisance, 233-26
strict liability, 229-30
vicarious liability, 230

Trafficking, 161-62
Trespass
to chattels, 217
to land, 216
Trial
civil actions, 259-61
defendant's rights at, 108
indictable offences, 112-19
jury, 111-12
summary conviction offences, 123-24
Trusts, 318

U
Ultra vires, defined, 26
Unemployment insurance, 551-52
Union, 536, 562
bargaining units, 564
Unlawful assemblies, 134-35

V
Vicarious liability, 230
Vicarious performance, 318
Vote, who may, 50

W
Warrant(s)
accused's right to examine, 92
search—See Search Warrant
Warranty
consumer law, 438-39
contract, 326
Wills, 415-24
age, 416
administrators, 427
clarity and reasonableness, 419
contents, 418-19
changes, valid, 420
dependants, 421
executors, 426-27
guardians, 423
mental competence, 416
residue, 419-20
signature and witnesses, 417-18
undue influence, 416-17
writing, 415
Writ of Execution, 262
Wrongful dismissal, 540-41

Y
Young children, incapacity of, 171-72
Young offenders, 124-27
criminal records, 127
rights, 126
sentencing, 126

Credits

Every reasonable effort has been made to find copyright holders of the following material. The publisher would be pleased to have any errors or omissions brought to its attention.

Unit 1: Opening Spread, Photo: Canapress Photo Service/p.9 (Fig.1-4) Reprinted with permission—*The Toronto Star* Syndicate (24 July 1983)/p.14 (Fig.1-6) *The Globe and Mail*, Toronto (21 April 1983)/p.27 (Fig.2-3) *The Globe and Mail*, Toronto (21 June 1983)/p.49 (Fig.3-2) *The Toronto Star* Syndicate/p.55 (Fig.3-4) The Canadian Press (5 January 1984)/p.74 (Fig.4-4) Courtesy of the Metropolitan Toronto Police/p.84 (Fig.5-1) RCMP Photo/p.98 (Fig.5-7) The Canadian Press (24 March 1983)/p.119 (Fig.6-5) The Correctional Service of Canada/p.142 (Cartoon, Ch.7) Reprinted by permission of Chronicle Features, San Francisco/p.146 (Fig.7-4) *The Globe and Mail*, Toronto/p.149 (Fig.7-5) RCMP Photo/p.188 Unit 2: Opening Spread, Photo: Nancy Halpin/p.192 (Fig.9-2) *The Globe and Mail*, Toronto/p.218 (Fig.10-2) Photo: Sidney Tabak/p.228 (Fig.10-6) The Canadian Press (27 January 1984)/p.260 (Fig.11-9) *The Globe and Mail*, Toronto/p.277 (Fig.12-4) Courtesy of the International Air Transport Association/p.341 Unit 3: Opening Spread, Photo, Fred Sonnega/p.348 (Fig.15-2) Reprinted by permission of the Queen's Printer, Manitoba/p.350 (Cartoon, Ch.15) Reprinted by permission of Chronicle Features, San Francisco/p.365 (Fig.16-2) C-56705 Public Archives Canada, B.J. Knight, Box 640, Ladysmith, B.C./p.369 (Fig.16-3) Miller Services Ltd./p.372 (Fig.16-4) The Canadian Press (17 February 1983)/p.400 (Fig.17-1) *The Globe and Mail*, Toronto (20 January 1984)/p.406 (Fig.17-2) Brian Gory, Copyright, 1983. Reprinted with permission/p.413 (Cartoon, Ch.18) Reprinted by permission of Chronicle Features, San Francisco/p.422 (Fig.18-2) The Canadian Press/p.435 Unit 4: Opening Spread, Nancy Halpin/p.447 (Fig.19-3) *The Globe and Mail*, Toronto (29 June 1983)/p.447 (**Fig.** 19-4) *The Globe and Mail*, Toronto (25 May 1983)/p.477 (Fig.20-3) *The Toronto Star* Syndicate/p.489 (Fig.21-2) *The Globe and Mail*, Toronto/p.490 (Fig.21-2) *The Globe and Mail*, Toronto/p.502 (Fig.21-5) *The Globe and Mail*, Toronto (21 February 1984)/p.515 (Fig.22-2) Miller Services Ltd./p.533 Unit 5: Opening Spread, Photo: Nancy Halpin/p.547 (Fig.23-5) Miller Services Ltd./p.550 (Fig.23-6) Courtesy of the Alberta Human Rights Commission/p.561 (Fig.24-1) Photo: Nancy Halpin/p.568 (Fig.24-3) *The Globe and Mail*, Toronto (23 April 1982)